BERND POLSTER

WALTER KNOLL

THE FURNITURE BRAND OF MODERNITY

teNeues

CONTENTS

FIRST **MODERNITY**

1865 TO 1945

SECOND **MODERNITY**

1945 TO 1993

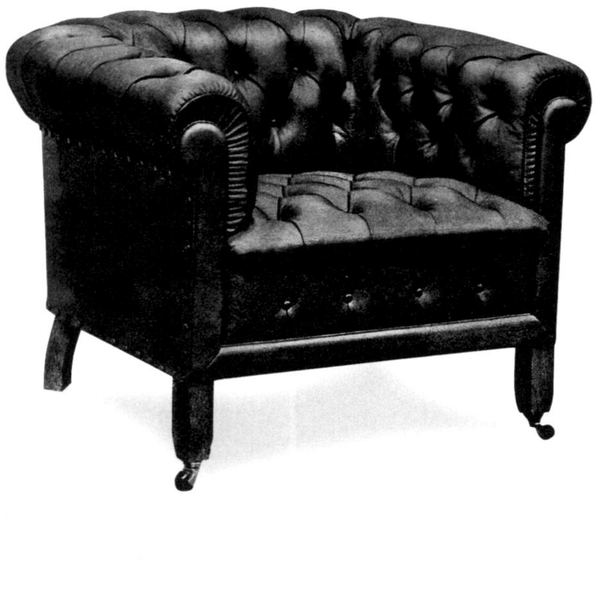

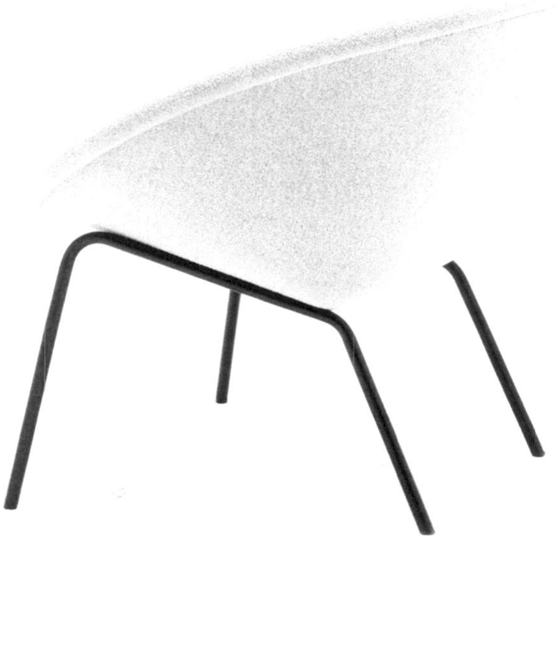

THIRD **MODERNITY**

1993 TO PRESENT

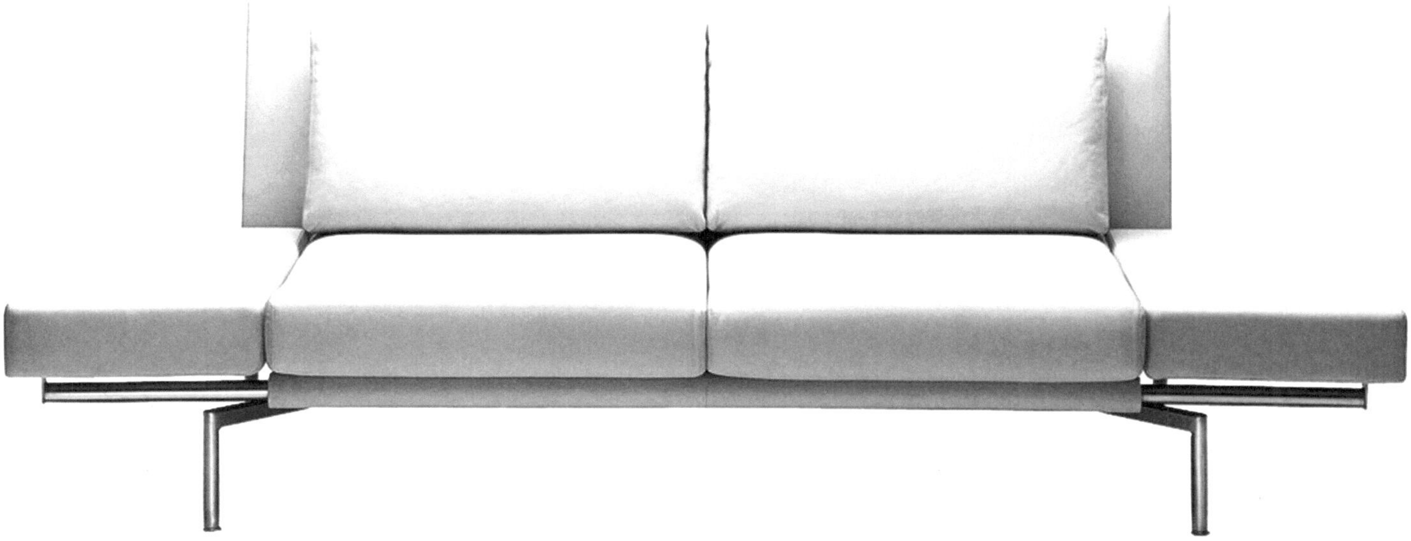

FOREWORD

The letter that Markus Benz wrote to me in late 2013 hung above my desk like a sibylline oracle: he was asking me if I would like to come to Herrenberg after the Cologne furniture fair as he just may have an idea. The riddle was solved the day I was first beguiled by the panoramic view of the Swabian Alb from the modern company headquarters of Walter Knoll. His idea was ambitious and therefore required a number of meetings. Markus Benz, CEO of Walter Knoll, wanted a book about the roots and relationships of the Knoll furniture dynasty and its place in modernity. He was not only interested in what happened but, above all, why it happened. It concerned the history of a family, design and the Stuttgart region, famously one of the world's most successful economic areas.

As we would soon discover while gaining an abundance of new insights, this region was also one of the strongest design regions throughout the 20th century. The companies of the Knoll furniture dynasty were among its flagships. In addition, the interactions between economy and culture that were actively promoted in Swabia – another particularity – acted as catalysts. Many positive outcomes are included here. Consequently, our project reveals a dialectic that goes well beyond a chronology of the company. The close link between the biography of the Walter Knoll brand and the stages of modernity is reflected in the book's structure. It is divided into three main phases, with the First, Second and Third Modernity forming a template for the unique history and rise of the company Walter Knoll. From the outset, two central motifs can be recognized: cross-border thinking and the primacy of innovation and quality – accomplishments that result from a mature corporate culture, and hard work.

Bernd Polster

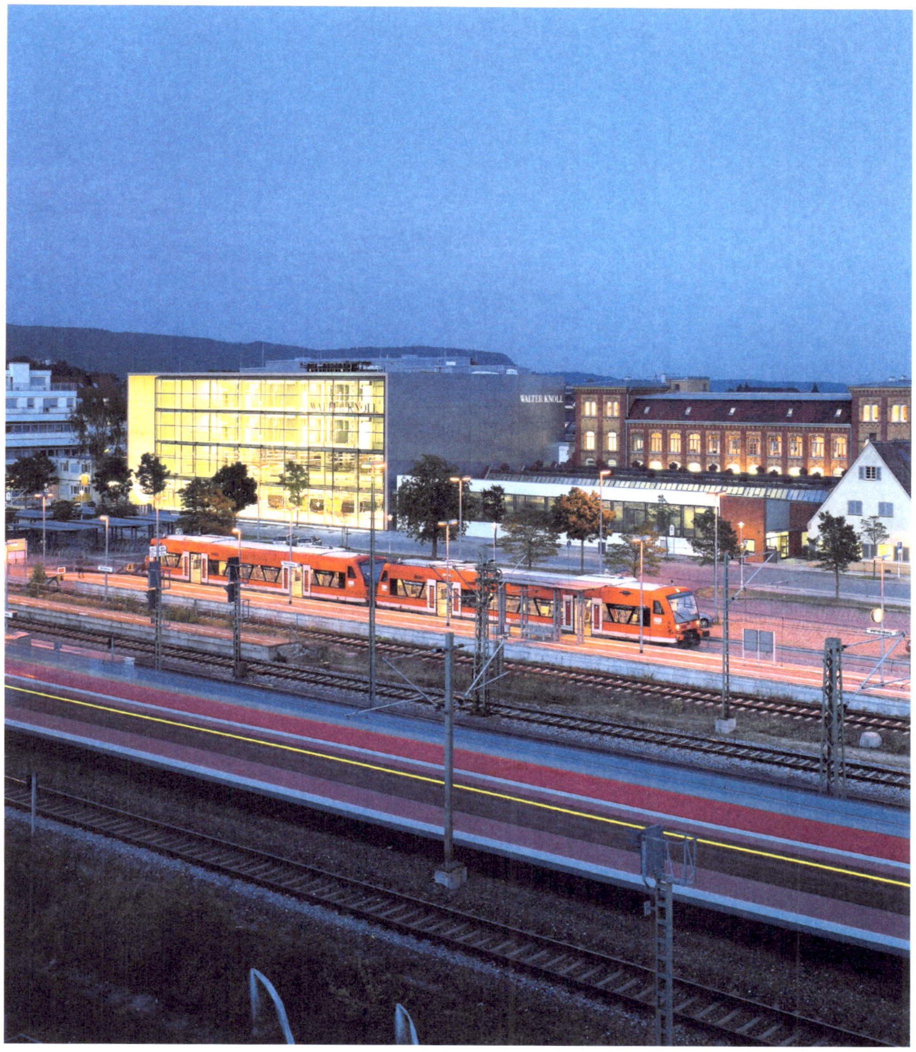
WALTER KNOLL

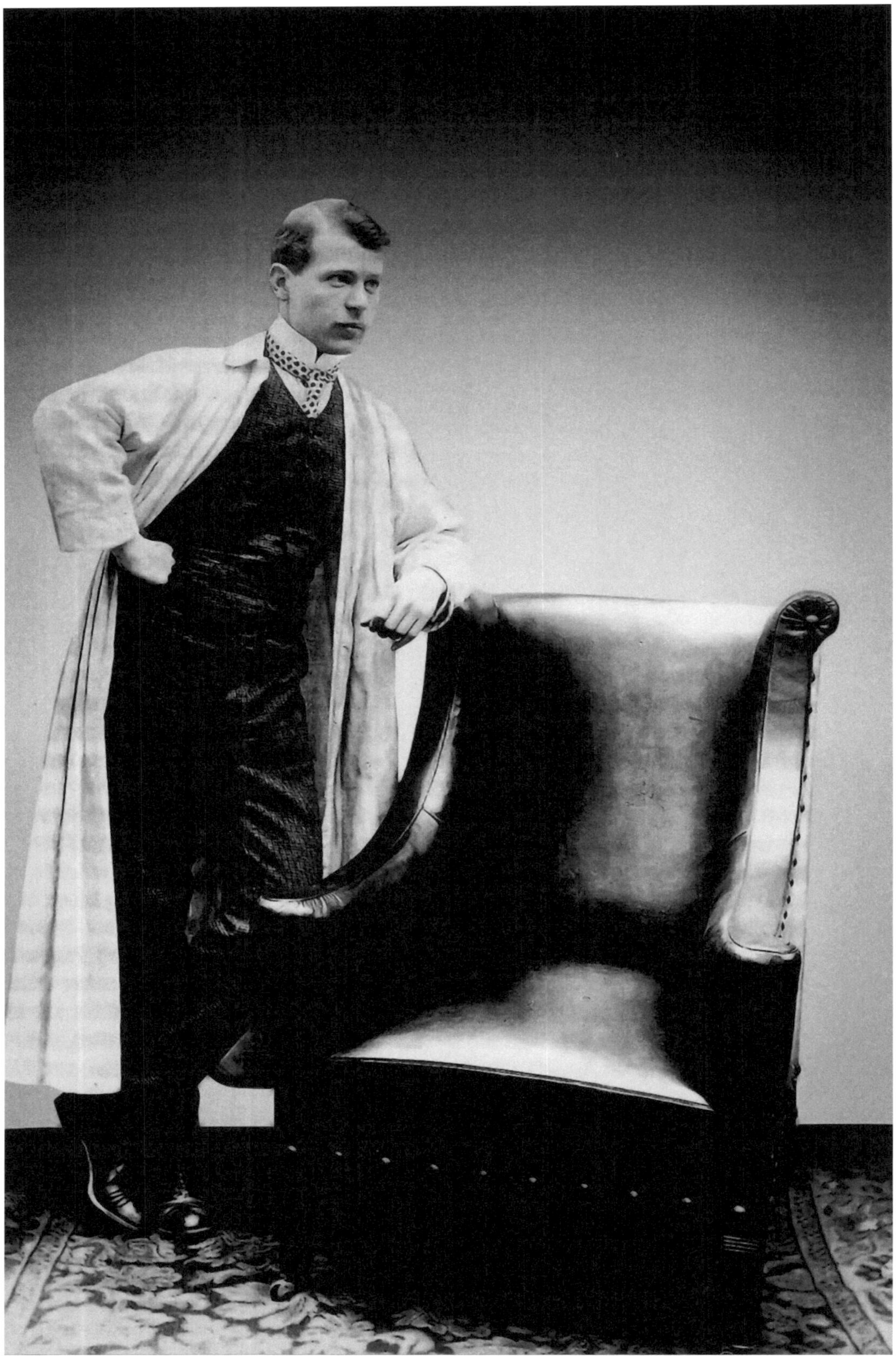

INVENTOR CULTURE
The 32-year-old Walter Knoll standing next to one of the early club chairs of his father's company (1908). Unlike his brother Willy, it is obvious that he was a German dandy and no dyed-in-the-wool upholsterer. His strengths lay elsewhere: he focused on modern sales techniques, had experience of America, and already thought in terms of the brand, as demonstrated by his slogan, "The psychology of sitting."

FIRST **MODERNITY**

1865 TO 1945

GRÜNDERZEIT

FOUNDERS AND INVENTORS

The story of the Knoll furniture family, the subject of this book, has an official start date. On June 6, 1865, an ambitious young man named Wilhelm Knoll placed a commercial ad announcing that he had just set up his own business and opened a leather shop in downtown Stuttgart – an event that would most likely have been forgotten, had it not marked the start of a dynasty. Knoll, a mere 26 years old, had previously completed an apprenticeship as a tanner and attended a commercial school in Stuttgart. But that was not enough for him, because afterward, he also spent over a year in Paris having a look around. At the time, the French capital was the world center of beaux arts, fashion, and luxury goods. This also included a highly developed leather industry, some of which still exists today.[1]

Paris gave forth the most refined shoes, bags, saddles and leather chairs. For the young Swabian, it was exactly the right place to compare himself with the best of his trade and experience the latest fashion. Here lay the beginnings of that "well-traveled leather specialist," as his son Walter later described him.[2]

Walter Knoll, who went on to found his own company – the story and prehistory of which are told here – was born in Stuttgart on October 20, 1876. On his birth certificate, "Walther" was written with an "h", which he later eliminated.[3] For a while, he added the abbreviation of his second name, Carl, which was his grandfather's first name, and called himself "Walther C. Knoll," a variant typical in America. Later on, both the "h" and the "C" disappeared from his name – a side note whose reasons we can only speculate about[4], but which continued to provide material for discussions right down to the recent past. So when it came time to put up the sign for the street named after him in the town of Herrenberg, of which he was an honorary citizen, opponents and proponents argued over the letter "h." The latter sited historical accuracy and, in this case, prevailed. Nevertheless, his name change is a historical fact, just like that of his famous namesake, Walter Gropius.

Walter Knoll, as he will be called here for simplicity's sake, was the oldest of six children born to Wilhelm and Emma Knoll.[5] According to Walter, his mother – a newcomer from the Bergisches Land region of Germany – was "capable, kind, and selfless" and showed a "sympathy for the individuality of her children."[6] This prudent and generous woman took care of the "thrifty management of the household"[7] and, when it came to raising the children, was a calm antithesis to her restless husband, a "genuine Swabian,"[8] who ventured into the wider world. A photograph shows an ambitious man with a serious expression seated at a table. He is holding a book with a leather binding, an indication of how important education and craftsmanship were to him. It is the image of an entrepreneur. Also unusual is the fact that his face is not turned towards the camera, but to the side. It is as if he were looking into his future and would not allow himself to be distracted by anyone (see photo below).

Wilhelm Knoll's ancestors came from Walheim, a winegrowing community located in a loop of the Neckar River, directly opposite Besigheim and not far from Heilbronn. This was one of the heartlands of Pietism, that particular form of Protestant belief in which God's favor is earned through hard work and abstinence. This ascetic movement attained great significance in Württemberg as of the early 19th century, although it has always remained a minority.[9] The turbulent fate of Walheim, whose origins reach back to the Roman period, is entirely typical of more recent Swabian history. Many of its numerous towns stopped developing at some point – which is why they later appeared to us as the epitome of the romanticist painter Spitzweg's idyll. Perhaps that is also one of the reasons why Swabia was able to become a cradle of romanticism.[10]

Another reason for Walheim's involuntary stagnation was that it was repeatedly beset by wars, floods, and famines over the centuries. For this reason, quite a few inhabitants abandoned their home town. In around 1800, several disasters befell the town in quick succession that resulted in a mass exodus. Many Walheim residents emigrated – some to America, others to cities in the surrounding area. One of them who moved first to Möglingen and then to Stuttgart was the shoemaker Carl Johann Knoll. Whether he went out of necessity or of his own free will is not known. This master shoemaker, who opened a workshop on Geissstrasse in the heart of the old city, was the father of Wilhelm Knoll, who would later become the company founder. Son Wilhelm grew up with the scent of leather in

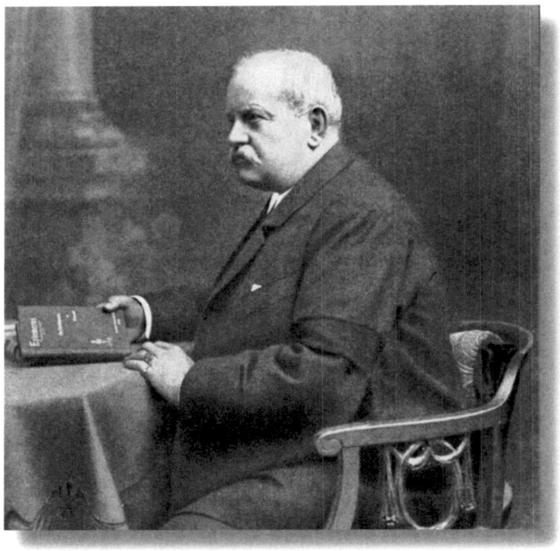

his nostrils, learned this profession from the ground up, and always remained true to it.

Wilhelm Knoll, to whom the current Walter Knoll company and the American subsidiary[11] can trace their roots, ultimately opened a leather shop on Stuttgart's Rotebühlstrasse, just a few doors down from his father's workshop. He was soon running his business on wholesale terms, becoming a merchant. Thus, he worked his way up the social ladder from workshop owner to businessman. After only four years, the eager young entrepreneur was already looking for new premises to accommodate his need for larger sales rooms. This was followed by further relocations based on the same necessity up until the turn of the century. Each time his family moved with him because, in those early days, it was still customary for home and business to be located under one roof. The frequent changes of location became necessary as Wilhelm Knoll took on new lines of business. The mid-1870s saw another milestone, when he began to produce his own leather. About a decade later, he became a supplier to the furniture industry, which was prospering in Stuttgart, an up-and-coming residential city. Finally, as his next step, Wilhelm Knoll also took on the prefabrication of furniture parts, including chair backs and seats. From there, it was only a small step to the company making its own furniture – but this was reserved for the next generation.

In those days, furniture was often richly ornamented. Decorated leather was therefore in great demand. The patterns were embossed or punched (see p. 15, 18, 19). While embossing was done with a roller or stamp, punching was an elaborate technique that placed high demands on craftsmanship. It could only be done using high-quality cowhide. The pattern first had to be drawn on, then cut, and finally, in a process of time-consuming manual labor, embossed stroke by stroke using a punching iron. Stuttgart developed into a stronghold for this type of embossed leatherwork. When an exhibition was held there in 1896 in the new "Landesgewerbemuseum," the local press reported it as a "specialty that can be called, without exaggeration, unique to Europe."[12] Nevertheless, even in those days, some were unable to resist "a certain dubious shaking of the head over the boldness of the forms."[13] Punched leather was seen as the epitome of upmarket craftsmanship and luxury, and was applied to virtually every object. Not only did it enhance fire screens, wall panels, cushions, chests, flower pots, and picture frames, but countless books were also transformed into magnificent volumes and commemorative publications. The public was able to admire such artfully punched objects at numerous exhibitions. Wilhelm Knoll, a specialist in furniture leather, was one of the top-ranking members of the Stuttgart punching industry, as was attested to by a very special award: the company was ultimately elevated to "Royal Court Supplier" – incontrovertible evidence that it was one of the best.

AFTER ONLY FOUR YEARS, THE EAGER YOUNG ENTREPRENEUR WAS ALREADY LOOKING FOR NEW PREMISES BECAUSE HE NEEDED LARGER SALES ROOMS.

Usually the leather was still dyed with stain to match the dark furniture that was very common at the time. For example, no respectable parlor was without a heavy buffet, often in the style of the Neo-Renaissance. At that time, this style was considered to be German or "Old German," which is why it soon spread, including to the field of architecture. By around 1830, immediately following the restrained Biedermeier period, lavish shapes and the copying of earlier styles had become the norm. The rest of the century was ruled by Historicism.

---

1 ▶ One example was the French family business Hermès.

2 ▶ Schnermann, in: Janssen, 1999, p. 392.

3 ▶ Walter Knoll himself distinguished between his personal name and the company name. When he applied for a building permit from the city of Stuttgart at the end of the 1930s, he appeared as Walther C. Knoll. Inventory of the Stuttgart City Archives No. Q 3/41.

4 ▶ No doubt, this was a simplification. The name sounds more businesslike, i.e. more modern. Perhaps there was a problem in America with the pronunciation of the "th" in the first name.

5 ▶ In 1872, Emma Sporket came from Barmen to Stuttgart and they married the same year. She was 19 years old and thus 14 years younger than her husband.
See: Schnermann, in: Janssen, 1999, p. 397.

6 ▶ Ibid.

7 ▶ Knoll, n.d., p. 3.

8 ▶ Ibid.

9 ▶ After the Reformation, Pietism is the most important reform movement in continental European Protestantism. In theological terms, Pietism is understood as a reflection on central concerns of the Reformation which, however, were transformed in a specific way by the inclusion of other strands of tradition. See: www.heiligenlexikon.de/Glossar/Pietismus.html (accessed on 12/7/2018).

10 ▶ The group surrounding the poet Eduard Mörike, who earned his living as a pastor, also shaped the image of the Germans as a people of poets and thinkers.

11 ▶ This refers to Hans G. Knoll Furniture Company, later Knoll Associates, then Knoll International, and now Knoll. The company was founded by Hans Knoll, the son of Walter and grandson of Wilhelm.

12 ▶ State Gazette for Württemberg, 1896, inventory of Stuttgart City Archive No. 1056/2.

13 ▶ Swabian Mercury, inventory of Stuttgart City Archive No. 1056/2.

THE METROPOLIS OF STUTTGART

In 1806, Württemberg became a kingdom and its capital a royal residence. Stuttgart developed into a major city. From a population of barely 20,000 at the beginning of the century, the number of inhabitants grew to almost 300,000 by the First World War. During the second half of the century, industry expanded. Specialized industries aimed at export were created, including mechanical and electrical engineering. As of 1868, there were horse-drawn trams, which were electrified in the 1890s.

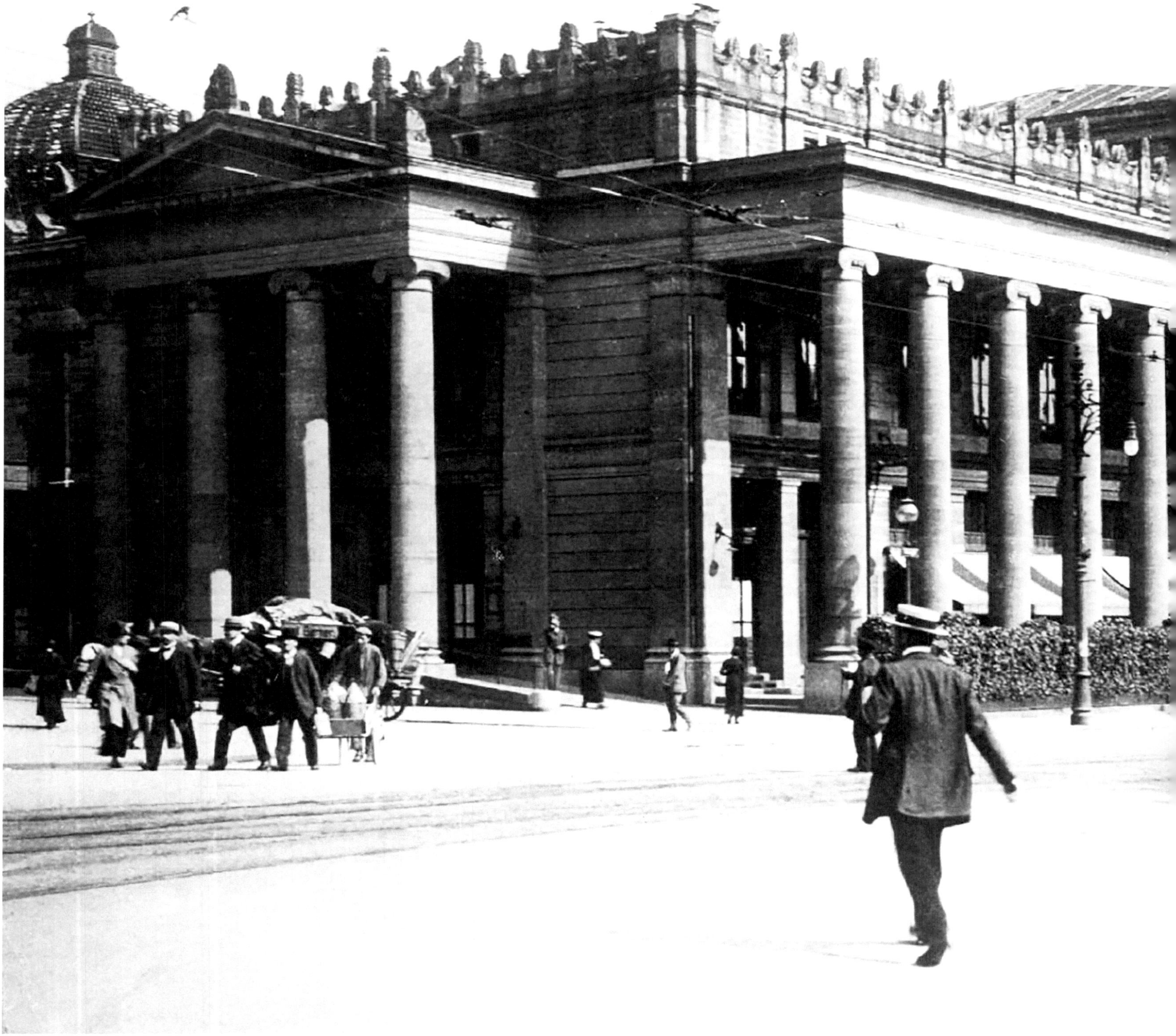

Königsbau,
Stuttgart,
around 1890

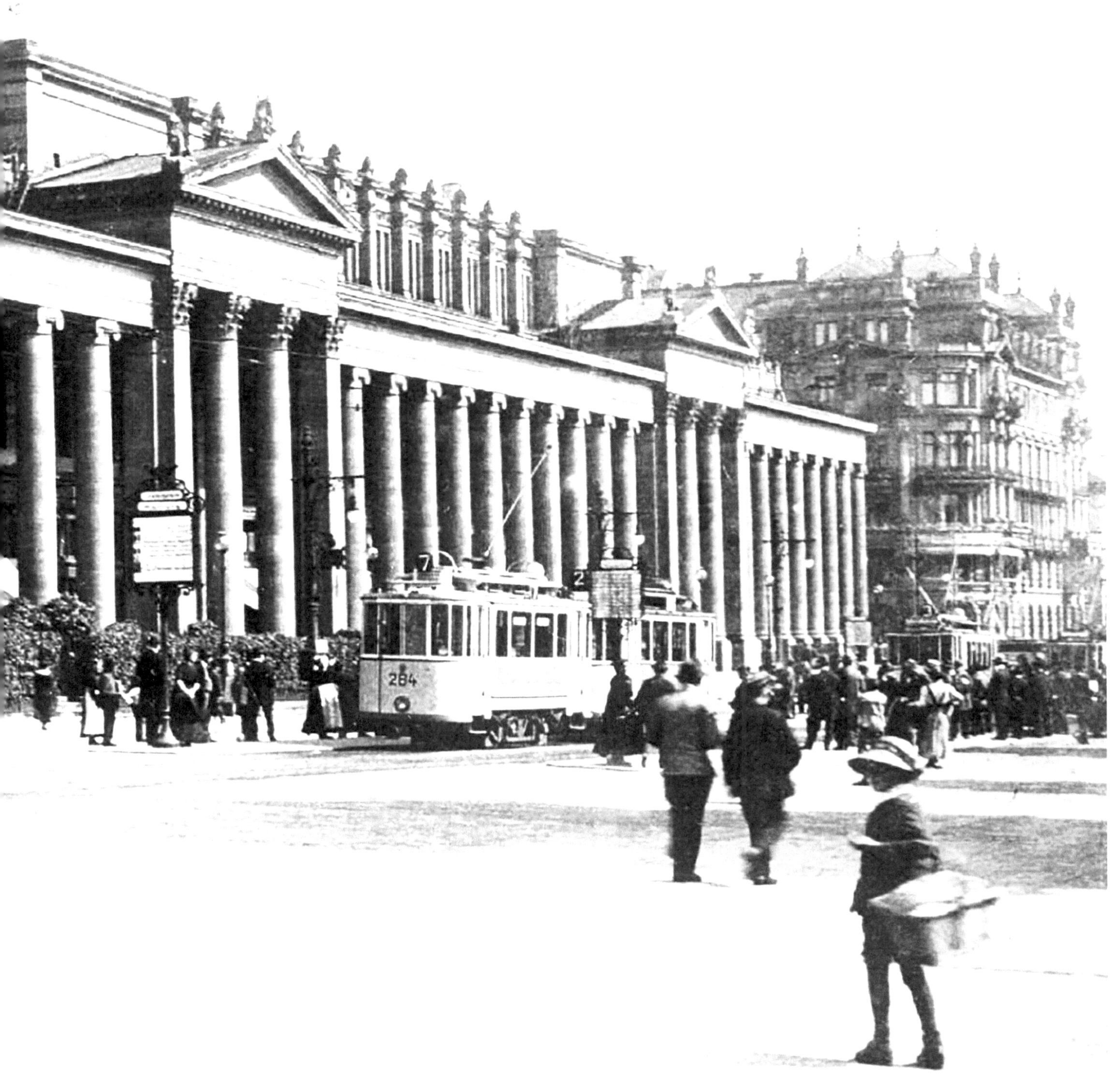

The up-and-coming bourgeoisie, often newly wealthy and stylistically uncertain, wanted to show off their attainments. Sophisticated "Knoll and Antique Leather" was a way to meet this need. People indulged in stylistic nostalgia, but made use of the latest technology to do so. Business was soon being conducted by telephone and telegraph as well. The communication age had begun. The telegram address was simply "Knolleder" (Knoll leather). This may not have been a brand in today's sense, but it soon became a common term in the industry, far beyond the borders of Württemberg.

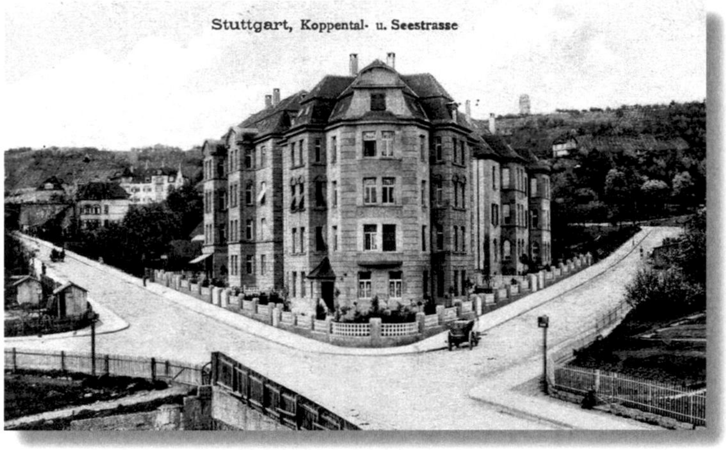

THE STEADY RISE OF KNOLL'S BUSINESS NICELY PARALLELED THE TREMENDOUS UPSWING THAT THE GERMAN ECONOMY EXPERIENCED AS A WHOLE IN THE SECOND HALF OF THE 19TH CENTURY.

The first company logo, which consisted of the initials "WK" and the abbreviation "ST" for Stuttgart, also dates back to this period. This combination of four letters, which expressed pride in the company's own name and city, would continue to be used later on. It was a simple signet that looked as though it had been punched with a leather stamp.

The leather expert Wilhelm Knoll belonged to the class that gave the period its name: *Gründer*, meaning founder. As a rule, this generally included businesspeople who took the expression "entrepreneur" very literally. Their achievement consisted not only of building companies from the ground up, but also of further developing them under what were often difficult conditions. The legendary *Gründerzeit*, the age of industrialization in Central Europe up until the great crash of 1873, was also an era of countless bankruptcies.

As for the steady rise of Knoll's business, it nicely paralleled the tremendous upswing experienced by the German economy as a whole during the second half of the 19th century. Compared to countries such as England or France, industrialization came late but was all the more rapid as a result. The race to catch up was even more turbulent in Württemberg and its capital city, Stuttgart, which was still just a small town at the beginning of the 19th century. The Reich's southwest corner was considered backward, with only a few scattered factories. To change all this, King Wilhelm I of Württemberg, an eminent pragmatist, founded the "Centralstelle für Gewerbe und Handel" (Central Office for Commerce and Trade) in 1846, which later became the "Landesgewerbeamt" (State Trade Office). It became the springboard for a clever and often unorthodox promotion of the economy. Founded on education and consulting, it transformed the state into one of the leading industrial regions within a matter of decades. How was this done?

Since no mineral resources were available, the focus had to be on human resources based, in large part, on the craftsmanship that still flourished in the old cities, with reliance on existing skills and new ideas. The fact that the "Centralstelle" established a collection of patents underscores the ambitious nature of this approach. The focus was on technical innovations – which included creativity and a marked tenacity, the precise qualities that we attribute to the now proverbial "Swabian tinkerer." It was indeed that lone wolf, with a tendency toward stubbornness and without whom nothing new could come into being, that paved the way for the very type of the highly motivated founder and inventor.

Further processing and refining resulted in new, sophisticated products whose uniqueness made them difficult to copy and, therefore, suitable for export. Wilhelm Knoll also pursued this strategy. The entire Swabian economy made a virtue out of necessity and at the same time developed an awareness that it was possible not only to catch up within a reasonable period of time, but also to reach the highest level. The secret to success was a Swabian can-do attitude that created positive momentum. Thus, this deliberately initiated structural change – an early form of economic miracle – was based on a unique combination of virtues that epitomize the Greater Stuttgart Area, making it one of the strongest locations in the world.

Other, more traditional influences also played a role in the transformation, such as a cosmopolitanism which, paradoxically, was accompanied by a strong attachment to the homeland. Emigration, as is so often the case in backward regions, was not considered unusual for Swabians at that time. Rather, it represented a realistic and viable alternative. Success was also based on a number of attitudes rooted in religion, described at that time by the sociologist Max Weber as the "Protestant ethics."[14] Weber was referring to the combination of qualities that were a driving economic force and became even more pronounced through the influence of Pietism. Swabians were reputed to be modest, thrifty, and ambitious. These virtues were not only preached from the pulpit, but became a general commandment for a way of life that was deeply engrained in the awareness and conscience of every individual. Even though the direct influence of the church has greatly diminished, these psychological characteristics of Germany's southwest economic region continue to make themselves felt up to the present day.

Although Wilhelm Knoll's exact association with the "Centralstelle" is unknown, he profited from the numerous exhibitions that were held in the Stuttgart Gewerbehalle and later in the Kunstgewerbemuseum. The family business of Wilhelm Knoll was basically a model of the special Swabian method and even in its early days demonstrated the effectiveness of precisely those principles that had now established themselves in the local economy. This applied both to the high-quality products made of fine leather, which required sophisticated craft techniques, and to the gradual expansion of business activities. It was carried out in incredible lockstep with the general economic development of Württemberg and the German Empire. The company's founding in the 1860s – just when the state was beginning to boom – was followed by the start of leather production in the mid-1870s. The Unification of Germany in 1871 gave additional impetus to the economy.

After Wilhelm Knoll also became a supplier to furniture manufacturers a decade later, the inevitable next logical step was to produce his own furniture. However, this would be reserved for Wilhelm's sons, Walter and Willy. Early exports to other European countries also fit the picture of a model Swabian company and made Wilhelm Knoll a frequent guest in First Class railway salons. Of course, such cross-border trade was possible only if the offer was competitive, as was obviously the case with "Knolleder." The company acquired excellent contacts in Holland, Belgium, and France. One important trading center was Saint Petersburg, at that time the residence and cultural center of the Tsarist Empire. Wilhelm Knoll often traveled there by steamer across the Baltic Sea. Wherever there was a concentration of Russia's nobility, there would also be a market for luxury goods.

The Wilhelm Knoll company was a prime example of a Swabian success story rooted in the middle class – accompanied by other characteristics, such as the previous generation's rural origins. Theodor Heuss, an intimate authority on and portraitist of his compatriots, associated this with characteristics such as the "gift of reaching for the ceiling" and "undaunted willingness"[15] Of course, Heuss did not neglect to mention the Protestant faith, which often appeared along the Neckar in its pietistic version, just as it did in Bergisches Land, the home of Wilhelm's wife, Emma Knoll, who was born in Barmen. The obligatory unison in matters of faith between the spouses did the rest. As the most important confidant of her sons Walter and Willy, Emma shaped their character and was also largely responsible for the well-being of the family and the company.

THE REFORM FROM THE HILLSIDE

The prototype of the Swabian entrepreneur was Robert Bosch, the enterprising inventor whose ingenious ignition device first made the automobile suitable for everyday use. He was the embodiment of early technical modernity. From his person, however, it was only all too clear that this was by no means limited to the development of devices. An unconventional thinker, Bosch understood his role as a manufacturer in a broader sense. He was regarded as a rebel and acted the part. As a Swabian outdoorsman, he rejected the conventions of his time: he was never seen in a tailcoat. Instead, for years he wore the woolen clothing designed by a certain Gustav Jäger and offered under the designation "normal clothing."

14 ▶ See the two essays from 1904 and 1905 in the periodical "Archiv für Sozialwissenschaften und Sozialpolitik" (Archive for Social Sciences and Social Policy). A version produced by Weber towards the end of his life was published in 1920 as a book entitled "Die protestantische Ethik und der Geist des Kapitalismus" (Protestant Ethics and the Spirit of Capitalism). It is one of Weber's most important contributions to sociology and is regarded as a key work on the sociology of religion.

15 ▶ Heuss, 1986, p. 81.

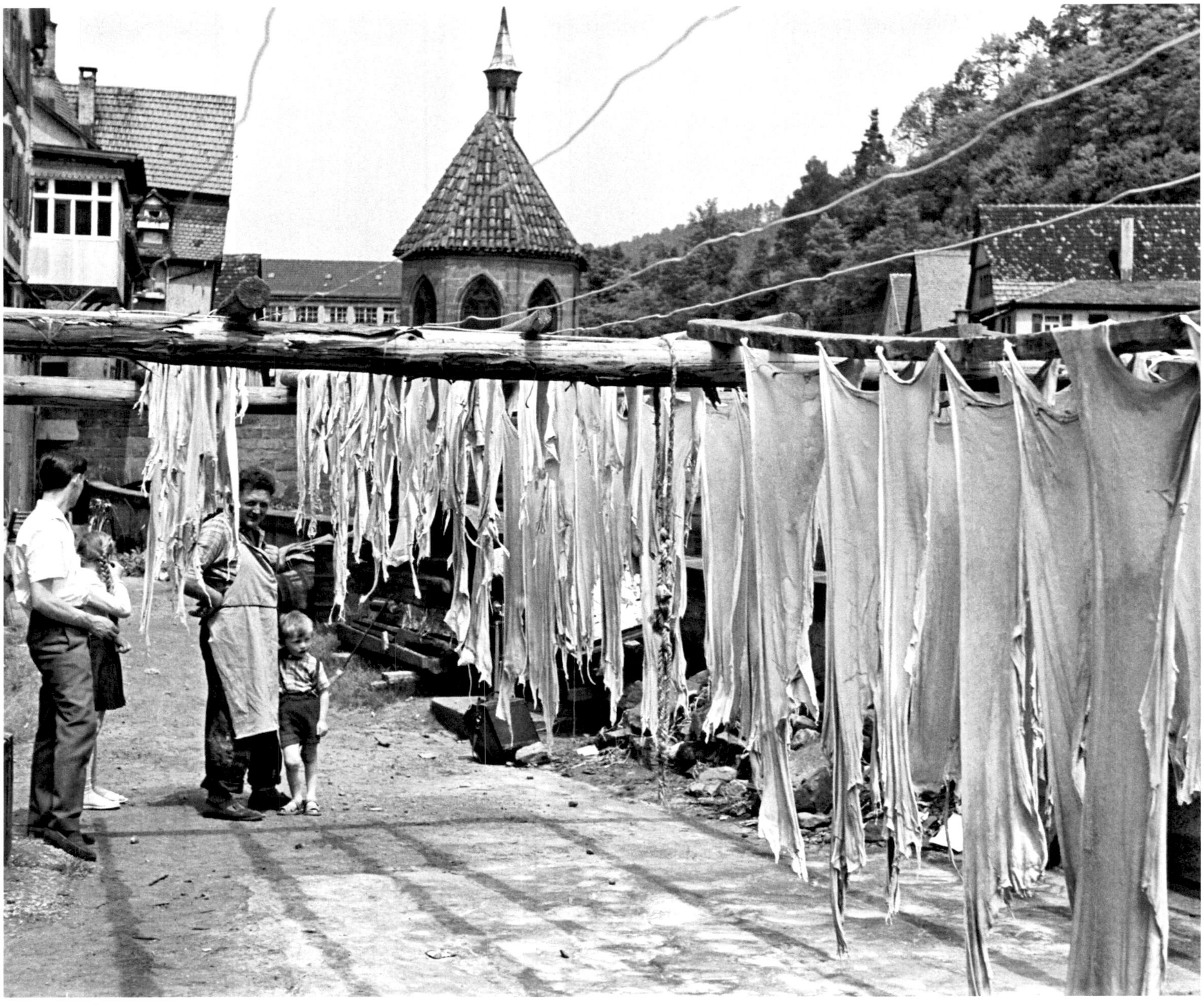

"KNOLLEDER"

The Stuttgart leather industry produced leather for sophisticated demands. The leather business founded by Wilhelm Knoll in 1865 was a leading company and eventually became a purveyor to the Royal Court. There was even a brand name: "Knolleder" (Knoll leather).

Tannery,
Calw an der Nagold,
around 1910

Punched leather,
exhibition at the
"Landesgewerbeamt"
(State Trade Office),
Stuttgart, around 1900

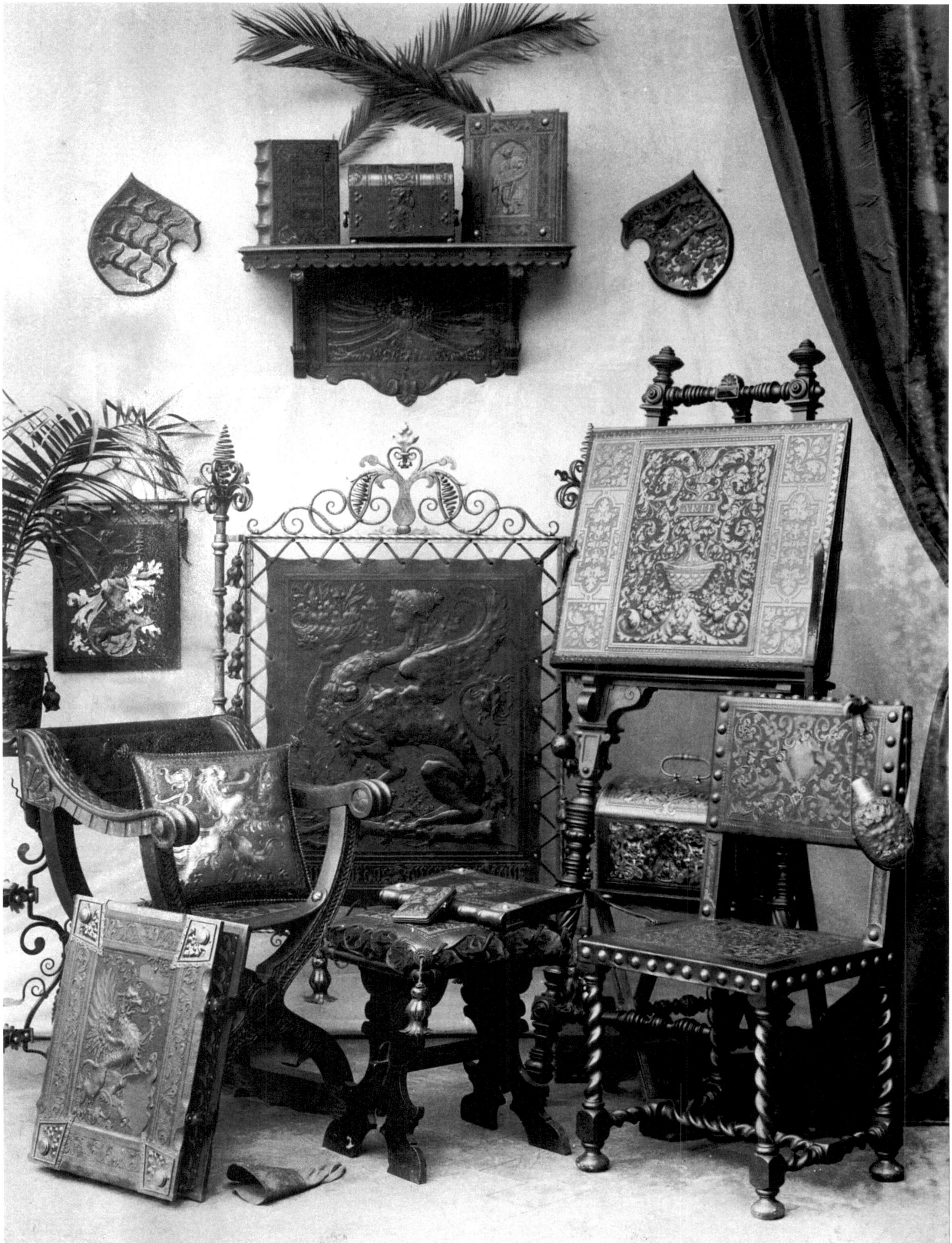

Like Bosch, Jäger was a life reformer[16]. As an entrepreneur, Bosch attached a great deal of importance to training and promoting talent. Responsibility for his workforce mattered to him. In this, he agreed with Eduard Pfeiffer, a banker from Stuttgart who, like Bosch, had a certain outsider status because of his Jewish faith. Pfeiffer was involved in social causes, including the construction of housing, which was urgently needed because Stuttgart's old city was hopelessly overcrowded at the time. As reformers, Bosch and Pfeiffer stood for a caring version of capitalism, the drawbacks of which were becoming clear. In the meantime, Stuttgart had also become a center of social democracy.

The millionaire Pfeiffer lived part of the time on Seestrasse, one of the hillside streets along which Stuttgart emerged from the confines of its valley. In this new residential quarter, he found neighbors befitting his social status, including the Vollmöller family of factory owners, which was quite obviously inspired by the philanthropist Pfeiffer. Company founder Robert Vollmöller, whose factory grew to

VILLA VOLLMÖLLER BECAME A PLACE OF INSPIRATION FOR WALTER KNOLL THAT GAVE HIS LIFE NEW DIRECTION.

become the largest hosiery factory in the world by the start of the First World War and who established several subsidiaries in the surrounding area – one of which was in Herrenberg –, did more for his workforce than usual. "In terms of light and air, the factory premises can serve as a role model,"[17] was the opinion of a visitor to the plant. The company owned more than a hundred employee apartments and a "girls' home" for foreign workers that was surrounded by a park. Like Bosch, Vollmöller was a caring factory owner. But he was also a romantic, which is why he bought Beilstein Castle near Heilbronn and had it converted into a palace with medieval towers and oriels.[18]

Bosch, Pfeiffer, and Vollmöller, all of whom belonged to the founding generation, were occasionally neighbors and knew each other well, forming a loose circle that might be called the hillside reformist group. In this environment, a Stuttgart version of the industrial revolution was created, enriched, and cushioned by various elements of modernity, including *Lebensreform*, or Life Reform – a social movement that emerged on the fringes of the bourgeoisie that questioned the strict customs of the German Empire and finally penetrated the heart of society.[19]

In those days, as Walter Knoll stated, "class differences were pronounced"[20] and usually insurmountable. For him, the son of a merchant and craftsman, it would have been impossible to move up into higher circles – which makes it all the more amazing that he actually did so. In the 1890s, Walter had become a smart young man who liked to go out on the town. His trademark was a walking stick, which earned him many a mocking remark. There began a time, he recalled later, when "taking students as role models, one went boozing once a week in a certain pub, sang songs, and gave vent to one's youthful exuberance through all sorts of pranks."[21] Walter possessed very special abilities in this regard. He was an excellent dancer and singer. So it came about that he performed humorous couplets "at every opportunity" and "dressed funnily" accordingly.[22]

Walter Knoll was an attraction and apparently extremely entertaining. It was a wonderful time, which was only a little clouded by the fact that his mother would not give him a house key. In 1895, after completing his apprenticeship and with military service still before him, the 19-year-old became attracted to a young woman at May Day celebrations who introduced herself to him as Maria Vollmöller. Later, she was to become "Maia" through the omission of a letter. She was the daughter of the well-known Stuttgart knitwear manufacturer and loved fun and dancing as much as Walter. Because they took an instant liking to one another, Maria invited her new acquaintance to her home, a villa on Hasenbergsteige, which was another of Stuttgart's prominent hillside areas. Thus the charming Knoll Junior entered a world that was actually closed to him. It would be another 14 years before he married Maria. But throughout the entire waiting period "Knoller," as he was sometimes called, was a regular visitor to the Vollmöllers' house. It became for him a place of inspiration that gave his life a new direction. The inhabitants read books in English and French, and even the children grew up multilingual. Besides the German nurses, all of whom came from the Swabian Alb, there was always a French housemaid and an English governess. Both conversed in their native language. In addition, English sports were extensively indulged, including croquet, badminton, and especially tennis. An "English lawn" had been laid especially for this purpose. This was all new to Walter. His parents lived a spartan life and he himself had left school early. Karl Gustav and Mathilde Vollmöller, Maria's older siblings, spoke English so well that they translated a book for the renowned Insel Verlag publishing house in Munich.

Maria finally introduced Walter to Mrs. Brown, an American who lived with her children in Stuttgart and in whose house he was now a frequent guest. Almost every week, a group of young people of both sexes gathered there, mainly to dance. It's no wonder that Walter was drawn there, as he later recalled, "with magic power."[23] As he cautiously expressed it, "at that time in Stuttgart, it was highly unusual for young people to be able to gather in a house and socialize so informally."[24] It was undoubtedly also due to the fact that Mrs. Brown was an American and did not take things too seriously. "Through her cultivated home life," she had "created an atmosphere that captivated me tremendously."[25] Walter also found "her foreign ways to be very special."[26] This piqued his curiosity and broadened his view of the world in an unconventional way. He was also able to meet up with Maria and her siblings, who came there often. And as the "favorite young friend"[27] of the Brown family, he also acquired the foundations of his English language skills. For someone who wanted to conquer the world, this was, of course, an enormous advantage.

When Walter first arrived at Villa Vollmöller, nine children between the ages of three and 21 lived there. He became friends with Karl Gustav, Maria's eldest brother, who was two years younger than him and was still in high school.[28] The two young men could hardly have been more different. Karl Gustav, who went on to become an explorer, writer, and globetrotter, was a child prodigy who read and recited the classics in the original ancient Greek just to amuse himself. The fact that Walter knew nothing about all this made no difference. A lifelong friendship developed between the two – almost complete opposites, but each in his own way a jack of all trades. For the young Knoll, whose parents did not even own a house at that time, it was an opportunity to immerse himself not only in an intellectual sphere but also in an atmosphere of great wealth. Through Eduard Pfeiffer, father Vollmöller maintained close contacts with banks in Frankfurt, London, Paris, and New York. Walter's new friend Karl Gustav had known the bankers from an early age, since they were mostly friends of the family in addition to being business partners. But it wasn't just the tremendous wealth that Walter Knoll first encountered here that impressed him so greatly. It was also and above all the cultural horizons that were opened up to him.

Karl Gustav Vollmöller became a universalist whose creative cosmos can only be hinted at. As an archaeologist, he participated in excavations. As a classical scholar, he translated classical texts. He shared his publisher, Samuel Fischer, with Thomas Mann, whom he knew well. The French novelist André Gide, the Italian futurist Gabriele D'Annunzio, and a raft of German poets were also among his acquaintances.[29] Karl Gustav Vollmöller, himself a literary figure, was already publishing articles in the satirical magazine "Simplicissimus" as an adolescent. His monumental dramatic work "Das Mirakel" (The Miracle) was staged by Max Reinhardt, with around 2,000 actors and some 30,000 spectators. It was a huge success, also in financial terms. Karl Gustav, a frequent traveler, often resided at his second home on Pariser Platz in Berlin, right next to the Brandenburg Gate.[30] He also enjoyed staying at the Palazzo Vendramin in Venice, right on the Grand Canal, where Walter occasionally visited him. Karl Gustav lived there for a while with his first wife, the Italian Maria Carmi – a genuine beauty who made an international career for herself as an actress.[31]

One link between the dissimilar friends was their Swabian origins, and another their sense of humor. Walter also formed friendships with other siblings of his future wife – for example, with the younger Hans, a technophile and flight pioneer who finally took the friend of the family on one of his early flight tests through the Neckar Valley. Mathilde, Karl Gustav's older sister, who was a talented painter, was also close to Walter. It was through her that he first came into contact with modern art. She had studied under Henri Matisse in Paris and later married the painter Hans Purrmann, an expressionist and also a student of Matisse. It was a milieu of modernity, whose facets were focused in the Vollmöller house as if in a magnifying glass. Walter Knoll later said that the house was where he "met people who had a decisive influence on the rest of my life," in that he "entered a new, extremely attractive atmosphere in which intellectual and cultural values had a special weight."[32] Without this reappraisal, his own company could not have developed in the way it did.

16 ▶ *Lebensreform* (Life Reform) was the expression of a movement towards the end of the 19th century that rebelled against the restrictive conventions of the time and advocated a natural way of life. It found a large following in Germany. In addition to organic food and nudism, its central concerns included clothing and housing reform. Nearly all alternative movements of the time originated from this.

17 ▶ Dillmann, 1999, p. 48.

18 ▶ The fact that he also made his fortune wearing the knitwear of life reformer Jäger completes the picture of the inspired entrepreneur.

19 ▶ See note 16.

20 ▶ Knoll, n.d., p. 15.

21 ▶ Knoll, n.d., p. 13.

22 ▶ Ibid.

23 ▶ Knoll, n.d., p. 19.

24 ▶ Ibid.

25 ▶ Ibid.

26 ▶ Ibid.

27 ▶ Ibid.

28 ▶ Interview with Michael Knoll, Walter's grandson, on 04/22/2015.

29 ▶ Among the writers that Karl Gustav Vollmöller was in contact with were Stefan George, Erich Maria Remarque, Rainer Maria Rilke, Arthur Schnitzler, and Frank Wedekind.

30 ▶ In the capital, he became co-founder and coordinator of the library committee of the "Deutsche Gesellschaft 1914," an exclusive club co-financed by Robert Bosch, in which everything of importance in business and culture was concentrated. See: Sösemann, in: Wilderotter, 1993, p. 169–178.

31 ▶ At the end of the 1920s, after Karl Gustav Vollmöller had written the text for the film classic "Der Blaue Engel" (The Blue Angel), he became friends with the leading actress Marlene Dietrich. See: Higham, 1978, p. 60.

32 ▶ Knoll, n.d., p. 17.

Leather book cover,
Stuttgart, around 1900

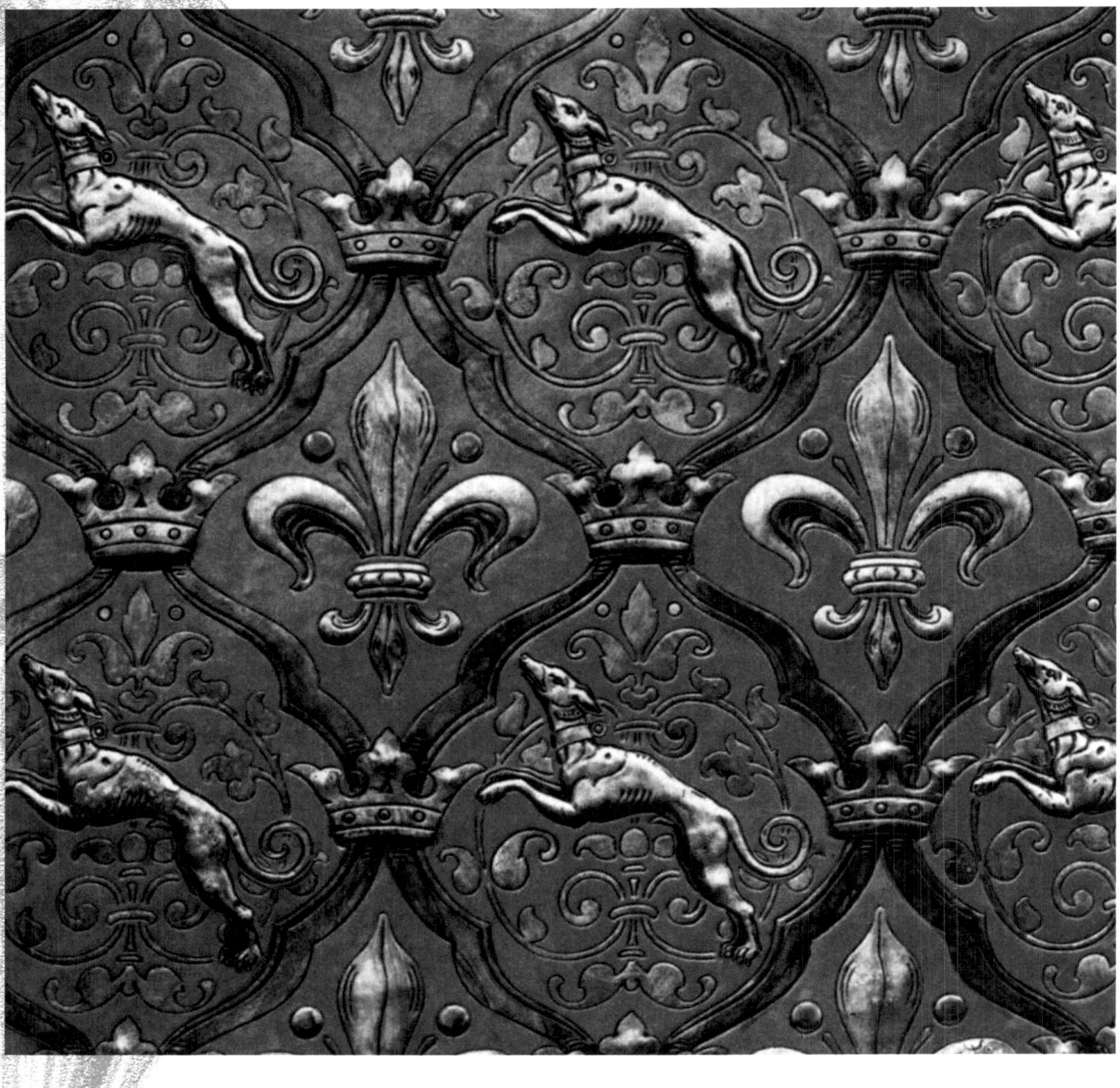

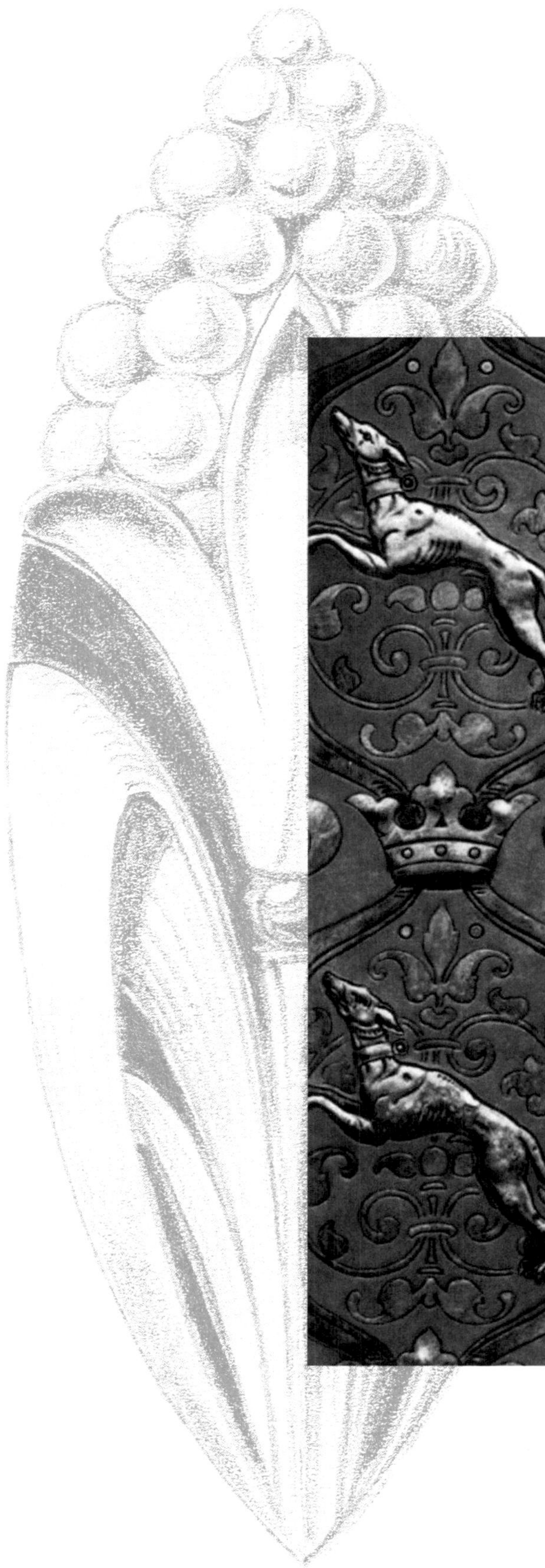

Sample drawing by a
cabinet maker,
Stuttgart, around 1910

PATTERN BOOKS

Elaborate techniques of leather processing such as punching were very popular. Pattern books contained the whole range of shapes used at that time.

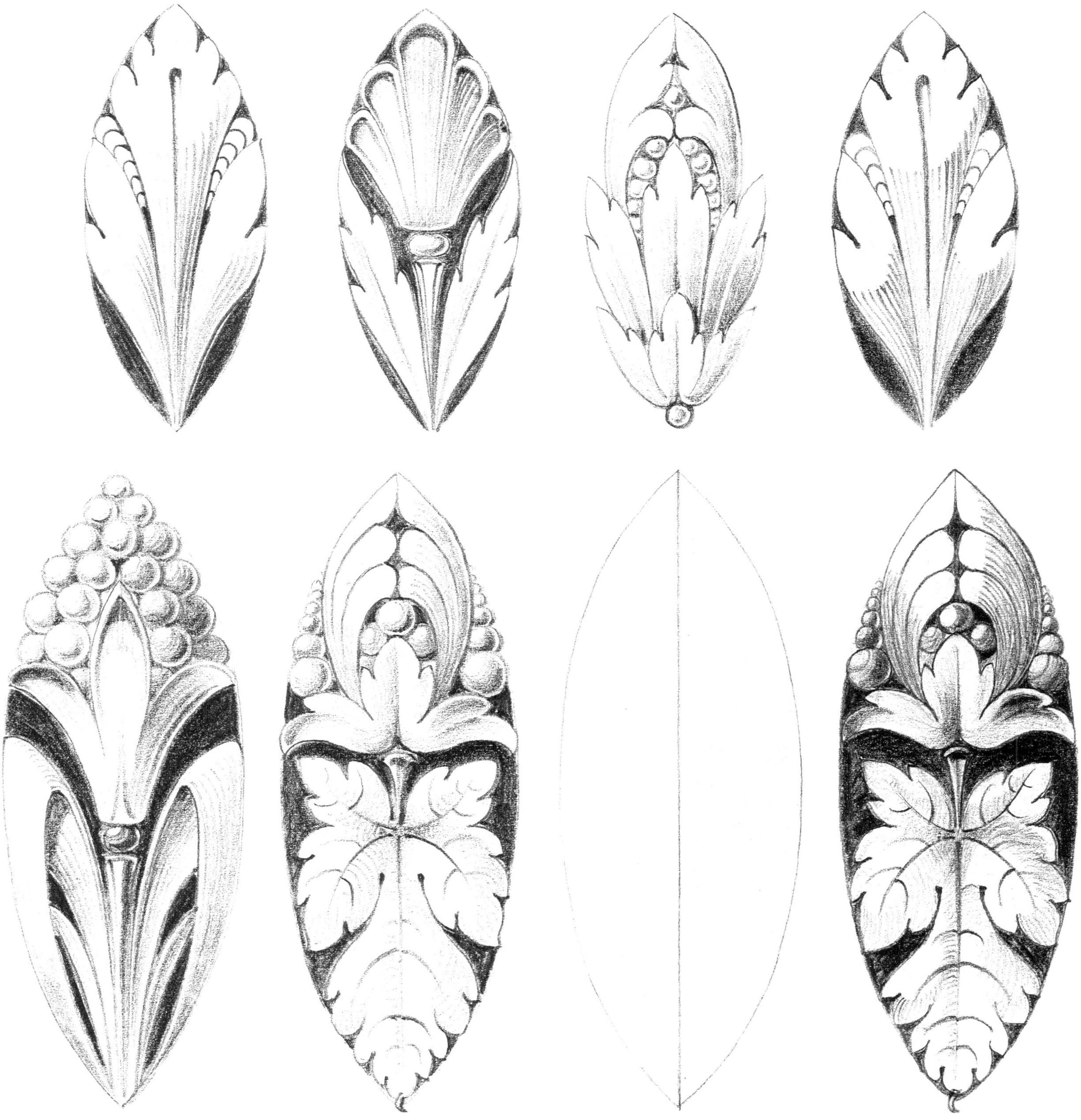

LANDESGEWERBEMUSEUM

Stuttgart's early economic miracle was largely based on clever promotion. The "Landesgewerbeamt" (State Trade Office), founded in 1848, advised companies and set up a patent archive. In 1896, it moved to a magnificent new building (today's "Haus der Wirtschaft"). Since then, top-class exhibitions have been held in the adjacent museum. Wilhelm Knoll produced his first furniture at this time.

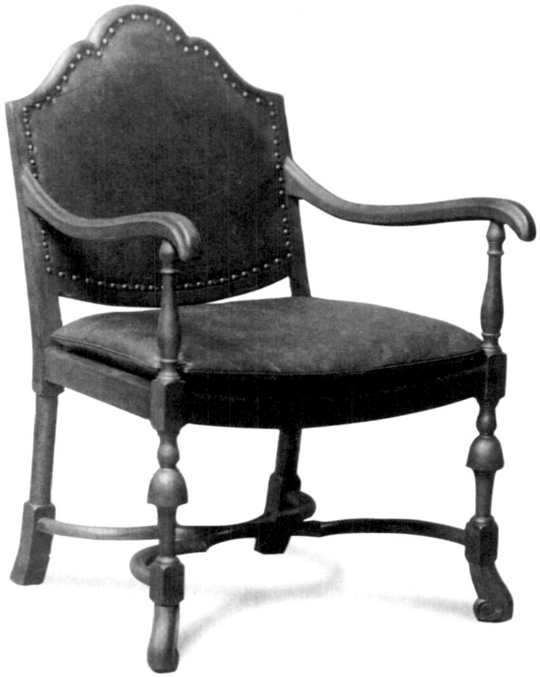

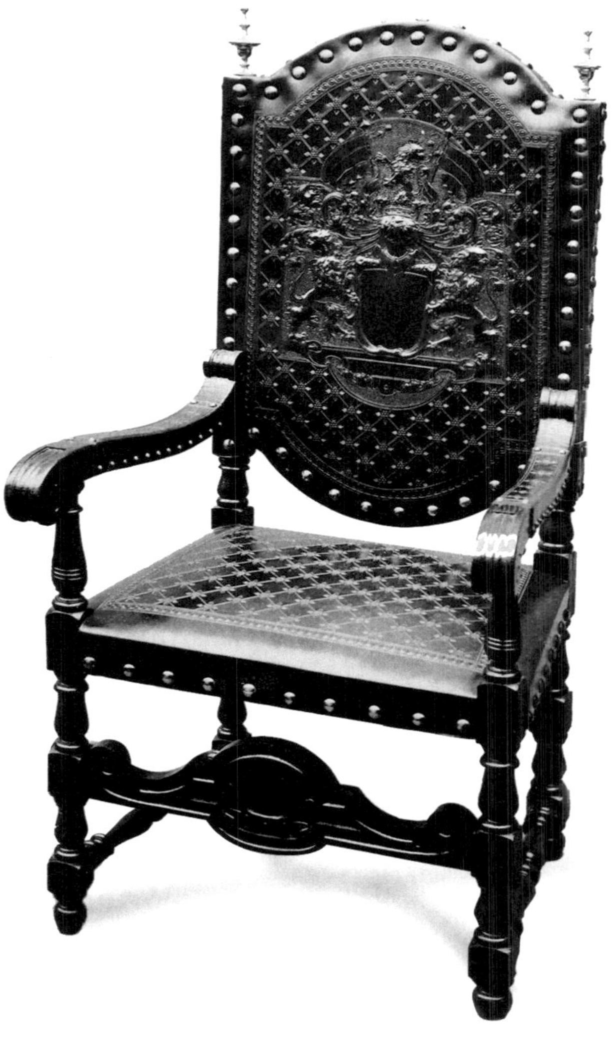

Armchair 3252, Wilhelm Knoll, Stuttgart, around 1900

Armchair 81, Wilhelm Knoll, Stuttgart, around 1890

Main entrance of the State Trade Museum, Stuttgart, around 1905

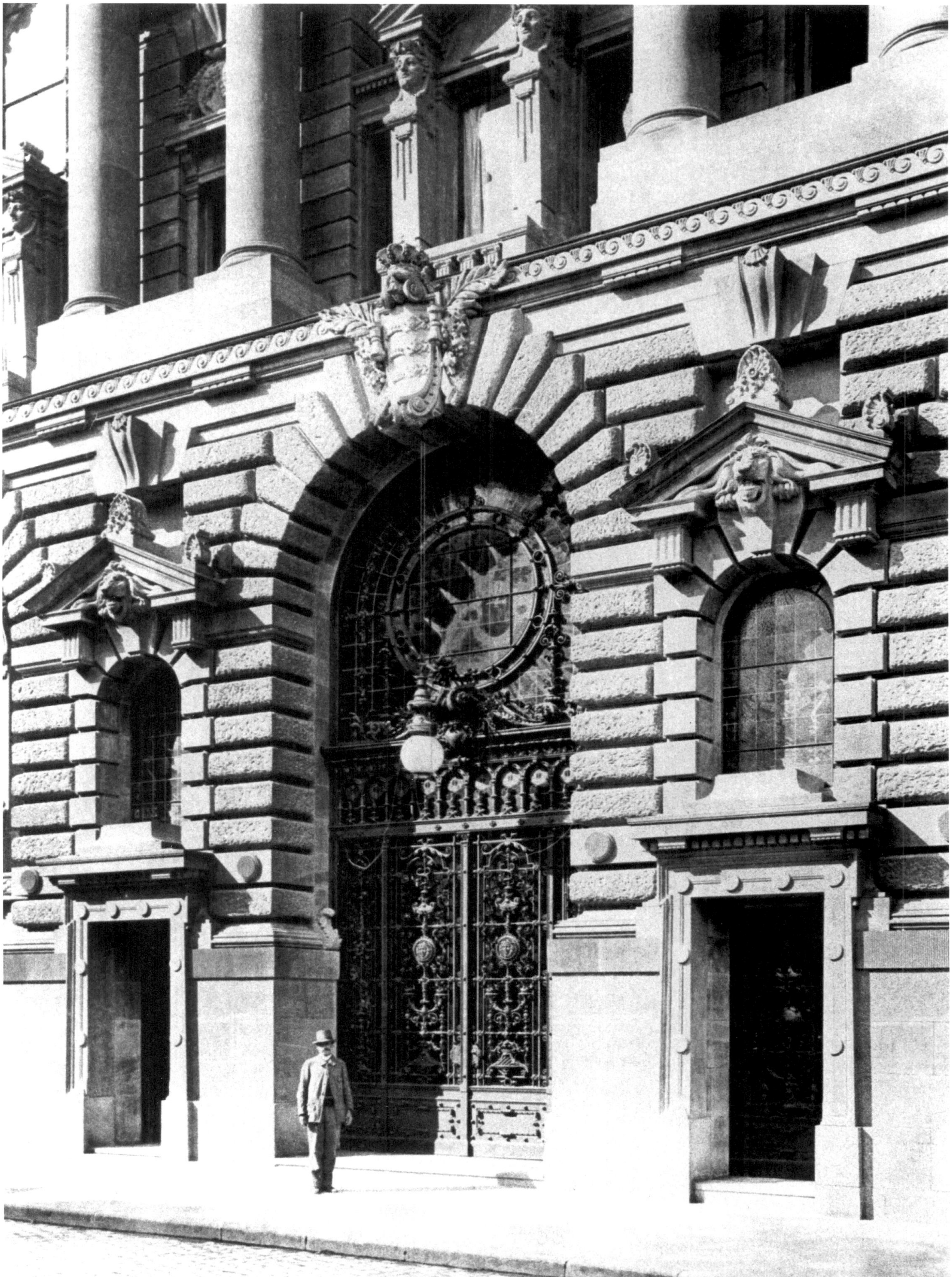

STYLE

In around 1900, Stuttgart-born Lucian Bernhard was one of the most successful graphic designers of the Reform Period and worked for numerous well-known companies. During this phase, Wilhelm Knoll also created chairs inspired by Art Nouveau.

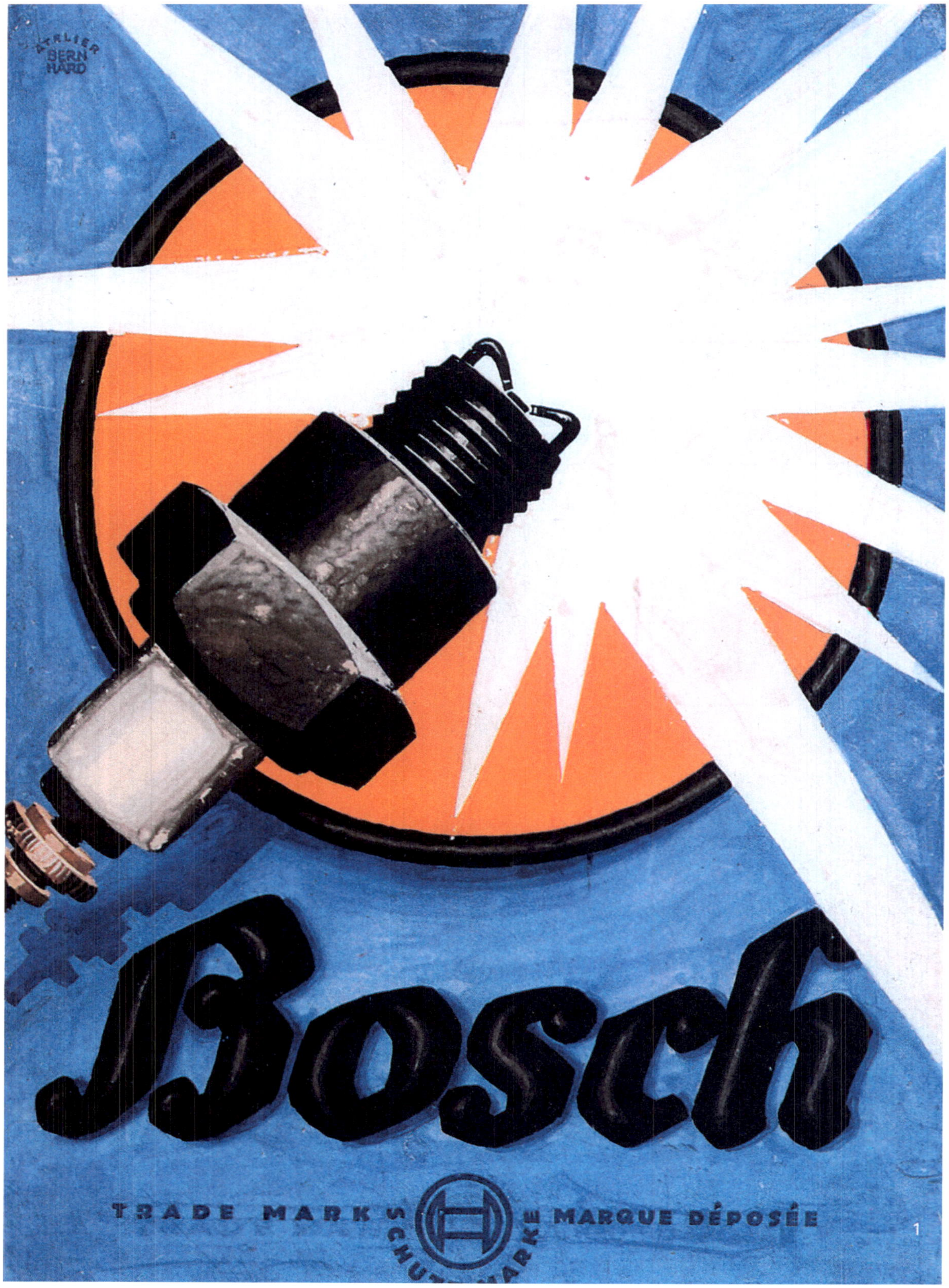

1

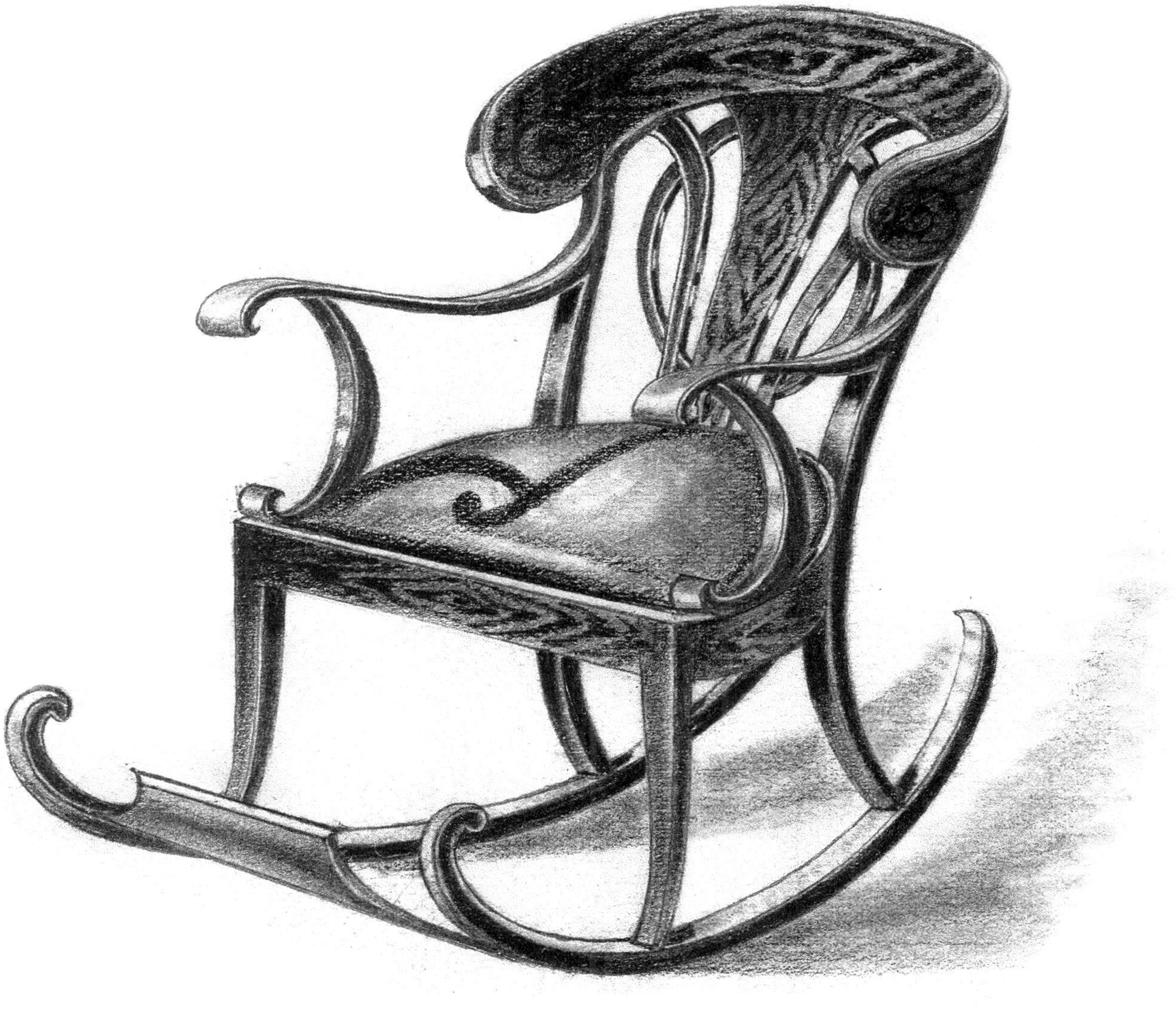

Advertising poster
designed by Lucian Bernhard,
around 1905

Sample drawing by a cabinet maker,
Stuttgart, around 1910

REFORM PERIOD

THE TRANSPOSED SUCCESSION

The enormous significance that immersion in the fascinating world of the Vollmöllers must have had for Walter becomes even clearer when we examine his background. He was one of countless victims of the merciless school system. He was a bad pupil – which, in those days, usually meant a double humiliation, both in class and at home. In addition, he was constantly compared to his older sister Helene and his younger brother Willy, who brought home nothing but good grades. That "naturally was a burden on my childhood soul," Walter remarked. The agony came to an end when he left school, the site of his ordeal, at the early age of 14. He then joined the Stuttgart-based company C. H. Burk, which was known for its peppermint-flavored "Kaiser pastilles" and also sold pharmaceutical products. There he completed a four-year apprenticeship, learning how to "manage the petty cash, register, run the postal service, address envelopes, and the like."[1] Life was certainly not easy. Nor did the fact that Walter was a life-affirming person bring him any solace. On the contrary, his father and his brother Willy, both believers well-versed in the Bible, found his talent for dancing and singing to be a rather alarming tendency. Wilhelm Knoll always spoke of Willy as "my star pupil," referring not only to school but also to succession. Under these circumstances, it was predictable that Walter, the older son, would lose out. That stung him and put a strain on his relationship with his father and brother.

WALTER HAD NOW BECOME A BIT OF AN ADVENTURER. HE WAS ALREADY EXPECTED ON THE QUAYSIDE IN MANHATTAN.

Walter's brief interlude as a traveling salesman for his parents' business came to an end in 1896. When Willy graduated from high school with honors the following year and then learned the leather business from the ground up, the circumstances were clear. In this muddled situation, a way out was finally found for the laggard, which was not so unusual at that time as it might seem today. Walter went to America to "prove it to his father," as he later said.[2] Already

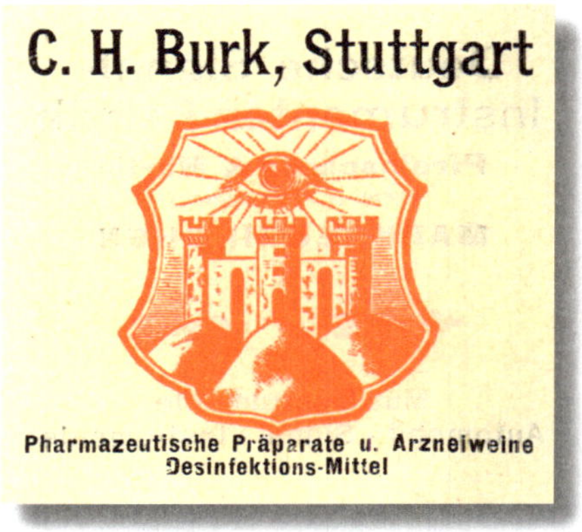

in the process of freeing himself from the shackles of his restrictive parental home, he ultimately succeeded in doing so on the basis of his experience and personality. In those days, problematic cases were often shipped overseas. That's why Walter Knoll was initially "slightly ashamed" – because he hadn't "done anything at all."[3] His father paid for the 21-year-old's crossing, the last time he spent any money on the son who had apparently turned out badly. Walter had now become a bit of an adventurer. He was already expected on the quayside in Manhattan. Mrs. Brown, who was once again living in New York, surprised her friend and helped the newcomer. The fact that there was a strong German ethnic group in America that played an important role in U.S. culture and economy also made things easier – if only in terms of language. In the beginning, Walter's English was anything but perfect. In New York, however, about one-third of the population lived in districts referred to at the time as "Little Germany."[4] Walter went to the German Club, met compatriots, and learned to box. He finally found a place with Schäfer, Schramm & Vogel, importers who sold Roeckl-brand leather gloves. So the job was also right. Walter was in charge of children's gloves. When he met Hermann Roeckl, the owner from Munich, Roeckl would have liked to have hired him permanently, but after two years, Walter returned home. Around the turn of the century, he worked for a while in his father's business, occasionally as a sales representative, only to learn that brother Willy, who had achieved considerable increases in sales since joining the company, now had the upper hand. Walter saw the writing on the wall and returned to America in 1901.

In those days, the U.S. was the land of progress and inventions, epitomized by Thomas Edison, to whom Robert Bosch had also been apprenticed a few years earlier. And it was no coincidence that the American and Swabian spirit of inventiveness entered into a liaison there. It was precisely this special connection between Stuttgart and New York that Walter Knoll attempted to exploit, particularly when he first tried his hand as an entrepreneur with the "Fortuna Machine Company." It was based on the company of the same name (that still exists today) founded by the Swabian Albert Hirth, an inventor who was also called the "Swabian Edison." Hirth, whose company was based in Cannstatt, owned numerous patents, including a gear cutter used by the watch company Junghans, among others, and an ignition device for Bosch. Robert Bosch saw Hirth as a pioneer in the mass production of precision instruments. Walter Knoll now pinned his hopes on Hirth's leather sharpening and cylindrical grinding machine: a piece of equipment that was to revolutionize shoe production. The following anecdote reveals the touching nature of the personal relationship between the Swabians on opposite sides of the Atlantic: once, when Walter visited Albert Hirth's factory at the end of the year, Hirth's wife asked him to take a Christmas parcel to her son in New York. When it was opened by customs, it was found to contain a hand-knit sweater and homemade biscuits. Walter successfully delivered the items. Walter Knoll became accustomed to the pace of the American way of life and felt quite at ease with it. In the meantime, a "Stuttgart clique" established itself in New York.

The young Swabian, initially insecure like all immigrants, now not only spoke perfect English but had also matured as a person. He made friends, including artists, and – what was very important to him – other "people who had little or nothing to do with the business."[5] Finally, he pursued his old passion and took singing lessons from an opera singer. At this time, he developed new business activities. He took charge of sales for the Stuttgart company Fein, a manufacturer of electric drills, and at the same time tried his hand at exporting American goods. In retrospect, they were, as he put it, "beautiful and stimulating times"[6] that made of him a different person. As a 30 year old, he was now familiar with the latest business methods, almost all of which came from the U.S. But his interests went far beyond that – which was and is a rare combination.

In 1907, when his father fell seriously ill, his brother Willy visited him in New York and was able to persuade him to return. Walter "gave up everything I had built up over six years,"[7] as he later noted with regret. His father died that same year and Willy took over the family business, which had recently relocated to Forststrasse 71. This remained the address of the head office for almost eight decades. For the first time, the company stood on its own property and, for the first time, the family lived in its own house. Willy Knoll quickly took the initiative, setting up his own dyeing and finishing plant[8] to ensure the quality of the products. A few years earlier, he had started producing leather upholstered furniture, a pioneering move that was to fundamentally change the company's character. It was now listed in the Stuttgart address book as a *Ledersitzmöbel-Fabrik* (leather seating furniture factory) and thus established a new segment. Since then, the most important products in the range have been modern armchairs and sofas.

WALTER KNOLL BECAME ACCUSTOMED TO THE PACE OF THE AMERICAN WAY OF LIFE AND FELT QUITE AT EASE WITH IT.

It soon became apparent to everyone involved that the fraternal quarrel would hardly allow for any fruitful cooperation. It was a lucky coincidence that the dynamic Willy had set up two new subsidiaries, one in St. Petersburg and one in Vienna. Brother Erich went to Russia. Walter and Maria Knoll, who were married that same year – Maria becoming "Maia" – moved to the city on the Danube in 1909. There, where their first son Robert was also born, they were to spend five happy years, despite Willy's "unfraternal conduct."[9] When they returned to Stuttgart in 1914, shortly before the outbreak of First World War, they moved to the comfortable Vollmöller estate on Hasenbergsteige. Their son Hans was born there that same year. The imperial villa, built by the now deceased father-in-law, was to be Maia and Walter's home for over forty years. There they raised their sons Robert, Hans, and Herbert, who were born between 1912 and 1919.[10]

---

1 ▶ Knoll, n.d., p. 12.

2 ▶ Schnermann, in: Janssen, 1999, p. 393.

3 ▶ Knoll, n.d., p. 26.

4 ▶ Winn 2013, p. 107.

5 ▶ Knoll, n.d., p. 45.

6 ▶ Knoll, n.d., p. 41.

7 ▶ Knoll, n.d., p. 47.

8 ▶ Leather that comes from the tannery is still damp and extremely unsightly. The last round before it can be included in the production process takes the leather to the finishing shop. This is the final treatment and includes drying, softening, and dyeing, as well as other refinements to the leather. See: Knoch, in: "Handbuch der Gerbereichemie und Lederfabrikation" (Manual of Tanning Chemistry and Leather Production), 1955, p. 42.

9 ▶ Knoll, n.d., p. 52.

10 ▶ Born in 1917, Walther died during his first year.

REFORM

Willy Knoll, Wilhelm's son, designed leather armchairs and sofas in the spirit of the Reform movement, which rejected everything plush. The title motif of Wilhelm Knoll's first catalog was created by the well-known graphic artist Lucian Bernhard.

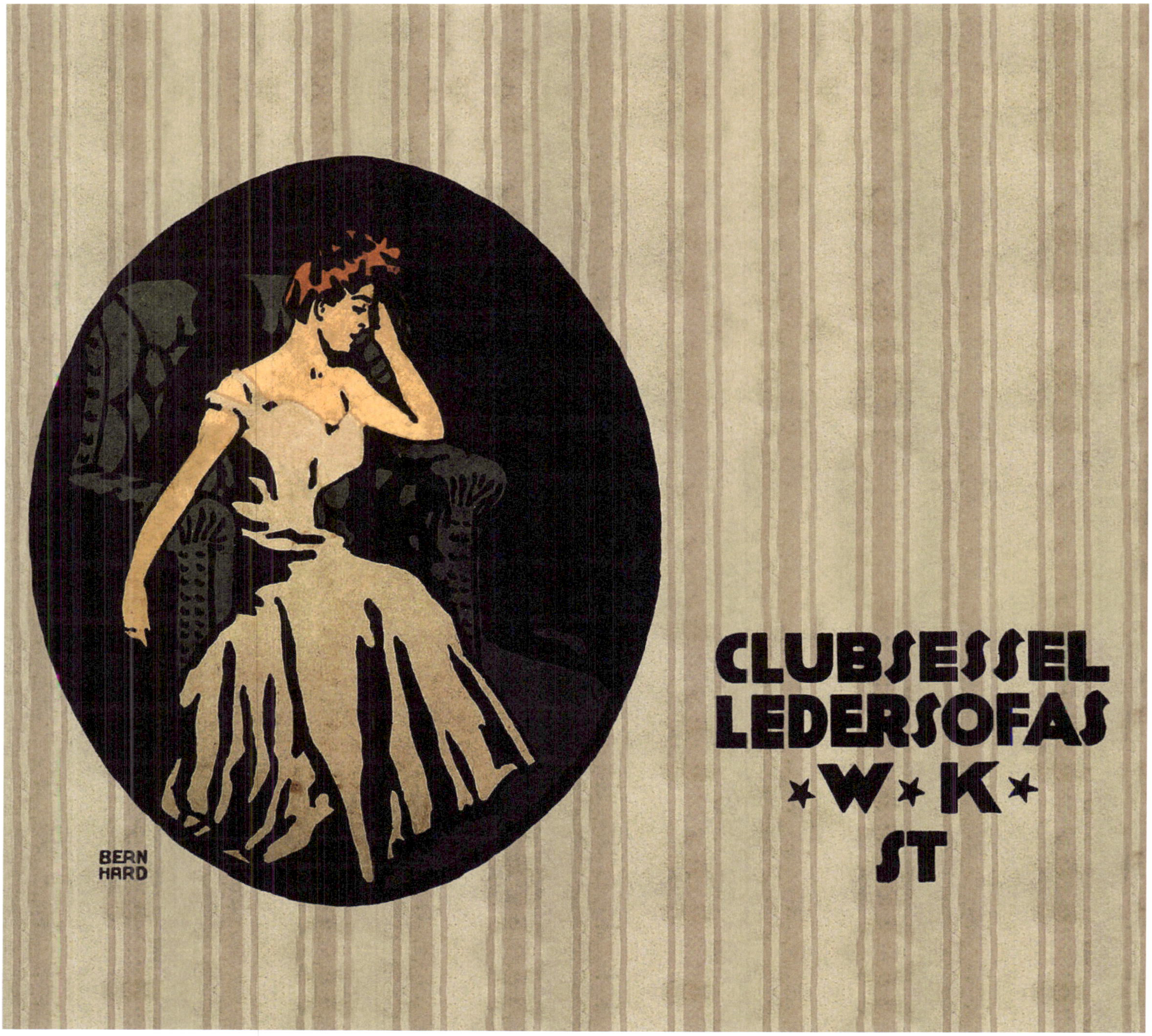

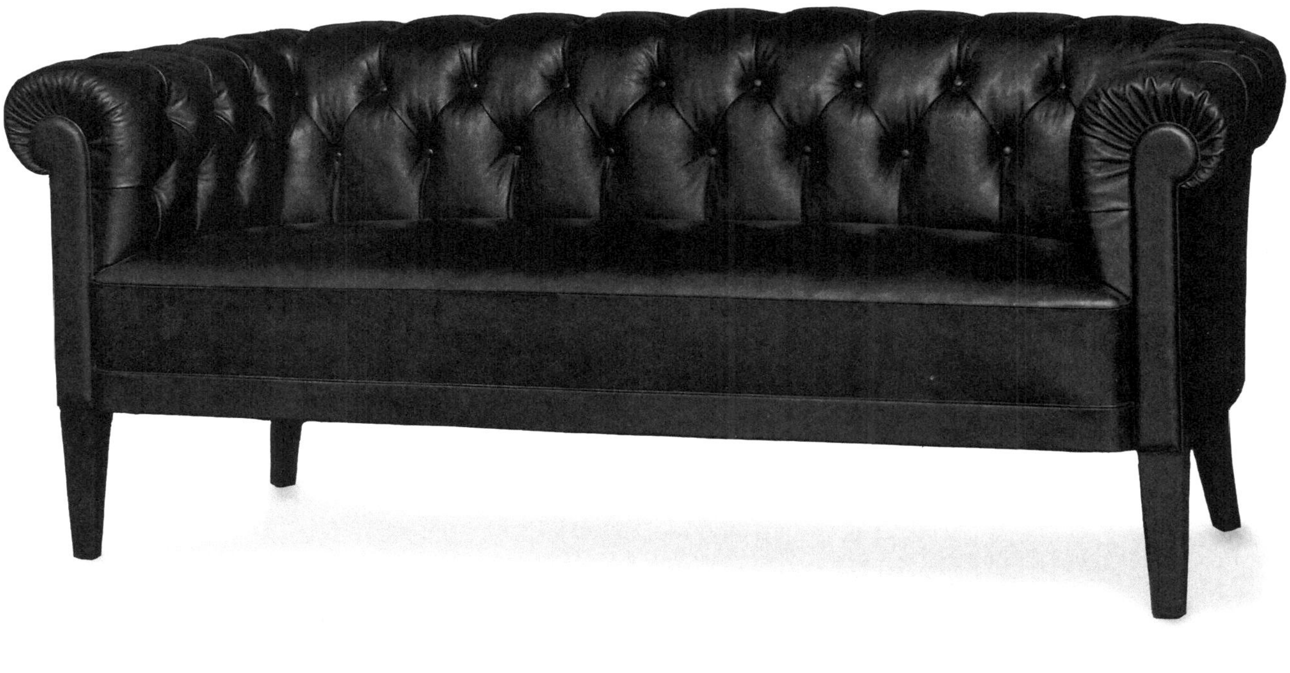

Catalog title, Wilhelm Knoll, design by Lucian Bernhard, Stuttgart 1908

Clubsofa 3215, Wilhelm Knoll, Stuttgart, around 1908

STUTTGART *WOHNUNGSKUNST*

Upon entering the room, one's eye was immediately drawn to the richly decorated wood paneling. It was adorned with a multitude of inlays, finely worked patterns that could be interpreted as natural motifs. The grand piano in the middle of the room also had ornaments on the top. The artistic originality and impressive quality of execution gave the room a festive atmosphere. This was the "Württembergisches Zimmer" (Württemberg Room) that the painter and interior designer Bernhard Pankok had designed on behalf of the Stuttgart "Centralstelle für Gewerbe und Handel" (Central Office for Trade and Commerce). Although not very large, it was evidently one of the highlights of the 1904 World's Fair in St. Louis, Missouri. It was a demonstration of Swabian *Wohnungskunst* (Art of Dwelling)[11], as it was then called, in which local trade and handicrafts entered into a symbiosis. Once

THE EARLY YEARS IN WHICH WILLY KNOLL HAD TO REORIENT HIMSELF AS A BUSINESSMAN CAME AT A TIME WHEN THE TECHNICAL REVOLUTION WAS JOINED BY ANOTHER REVOLUTION: THAT OF ART AND ESTHETICS.

again the "Centralstelle," which had since been renamed the "Kunstgewerbeamt" (Arts and Crafts Office), had set the right course and the artist Pankok had succeeded in taming the enormous variety of shapes by means of formal austerity. "Everything is subordinated to the great," praised one critic.[12] Thus an overall work of art was created of the kind that even normal citizens in possession of the necessary small change were striving to create in their own homes.

Not only did the German Reich lag far behind during industrialization, but it was also a straggler in terms of style and had been embarrassed time and again by patriotic kitsch at the World's Fairs of the late 19th century. On a relentless search for its own German style, it had not found it. In St. Louis, it was different. The German pavilion was a success. And it was precisely "the German arts and crafts exhibition that was to leave its mark as one of the main attractions."[13] The extensive presentation of new types of furnishings was "a milestone in the development of modern German *Wohnungskunst*" that "eclipsed the exhibitions of all the other countries."[14] Even if the chauvinism typical of the time was also blowing off steam, there was still some truth to it. Around the turn of the century, there had been an esthetic fracture in Germany that was later referred to as a "style revolution." Although "particularly in the case of elegant villas, architects still adhered to older shapes, this direction noticeably gave way to a more simple stylistic idiom,"[15] as was stated in the German catalog of the World's Fair, which itself was a striking example of the trend towards simplification.[16] The reduced Reform Style prevailed.[17] In St. Louis, it now became the official direction of the German Reich. The "Württembergisches Zimmer" (Württemberg Room) was an impressive example of this revolution.

The work done on Pankok's sensational room was carried out exclusively by local companies. The well-known Wölfel intarsia workshop, the Schiedmayer "Pianofortefabrik," the watchmaker Mauthe, and Georg Schöttle, Stuttgart's leading furniture store, were all involved. For the Wilhelm Knoll company, on the other hand, St. Louis came too early. Embossed leather was now considered old-fashioned and furniture production was still in its infancy. But Willy Knoll, now in his mid-twenties, was far too ambitious to miss the boat. He observed the changes around him closely. As someone who was about to enter the furniture business, he probably modeled himself after a top dog like Schöttle, especially since this long-established company was now a supplier of "Furniture and Spatial Art," which was just another way of saying *Wohnungskunst* (Art of Dwelling). He also noticed that Schöttle was trying to get close to Pankok.

The early years in which Willy Knoll had to reorient himself as a businessman came at a time when the technical revolution was joined by another revolution: that of art and esthetics. During the phase between the turn of the century and the First World War known as the Reform Period, a "simple stylistic idiom" prevailed in Germany that overcame not only the exaggerations of historicism but also the scarcely less exalted Art Nouveau. And Stuttgart, a stronghold of technical modernity, set out to become a center of artistic upheaval and combine the two. The all-round artist Pankok became a key figure in this complicated operation.

Bernhard Pankok, born in Münster in 1872, had studied painting in Munich in the 1890s, just as Art Nouveau was starting to emerge. He immersed himself in the Schwabing bohemic and became a co-founder of "Vereinigte Werkstätten" (United Workshops) in 1898.

This was an initiative of young painters who, inspired by Art Nouveau, switched to Applied Art, setting an avalanche in motion. Such ambitious alternative companies were soon established in numerous cities with the aim of redesigning everyday objects and furnishings according to artistic standards. These workshops became laboratories of the style revolution and at the same time were part of an even more comprehensive movement.

The German Reich was a land full of contradictions. Despite rapid changes, old habits died hard. The nobility and the military still set the jarring tone. The more unbearable these disparities became, the more frustration grew. Many people finally tried to escape the corset of Wilhelmine conventions. From this came a grassroots revolution that strove for a natural life and questioned everything that was sacred to the respectable citizen. Young people left the city like "migrating birds." Others ate organic food (which was soon available from the *Reformhaus* (health food store)), practiced nudism, or wore "Reform clothing." Consisting of countless small groups and cloaked in esotericism, a catchword was adopted that united the fragmented movement: *Lebensreform* (Life Reform).[18] From its bourgeois pole emerged the workshop movement, creating a new everyday esthetic in the form of furniture and other utensils and thus moving housing reform to the top of the social agenda. The enormous popularity of its protagonists alone shows how successful this movement was. Founders of Munich's "Vereinigte Werkstätten," such as the former painters Peter Behrens and Richard Riemerschmid, were no less famous than today's star architects and designers, and were soon overwhelmed with commissions from industry.

The Reform Style became a location phenomenon. And because Stuttgart already had an excellent understanding of location policy at that time, one of the important innovators was enlisted: Bernhard Pankok. In addition, the enterprising "Centralstelle" wanted to attract not only him but also the entire operations of the "Vereinigte Werkstätten" from the Isar to the Neckar. This ended in failure, not only because of the tight budget but also because of the resistance of the wary local trade. Nevertheless, in 1902, the 30-year-old Pankok was himself able to set up a "Lehr- und Versuchswerkstätte" (Teaching and Experimental Workshop) – a laboratory for the Reform Style – with royal approval. The fact that it was housed in a former prison was a source of various jokes for the enemies of change, who were to be found in abundance. Finally, in 1913, Pankok – who had already been in Stuttgart for ten years – moved to the new "Kunstgewerbeschule" at the Killesberg as its director. Its simple, unadorned architecture, which Pankok had to push through in the face of tough opposition, wasn't its only resemblance to the Weissenhofsiedlung (Weissenhof estate), which was built within sight of the school 14 years later.[19] Its teaching program was also focused on the future. Like the Bauhaus, it was based on the workshop principle and thus set the trend for other art and design colleges. Pankok's versatility made him a key figure in the cultural transformation of the city, which he as an architect enriched with further modern buildings.[20]

BERNHARD PANKOK EMBODIED THE SOLIDARITY BETWEEN ART AND TRADE.

Because he was also an outstanding portrait painter, his studio was a frequent haunt of Stuttgart's celebrities, including Robert Bosch and Graf von Zeppelin. The latter had previously commissioned him to furnish an airship gondola.[21] His design for a Lake Constance ferry was similarly spectacular. Ultimately, the very busy man was also enlisted by industry. He designed a series of models for Mauthe, a major Swabian watchmaker with well over a thousand employees. Bernhard Pankok embodied the solidarity between art and trade. It goes without saying that he was also a member of the "Deutscher Werkbund" (German Association of Craftsmen), which was established in 1907 at the height of the Reform Period and promoted this very symbiosis.

---

11 ▶ Muthesius, 1905, p. 209.

12 ▶ Klein, in: "Stuttgarter Mitteilungen über Kunst und Gewerbe" (Stuttgart Communications on Art and Trade), 1904/05, p. 154.

13 ▶ Muthesius, 1905, p. 209.

14 ▶ Ibid.

15 ▶ German Reich / World's Fair, St. Louis, 1904, p. 161.

16 ▶ Catalog designer Peter Behrens even set all the advertisements in the same typeface which he, of course, had created.

17 ▶ Polster et al. 2009, p. 16 et seq.

18 ▶ Gustav Jäger and his "normal clothing" formed a new ethic in Reform fashion. Thus the nature apostle Gustav Gräser lived among the vineyards around Stuttgart, a preacher against civilization who became an early ancestor of the hippies, including flowing clothing and long hair. Rudolf Steiner, pioneer of Reform pedagogy, set up a kindergarten for the Stuttgart cigarette factory Waldorf.

19 ▶ This dispute was also called the "Pankok scandal."

20 ▶ Among other things, the studio for the "Württembergischer Kunstverein" and Haus Rosenfeld, a villa that he made into a complete work of art and that is regarded as his most important work.

21 ▶ His designs of tubular metal armchairs and couches (made of lightweight aluminum) failed due to the resistance of conservative engineers.

CLUB CHAIR

Simple models in sophisticated execution: the club chair was Wilhelm Knoll's first furniture innovation and a tribute to the Reform Period before the First World War.

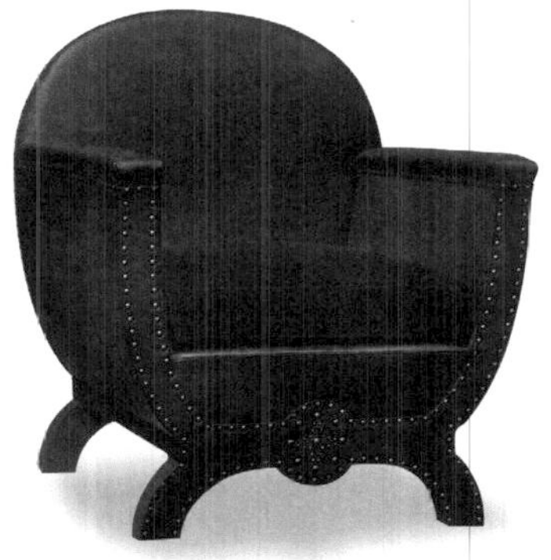

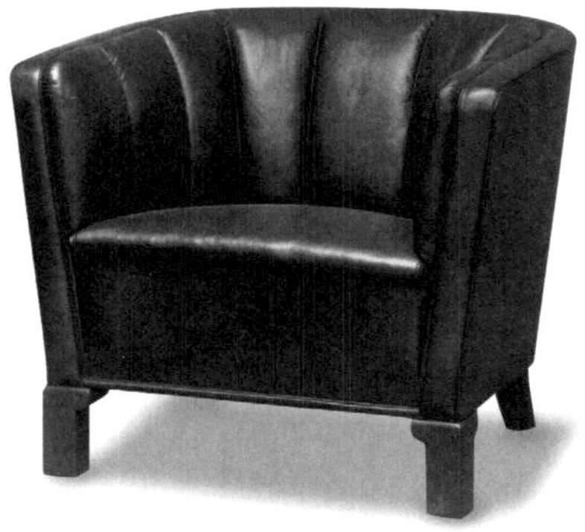

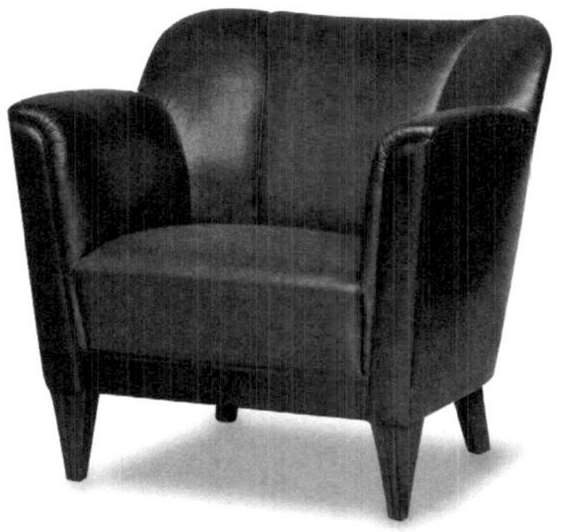

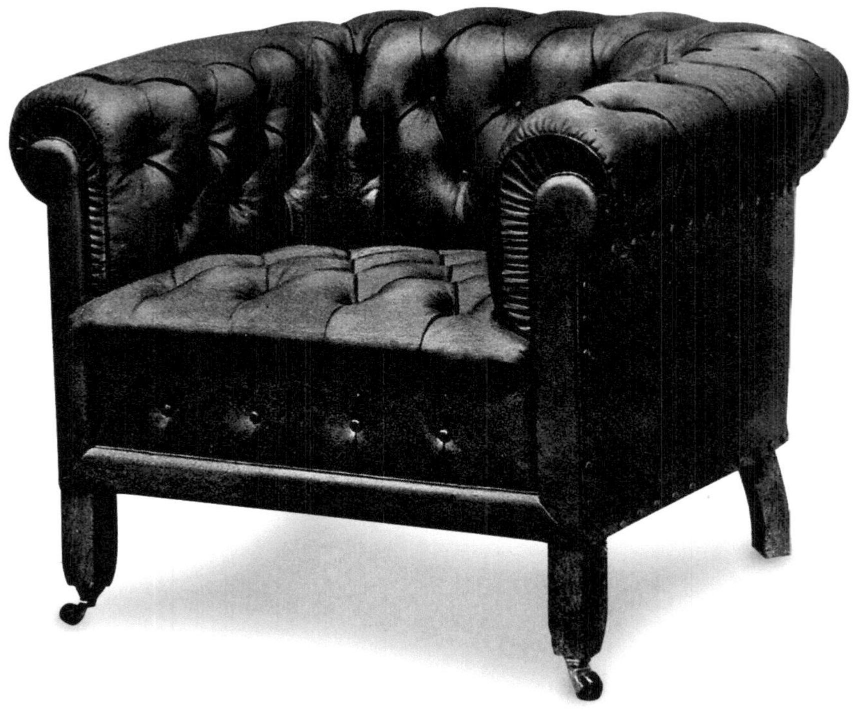

Chair 3114, Wilhelm Knoll, Stuttgart 1912

Chair 3173, Wilhelm Knoll, Stuttgart 1910

Chair 3207, Wilhelm Knoll, Stuttgart 1912

Club chair 3212, Wilhelm Knoll, Stuttgart 1907

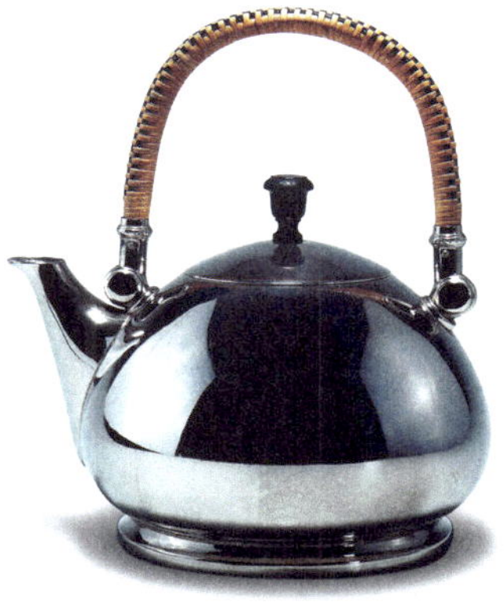

The kettle designed in the Reform Style by Peter Behrens for AEG in 1909 is regarded as an early highlight of industrial design.

Bernhard Pankok created the interior design for the Rosenfeld house in Stuttgart in 1910. That same year, Willy Knoll published his catalog of club chairs.

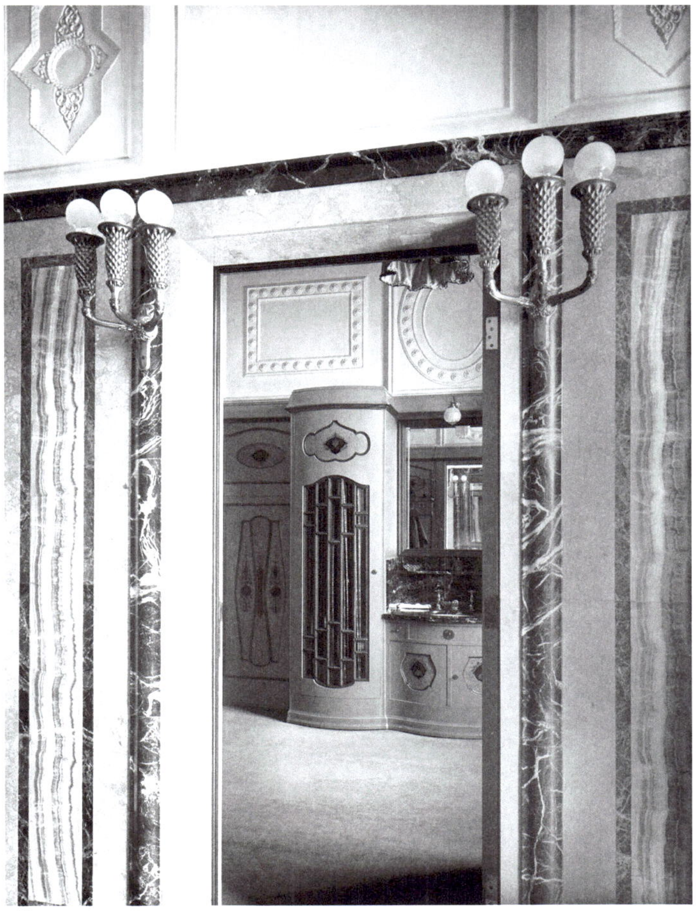

The currents of the Reform Period came together in this influential institution, which was then headed by the Swabians Bruckmann and Heuss. So improbable does it seem to us today that living, including furniture and household effects, was at the center of all this, that it's worth repeating here. The fact that seating furniture is still regarded today as the premiere league of design is probably also a legacy of this early period.

In addition to the "Kunstgewerbeamt" (Arts and Crafts Office), the "Kunstgewerbeschule" (School of Arts and Crafts), and the "Werkbund" (Association of Craftsmen), there was another institution in Stuttgart that intensified the esthetic upheaval: the "Landesgewerbemuseum" (State Trade Museum) founded shortly before the turn of the century, it received a new director in 1906: Gustav Pazaurek. This art historian from Bohemia had the brilliant idea of launching an original and completely new educational campaign by showing negative examples of design. In 1909, he set up a department for "Misapprehensions of Taste in Arts and Crafts," popularly known as the "Kitsch Museum." It was a resounding success. There were now also dedicated magazines

THE STYLE REVOLUTION OF THE REFORM PERIOD WAS NO MARGINAL PHENOMENON, BUT NEITHER WAS IT AN ATTEMPT TO OVERTHROW EVERYTHING, AS WAS ART NOUVEAU.

for the dominant reformist-artistic style. The two most important were "Innen-Dekoration" (Interior Decoration) and "Deutsche Kunst und Dekoration" (German Art and Decoration). Both titles were published by Alexander Koch, who had moved his headquarters from Stuttgart to Darmstadt around the turn of the century because the world's first model estate had been built there in 1901. It had been completely designed by artists, and a quarter of a century later was also a model for Weissenhof. As early as 1898, Koch, together with the furniture stores Schöttle in Stuttgart and Buyten in Düsseldorf, had organized a "prize competition" for "dignified, simple modern designs for real furniture intended for everyday use"[22] and advertised it in his magazines. The prize money was an impressive 2,000 Marks, equivalent to a good annual salary. For all those who wanted to know what was happening on the Reform scene, Koch's magazines were compulsory reading. Willy Knoll also read them, of course, and carefully studied the many photos showing modern "Spatial Art." In the next generation – and in the one that followed during the Second Modernity after 1945 – the Knoll family of factory owners and the Koch family of publishers, both now back in Stuttgart, were close friends.

The style revolution of the Reform Period was no marginal phenomenon, but neither was it an attempt to overthrow everything, as was Art Nouveau. It took place gradually, but inexorably. After all, even in "conservative circles, one felt the need for simple and smooth furniture," but still "turned to the Empire style, primarily the English form of the same intended for the town house."[22] The manufacturers responded to the new preferences. "Seating furniture is given a variety of shapes, the designs of different bodies are given nestling forms," wrote an industry expert at that time, "and everything is kept so lightweight that the furniture can be grouped according to the need of the moment. Invention in this field has been so active that it has not yet become a fixed type."[23] This reads as though Willy Knoll had used Reform trends as an instruction manual for his own upholstery collection. He largely dispensed with ornaments in sharp contrast to the exuberantly decorative era before the turn of the century. He almost exclusively used smooth leather, preferably in a serious, masculine black. Although most Knoll armchairs of this early period were anything but lightweight, they were mostly fitted with casters so that they could be easily moved. In fact, in terms of shapes and proportions, Wilhelm Knoll also did a lot of experimenting. The range of armchair and sofa models was correspondingly wide. Nevertheless, the furniture newcomer Knoll soon managed to accomplish what was otherwise scarcely possible during this phase of reorientation – to establish a type. The club chair, also initially called the "Clubfauteuil," was a new concept in the furniture industry from which "the Stuttgart leather furniture industry developed."[24] The original came from Wilhelm Knoll.

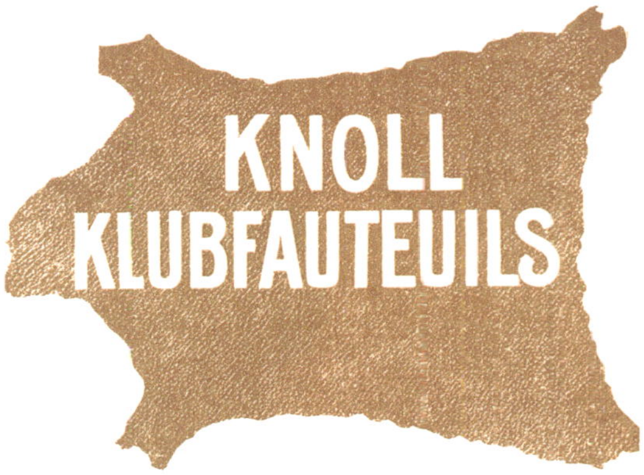

The term "fauteuil" refers to the origin of this innovation: it is the Austrian or Viennese word for armchair – borrowed, of course, from the French. The term migrated, so to speak, from Versailles to Schönbrunn. Vienna, with its Reform workshops and art secessionists, was now also a hub of creative upheaval. Josef Hoffmann, one of the most prominent representatives, designed a leather armchair in 1910, which is now sold as a Club and was most probably originally also called a Clubfauteuil because Hoffmann, a professor at the "Kunstgewerbeschule" and member of the Secession, was of course Austrian. At that time, Walter Knoll had been head of the Vienna subsidiary for just one year. He later indicated that a Viennese named Löbl had developed the first club chair for the Wilhelm Knoll company in 1908. There is also a photo from that same year that shows him posing beside a club chair, supposedly the first one by Wilhelm Knoll. It makes Walter look as chic as a German dandy, despite his white smock (see p. 6). The armchair bears little resemblance to what we imagine nowadays to be a club chair. So if the inspiration did come from Vienna, Walter may have been the mediator. In fact, models soon appeared in the Wilhelm Knoll catalog that were reminiscent of designs created in the vicinity of the "Wiener Werkstätte" (Vienna Workshop). These included an armchair reduced to the geometry of a cube, which was daring for the time, and was exactly what brought Josef Hoffmann his fame.

The word "club" is of English origin and had positive connotations, above all in better and more conservative circles, and especially in the area of seating furniture. In fact, clubs were also very popular in Germany in around 1900 as a meeting place for men. They acted as points of contact for those who had influence and wanted to be on their own. The word "club" signals this exclusivity, unlike the German term "Verein" (association). London's "gentlemen's clubs," where manners were supposedly as sophisticated as the upholstery or leather furniture, acted as approximate models. Comfortable furnishings in the club rooms were naturally a part of this. And because the gents wanted to make themselves comfortable with small talk and whisky drinking, they preferred to sink into upholstered furniture of the finer sort. However, it is incorrect to conclude from this that club chairs had already existed in England in a certain, standardized form before the First World War. Not even the word existed in English-speaking countries.

The allegedly classic "Chesterfield," the quilted version with connected backrests and wings of the same height and the typical decorative button trimming that we consider to be the club chair par excellence is actually one of many. The brand is in any case a much later phenomenon, dating back to the 1930s. So this is a backward projection, a typical example of an "invented tradition"[25] such as is commonly found in English culture of the early 20th century. In fact, it appears that it was Willy Knoll who deliberately introduced the name "Clubsessel" (club chair). Subsequently, it became such a familiar German expression for a period of several decades that even Marcel Breuer used it for his first tubular steel chair, although everyone thought and still thinks of it as typically English.

THE CLUB CHAIR WAS A NEW CONCEPT IN THE FURNITURE INDUSTRY. THE ORIGINAL CAME FROM WILHELM KNOLL.

Willy Knoll's willingness to open himself up to new trends was unmistakable – without his already belonging to the circle of modernists. Shortly before the First World War, however, he finally came into direct contact with the Reform scene. The first external artist of

---

22 ▶ German Reich / World's Fair, St. Louis 1904, p. 162.

23 ▶ Ibid.

24 ▶ Knoll, n.d., p. 36.

25 ▶ The historian Eric Hobsbawm coined this term. See: Hobsbawm and Ranger, 1992.

ARTS AND CRAFTS

Opened in 1913, the "Kunstgewerbeschule" at Weissenhof finally turned Stuttgart into a center of modernity. Its architect and first director, the painter Bernhard Pankok, was a leading representative of the Reform movement. He designed houses as complete works of art in which all the details were coordinated.

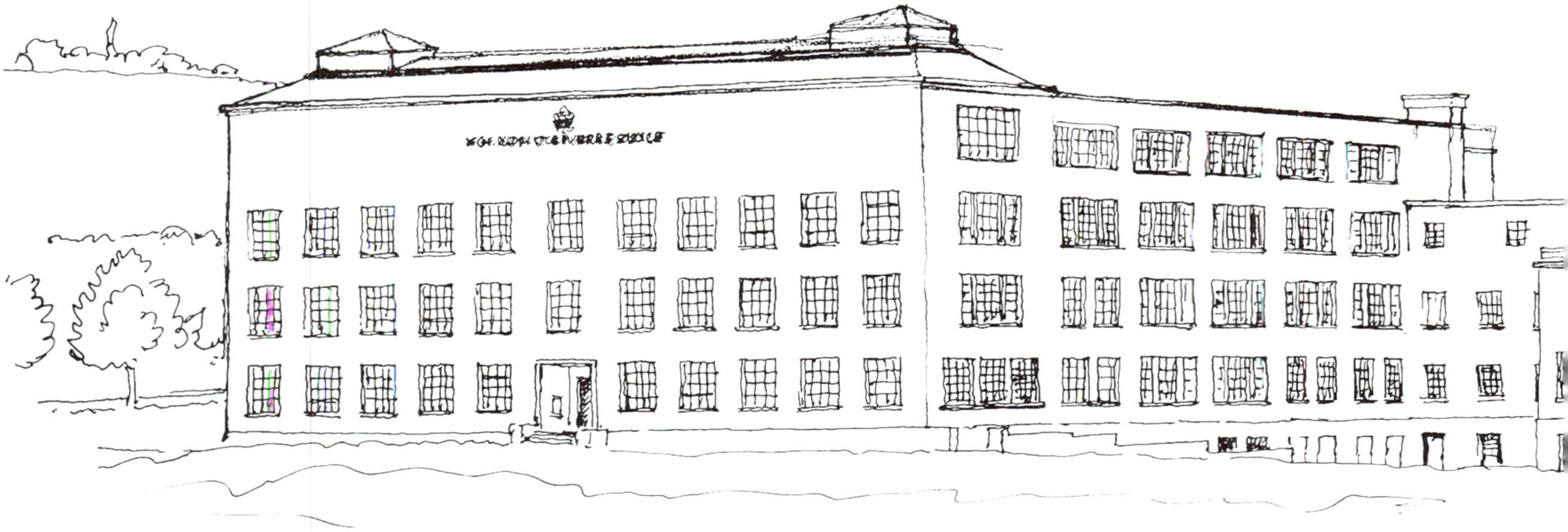

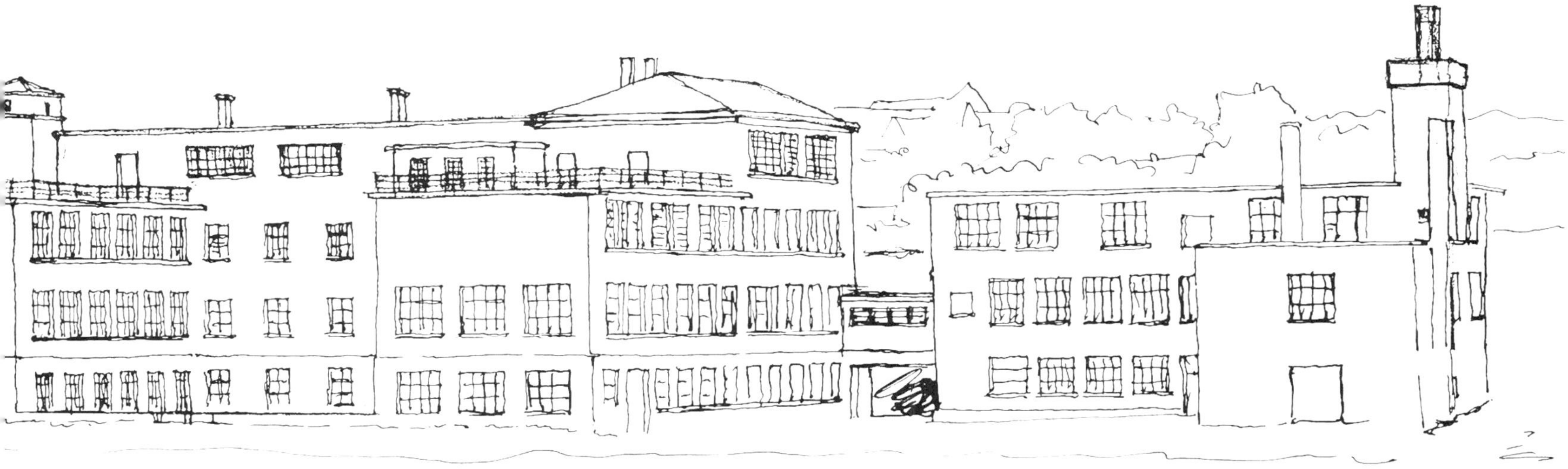

Sketch of the "Kunstgewerbeschule"
from the east,
design by Bernhard Pankok,
Stuttgart 1912/13

KNOLL
Leder · Ledermöbel

note to work for Wilhelm Knoll, the graphic artist Lucian Bernhard, was of an extremely high caliber. The Stuttgart-born artist, who had studied art in Munich, first made his name in Germany, and later in the U.S. His distinctive visual style made Bernhard perhaps the most famous graphic artist of the Reform Period. He invented important typefaces and created a new, expressive visual language, especially on his posters, which was characterized by simplicity, strong color contrasts, and the thrifty but effective use of typography. Posters that he designed for well-known brands became icons, including some motifs for Bosch, which are considered classics (see p. 22). Ultimately, this highly sought-after artist also worked for Wilhelm Knoll, a lightweight in terms of capital compared to his other customers from heavy industry. It is highly probably that the connection was made through Bosch or other reformers on the hillside. Perhaps Walter acted as a messenger. In 1908, Bernhard designed a cover for a furniture catalog featuring the main products at that time, club chairs and leather sofas (see p. 26). Thus, Willy Knoll used the term as a type two years before Hoffmann brought out his version. The catalog shows the high-contrast, abstract outlines of a woman seated on a quilted armchair whose facial appearance and hairstyle resemble the "Gibson Girl," an ideal of beauty at the time. In addition, he had set the title entirely in uppercase letters in a clear, uniform, solid typeface. The narrow "S" with slanted ends, which clearly falls outside the grid, is unusual. Below it are the letters "WK" and "ST," the abbreviation for "Wilhelm Knoll Stuttgart," which had already been used before. Here, however, it appears as a stylized trademark, at that time a novelty for the company. Although this graphic masterpiece signaled brand-new approaches to the company's image, the collaboration was apparently not continued. Perhaps it fell victim to the sharp pencil of the Swabian merchant Willy Knoll, because Bernhard certainly understood his own value and would not have come at a bargain price.

Or perhaps the young entrepreneur Willy Knoll simply had other priorities. At that time, he placed ads for a new product, the Derby armchair. It was "easily adjustable by pressing the button from the seat," a small mechanical marvel from the Swabian inventor's workshop. Such technical refinements – including heavy armchairs that could be disassembled for transport using a sophisticated plug-in system – became a specialty. Thus, Wilhelm Knoll distinguished itself from the usual crowd of upholstered furniture manufacturers. The fact that Wilhelm Knoll's furniture now bore a name that would lend it significance was not at all to be taken for granted. It underscored its exclusivity. With the model name Derby, which Willy Knoll protected as a registered design, the company once again relied on the English card, as it had previously done for the club chair. Now the allusion to horse racing was added, including associations with sport, ladies, and dandies. The main clientele was high society. Furniture by Wilhelm Knoll had to be sophisticated but by no means old-fashioned.

Shortly before the First World War, Nestra arrived, a project that was to mark the start of a new era. In 1912, a separate company was even founded for this purpose – Nestra-Gesellschaft. The meaning of this neologism is unknown. Nevertheless, Nestra was a novelty, a brand within a brand. This principle by means of which Wilhelm Knoll set itself apart from the rest of the industry became the leitmotif of the company's history. The practical purpose of this spin-off can only be surmised. It certainly reflected the importance that Willy Knoll attached to the project. It was all about innovative armchairs that fundamentally differed from the previous, fully upholstered models, because their sales were declining. Willy Knoll himself now wanted to develop seating as he knew it from Reform magazines. He by no means copied it but sought his own way, with his own company.

Although these armchairs were not to be around for long, they changed the Knoll project forever. The process was extremely systematic. It started with penetrating the interior of the furniture, so to speak, and breaking it down into its components, analytically and practically. The upholstery and the wooden frame were designed separately. At Nestra, the aim was to combine the technical and esthetic aspects of design. This was also supported by the fact that they were also working on improving the suspension. That the frames were now partially visible was a side effect. There were two other decisive benefits: the simplification of the manufacturing process and the possibility of accelerating the development of new models. It was now also easier to change the details of the design, thereby varying models and being able to respond to special requests. In addition, this new seating furniture gave the impression of being much lighter-weight, thus corresponding to the Reform Period's ideas of functional furniture. From a typological point of view, the Nestra models were based on the women's armchair, which was smaller and lighter, and now moved to the center of the range under a different name. Casters could also be eliminated. The armchairs created during this period, with their flat down cushions and wooden bodies mostly covered in leather, looked as modern as the young men of the time with their smoothly shaved chins. The long beards of the imperial period were dispensed with.

In June 1914, the three Knoll brothers – Erich, Willy, and Walter – met at a café in Munich's Hofgarten to discuss the future. Suddenly, the papers issued special editions: "murder of the Austrian heir to the throne Franz Ferdinand and his wife," shouted the newspaper boys. It was not a good omen. The First World War, which began soon afterward and buried the supposed glory of the empire forever, also marked a turning point in the history of the Knoll furniture family. Production was forced to switch to items that could be used for military purposes, such as ammunition bags and horse saddles. Clearly, in contrast to the general martial rage, neither Walter nor

IN JUNE 1914, THE THREE KNOLL BROTHERS – ERICH, WILLY AND WALTER – MET AT A CAFÉ IN MUNICH'S HOFGARTEN TO DISCUSS THEIR JOINT FUTURE.

Willy Knoll felt inclined to add to the glory of the fatherland on the battlefield. Willy Knoll, initially commissioned by the Württemberg War Ministry to head a leather cutting factory, withdrew from further deployment by moving his residence to Switzerland – then the traditional emigration destination for Germans who wanted to avoid the draft, including numerous avant-garde artists. The fact that Willy Knoll founded a company there and did not return home until 1921 demonstrates how serious a matter this was for him. One plausible explanation for his temporary emigration was his strong religious conviction, which did not allow him to carry a weapon. This, of course, ran contrary to the patriotic frenzy that was now gripping the whole of Germany. Switzerland was neutral and, like Swabia, a stronghold of Pietism.[26] The Swiss episode is not mentioned in any company chronicle. Nor is it possible to find out who was in charge of Forststrasse in Stuttgart in the interim.

It cannot have been Walter, the older brother. He was recalled from the Belgian front, where he served for a short time, as no longer "fit for field service." Thereafter, however, he took over the management of an "inspection office" vital to the war effort at the Daimler works in Untertürkheim. Here, among other things, he was involved in the construction of a body shop. The reasons for his probably life-saving transfer at this stage are unknown. When Germany was defeated and the war was over, the Württemberg king, like all other German monarchs, stepped down silently from his throne. As far as the leather business was concerned, important foreign relations were disrupted. In view of the shortage of materials and the collapse of the old system, the economic prospects seemed extremely bleak.

26 ▶ Knoll, n.d., p. 62; spoken interview with Michael Knoll on 04/22/2015.

SPATIAL ARTISTS

The modern furnishing of a home is now called "Spatial Art." The spatial artists of the Reform Period were the first designers. The shapes of the Wilhelm Knoll company's leather armchairs also became clearer.

Reform armchair 2176, Wilhelm Knoll, Stuttgart 1913

Kitchen in Villa Rosenfeld, design by Bernhard Pankok, Stuttgart 1911

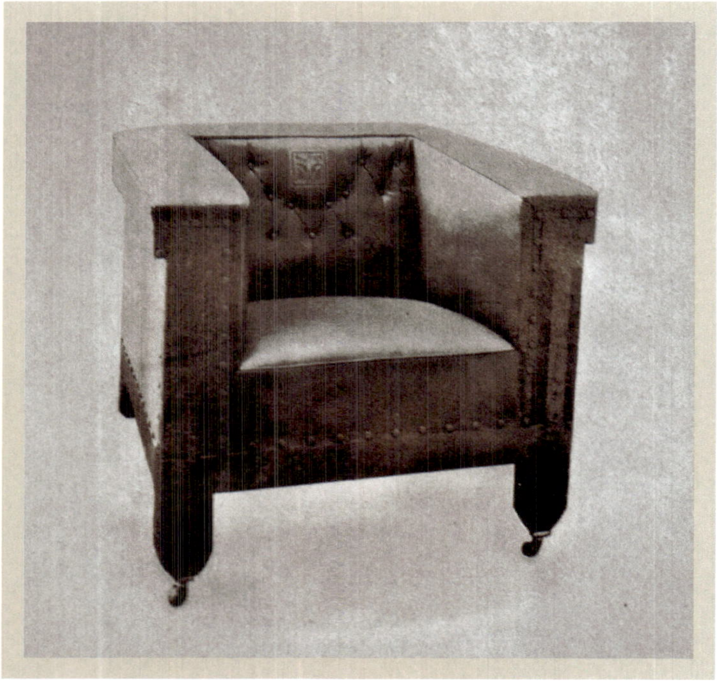

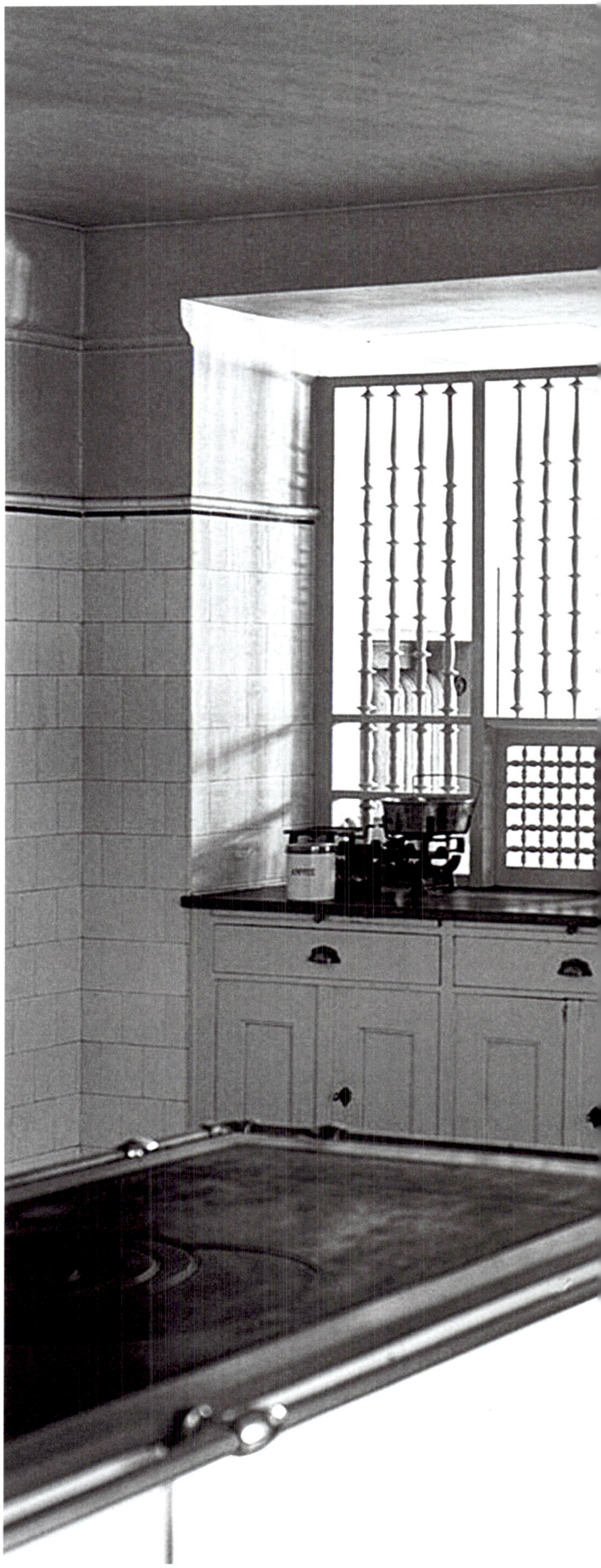

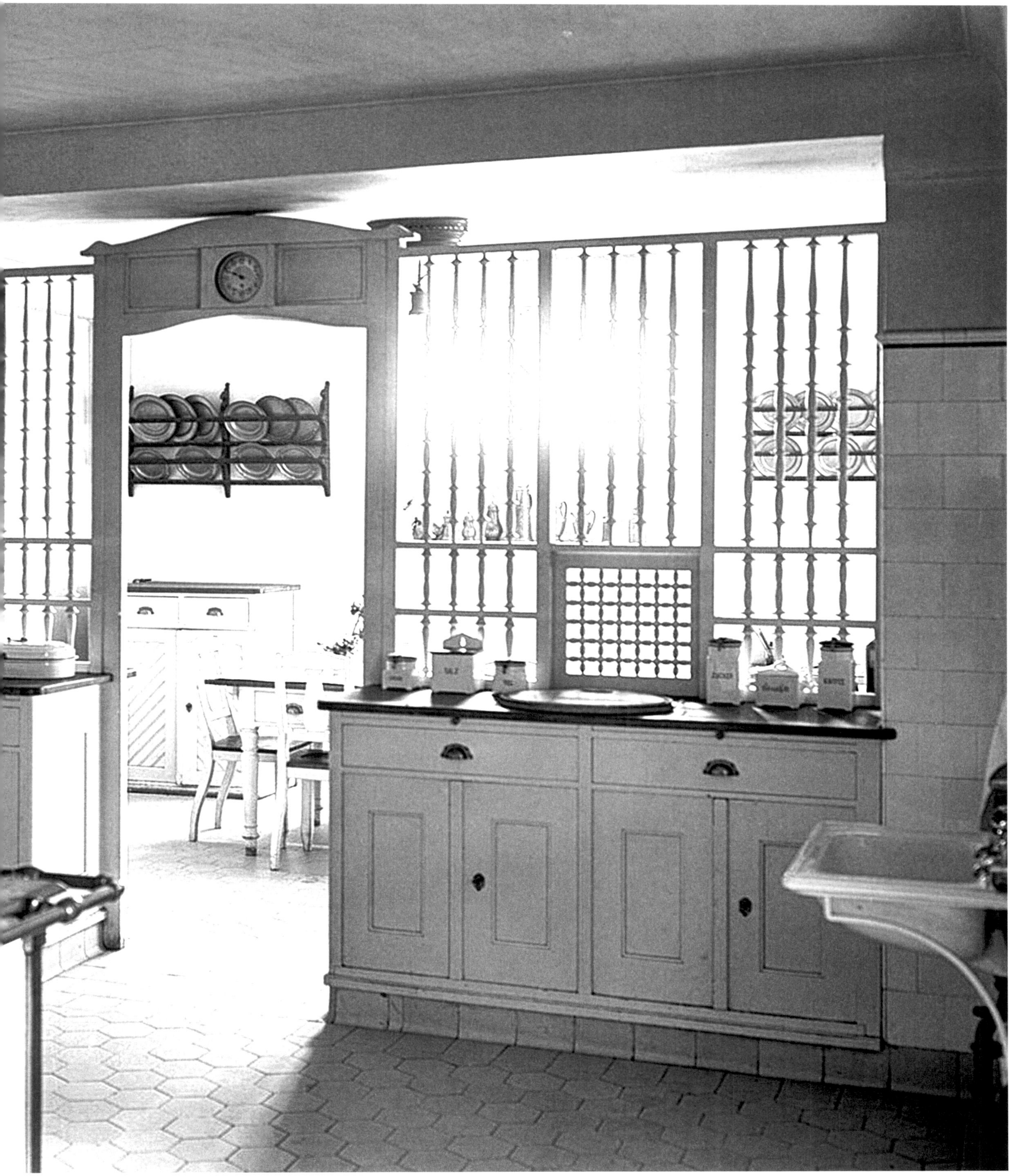
SALZ
ZUCKER
KAFFEE

ADJUSTABILITY
The equipping of seating furniture with additional functions through folding and pull-out mechanisms was an early specialty of Wilhelm Knoll. They were now also advertised in newspapers.

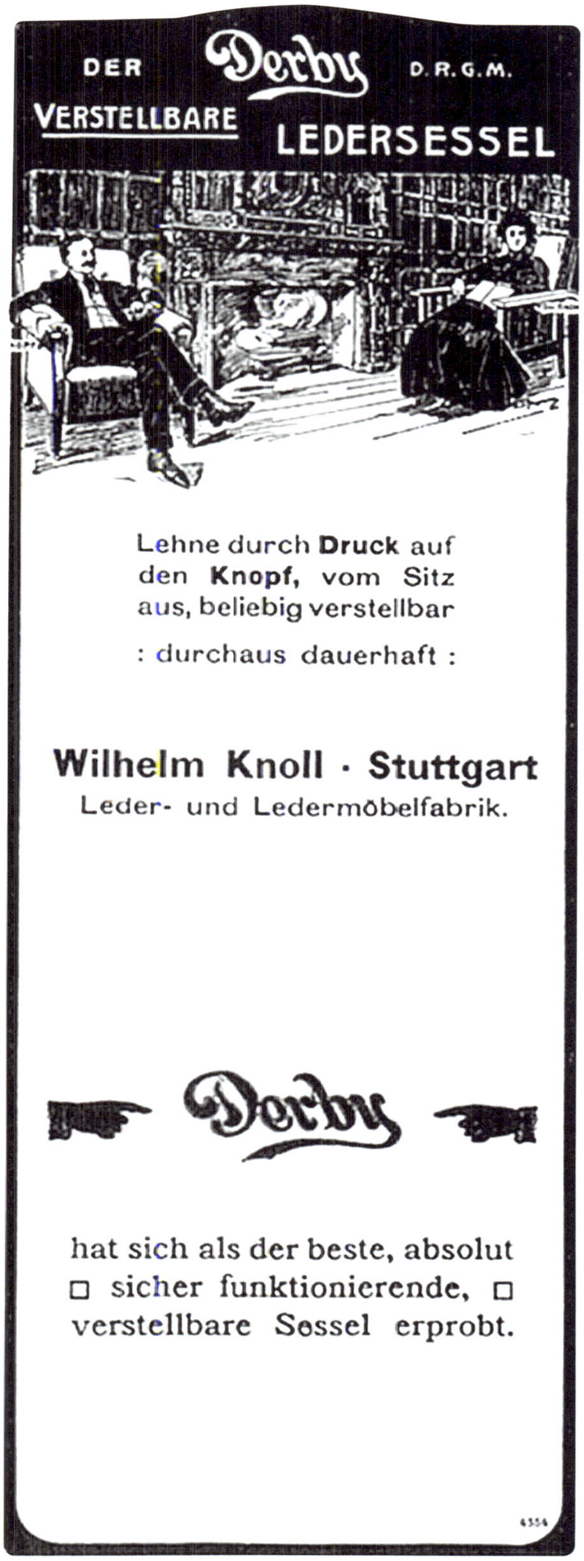

Advertisement for Derby,
Wilhelm Knoll,
Stuttgart, around 1910

Armchair 2280 with folding function,
Wilhelm Knoll,
Stuttgart 1909

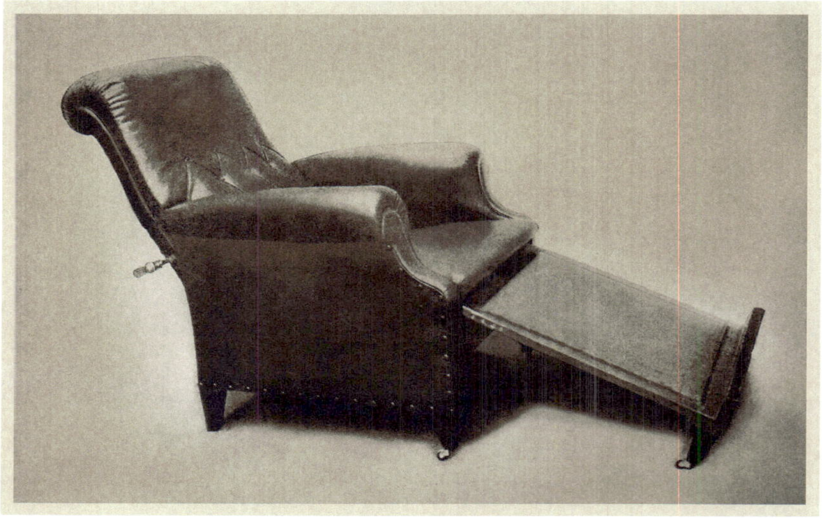

GLOBETROTTER

Karl Gustav Vollmöller, Walter Knoll's brother-in-law and friend, was a restless spirit and had several homes. One of them, Palazzo Vendramin, stood in Venice, right on the Grand Canal. Karl Gustav lived there with his wife, the actress Maria Carmi. Walter visited him there on occasion.

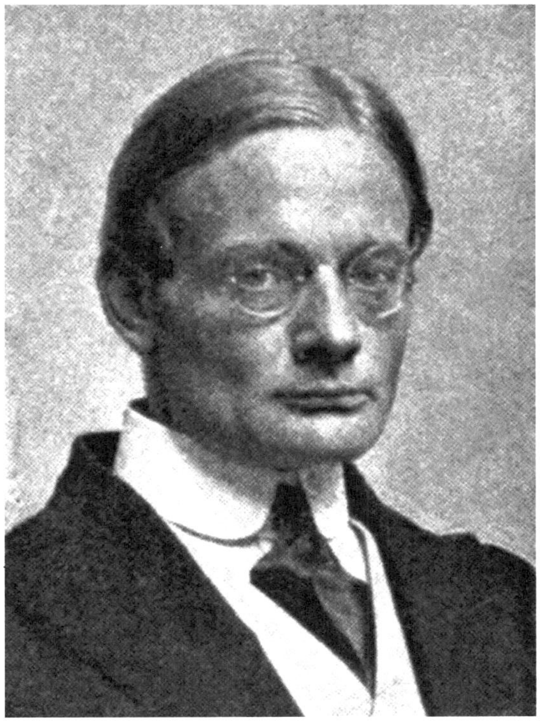

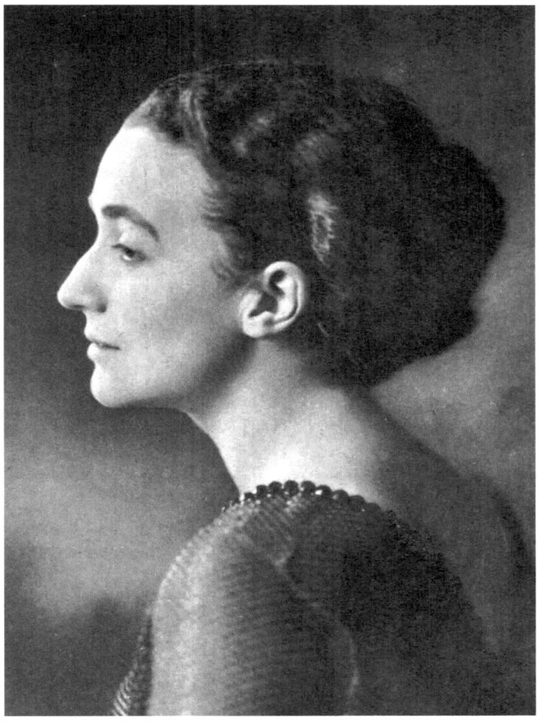

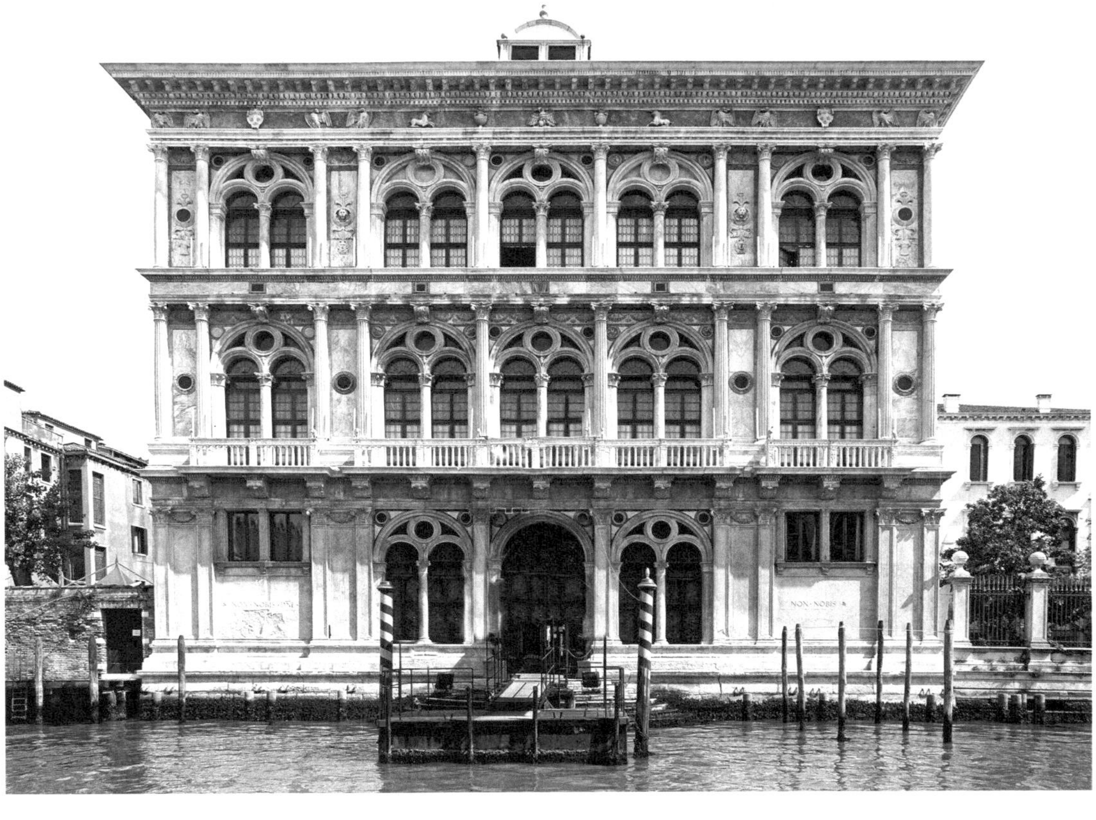

Karl Gustav Vollmöller, archaeologist, writer, and man of the world, friend and brother-in-law of Walter Knoll, around 1910

Maria Carmi, actress, wife of Karl Gustav Vollmöller, postcard, around 1916

Palazzo Vendramin-Calergi in Venice, design by Mauro Codussi, built in 1509, photo from 2011

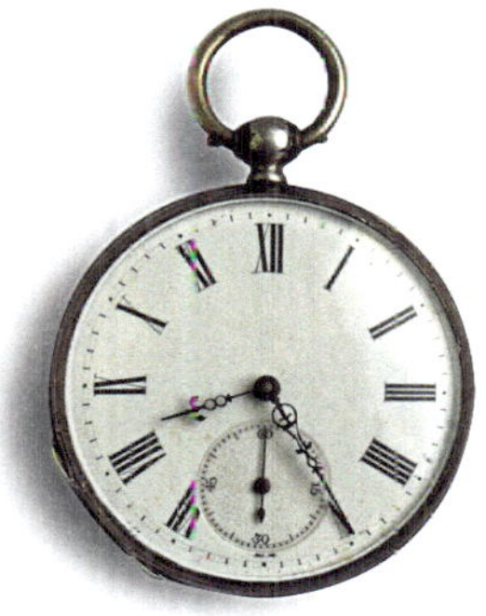

Even the pocket watch – the smartphone of the early 20th century – now appeared in the spare Reform Style.

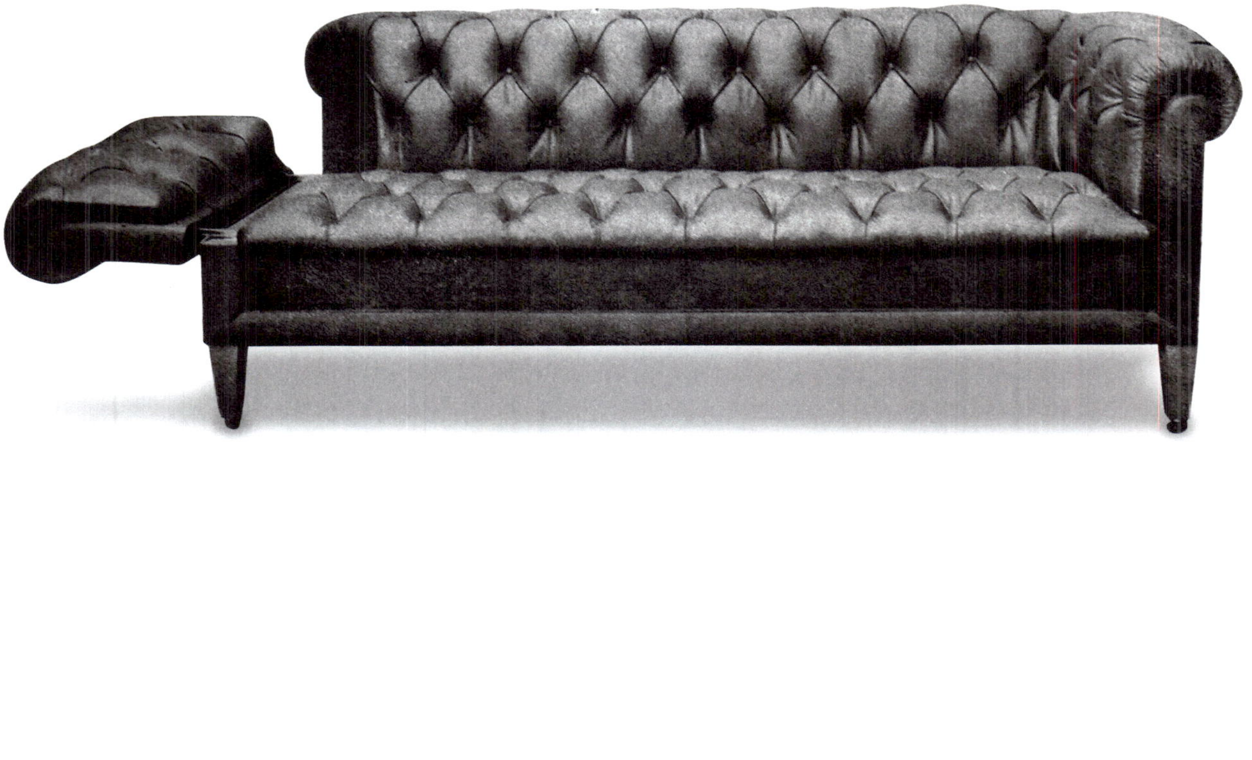

Sofa 2298, Wilhelm Knoll, Stuttgart, around 1910

FURNITURE TECHNOLOGY

The mechanization of seating furniture extended all the way to plug-in functions that enabled it to be disassembled for transport.

Dismountable armchair 2406,
Wilhelm Knoll,
Stuttgart 1908

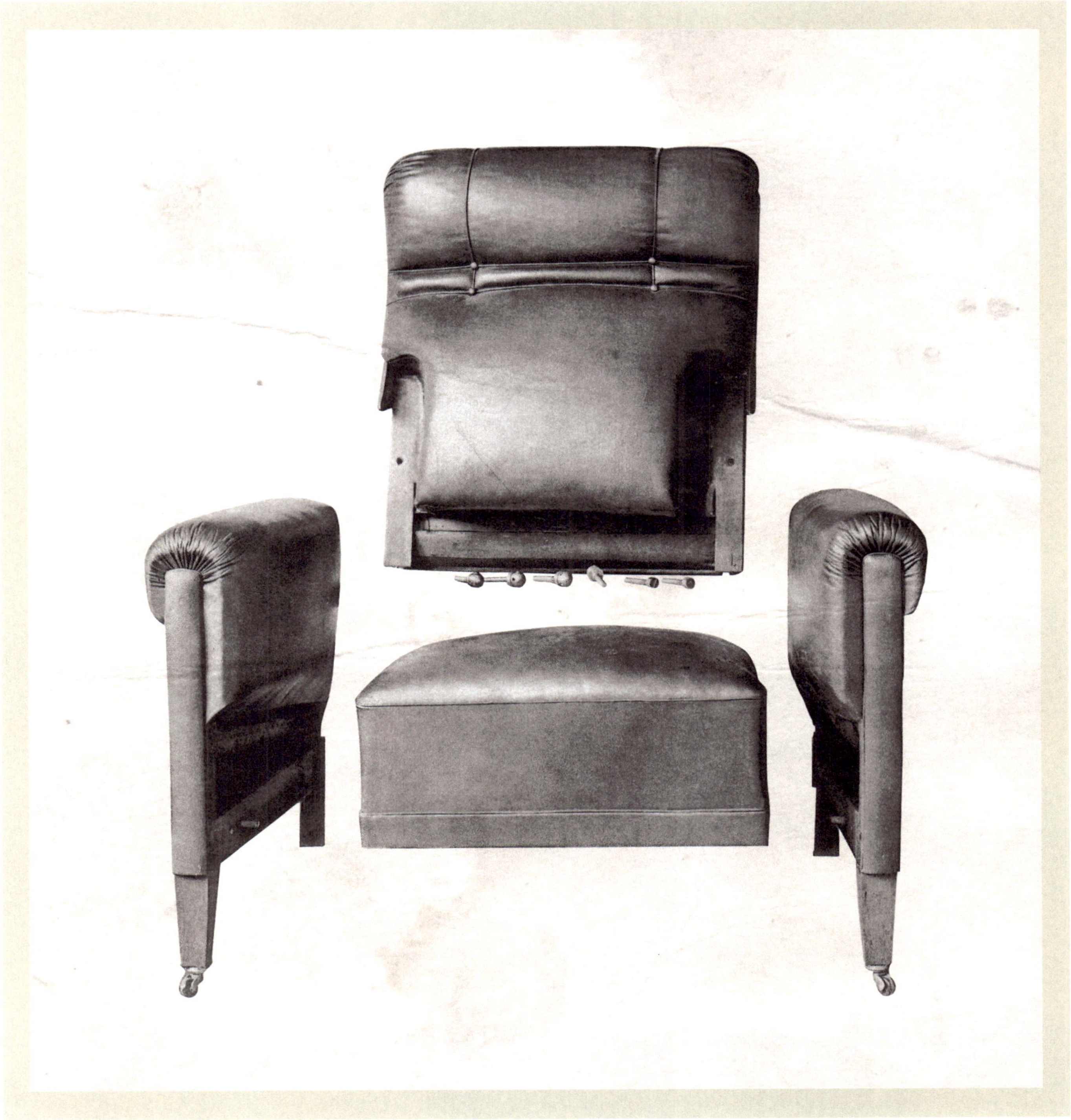

Chair Nestra 3390, Wilhelm Knoll,
Stuttgart, around 1913

Armchair Nestra 101, Wilhelm Knoll,
Stuttgart, around 1910

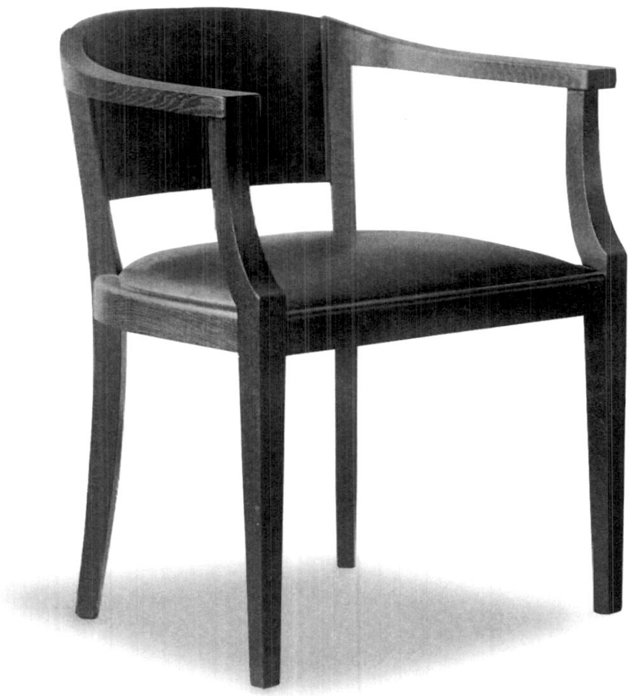

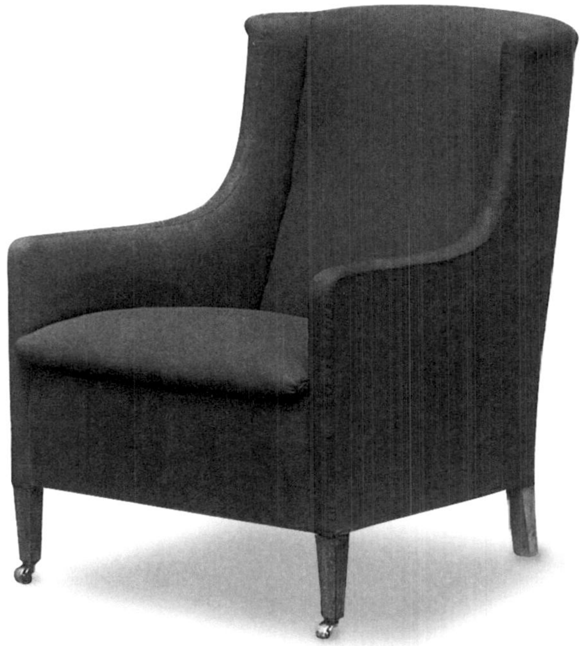

NESTRA

The hybrid furniture of the Nestra series – half chair, half armchair – was also invented by Willy Knoll.
This basic idea was to recur even more frequently in the model history of the Knoll dynasty.

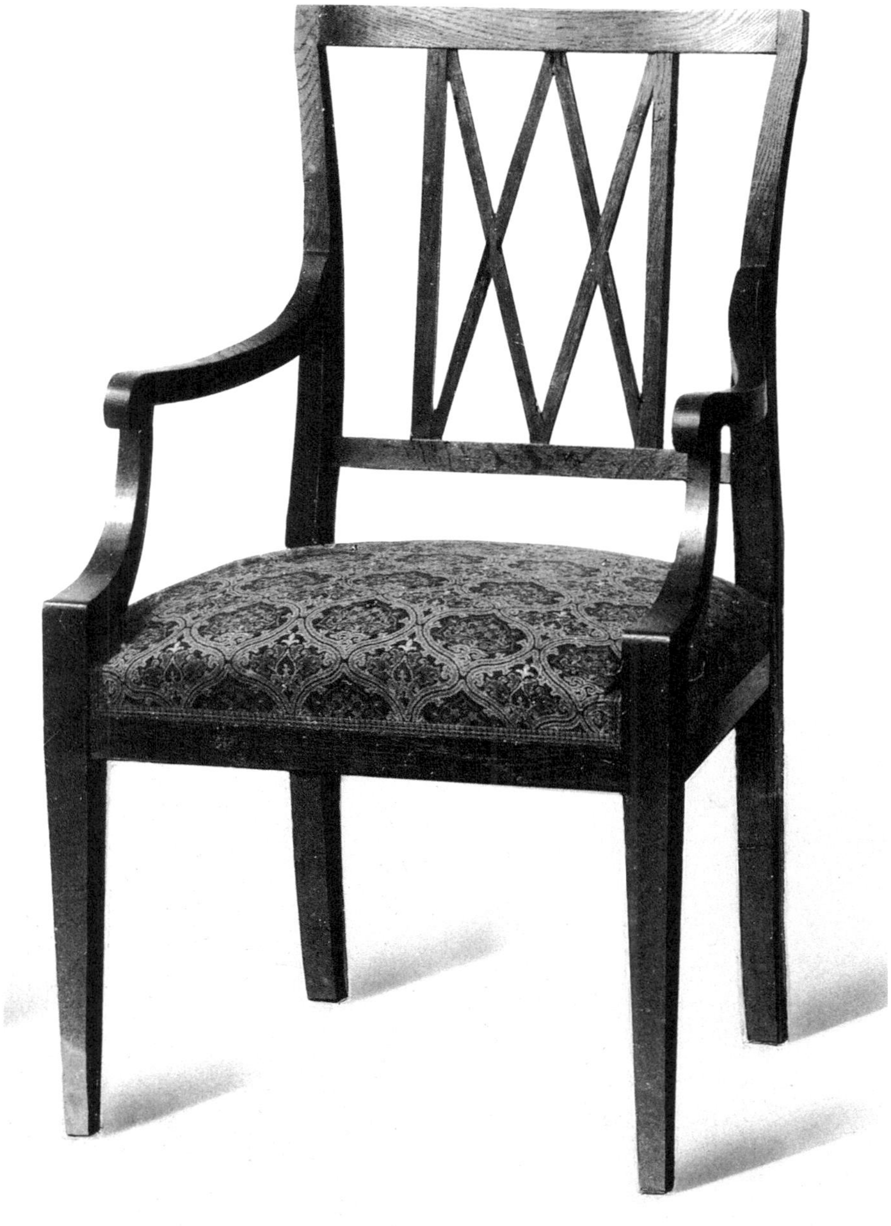

Chair Nestra 2922,
Wilhelm Knoll,
Stuttgart, around 1913

REFORM STYLE

Re|form| style, the replaced Art Nouveau. Also called "style revolution," "spatial art," or "machine style," it is not a commonly used generic term. It emerged from the Reform movement in around 1900, whose aim was to achieve objectivity in design. Early representatives were the "Vereinigte Werkstätten" in Munich, the "Deutsche Werkstätten" in Dresden, and the "Königliche Lehr- und Versuchswerkstätte" in Stuttgart. Its director, Bernhard Pankok, was a co-founder of the "Werkbund" and the creator of unadorned interiors. Other important representatives of the Reform Style included Peter Behrens, Lucian Bernhard, Bruno Paul, Richard Riemerschmid, and Henry van de Velde. The reform style first prevailed in residential institutions, but was soon transferred to other areas such as architecture, graphics and typography. Magazines such as "Deutsche Kunst und Dekoration" (German Art and Decoration) and "Innen-Dekoration" (Interior Decoration) disseminated the new trend. The new style was propagated in the "Landesgewerbemuseum" in Stuttgart, which set up a department for bad taste with deterrent examples. It was a typical feature of this unnamed era that lasted from the turn of the century until the First World War and is here referred to as the "Reform Period." When Wilhelm Knoll launched its first series of upholstered furniture under the name club chair – or Clubfauteuil – this was not only a new type of furniture but also the Reform Style's breakthrough into upholstered furniture. It was certainly no coincidence that Lucian Bernhard, one of the leading graphic designers of the period, designed the catalog.

1907
The Wilhelm Knoll company introduced the club chair – or Clubfauteuil – as a type of furniture in Germany. The invention of folding and pull-out mechanisms also corresponded to the new direction.

1910
Wilhelm Knoll's first catalog for the club chair collection was designed by Lucian Bernhard, one of the leading graphic artists of his time.

1912
Lightweight armchairs from the Nestra series entered production at Wilhelm Knoll.

1913
Opening of the "Kunstgewerbeschule" at Weissenhof, a stronghold of the Reform Style under its director Bernhard Pankok.

THE GOAL OF OUR EPOCH SHOULD BE A DESIGN APPROPRIATE TO THE MACHINE.
PETER BEHRENS

Typeface,
design by Lucian Bernhard,
Hellerau, around 1920

Drawing by Bernhard Pankok,
catalog of the World's Fair
St. Louis 1904

Reform sofa 2113,
Wilhelm Knoll,
Stuttgart, around 1910

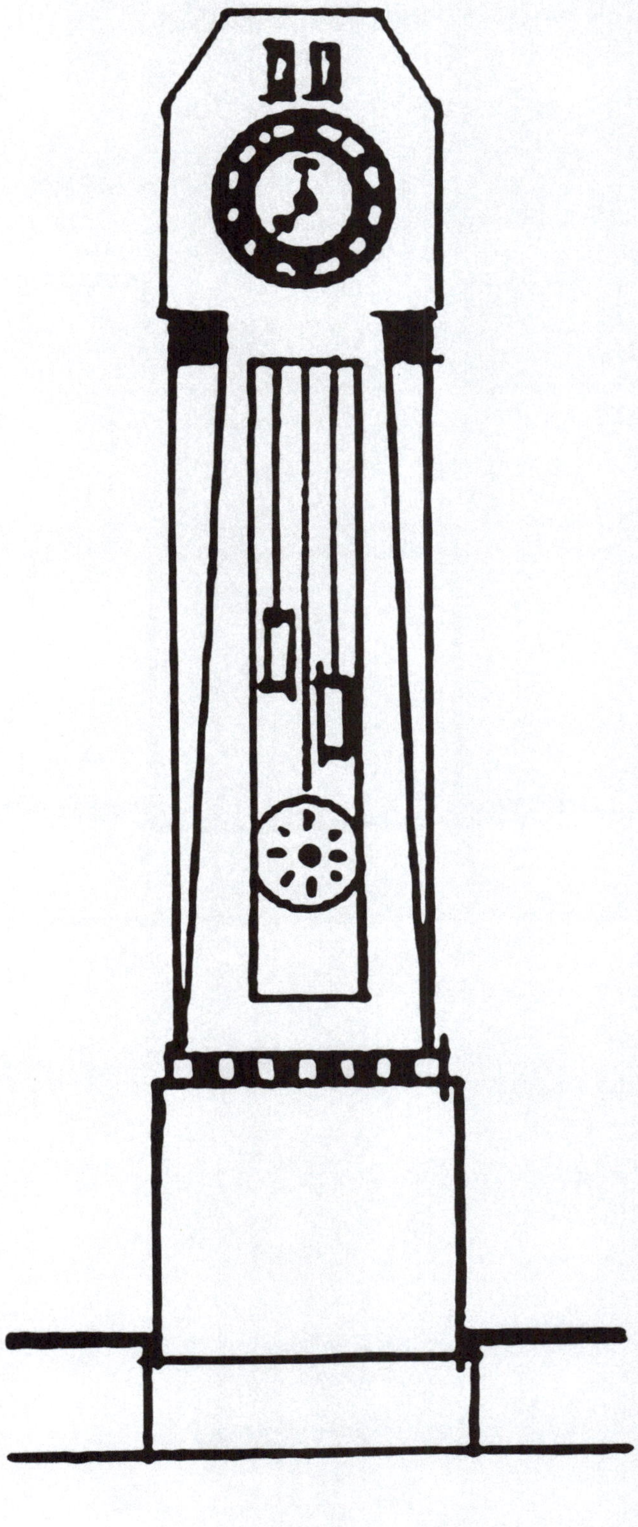

Stuttgart

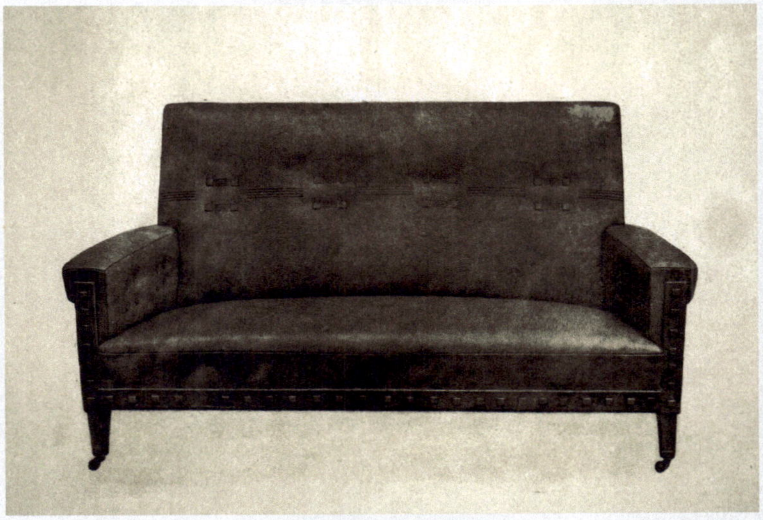

THE 1920s

KNOLL TIMES TWO

In the wake of the war, nothing remained the same as it was before. There were shortages of everything. Even at the magnificent Vollmöller villa on Hasenbergsteige food was now scarce. Walter Knoll, now the head of the household, lived there with his wife Maia, 4-year-old Hans, 6-year-old Robert, and Herbert, their newborn baby. Walther, who was born during the war, died as an infant. All the boys lived through the difficult war and post-war years during their childhood. To deal with the shortages, the family had to make do with unconventional means. The garage was re-purposed as a chicken coop and also housed a cow to provide milk for the children. The tennis court was turned into a vegetable garden. And in the surrounding area there was a plot of land that the family used as a potato field.

The feudal lords had relinquished their privileges. The country, now a democracy, was in a state of shock induced by the defeat and was starving. The short episode of a half-hearted revolution – Daimler workers in Untertürkheim also rebelled – was followed by hyperinflation, accompanied by uprisings in all corners of the German Reich, though

WILHELM
KNOLL

these only flared up briefly in Württemberg and its capital city. It was a time of great turmoil. In historical accounts, it is often regarded as a period of transition that was doomed to failure from the outset. It is indisputable, however, that this chronically unstable era progressed at an unprecedented pace. This also gave rise to the reputation of the proverbial "roaring twenties" as a "golden" era. The floodgates of modernity had been opened. The buzzwords of the day were *Neues Bauen* (New Building), *Neue Typografie* (New Typography) and – not least – *Neues Wohnen* (New Living). Radical trends that swept away conventions and broke free from antiquated customs were triumphant in virtually all areas of life. *Neue Sachlichkeit* (New Objectivity), *Neue Stadt* (New City), and even *Neue Frau* (New Woman) were declared. And the still devastated Germany, forced to make a new start, took center stage in this all-encompassing upheaval.

In this period of breaking away from the past, in which the old became obsolete but the new was still unknown, the Wilhelm Knoll company also faced considerable uncertainty. At the end of the war, company director Willy Knoll remained in exile in Switzerland. Walter, who took an extremely critical view of his brother's activities there[1], managed the business in his absence during the post-war chaos. Albeit in the knowledge that he would have to vacate the manager's office again upon Willy's return. Their mother, Emma Knoll, died in a traffic accident in 1919. This was a severe loss for both brothers and also tragic, since without the gentle authority of their mother their reconciliation became even more unlikely. In 1921, Willy Knoll, having barely returned from his seven years of emigration, had the family name "Knoll" protected as a trademark, a wise move with far-reaching consequences. Although the brothers were now in collaboration, reflecting their recent experiences, their working relationship "did not prove harmonious"[2], as Walter diplomatically put it. The two stubborn Swabian mules, cut from the same Knoll cloth but very different in nature, collided head-on. Walter, the elder brother, having been made co-partner by Willy, soon returned his shares and left the family business the same year. For good.

What was actually behind the irreconcilable conflict between these two brothers who, despite their differences, also had much in common? Walter and Willy were the sons of a company founder who reinvented his business multiple times. They learned the fundamentals of creative, future-oriented business management from a young age. Consequently, the pair did not just become businessmen, but entrepreneurs. Both second-generation Knolls were heavily influenced by their Swabian environment. Its values, such as proficiency and self-discipline, were as much a part of them as their relentless pursuit of better solutions. Furthermore, like their father, they were strict patriarchs who conferred the same caring attitude towards the company and its workforce as they did with their own family. And, of course, they were old-school businessmen and devout protestant men in any event. There was another similarity. Both Knoll brothers were high achievers, although with very different motivations. The reason for this lay in their respective relationships with their father, as well as their life experiences. While Willy, daddy's "star pupil," was a brilliant student, Walter not only suffered as a result of his poor grades but also from the affront this caused. While for Willy, a leather virtuoso like his father, success itself made him a high-flyer, for Walter it was the other way round. He was driven by a burning ambition to become one. Willy knew his path, Walter first had to find it. That he succeeded with flying colors is the extraordinary quality of his biography. His experiences in America as a young migrant and the positive culture shock he experienced in

WALTER
KNOLL
& CO. G.M.B.H.

the extravagant milieu of the Vollmöllers opened up the necessary perspectives for him. For all these reasons, both Walter and Willy were anything but average businessmen. They were captivated, often even obsessed, with their mission. And they were both committed modernists, although with a clearly differing perspective on modernity.

Willy Knoll picked up where he left off before the war had interrupted him. The leather expert had the tannery, dye works and finishing plant modernized and in 1922 was listed in the Stuttgart address book as the *Wilhelm Knoll Lederwerke* (Wilhelm Knoll Leather Factory), which produced "all kinds of leather for furniture, portfolios, automobiles, hats, and clothing."[3] At this point, upholstered furniture was just one product among many. Up to 60 hides were produced each day, excellent "provenances," mostly from the Balkans, but also Australia. According to a method devised be Willy Knoll himself, a variety of leather was produced that was particularly suitable for purses and wallets. Customers included large companies in Offenbach, the center of the German leather industry. Customers in North America were also soon acquired. The "Vachettin" leather care product was a resounding sales success, making the Wilhelm Knoll company known across the country. The name was derived from the French word "vache," meaning cow. Vachette leather, in its natural color or dyed, is often used for suitcases, bags, and saddles. At that time, however, it was also used as automobile or furniture leather, frequently pigmented or embossed. Willy Knoll developed and patented countless such methods, following in the footsteps of his father and even surpassing him.

Eventually, Willy Knoll also began to revive armchair production as a second economic pillar. To this end, for the first time, he sought the assistance of a specialist who he hoped would provide him with stylistic inspiration. The interior designer Karl Pullich, born in 1884 and therefore a couple of years younger than his new employer, worked for Willy Knoll as an independent artist throughout the 1920s. Born and raised in New York as the child of German parents, Pullich was no stranger to the industry. Prior to the war, he first went to Munich and London and eventually arrived in Stuttgart where he worked for Georg Schöttle, the top furniture store in the city at the time. Furthermore, he had a consultancy agreement with Württemberg's furniture industry. The work of this highly esteemed "spatial artist" was repeatedly publicized in the journal "Innen-Dekoration" (Interior Decoration). He favored "the constructive"[4], the journal acknowledged, and was an expert in "the solid assembly of rooms and furniture, which he put together with pure skill."[5] Furthermore, he was a "master of small furniture items."[6] Pullich, not yet stylistically established or particularly familiar with historic furniture designs, represented the accomplished tastefulness that had emerged in the Reform Period. He was someone who mastered his craft with virtuosity and possessed a "fighting spirit"[7], for he had no intention of submitting himself to a particular school.

TWO STUBBORN SWABIAN MULES, CUT FROM THE SAME KNOLL CLOTH BUT VERY DIFFERENT IN NATURE, COLLIDED HEAD-ON.

In terms of technical expertise and character, he seems like the perfect counterpart to Willy Knoll. Although he was also a staunch innovator, Willy remained open-minded and undogmatic as far as style was concerned. In Pullich, he had found someone with whom he could push things forward, but who, like himself, did not take things to esthetic extremes.

Pullich, the first artistic specialist at the Wilhelm Knoll company, immediately produced a whole series of seating furniture. Its name, "Handi," referred to the first syllables of the name Hans-Dieter, the son of Willy Knoll, but was also intended to have a slightly English sound. Inspired by the Nestra series of the pre-war period, these were relatively lightweight chairs. Their distinguishing feature was the combination of fabric and leather in interwoven straps. Both materials were processed in a special way to form a mesh and, of course, were patented. In the case of such "strap webbing chairs," the design was a product of the construction method. The Handi was also exported, in particular to the Netherlands according to company records.[8]

The eclectic Pullich was in his element. The decorative eccentricity of some of his drafts (which, due to their complexity, were never put into series production) evoke the so-called "revolution style" of the post-war years, which was, in turn, a close relation of expressionism. Other, subsequently created models could be classified as "Art Deco." Though this style, launched at the 1925 trade exhibition of the same name in Paris, also escapes easy definition. In any case, far more important than any particular style, is the fact that the collaboration

---

1 ▶ Knoll, n.d., p. 62.

2 ▶ Schnermann, in: Janssen, 1999, p. 397.

3 ▶ Knoll, 1965, p. 17.

4 ▶ Häuselmann, in: Innen-Dekoration, 1917, p. 247.

5 ▶ Ibid, p. 251.

6 ▶ Ibid, p. 254.

7 ▶ Ibid, p. 248.

8 ▶ Knoll, 1965, p. 19.

NEW STUTTGART

During the time of the Weimar Republic, crisis-ridden Germany experienced a push for modernization. In the Stuttgart cityscape, still largely characterized by timber framing, department stores sprung up, which were perceived as "glass palaces" due to their bands of windows. Pictured, the inauguration of the Breuninger department store on the market square in the early 1930s.

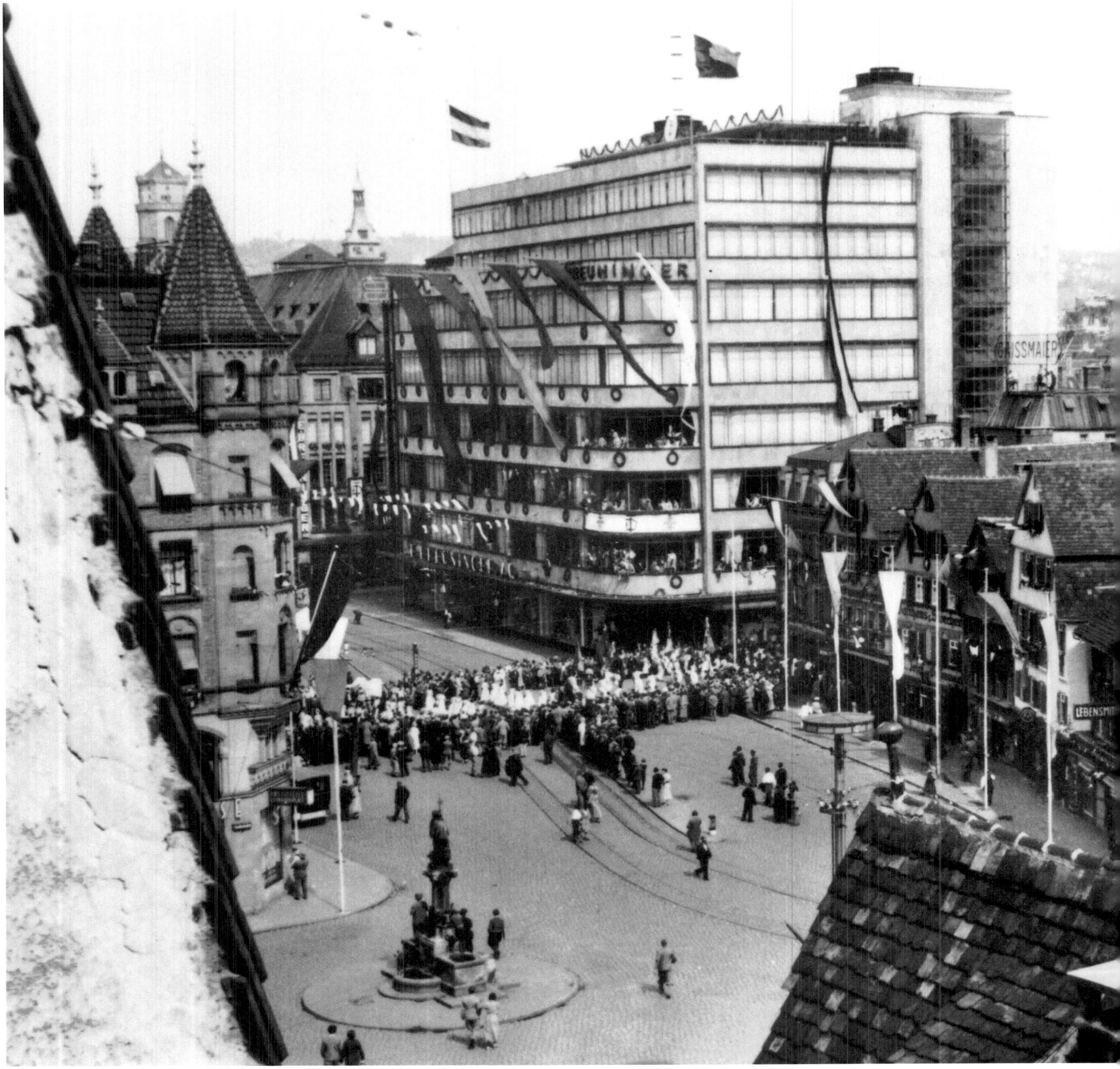

Breuninger department store,
Stuttgart, around 1930

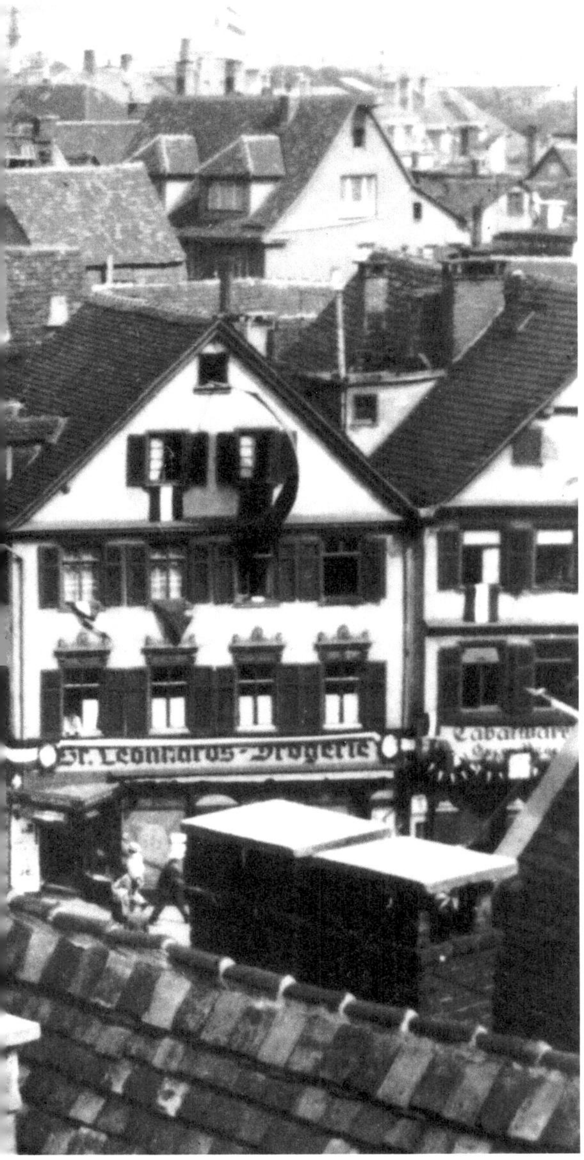

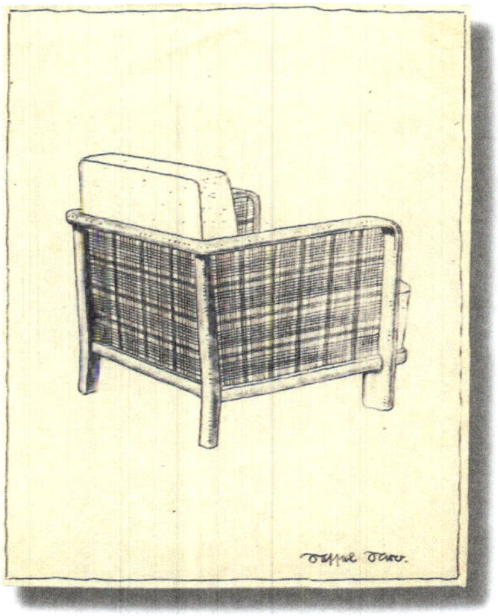

between Wilhelm Knoll and Karl Pullich, a congenial entrepreneur-designer pair,[9] featured technical solutions as a starting point in the development of new models. This systematic and, simultaneously, undogmatic approach, with which the two swam the channels of Swabian designer culture, which treats patents as trophies, would soon provide the foundation for an astonishing chapter of success in the company's history. However, this would take another couple of years.

Following the falling-out with his brother, whom he had experienced as a "domineering character,"[10] Walter Knoll took a position at Vollmöller, the company owned by his wife's family. However, his role as a member of the supervisory board of the "Vereinigte Trikotagenfabriken" (United Hosiery Factories), a position he held for approximately a year, appears to have been just as unsatisfactory as his subsequent activities in the financial sector. He established the "Württembergischen Privatbank" (Württemberg Private Bank), also with the participation of the Vollmöllers, in May 1923, which proved to be entirely inopportune timing. Inflation was sweeping over Germany like a hurricane and literally destroyed all value before it. After just one and a half years, the newly founded financial institution was dissolved again.

At this point, Walter Knoll seems to have returned to his familiar roots. He prepared to establish his own furniture company. Its name: Walter Knoll & Co. The funds for the small factory building that was completed in the Feuerbach district in the summer of 1925 likely also originated from the Vollmöllers. However, the almost instantaneous success that established the new company in leading furniture stores countrywide within just a year was down to his own ideas. Walter Knoll, already approaching 50, had plenty of experience, including disappointments, and wanted to try again. It pretty much looked like his last chance. His decision, like Willy, to bring an artistic advisor into the company would prove a wise move. Especially since he would be dealt an equally good hand as his brother in the selection of a partner. Paul Hahn, his new creative force, would likely have aroused skepticism among modern-day personnel managers with his extraordinary, zig-zagging résumé. Not least because he was a political activist. The son of a locksmith, born in Obertürkheim in view of the gates of the Daimler factory and raised in the working-class city of Esslingen, he initially became a teacher. He then discovered his true passion: artistic studies, first at Pankok's *Versuchs- und Lehrwerkstätte* (experimental and apprentice workshop), then at the Stuttgart State Academy of Fine Arts. Hahn then became self-employed and, within a short period of time, managed to establish himself as a commercial artist and painter. He also asserted himself as a soldier in the First World War, rising to the rank of lieutenant. The extent of the charisma that the working-class boy and social democrat Hahn must have exuded is demonstrated by the following events. As the revolution took him by surprise at the military hospital in Isny, his comrades elected him chairman of the local soldiers' council, one of many that were forming everywhere at the time. Sent to the "Landesausschuss der Soldatenräte" (National Committee of Soldiers' Councils) convening in Stuttgart, Hahn developed a plan to defend the Republic using "security forces." He personally assumed responsibility for their central direction.[11] He came to local prominence not least because of the drastic measures he took in the post-war chaos. He set up his command center in the tower of the not yet fully complete Stuttgart Central Station. In 1920 he was appointed "chief police officer" at the Ministry of the Interior, but lost his post soon thereafter. He then wrote his memoirs, which turned him into a local legend, living on to this day under the self-invented name *Roter Hahn* (The Red Rooster).[12] In this situation, Walter Knoll gave him the opportunity to become head designer and also partner at his new company. Hahn, in his early 40s, was charismatic and assertive and endowed with that extremely rare combination of both organizational and artistic talents.

It is not documented who first connected Paul Hahn and Walter Knoll, these partners with an eventful history. It may have been Carl Koch, an art historian who in 1921 came from Berlin to Stuttgart where he worked as a curator at the "Staatsgalerie" (Stuttgart state gallery). Hans Purrmann, the husband of Walter's sister-in-law Mathilde Vollmöller and, at the time, a renowned modern painter, had invited the newly arrived Koch to his family home on Hasenbergsteige and also introduced him to Walter Knoll. At the time, he was fairly shaken up by the conflict with his brother and was delighted to have someone to pour his heart out to. A deep, lifelong friendship subsequently developed between the two, also involving their wives. The somewhat younger Koch was an art connoisseur who was surely also aware of the artistic past of ex-chief police officer Hahn. Koch may, therefore, have given his new friend the all-important tip. After all, he had by now become his "mentor,"[13] as Walter Knoll retrospectively wrote.

"NO BAUHAUS WITHOUT STUTTGART." A PERFECTLY JUSTIFIED EXAGGERATION.

He remembered thankfully that he, who had not studied, had here "for the first time, the opportunity to form a bond with someone who was professionally at home in the field of art."[14] And furthermore, unlike his first mentor, Karl Gustav Vollmöller, this person was not constantly on the move. Koch had an influence that Walter Knoll later considered to be of great importance, both for his world view and his professional ethos. He became interested in art books and they soon filled the shelves of his home. Mostly recommended by his new friend, they were the trigger for animated discussions. This impulse would continue over future generations of Knolls.[15] Carl Koch gave Walter Knoll an understanding of modern art. This was bound to have implications for the way in which he managed his company. In the end, he himself sought contact with artists.

Although not widely recognized, Stuttgart was, at the time, not only a thriving industrial city, but was also developing into a center of modern art. The painter Adolf Hölzel played a key role in this. Born in Moravia in 1853, his name is known only among experts nowadays. However, Hölzel was a pioneer of abstractionism. The co-founder of the Munich Secession, who formed the Dachau art colony in around 1900, was appointed by the State Academy of Fine Arts in Stuttgart in 1905. Alongside Pankok, he was immediately regarded as a strong personality in the local art and cultural scene. This is demonstrated, not least, by the large number of students that he taught. Countless artists, who would soon crop up in the environment of the Berlin Expressionists and go on to have an influence on Bauhaus, emerged from the "Hölzel circle." One might say "no Stuttgart, no Bauhaus," which, although a slight exaggeration, would certainly not be without justification.[16] This unquestionably includes the artist friends Johannes Itten and Oskar Schlemmer. The latter, born in Stuttgart, where he took his first artistic steps at the renowned Intarsienwerkstatt Wölfel & Kiessling[17], also performed his world-famous Triadic Ballet there. In the post-war period, Schlemmer was part of the avant-garde underground. He also met Willi Baumeister there, another of the young, wild early modernist artists, who, like him, had an unmistakable Swabian accent. Baumeister belonged to the Stuttgart Secession, a splinter group of the conservative *Künstlerbund* (Association of Artists).[18] The fact that the Secessionists drew upon the art academy, as well as the ranks of the free artists and the school of applied arts, for its personnel is indicative of how things were in flux at the time and could no longer be held back. Of course, these relationships, much like the accompanying fierce conflicts[19], can only be roughly outlined here. Nevertheless, the married couple Lily and Hans Hildebrandt, two art history experts and fervent proponents of the avant-garde, whose house became a meeting point for all inspired artists, should not go unmentioned.[20] Was Walter Knoll ever a visitor there? His friend Carl Koch certainly was and at the very least told him about it. Stuttgart was home to a cultural life that was an equally close-knit and far-flung network. The impulses resulting from this were in no way limited to art in the narrow sense of the term. Interactions between neighboring fields such as architecture, design, fashion, and advertising, were in fact, as previously in the Reform Period, virtually a hallmark of this development. Behind this was the interdisciplinary vision of an all-embracing modernity, as found expression in "Spatial Art" and the endeavors of the "Werkbund" (Association of Craftsmen). The technical-industrial and artistic sides were complements to each other. The topic where they naturally overlapped and that, like before the war, aroused remarkably strong public interest, was modern living. Here, the avant-garde reached right into in the private sphere. The issue at stake was nothing less than an esthetic evolution, or even revolution, within one's own four walls.

In the course of the 1920s, a whole series of trailblazing exhibitions were held in Stuttgart. It began in 1923 with the first exhibition

9 ▶ The occurrence of such "pairs," representing strokes of luck in industrial and design history, has thus far garnered little attention.

10 ▶ Knoll, n.d., p. 36.

11 ▶ This involved the Württemberg version of the *Freicorps* (Free Corps), consisting of around 11,000 men.

12 ▶ With his autobiography, published under the title "Der rote Hahn" (The Red Rooster), he established a local topos and his own legend. See: Hahn, 1922.

13 ▶ Knoll, n.d., p. 160.

14 ▶ Ibid.

15 ▶ The fact that Michael Knoll, Walter Knoll's grandson, ultimately studied art must undoubtedly be considered in this context.

16 ▶ Johannes Itten is considered to be the actual originator of the pioneering Bauhaus education model.

17 ▶ The Wölfel & Kiessling company provided the inlays for Pankok's "Württembergisches Zimmer" (Württemberg Room) at the 1904 World's Fair in St. Louis.

18 ▶ Likewise Ida Kerkovius, a student of Hölzel and teacher of Itten.

19 ▶ These developments ultimately led to Hölzel's departure.

20 ▶ Lily Hildebrandt, also Hölzel's master student, was a fascinating person (whose portrait was painted by Bernhard Pankok). It was this intelligent woman who first set *Bauhaus* founder Walter Gropius on the path of *Neues Bauen*, to name just one example. She discovered and translated early texts of Le Corbusier for Gropius, with whom she entered into a relationship.

HANDI

In the early 1920s, a range of lightweight chairs went into production, with designs reminiscent of modern artistic styles and which – like Nestra – also had its own brand name.

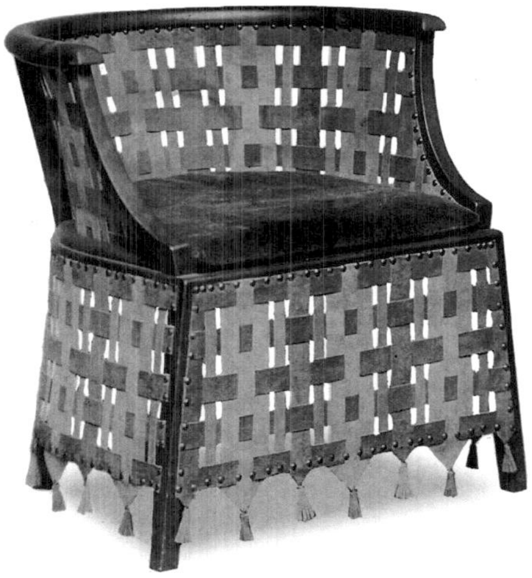

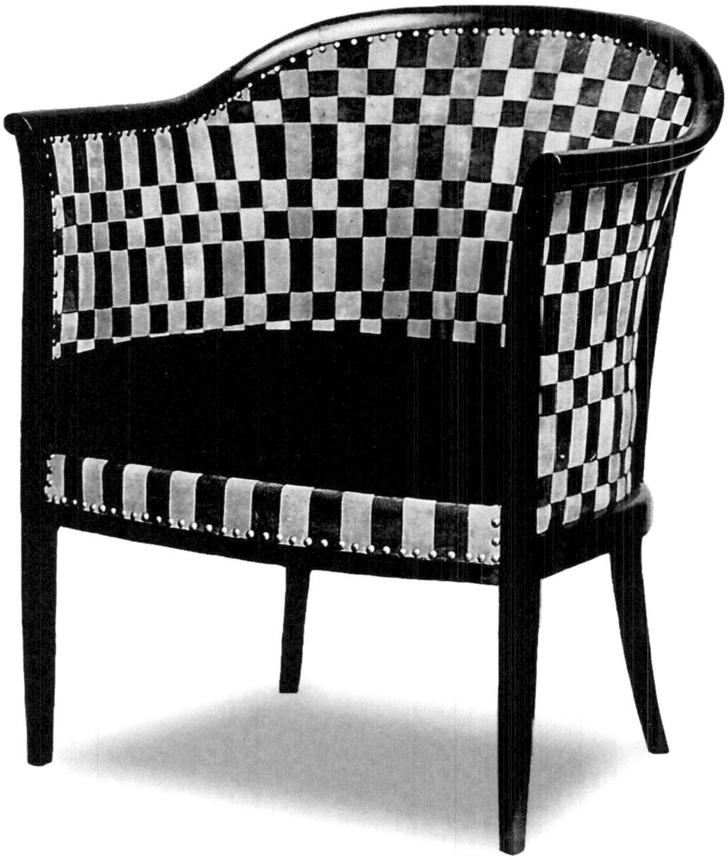

Chair Handi 1,
design by Karl Pullich, Wilhelm Knoll,
Stuttgart, around 1920

Chair Handi 12,
design by Karl Pullich, Wilhelm Knoll,
Stuttgart, around 1920

Chair Handi K-F 502,
Wilhelm Knoll,
Stuttgart, 1923

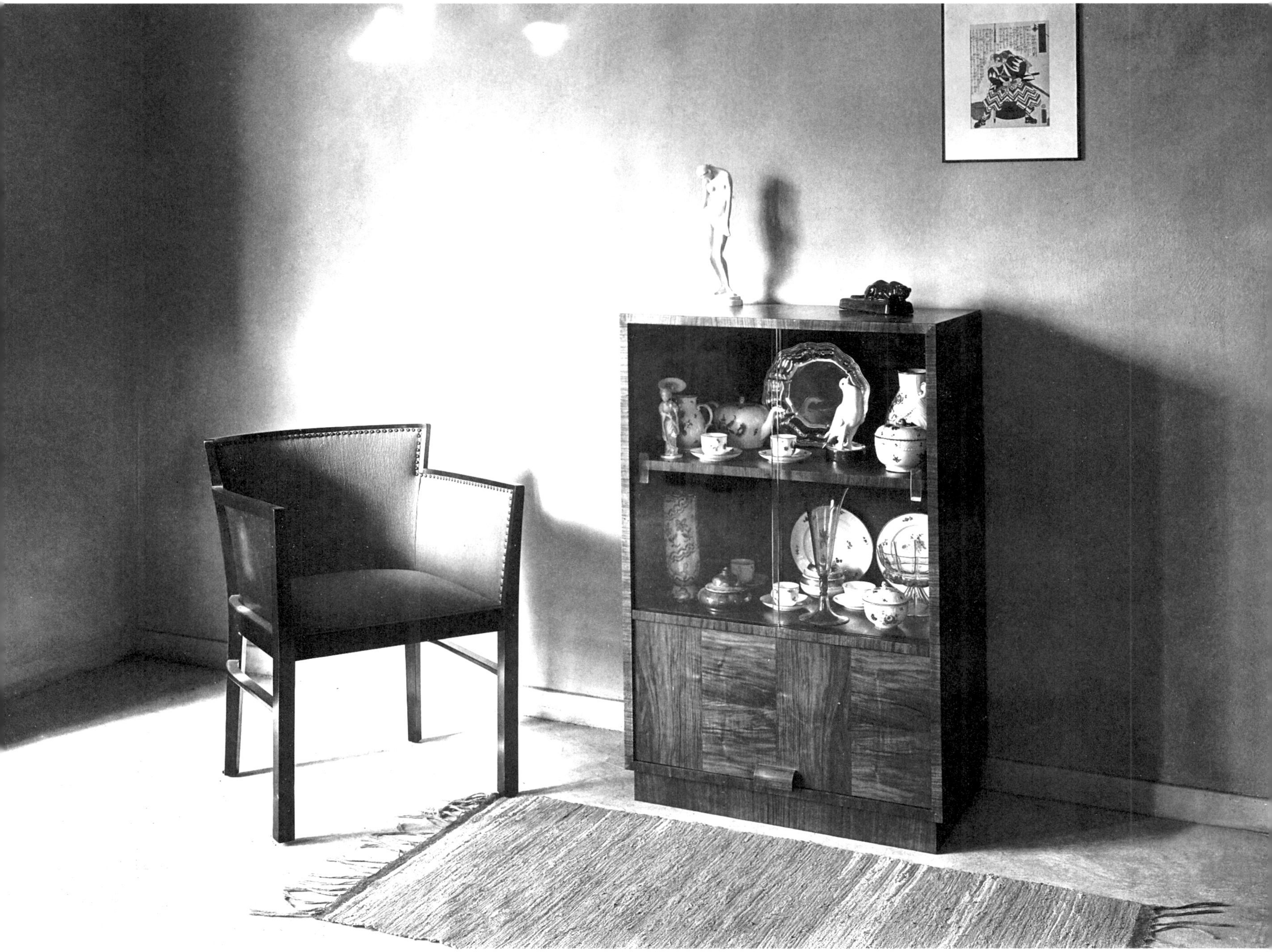

THE FACT THAT WALTER KNOLL INTERPRETED HIS FURNITURE AS A PRACTICAL "PSYCHOLOGY OF SITTING," WAS NOT ONLY RATHER COURAGEOUS, BUT ALSO DEMONSTRATED THAT HE WAS ALREADY THINKING IN BRANDS.

of the newly formed "Secession," which subsequently took place virtually every year up until 1932. On each occasion, it was a major event, which Carl Koch and Walter Knoll would not have wanted to miss. An ongoing conflict developed between the forwards-charging avant-garde and the resisting forces. At the time of the Weimar Republic, Stuttgart was one of its preferred battlegrounds, not least in the field of architecture, where a group of conservatives at the technical university led by Paul Bonatz, architect of the central railway station, made a name for themselves as the *Stuttgart School*.

An event that once again caused tempers to flare was the exhibition titled "Die Form" (The Form).[21] At this acclaimed show, held in 1924 at the newly completed exhibition and trade fair center in Stuttgart, the Württemberg branch of the "Werkbund"[22] presented furniture and household items, though expressly "without ornament." Although the idea of radical simplicity was in no way new, it had never before been presented so aggressively. The driving force was the long-serving chairman of the "Werkbund," Peter Bruckmann, a silverware manufacturer from Heilbronn. Adolf Schneck, who taught as a lecturer on furniture making at the "Kunstgewerbeschule" (School of Arts and Crafts) in Stuttgart, served as curator. The dedicated professor, born in Esslingen in 1883, would take the opportunity to bring his specialist topic to the fore more frequently in the coming years. Willi Baumeister contributed the cover of the exhibition catalog, a simple typographic design. The short-titled exhibition caused a stir well beyond Stuttgart. It was an expression of an "ethos that considered ornamentation to be distracting, indecent, tasteless," wrote the magazine that still bore the name "Deutsche Kunst und Dekoration" (German Art and Decoration), and attested to the heightened "sense of technical beauty" of the time. This celebration of the pure, unadorned form was a precursor to the renewed "change in style" that would soon eliminate all romantic baggage from the esthetics of art and everyday life. This unromantic movement was still lacking a name. It was finally provided by an exhibition that took place the following year in the Kunsthalle Mannheim. Its title: "Neue Sachlichkeit" (New Objectivity). In all areas of life, right through to architecture and the design of everyday items, the functional and unsentimental was gaining the upper hand. There were even objective romances.

The exhibition "Die Form" arrived as the factory in Feuerbach was already under construction and Walter Knoll, together with his partner Paul Hahn, had to think about how they would make a success of their start together. His principles, which he also fixed in writing, included the idea that "our product range must significantly deviate from that of other companies."[23] Naturally, his brother's company was not far from his thoughts when writing this. Consequently, their focus would be on "not leather furniture, but upholstered furniture"[24]. This renunciation of the bourgeois form of the leather chair can, by all means, be understood as an expression of *Neue Sachlichkeit*. He was meticulous in his realization of a modern image. For the company, he dropped the "h" from his name. Walter Knoll & Co. sounded leaner and fresher. Of course, America beckoned, and he turned his attention to effective sales and advertising. He pursued an offensive strategy, as he had learned during his formative years in New York. The fact that he interpreted and sold his furniture as a practical "psychology of sitting," was not only highly imaginative and rather courageous, but also demonstrated that he was already thinking "in brands." After just a year, the turnover of the market entrant had already doubled and was approaching half a million Marks. Knoll company number two was already present in specialist stores in 30 German cities. In addition, there were another three stores in Switzerland. Walter Knoll attempted to combine the production of smaller series with "good designs and a strong emphasis on quality."[25] If not always strictly unadorned, then definitely modern. For example, geometric patterns were preferably used for the cover fabrics, in keeping with the spirit of a rigorous, but moderate, form of modernity. This concept suited the tastes of an open-minded clientèle, one that danced the Charleston, went to the movies and read the poetry of Erich Kästner. And it also appealed to those who back then, as today, acted as the guardians of style: the architects. Those were specifically seeking suitable furnishings for the modern buildings inspired by *Neues Bauen*, examples of which were now appearing everywhere in the cityscape.

Though the start of his company had been progressing very satisfyingly, the new entrepreneur would soon be able to celebrate a real triumph. After just two years in the business, he held his own in the face of strong competition at the legendary Weissenhof exhibition in 1927. One year after the opening of the Bauhaus building in Dessau, this major event, which attracted half a million visitors to Stuttgart, once again directed the attention of the international public towards modernity in Germany. And, as stated in the "official catalog," Walter Knoll & Co. was among the best represented furniture companies here on the Killesberg.[26] The loosely scattered model estate on the hillside, which looks positively idyllic nowadays, consisted of around thirty residential buildings of varying size, designed by 17 mostly young and still largely unknown German and international architects, some of whom would, however, soon embark on global careers. Today, the list of contributors reads like a who's who of modern architecture in the early 20th century. It includes the Swiss Le Corbusier (whose buildings at Weissenhof have since become world heritage sites), the Belgian Victor Bourgeois, the Hungarian Marcel Breuer, the Austrian Josef Frank, and the Dutchman J. J. P. Oud. Furthermore, there were leading representatives of *Neues Bauen* in Germany, such as Bruno Taut, Hans Poelzig, Walter Gropius, and Ludwig Mies van der Rohe, who oversaw the exhibition. And not forgetting a number of progressive architects from Stuttgart itself,

A REAL TRIUMPH: AFTER JUST TWO YEARS IN THE BUSINESS, WALTER KNOLL HELD HIS OWN IN THE FACE OF STRONG COMPETITION AT THE LEGENDARY WEISSENHOF EXHIBITION IN 1927.

namely Richard Döcker, Hermann Gretsch, Richard Herre, and Adolf Schneck, the professor at the school of applied arts who had already excelled in previous years as a furniture reformer and organizer of visionary exhibitions. It was the uniform esthetics, the geometric discipline, the unusual flat roofs, and the numerous dazzling white facades that made the estate so impressive, but also shocking. Today though, given the beauty of the estate, it is difficult to explain the uproar that prevailed at the time. Such examples of *Neues Bauen*, some of which were much larger, already existed in many other cities. However, the massive presence of the construction avant-garde and the associated progressive impetus made the Weissenhof experiment unique[27] and a favorite target for the sometimes scathing criticism. It was deplored not least by the conservative *Stuttgarter Schule* (Stuttgart School), whose best-known exponents taught at the technical university.[28] Thus, the issue of residential housing had become a question of world view in Germany. Consequently, the matter-of-fact title of the exhibition –"Die Wohnung" (The Dwelling) – must also be understood programmatically. As Ludwig Mies van der Rohe, its director, observed in the preface to the catalog, "the battle for the new dwelling is a battle for new ways of living."[29] Stuttgart became the stage for this "battle" as well as the location where modern living for the first time manifested itself in such a comprehensive and spectacular manner.

Besides the estate with its new style of living, which caused a worldwide sensation back then, two other events took place: a trade fair for furniture and household items at the commercial hall in the city garden and an architecture exhibition near the palace. The fact that Stuttgart was the setting for this demonstration of modernity was anything but a coincidence. Once again, the strong Swabian faction in the "Deutscher Werkbund" (German Association of Craftsmen) had set things in motion. Peter Bruckmann and Adolf Schneck, who had already initiated home and industrial exhibitions in Stuttgart in previous years, were driving forces, as was "Werkbund" secretary Theodor Heuss. Other actors, such as the architect and professional visionary Bodo Rasch, were also involved.[30] Rasch had signed up his friend Mies van der Rohe, who was also on the board of the "Werkbund," for the project, which, although international in nature, would have been inconceivable without Stuttgart's avant-garde milieu. The catalog was designed by Willi Baumeister, a former student of Hölzel.

As previously in the Reform Period, the topic of living was the focus of public interest and, scarcely imaginable nowadays, sometimes provoked heated debates. A major event like Weissenhof acted as a catalyst that caused controversial opinions to boil over. At the time,

---

21 ▶ The title was identical to that of the "Werkbund" magazine, which appeared for the first time in the spring of 1922.

22 ▶ The organizer was the "Arbeitsgemeinschaft des Werkbunds Württemberg" (Württemberg Working Group of Deutscher Werkbund).

23 ▶ Votteler, 1990, p. 83.

24 ▶ Ibid.

25 ▶ Ibid.

26 ▶ Only Adolf Schneck from the school of applied arts, the chair specialist and exhibition organizer of previous years, was represented by a similar number of objects.

27 ▶ The "Werkbund" estate at Weissenhof, directly beside the "Kunstgewerbeschule" (School of Arts and Crafts), inspired a whole series of similar projects, including in Vienna and Wrocław.

28 ▶ In particular, the advocates of the "Stuttgarter Schule", a group of conservative architects at the technical university in Stuttgart, excelled in this area.

29 ▶ "Deutscher Werkbund," 1927, p. 5.

30 ▶ To name just a few.

FURNITURE DYNASTY

In 1925, Walter Knoll ventured on a new beginning with his "Polster-Möbel-Fabrik" in the Stuttgart suburb of Feuerbach. Of note: he soon had to change the logo and company sign as his brother possessed the rights to the family name. Another critical juncture for the Knoll dynasty.

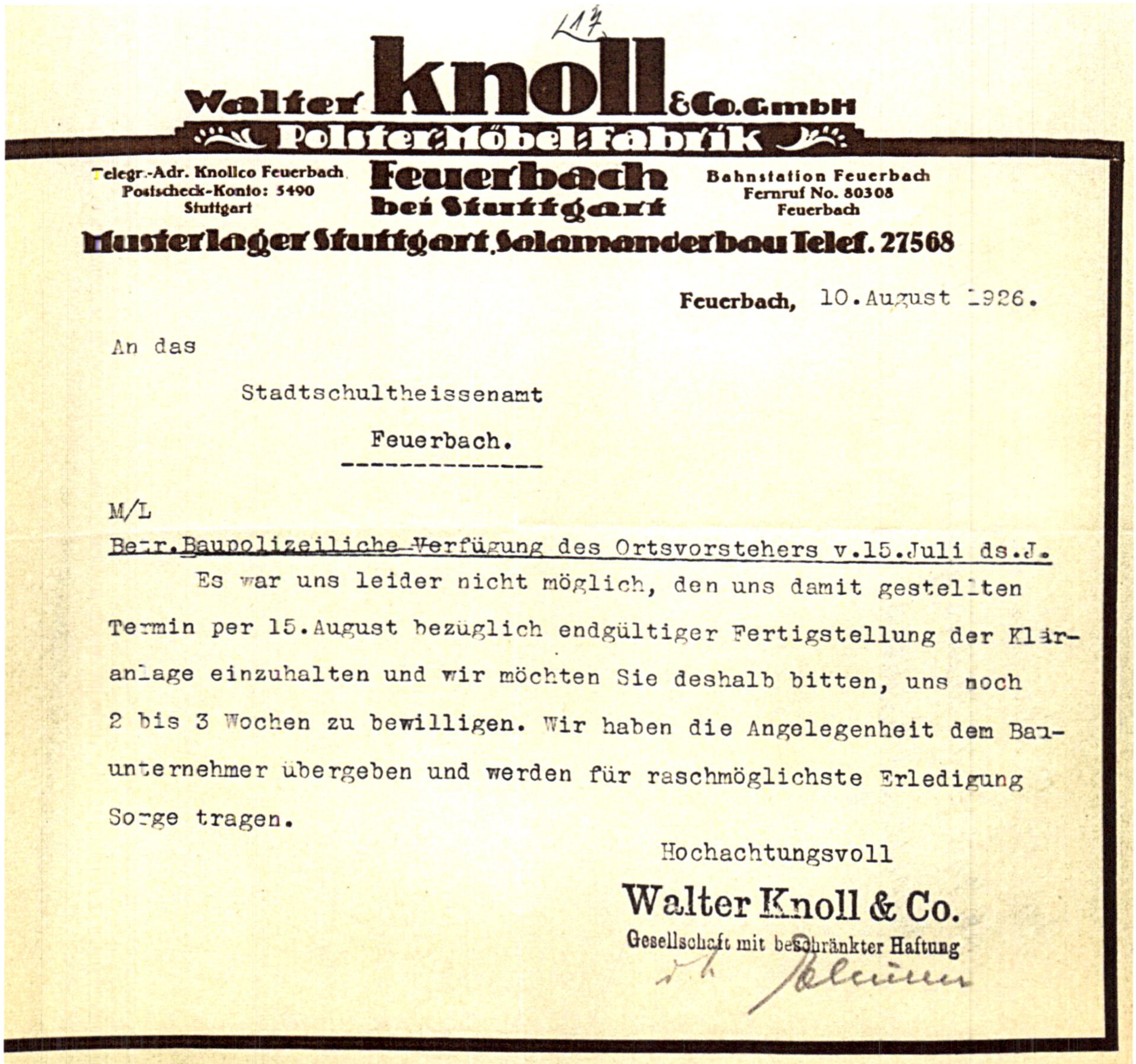

L17

Walter Knoll & Co. GmbH
Polster-Möbel-Fabrik

Telegr.-Adr. Knollco Feuerbach
Postscheck-Konto: 5490
Stuttgart

Feuerbach
bei Stuttgart

Bahnstation Feuerbach
Fernruf No. 80308
Feuerbach

Musterlager Stuttgart, Salamanderbau Telef. 27568

Feuerbach, 10. August 1926.

An das

Stadtschultheissenamt

Feuerbach.

M/L

Betr. Baupolizeiliche Verfügung des Ortsvorstehers v. 15. Juli ds. J.

Es war uns leider nicht möglich, den uns damit gestellten Termin per 15. August bezüglich endgültiger Fertigstellung der Kläranlage einzuhalten und wir möchten Sie deshalb bitten, uns noch 2 bis 3 Wochen zu bewilligen. Wir haben die Angelegenheit dem Bauunternehmer übergeben und werden für raschmöglichste Erledigung Sorge tragen.

Hochachtungsvoll

Walter Knoll & Co.
Gesellschaft mit beschränkter Haftung

Business letter, Walter Knoll,
Feuerbach (now Stuttgart), 1926

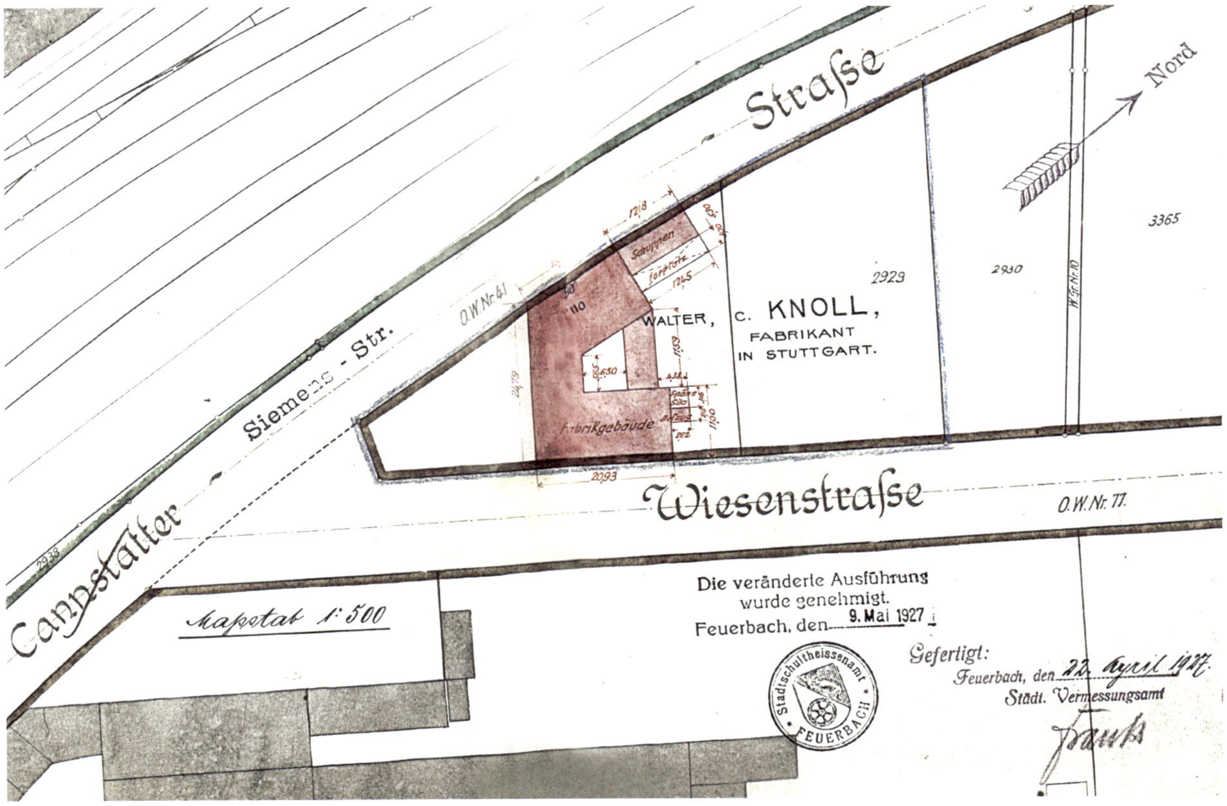

Architectural drawing, Walter Knoll,
Feuerbach (now Stuttgart), 1927

numerous illustrated books appeared, bearing unambiguous titles such as "Die Neue Wohnung" (The New Dwelling) or "Befreites Wohnen" (Liberated Living)[31] and propagating the furnishings revolution initiated by *Neue Sachlichkeit* in rich imagery. Such a book was also published for the Weissenhof exhibition. "Innenräume" (Interiors), its decidedly simple title, was as significant a feature as the plain typesetting and the emptiness that prevailed in the depicted rooms. The extremely sparsely furnished rooms with their bare walls, spotless linoleum floors, and bright light, which fell through the unusually large windows, contradicted every traditional notion of homeliness. One person might welcome this with a huge sense of relief, while another would be reminded of a hospital room. The rooms in the Weissenhofsiedlung (Weissenhof estate) were laboratories of modernity, and the furnishings were instruments of a radically altered lifestyle. Walter Knoll had managed to assert himself in this ambitious environment.

"MORE AND MORE, THE MODERN INTERIOR WILL BREAK AWAY FROM THE TRADITIONAL MODEL."
WALTER KNOLL

The fact that, now in his mid-50s, he saw himself as an innovator was a vital prerequisite for this. "More and more, the modern interior will break away from the traditional model," he noted in an artistic manifesto at the time of the company's founding.[32] Although the offspring of a furniture family, he was not a trained upholsterer, representing a new type of furniture manufacturer. His years in America and his friendships with esthetes such as Karl Gustav Vollmöller and Carl Koch did not fail to leave their mark. He felt a deep affinity with the avant-garde that had gathered in Stuttgart and purposely sought out contacts. A key difference from his brother Willy, who was rather a lone Swabian wolf. Furthermore, Walter had little trouble initiating conversations with artists and architects. And this was not only due to the fact that many of them also spoke the Swabian dialect. Others were also able to make use of this home advantage. In any case, Walter Knoll grasped the opportunity with both hands. His cheerful nature was certainly a help. As someone who loved public appearances, reached out to people, and had the ability to be extremely charming, personal contact was always a part of the job for him from the start. Consequently, it was no wonder whatsoever that he also had such a good

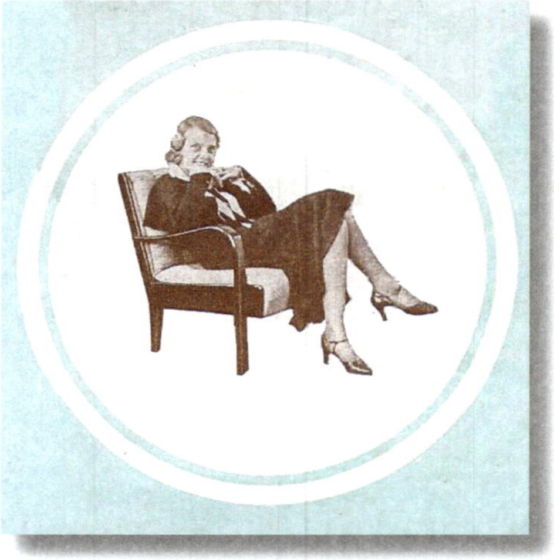

rapport with Mies van der Rohe, who copiously availed himself of his product range and, incidentally, was also of a fun-loving nature. The exhibition director placed upholstered furniture from Walter Knoll in five of his apartments, more than from any other company. The fact that they shared a predilection for noble elegance undoubtedly also played a role.[33] Four other architects from the leading group of *Neues Bauen* also opted for furniture from Walter Knoll, namely Ludwig Hilbersheimer, Adolf Rading, Hans Scharoun, and Adolf Schneck. The young enterprise was thus represented in nine apartments and, with this extremely strong presence, had eclipsed even traditional companies, not least that of his brother. Although Willy was able to exhibit his product range in the central hall 8, designed by Bernhard Pankok, together with other renowned Stuttgart furniture companies, and was thus part of the establishment, he had a presence in just one house in the model estate. A setback that must have somewhat rankled the notoriously ambitious entrepreneur.

Walter Knoll, who sought proximity to the avant-garde, made numerous acquaintances, including a certain Franz Schuster. Although this Austrian architect had not himself designed a house in the estate, he had excellent contacts and was, moreover, an experienced furniture designer. Schuster, born in Vienna in 1892, a student of Heinrich Tessenow, the godfather of reform architecture, emerged from the settlement movement and later worked in Dresden-Hellerau, the Valhalla of lifestyle reform. Eventually, he also designed a *Gemeindehof* (municipality building) in "Red Vienna," which was by far the largest of all the communal housing programs. As this explorer of the modern movement visited the Weissenhofsiedlung, he was precisely halfway to *Neues Frankfurt* (New Frankfurt), where a whole city in the spirit of *Neues Bauen* was being planned. There, Schuster was responsible for designing the objective furniture.[34] His *Aufbaumöbel* (assembly furniture), produced by the Erwin Behr company in Wendling, can be considered a prototype of modern wall cabinet systems. An alliance of kindred spirits developed between Knoll, Behr and Schuster, with

Paul Hahn also joining the ranks. In fact, Schuster then not only showcased his own combination cabinets, but also upholstered furniture from Walter Knoll, in the "Frankfurter Register," a goods catalog and a kind of handbook for *Neues Wohnen*. Thanks to the respectable showing at Weissenhof, Walter Knoll had become an established name overnight. However, Willy Knoll took this as an opportunity to sue his brother over the use of the family name, for which he held the sole rights. As a result, despite all the successes, Walter chalked 1927 up as "the difficult year." He fell ill over the matter and spent a few weeks in a sanatorium. The matter did not come to trial, however, as Erich, the youngest of the brothers, intervened and ensured that a settlement was reached.

ANTIMOTT AND PRODOMO – THE INVISIBLE REVOLUTION

The Weissenhof failure and the fraternal dispute did not hold Willy Knoll back for long. At least since the Nestra chairs of the pre-war period, his thoughts had continually returned to improving upon traditional upholstered furniture. Innovation, as one would say today, was his central theme. The Handi series, which propagated the padded chair, had already taken a further step away from the traditional full upholstery that dominated the market and living rooms at the time. With their visible structural design, the lightweight Handi chairs were a hybrid between a regular chair and an armchair, thus conforming to the spirit of the avant-garde. They were, nevertheless, only a precursor to a truly groundbreaking innovation, with which Willy Knoll would enjoy great success. Yet again, the appropriate stage for the premiere of this innovation would be provided by a pioneering Stuttgart exhibition. It was held at the "Kunstgewerbemuseum" in 1928, just one year on from "Die Form" and "Die Wohnung." The topic was an aspect of modern living that had, as yet, never been showcased to such an extent. And, unsurprisingly, it also bore a laconic title. The exhibition "Der Stuhl" (The Chair) featured "primarily simple, functional and comfortable models," claimed the preface to the catalog.[35] Adolf Schneck, who had also been involved in the two preceding exhibitions and was now able to apply himself to his area of expertise, chair design, acted as curator. Around 400 exhibits from German and international manufacturers provided a panorama of the various innovations of recent years. The avant-garde convened, among them Marcel Breuer, Le Corbusier, Ludwig Mies van der Rohe, Gerrit Rietveld, and Mart Stam. Not least the tubular steel chair, which had been presented for the first time almost two years prior at the opening of the Bauhaus in Dessau and celebrated as a sensation at Weissenhof, once again caused a stir. However, Willy Knoll's invention of a new kind of seat suspension, though far less spectacular purely in terms of external appearance, was also a hit, albeit mainly among the specialist public. The Antimott spring, which Willy Knoll was now having fitted in his latest models, did not change seating furniture with a new frame or a spectacular outer appearance, but from within through a technical principle. It was unseen, concealed beneath the flat, removable upholstery. The traditional principles of upholstery had been discarded. The structure now consisted of a series of enmeshed metal springs, which stretched between the seat and the backrest, forming an elastic supporting surface. This simple and space-saving system allowed for lightweight constructions (with a simplified production process) and solved a major problem that was pervasive at the time, namely the menacing disintegration of upholstered furniture by pests, in particular moth infestation. These ravenous flying insects all too readily nested inside seating furniture and destroyed it from within. The name "Antimott" took aim at this scourge and was immediately understood by everyone.

The Antimott was a real innovation and brought about a paradigm shift for upholstered furniture. The special springs required were not readily available in shops. They had to be developed for the new upholstery system, as did the necessary machinery. In the process, Willy Knoll, himself the prototypical Swabian inventor-entrepreneur, made use of the advantages offered by the region. After all, it was akin to the Silicon Valley of metalwork and mechanical engineering of the time. Willy Knoll, who had no experience in this area, relied on the help of a technology developer. Hellmuth Hirth, son of Albert Hirth, the Swabian Edison from Cannstatt, whose exporter in America Willy's brother, Walter, had intended to become prior to the war, was brought in to work on the Antimott. Hirth junior was in no way inferior to his father and had, incidentally, already gone to the U.S. as a 17 year old (Walter brought him a Christmas package from his parents). There, he was actually employed by Thomas Edison and also found work as a racing driver, among other things. On his return to Stuttgart, Hellmuth Hirth became an in-demand engine designer and a record-breaking aviation pioneer whose name would soon be known by every child in Germany. This acclaimed hero of the skies and horsepower founded the "Hirth Versuchsbau" company together with the brothers Ernst and Hermann Mahle. It was at the leading edge in everything to do with mechanics and metalwork. And Willy Knoll now turned to this

31 ▶ The authors were Bruno Taut ("Die Neue Wohnung," Leipzig, 1924), Sigfried Giedion (Befreites Wohnen, Zürich, 1929) and Mia Seeger (Der neue Wohnbedarf, Berlin, 1932).

32 ▶ Votteler, 1990, p. 83.

33 ▶ Mies van der Rohe, who is today seen as the sole representative of the tubular steel fraction, had designed a wooden set of furniture for his own house the previous year.

34 ▶ Ferdinand Kramer and Grete Schütte-Lihotzky were among his employees.

35 ▶ Votteler, 1983, p. 38.

SEATING INNOVATION

The patented Antimott system, which was based on metal springs and combined slim upholstery with high sitting comfort, was a groundbreaking invention that racked up rapidly increasing sales.

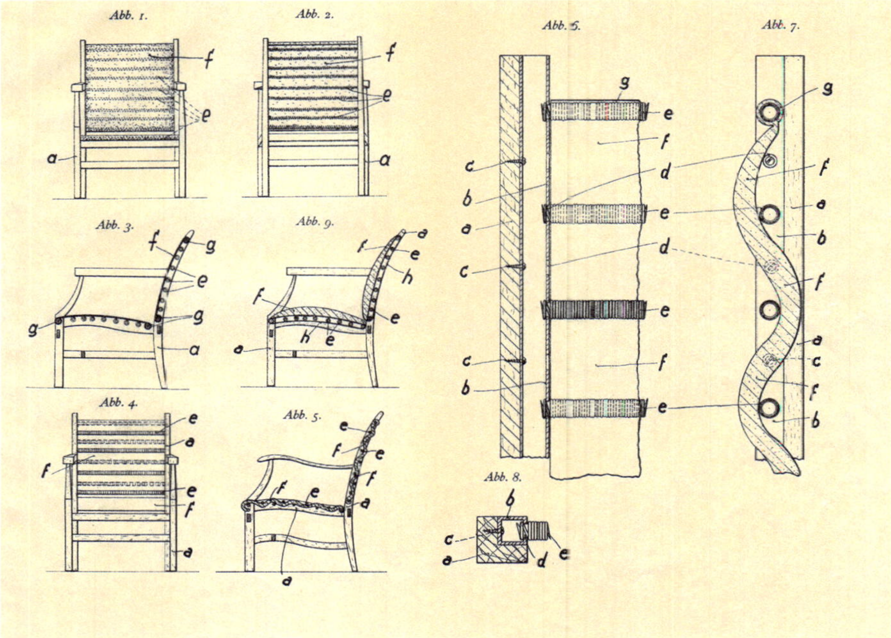

Chair Antimott SO 91, Wilhelm Knoll, Stuttgart, 1927

Patent specification No. 482145 for a "Upholstery and suspension for seating and loungers of all kinds," Wilhelm Knoll, Stuttgart, 1928

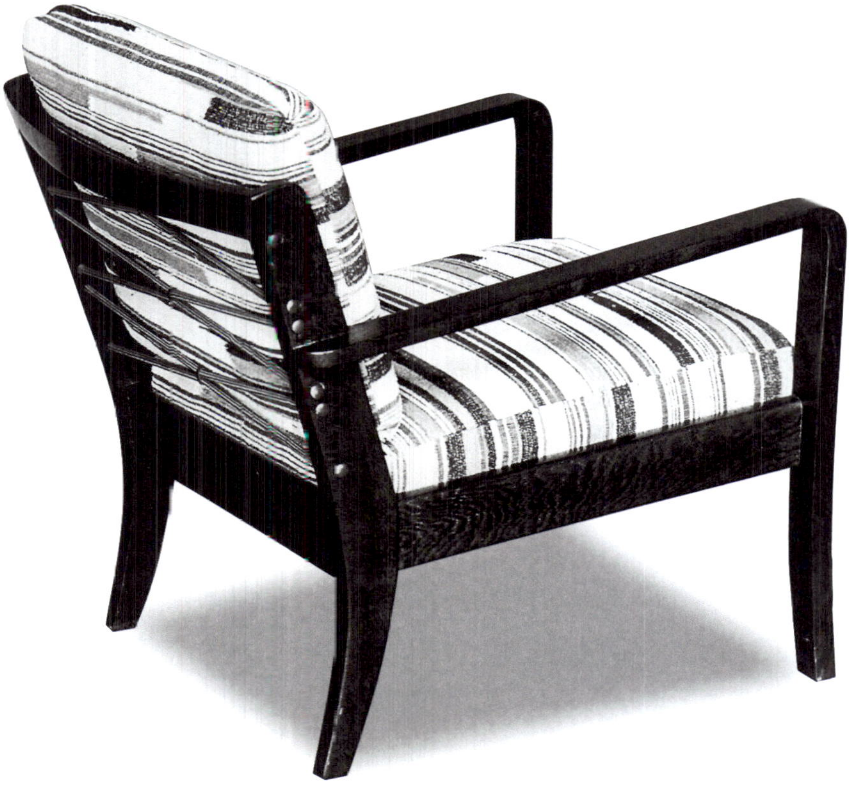

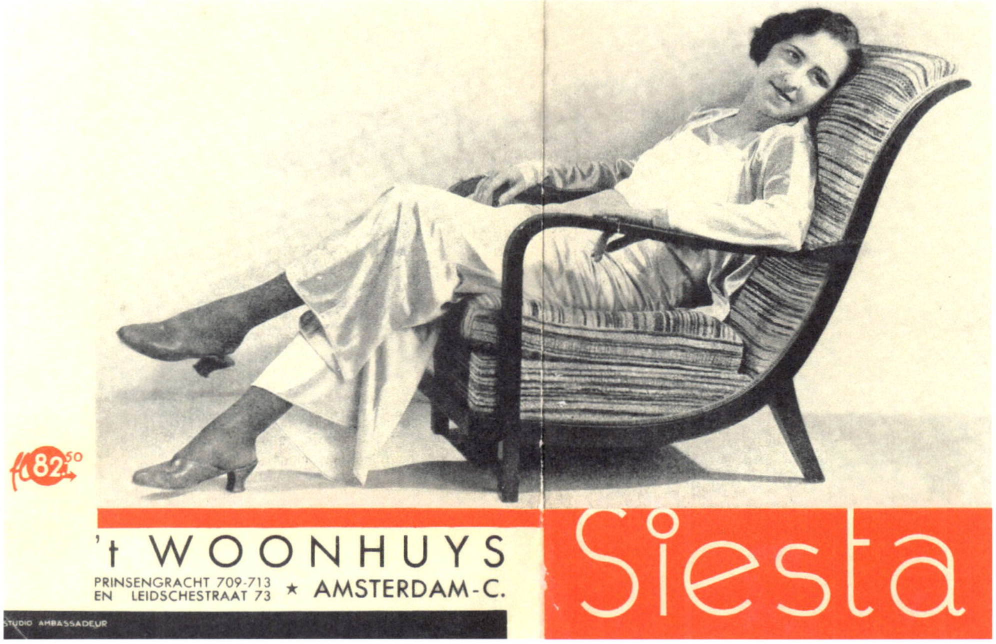

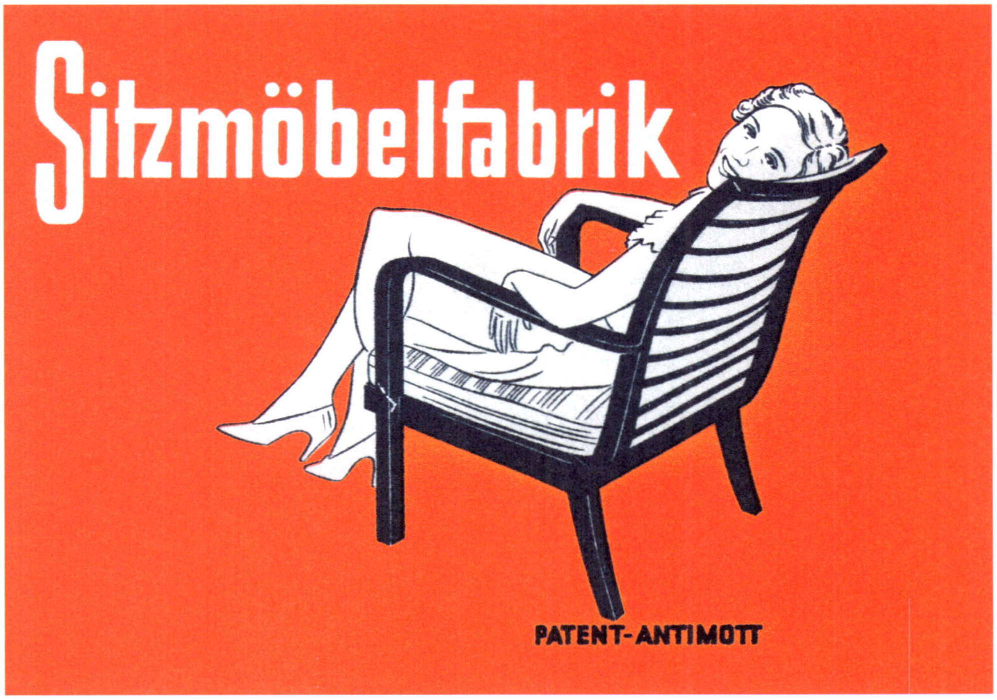

Advertisement of a Dutch
Antimott licensee, around 1930

Catalog of an Antimott licensee,
Zurich, around 1930

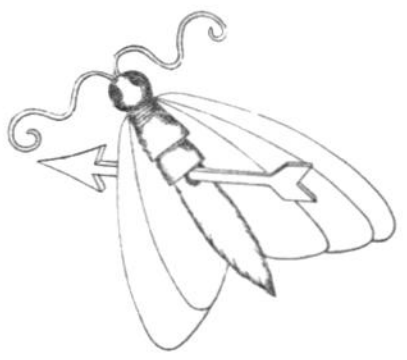

Swabian hotbed of innovation for his Antimott idea. To this end, he needed two machines; one to produce the springs, the other to spin fabric around them. The Antimott patent was by far the most important in the Knoll story, and likely also the most important in the upholstered furniture industry overall in the early modernist period.

Willy Knoll also had a logo designed for the new product, vividly demonstrating one of the main advantages of this innovative seating furniture: a stylized moth pierced through with an arrow. This graphic, somewhat savage emblem suited the memorable name. When coining the artificial word "Antimott," Willy Knoll was not only thinking about the technical aspects of the products, but also their communication. The success proved him right. Sales went through the roof. And not only in Germany. Exports also went into full swing. Parallel Antimott patents were registered in numerous countries. Eventually, a factory was constructed in Malmö, specially for Antimott models. As a result, Wilhelm Knoll was among the first German furniture companies

THE ANTIMOTT WAS A REAL INNOVATION. FROM A TECHNICAL POINT OF VIEW, THE PRODUCT RANGE WAS THE FIRST EXAMPLE OF MODERN UPHOLSTERED FURNITURE.

to have production facilities abroad. All of Scandinavia was supplied from southern Sweden. At the same time, successful partnerships were being entered into in other European countries, such as with Parker & Sons in England and Merchi in Italy.[36] Such a degree of internationalization was unique in the industry in those days.[37]

Although Antimott was virtually a sure-fire success, advertising was also used. "Durable, hygienic, maximum comfort at the lowest possible price"[38], the advantages were recited somewhat matter-of-factly. A head-turner ultimately emerged in the form of an image motif, the "chair with lady."[39] The highlight: the young lady in the Antimott chair was not shot from the front as was accustomed, but from behind. Consequently, she smiled at the viewer over her shoulder and the backrest of the chair (see p. 63). This advertising icon, the first of the furniture industry, had many faces in various countries. It was every bit as new and unusual as the seating technology of the Antimott. With the groundbreaking springs, a suitable design for the padded chair had been found and, consequently, established no more and no less than a new class of seating furniture, as had already been previously achieved with the club chair and the Handi series.

However, Willy Knoll, the father of all these innovations, had also understood that there was much more to be made of the new invention, specifically the development of further types of armchair. As a result, a kind of variable folding chair was produced with a stool, which could be used to stretch out on. To place even greater emphasis on its newness, it was also given a new invented name "Lieger" (The Lounger). The success of the Antimott was reflected in the unanimous praise of the expert community, but above all in the fantastic sales figures. It was almost beyond belief. In the middle of the Great Depression, while corporate collapses were the order of the day and millions of German were losing their jobs, the Wilhelm Knoll company was enjoying an expansion of incredible proportion thanks to the Antimott. The workshops in Forststrasse quickly became too small. In 1930, at a time when people were taking "emergency measures" in Württemberg[40], Willy Knoll purchased the former Tivoli brewery in Stuttgart as an additional new production site. But even this only sufficed in the short term. Eventually, in 1932, a vacant building was first rented in Gaildorf am Kocher, around 45 miles from Stuttgart, with a new factory being built next door soon thereafter. This site would later evolve into Wilhelm Knoll's main production facilities. By 1937, "Bauteil III" (Building Unit III) had already been constructed there, and no longer just at ground level, but multi-storey. Initially, Willy Knoll himself traveled to the Franconian Gaildorf every week, not least to personally train the upholsterers there. They were, of course, unfamiliar with the Antimott method. The joinery was steadily expanded. This was necessary in order to manage the increasingly expansive Antimott product range. By now, hardly any unemployment existed in Gaildorf.

By 1930, the innovative upholstery had already captured another area of application. Opel in Rüsselsheim had car seats produced according to the Antimott principle fitted in two of its latest models. Special patents for this development could also be registered in various countries. The positive press response that the Antimott chair had provoked could soon be used for advertising purposes. It was a wholly "new class of seating furniture"[41], one would read. In short, the Wilhelm Knoll company had discovered the "Egg of Columbus" of the upholstery industry.[42] The question remains, though, why such a quantum leap in the history of modern furniture has thus far received so little acknowledgment. Not to mention the design historians, who have evidently been completely eluded by this paradigm shift, in which technical

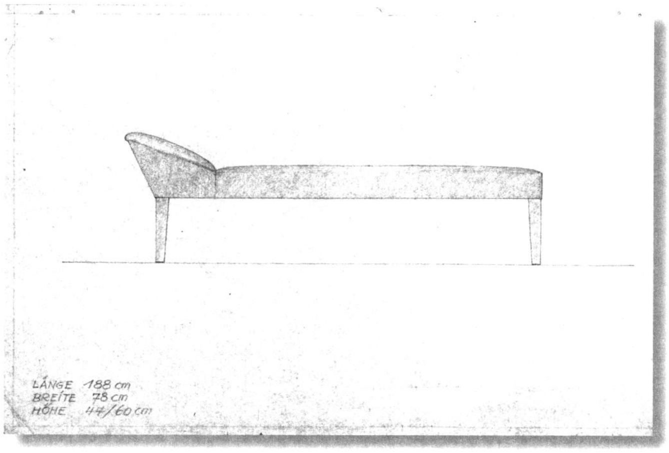

and visual advances complemented one another without restraint. Attention was, and still is until today, primarily focused on the architectural avant-garde. The equally pioneering, esthetically "tasteful" and incredibly commercially successful Antimott variant, by contrast, has remained a blank spot on the map of the modern furniture landscape.

For Wilhelm Knoll, padded chairs, sofas and loungers were now the focus of production. There was also another form of seating furniture that would turn out to be a sales driver. The couch was popular during this period. Here, the use of seat and back cushions was also typical for Wilhelm Knoll. There was, however, yet another idea, which was also made possible by an open design: the further development of the folding couch. Around 1930, Martha Knoll, Willy's wife, devised folding mechanisms. They gave versatility to the couch by allowing the seat to be adjusted and used as a reclining surface in its folded state. This was enabled by folding or extendable side parts (also double-sided) and adjustable seat backs. Such mechanisms are a part of the Knoll tradition that has been continued to the current day. The Knoll dynasty was characterized by an atmosphere of innovation. Furniture with smart conversion options also occupies a prominent place in the current Walter Knoll product range.[43]

The technique of conversion runs like a thread through the company's history. Extendable chairs that mutated into relaxing armchairs when required had already been included in the product range before the First World War. This conversion principle was now transferred to the couch. Magazines such as "Mode und Heim" (Fashion and Home) and "Elegante Welt" (Elegant World) extolled the benefits of the "wider relaxation couch."[44] The new furniture was a hybrid, a couch and bed in one. This was occurring at a time in which living space was tight and expensive. Even among bourgeois circles, people often had to live in confined space and, therefore, contemplated *Die Wohnung für das Existenzminimum* (The Dwelling for Minimal Existence)[45]. In terms of her ingenuity, Martha Knoll, a smart woman who is mentioned here for the first (and also the only) time, was certainly capable of going head-to-head with the avant-gardists of the time. However, the invention of the modern folding sofa is attributed to the Finnish architect Alvar Aalto.[46] Which is clearly dubious. The couch, which was variable and no longer prescribed a particular sitting posture, offered a greater degree of freedom. Fashion provided the complementing items of clothing. Men slipped on casual pullovers. Women wore short, above-the-knee skirts with a concealing, loose fit at the waist that did not inhibit movement. The variable couch was a challenge for designers. This form of hybrid furniture opened up an endless field of technical and layout improvements for them. A task that would occupy them right until the present day. And although it would soon be present in virtually every home, the folding couch is treated as a wallflower in design history.

As the Wilhelm Knoll company proudly announced, the Antimott was "a revolution in the market."[47] For it did not take long before there were attempts to ride the coattails of this success. By 1929, a type of upholstery that was based on the same basic idea as the Antimott had already emerged, though using steel strips instead of spiral springs. The manufacturer was none other than Walter Knoll, Willy's own brother. He also came up with a similarly striking artificial word for his patent: "Prodomo."[48] Furthermore, in addition to the simplified production and high sitting comfort, it also enabled the construction of remarkably slimmer furniture. An elastic steel band suspension for the seats and backrests was integrated into the respective seating furniture, taking up the smallest of spaces. Franz Schuster was given the job of designing numerous Prodomo models. They were characterized by their flat

36 ▶ This Antimott furniture was then marketed under the names Parker-Knoll and Meroni-Knoll respectively. Parker-Knoll was a licensee. The company exists to this day.

37 ▶ Another example of early international networking was the bentwood chair manufacturer Thonet.

38 ▶ Knoll, 1965, p. 24.

39 ▶ Ibid.

40 ▶ Landesarchiv Baden-Württemberg, record E 130 b Bü 3219. Among other things, this involved the construction of the Rhine-Neckar canal and "winter aid" for families in need.

41 ▶ Knoll, 1965, p. 24.

42 ▶ Newspaper "Württemberger Zeitung," 9/25/1928, advertisement for the exhibition "Der Stuhl" (The Chair). With a Swabian sense of modesty, this was not too heavily accentuated. It was surely also up to the company to report on this – but this is precisely what did not happen.

43 ▶ E.g. the Living Platform or Living Landscape series by Walter Knoll.

44 ▶ Knoll, 1965, p. 25.

45 ▶ *Die Wohnung für das Existenzminimum* (The Dwelling for Minimal Existence) became a slogan of *Neues Bauen*.

46 ▶ Giedion, 1982, p. 472.

47 ▶ Knoll, 1965, p. 24.

48 ▶ It was even quite possible to deduce a reference to protection against the threat of moths.

SPRING MECHANISM

Special machines were required to produce and wrap the Antimott springs. In the process, the partnership between Willy Knoll and the inventor Hellmuth Hirth proved successful.

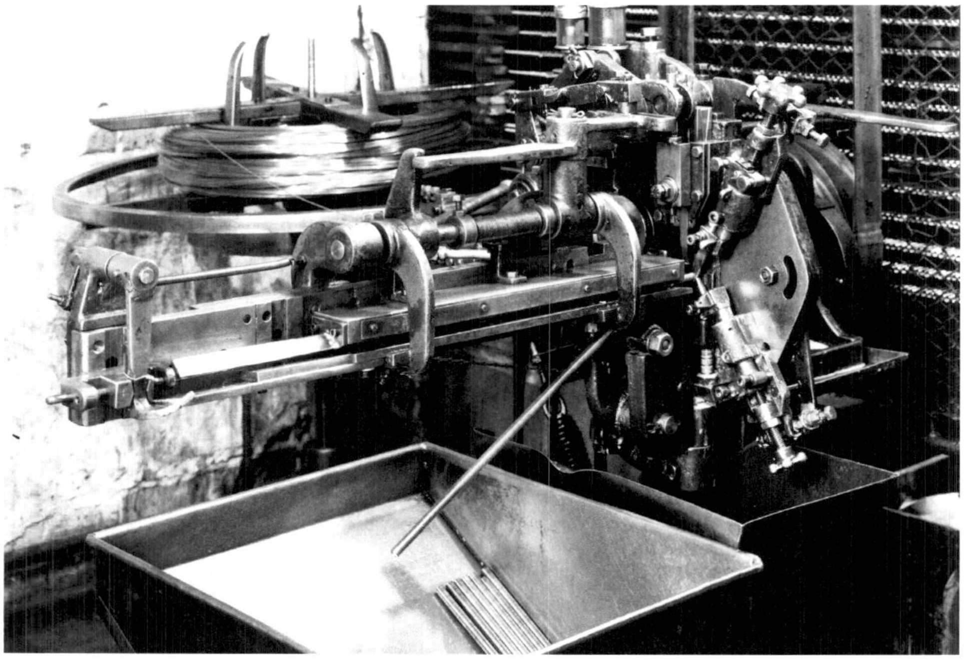

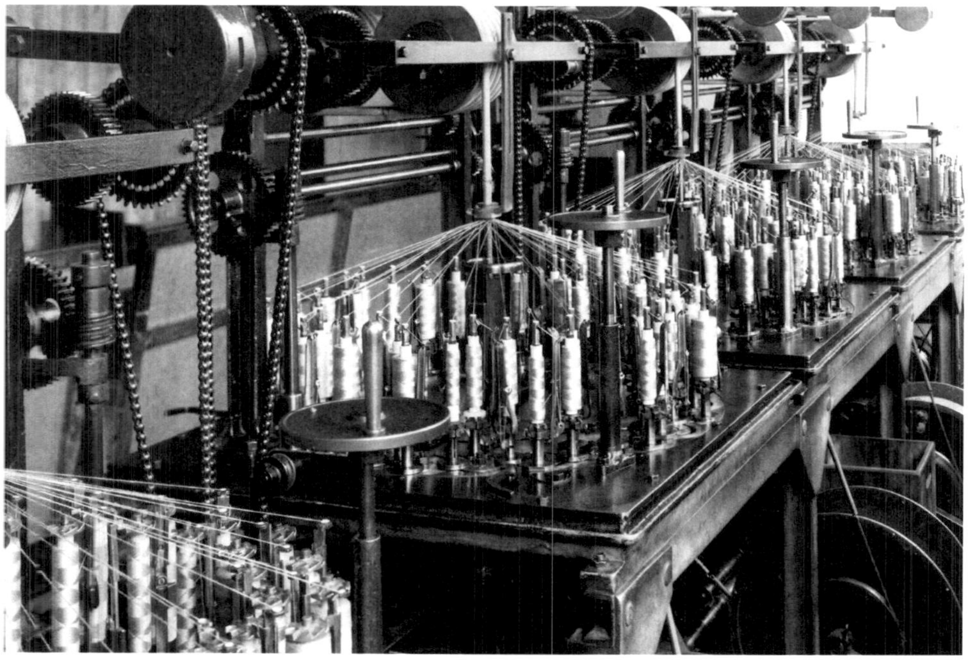

Machine for the production of Antimott springs,
Wilhelm Knoll,
Stuttgart, around 1930

Machine for wrapping Antimott springs,
Wilhelm Knoll,
Stuttgart, around 1930

Aviation and technical pioneer Hellmuth Hirth in a plane by Albatros Werke, Berlin 1915

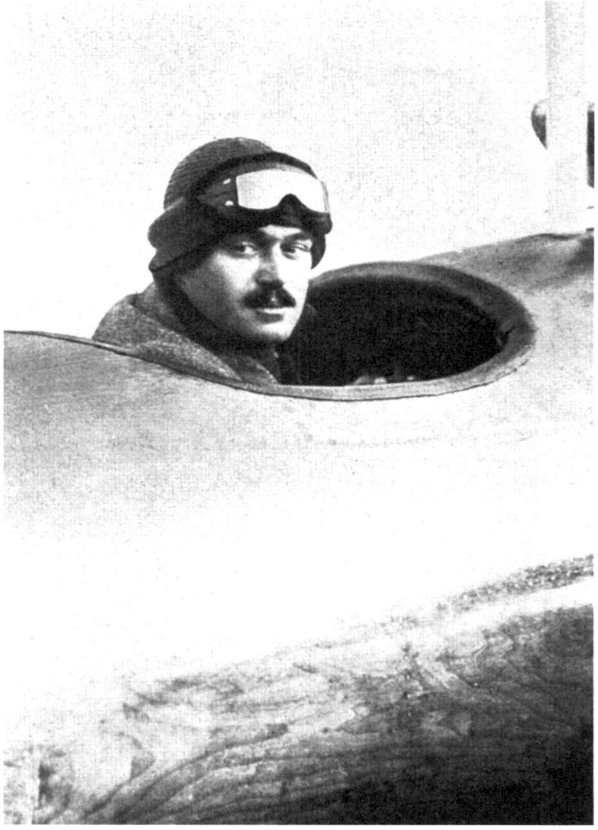

Willy Knoll,
Stuttgart, around 1925

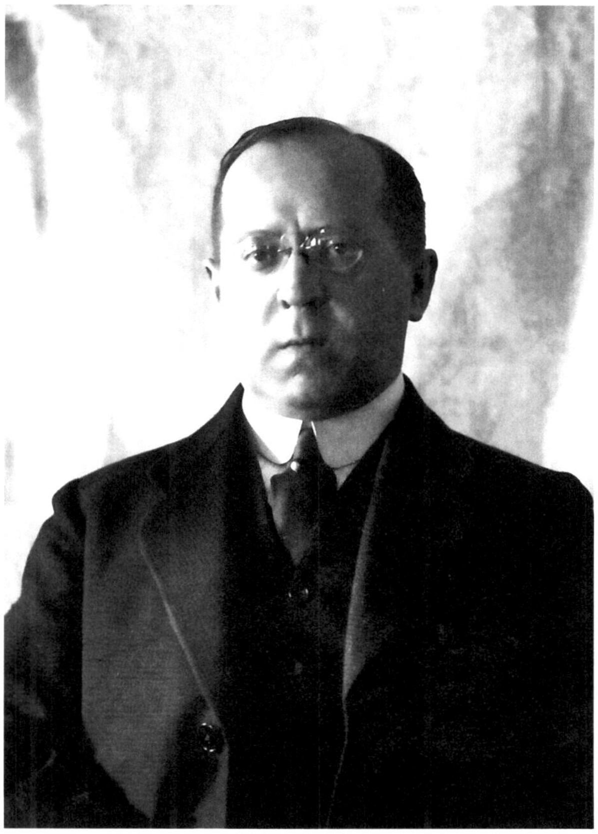

padding and wooden frame in elegant black. "The solution to one of the problems of the time and of your home," simply "essential for bachelors" and "the working woman,"[49] Walter Knoll had printed on his advertising brochures. All this could hardly have been pleasing to Willy Knoll. The fact that his brother then also launched a "Prodomo couch-bed" with a specially designed folding mechanism represented a further setback to the prospects of a fraternal reconciliation.

The English name, which – then as now – sounded intrinsically modern, played no insignificant role in the triumph of the couch. The economic recovery beginning in the mid-1920s was accompanied by a change in mood. And it had an irresistible rhythm, namely that of jazz from the U.S. One dance craze after another swept in from across the Atlantic, which, from the Shimmy[50] to the Charleston, all bore English names. On the dance floor, the population moved to the tempo of the city. The urban landscape was also becoming Americanized. In 1928, just one year after the exhibition at Weissenhof, the Tagblatt Tower, Stuttgart's formidable first high-rise at 18 stories high, was unveiled in the inner city.[51] Like the Weissenhofsiedlung, it is now considered an outstanding testimony of *Neues Bauen* and caused a similar amount of controversy at the time. At night, the contours of the office tower were highlighted in neon strips to great effect. New buildings were a manifestation of modernity and were made all the more striking by the contrast with the facades of the historic city center. One example was the Breuninger menswear department store with its circumferential bands of windows, a white block whose nine stories now towered far above the roofs of the old city. As ever, the commercial palaces competed with regard to their architecture. The bold glass facade of the Schocken department store, a design by renowned Berlin architect Erich Mendelsohn, which sprung up at around the same time, was likewise a potent symbol of progress and received extensive attention beyond Stuttgart.[52] The city was being refurnished.

Walter and Willy Knoll were now in direct competition. Whereby the latter benefited from a particular advantage that was not to be underestimated. He possessed the rights to the name "Knoll." This meant that his brother was not permitted to use it. And from precisely this conflict emerged a particular dynamic. As a result, a new brand name, consisting of the uppercase letters "K" and "F," began to appear in Walter Knoll's catalogs towards the end of the 1920s. "K-F" was an acronym standing for Knoll and Feuerbach, i.e., the family name plus the location, the two fixed points in the company's identity.[53] This principle had already been applied once in the early stages of the company around 1900. Back then it had been "WK" and "ST" for Wilhelm Knoll and Stuttgart. In any case the Prodomo name had by now effectively become Walter Knoll's most important figurehead. The sonorous artificial word with a resounding triple "o" was striking in a way similar to Wilhelm Knoll's Antimott – with its crackling double "t." Both are successful examples of applied onomatopoeia. But that's not all. Putting such a sub-branch in the spotlight in such a way has otherwise been a rare occurrence in the industry, and has since almost become a Knoll specialty. The genesis of the brand names of the furniture family Knoll, with all their ramifications, is a unique and as yet, in all its originality and diversity, undocumented phenomenon. This communicative aspect of the company's history clearly reflects the character of the Knoll furniture dynasty and enabled it to become the furniture brand of modernity.

„PRODOMO" SESSEL

THE PASSENGER ROOMS IN THE EXTREMELY SPACIOUS GONDOLA OF THE HINDENBURG WERE FURNISHED WITH "ANTIMOTT LIGHT METAL CHAIRS."

The fact that Walter and Willy Knoll got in each other's way did nothing to hinder their success. Quite the contrary; during this period both won contracts of a prestige that was hard to beat. In 1929, Walter Knoll provided furnishings for the Do X, a legendary aircraft. By far the world's largest aircraft at the time, with its twelve monstrous 600 hp engines mounted on the wings, it was unmistakable and awe-inspiring, ensuring that crowds gathered wherever it made an appearance. This giant of the skies was built by the Dornier company in Lindau on Lake Constance. For the exclusive circle of passengers, only the best was good enough. The exquisite interior design consisted of Prodomo furniture, which was ideal for this purpose due to its compact lightweight design. Although the flying boat, which took off and landed on water, never went into regular service, the advertising impact was huge.

In the same year, 1929, the "Bremen" passenger liner was awarded the "Blue Riband" for the fastest Atlantic crossing. This success was a balm for the collective German soul. A technical masterpiece (ensured by 30 engineers who were constantly on board), the passenger ship was then the world's most advanced fast steamer, with a level of comfort and luxury that was also unparalleled. In first class, glamorous passengers could take their seats in upholstered chairs from Walter Knoll. He later recalled that it was far from easy to gain a foothold in this exclusive terrain. Despite multiple trips to Bremen and the delivery of sample models, the gentlemen from the Norddeutscher Lloyd shipping company were seemingly incapable of reaching a decision: the contract would almost have been awarded to a Bremen-based company were it not for the intervention of Paul Hahn, whose powers of persuasion were considerably above average. Walter Knoll was now a brand with a presence in the luxury segment.

At the time, there were also other German-built transportation behemoths that caused a sensation, not least the zeppelins. When they appeared in the sky, it was not only children who went into raptures. The Swabian origins of the Graf von Zeppelin as well as the location of his airshipyard in the city of Friedrichshafen on Lake Constance induced a certain amount of local pride. Airships seemed to be the future. The "Hindenburg," one of the largest aircrafts ever built, took to the skies in the mid-1930s.[54] This prestigious project presented Willy Knoll, long known as a furniture innovator, with an opportunity. The passenger rooms in the extremely spacious gondola were furnished with "Antimott light metal chairs."[55] These were aluminum models that were suitable for aviation thanks to their low weight and presumably were specially developed for this purpose.

By around 1930, both Knoll companies had included tubular steel furniture in their product range. This innovation of the late 1920s, which made its breakthrough at the Weissenhof exhibition and would go on to become the epitome of modernity, reached a wider audience in the 1930s.[56] Paul Hahn, Walter Knoll's man for in-house designs, recognized the design possibilities that a frame of bent tubes offered and developed numerous variants. Not only were armchairs and sofas produced in varying designs. Chairs, footstools and tables with metal frames also found their way into the catalog, which – itself an indication of its great significance – was printed specially for the tubular steel range. Despite the fact that Marcel Breuer and Ludwig Mies van der Rohe had claimed the rights to seating furniture on skids as well as cantilever chairs, there was no break in contact with the two former Bauhaus masters, although the situation did give rise to frequent heated discussions.[57] Judicial disputes, which commonly revolved around this issue in those days, were nevertheless avoided. Tubular steel, this central myth of the First Modernity, later became a fruitful ongoing theme in all branches of the Knoll dynasty right through to the present day.

In the spring of 1929, a crash on the New York Stock Exchange plunged first the USA, and then the rest the world, into an economic

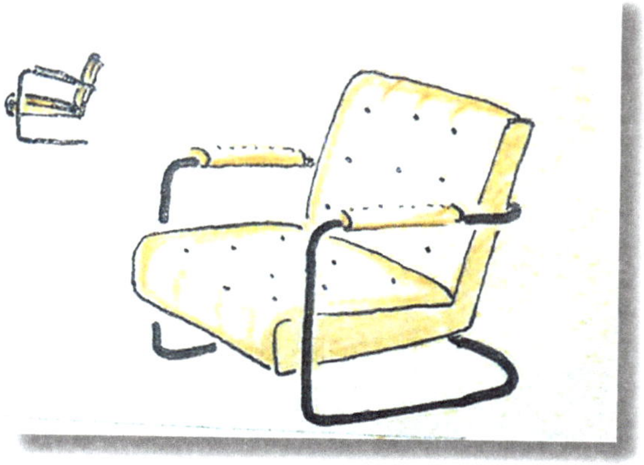

abyss. Germany, which was living on credit, was hit particularly hard. Just ten years after the post-war collapse, the economy slid into its next severe crisis. Extremists exploited the precarious situation to their own benefit. Governments collapsed on a weekly basis. At the Stuttgart-based Vollmöller corporation revenues dropped by a quarter in 1930 alone. Karl Gustav Vollmöller, now majority shareholder and senior member of the supervisory board, for the first time had to assume entrepreneurial responsibility for himself and his siblings. In the attempt to open up new markets, he eventually succeeded in arranging a partnership with the American textile firm Jantzen Knitting Mill, a leading manufacturer of swimsuits. A cooperation and licensing agreement was signed in 1932. During the negotiations, which were conducted with Jantzen's British branch in London, his brother-in-law and friend Walter Knoll was by his side.[58] The Jantzen deal marked a turnaround in fortunes for Vollmöller. And the resulting transatlantic relations would prove to be a remarkable stroke of luck for the further evolution of the Knoll dynasty.

---

49 ▶ Flyer, around 1930.

50 ▶ Eichstedt and Polster, 1985, p. 35 ff.

51 ▶ The first exposed concrete building in Germany with the world's highest paternoster, constructed in 1927/28 under the direction of local architect Ernst Otto Oßwald.

52 ▶ The design originated from Erich Mendelsohn, one of the leading figures of *Neues Bauen* (New Building). There were, however, also great talents among the Stuttgart-based architects such as Richard Döcker, Paul Laszlo, and the brothers Bodo and Heinz Rasch.

53 ▶ "K-F" is not mentioned anywhere in the company's history. That alone speaks volumes about the repressed conflict.

54 ▶ The "Hindenburg" (official designation LZ 129) exploded in spectacular fashion upon landing in New York. The disaster resulted in 36 fatalities.

55 ▶ Knoll, 1965, p. 26.

56 ▶ Similar to the *Bauhaus* wallpaper collection.

57 ▶ Although legal disputes concerning tubular steel were far from a rarity in those days, Walter Knoll managed to avoid them.

58 ▶ Founded in Oregon as the Portland Knitting Company in 1910, the firm developed into a major producer of swimwear. It is highly likely that the German origins of the company founders John A. Zehntbauer and Carl Jantzen also played a role in the business relations with Vollmöller.

SITTING FREEDOM

The couch, a furniture innovation of the 1920s, was simple, modern and egalitarian. Women were also able to sit back and relax. A new freedom of sitting prevailed.

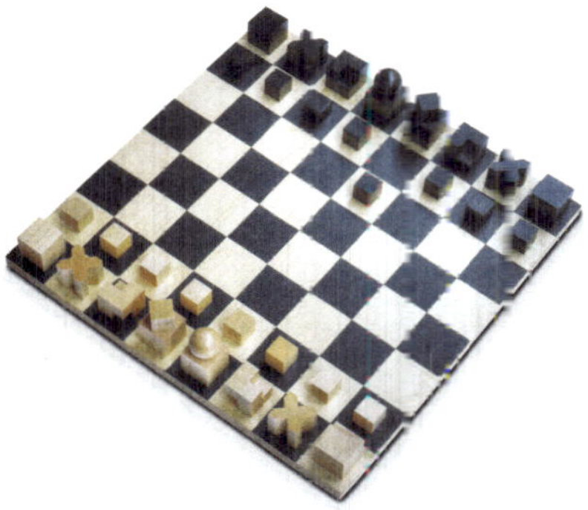

Chess set,
design by Josef Hartwig,
Bauhaus, Weimar, 1924

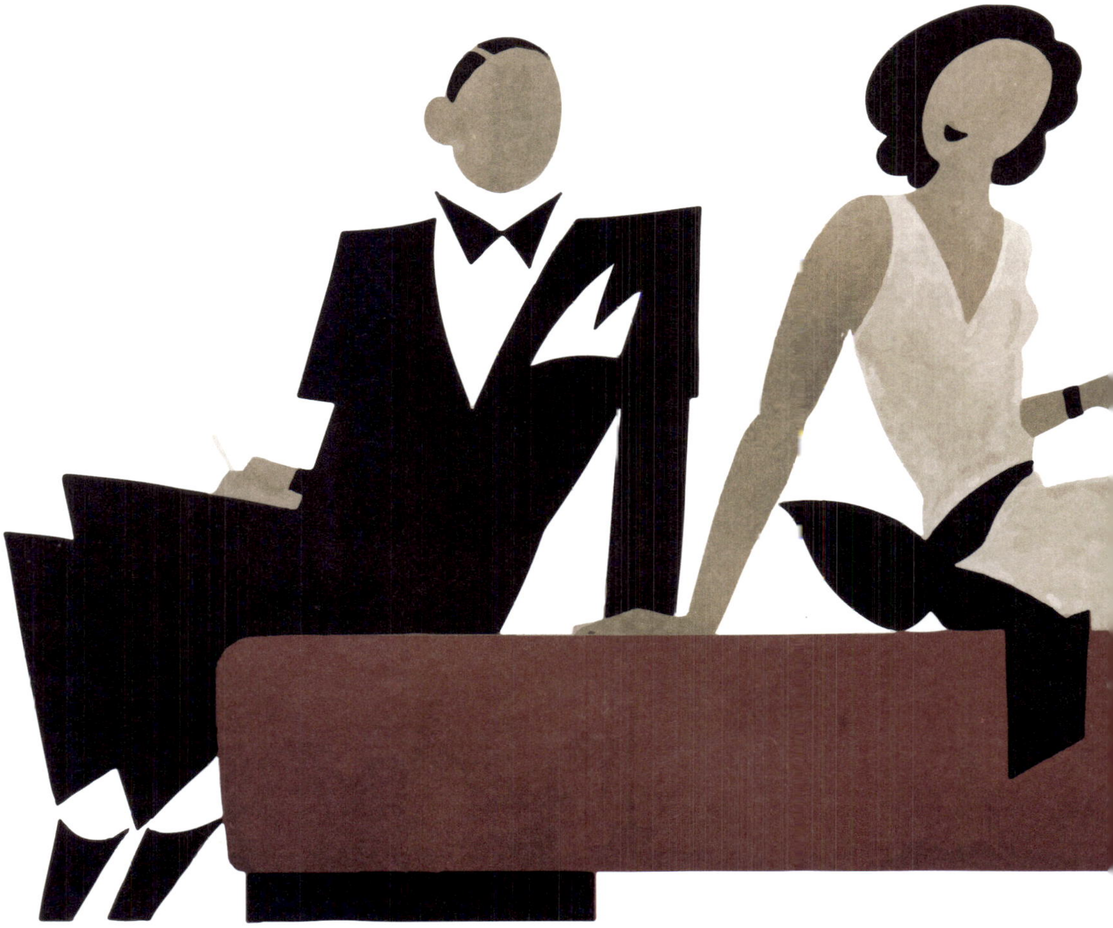

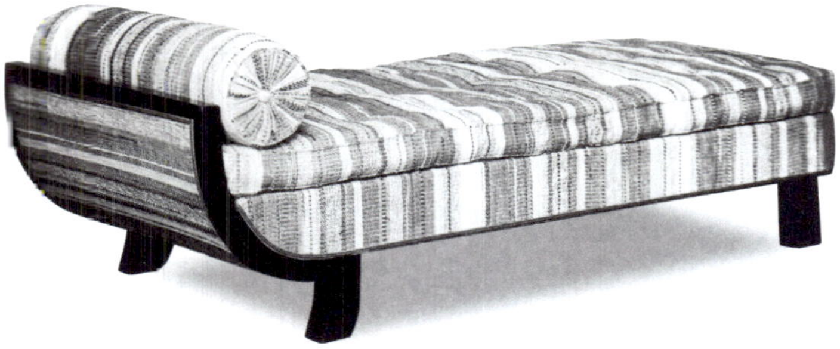

Advertisement,
Wilhelm Knoll,
Stuttgart, around 1930

Chaise longue 761,
Wilhelm Knoll,
Stuttgart, around 1930

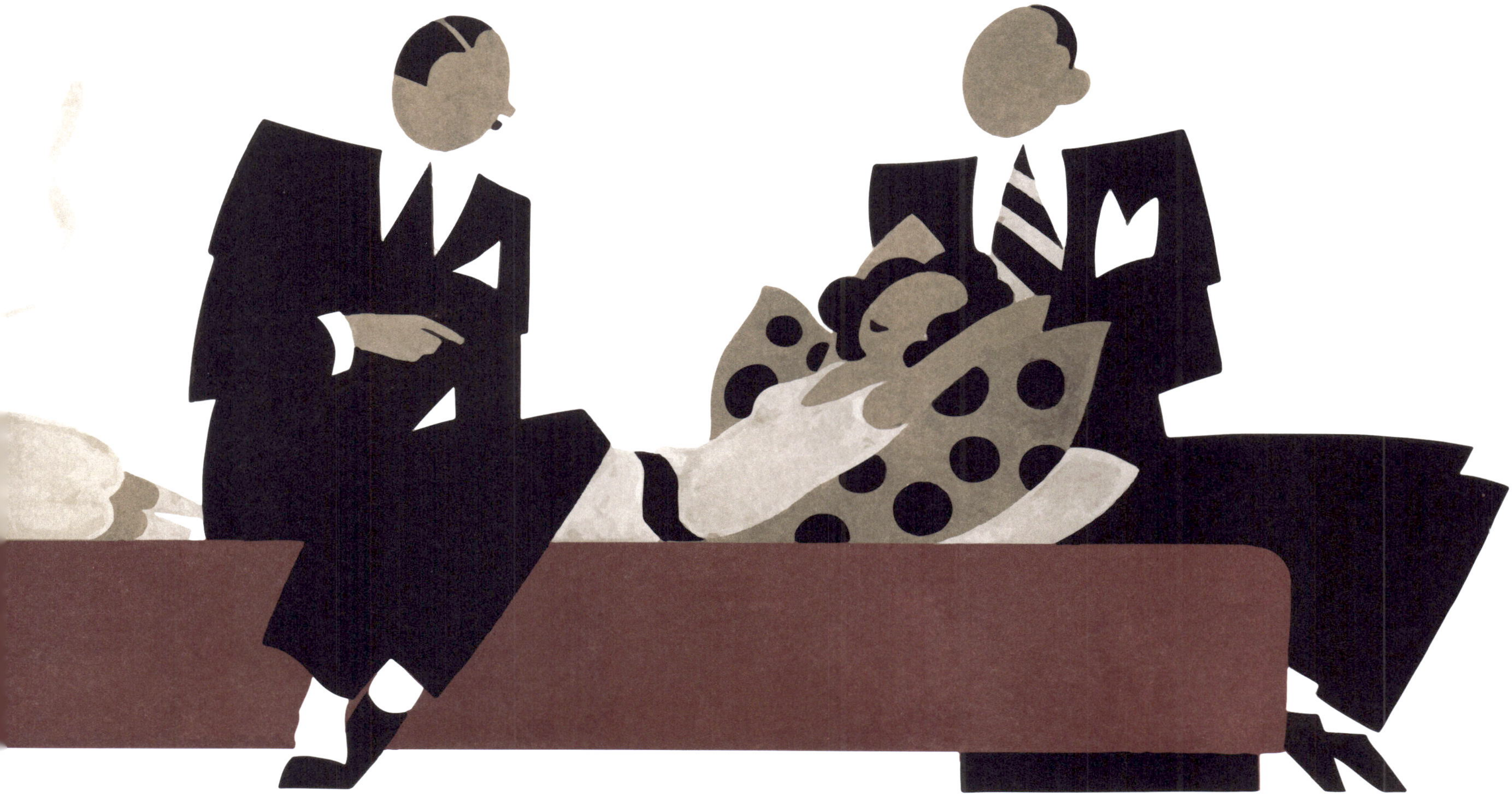

FURNITURE INVENTOR

For the development of the Antimott spring, Willy Knoll sought the assistance of inventor Hellmuth Hirth, a Stuttgart-based expert in metal and engines. His Versuchsbau company had been a successful Swabian think tank.

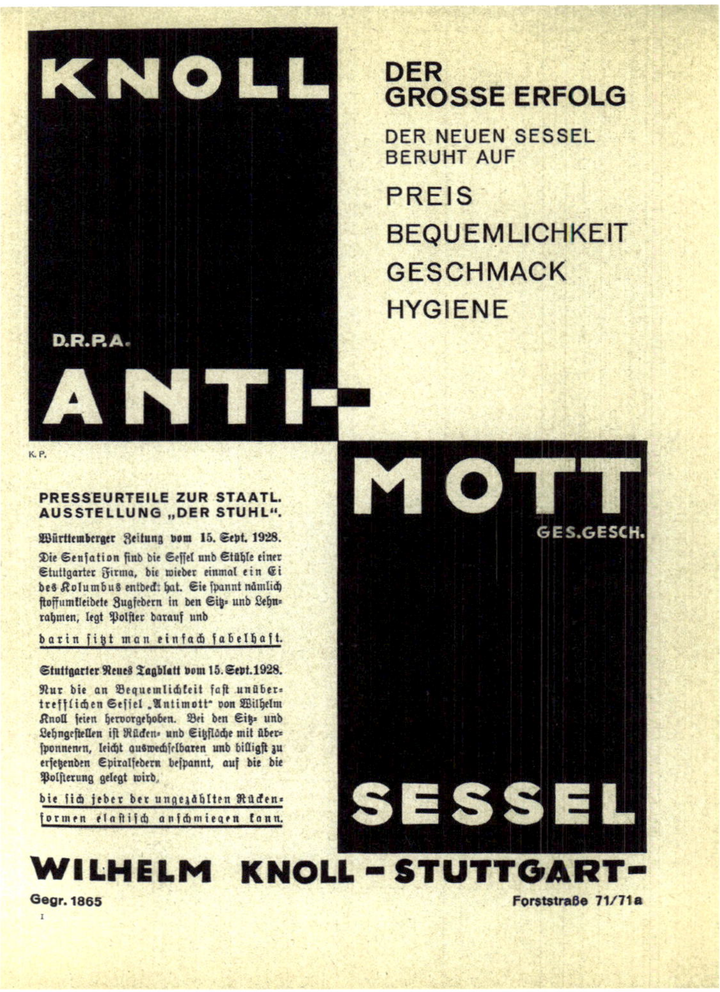

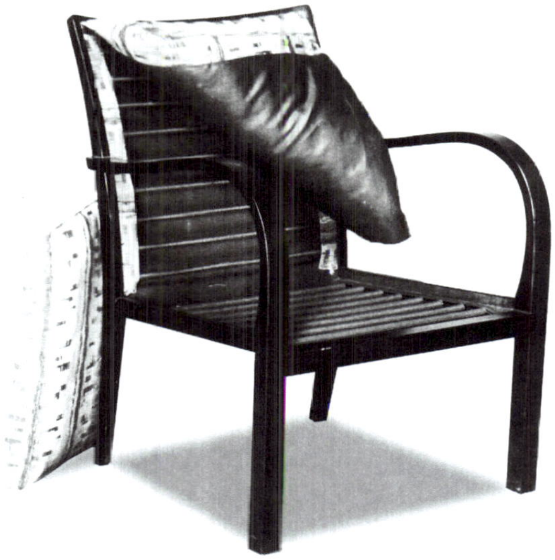

Advertisement,
Wilhelm Knoll,
Stuttgart, 1928

Chair Antimott 595,
Wilhelm Knoll,
Stuttgart, 1928

LOUNGER

With the Antimott technology, Willy Knoll wanted to create new types of furniture. Such as this relaxing armchair with an adjustable sitting position and a memorable name.

Advertisement, Wilhelm Knoll, chair design by Karl Pullich, Stuttgart, 1927

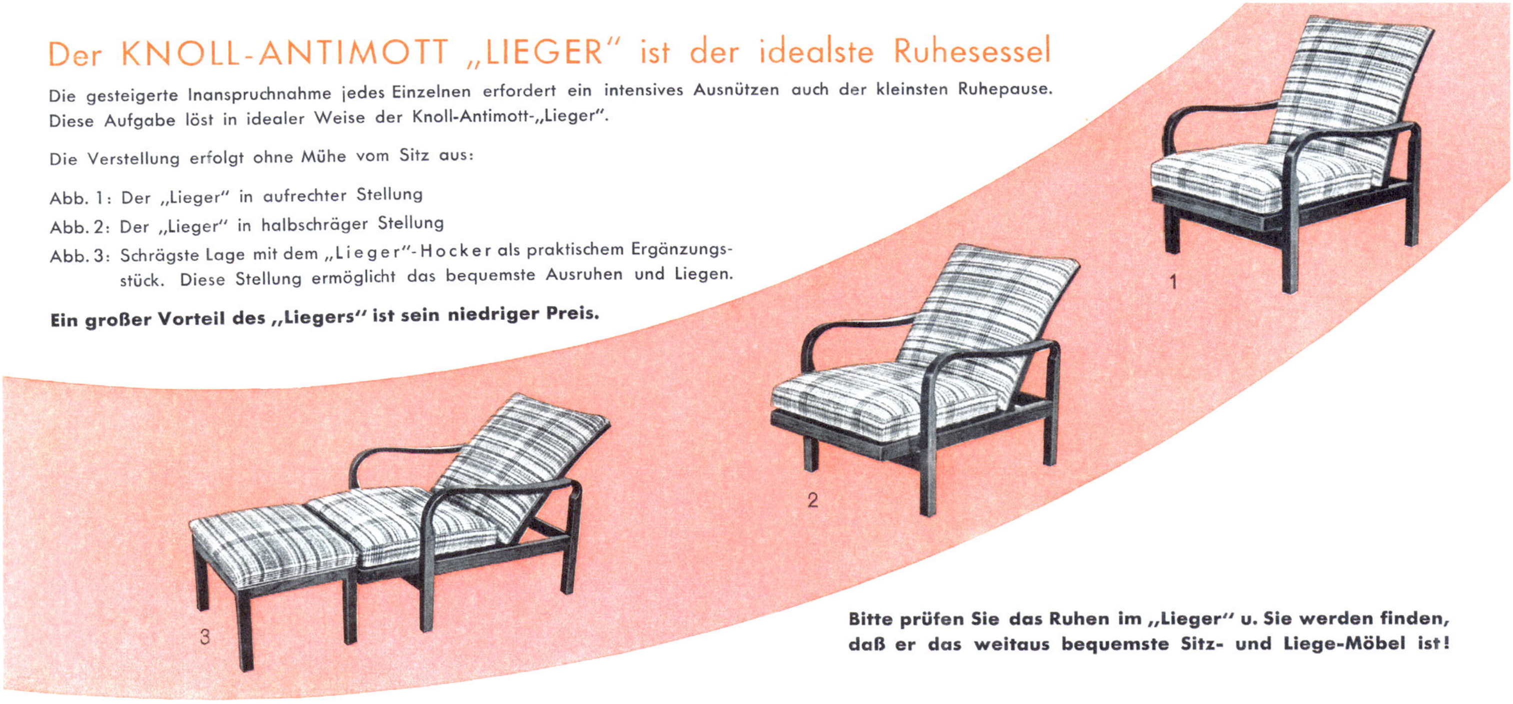

MODEL ESTATE

The Weissenhofsiedlung (Weissenhof estate) in Stuttgart was a demonstration of *Neues Wohnen* (New Living). Architects who are now world-famous, such as Le Corbusier and Walter Gropius, were involved. The at the time still young Walter Knoll company had the strongest presence with its furniture.

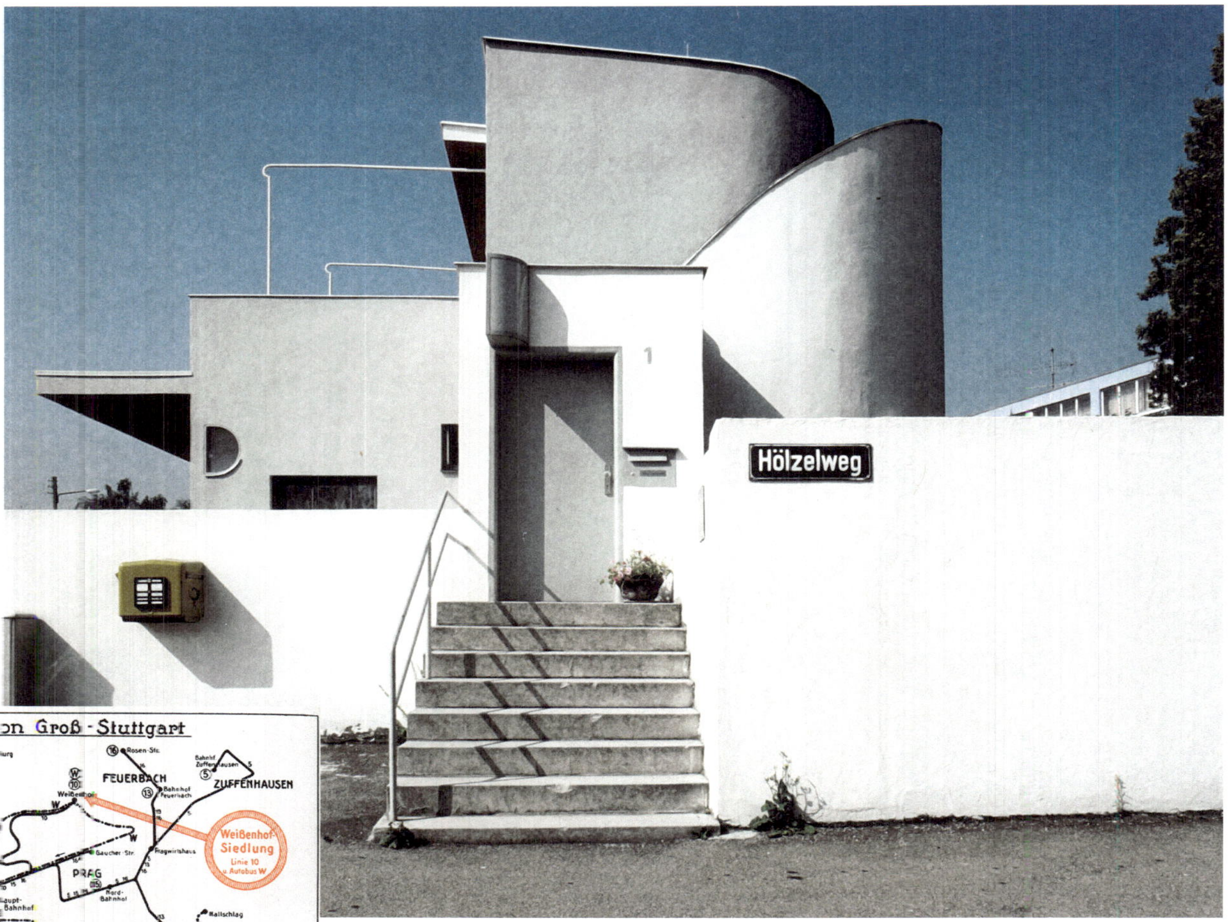

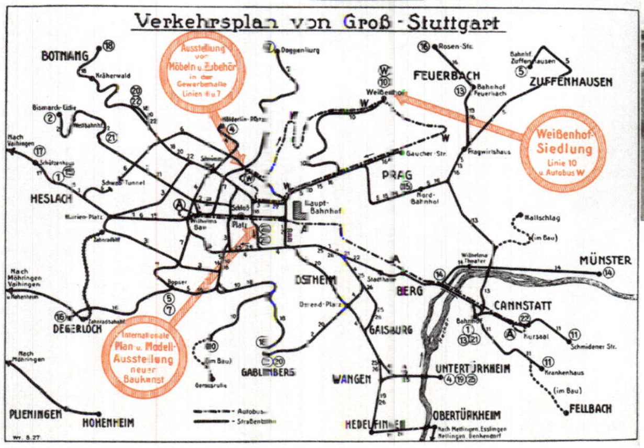

Weissenhofsiedlung, house 33,
architect Hans Scharoun,
Stuttgart (built in 1927)

Network map,
Stuttgart, 1927

Weissenhofsiedlung, house 33,
architect Hans Scharoun, photo from the
illustrated book "Innenräume" (Interiors),
Stuttgart, 1927

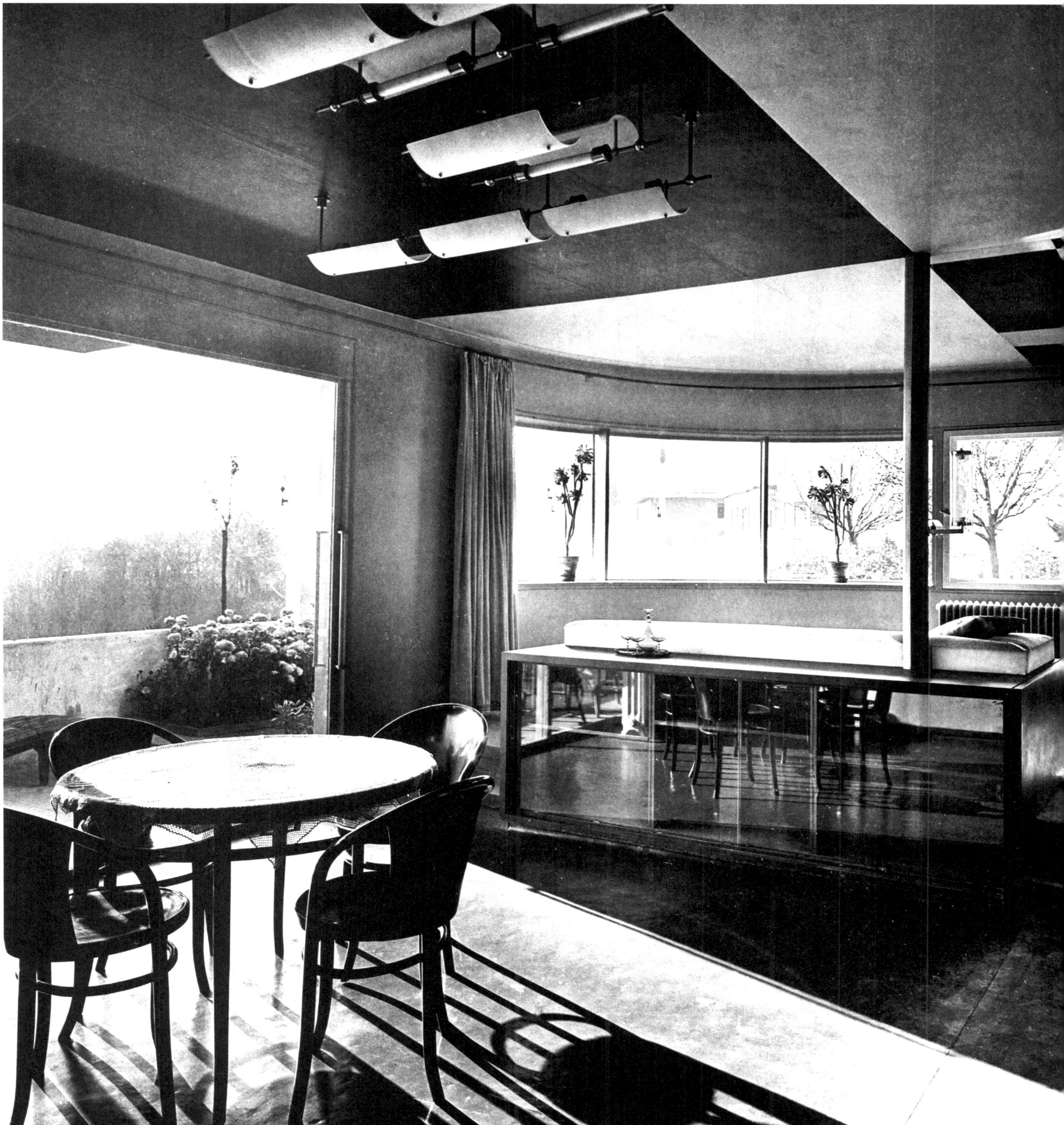

EXHIBITS

The exhibition director Ludwig Mies van der Rohe, avant-garde architect and later director of the Bauhaus, had a pronounced taste for upholstered furniture from Walter Knoll. It stood in five of his sparsely furnished show apartments and in four other model dwellings in the Weissenhofsiedlung.

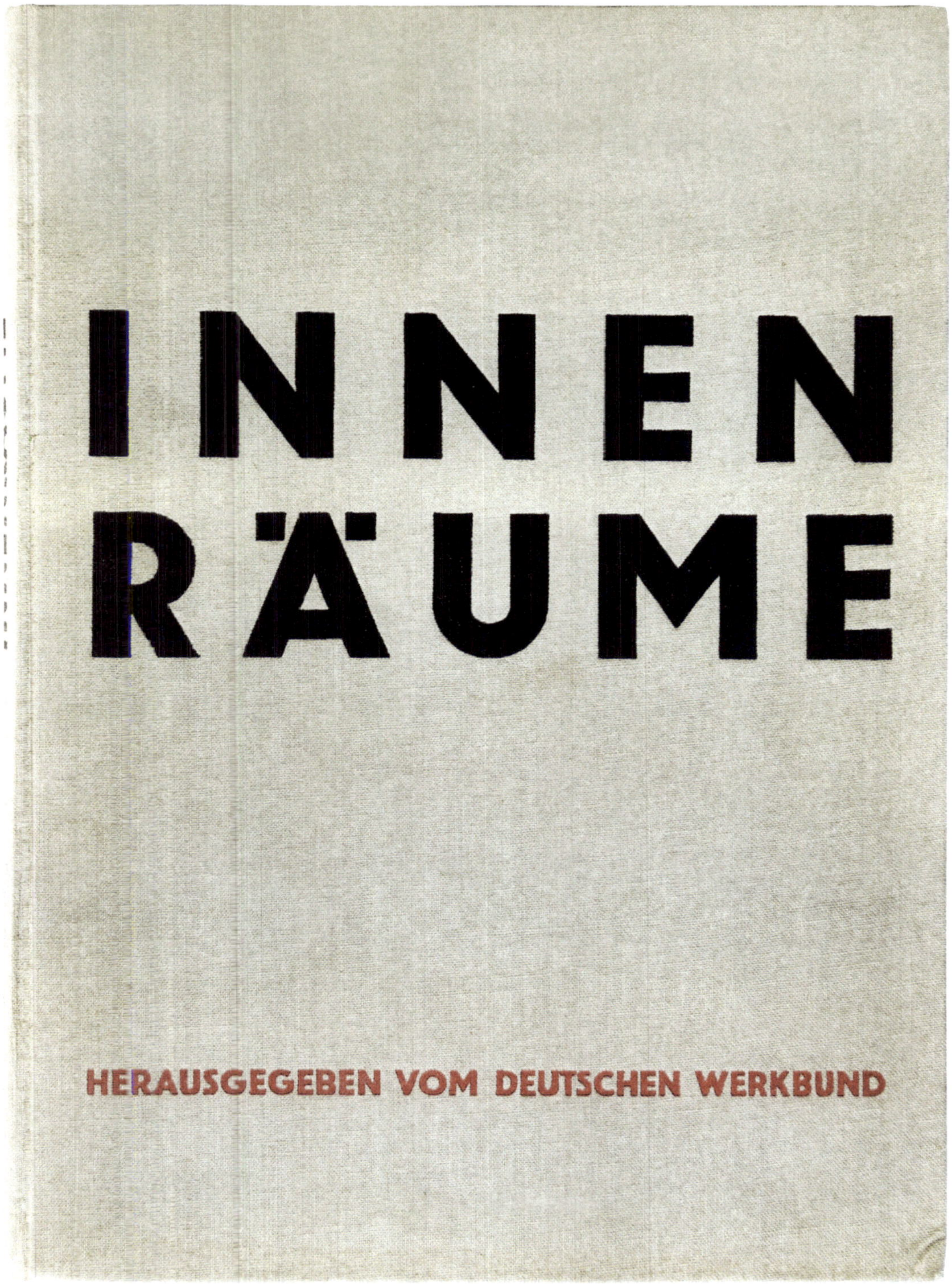

Illustrated book,
Stuttgart, 1928

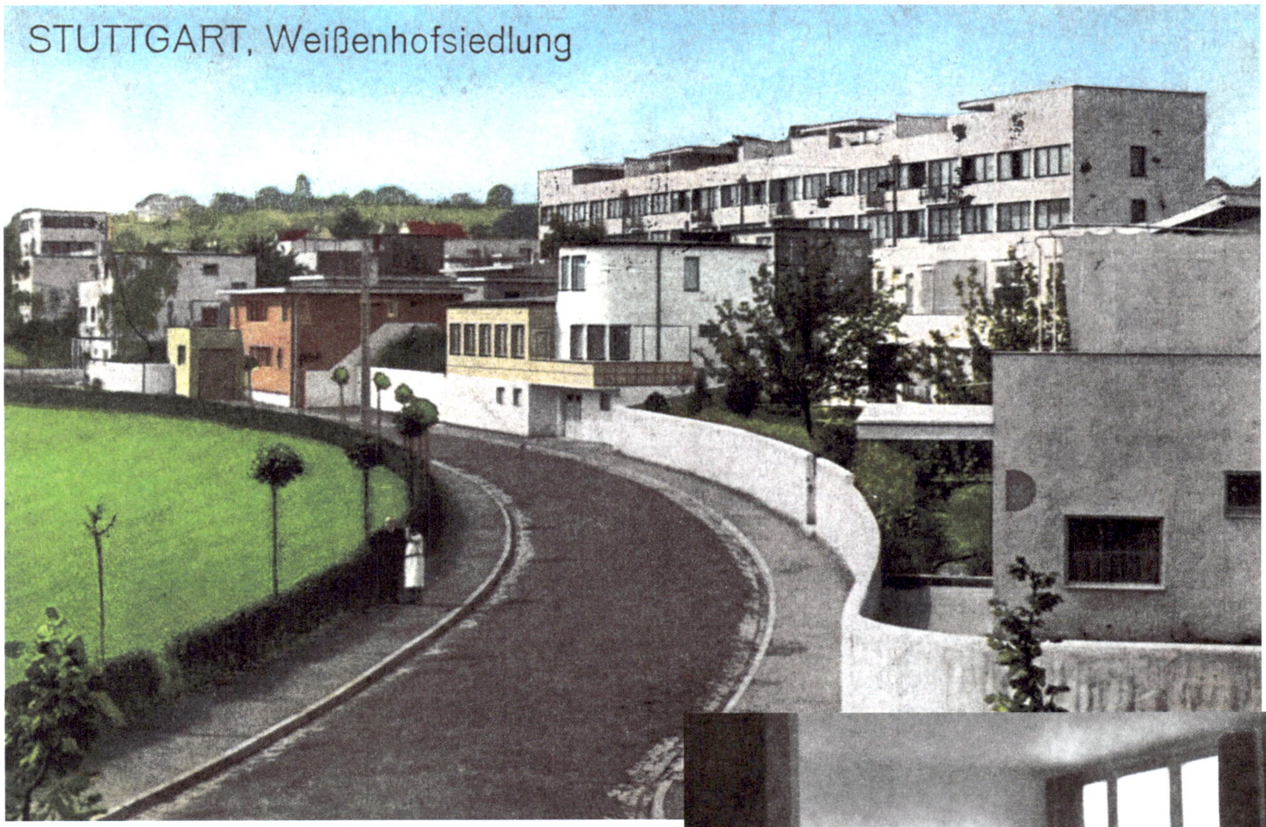

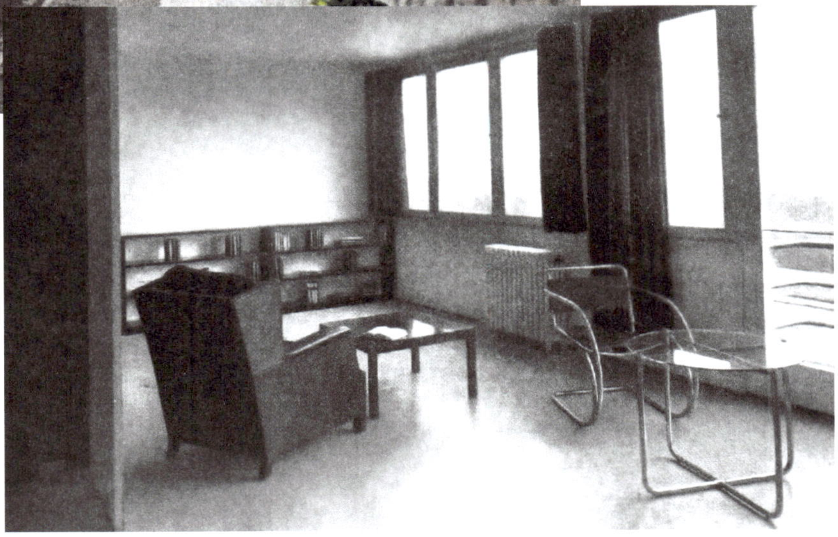

"Werkbund" exhibition "Die Wohnung" (The Dwelling) at Weissenhof, postcard, Stuttgart, 1927

Weissenhofsiedlung, houses 1–4, architect Mies van der Rohe, photo from the illustrated book "Innenräume" (Interiors), upholstered armchair by Walter Knoll, Stuttgart, 1928

LIVING FREEDOM

In the sparsely furnished interiors of the Weissenhofsiedlung, the few well-chosen items of furniture were the center of attention. The dialectic of emptiness was an important aspect of *Befreites Wohnen* (Liberated Living).

Chair 557, Wilhelm Knoll, Stuttgart, around 1925

Weissenhofsiedlung, house 33, architect Hans Scharoun, photo from the illustrated book "Innenräume" (Interiors), upholstered sofa by Walter Knoll, Stuttgart, 1928

Weissenhofsiedlung, house 25, architect Adolf Rading, photo from the illustrated book "Innenräume" (Interiors), chaise longue by Walter Knoll, Stuttgart, 1928

Weissenhofsiedlung, houses 1–4, architect Mies van der Rohe, Stuttgart (built in 1928)

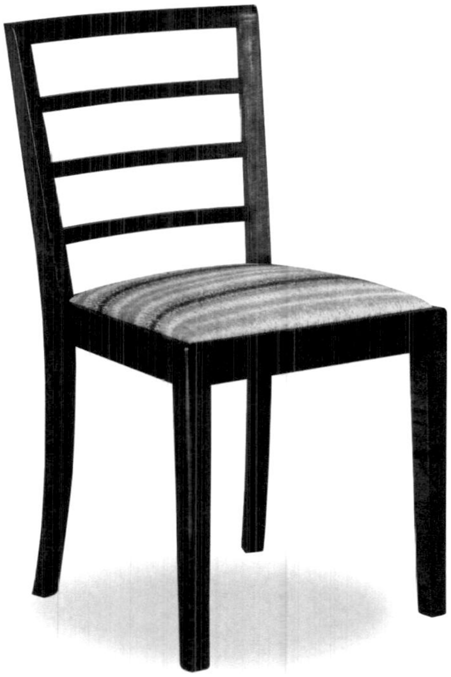

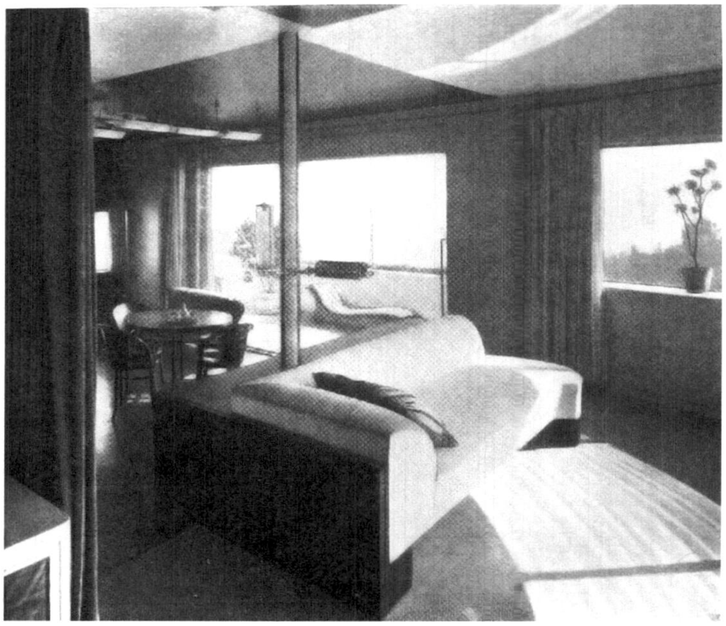

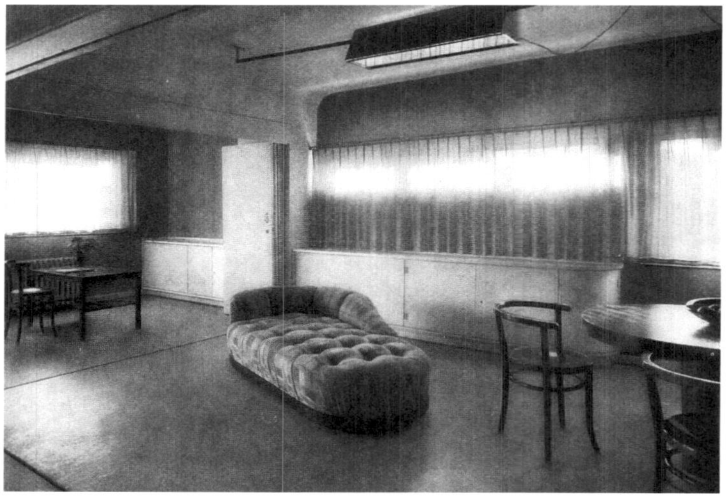

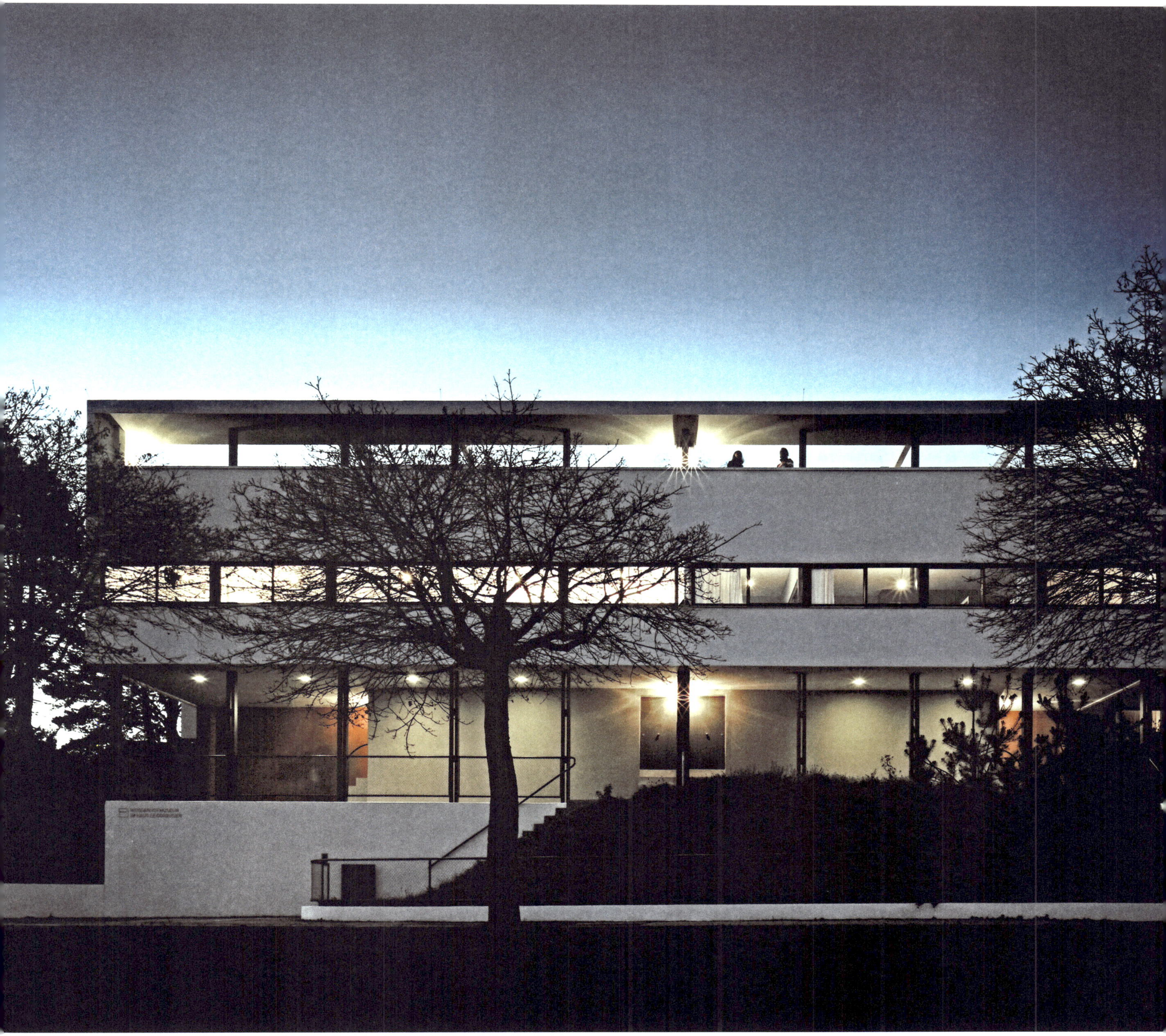

OBJECTIVITY

The industrial esthetics, represented by steel and glass, permeated daily life. The Schocken department store in Stuttgart (architect Erich Mendelsohn) was a prime example of this. Walter and Wilhelm Knoll both brought out metal furniture.

Tubular steel table, Walter Knoll, Feuerbach (now Stuttgart), 1928

Schocken department store, architect Erich Mendelsohn, Stuttgart, 1928

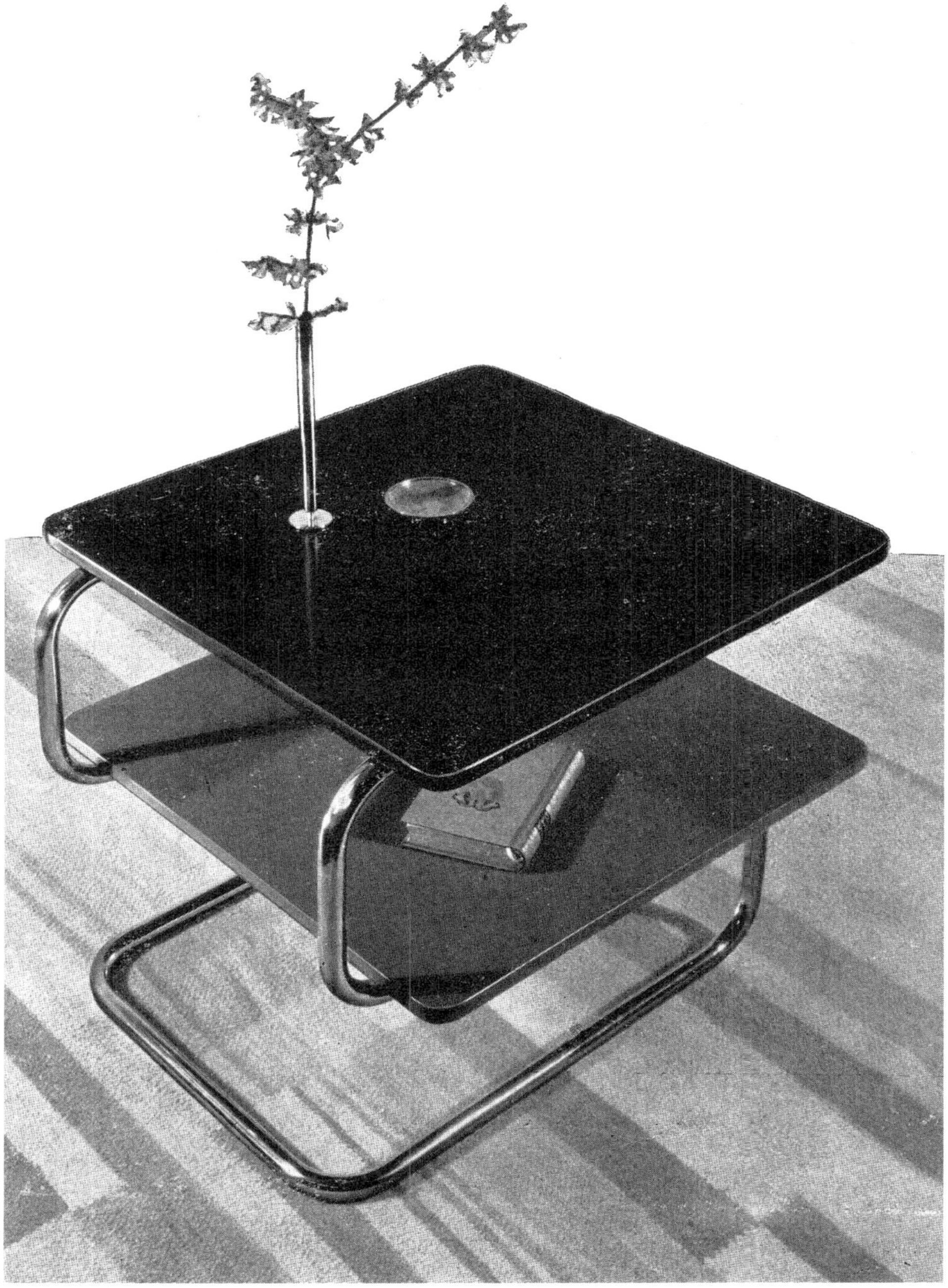

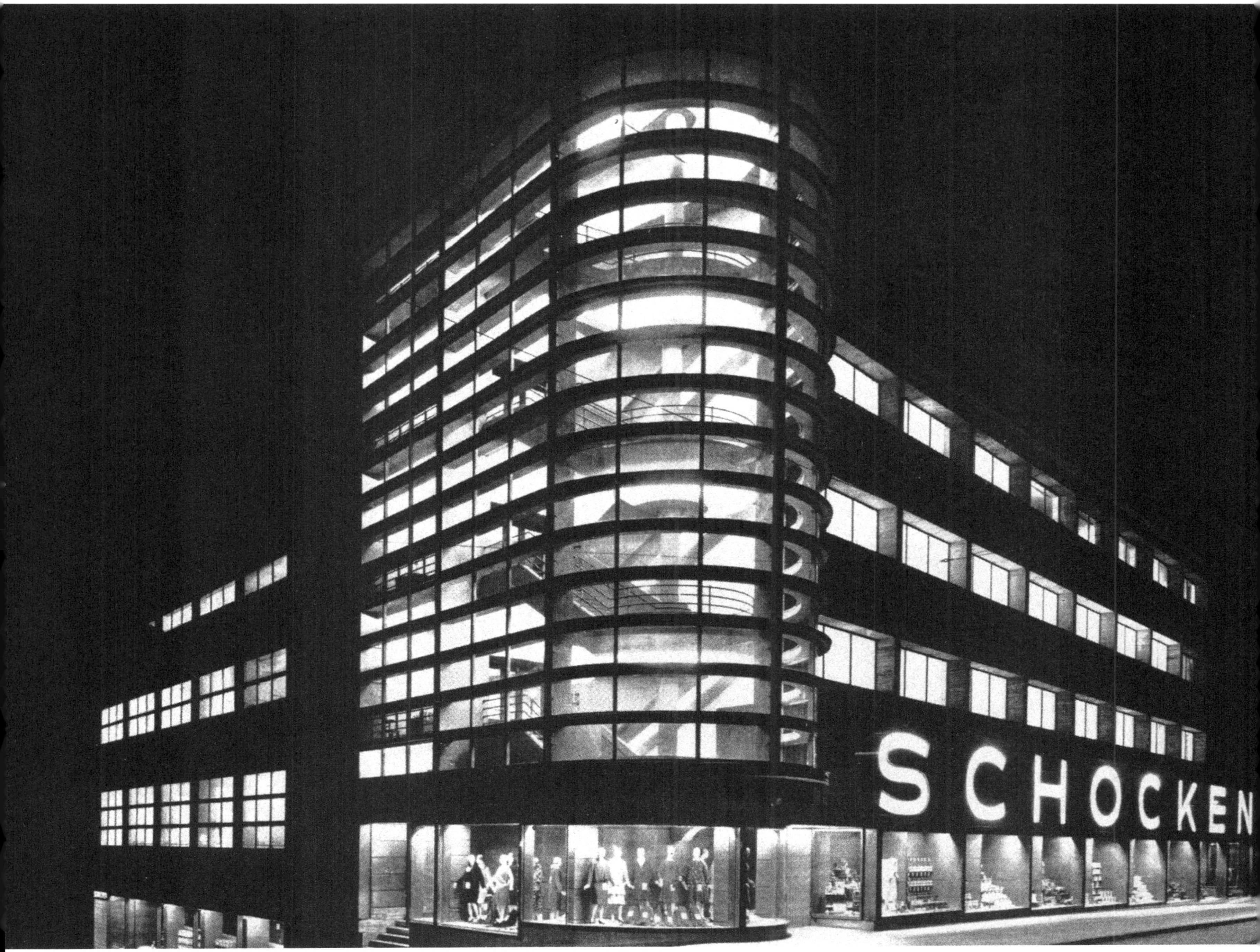
SCHOCKEN

AVIATION FURNITURE

In 1929, the Do X, the world's largest aircraft at the time, made its maiden flight. The passenger rooms were furnished with lightweight seating furniture from Walter Knoll's Prodomo series.

Pilot of the Do X,
cover photo of "Das illustrierte Blatt,"
Frankfurt am Main, 1930

Interior of the Do X featuring
Prodomo furniture by
Walter Knoll, 1929

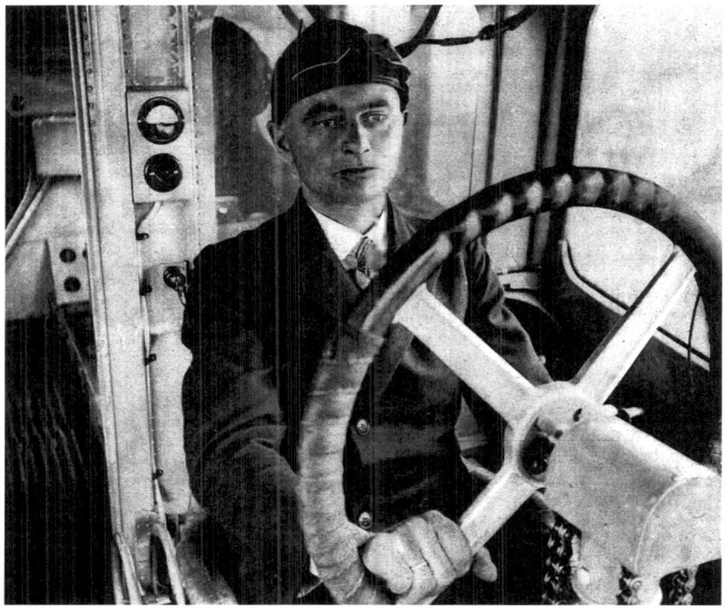

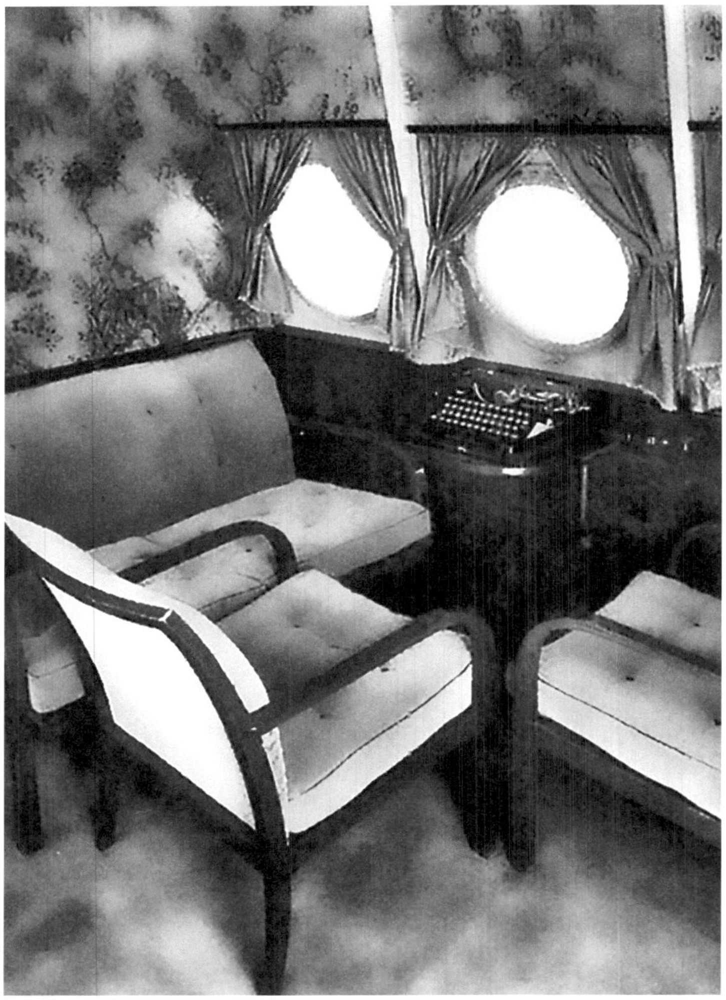

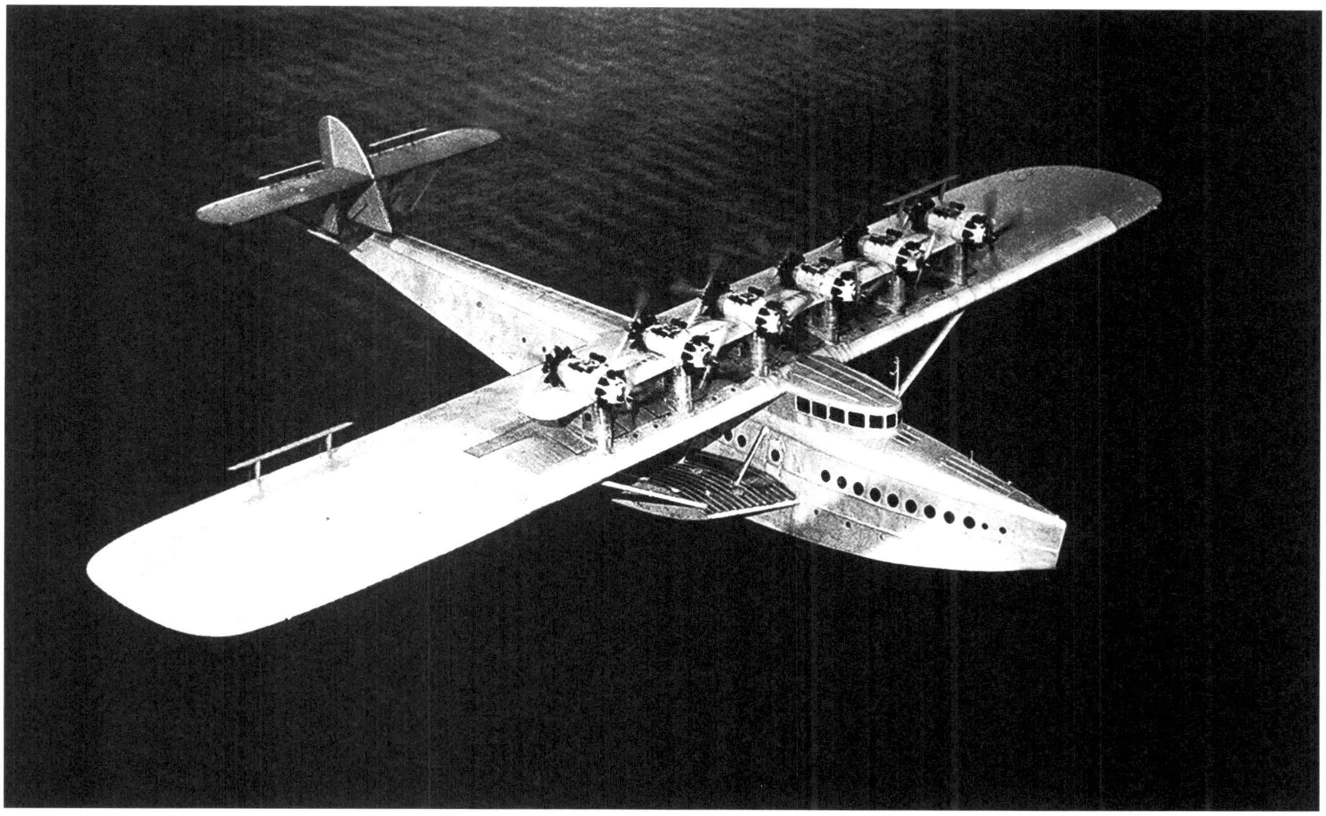

Flying boat Do X, 1929

Advertisement, Walter Knoll, Feuerbach (now Stuttgart), 1929

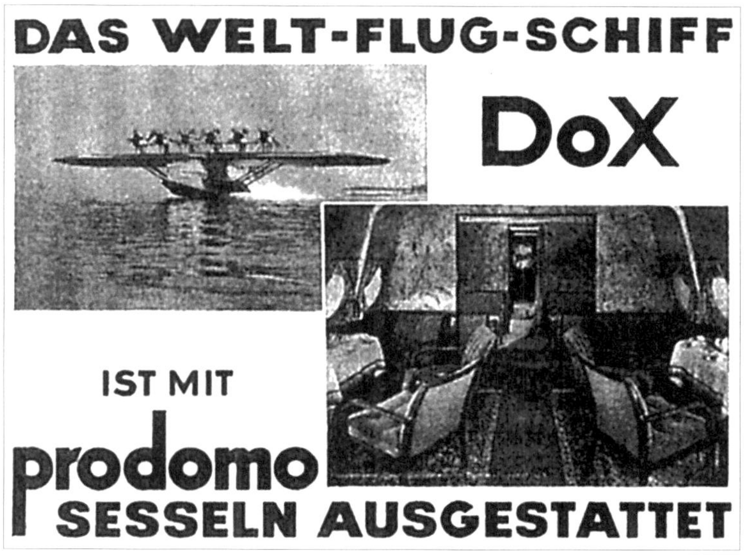

PRODOMO

Walter Knoll placed the patented Prodomo technology at the heart of his offering and turned it into its own brand. Whether for tubular steel, skid-base or reclining chairs, it was universally applicable.

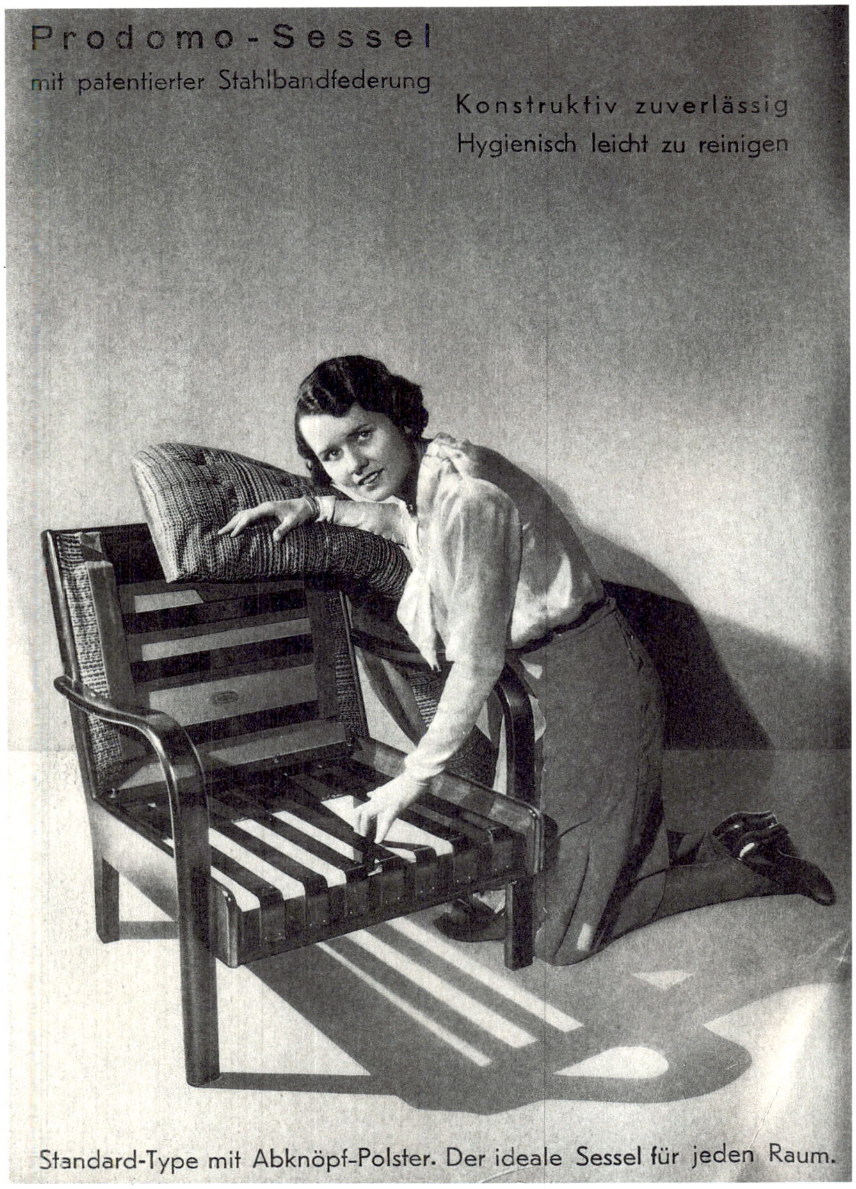

prodomo
K-F
SESSEL
FÜR JEDERMANN

Advertisement, Walter Knoll,
Feuerbach (now Stuttgart), around 1930

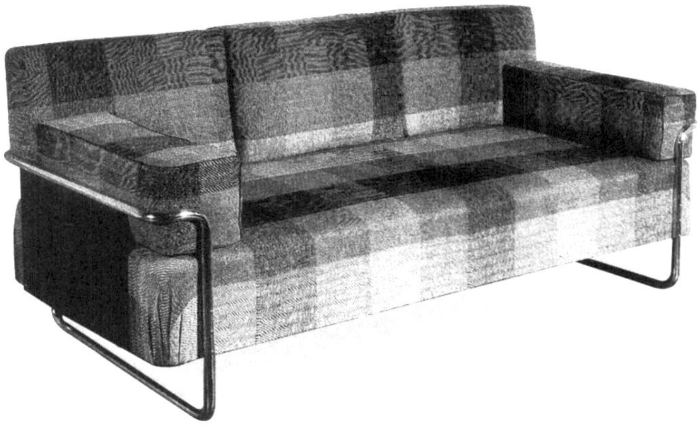

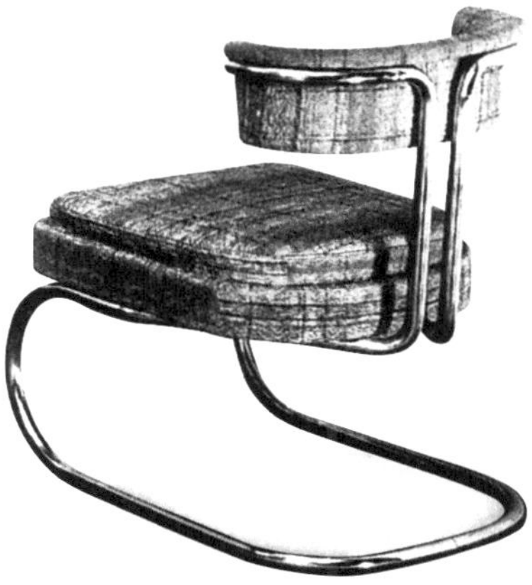

Tubular steel sofa Prodomo K-F 402, Walter Knoll, Feuerbach (now Stuttgart), 1930

Tubular steel chair Prodomo K-F 428, Walter Knoll, Feuerbach (now Stuttgart), 1930

Advertisement, Walter Knoll, Feuerbach (now Stuttgart), around 1930

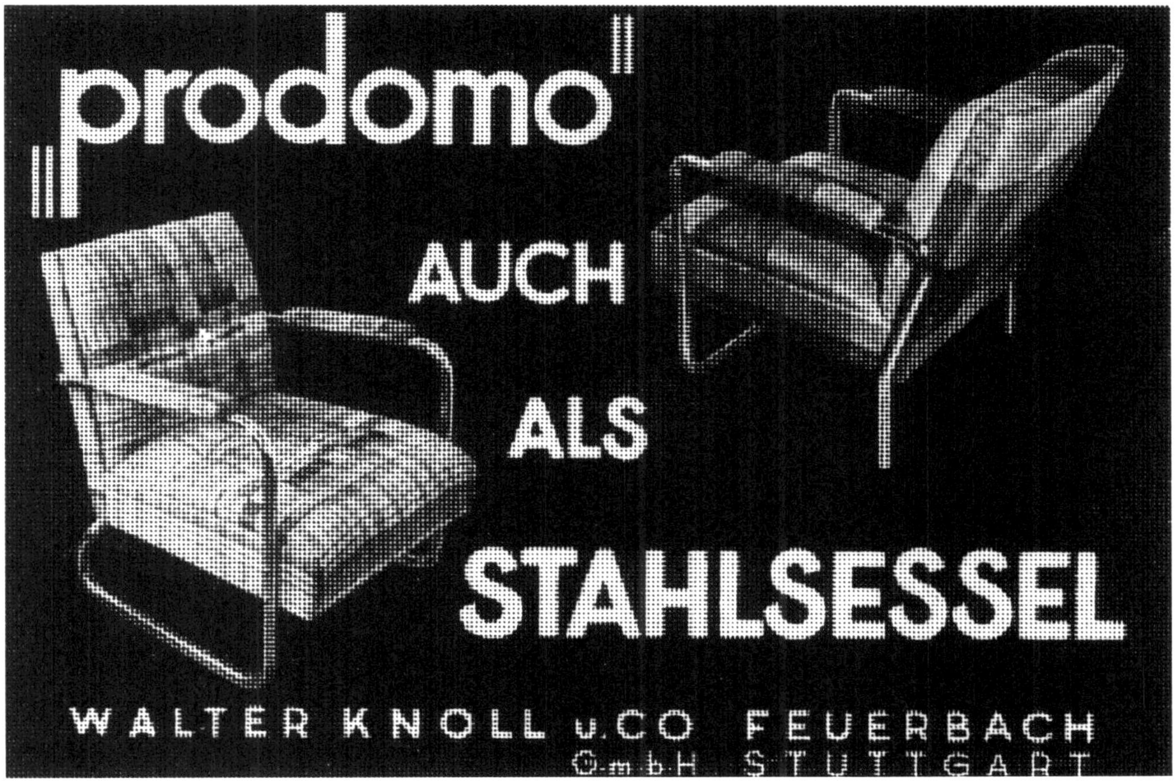

NEUE SACHLICHKEIT – NEW OBJECTIVITY

New | Obje | ctiv | ity, the. The exhibition of hyperrealistic paintings that the Kunsthalle Mannheim organized in 1926 under the title „Neue Sachlichkeit" (New Objectivity) was a concept-defining event. Once again – as before with expressionism – an art movement gave its name to a whole stylistic direction. *Neue Sachlichkeit* not only referred to various art forms, but also gave expression to a general atmosphere of the time. In particular, architecture and furniture design, referred to as *Neues Bauen* (New Building) and *Neues Wohnen* (New Living), attracted a great deal of attention. Both made their breakthrough a year later at the "Werkbund" exhibition at Weissenhof in Stuttgart. The avant-garde was represented there by Peter Behrens, Richard Döcker, Josef Frank, Walter Gropius, Le Corbusier, Ludwig Mies van der Rohe, J. J. P. Oud, Hans Poelzig, and Bruno Taut. The cubic form, the flat roof, large windows, and white walls were icons of "classical modernity." The companies of the Knoll dynasty played a central role in the objectivist-functional reinvention of upholstered furniture. Wilhelm Knoll's lightweight seating furniture, featuring the innovative "Antimott" technology, and Walter Knoll's "Prodomo" system revolutionized the industry. Ultimately, the metal chair – whether in steel or light metal – became a symbol par excellence of *Neue Sachlichkeit* and the early modernist period. Wilhelm and Walter Knoll were also at the forefront from the outset with a variety of models.

1925
The newly established Walter Knoll company opts for strict modernity. Marcel Breuer designs the club chair B3, the first example of modern tubular steel furniture.

1927
The companies of Walter and Wilhelm Knoll are represented at the "Werkbund" exhibition at Weissenhof.

1928
Wilhelm Knoll brings the patent-protected Antimott upholstery system to market.

1929
Walter Knoll's patented Prodomo upholstery system is used in the "Do X," at the time the world's largest aircraft.

1930
Wilhelm Knoll opens Antimott factories in the Franconian Gaildorf and the Swedish city of Malmö.

NOTHING IS MORE SURPRISING THAN THE SIMPLE TRUTH, NOTHING IS MORE EXOTIC THAN OUR ENVIRONMENT, NOTHING IS MORE IMAGINATIVE THAN OBJECTIVITY.
EGON ERWIN KISCH

Title of the official catalog, design by Willi Baumeister

Tagblatt Tower, architect Otto Oßwald, Stuttgart, 1928

Model drawing, chair H – S 511, Wilhelm Knoll, Stuttgart, around 1929

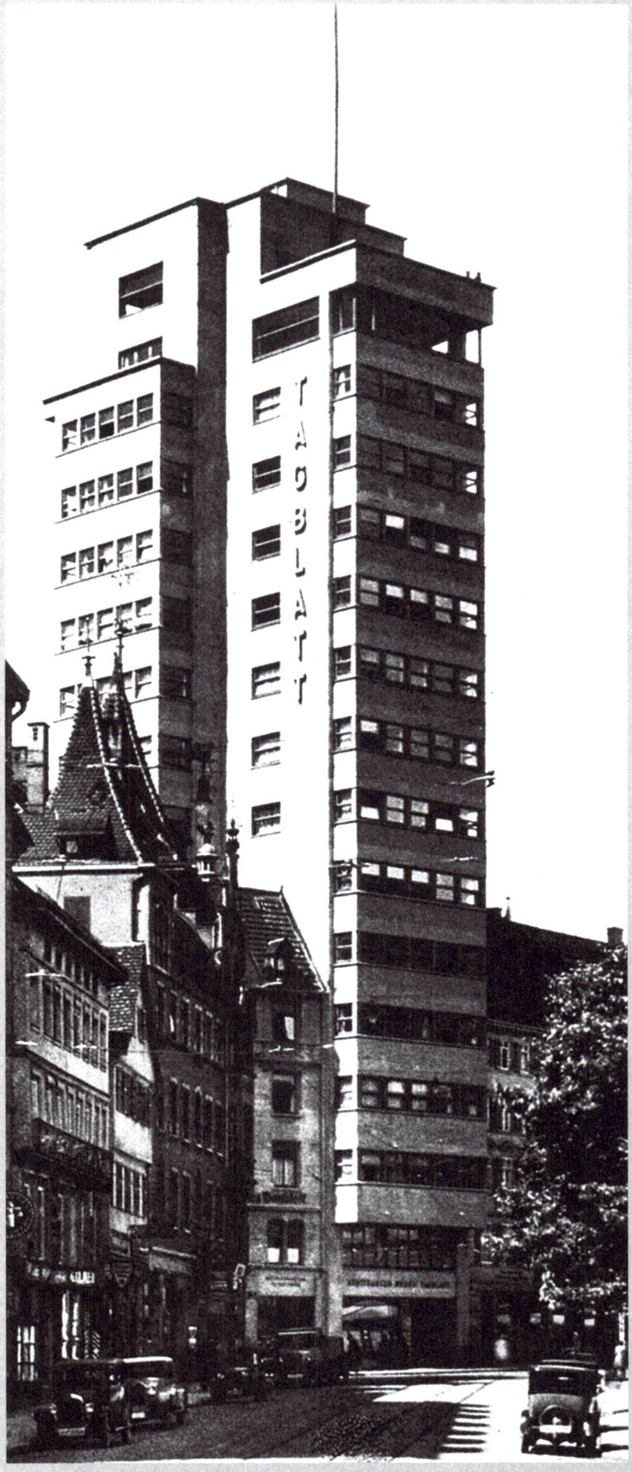
TAGBLATT

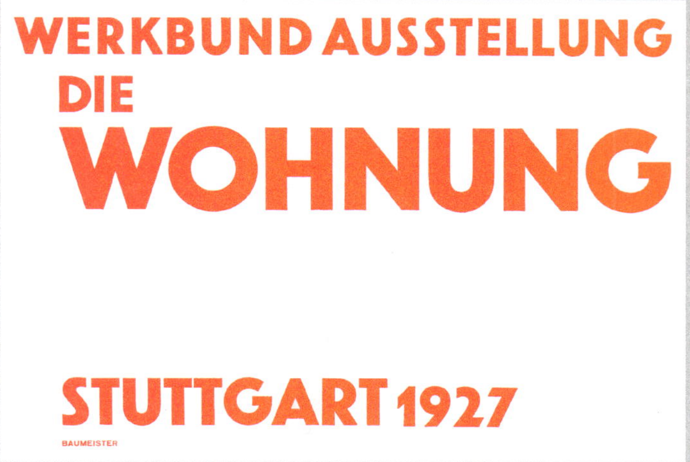
WERKBUND AUSSTELLUNG
DIE
WOHNUNG
STUTTGART 1927
BAUMEISTER

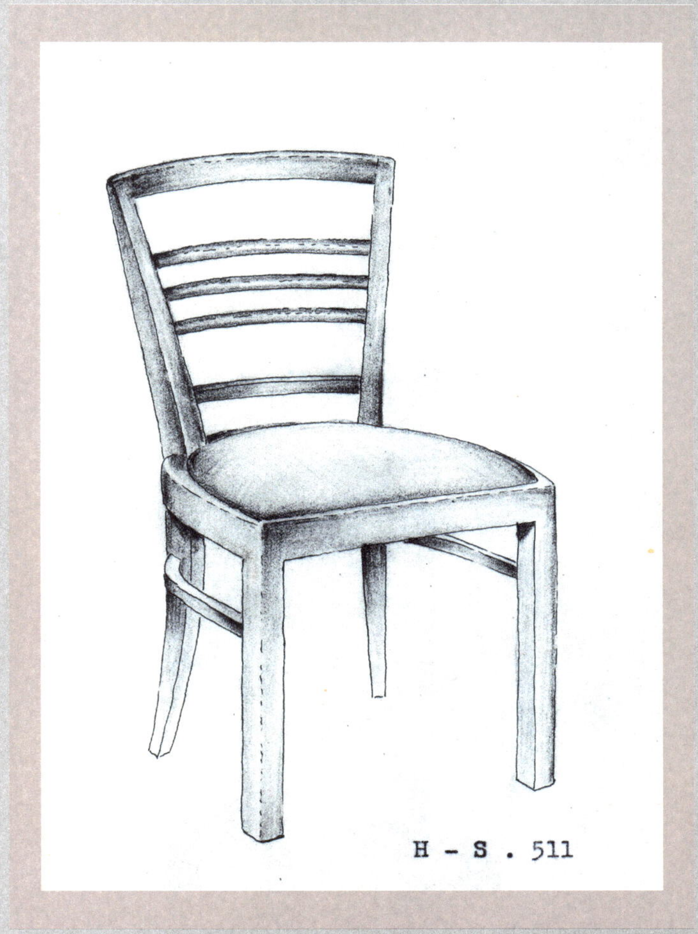
H - S . 511

THE 1930s

EXTREME TIMES

In 1935, when Germany had been a dictatorship for two years, Paul Hahn left Walter Knoll for no readily apparent reason. It was the end of a ten-year, successful collaboration in which the two congenial men at the top had practically emerged from nowhere into the elite of German furniture manufacturers. However, the current situation seemed abominable. The company was still suffering from the economic crisis and its future development appeared uncertain, especially for a manufacturer of modern furniture. For Hahn, now aged 52, this was true to an even greater extent. The abrupt separation was probably also due to the fact that he, a prominent Social Democrat, was high on the black list of the National Socialists.[1] The fact that Robert Bosch was subsequently protective of him and that Hahn had to serve a prison sentence for his contacts with the resistance also supports this conclusion. Paul Hahn was not the only one in Walter Knoll's circle to suffer reprisals. Hans Purrmann, the painter and husband of Walter's sister-in-law, Mathilde, initially fled with his wife to Florence when his paintings were branded "degenerate" and removed from museums.[2] Even Karl Gustav Vollmöller rarely stayed in Germany after 1933. He, a man of the world and esthete who, like so many others, had not seen the disaster coming, commuted for a while between Venice, Paris, and Hollywood.[3] When, at the instigation of Joseph Goebbels, Hitler's Minister of Propaganda, the Mussolini government had Palazzo Vendramin confiscated in 1937 along with Karl Gustav's million-dollar collection of paintings, books and antiquities, he went into exile in America. He died there impoverished shortly after the end of the war.

America, always an option for those who lived in the valleys of Swabia, once again became a place of refuge. Hans Knoll, Walter Knoll's second eldest son, also left his parents' house during this dark period and ventured a new beginning on the other side of the Atlantic. Born in 1914, Hans grew up with his brothers in the upper middle-class

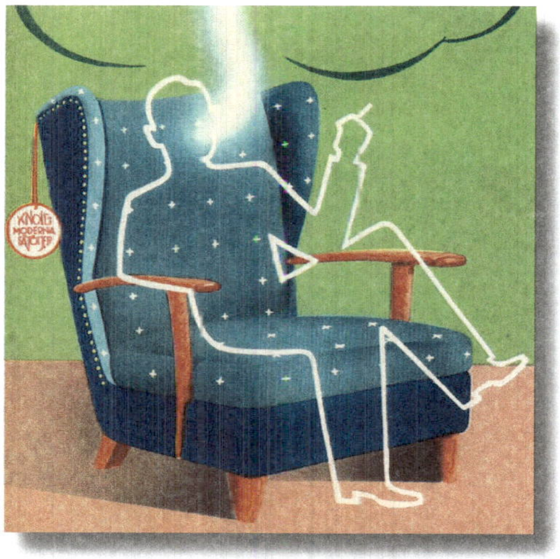

setting of the Vollmöller villa on Hasenbergsteige, where wealth – both intellectual and financial – seemed limitless. As a boy, he experienced his father's successful new start, achieved in tandem with his partner Paul Hahn. When the factory in Feuerbach opened its doors, Hans was 11; when modernity manifested itself at Weissenhof, he was 13. One might say he was raised to be an avant-gardist. His own life, too, knew extremes from the very beginning. At a young age, blond Hans was considered to be "everyone's darling."[4] But besides being a sunny child, he was also a "problem child"[5] with whom, according to his father, there were "difficulties upon difficulties"[6] at home – not least because of his "unrestrained nature."[7] Like his father, Hans was a bad pupil and therefore changed schools "on a regular basis."[8] This was another reason why he was his father's unbeloved son, experienceing exactly what his own father had experienced at home. And just as Walter's mother, Emma Knoll, had loved him unconditionally, Maia Knoll loved her son Hans. Between these poles – the father's disregard and the mother's total devotion – the character of both Walter and Hans developed. Thus ego and ambition were able to take on oversized forms. Before he was 18, Hans Knoll spent some time in a Swiss sanatorium because of a dangerous lung condition, probably tuberculosis. When he then went to London in 1934, just after turning 21, to work at the English subsidiary of the Jantzen company, he again paralleled his father's experience in some respects. Like Hans, Walter was an extraordinarily sociable person, but also like Hans, he had to endure crises as a young man. And when he saw few opportunities for himself at home, he had also gone abroad to stand on his own two feet. Whether Walter Knoll drew these parallels or unconsciously prescribed for his son the same cure that he had undergone is irrelevant. It worked brilliantly in both cases. Hans Knoll spent about two years at Jantzen, whose owners were of German descent and became his friends[9]. During this time he underwent an amazing transformation, as one visitor observed at the time. He had "noticeably matured"[10] and developed from a chronically erratic teenager into a self-confident young man. And when he was close to death, he was healed as if by a miracle. During this time he became a different person.

Finally, Hans focused on the career for which he was destined. He became an employee of Plan Furniture, a small company that had only existed for a few years and had something to offer that did not exist anywhere else in England: modern furniture that came from Germany – including from Walter Knoll. The company was an exotic flower in the midst of British traditionalism, where it experienced only a brief period of prosperity but left behind a remarkable footnote in the annals of modernity.[11] The founder, Serge Chermayeff, was also a rare specimen. This "aristocratic Russian,"[12] as tall as a tree with wild curls, was sent by his parents to Harrow, one of the posh English boarding schools (from which he had dropped out). The "irresistible Gigolo"[13] who "only wore suits that clearly came from the Savile Row,"[14] as he was later

THE COMPANY WAS STILL SUFFERING FROM THE ECONOMIC CRISIS AND ITS FUTURE DEVELOPMENT APPEARED UNCERTAIN, ESPECIALLY FOR A MANUFACTURER OF MODERN FURNITURE.

described by a friend, the painter Peter Blake – was a self-educated man who was in the process of inventing himself. This was not the only way in which he resembled Hans Knoll, his new colleague from Germany. The two young and exceptionally good-looking daredevils (who, it can be assumed, were also heartbreakers) now became partisans of modernity. Chermayeff, who went on to become one of the leaders of the modern movement in America, a professor at Harvard, and a director of the Institute of Design in Chicago (whose patrons included his friend Walter Gropius), tended toward extremes and was not unlike Hans in this respect. In the 1920s, he landed in the furniture industry more by chance – probably in part because of his good taste – and finally worked for an elegant furniture store on Oxford Street where he ran the "Modern Art Studio."[15] However, he had to procure the necessary pieces of furniture abroad, which inevitably brought him to Germany, then the stronghold of *Neues Wohnen*. On one of his shopping trips, which also took him to *Neues Frankfurt*, he met Franz Schuster, the inventor of the modular closets manufactured by Behr in Wendlingen – not so far from Stuttgart. Schuster must have recommended Walter Knoll, who was able to supply the matching seating furniture. Schuster's wardrobes and Walter Knoll's tubular steel furniture, the Prodomo brand, eventually became the basis for Plan Furniture, Chermayeff's own business. He promoted the unusually versatile furniture made in Germany under the banner "Design your own furniture! No two Plan-furnished homes are ever alike."[16] Hans Knoll, who started out at Chermayeff in 1935, was also the natural liaison to his suppliers. Economically speaking, Plan was not a success story and soon went bankrupt. But the two years during which the foreigners worked together were an exciting and formative time for both of them. They never lost touch with the euphoria of belonging to the avant-garde. And this was further reinforced by the current environment.

In those days, London was a preferred destination for German emigrants, including top-class scientists, artists, and architects. One of these was Erich Mendelsohn, perhaps the most brilliant among the architects of *Neues Bauen* (New Building), who had been forced to leave Germany because he was Jewish. Chermayeff, also a Jew, helped him gain a foothold in London and, in turn, trained as an architect under Mendelsohn.[17] Hans Knoll, who witnessed all this, also frequented the Isokon Building, the epicenter of London's modernist scene (and also the residence of Gropius and his wife, among others). A larger dose of avant-garde was hardly conceivable. It was a turning point in Hans's life, but also a special moment in recent cultural history. The modernist ship, which had sailed under full steam in Germany at the beginning of the 20th century, now lay at anchor in England for a short while before setting its course for America. Hans Knoll was a young passenger on this visionary ship.

By the time Hans Knoll returned to Stuttgart in 1937 after four years in London, he had become a different person. But conditions in Germany had also changed drastically, and the two were no longer compatible. Hans, who held only a subordinate position in the company below

---

1 ▶ The fate of the Stuttgart architect Karl Beer, who was involved in the Weissenhofsiedlung on the outskirts and whom the new rulers first propelled into a mental hospital and then drove into exile, serves as an example of what could befall an SPD member.

2 ▶ After participating in the funeral of the Jewish painter Max Liebermann in February 1935, he was shadowed by the Gestapo.

3 ▶ In Hollywood, he was friends with the director Josef von Sternberg, who discovered Marlene Dietrich. The National Socialists are said to have offered him several high offices, and finally that of Prussian Minister of Culture. But Karl Gustav Vollmöller always refused in disgust.

4 ▶ Knoll, n.d., p. 66.

5 ▶ Ibid.

6 ▶ Knoll, n.d., p. 109.

7 ▶ Knoll, n.d., p. 66.

8 ▶ Ibid.

9 ▶ Martin, 2011, p. 99.

10 ▶ Ibid.

11 ▶ The Plan company was in existence from 1932 to 1939, until its founder Serge Chermayeff went bankrupt and emigrated to America.

12 ▶ MacMahon, 2014, p. 121.

13 ▶ Ibid.

14 ▶ Ibid.

15 ▶ Chermayeff's father-in-law, a well-known contractor, introduced him.

16 ▶ Plan Furniture catalog.

17 ▶ Chermayeff became an architect only after he entered into a business relationship with the experienced Mendelsohn – who, of course, also became acquainted with Hans Knoll.
This resulted in excellent buildings that are now listed as historical monuments. The best example is the De La Warr Pavilion in the English seaside resort town of Bexhill-on-Sea, built in 1935.

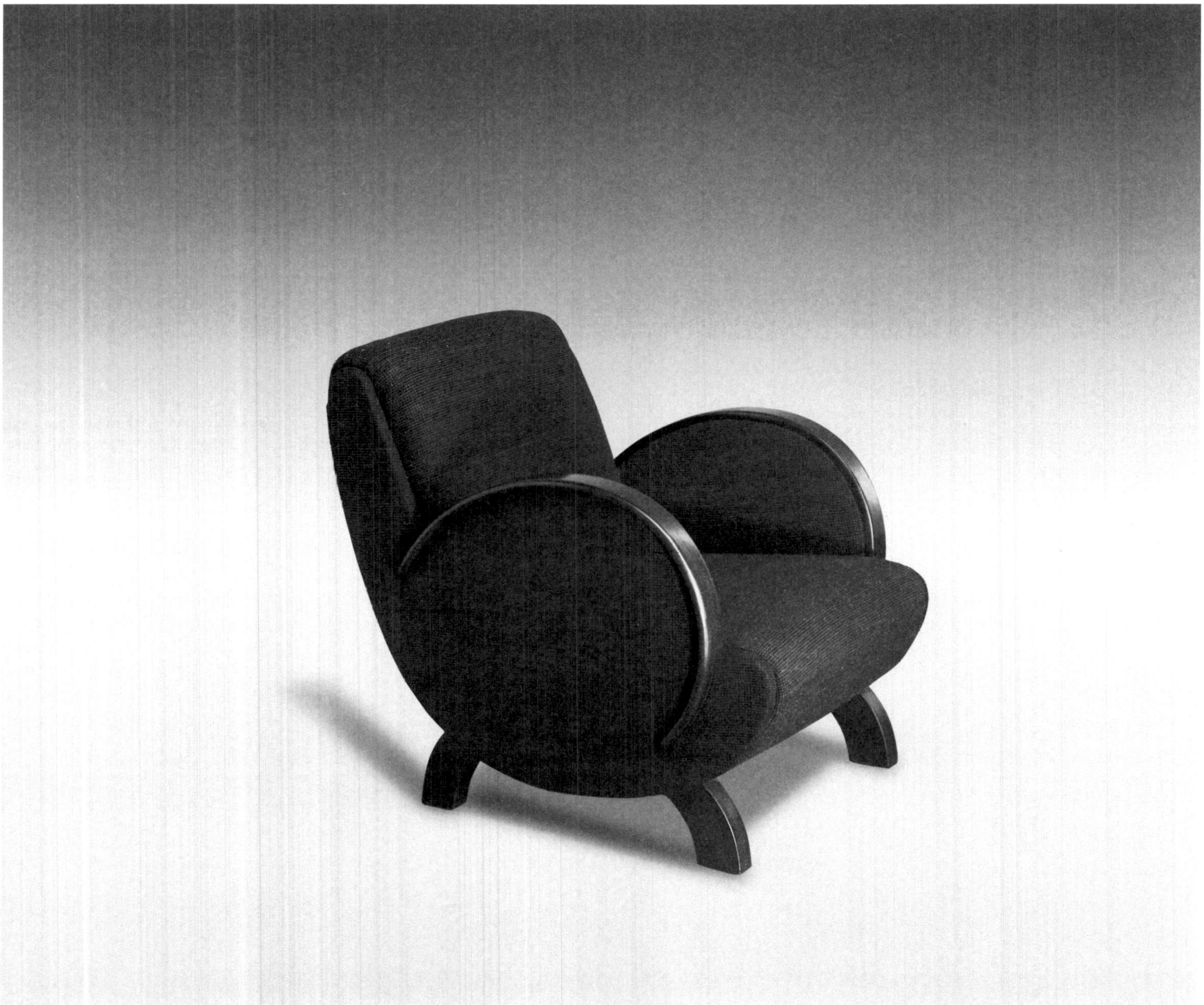

ALTEA

Walter Knoll turned a small "women's armchair" into a series of compact models with high recognition value.

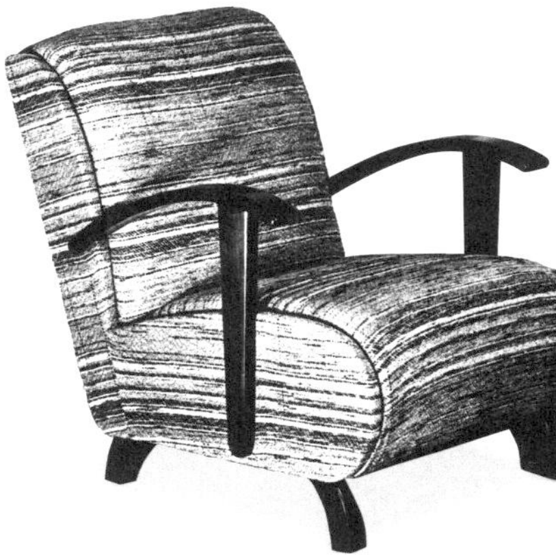

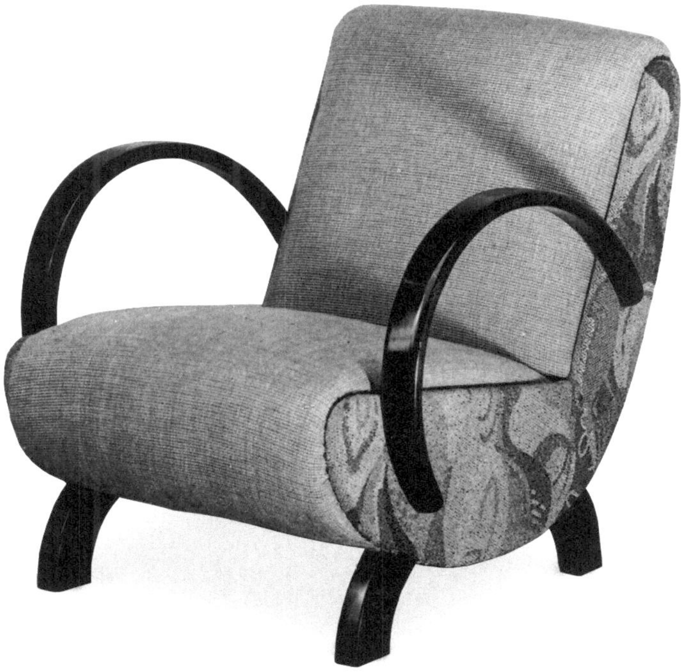

Armchair Altea 802a, Walter Knoll, design by A. C. Rüdenauer, Feuerbach (now Stuttgart), 1934

Armchair Altea 800, Walter Knoll, design by A. C. Rüdenauer, Feuerbach (now Stuttgart), 1934

Armchair Altea 802, Walter Knoll, design by A. C. Rüdenauer, Feuerbach (now Stuttgart), 1934 his father and older brother Robert, now had other, far more serious concerns. The fact that he no longer wanted to do without life in a cosmopolitan city was the least of his problems. The avant-garde, which had become the center of his life, was banished from the Third Reich. The fate of the Jews was also clearly on his mind, not least because of his relationship with Chermayeff and Mendelsohn.[18] What made things worse was that the demon of the new era penetrated his own family. His brothers Robert and Herbert, aged 25 and 18, were infected by National Socialism. The Knoll boys, who were now young men, all belonged to the generation that had experienced the First World War and Germany's humiliating defeat as children. This drove them towards National Socialism. "Here lies the root," wrote the journalist Sebastian Haffner, who belonged to the same generation, "not in the 'experience of the Front,' but in the war experience of the German schoolboy."[19] Robert was 7 years old when the so-called "dictated peace" of Versailles was concluded and was experienced as an even deeper humiliation. He was obviously among those who were unable to rid themselves of this thorn until much later after the Second World War. Hans, who was also part of the First World War generation, went off in a completely

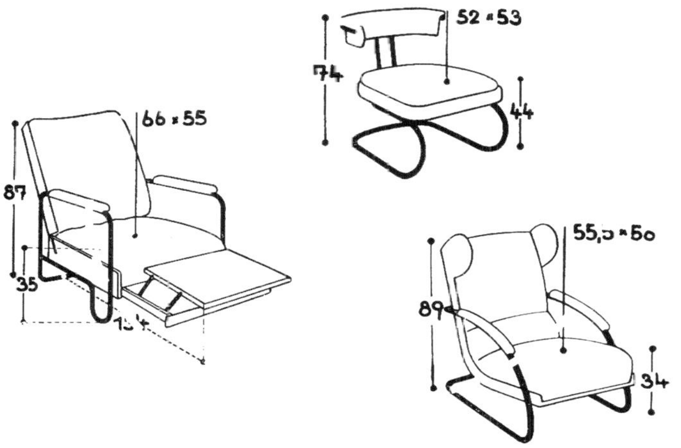

different direction. For a long time, it had looked as though he were the black sheep of the family. At home, he was regarded as "morally unstable".[20] But the tide finally turned. The renowned New York lawyer Bronson Winthrop – a "father figure"[21] who had met Hans in the Swiss sanatorium and who had also visited him in London – took care of him. The reasons for the great affection between such unequal men are obscure.[22] Ultimately, Hans Knoll's patron even paid his passage to America. This was Hans's way out of a precarious situation and the beginning of his legendary ascent under the initial tutelage of Winthrop. Because emigration to the U.S. was a quite typical solution for both Swabians and his family, it met with his father's immediate approval. Hadn't he himself sown his wild oats in the U.S. a few decades earlier and thus developed as a man? And hadn't he also wanted to prove to his own father that he could do it alone? So when Hans boarded a ship to New York in 1937, Walter understood him well and probably even envied him. The ship was the SS American Farmer, a freighter. The Jantzens had made arrangements for the ship and Bronson Winthrop had paid for the crossing. But uncle Karl Gustav, with whom Hans initially lived in Manhattan, also took the young arrival under his wing.[23]

The year 1937 marked another important event in the company's history: the relocation of Walter Knoll to Herrenberg. Conditions had become increasingly cramped at the corner property in Stuttgart-Feuerbach. Work had to be outsourced. Therefore, the relocation of production to a former Vollmöller factory that had been shut down years before appeared to be the ideal solution. It was probably also a friendly gesture on the part of Karl Gustav, who was still in charge of the Vollmöller group at that time. There was twice as much space available in the new factory halls. Although Herrenberg, a small country town in the foothills of the Black Forest and strongly influenced by its rural surroundings, had not quite arrived in the 20th century, it did have a railroad connection, and the train station was and still is located directly opposite the factory. The move also required a change in the brand's strategy. Instead of "K-F" (for Knoll Feuerbach), the phrase "Herrenberger Sitzmöbel" (Herrenberg seating furniture) now appeared, which emphasized the location and adorned the catalogs well into the post-war period. In the mid-1930s when the economic crisis was finally over, the furniture industry was also able to breathe a sigh of relief. The Prodomo line now did so well that it was advertised directly in the press, a novelty at the time. "No failure, no rust, no vermin," were the advantages listed in one advertisement for this still innovative upholstery.[24] Another innovation was a series of compact armchairs called Altea. The curved upholstery, together with the black wooden frame, created a calculated look.

The National Socialists had taken up the fight against modernity. Modern architecture, like jazz and modern art, was also denigrated as "cultural Bolshevism." Famous examples of *Neues Bauen* architecture, such as the Bauhaus in Dessau and the housing estate in Stuttgart-Weissenhof, were objects of hatred and considered "un-German." However, the German style that was sought for unsuccessfully in the 19th century had never existed, nor could anyone even say what "German furniture" was supposed to be like. Of course, reality looked somewhat different. In the Third Reich, a deeply "divided consciousness"[25] prevailed as far as modernity was concerned. This was evident in the relationship with America. It was true that hatred was incited against "nigger jazz." The poster for the "Entartete Musik" (Degenerate Music) exhibition in 1938 showed a black saxophone player with a face distorted into a grimace. At the same time, however, swing music from the U.S. had long since conquered German dance halls. Above all, it was popularized by American movies, which were shown regularly in

THE YEAR 1937 MARKED AN IMPORTANT EVENT IN THE COMPANY'S HISTORY: THE RE-LOCATION OF WALTER KNOLL TO HERRENBERG.

German theaters. The dream worlds from Hollywood influenced style, fashion, and home living. The esthetics of the 1930s were by no means "synchronized." Quite the opposite. There were even some very different styles in existence simultaneously. One of the newer trends was the streamline, which was particularly striking in car bodies – both in its American version, and in the German "Silver Arrows." At the same time, there were different versions of the Reform Style, in which ideas of the "Deutscher Werkbund" (German Association of Craftsmen) continued to have an influence, despite its prohibition. Even elements of *Neues Wohnen* (New Living) occasionally survived. Thus the *Volksempfänger* (NS-era radio) that was introduced for propaganda purposes was a flawless example of the *Neue Sachlichkeit* (New Objectivity). A generally widespread cautiousness and a clear trend towards the conservative that had taken hold in the 1930s – not only in Germany but elsewhere as well – finally produced a "solid" modernity. It was no coincidence that the results strongly resembled the Reform Style of the imperial era which, incidentally, was anything but uniform.[26]

A prime example of these ambivalent tendencies was the "Deutsche Warenkunde" (German Commodity Science) of 1939, a compendium of stunningly designed products modeled after the predecessor of the same name from 1915. The authors were former members of the "Werkbund" (Association of Craftsmen), and included Hermann Gretsch, Hans Schwippert, and Mia Seeger, all of whom had studied in Stuttgart. Continuity was also maintained as far as the strong influence of the southwest was concerned. Gretsch, who had furnished three rooms in the Weissenhofsiedlung, carved out a career in the Nazi state, became director of the "Kunstgewerbeschule" (School of Arts and Crafts) in Stuttgart, and promoted the moderate Reform Style.[27] The architect Schwippert and the publicist Seeger later numbered among the prominent representatives of the Second Modernity in the Federal Republic of Germany.

During the six years between Hitler's seizure of power and the Second World War, an astonishing variety of styles prevailed. This juxtaposition of different paradigms was also reflected in the product range of the companies of Wilhelm and Walter Knoll. Even models from the 1920s continued to be produced, including tubular steel furniture. At the same time, there was a strong tendency to return to full upholstery – larger and heavier than ever. The lightweight furniture of the Prodomo and Antimott collections provided a contrast. Based on the persistent popularity of Antimott, Wilhelm Knoll continued to ride on the wave of its success, which had now lasted ten years. In 1938, another factory subsidiary was opened in Coburg.[28] It employed around 150 upholsterers, carpenters, and picklers who were now exclusively engaged in the production of Antimott. For contemporary designs, Willy Knoll had secured the interior designer Hans Hartl as a freelance employee – a versatile man like Karl Pullich and also, like Pullich, no stranger to the trade. In the early stages of his career, Hartl – born in 1899 and thus a good twenty years younger than his new employer – had spent a few years working for the "Deutsche Werkstätten" in Dresden-Hellerau, one of the most renowned manufacturers of modern, industrially manufactured furniture. Grandmasters of the Reform Period such as Bruno Paul and Richard Riemerschmid, who inspired Hartl, worked for the "Deutsche Werkstätten," or DW.[29] The native of Munich designed a number of solitaires for Wilhelm Knoll, including a light wood armchair with webbing that might have been a throwback to the early Handi series, but was perhaps also influenced by the ultra-modern models of the Swede Bruno Mathsson – a secret tip at the time. Ultimately, Hartl produced an entire range of couches, sofas, and armchairs. All of them were large-format, fully upholstered, and often of asymmetrical shapes. Some are reminiscent of the streamlined car bodies of those years and can easily be imagined in the bar of a luxury liner or on a film set.

---

18 ▶ For this reason Chermayeff, whose name was actually Issakovitch, had even changed his name in the mid-1920s. See: McMahon, 2014, p. 119.

19 ▶ Haffner, 2000, p. 22. It continues: The "real Nazi generation" were those who "experienced the war as a great game, completely undisturbed by reality." And their children's hearts, it must be added, were easy prey for chauvinist propaganda. They could never overcome the sudden, completely inexplicable defeat. National Socialism, with its exaggeration of Germanness, offered the possibility of compensation.

20 ▶ Knoll, n.d., p. 71.

21 ▶ Knoll, n.d., p. 111.

22 ▶ Bronson Winthrop was already nearly 70 years old when he met 19-year-old Hans at the Swiss sanatorium.

23 ▶ Martin, 2011, p. 76.

24 ▶ Walter Knoll company archive. In the following: WK archive.

25 ▶ That was the title of a study by Hans Dieter Schäfer in which the phenomenon was first presented in 1984.

26 ▶ Illustrative of the elegant, conservative style of the *Vereinigte Werkstätten* (United Workshops for Arts and Crafts) in Munich, that primordial cell of the Reform movement.

27 ▶ The ceramicist Hermann Gretsch had studied at the Stuttgart Technology University of Applied Sciences under the architect Paul Bonatz. In 1931, he designed Service 1382 – one of the most popular pieces of its time – for the Arzberg porcelain factory.

28 ▶ This company was Forchheimer & Co.

29 ▶ In Dresden, it was possible to pursue a restrained, "dignified" modernism, despite the National Socialists' "enforced conformity."

ESTHETICS AND MECHANICS

The chrome-plated frames and modern fabrics made a highly elegant impression, but new technical solutions were also found. Since the early days, folding functions had been a specialty of Wilhelm and Walter Knoll.

Catalog brochure,
tubular steel chairs Prodomo K-F 425,
K-F 423 and K-F 410, Walter Knoll,
Feuerbach (now Stuttgart), around 1930

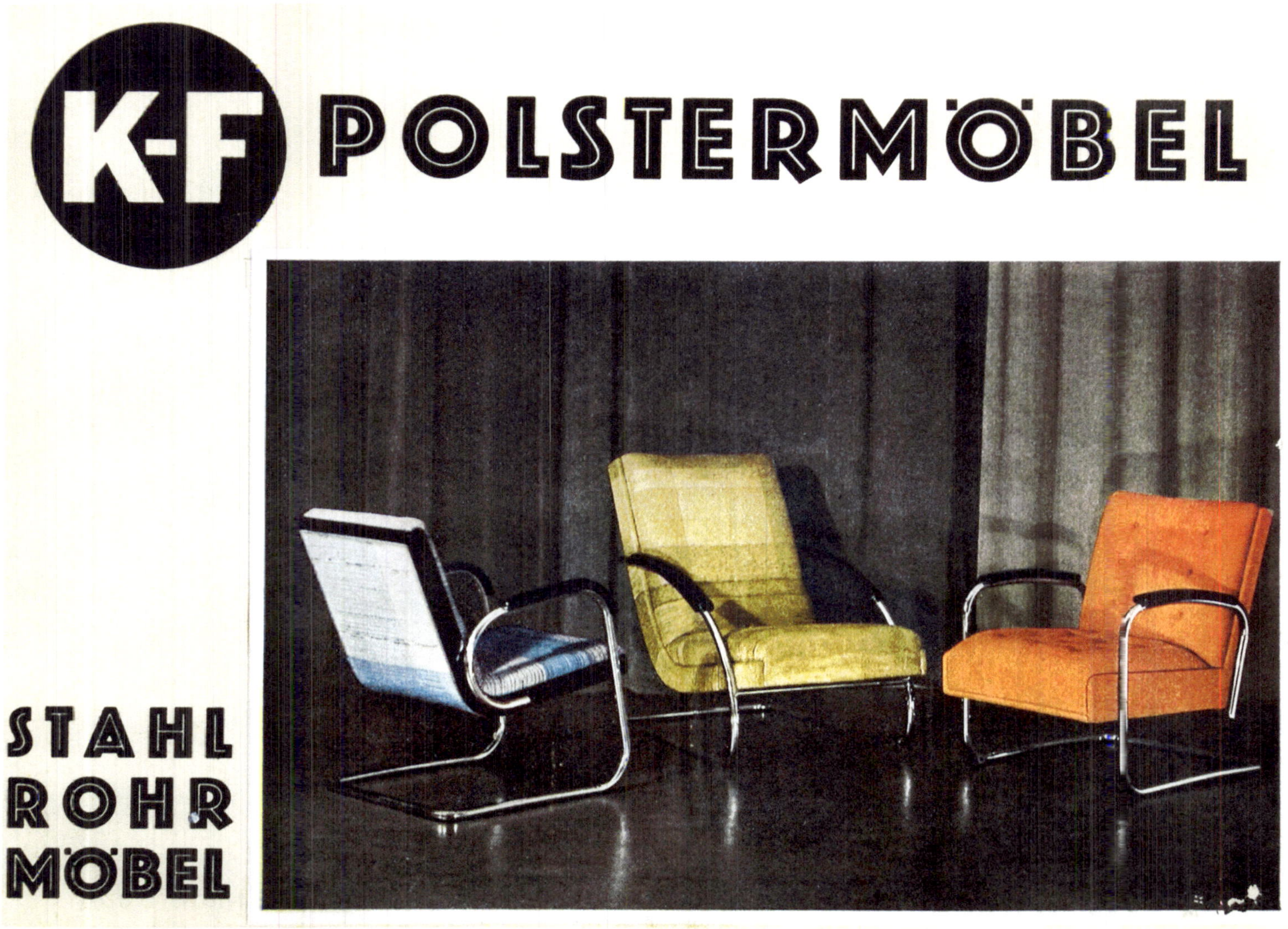

Tubular steel furniture,
Stool Prodomo 408 and
Table Prodomo 429, Walter Knoll,
Feuerbach (now Stuttgart), around 1930

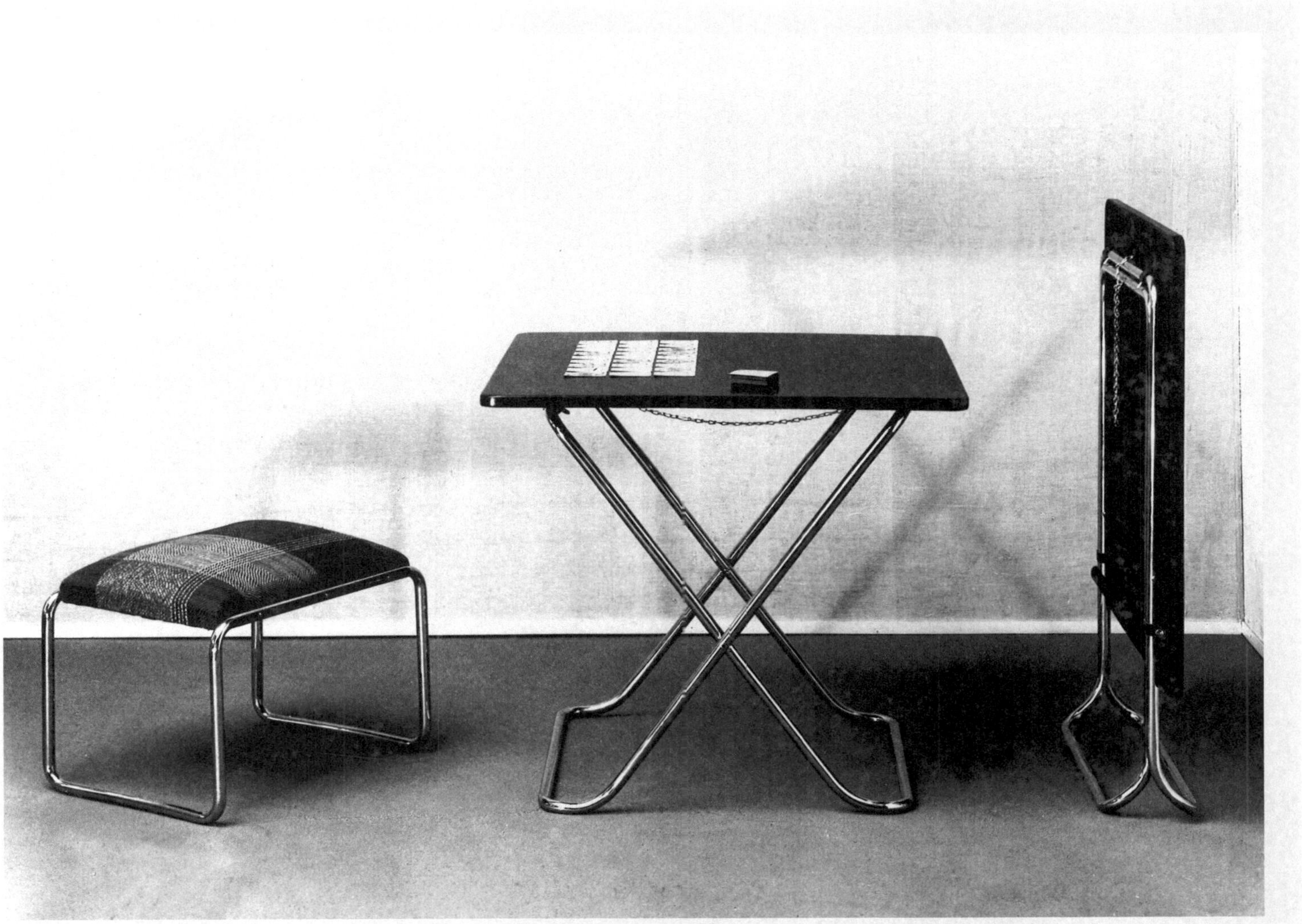

The divergent picture of those years can also be seen in the latest edition of *"Die schöne Wohnung"* (The Beautiful Dwelling), a series of books by the renowned Munich publisher Bruckmann Verlag. Approximately every five years, a book would appear with this same title but completely re-illustrated, the fourth time being in 1941. This unofficial style guide for interior designers looks like a regression to the days before *Neues Wohnen* and radiates the solidity typical of the Reform Style before the First World War, including bourgeois and feudal reminiscences. In addition to several interiors furnished with period furniture, it also contains numerous examples of a restrained modernity in turmoil. Even tubular steel is not entirely left out. Some of the rooms pictured include seating furniture by Walter Knoll. An armchair is shown from several different angles. It is a light

AT THE END OF THE 1930S, WALTER AND WILLY KNOLL WERE SUCCESSFUL BUSINESSMEN AND HIGHLY RESPECTED IN THEIR HOME TOWN OF STUTTGART.

wood construction with a large wickerwork area and inlaid cushions that conform to the rounded shape of the frame. The function of the rear legs is taken over by a centrally placed and intrinsically curved wooden plate. This original and coherent design, devoid of right angles, appears lightweight and elegant. It reveals a further development in the Reform Style as well as attempts at the streamline. The armchair was designed by the Stuttgart architect Adolf C. Rüdenauer, a typical representative of those years. Rüdenauer was a conservative modernist, similar to Hans Hartl, who recommended a "calm serenity" in matters of style that above all recognized "the essence of German home decor."[30] In the 1950s, he became one of the advocates of the Second Modernity.

Hans Knoll, who initially intended to stay in America for only a year to sell his father's Prodomo models, soon changed his mind. In 1937, scarcely having arrived, he founded the Hans G. Knoll Furniture Company, rented an office in Manhattan, and posted the sign "Factory No. 1" on the door. But that wasn't much more than the symbolic gesture of a hopeful entrepreneur. In the beginning, Hans worked as a representative of a furniture wholesaler – a job that was boring and badly paid, but good for making contacts. It was no coincidence that many of the names sounded German (including that of his employer, George Ditmar). "Little Germany," the local German community, was still functioning. Hans also visited the Mueller Furniture Company in Grand Rapids, Michigan, America's *furniture city*. Its boss, Frederick H. Mueller, was an industry leader[31] who produced high-quality upholstered furniture and employed artists, such as Kem Weber, to create it. Weber, born in Berlin and known for his streamlined furniture, was considered a leading exponent of American Modernism, a collective term for alternatives to America's conservatism. Hans Knoll successfully offered Mueller the Prodomo range, but the deal fell through due to the war.

America was still deep in the Great Depression and hoping for a miracle. It was the hour of the designers, who now invented themselves as a profession and promised to stimulate the economy through beauty. The panacea was called Streamline and the World's Fair in New York was the victory parade of those designers.[32] Among the highlights of this show of superlatives (at which Germany was not represented) were the pavilions of the Scandinavian countries – Alvar Aalto's Finnish pavilion, and Josef Frank's Swedish pavilion – which were early forerunners of Scandinavian design.[33] When Hans Knoll became a representative of Artek, Aalto's distribution company[34], he also became acquainted with the Dane Jens Risom. Risom, who was about the same age and is now considered to be one of the greats of the Second Modernity, was an immigrant like Hans.[35] He had studied furniture making at the School of Arts and Crafts in Copenhagen and then designed furnishings for Sweden's finest department store, Nordiska Kompaniet, in Stockholm. The young man was so gifted that he finally met the idols of his trade, the Swede Bruno Mathsson, who was famous for his webbing chairs, and Alvar Aalto. And so the circle

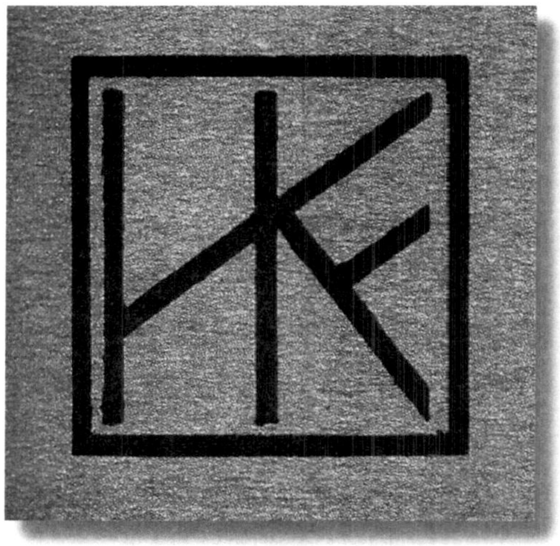

was closed. Hans Knoll had found what he was looking for: a creative man who knew something about modern furniture that he could sell. "We needed each other," Risom later recalled.[36]

The two men, who complemented one another so perfectly – and thus strongly resembled the duo of Walter Knoll and Paul Hahn –, created a constellation from which something new could emerge. Here again, in line with the creative tandem principle, Hans followed – whether consciously or intuitively – in his father's footsteps. The German Hans and Danish Jens first crisscrossed the U.S. as in a road movie while familiarizing themselves with the country and its furniture landscape. It took a few more years before a catalog of Hans Knoll Furniture was published in 1942 under the trademark "HKF." The resemblance to "K-F," the former logo of the father's company, is difficult to ignore. Yet again, Walter was his role model. The partnership with Risom had another advantage. Because the U.S. was on the opposite side in the war, antipathies against Germans increased significantly. The fact that Hans relied on the Scandinavian connection could only be considered a positive thing. Ironically, the blond-haired Hans managed to do something that no one before him had ever been able to do, particularly in this delicate situation. He was the first, and for a long time "the only person who ever managed to successfully sell modern furniture in America."[37] That is how one of the Swedish business partners summed up Hans's achievements as an entrepreneur and pioneer of modern furniture. The fact that the young company's first showroom exhibited an *authentic Swedish room* also fits the picture. And so, in the middle of the war and on the other side of the Atlantic, the third branch of the Knoll furniture dynasty assumed a concrete shape.

At the end of the 1930s, Walter and Willy Knoll – now both around 60 – were successful entrepreneurs who were highly regarded in their hometown of Stuttgart, but who had gone their separate ways since the death of their parents. Thus they formed two geographically close but completely independent branches of the Knoll dynasty. Walter and Willy, two entrepreneurs with a passion and, as such, both exceptions in their profession, continued their father's legacy each in their own way according to their different biographies and temperaments. Decisive for both men was the examples set by their father Wilhelm, who stepped away from his Stuttgart-based leather workshop and continued his father's legacy in his own way, and by Emma Knoll, wife and self-sacrificing mother, who gave her children emotional security and thereby an unshakable self-confidence. Would the history of the Knoll furniture dynasty have been different if she had not died so early and had used her authority and conciliatory manner to mediate between her sons? While the energetic Willy, who found strong support in his faith, reinvented upholstery as a much-traveled leather and furniture expert, the sociable Walter had other priorities. The Vollmöllers, his wife's family, and his years in America had introduced him to the wider world. For this reason, he sought proximity to the cultural milieu of modernity and also explored new horizons as a businessman. Until his separation from Paul Hahn in 1935, he had an experienced man on the premises. In the years that followed, moderate modernists such as Adolf C. Rüdenauer and Franz Schuster filled the gap.

In January 1939, Maia and Walter Knoll received a telegram from New York in which their son Hans informed them he would soon be married. In May, his parents crossed the Atlantic on the passenger steamer "Hamburg." At the same time, his brother-in-law Karl Gustav Vollmöller traveled on the "Bremen." The bride's name was Barbara Southwick. She was the daughter of an engineer who had traveled around Europe professionally and spoke fluent German. According to Walter, the Southwicks were highly "cultivated people."[38] Barbara had lived in Paris for a while and showed "a talent for painting."[39] She was to give birth to their two children, Maja and Peter – which did not prevent the imminent breakdown of their marriage. Hans's business was in an embryonic state at that time when he had no collection of his own. But Walter Knoll felt that the right course had been set. A visit to Bronson Winthrop's stately manor on Long Island convinced him of this. Winthrop, now 76, was the father figure who had known Hans since his time at the Swiss sanatorium and had treated him as his protégé ever since. "A fine old gentleman," said Walter Knoll, "a model of the highly civilized American, prominent as an attorney and bearer of an old family name."[40]

30 ▶ Rüdenauer, in: "Innen-Dekoration" (Interior Decoration) 1937, p. 341–345.

31 ▶ In the 1950s, Mueller became Secretary of Commerce in Eisenhower's second cabinet.

32 ▶ It was a relatively small group that included Henry Dreyfuss, Walter Dorwin Teague, Russel Wright, and Raymond Loewy, the latter having introduced the concept of design.

33 ▶ The Finnish pavilion was designed by Alvar Aalto and the Swedish pavilion by Josef Frank, the Viennese architect who was already involved in the Weissenhofsiedlung estate, was now living in exile in Stockholm, and exerted enormous influence.

34 ▶ Aalto caused a sensation with the Finnish pavilion and was one of the first to have a solo exhibition at the Museum of Modern Art.

35 ▶ The American magazine Playboy showed Jens Risom in the July 1961 issue in a photograph with George Nelson, Edward Wormley, Eero Saarinen, Harry Bertoia, and Charles Eames – almost the entire American design elite of those years.

36 ▶ Martin, 2011, p. 77.

37 ▶ Martin, 2011, p. 94.

38 ▶ Knoll, n.d., p. 76.

39 ▶ Ibid.

40 ▶ Knoll, n.d., p. 77.

RICH IN VARIANTS
Tubular steel was a material that offered many possibilities. The collections of Wilhelm and Walter Knoll became the testing ground for design.

Sketch, chaise longue 3762, Wilhelm Knoll, design by Wilhelm Renz, Stuttgart, around 1935

Chaise longue 3762, Wilhelm Knoll, design by Wilhelm Renz, Stuttgart, around 1935

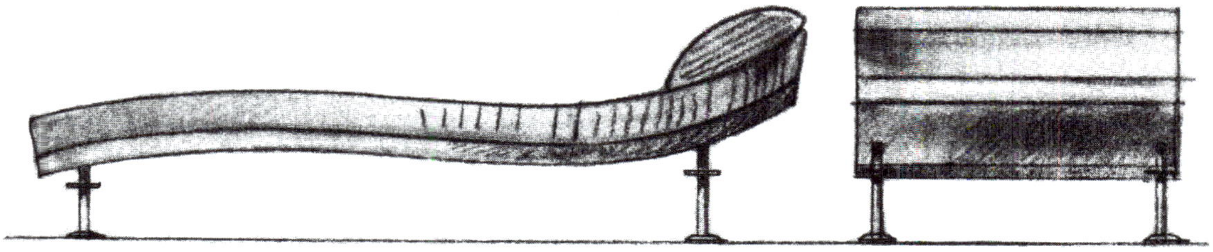

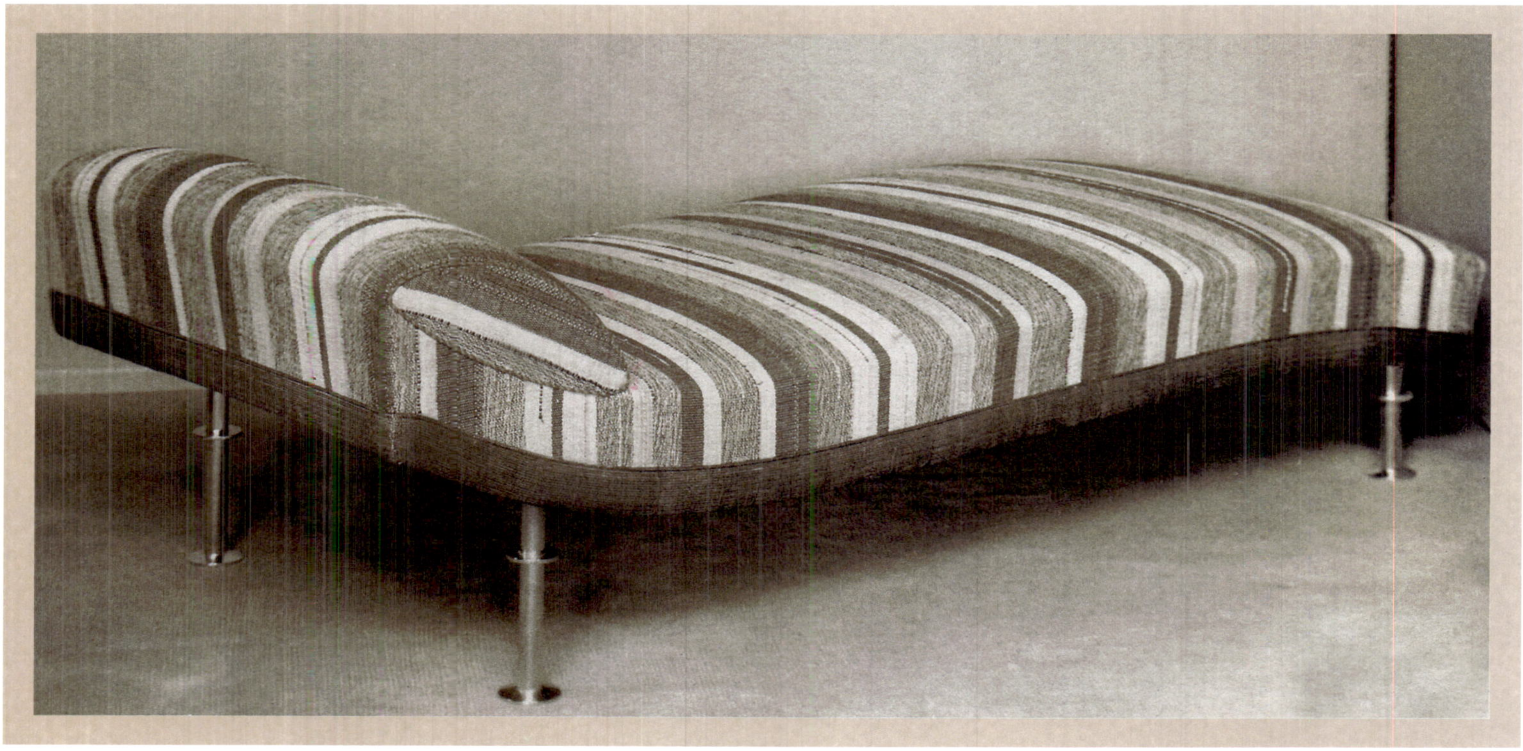

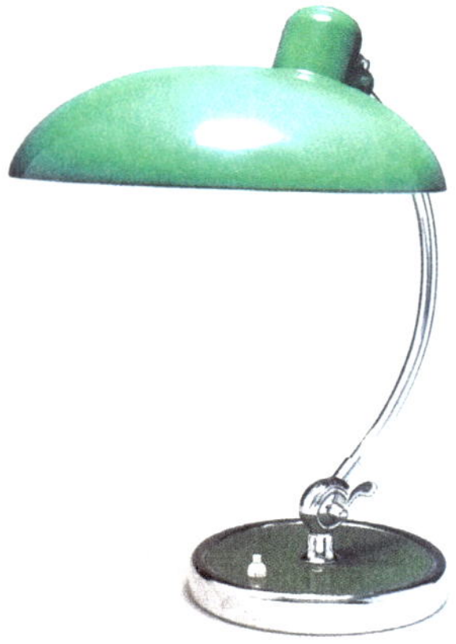

Christian Dell's desk lamp from 1930 is an obvious and extremely successful application of metal tube technology.

Tubular steel chair, K-F 87, Walter Knoll, Feuerbach (now Stuttgart), around 1935

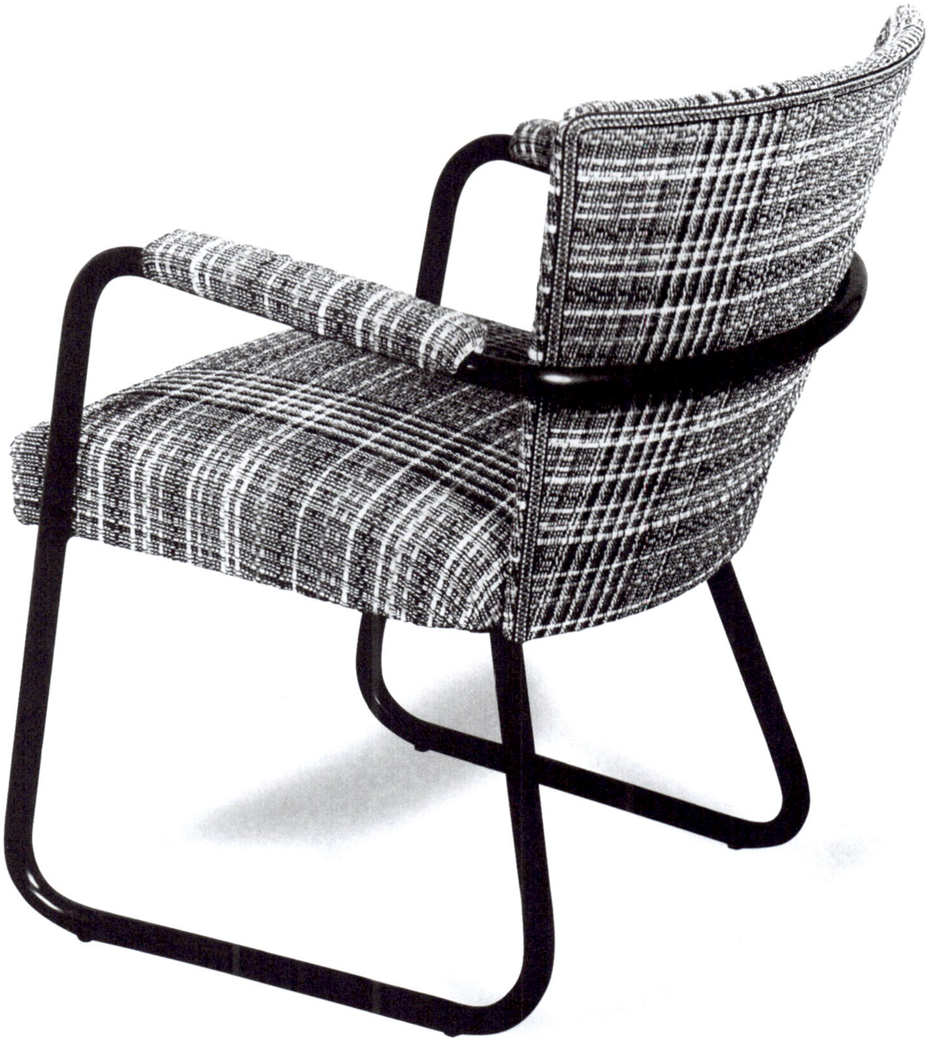

IT WAS THE MOMENT IN WHICH HANS BECAME A BEARER OF HOPE FOR HIS FATHER.

This gentleman, who so touchingly looked after Hans and introduced him to the very highest circles of New York society, also spoke about his good friend and lawyer colleague Henry Stimson, the former Secretary of State, who was to become Secretary of War the following year. There is film footage of the day of this visit, which shows Hans and Walter treating each other almost lovingly.[41] It was the moment when Hans, the "problem child" and supposedly lost son, became a bearer of hope for his father who now helped him to realize his own American dreams.[42] In fact, Walter literally met old friends in New York. Otherwise, as in the past, there were "many invitations and a number of new acquaintances".[43] Walter Knoll was in his element. There was another important item on the agenda: the World's Fair, which was currently being held in Queens, a borough of New York. Hans had succeeded in introducing Prodomo into one of the exhibitions there, which was ironically called "America at Home" – not bad for a 25-year-old immigrant – and it made his father even prouder. The world seemed to be in order and yet faced with catastrophe.

When the Second World War broke out in September 1939, there was little evidence of the rejoicing seen at the start of the First World War. The event was hardly perceived as a watershed, especially since people also believed that the war would once again come to a swift end. Of course, the impression of normality was an illusion. Wilhelm Knoll's production line was soon converted to arms-related goods, which did not include armchairs and sofas.

The clever Willy Knoll, who had remained in the country this time because his age exempted him from the draft, did manage to ensure that the new products also included furniture in the broadest sense of the term. He now produced beds for military hospitals and air-raid shelters as well as airplane cushions for the Heinkel company. In this way, the factory was even able to basically maintain "its old program by and large."[44] Walter Knoll was also able to continue making furniture, albeit under tougher conditions, because the number of men who were drafted as soldiers cut the original workforce in half. Among those who were compelled to go to the Front early on were Walter Knoll's sons, Robert and Herbert. A real turning point, both personally and on the battlefield, came in 1941. This was the year in which Walter Knoll had to sell the Vollmöller's villa, where he had lived with his wife for over a quarter of a century and which was their sons' parental home. The family then moved to Herrenberg. The entrance of the U.S. into the war in December of that same year was a veritable bombshell – an event whose significance Walter Knoll recognized more clearly than most, probably in part because of his special relationship with America, which he had just renewed. And, of course, it made contact with Hans even more difficult. For two years they knew nothing of one another, until a Swedish friend brought news. It was quite surprising. There had been drastic changes in Hans Knoll's life. After falling in with the Russian Chermayeff and the Dane Risom, he had another fateful encounter – this time with a woman.

The phenomenal story of the American branch of the Knoll dynasty has a genuinely European background and is unimaginable without the unusually gifted and emancipated woman named Florence Knoll. The daughter of a wealthy Swiss family from Saginaw, Michigan, named Schust (hence her nickname, "Shu"), she attended a boarding school for girls near Detroit following the early death of her parents in 1931 when she was only 14. The school was on the campus of the Cranbrook Academy, which at that time was developing into a training ground for American design under the leadership of Eliel Saarinen of Finland and his wife Loja. Florence, who was ultimately adopted by the Saarinen family, experienced her professional revival as an interior designer here in the mid-1930s. She subsequently studied in New York, Munich, and London, and then began her apprenticeship with various ex-Bauhaus members who had emigrated from Germany – those grandmasters of modernity who had just introduced *Neues Wohnen* (renamed International Style) to America, and included none other than Herbert Bayer, Marcel Breuer, Walter Gropius, and Ludwig Mies van der Rohe. Finally, she was a guest of the Frenchman Raymond Loewy, Streamline guru and jack-of-all-trades among the American designers.

So when Florence and Hans met in New York in 1941, the petite 24-year-old already had a storybook education behind her. A higher

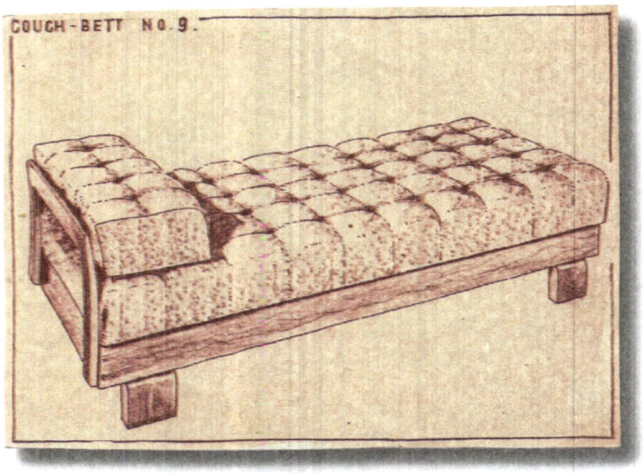

dose of European modernity was hardly possible. One of their first joint commissions, mediated by Bronson Winthrop, was an office suite for Henry Stimson, the new Secretary of War. This work for the Pentagon resulted in further direct contacts with government circles. In 1943, Hans Knoll, who now employed over a dozen people, founded H. G. Knoll Associates. His partner, Jens Risom, had to join the U.S. Army to fight Nazi Germany in Europe. A little later, when Hans Knoll was already divorced from his first wife, New York's Bloomingdale's department store exhibited his collection. It was a great success, but a financial fiasco. Florence Schust stepped in and paid the debts, [45] thus becoming a de facto owner – which found expression in the renaming of the company as Knoll Associates, without the founder's initials. Shortly thereafter, Florence and Hans were married. The marriage remained childless. For one turbulent decade, they became the number-two dream couple of American design alongside Ray and Charles Eames and laid the foundation for the third, soon to be strongly burgeoning branch of the Knoll furniture dynasty.

The first bombs were dropped on Stuttgart in August 1940. For the population, this marked the beginning of a martyrdom set to the tune of howling sirens. The city – which was one of the most important industrial centers in Germany and the focal point of modern sectors such as the electrical and automotive industries, as well as precision mechanics and mechanical engineering – was subsequently the victim of more than 50 air raids, consisting of up to 800 airplanes in a single night. Large parts of the city were destroyed, including the historic center. Only ruins remained of the headquarters of the Wilhelm Knoll company on Forststrasse. In idyllic Herrenberg, situated in the outskirts of Stuttgart, residents also had to accustom themselves to the sound of bombers' engines. Walter Knoll reported how, on a train ride from Herrenberg to Stuttgart, the train was strafed by a low-flying airplane and he and his wife Maia had to flee to the meadows. It was at this time that the two received bad news. Their youngest son Herbert, who was stationed on the Western Front, had died in an accident.

In 1943, "total war" was declared in Germany. In that same year, according to Walter Knoll, "the factory had to be completely vacated by order of the army command."[46] The company discontinued operations. The Klemm aircraft company from Böblingen now moved into the premises and took charge of the business and its personnel, which included prisoners of war. Walter Knoll worked on site as a "workshop manager" for Klemm. While he had frequently visited his company during the transition period, he "had become completely inactive in the last year of the war."[47] In April 1945, when the war was almost over, Herrenberg experienced its most severe air raid, which was to paralyze train traffic and hit the factory building directly adjacent to the train station. Rural Gaildorf, to which Willy Knoll

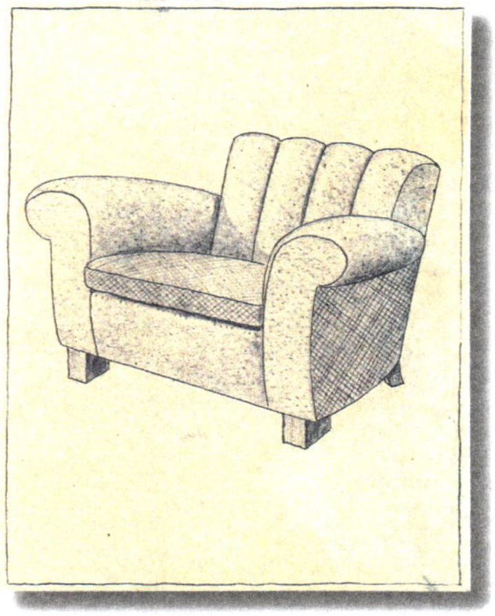

had almost entirely relocated production, also fell victim. Shortly before the end of the war, a contemporary witness reported that "a hit caused window damage in the carpenter's workshop and removed most of the roof from Building B."[48] But "the incendiary ammunition dropped during low-flying attacks did not cause any major damage, because courageous factory personnel nipped any fires in the bud."[49] This made it possible for "all the minor damage to be repaired even before the occupation."[50] Thus, reconstruction had already begun before the war's end.

41 ▶ Interview with Brian Lutz on 05/23/2016.

42 ▶ Knoll, n.d., p. 76.

43 ▶ Ibid, p. 77

44 ▶ Knoll, 1965, p. 34.

45 ▶ It was a matter of some 50,000 U.S. dollars. See: Martin, 2011, p. 88.

46 ▶ Knoll, n.d., p. 81.

47 ▶ Ibid.

48 ▶ Knoll, 1965, p. 35.

49 ▶ Ibid.

50 ▶ Ibid.

ZEPPELIN

Airship LZ 129, the "Hindenburg," then the largest and most modern airship of its kind, was equipped with lightweight metal furniture from Wilhelm Knoll's Antimott range. Nothing could be more modern.

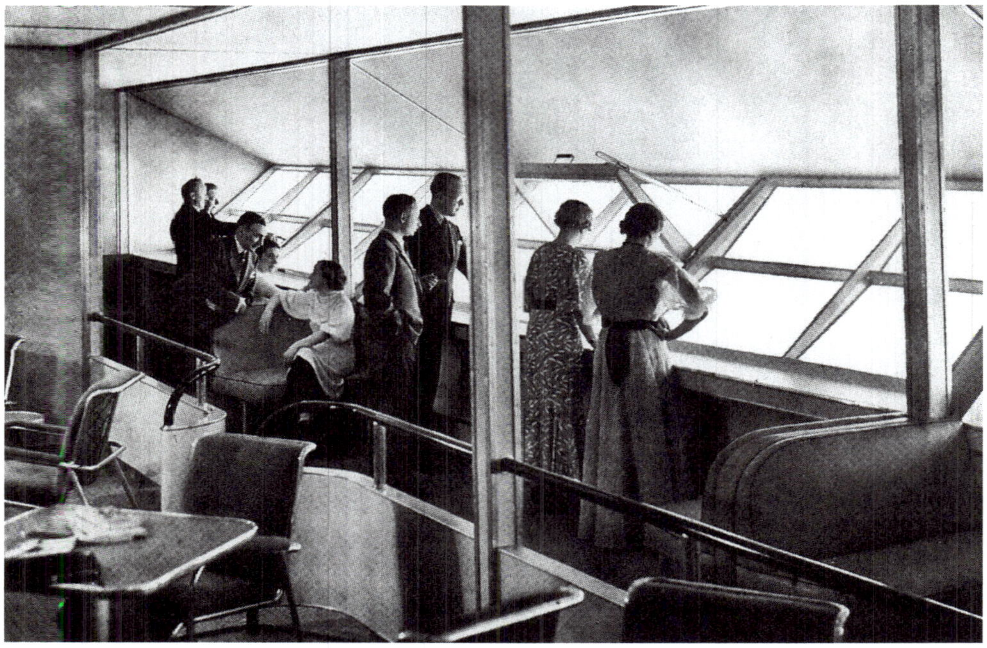

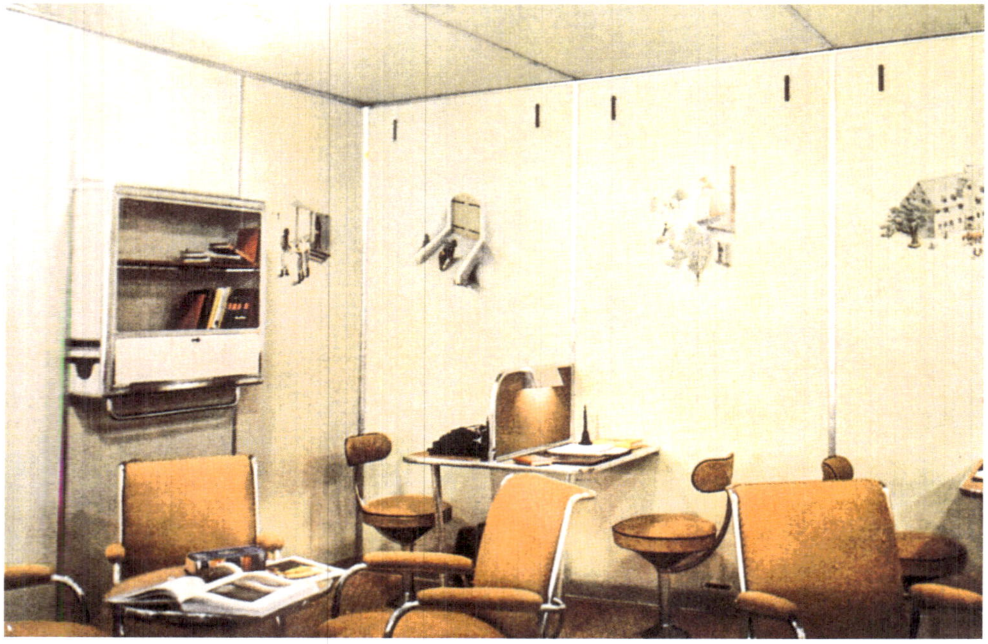

Airship LZ 129 with
Antimott light metal chairs,
Wilhelm Knoll,
design by F. A. Breuhaus,
Friedrichshafen, 1936

Postcard, 1937

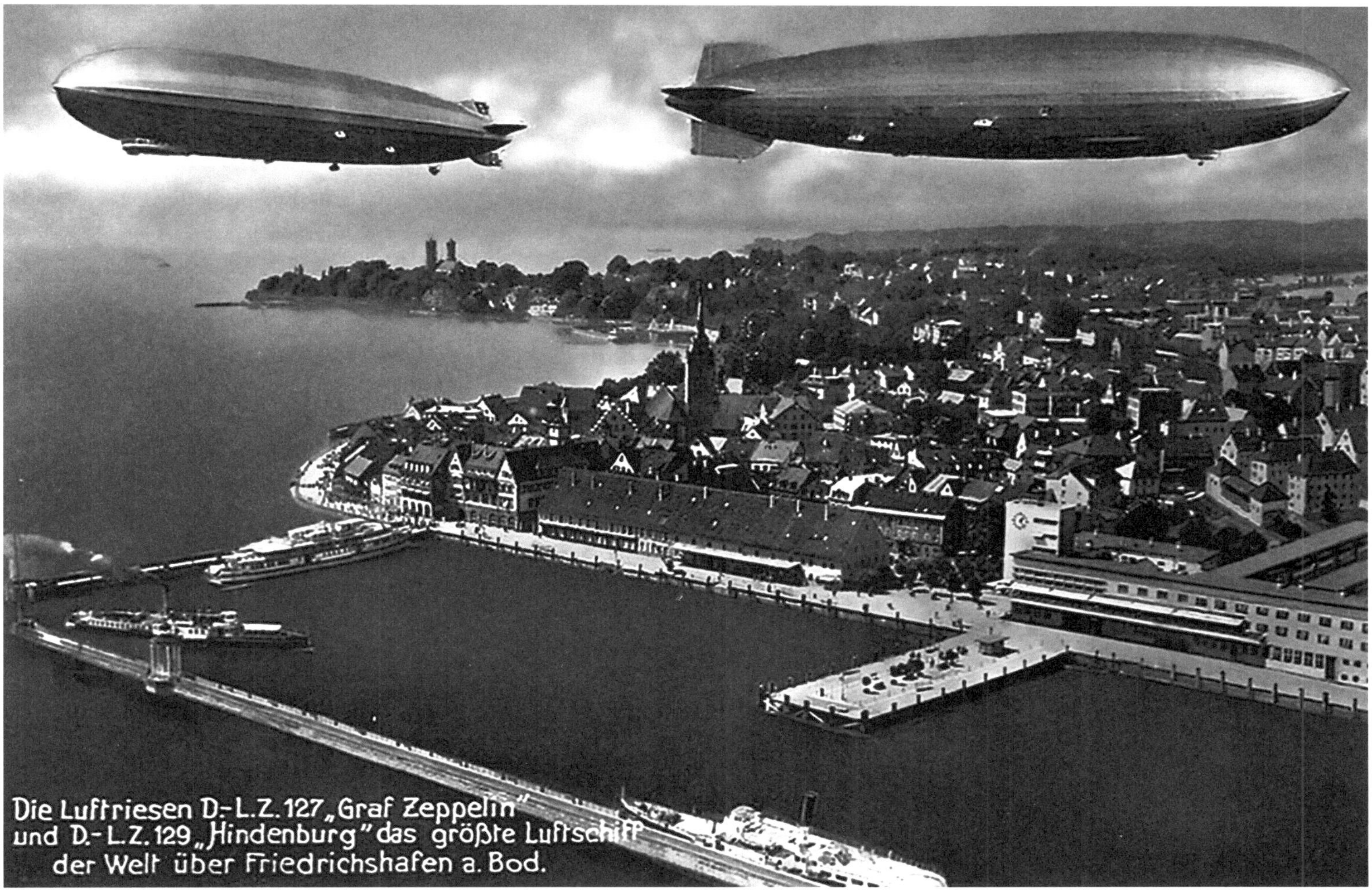

ZEITGEIST
"Metal furniture," which was still considered avant-garde in the 1920s, became a status symbol for modern living in the next decade.

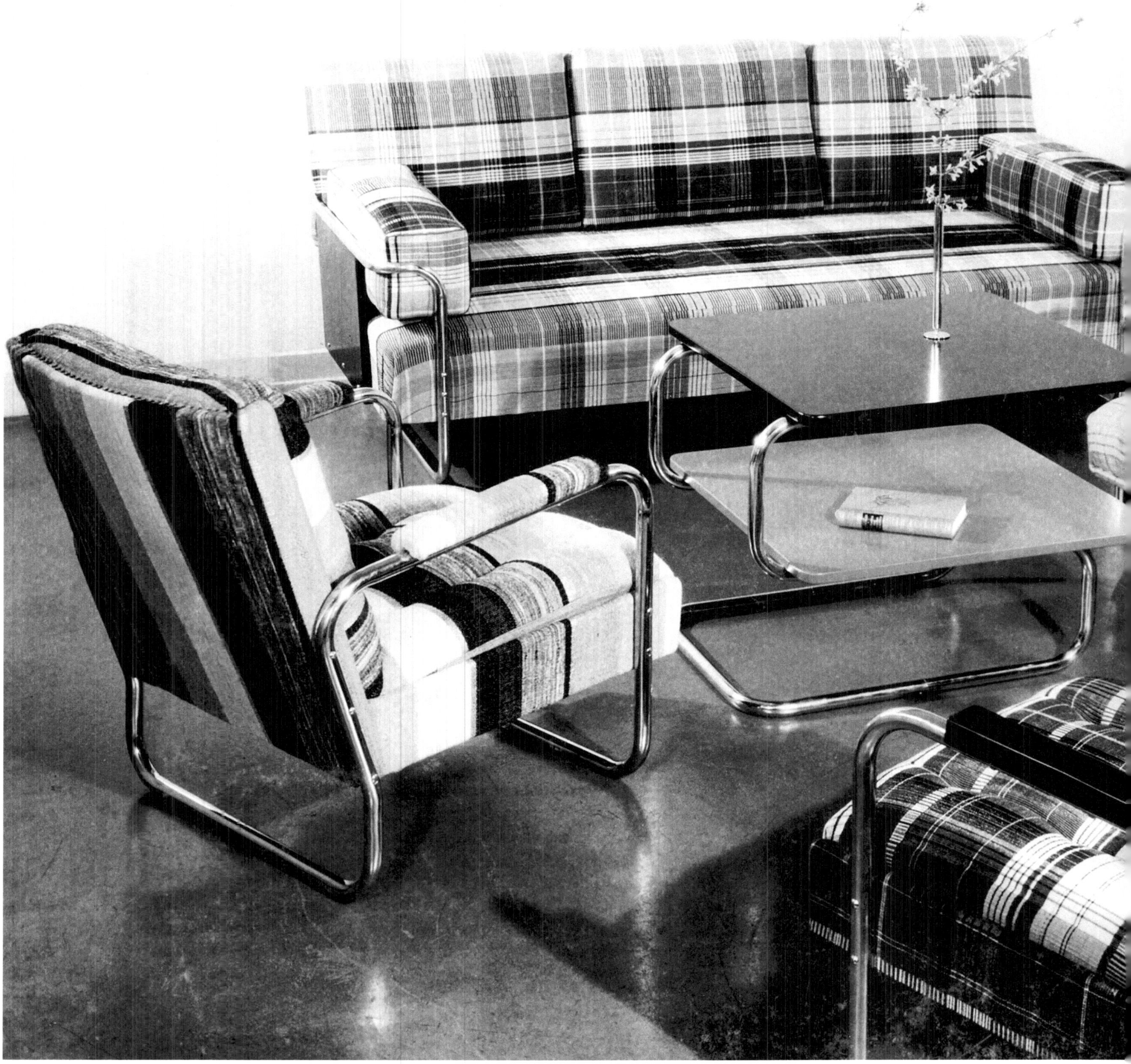

Tubular steel furniture,
sofa Prodomo K-F 402,
armchairs Prodomo K-F 406, K-F 403,
K-F 425 and table Prodomo K-F 407,
Walter Knoll, Feuerbach (now Stuttgart), 1930

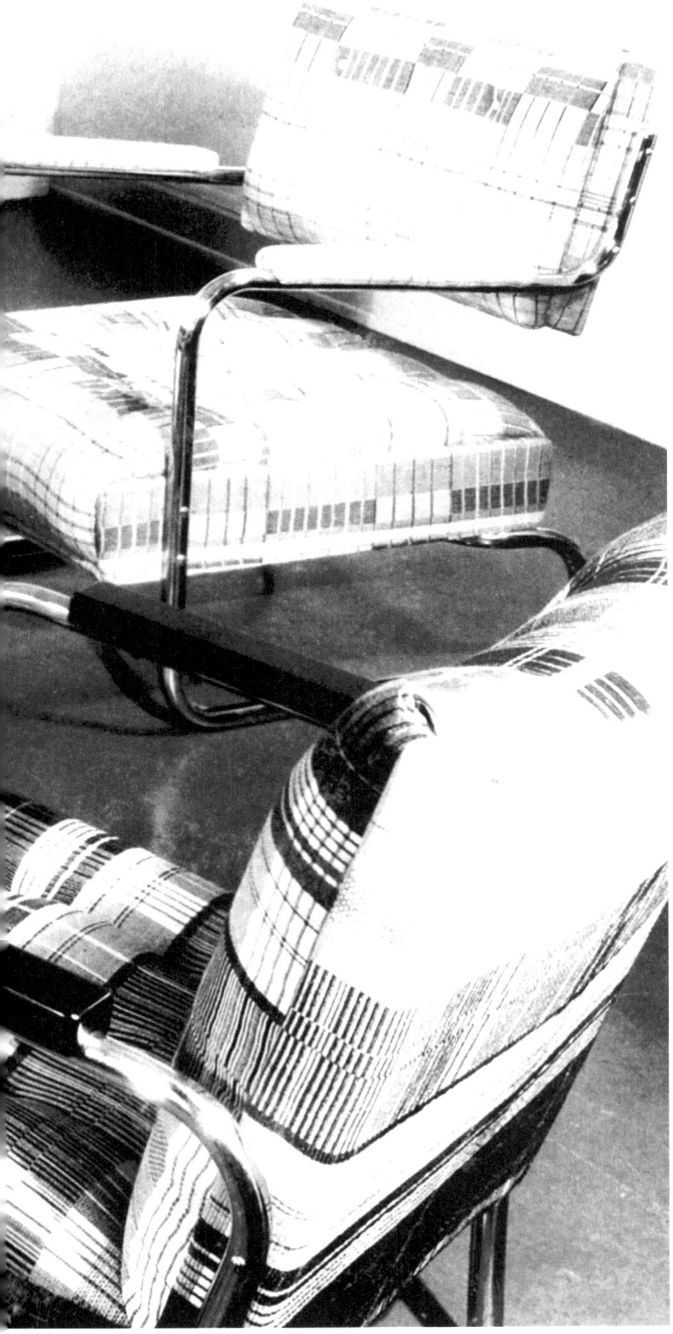

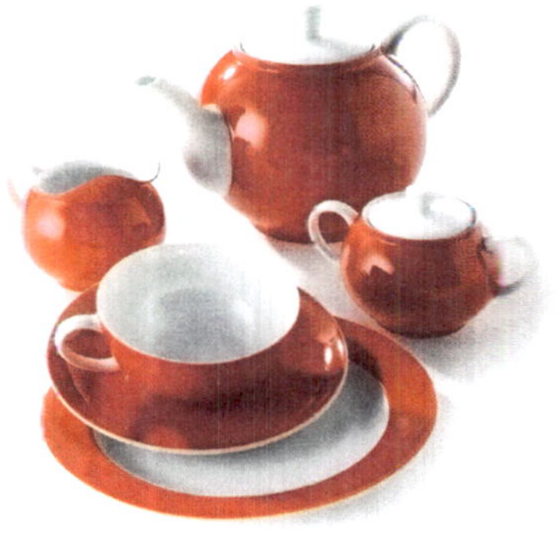

The tableware designed by Hermann Gretsch in the early 1930s was a bestseller and an archetype of moderate modernity.

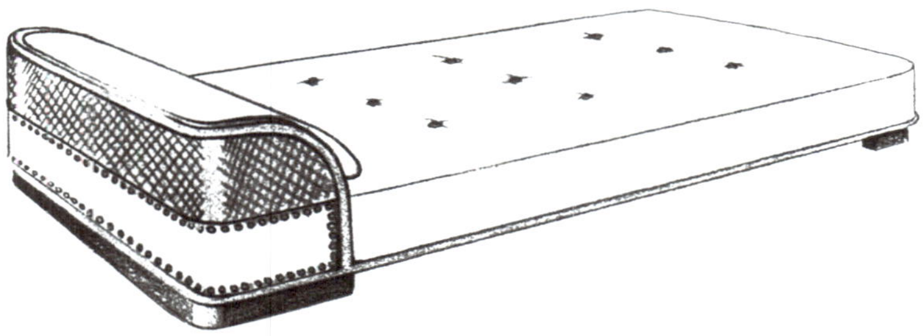

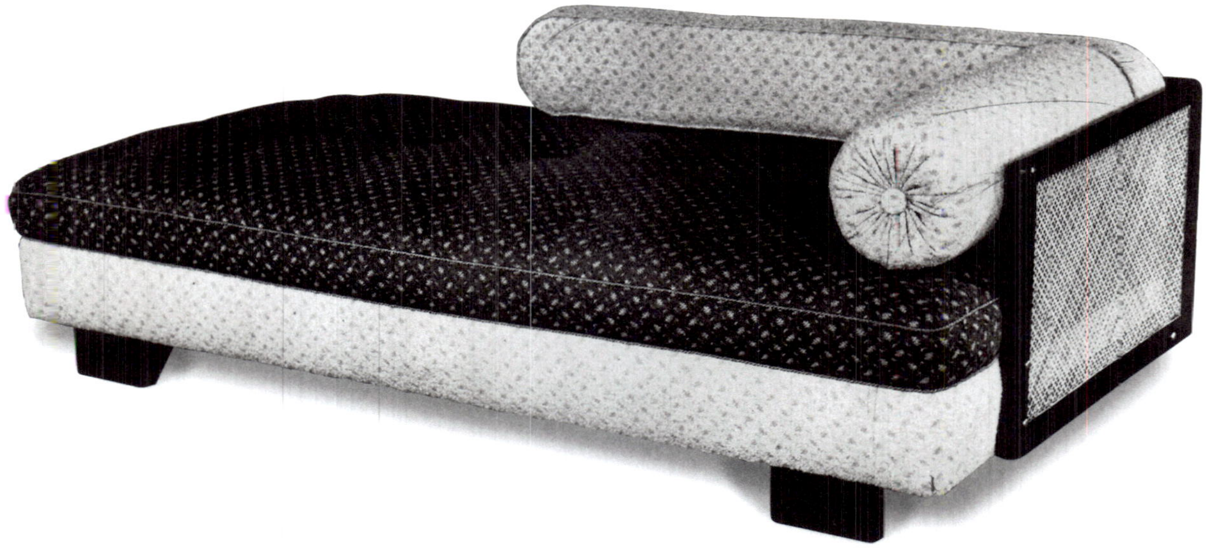

Model drawing, chaise longue 377, Wilhelm Knoll, Stuttgart, 1936

Chaise longue 374, Wilhelm Knoll, Stuttgart, 1936

Armchair WK 303, Wilhelm Knoll, Stuttgart, 1938

LINES
In the 1930s, Streamline also entered the living room.
Walter and Wilhelm Knoll created upholstered furniture that fell between "Silberpfeil" (Silver Arrow) and bourgeois modernity.

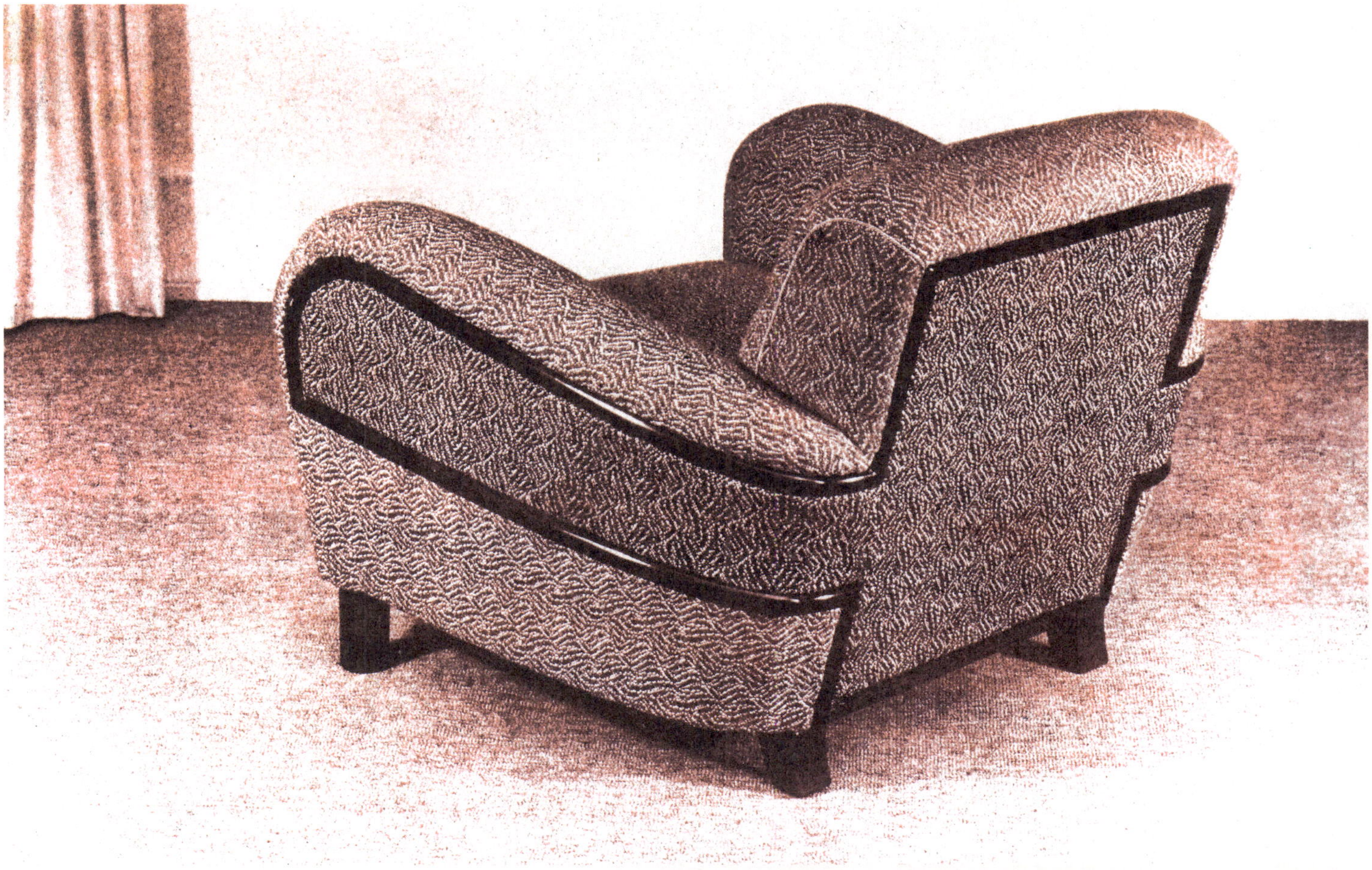

SEAT PATENTS

The invention of the Antimott spring was protected by patents. This also included a car seat for Opel, then Germany's largest car manufacturer.

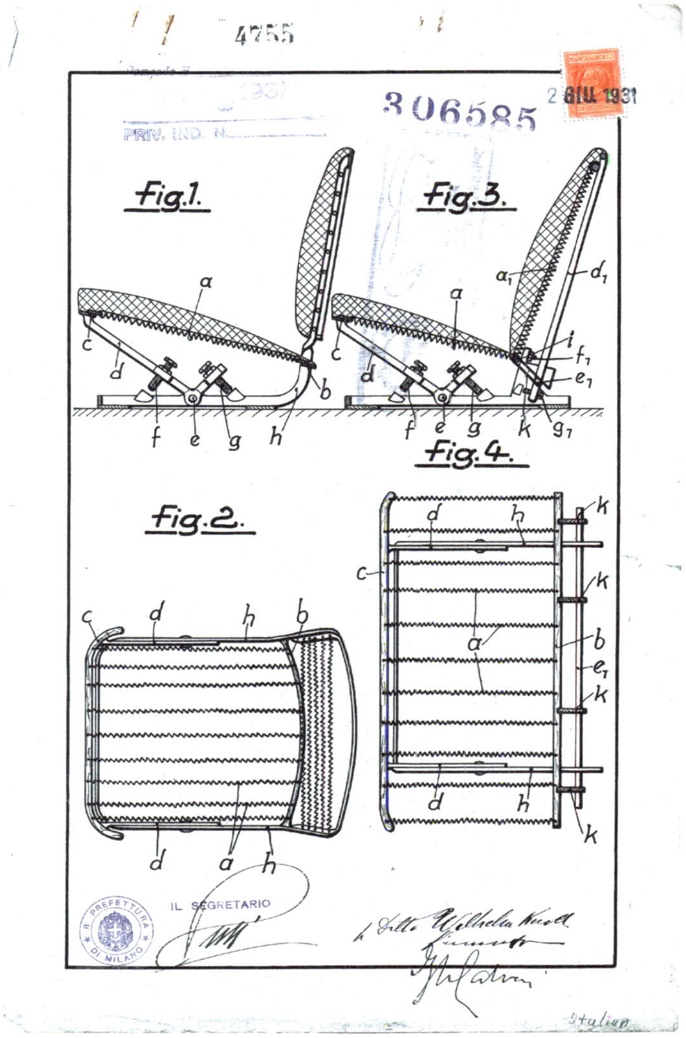

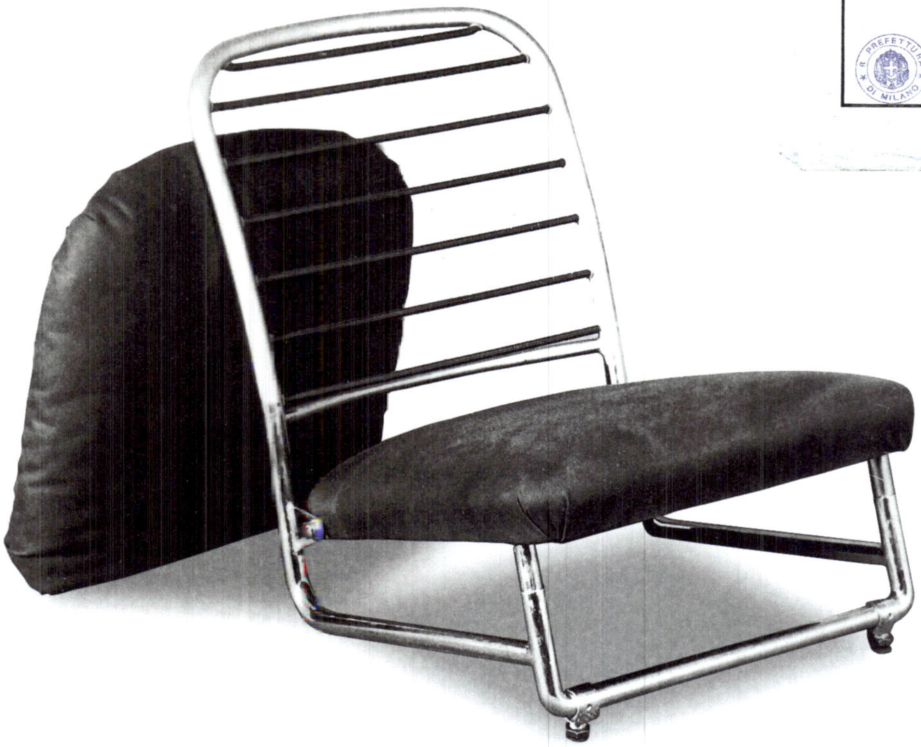

Italian patent No. 306585, for Antimott car seat, Wilhelm Knoll, Milan, 1931

Leather car seat for Opel, Wilhelm Knoll, design by G. Guevrekian, Stuttgart, 1929

Patent no. 629125 "Sprung seat, especially for motor vehicles," Wilhelm Knoll, Stuttgart, 1930

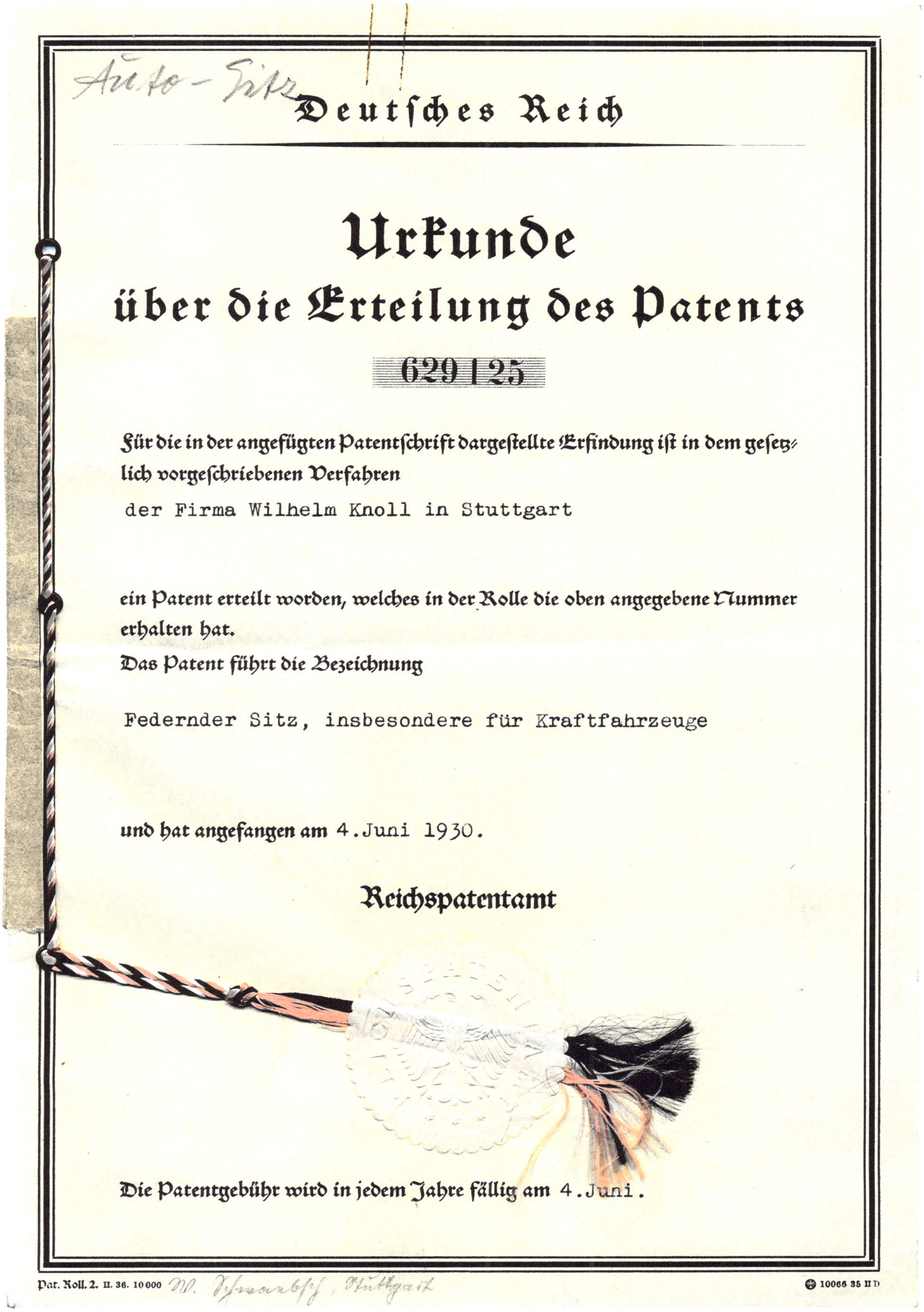

Auto-Sitz

Deutsches Reich

Urkunde
über die Erteilung des Patents
629 125

Für die in der angefügten Patentschrift dargestellte Erfindung ist in dem gesetzlich vorgeschriebenen Verfahren

der Firma Wilhelm Knoll in Stuttgart

ein Patent erteilt worden, welches in der Rolle die oben angegebene Nummer erhalten hat.

Das Patent führt die Bezeichnung

Federnder Sitz, insbesondere für Kraftfahrzeuge

und hat angefangen am 4. Juni 1930.

Reichspatentamt

Die Patentgebühr wird in jedem Jahre fällig am 4. Juni.

Pat. Roll. 2. II. 36. 10000   10066 35 II D

ENGLISHNESS

The partner company Parker-Knoll opened up the British market for Antimott. It demonstrated the innovation at important industrial trade fairs.

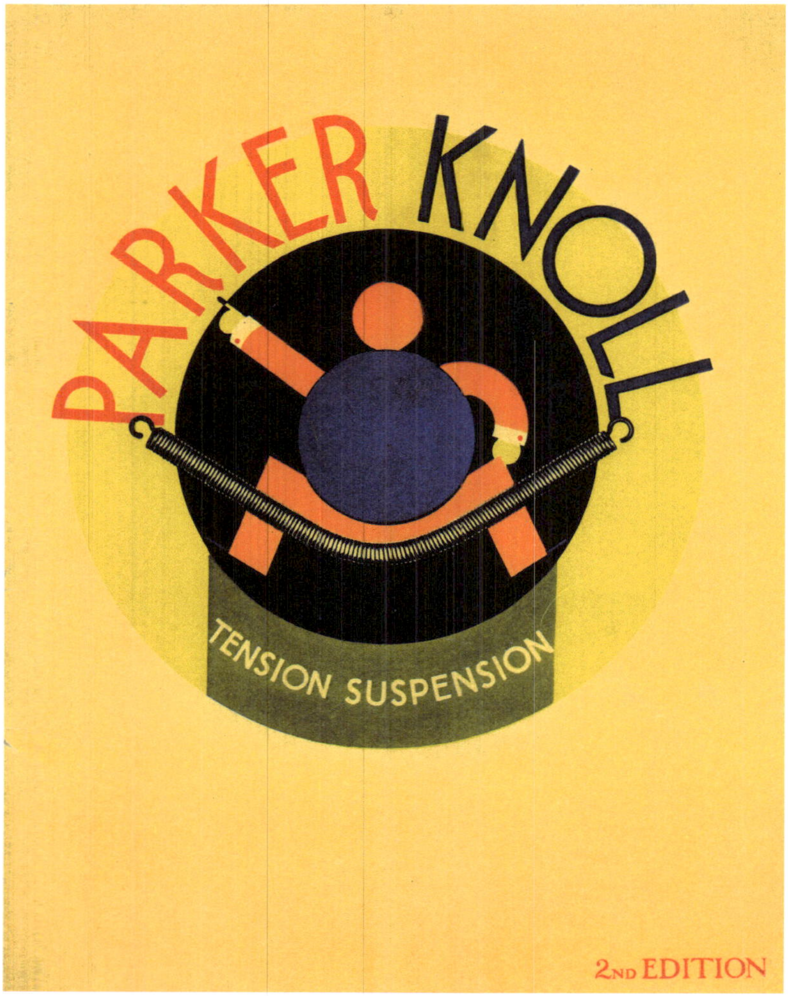

Catalog of the English licensee, London 1936

Invoice, Parker-Knoll, London, 1936

Advertisement for a trade fair, Antimott licensed furniture

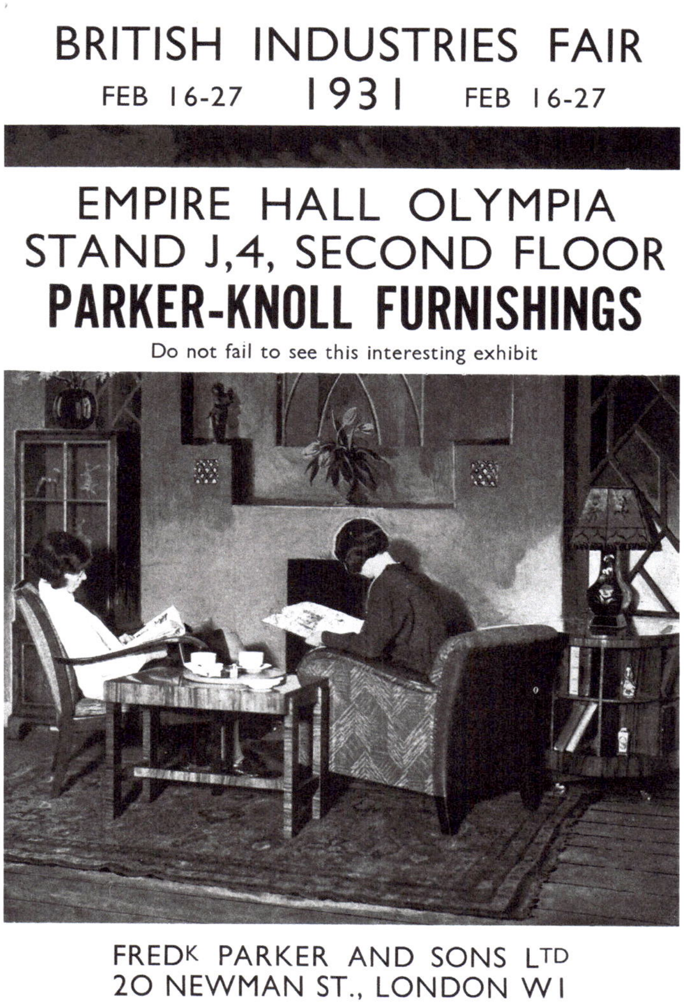

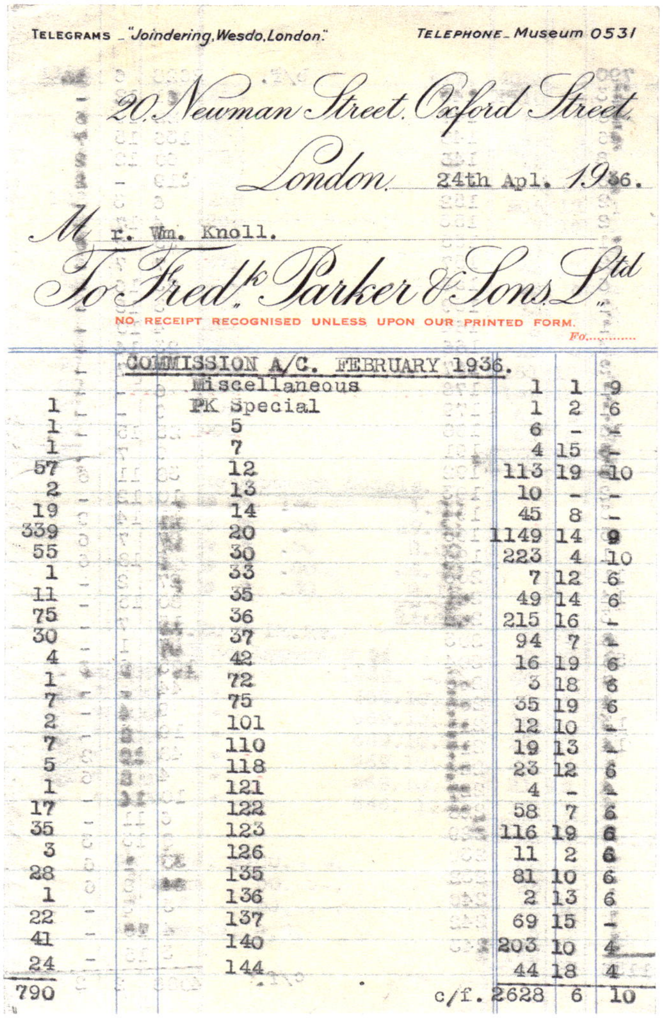

TELEGRAMS _ "Joindering, Wesdo, London." TELEPHONE _ Museum 0531

20, Newman Street, Oxford Street,
London, 24th Apl. 1936.

Mr. Wm. Knoll.

To Fredk Parker & Sons Ltd

NO RECEIPT RECOGNISED UNLESS UPON OUR PRINTED FORM.

Fo.........

	COMMISSION A/C. FEBRUARY 1936.			
	Miscellaneous	1	1	9
1	PK Special	1	2	6
1	5	6	-	-
1	7	4	15	-
57	12	113	19	10
2	13	10	-	-
19	14	45	8	-
339	20	1149	14	9
55	30	223	4	10
1	33	7	12	6
11	35	49	14	6
75	36	215	16	-
30	37	94	7	-
4	42	16	19	6
1	72	3	18	6
7	75	35	19	6
2	101	12	10	-
7	110	19	13	-
5	118	23	12	6
1	121	4	-	-
17	122	58	7	6
35	123	116	19	6
3	126	11	2	6
28	135	81	10	6
1	136	2	13	6
22	137	69	15	-
41	140	203	10	4
24	144	44	18	4
790	c/f.	2628	6	10

LUXURY LINER
The "Bremen" won the "Blue Riband" for the fastest crossing of the Atlantic and broke other records besides. First Class passengers sat in Walter Knoll's armchairs.

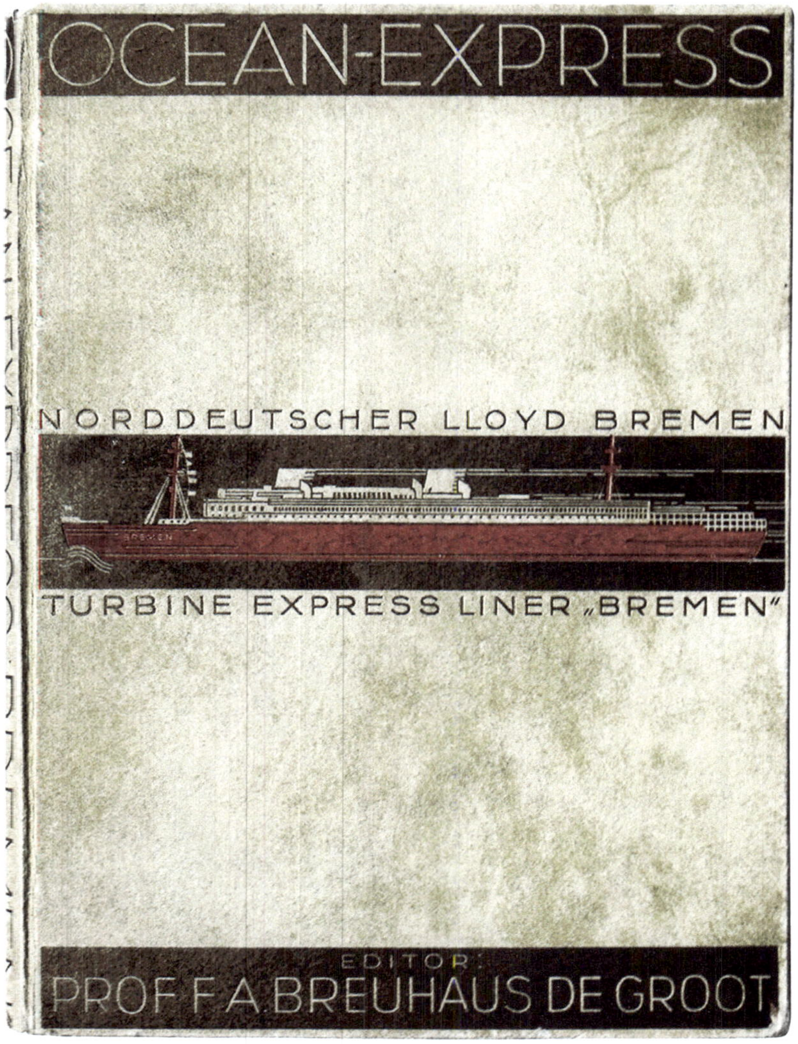

Illustrated book about the passenger steamer "Bremen," Munich (built 1929)

First Class lounge on the "Bremen," upholstered armchair by Walter Knoll, Bremen, 1929

Preparing to launch an aircraft by means of a catapult, deck of the "Bremen," 1929

Leather armchair SO 111, Wilhelm Knoll, Stuttgart, around 1930

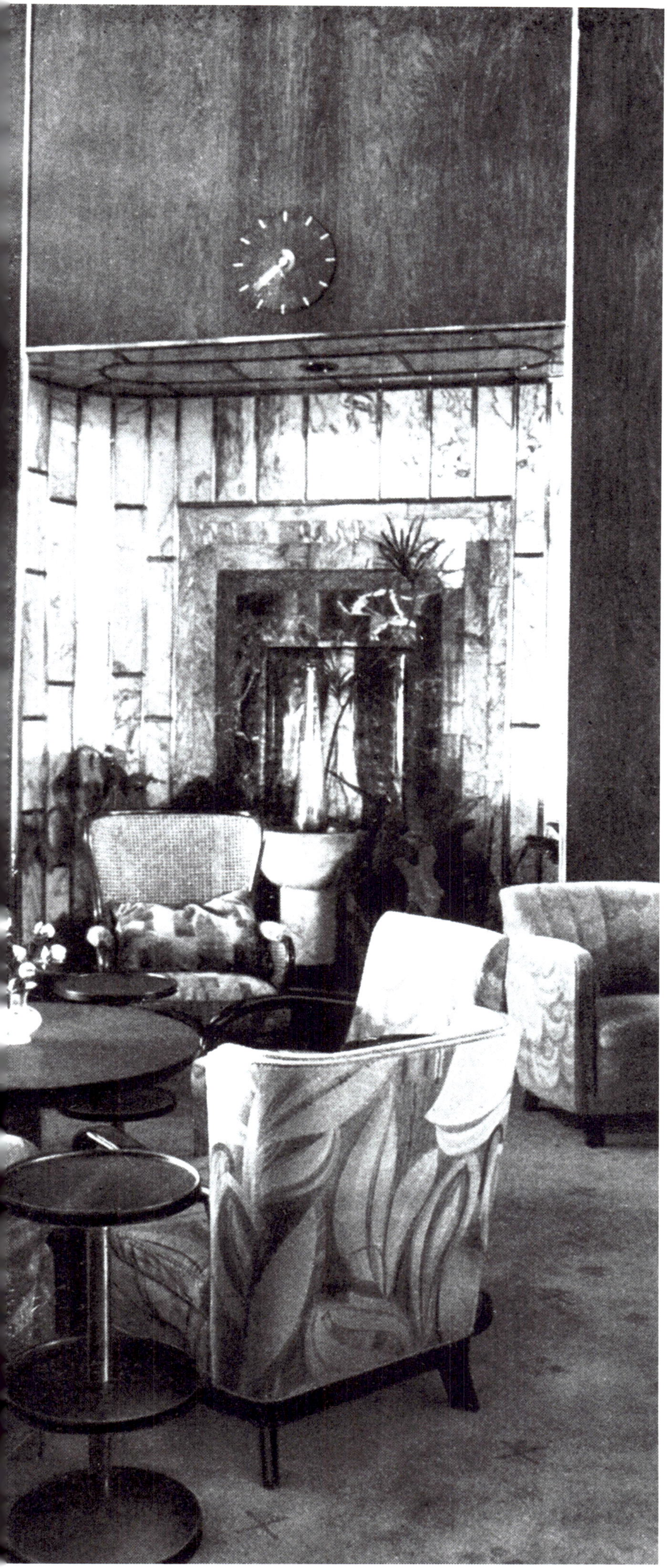

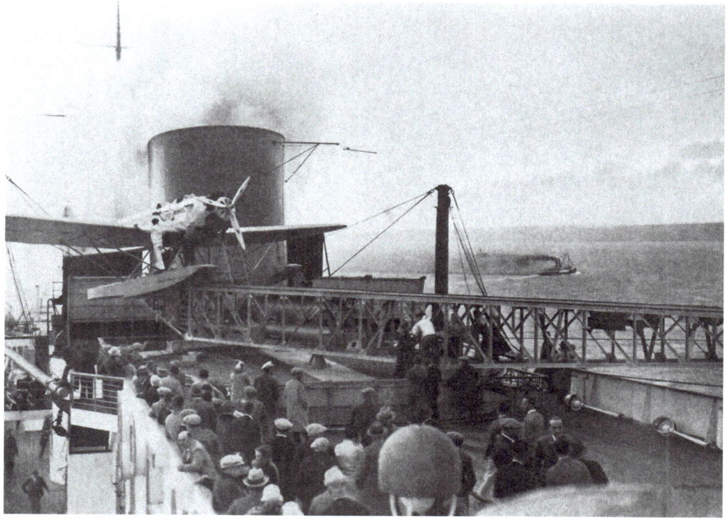

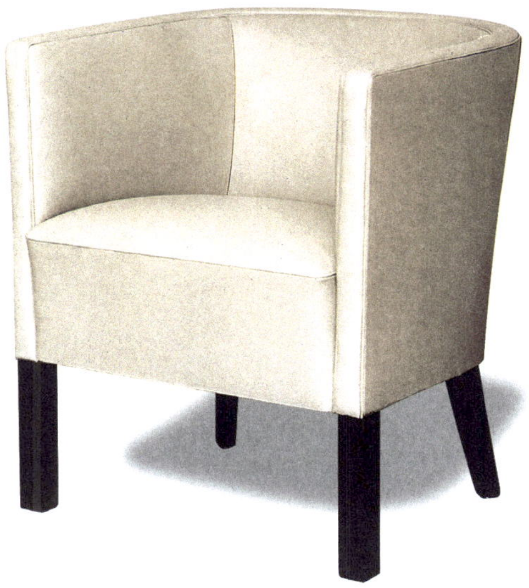

CANTILEVER CHAIR

Tubular steel furniture became an icon of the 1920s and 1930s – for example, in the form of a "cantilever chair without rear legs." Despite the complicated terms, they represented a sophisticated attitude toward life. Both Walter and Wilhelm Knoll had "metal furniture" in their product range.

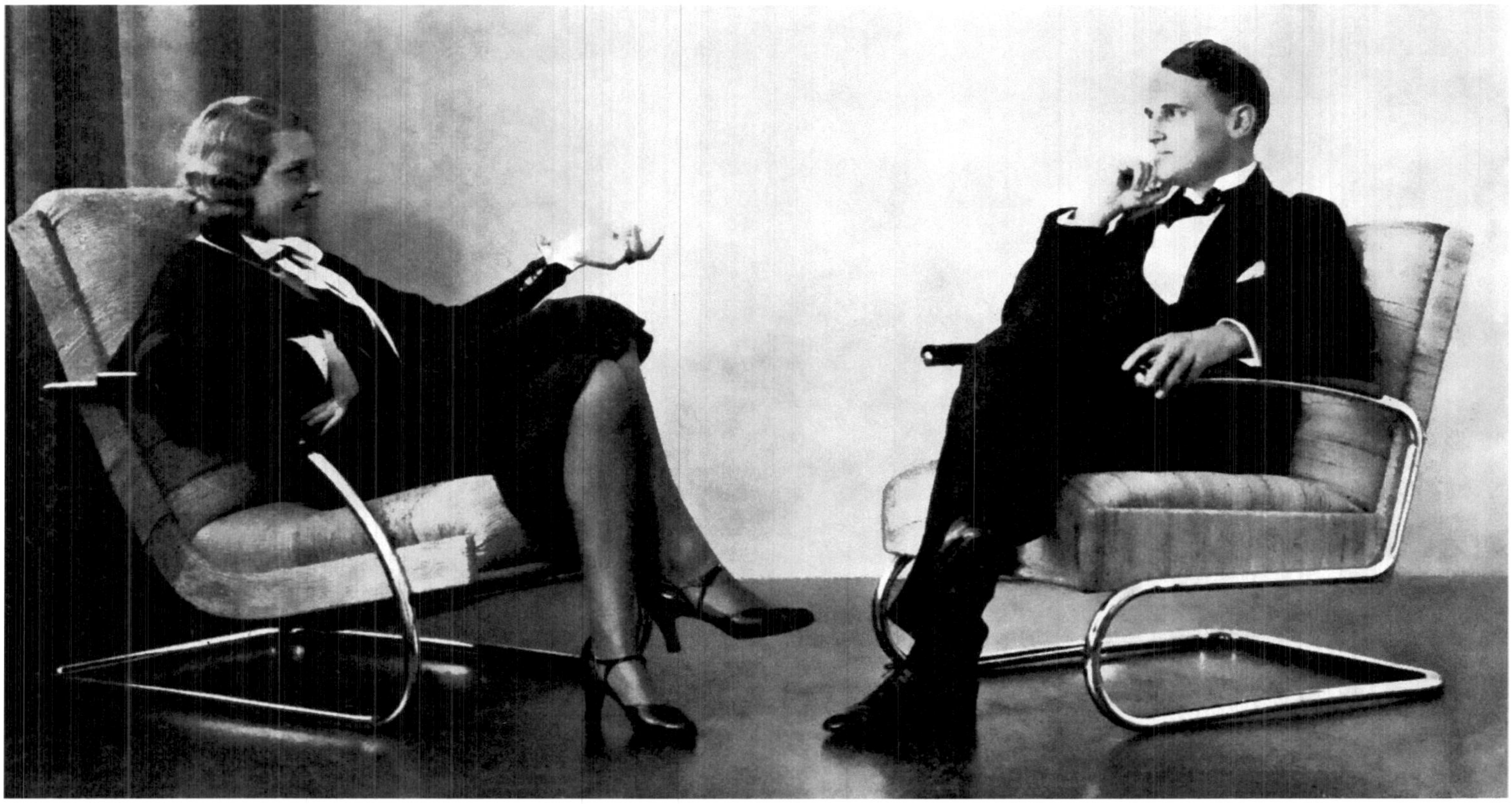

Advertisement, tubular steel chairs K 423 and K 411, Walter Knoll, Feuerbach (near Stuttgart), 1931

HIGH-RISE

The 18-story Tagblatt Tower of 1928, Stuttgart's tallest building at the time, stood out from the rest of the cityscape. It was a modern landmark and a manifesto of *Neues Bauen* (New Building).

Eberhardstrasse with Tagblatt Tower, Stuttgart, 1936

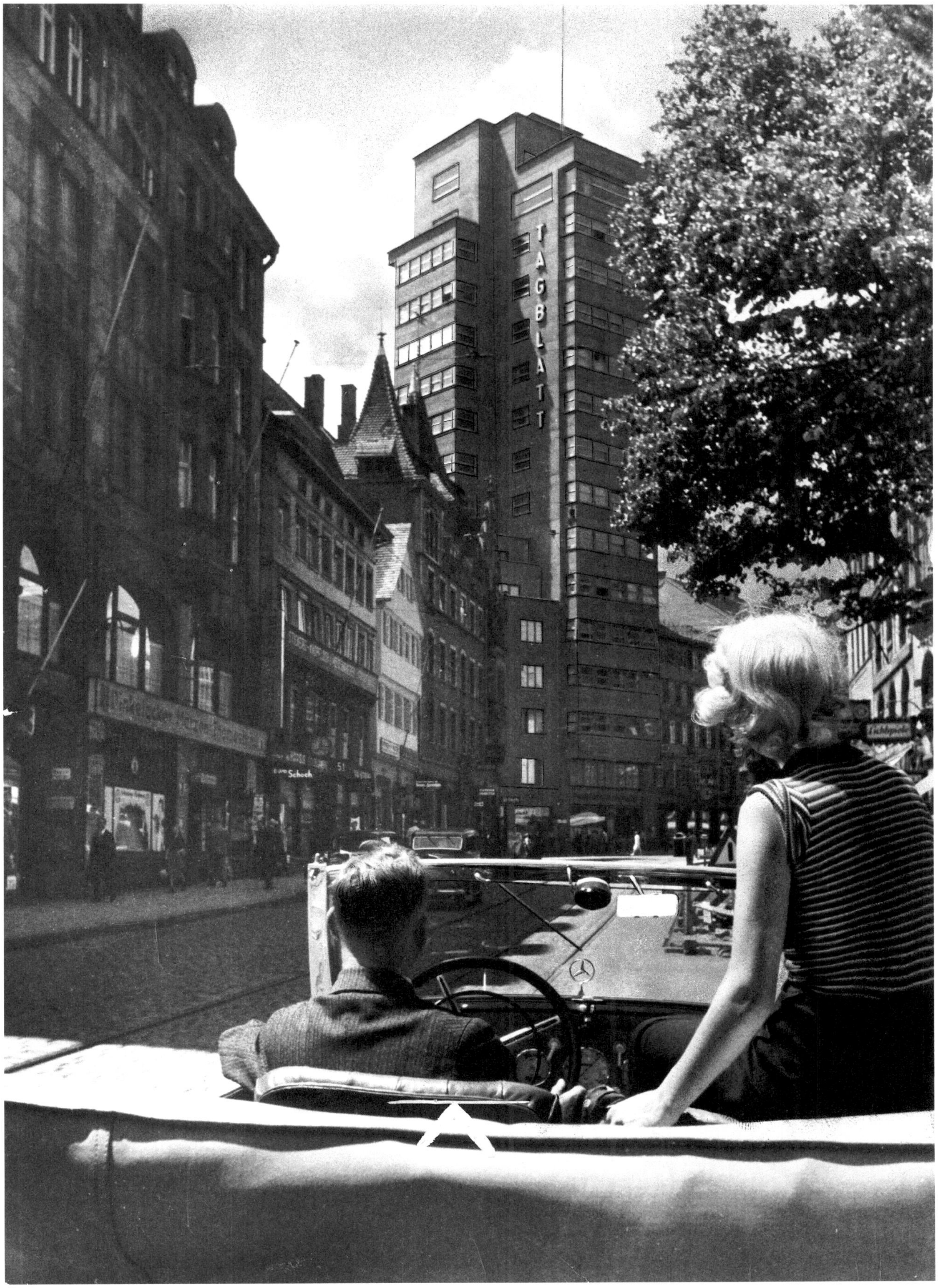

STREAMLINE

Stream | line. The technical principle of wind slip, which has reduced air resistance in cars and other means of transportation since the early 20th century, eventually became a fashion: the streamlined shape. At some point, the droplet shape was applied not only to radiator hoods, passenger steamers, and locomotives, but also to such objects as lamps, radios, and refrigerators. The streamlined German racing cars, the "Silver Arrows," became legendary. The smooth surfaces and large volumes associated with them were both modern and elegant. So it was only a matter of time before the style was transferred to upholstered furniture, the most representative genre of home furnishings. Never before had there been such an explosion of shapes and proportions. It has remained largely unnoticed to this day, a blank spot in the history of design. There were crossovers to the sophisticated "steamer style," named after the furnishings on luxury liners, but the lavishly staged films from Babelsberg and Hollywood were also an inspiration. The brother companies, Walter and Wilhelm Knoll, already had these types of streamlined models in their range in the mid-1930s. Recurring features were slants and asymmetries as well as the use of different materials. Seldom before had furniture designers been called upon to invent such original shapes.

1934
Streamlined racing cars from Mercedes and Auto Union start as "Silver Arrows" on the Avus in Berlin.

1936
The Summer Olympics are held in Berlin.

1937
Walter Knoll moves into a former textile factory in Herrenberg. Hans Knoll moves to the U.S. and founds the Hans Knoll Furniture Company.

UGLINESS DOESN'T SELL.
RAYMOND LOEWY

Schocken department store, sketch by Erich Mendelsohn, Stuttgart, 1928

Upholstered armchair K-F 211, Wilhelm Knoll, Stuttgart, 1937

"Silver Arrow" Mercedes-Benz 12-cylinder, record-breaking car W 125 Stuttgart, 1938

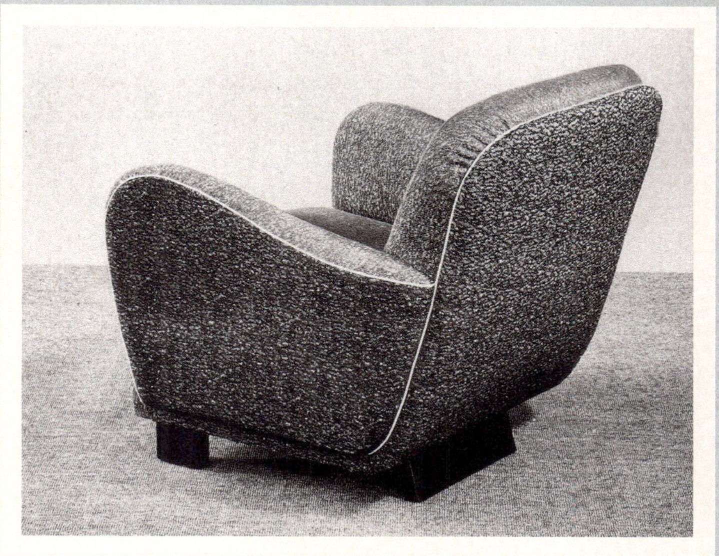

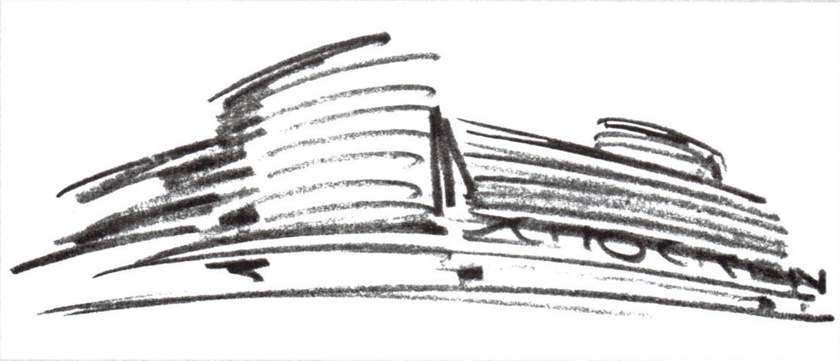

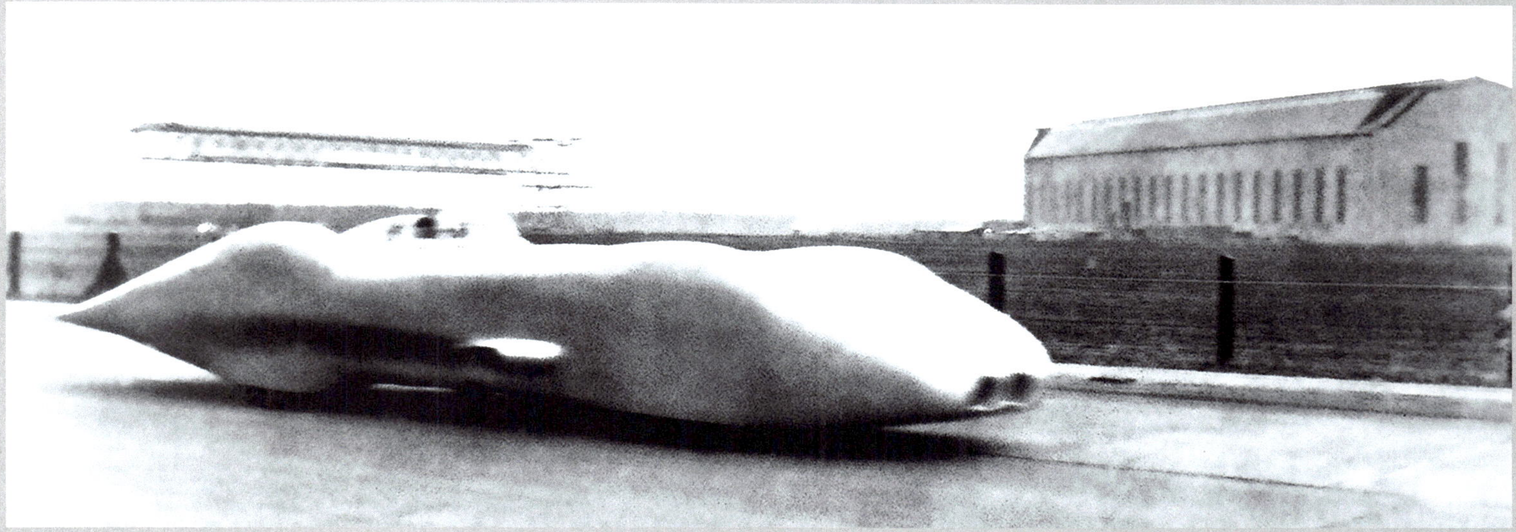

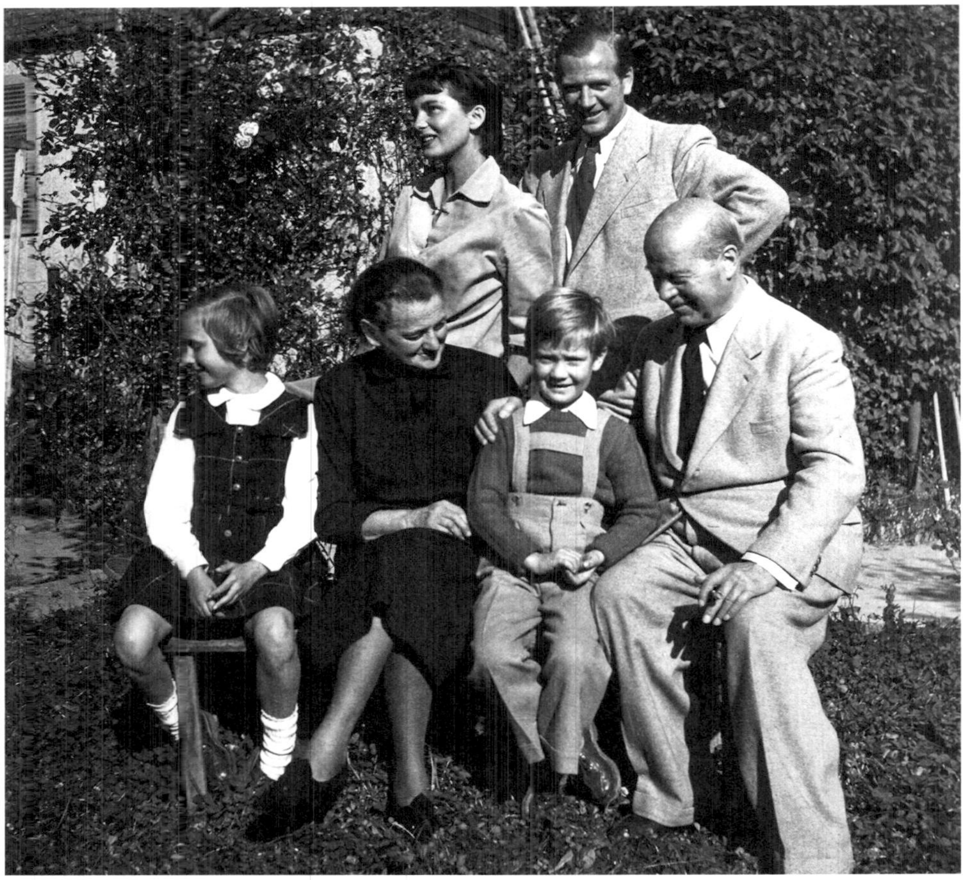

Standing: Bruni and Robert Knoll.
Sitting: Walter Knoll and his wife
Maria with grandchildren Kristina
and Michael.

SECOND **MODERNITY**

1945 TO 1993

THE 1950s

THREE BRANCHES OF THE KNOLL DYNASTY

As the director of "Süddeutscher Rundfunk" (South German Broadcasting) ceremoniously opened the Stuttgart Television Tower on 2/2/1956, a large number of celebrities had gathered in the hall at lofty heights.[1] With its circular restaurant, the icon, over 200-meter high structure was a world first and would be a model for similar broadcasting towers in Germany and numerous other countries. Just a decade after the war, Stuttgart had a new landmark, situated on one of the nearby hills and therefore visible within the city itself, and also far beyond in the region. It was a monument to a new beginning. The Second Modernity had begun. As a technical masterpiece, the Television Tower also represented the proverbial ingenuity of Swabian engineering. Its creator, the Stuttgart-born Fritz Leonhardt, was no architect, but a structural engineer. Like before with the Weissenhofsiedlung estate and as always whenever something new is radically breaking ground, bright enthusiasm and stark disapproval also collided on this particular occasion. Like the "white modernity" of the 1920s, the massive concrete tower shocked thanks to its deliberate lack of decoration. There was yet another significant parallel to be drawn. As before, the design of the interiors was an integral element of the construction. Consequently, the furniture also had to be uncompromisingly modern. And like at Weissenhof, the Walter Knoll company was prominently represented. The chairs in the tower restaurant came from Herrenberg. They were Forum 363 models. The all-purpose chair with its lightweight tubular steel frame, like the tower itself, is the epitome of functionality. The iconic chair, universal both in terms of use and its ubiquity, was designed by Herta-Maria Witzemann, the interior designer of the Television Tower. As a result, everyone who visited this synthesis of the arts also sat on chairs from Walter Knoll.

The world had entered a new era. The Americans called it the *Golden Age*, the French *les Trente Glorieuses*, and for the Germans it was the *Wirtschaftswunder*. In the quarter-century following 1945, as production figures rose at breakneck speed and the phrase "living standards" made sense for the first time for most people, after all everyone believed they were on the way to the land of milk and honey. But did it not already exist on the other, better side of the Atlantic? The United States had not only won the war and unquestionably become the leading western power, they also seemed to possess the recipes for a glorious future. Whether in terms of the economy, science or art, America appeared superior in all areas.[2] The American age had begun, although on closer inspection it was not at all one-sided, but actually transatlantic. Design is a perfect example of how reciprocal exchange took place across the ocean. As before in the First Modernity, furniture design, and more specifically seating furniture, once again served as a kind of aesthetic barometer of progress and received the most attention. Like advertising or marketing, design is part of the "Made in USA" economic instruments that have since spread from there across

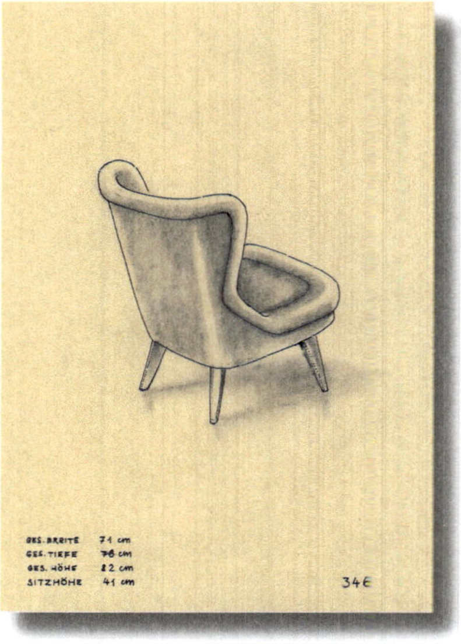

the globe.[3] However, Europe also had something to offer and made a crucial contribution. The old continent supplied the ideas of modernity, the schools, styles and trends. Immigrants, including scores of Germans, brought these to the new world in their suitcases during the inter-war period.[4] Among them was Hans Knoll, the Swabian entrepreneur, who would almost single-handedly get modern furniture off the ground in America. Hans of all people, the former problem child, who at first seemed quite unsuited to the role of continuing his father's legacy, would go on to be a real triumphator. And precisely in this respect, in the fundamental transformation that he himself helped to bring about, his life resembles that of his father's.

There is a recurrent theme throughout the family and company history of the Knolls: the father-son dialectic. Like other dynasties, the development of the Knoll furniture dynasty was also driven to a considerable extent by the dynamics that arose in the transition from one generation to the next and, in this case, particularly by the relationship between fathers and sons. The pattern could already be observed when Carl Knoll, the forefather of the dynasty, turned his back on his hometown in the mid-19th century and went to Stuttgart. Although venturing to the city to make a fresh start was the trend of the time, it was by no means a matter of course for the individual. His son Wilhelm continued in this vein. He left the shoemaker's workshop of his father, opting not to become a shoemaker himself, instead becoming a renowned, internationally trading leather expert and even a "Royal Court Supplier." He was the Knoll family's first entrepreneur and is therefore also considered the founder of the later dynasty. How might Wilhelm's father have reacted to his son's ascent? He was most probably very proud, although he may also have sometimes had mixed feelings about this meteoric rise. No details are known about the pair or their relationship.

It was the process of the son separating from the father that, in more or less difficult circumstances, would lead to completely new developments on an almost regular basis in the coming generations. Inevitably, these dynamics also involved dynamic personalities. This likely applies to Carl, most certainly to Wilhelm, and likewise to his son Willy, who was his crown prince. After the premature death of his father in 1907, Willy Knoll had a free hand to realize his own plans. He achieved this with distinction. With immense energy and a firm will, it was he who turned the company into a furniture manufacturer. And in the process, as a model Swabian, he relied on innovation as a driving force from the outset. Willy Knoll was the prototypical entrepreneur. He demonstrated this right from the start in the Reform Period with the introduction of the club chair, and subsequently continued with huge success in the 1920s with Antimott. This invention made the company the region's first furniture manufacturer to have foreign licensees and multiple production sites, including one outside Germany. If Wilhelm Knoll, the eponym of the company, had lived to see this, he would have rubbed his eyes in disbelief.

There is another variant of the above-mentioned pattern: the father-son conflict. In three successive generations, namely Walter, Hans and later Michael (son of Robert Knoll, Hans' brother), this played a key role in the development of the family and the company. In the case of Walter Knoll and Hans Knoll, several obvious and highly grave parallels can be drawn. As a result of conflicts with their fathers, they both left the family and the family company at an early age – both were in their early twenties – and then sought their luck abroad. Both went to America (as did Michael Knoll later). Walter Knoll and Hans Knoll wanted to prove to their fathers, themselves and the world that they were capable of creating something significant of their own. That was their strongest motivation. And they both succeeded. And in both cases, cutting the cord led to the establishment of new companies, in 1925 for Walter and 1938 for Hans. Even the names of their companies – Walter Knoll & Co. and Hans Knoll Associates respectively – are somewhat similar. New branches of the Knoll furniture family came into being as a result. Only then did it become a dynasty.

However, that is not the end of the similarities. Just as Walter and also Hans Knoll acted on the basis of a father-son conflict, another, no less crucial, even fundamental factor also contributed to their motivation. Meant here is the love for their mother, who loved them just as much. Whether Emma Knoll for Walter, Maia Knoll for Hans, or later also Bruni Knoll for Michael, with their unconditional love, the mothers always assumed a central and indispensable role for the emotional well-being of their sons and for the solidarity of the family. Here was a further source of strength that the Knoll entrepreneurs unquestionably needed for their respective fresh starts. After all, both established anything but ordinary furniture companies. Rather, as entrepreneurs are wont to do, they set their own, higher aims for their new companies and exceeded

THE AMERICAN AGE HAD BEGUN, ALTHOUGH ON CLOSER INSPECTION IT WAS NOT AT ALL ONE-SIDED, BUT ACTUALLY TRANSATLANTIC.

the ambitions of their fathers. Walter Knoll created the furniture brand of modernity, which was linked with the avant-garde from the beginning. Hans Knoll did exactly the same. However, he also upped the ante – like his father, he was transatlanticist and turned the Knoll name into a global brand.

TRANSATLANTICISTS

Another prerequisite for the development of the Knoll furniture dynasty was its nomadic genes. In London, where his father had done business with the Russian migrant Serge Chermayeff, this later design visionary would turn Hans into a furniture cosmopolitan.[5]

---

1 ▶ Fritz Leonhardt, the designer of the tower, was not reserved a place for its opening. As compensation, he received a free pass for life.

2 ▶ Hobsbawm, 1995, p. 324 ff.

3 ▶ Polster, 2002, p. 233.

4 ▶ Polster, 2002, p. 231.

5 ▶ Hans Knoll's "German connections" were a constitutive element in his career. For one thing, this broadly related to his business ties in the USA, which were initially established via the Vollmöllers, his mother's family, and heavily drew upon entrepreneurs of German origin. And this also applied to the central objective of making a mark as a company of furniture modernity, which, to a large extent, also had its origins in Germany, and the breakthrough of which Hans Knoll had experienced at first hand during his youth in the Stuttgart of the late 1920s.

RUBBLE-FREE
Stuttgart was one the most devastated German cities, but also the first to be completely cleared of rubble in the post-war period. For a long time, ruins and makeshift buildings dominated the urban landscape of the downtown. Many people had to live in cellars.

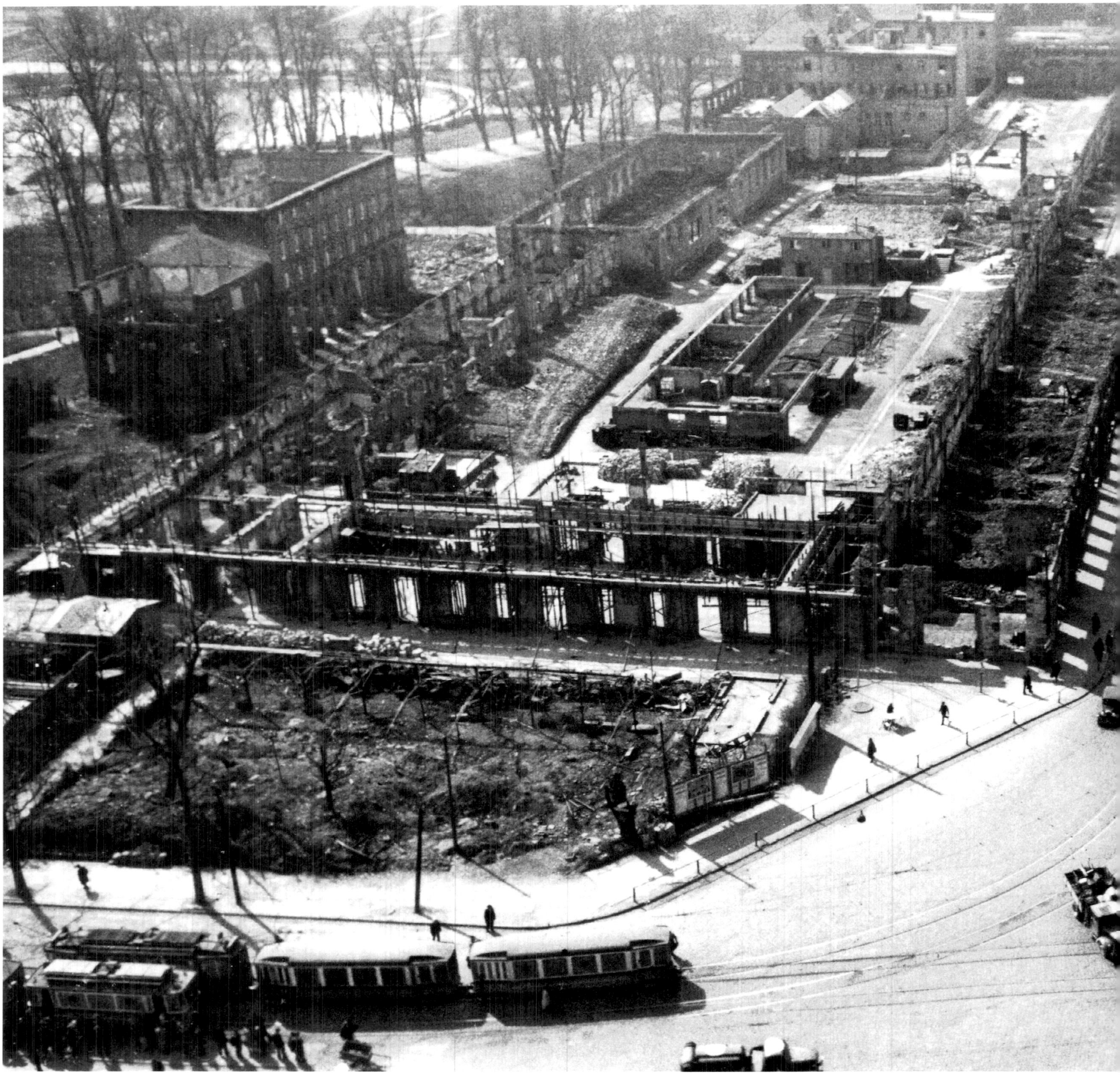

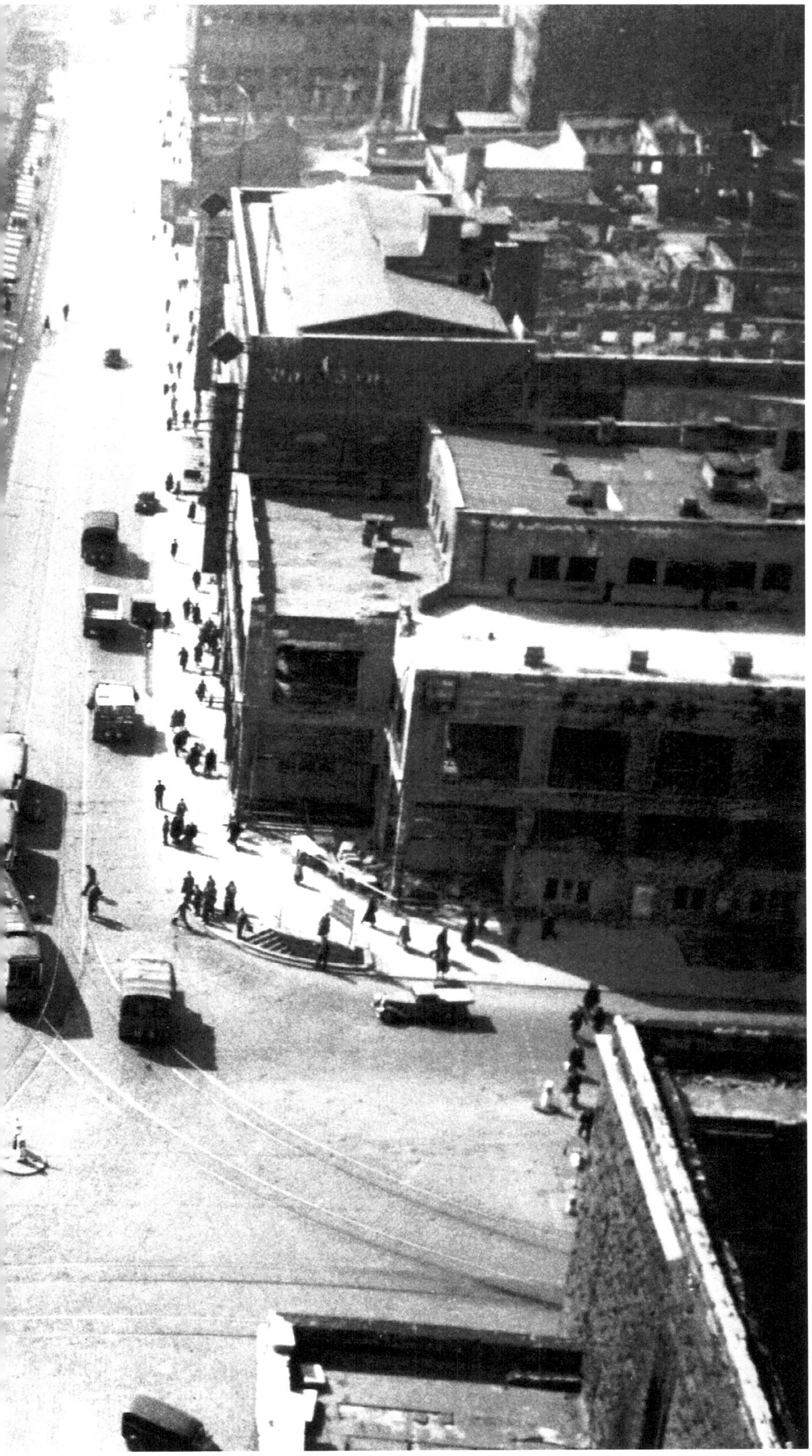

Königstrasse photographed
from the central railway
station tower,
Stuttgart, 1946

Eventually, just a few years later, he would succeed in realizing even greater ambitions on the other side of the Atlantic. Of course, it was extremely helpful that so many architecture and design emigrants from Europe were living in the USA at the time, including virtually the entire Bauhaus leadership.[6] Of equal significance was the fact that his second wife Florence was also a cosmopolitan in matters of design. Her ancestors came from Switzerland, which borders Swabia, as is well known, and where a stricter variant of Protestantism, demanding diligence and ambitiousness, is also widespread.[7] Florence Knoll, née Schust, who lost her parents at an early age, enjoyed a fairytale career. The daughter of a good family, she studied at the Cranbrook Academy, the elite school of American post-war design.[8] What's more, she was adopted by its director, the Finn Eliel Saarinen, and his wife Loja, who was also a designer. Eero Saarinen, one of the most successful post-war architects, became her brother. Like Hans, Florence was also raised in an aesthetically highly sensitized environment of modernity. She was right at the heart of the action.

But that's not all. She later became an apprentice to leaders of the Bauhaus, sat in at the offices of Marcel Breuer, Walter Gropius and Ludwig Mies van der Rohe. All this fitted perfectly with Hans Knoll's own plans like pieces of a puzzle. Anyone who reads the list of designers who worked for Knoll Associates encounters Scandinavian, Italian, Japanese, German and Hungarian names. This includes Franco Albini, Isamu Noguchi and Ludwig Mies van der Rohe, to name just a few. The internationality that shaped the company from the start is key to understanding the company Knoll Associates, which was renamed Knoll International some years later, and is today known as Knoll Inc. The Dane Jens Risom, Hans' first partner and creative director, was, of course, also an immigrant. And then there was also a certain Ralph Rapson who worked in Saarinen's office at Cranbrook and eventually taught at the Institute of Design in Chicago under director Serge Chermayeff. He evidently understood how to develop networks and, at the same time, establish a good and also personal relationship with his employees, among them many independent collaborators. Those who knew the young, blond, splendid-looking German, around 30 years old, whom everyone amiably addressed as Hans, describe him as having an extraordinary effect on people, including in personal contact. The design entrepreneur Hans Knoll not only dealt in very special goods, he was also a gifted communicator and converted all this into an entirely new business model. "He could sell virtually anything. He was actually always selling himself, his product, and the company," said Murray Rothenberg, a former employee, describing his charismatic boss.[9] "He had a relaxed demeanor. A man with whom things were not always easy. But he was admired and respected."[10] His personality combined the inherited passion for modernity with an, in a positive sense, engaging nature. His special talent for cultivating friendships with men took him all the way to the highest circles. His wondrous transformation from problem case to beacon of hope coincides precisely with his departure from Germany. In America, where a more relaxed and warmer approach was already common practice then, he was able to express his personality in his professional life too and, in this way, nourish talents that would ultimately shape a highly creative milieu. Many factors interacted to eventually put Hans Knoll in a position to actually achieve the incredible success that, though far from guaranteed, he believed he was capable of. Another factor was his loyal friend and sponsor Bronson Winthrop, the respected lawyer, who opened many doors, giving Hans access to major clients. Behind one of these thick doors sat Henry Stimson, a good friend of Winthrop, U.S. Secretary of War during World War II and, it may be hard to believe, an avowed Germanophile. He is regarded as one of the inhibitors of the Morgenthau Plan proposed by the U.S. government, which would have turned Germany back into an agrarian country after 1945. And this man Stimson had his office in the Pentagon, the new building of the Department of Defense, furnished by the small, completely unknown company Knoll Associates. The company later received a great number of other government contracts, including for several U.S. embassies. The Dane

HANS KNOLLS WONDROUS TRANSFORMATION FROM PROBLEM CASE TO BEACON OF HOPE COINCIDES PRECISELY WITH HIS DEPARTURE FROM GERMANY.

Jens Risom, who had experienced Knoll Associates in the middle of the difficult war and post-war years, also played a significant role in the upswing. Hans Knoll made use of his good connections to neutral Sweden. In this way, he was able to keep his German origins somewhat under wraps and maintained at least sporadic contact with home via a Swedish friend. At the same time, Hans Knoll anticipated the Scandinavian boom by a whole decade. The fact that Risom's first chair designs, inspired by Swedish and Finnish models, would soon be produced by Walter Knoll in Herrenberg and sold there under the Latin brand name "Vostra," triumphing in around 1950 in post-war Germany of all places, is nowadays a surprising and virtually forgotten stroke of fate in the history of furniture and design. It was, however, nothing less than a prelude to the Second Modernity of furniture.

The importance of America was demonstrated alone by the family's busy travel habits in the immediate post-war years. Since 1947, Hans Knoll had been a frequent guest in Stuttgart and Herrenberg. The focus was on his transatlantic business model, an axis of modernity between the old and new worlds, as well as between father and son. The fact that his father already made a reciprocal visit in 1949 shows that something was gaining momentum. For Walter Knoll too, who had been fascinated by America since his time living there, the trip was not merely a private matter. The senior, now in his mid-seventies and proud of the success of his once unloved son, wanted to try again himself, and closely examined his son's operations. Together with his son Hans, he met Ludwig Mies van der Rohe in Chicago, whom he had known since the days of the Weissenhof exhibition. Mies, in good spirits, talked about a new motor-driven band-saw and the Black Forest liquor that he cherished. Walter Knoll sent him a couple of bottles of it upon his return. Hans and Walter did not leave out the Cranbrook Academy. They visited the Saarinens, where "a degree of art and culture never before experienced"[11] awaited the father. The fact that he flew to America – with a stopover in Newfoundland – was quite unusual and suggests that some good connections were also at play. Even Chancellor Adenauer would travel by ship on his first state visit to the USA years later. Just like Willy Knoll, Walter's brother, who had by now also been gripped by America fever. In the late 1940s, he had already booked passage to New York, a city he was still familiar with from visiting his brother. He subsequently traveled to the promised land another three times. No further details are known. In any case, his endeavors do not appear to have produced measurable results.

The contrast between the two sides of the Atlantic could hardly have been greater than they were towards the end of the 1940s. While America, unscathed by the war, was enjoying a flourishing economy and the blessings of an affluent society, post-war Germany was living through what was colloquially known as "the bad times." Life among the ruins was strictly rationed. Everything was scarce. The black market reigned. Willy Knoll, who had to resume production in rented premises, reconstructed the original company building in Stuttgart's Forststrasse "using the still existing foundation walls."[12] Not much else of it remained. It was "built smaller,"[13] however, with just two stories instead of four. In times of scarcity, in which money had no value and material was extremely hard to come by, cut-backs were necessary. However, when making this decision, Willy Knoll had probably already been considering a complete shift in production to the main plant in Gaildorf some day. After four decades of running his company, as the world lay in ruins, he was already planning for the future once more. His brother Walter also managed to get his company operational again by 1946, if only temporarily at first. At this point, his eldest son, Robert, returned from captivity as a prisoner of war of the Russians.

Stuttgart was the first major German city that was able to declare itself rubble-free. This was not least thanks to the new mayor Arnulf Klett. He was a *Schaffertyp* (a man of action), as the Swabians say, who was not afraid to get amongst the ruins and break stones. This pragmatist at city hall would put his personal stamp on the capital of the new state of Baden-Württemberg throughout the "golden years." So when Hans Knoll first visited his family again in 1947, ten years after his expatriation, the rubble had already been cleared. Nevertheless, Stuttgart still resembled a ghost town where the remnants of walls rose to the sky and people resided in poorly heated cellars. This inhabited sea of debris that was his home city must have had a very depressing affect on the 35-year old – although, as a clear-thinking entrepreneur, he naturally also saw the opportunities for furniture manufacturers that lay in the forthcoming reconstruction. In particular for him, who could pay in hard dollars. In addition, Stuttgart was now occupied by the Americans, with whom Hans, himself now the holder of an American passport, had excellent relations. Hans Knoll, the proverbial "rich uncle from America," came bearing many gifts, including jeans and chocolate for the children, of course. There was, however, one more extra special souvenir: samples from his first furniture collection. He had these shipped from the USA to Herrenberg, which, given the circumstances at the time, was essentially an impossibility, and could only have worked with special authorization from the military government.[14] But he managed it. However, Hans' plans to have these models produced at his father's factory only began to make sense when the Deutsche Mark was introduced the following year. In 1949, the Federal Republic of Germany was formed from the three western zones of occupation. By this point, the "bad times," were already over.

There were now two German states, and a shift in power from east to west took place.[15] It was no coincidence that the new federal capital of Bonn was located on the westernmost edge of the republic.

---

6 ▶ The reproduction of the Barcelona chair by Ludwig Mies van der Rohe by Knoll Associates in 1948 – the very first new version of a furniture icon from the days of *Neues Wohnen* (New Living) – is one example that would, however, long remain an isolated case. Not until the 1960s would this be turned into a business model as a result of the takeover of the company Gavina.

7 ▶ Both countries are shaped by protestant ethics

8 ▶ The Cranbrook Academy is considered the crucible of modern design in America.

9 ▶ Fehrmann, 2009, p. 66 (copy: Cherie and Kenneth Fehrmann, "Interior Design Innovators 1910–1960").

10 ▶ Ibid.

11 ▶ Knoll, n.d., p. 94.

12 ▶ Knoll, 1965, p. 38.

13 ▶ Ibid.

14 ▶ An American officer named Bill (William) Mosetti, who also frequently visited Walter Knoll in Herrenberg at the time, played an instrumental role. William Mosetti was, among other things, general director of Mercedes-Benz Argentina after the Second World War. See: Knoll, n.d., p. 93.

15 ▶ The fact that, in Adenauer and Heuss, a Rhinelander and a Swabian now held the highest offices of state was a clear indication of this.

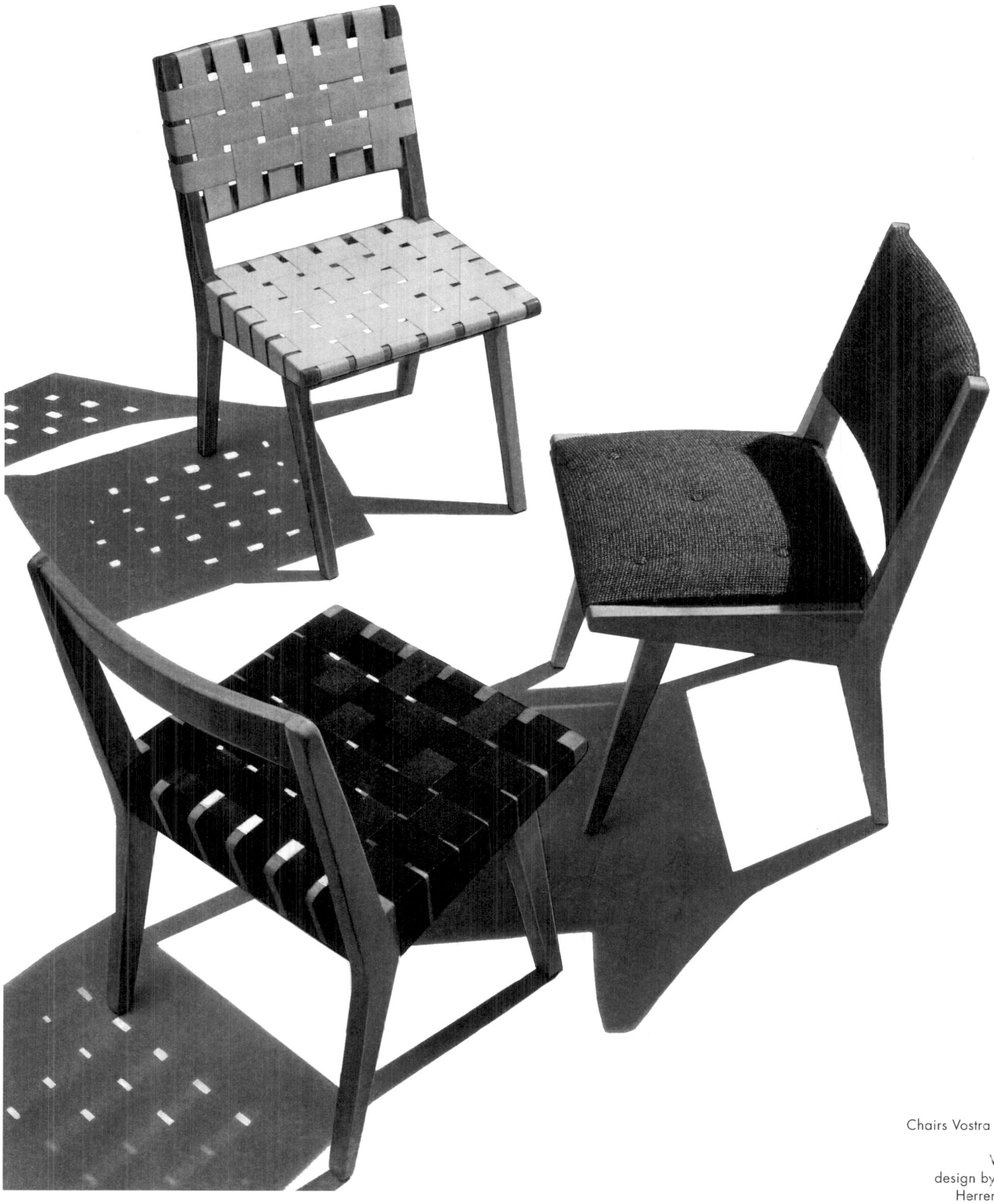

Chairs Vostra 605 L, 605,
and 605 P,
Walter Knoll,
design by Jens Risom,
Herrenberg, 1948

TRANSATLANTICIST
As soon as it was possible, Hans Knoll visited his parents after the war had ended. As a special gift from the USA, he brought with him belted armchairs and chairs designed by Jens Risom, which were now being produced in Herrenberg as Vostra models.

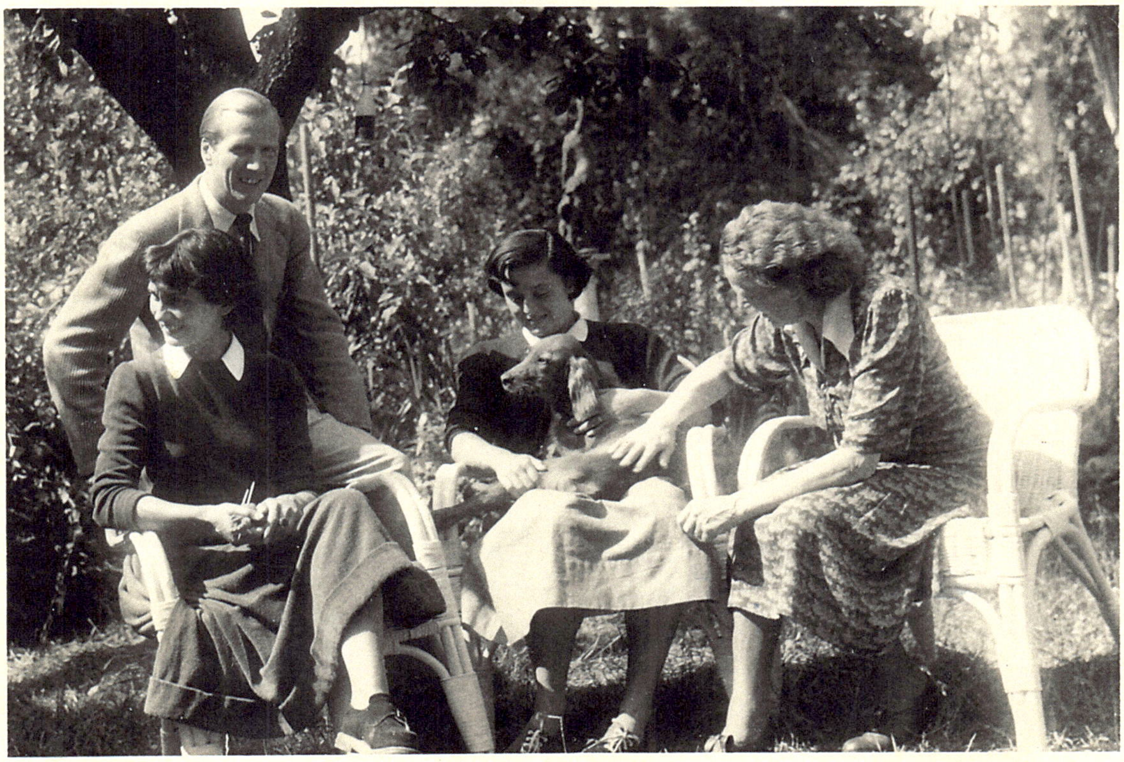

Hans Knoll with his daughter Maja, his wife Florence and his mother Maria (f.l.t.r), Herrenberg, 1950

WIE WOHNEN? – HOW TO LIVE?

949, the reconstruction had begun, and two pioneering exhibitions took place: "Wie wohnen?" (How to live?) in Stuttgart and "Neues Wohnen" (New Living) in Cologne. Vostra chairs from Walter Knoll created a furore on both occasions.

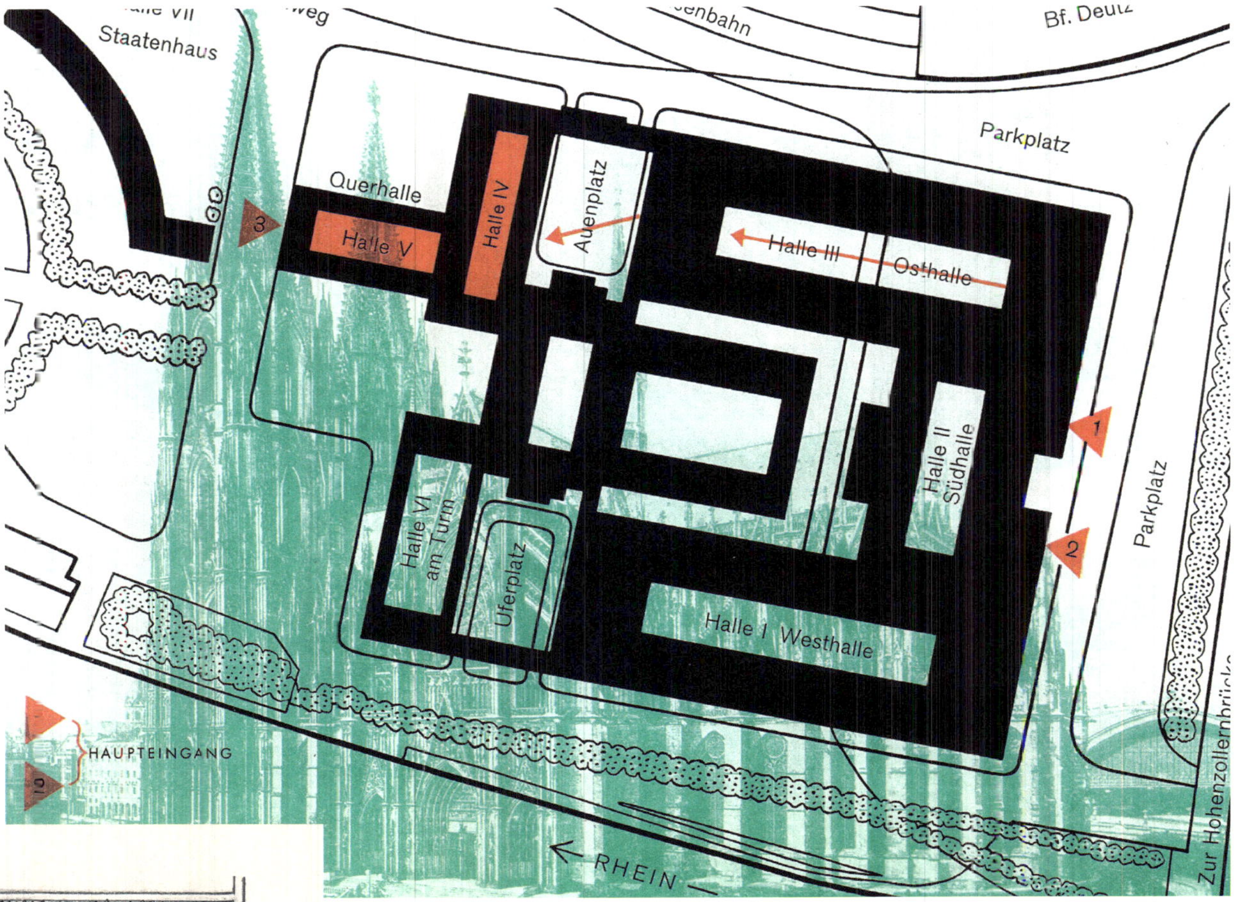

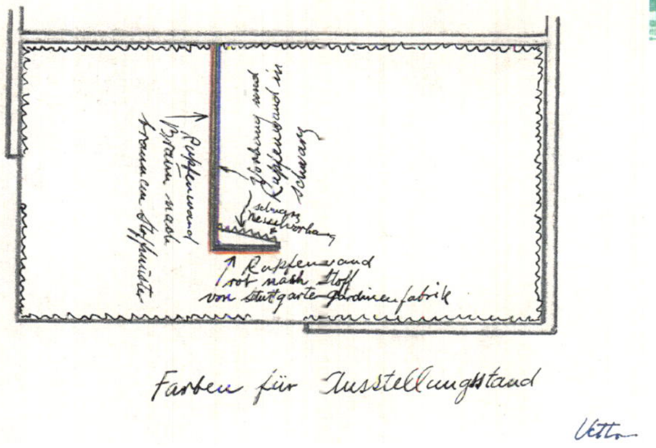

Leaflet for the furniture fair in Cologne, 1950

Drawing "Farbplanung für den Ausstellungsstand zur Kölner Möbelmesse" (Color plan of the exhibition stand for the furniture fair in Cologne), Walter Knoll, design by Arno Votteler, Herrenberg, 1952

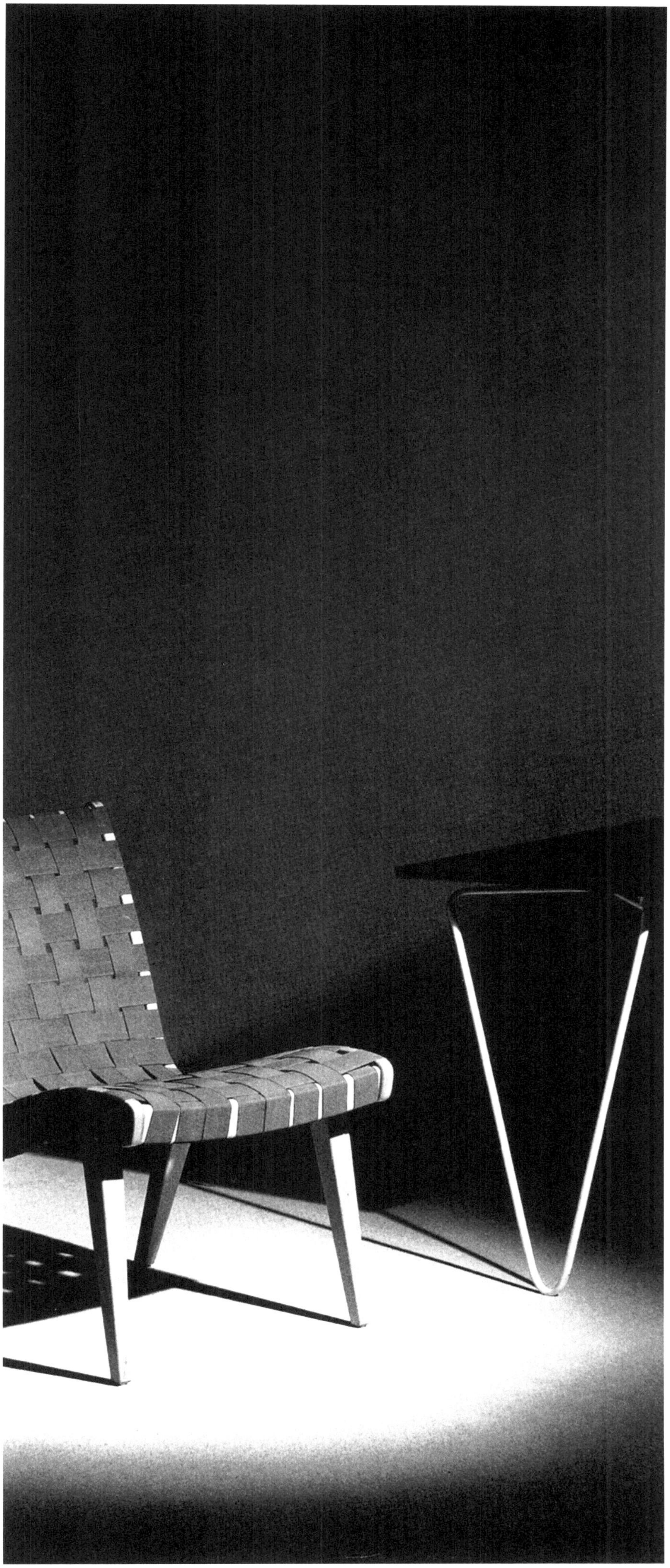

Catalog for the exhibition "Wie wohnen?" (How to live?), cover with armchair Vostra 601, Walter Knoll, photograph by Franz Lazi, Stuttgart, 1949

The already highly developed southwest was able to further benefit from the shift in balance. The mass exodus from the east also involved the relocation of entire industries such as the central German automobile industry, which was re-established in Bavaria and Swabia.[16] The Stuttgart region, already home to Daimler-Benz and major suppliers such as Bosch, was now transforming into one of the world's leading centers for the automobile industry. The establishment and expansion of global American corporations including IBM and Kodak, further strengthened the *Ländle* (literally "small state;" informal designation of the Swabians for their federal state). In an emotional sense, Württemberg, where the military radio station AFN was broadcasting the latest American pop music every day, was now closer to the USA than the "zonal border" of barbed wire that now separated East and West Germany, the German part of the Iron Curtain.

1949 was not the first pivotal year. Previously in the mid-1920s, Walter Knoll had been in the process of establishing his company, when the veil of crisis was suddenly lifted after times of war and inflation. Back

BETWEEN BARE WALLS AND TEMPORARY SCAFFOLDING, EXHIBITIONS WERE ONCE AGAIN TAKING PLACE, INCLUDING ONE THAT WOULD BECOME A LEGEND.

then too, the upswing began virtually overnight and likewise after a currency reform. Walter and Willy Knoll, who witnessed all this as entrepreneurs, must have had a sense of déjà-vu. And exactly like before when the world of tomorrow was being presented at Weissenhof, acclaimed exhibitions were once again paying homage to the future. Even the same organizers were involved, namely the "Deutscher Werkbund" (German Association of Craftsmen) and the "Landesgewerbeamt" (State Trade Office) in Stuttgart. And, hardly surprising, Walter Knoll was also involved again.

WIE WOHNEN? – HOW TO LIVE?

In Germany's so-called *Stunde Null* (Zero Hour), while scarcity reigned and the future looked bleak, Stuttgart once again relied on a proven virtue: the liaison between industry and culture. At the "Gewerbemuseum" (Industrial Museum), the location of the "Landesgewerbeamt" (State Trade Office), the plaster was still peeling off the walls. The devastation of the bomb war was still visible. Nevertheless, between bare walls and temporary scaffolding, exhibitions were being held once again, including one that would become a legend. Perhaps also because this bizarre time seems so distant nowadays and so little is known about it. The title posed one of the most burning and, therefore, most commonly asked questions of the time: "Wie wohnen?" – How to live?[17] As before at Weissenhof, the exhibition was thematically highly diverse, and the majority of the companies came from the region this time too. Once again, new methods of housing construction were exhibited, which, as numerous catalog photos clearly show, was already in full swing. The entire spectrum of home furnishings was represented in the main exhibition. Whereby by far the most space was devoted to furniture (alongside timepieces, porcelain, glass, silverware and fabrics). This included a great deal of steel tube and, as a result of cramped living areas, space-saving solutions with pull-out and folding mechanisms. This had always been one of the specialties of the Wilhelm Knoll company. Consequently, the company was also represented with a convertible sofa bed and a folding chair. The sofa integrated into a wall unit had back cushions that could be extended and used as a mattress; a simple principle that is still used to this day.[18] Walter Knoll exhibited a curved variant of Risom's lightweight, belted wooden chairs, which originally came from Hans Knoll's collection.

In the preface to the exhibition catalog of "Wie wohnen?" (How to live?), Josef Thuma, president of the State Trade Office and driving force of the exhibition, spoke out against the "pretentious furniture of yesterday" and in favor of an "appreciation of the functional and well-formed household appliance."[19] Thuma, an ardent modernist, had outstanding employees at his disposal for his educational work, among them Herbert Hirche, Heinrich Löffelhardt and Wilhelm Wagenfeld, whose own work would soon be the focus of exhibitions.[20] The fact that such luminaries were now concentrated in Stuttgart was not without reason. After all, an infrastructure of modernity was established here at the interface between culture and technology, which was unique in Germany; and therefore attracted talent. It was now being revitalized. Hirche and Wagenfeld, who had until that point been working in Greater Berlin, had only just relocated. The latter, known as the creator of the Bauhaus lamp, founded one of the first independent design studios in Stuttgart.[21] He became known, among other things, for his work for the Württembergische Metallwarenfabrik (WMF). There, even simple salt shakers ended up being classics. Hirche, a former Bauhaus student like Wagenfeld and a long-time assistant to the architect Egon Eiermann, would himself later become an architect, professor at the Stuttgart State Academy of Art and Design (Stuttgart Academy) and one of the most influential designers of his time. This was in no small part due to the works that he produced in the mid-1950s for the radio business Braun and also for Walter Knoll at around the same time. Heinrich Löffelhardt, the third member of the group, was a Swabian. The skilled sculptor, who would later become known for the porcelain tableware that he designed for Arzberg, came from Heilbronn. There, he apprenticed at the silverware factory of Peter Bruckmann, the initiator of the Weissenhof project. This demonstrates just how closely interlinked creative networks were in the Southwest. The "Landesgewerbeamt" (State Trade Office) in Stuttgart was an important connecting point. It is hard to believe nowadays that a "government agency" could simultaneously be part of the avant-garde. Walter Knoll and his son Robert, who personally knew all the actors mentioned here and were also close friends with some of them, were part of the inner circle in this milieu of modernity.

Other high-caliber talents joined the team at the State Trade Office or, in some cases, their talent was first discovered there: for example, the graphic designer Herbert W. Kapitzki and the photographer Franz Lazi, young men who, having returned from the war, had a thirst for the new age that was dawning. Kapitzki, who had been displaced from East Prussia, studied under Willi Baumeister at the Stuttgart Academy. He would go on to win the prize for best German poster several times and taught visual communication at the "Hochschule für Gestaltung Ulm" (Ulm School of Design), a new field, of which he was among the originators. Lazi was from the Black Forest, and had just returned from American war captivity.[22] His large-format black and white photographs were among the attractions of "Wie wohnen?" (How to live?). For his newly established studio, he acquired a swiveling large-format camera, which enabled unusual perspectives and produced images that were razor-sharp, even when extremely enlarged. "Wie wohnen?" (How to live?), Franz Lazi's first work, became a permanent exhibition, extended each year with special themes such as glass, household appliances, and lastly – as a manifesto of modernity – the beauty of technology, a special exhibition curated by the pugnacious Hirche.

Lazi, by now house photographer at the State Trade Office, developed his own innovative and expressive visual language. The abstracting black and white that he used to capture subtle lighting and lines was ideal for utilitarian objects, not least for furniture in the room.[23] His dramatic imagery and the method of staging would soon find their way into company catalogs, including at Walter Knoll. Although he was not employed there, other representatives of the objective-expressive school were, such as Willi Moegle. In keeping with the zeitgeist, an existential emptiness pervaded the stylized rooms of the catalog photographs. Some scenes resembled a stage set from a play by Jean-Paul Sartre. The cover image of the "Wie wohnen?" (How to live?) catalog is one of Franz Lazi's strongest photographs (see p. 129). Here, the observer's gaze is drawn through an open door, framed in deep black, falling on two modern pieces of furniture, an armchair and a table. They are only partially shown, giving the scene a little extra mystery. The main subject of the cover image, a dainty armchair made of light wood and a belted seating surface, is none other than the Vostra from Walter Knoll, the model with Danish-American roots that was now being produced in Herrenberg. The design, in which the seating surface and backrest merge together in a gentle curve, served as a symbol of a future living aesthetic. Lazi's cover photo, like the chair itself, is an abstract composition. This comes as no surprise. One of Lazi's best friends was Willi Baumeister, the Swabian Picasso.[24] When Theodor Heuss was Minister of Education and Cultural Affairs in Württemberg shortly after the war, he had brought him to the Stuttgart Academy. Baumeister, who – as a student of Hölzel – epitomized the avant-garde, became an idol for a young student generation. At the same time, he valued free and applied art in equal measure. Back in the 1920s, he had created new objectivist graphics, including exhibition posters and the Weissenhof catalog. The artist Willi Baumeister, the photographer Franz Lazi, and the businessman Walter Knoll were all players in the same environment. This was the Second Modernity, whose networks would develop particularly well in Stuttgart.

---

16 ▶ This is the reason for the existence of the modern-day Audi (formerly Auto-Union) plant in Heilbronn. In addition, the Porsche design office was converted into a sports car factory.

17 ▶ The associated catalog "Wie wohnen: Bautechnik, Möbel, Hausrat. Gedanken und Bilder zur Ausstellung" (How to live: Structural engineering, Furniture, Household goods. Thoughts and images of the exhibition) published by Gerd Hatje has since become a rarity. Stuttgart and Karlsruhe, 1949.
A catalog titled "Wie bauen?" (How to Build?) was published by the Stuttgart-based architects Bodo and Heinz Rasch for the Weissenhof exhibition in 1927, Marta, 2014, p. 18.

18 ▶ Baden-Württemberg State Trade Office (ed.), 1949, Nos. 62 and 63.

19 ▶ Baden-Württemberg State Trade Office (ed.), 1949 (without page numbers). At this time, Thuma was still deputy director of the State Trade Office, which he would assume control of a couple of years later.

20 ▶ Exhibitions on Wagenfeld (1965) and Hirche (1978) took place at the State Trade Office in Stuttgart. Löffelhardt's work was displayed in the State Museum of Baden in Karlsruhe (1980). The division of labor was roughly as follows: the concept of the exhibition likely stemmed from Hirche; Löffelhardt and Wagenfeld, who both worked in the Department of Industrial Design at the State Trade Office, handled the catalog, and the selection of exhibits.

21 ▶ The legendary "Werkstatt Wagenfeld" (Wagenfeld Workshop).

22 ▶ His father, Adolf Lazi, had also been a photographer and was a notable representative of *Neue Sachlichkeit* (New Objectivity) in the pre-war period. In 1950, Adolf Lazi established the Lazi Academy in Esslingen, where newcomers to the design, film and media industry are still trained today.

23 ▶ Architects like Hirche and Eiermann also had their buildings and interiors documented by Lazi. He was also later successful as an advertising photographer and documentary filmmaker.

24 ▶ Willi Baumeister was a student of Adolf Hölzel; he designed the Weissenhof catalog.

SWINGING

Vostrc chairs from Walter Knoll, which were available in assorted variants, became a brand name in itself – an anomaly in the industry that already had tradition in the Knoll furniture dynasty. The upholstered variant of the Vostra from 1949 evolved into a successful model for Walter Knoll.

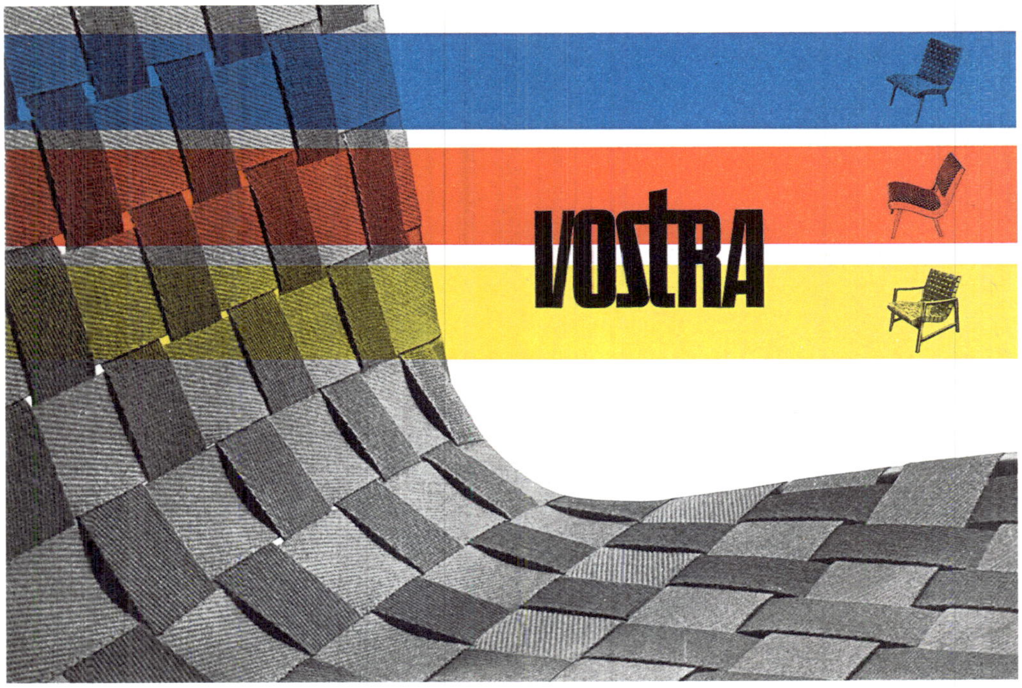

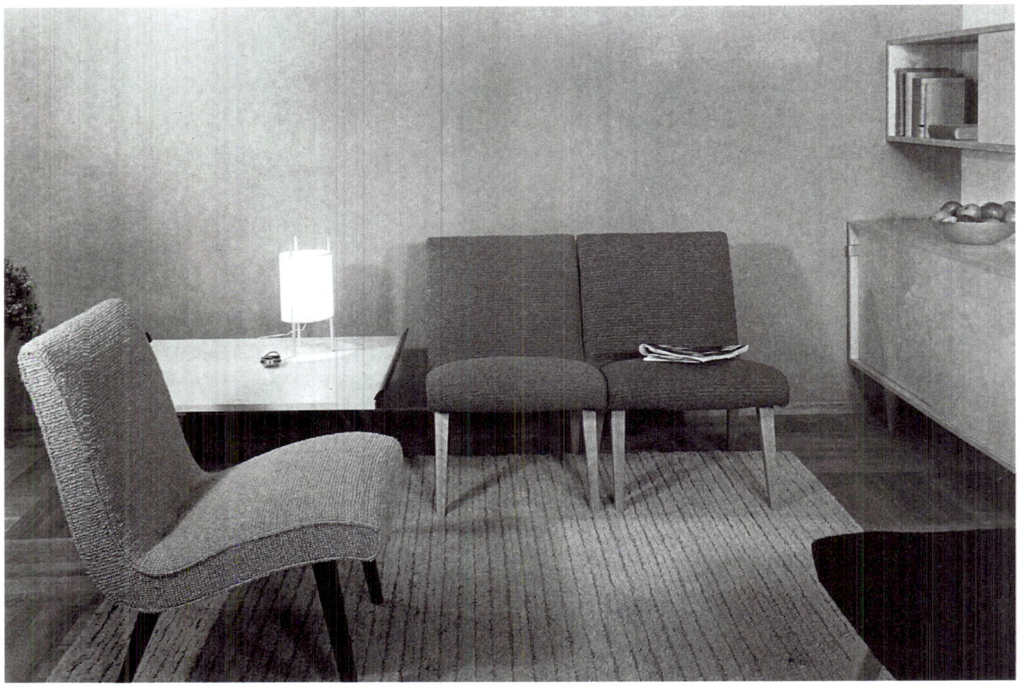

Brochure cover photo,
armchair Vostra 601, Walter Knoll,
design by Jens Risom,
Herrenberg, 1954

Armchair Vostra 607,
Walter Knoll,
Herrenberg, 1949

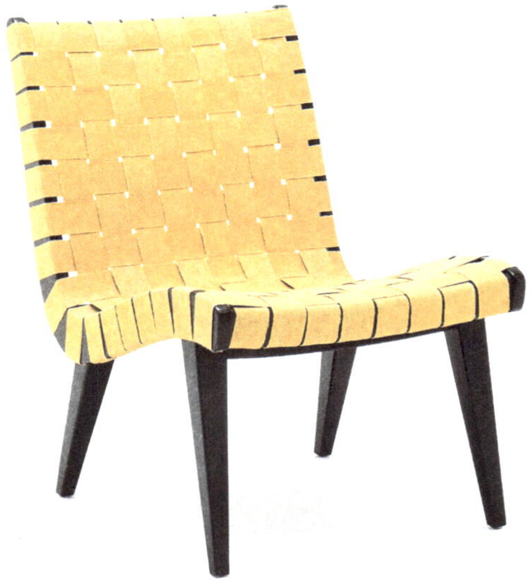

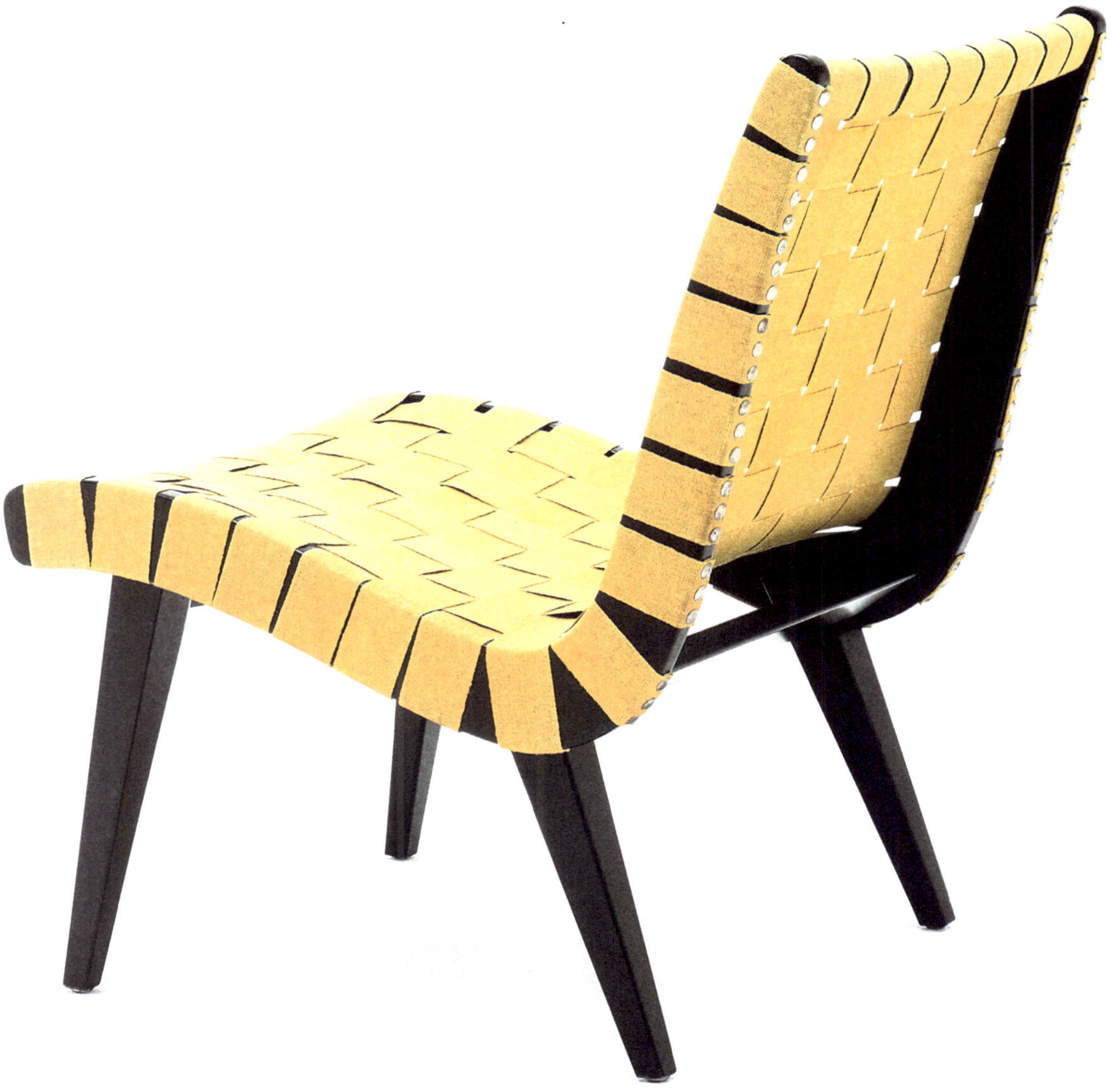

Original chair Vostra 601,
Walter Knoll, design by Jens Risom,
Herrenberg, 1954, restored in 2015

FURNITURE CULTURE

In Stuttgart, exhibitions that fell somewhere between art and industry created an open culturcl milieu. Artistic product and catalog photography also experienced an upswing.

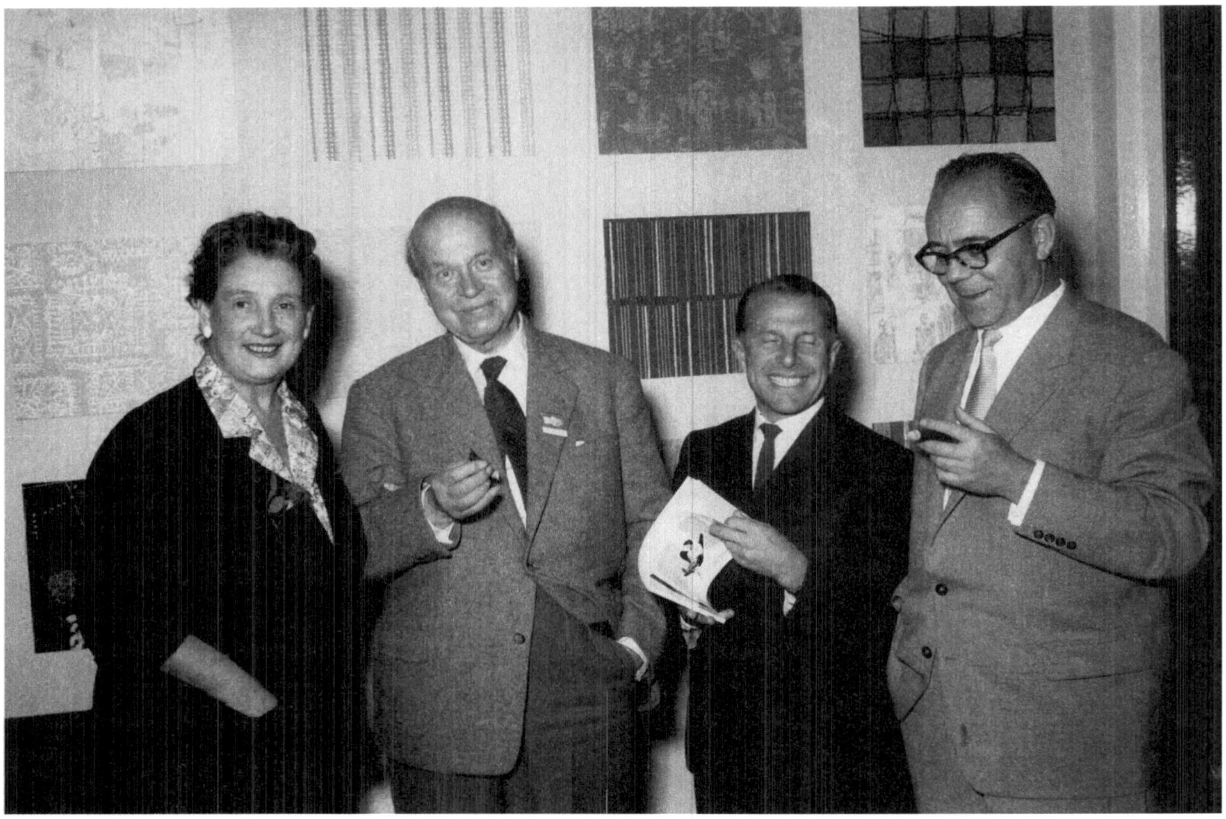

Exhibition at the State Trade Office, Walter Knoll with Mia Seeger, architect Hans Schwippert (right), and an unknown catalog reader, Stuttgart, around 1950

Chair Vostra 610, Walter Knoll, Herrenberg, around 1950

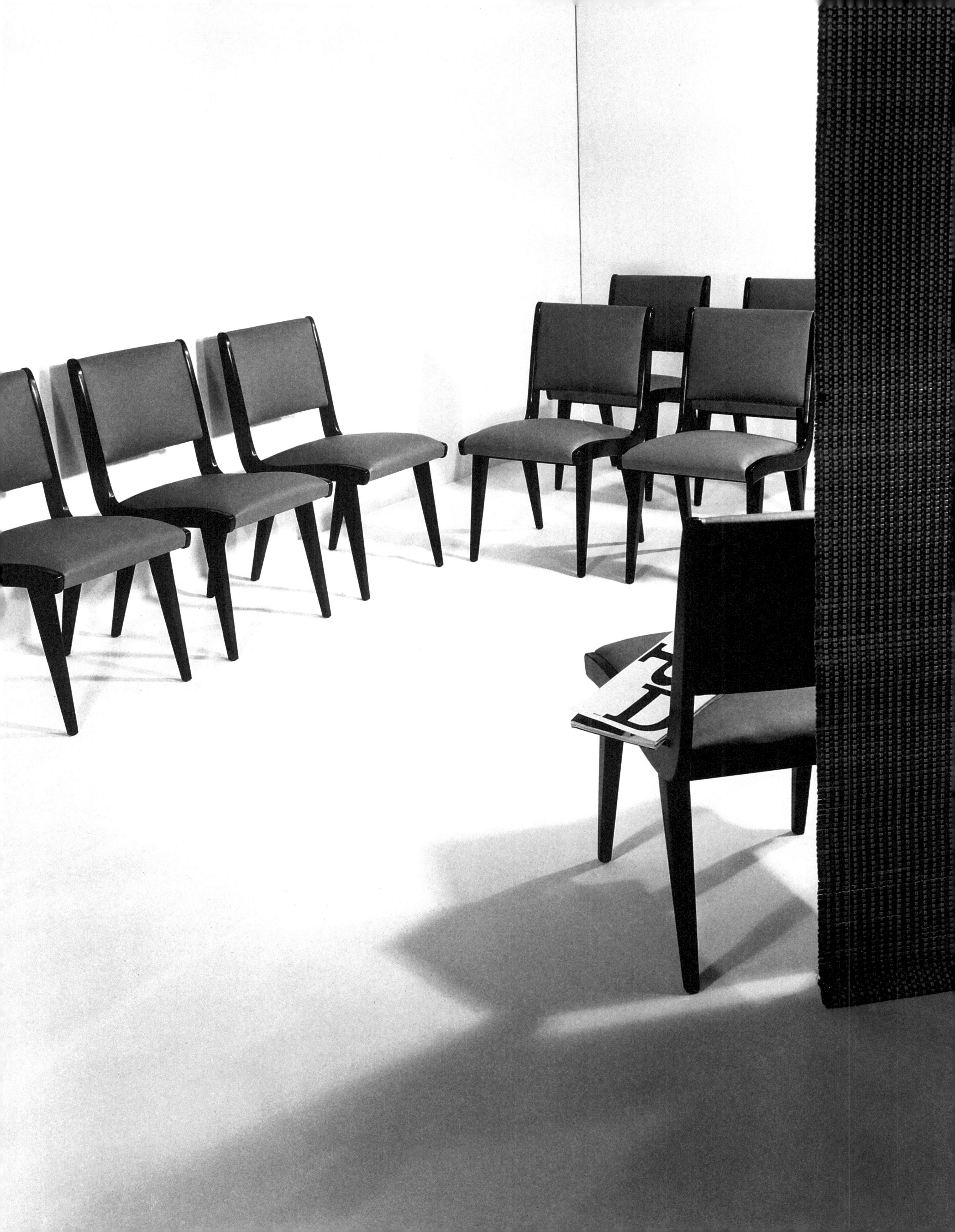

GOOD DESIGN IN BAD TIMES

Never had the question of how to house oneself been more relevant than in this time of extreme housing shortage, during which many Germans were still *Kellerkinder* (Cellar Children).[25] Another visionary exhibition took place in the trade fair halls of Cologne, like Stuttgart still a sea of debris, in the pivotal year of 1949. The title was an expression borrowed from the 1920s: *Neues Wohnen* (New Living). A battle cry, with which designers renounced fluff and frills and emphasized their affinity with the avant-garde. This evocative choice of words originated within the "Deutscher Werkbund" (German Association of Craftsmen), which, having been dissolved by the Nazis, was now in the process of being re-established and wanted to ensure continuity. The term *Neues Wohnen* (New Living) had by now become old hat. But it would soon be replaced. Parallel to the Cologne home show, a special exhibition was held. The Swiss artist Max Bill, another former Bauhaus member and soon to be a founding director of the "Hochschule für Gestaltung Ulm" (Ulm School of Design), which was

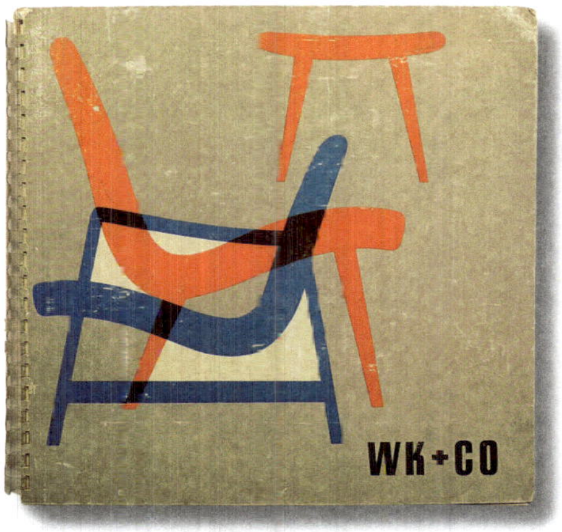

intended to be a continuation of the Bauhaus, preached the idea of *Die gute Form* (meaning "Good Design") – hence the title of his photo exhibition (though the exhibition was given the English title "View of Things"), where he displayed unusual images in a large format, including, among other things, a whirlpool and a mushroom cloud. What sounded harmless would, however, soon ignite. *Gute Form* (Good Design), like *Lebensreform* (Life Reform) and *Neues Wohnen* (New Living) before it, would turn into a rallying cry for world improvement and aesthetic asceticism.

The involvement of the Walter Knoll company became the subject of correspondence between Cologne, Herrenberg and America in the weeks prior to the start of exhibition. Hans Knoll conducted this correspondence in English, even with his father, who had a good command of the language.[26] Walter Knoll had made it clear to the trade fair and exhibition company that he intended to "claim a maximum floor space of 10 m² and pay a maximum sum of DM 300 for it."[27] As yet, he had no experience whatsoever with trade fairs. But that would change very soon. Confronted with such thrift, exhibition director Heinrich König did not falter. König, the new founder of the "Deutscher Werkbund" (German Association of Craftsmen) in Württemberg, was familiar with the Swabian mentality. In addition, he had contacts in the USA, most notably his friend Walter Gropius.[28] Gropius, or rather his wife Ise, had brought the furniture innovations of Hans Knoll to the attention of their old friend. "Dear Mr. Knoll," König subsequently wrote to Herrenberg, "I have just received the enclosed magazine pages from Mrs. Gropius in South Lincoln. I do not need to tell you how exceptionally important it would be for us to have these photos scaled up for our exhibition. I would therefore suggest writing an airmail letter immediately."[29] What had enthused König was none other than the curved form of the Vostra chairs. He suggested using them for the seating of the Ehrenhof, a central exhibition area. 18 pieces were actually displayed at the exhibition in Cologne, more than of any other model. Once again, the Vostra was an eye-catcher. This was in part a result of its transcultural charm, but was also due to the receptive Germans, who now intended to satisfy their pent-up demand for *Gute Form* (Good Design). The S-shaped Vostra became the first iconic chair of the Second Modernity, a success of the Knoll father-son alliance. When the illustrated book "Die schöne Wohnung" (The Beautiful Dwelling), a bible for interior designers, appeared shortly thereafter in its fifth – once again completely revised – edition, it was not entirely by chance that an original Vostra should adorn the cover.[30] The diminutive armchair was a star and seemed made for cover photos.

There was yet another aftereffect. In 1950, as a consequence of the highly successful home exhibition in Cologne the previous year, an entirely new event was launched. For the first time, a furniture trade fair, the present-day "imm cologne," an international furniture and interiors fair, was held in the cathedral city. It was the first of its kind anywhere in the world. From very humble beginnings, it would evolve into the most important event of the whole industry in an incredibly short period of time and, from the outset, would serve two functions that would always remain inseparable, but could never be completely united. This, of course, refers to buying and selling. However, at the same time, it was also always a trading center for ideas and a seismograph of styles. "Furniture from Württemberg" was a peculiarity in relation to other regions in that it was represented by a joint stand from the start. The collective appearance was once again organized by the State Trade Office in Stuttgart. It recognized the great opportunity

VOSTRA BECAME THE FIRST ICONIC CHAIR OF THE SECOND MODERNITY, A SUCCESS OF THE KNOLL FATHER-SON ALLIANCE.

that the trade fair offered to further reinforce the reputation of the Southwest as a site of modernity.

INFRASTRUCTURES OF MODERNITY

Whenever Hans Knoll returned home to visit, he looked forward to one happening in particular. Every Saturday afternoon after shopping downtown, the Knoll and Vollmöller families would meet at the Café Föhl, a Stuttgart institution. This inner-city café had also been bombed out and was therefore housed in a barracks during the post-war period. Here, news was exchanged over pretzels and ground coffee. Everyone was there, including his brother Robert Knoll and his wife Bruni, along with their son Michael who was as blond as his father. Walter Knoll's grandson had just started school and, as everyone here assumed, would later enter the company. This was therefore a meeting of the past and the future. And it was as if the last cusp of the past was protruding into the present. Sometimes aunt Liesl also traveled there from Beilstein, where she inhabited the large mansion that her father, the founder of the Vollmöller hosiery factory, had built in a mock-castle style among the vineyards of Heilbronn in around 1900. It would still serve both families as a getaway and holiday residence for some time yet, until this relic of bygone times would also be lost as a result of the gradual disintegration of the Vollmöller corporation.[31]

In 1950, Walter Knoll was able to celebrate the 25th anniversary of his company. Many well-wishers came to Herrenberg for the occasion, including Paul Hahn, his former partner, whose name was still known by every child in Stuttgart. This year, in which Café Föhl also moved into a new building, marked the end of the post-war period. It was the beginning of a new era. There was already a suspicion that it would turn out golden. In this historic moment, a new chapter in the saga of the furniture family Knoll was also beginning. Hans Knoll, the Swabian-American entrepreneur, ventured back across the Atlantic at a double pace. In 1951, he established a German branch of his U.S. company under the name Knoll International, a limited company with its head office in Stuttgart. This offshoot, whose name would not be applied to the entire company until much later, had a primary purpose: it would, as the name suggested, be the headquarters for his operations overseas. Stuttgart was an obvious choice. Love of his native city was surely not the most important reason; more likely the bond to his family was. Consequently, his brother Robert assumed control of the new company. He would set up European business operations. His sister-in-law Bruni was put in charge of designing the showrooms, which would soon receive national attention. There was naturally a resemblance to the congenial partnership he formed with his own wife Florence. Bruni and Robert Knoll took to their new task with great zeal. The idea of entrusting it to his brother, was part of Hans' strategy. He saw the Knoll furniture dynasty as a whole and wanted to link its parts together. By now a transatlanticist himself, he intended to forge a family-based axis of modernity across the pond. And Stuttgart, where modernity had tradition, was exactly the right location. There were, however, also other reasons. By a stroke of good fortune, Stuttgart was located in the American zone of occupation. Direct access to by far the most important of the Allies, with whom he was already maintaining good relations in the USA, would soon yield results. Among the most spectacular was the commission to furnish the "Amerika-Häuser" (America Houses) that was granted to Knoll International. These were cultural centers, over a dozen in number, which gave post-war Germans in all major cities an understanding of that way of life for which they so envied the Americans. The "Amerika-Haus" that opened in Stuttgart in 1950 was one of the first. Here, everyone now had the opportunity, while browsing books or magazines in the large library, to listen to cool jazz music and, at the same time, sit on equally cool Knoll furniture. Which part of the Knoll family was concerned, however, may have been somewhat less clear. In any case, Walter Knoll very much welcomed "the close relationship with my son"[32] – meaning Hans – that the pair enjoyed at the time. Assigning products to the various subsidiaries – Walter Knoll, Knoll Associates and Knoll International – which now truly overlapped, was also no longer straightforward. The mesh of companies and names is still occasionally a source of confusion to the present day.

---

25 ▶ "Wir Kellerkinder" (We Cellar Children) is a movie from 1960 that satirically dealt with the German post-war period.

26 ▶ Knoll, n.d., p. 92 ff.

27 ▶ Letter from 03/28/1949, WK archives.

28 ▶ König had worked as an adviser to Gropius at the Bauhaus in Dessau.

29 ▶ Letter from 3/31/1949, WK archives.

30 ▶ Harbers, 1951.

31 ▶ After multiple changes of owner and board members, Vollmöller AG slipped into the red during the crisis of the German textile industry of the 1960s, and was sold and liquidated in 1971. The main plant was almost entirely demolished.

32 ▶ Knoll, n.d., p. 100.

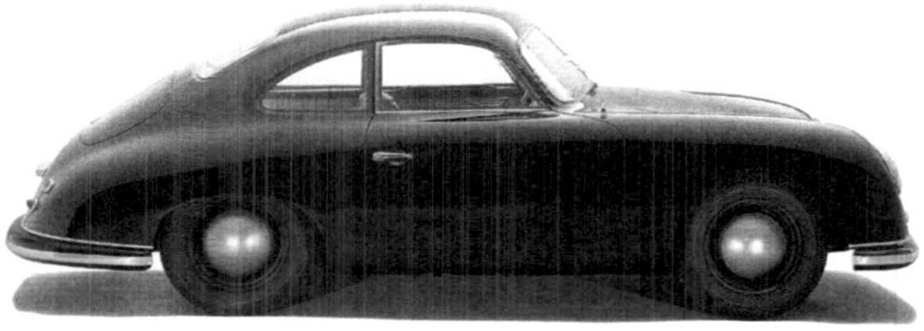

The organic aesthetic also found its way into other fields. The first Porsche was the original bucket of automobile design.

Patent drawing, PA 104021,
bucket seat 350,
Walter Knoll,
design by Arno Votteler,
Herrenberg, 1954

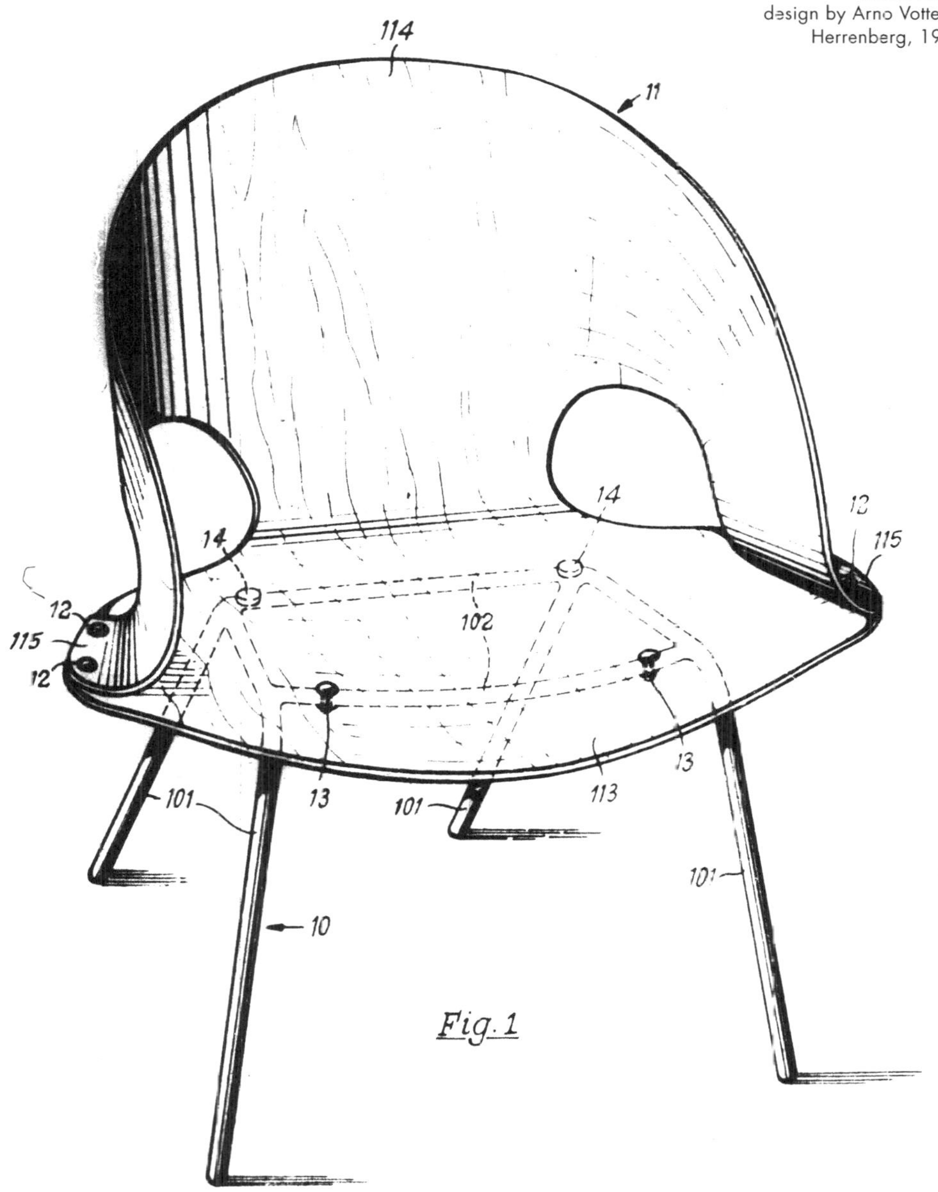

DOUBLE BUCKET

In the 1950s, new materials changed seating design. The bucket seat made of plywood became a symbol of the Second Modernity. Walter Knoll filed a patent application for Arno Votteler's design with a double bucket.

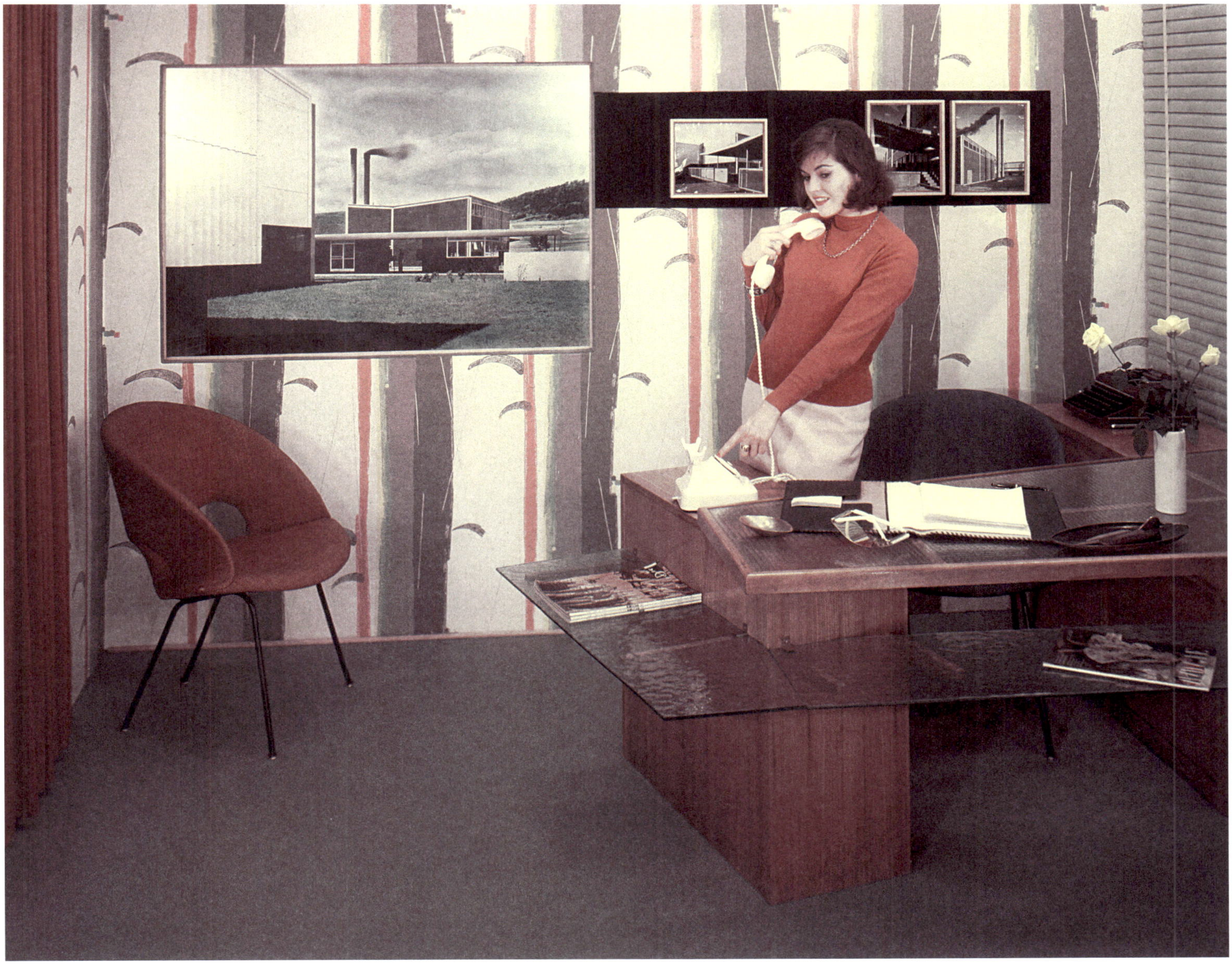

Bucket seat 350,
Walter Knoll,
design by Arno Votteler,
photograph by Franz Lazi,
the photographs in the
background likewise,
Stuttgart, 1954

NEW GROUND

Variants of a new type of furniture were developed by both Wilhelm and Walter Knoll: on the bucket seat, an icon of its time that was made possible by new materials and the invention of plastic, traditional elements such as armrests and backrests merged into one another.

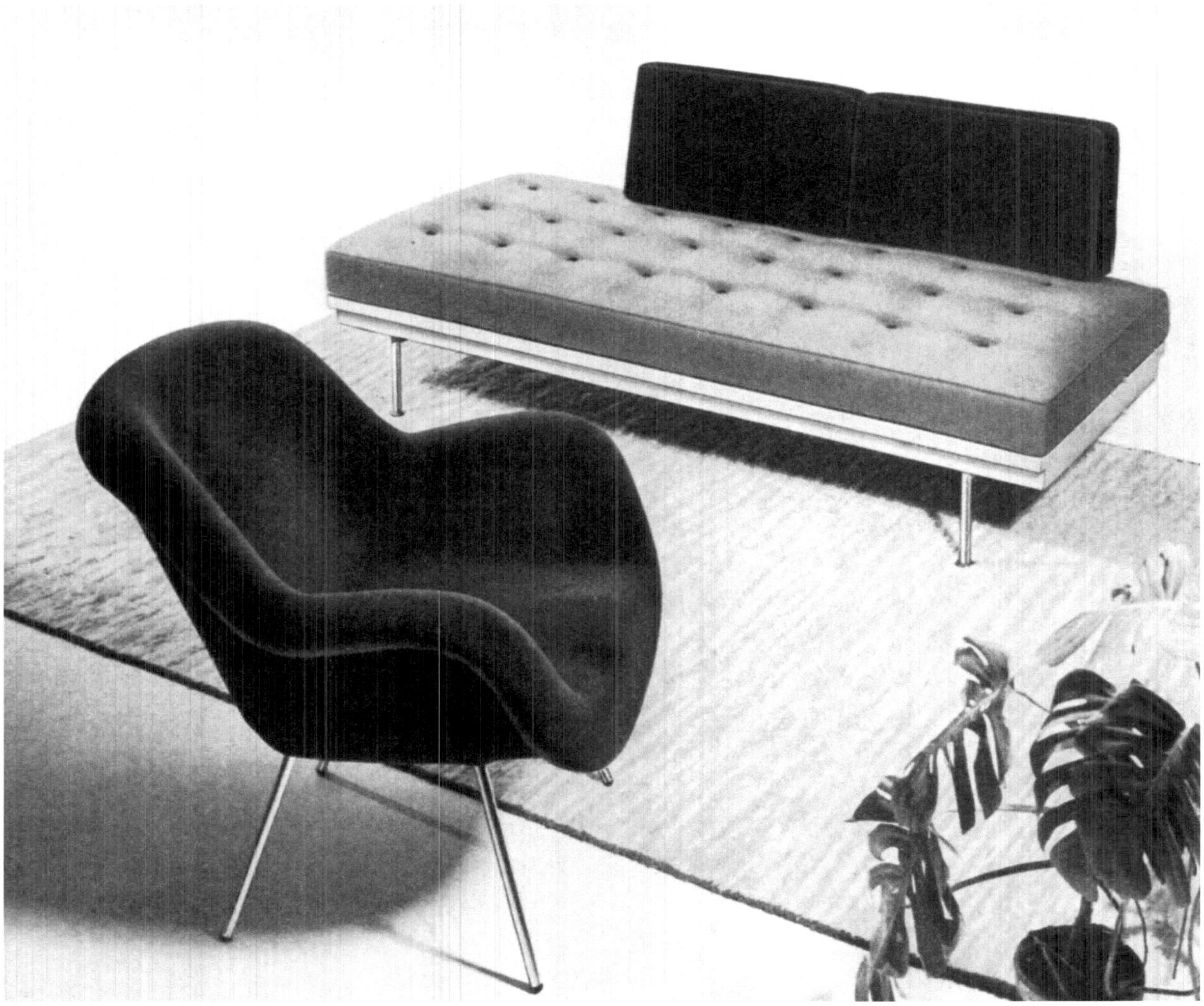

Catalog photo, armchair Antimott 601 and sofa Antimott 190, Wilhelm Knoll, Stuttgart, 1956

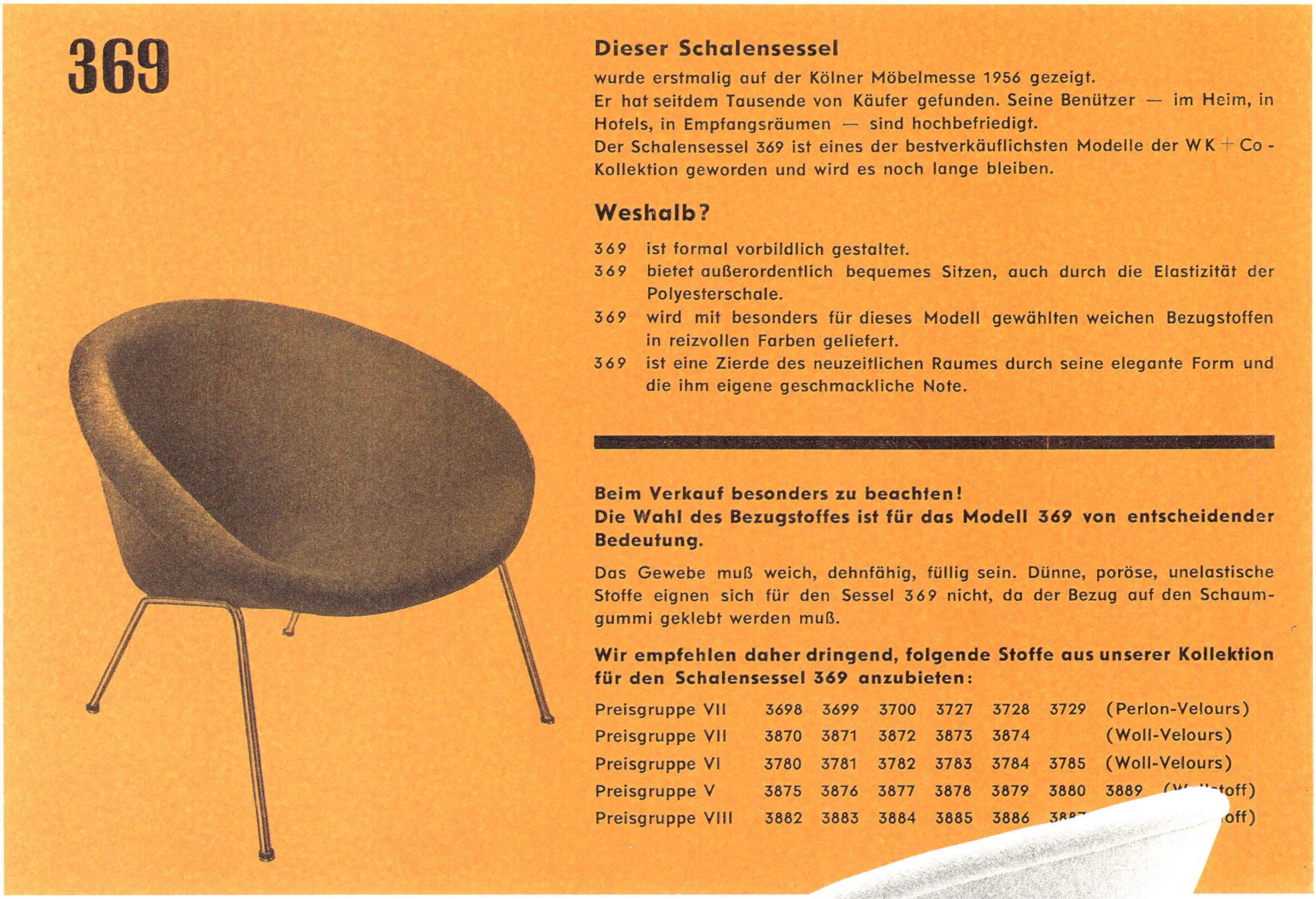

369

Dieser Schalensessel

wurde erstmalig auf der Kölner Möbelmesse 1956 gezeigt.
Er hat seitdem Tausende von Käufer gefunden. Seine Benützer — im Heim, in Hotels, in Empfangsräumen — sind hochbefriedigt.
Der Schalensessel 369 ist eines der bestverkäuflichsten Modelle der WK + Co - Kollektion geworden und wird es noch lange bleiben.

Weshalb?

369 ist formal vorbildlich gestaltet.
369 bietet außerordentlich bequemes Sitzen, auch durch die Elastizität der Polyesterschale.
369 wird mit besonders für dieses Modell gewählten weichen Bezugstoffen in reizvollen Farben geliefert.
369 ist eine Zierde des neuzeitlichen Raumes durch seine elegante Form und die ihm eigene geschmackliche Note.

Beim Verkauf besonders zu beachten!
Die Wahl des Bezugstoffes ist für das Modell 369 von entscheidender Bedeutung.

Das Gewebe muß weich, dehnfähig, füllig sein. Dünne, poröse, unelastische Stoffe eignen sich für den Sessel 369 nicht, da der Bezug auf den Schaumgummi geklebt werden muß.

Wir empfehlen daher dringend, folgende Stoffe aus unserer Kollektion für den Schalensessel 369 anzubieten:

Preisgruppe VII	3698	3699	3700	3727	3728	3729		(Perlon-Velours)
Preisgruppe VII	3870	3871	3872	3873	3874			(Woll-Velours)
Preisgruppe VI	3780	3781	3782	3783	3784	3785		(Woll-Velours)
Preisgruppe V	3875	3876	3877	3878	3879	3880	3889	([illegible]stoff)
Preisgruppe VIII	3882	3883	3884	3885	3886	[illegible]	[illegible]	[illegible]off)

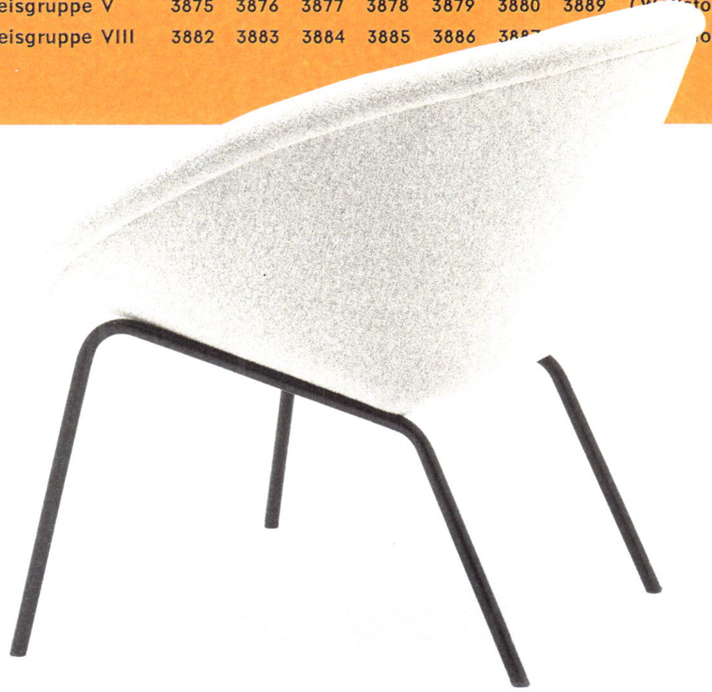

Catalog page,
armchair 369,
Walter Knoll,
design by Rolf Grunow,
Herrenberg, 1956

Original armchair 369,
Walter Knoll,
design by Rolf Grunow,
Herrenberg, 1956

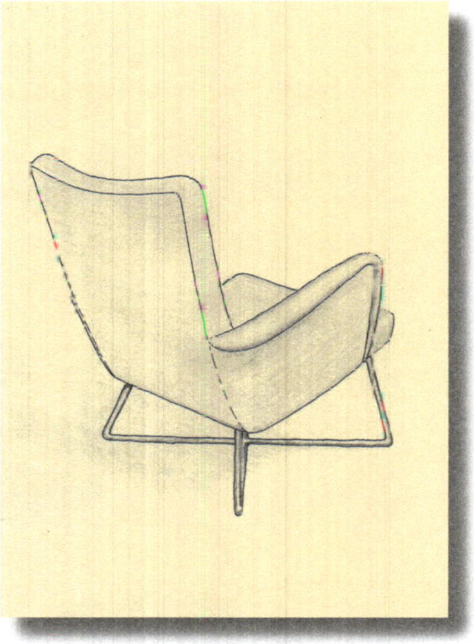

Hans, who had acquired sawmills and played a part in the emerging design scene of Federal Germany, used his father's operations in Herrenberg for production purposes, further evidence of an overarching strategy.

Everything seemed to be going well. At some point, however, Walter Knoll decided to bring his son Robert back to Herrenberg. Although Robert, clearly in a quandary, complied with his father's request, he did not want to give up on the recently started project and the independence that he had gained there. So for a while he commuted back and forth between Stuttgart and Herrenberg. This was, of course, doomed to failure. The euphoric mood of Bruni and Robert, who had thrown themselves into the Knoll setup with enthusiasm, was also severely deflated, which did not make things any easier for their marriage. In fact, Robert Knoll subsequently relinquished his executive chair at Knoll International in Stuttgart after around just two years. Hans Knoll would have to find himself another managing director whether he liked it or not. At this point in time, nobody could have realized that this step would fundamentally alter the character of the furniture family Knoll and even threaten the survival of the dynasty as a whole. Hans Knoll, who was simultaneously thinking in international and dynastic terms and who, as it looked at the time, would sooner or later go on to dominate the Knoll dynasty, held fast to his far-reaching goals. After all, there were plenty of solid reasons for his transatlantic master plan. For a businessman who could do the sums, there was another particularly compelling argument. Labor was low-priced in Germany. In fact for an American it was dirt cheap. And top quality was delivered. What more could one want? The concept of Knoll International was based on virtually ideal conditions. Last but not least, Stuttgart's strong foothold in modernity, which the furniture family Knoll had already been contributing to for decades, was naturally also a deciding factor. The infrastructure of modernity was surely incomparably better than in East Greenville, Pennsylvania, the new location of Knoll Associates, and, especially where furniture and design was concerned, could certainly also measure up to New York. What Stuttgart lacked was the image, the glamorous name, and, of course, also a certain amount of coolness. For a moment, however, it almost looked as though the Neckar metropolis could actually become a "Little Paris" of the furniture design world. The showroom of Knoll International, already a sensational innovation in itself, played a not inconsiderable role in this. For a while it would become a small, but fascinating, stage for the Second Modernity, with showcases that would cause passers-by to press their noses against the shop windows to admire the Knoll furniture. That the origins of this "Made in USA" coolness, which could be viewed there for free, lay in large part on the hills of Weissenhof was, of course, known only to a very few. After all, shrouded in the twelve dark years of Nazi rule the Germans now had a problem with their own past. The handling of the Weissenhofsiedlung, which was criminally neglected by the city of Stuttgart, is a good example of this. Pride at having played an important role in modernity, as was common in other countries (such as in France, Finland or Italy), is not part of the collective consciousness in Germany, even up to the present day.

The last of the ruins in Stuttgart disappeared in the early 1950s. The city was now a permanent building site and was gripped by construction fever. In the capital of the new dual state of Baden-Württemberg, a highly pragmatic, but certainly also art-loving, city leader diligently encouraged a boom. From the outset, the non-party affiliated mayor Arnulf Klett, in office for a small eternity from 1945 to 1974, pressed ahead with substantial construction projects that would become symbols of the new beginning. These prestigious buildings of economic miracle architecture were now the jewels of the cityscape, above all the Television Tower but also the "Neue Liederhalle" (New Concert Hall), the "Süddeutscher Rundfunk" (South German Broadcasting) studio and the university, to name just a few prominent examples. In the ideological battle, which had already been waged here between the modernists and the conservative "Stuttgarter Schule" (Stuttgart School) in the 1920s, the traditionalists came up short this time.[33] A new guard of architects, among them Egon Eiermann, Rolf Gutbrod, Hans Volkart and many others, prevailed and practically seized a monopoly on style. Naturally, these architects wanted to fit out their new, modern buildings with the appropriate furnishings. The demand was huge. Architects and furniture manufacturers were part of the environment of the Second Modernity that was rapidly developing in Stuttgart. There were gatherings at the Rotary Club, for example, which held weekly meetings in the "Neue Liederhalle." Walter Knoll had been a proud member since 1930 (likewise his son Robert), and he would only miss this happening in exceptional cases. As a result, Stuttgart had, in just a few years, also become a city of the Second Modernity on the outside – and in as "car-friendly" a manner as possible, as the saying goes.

WHENEVER THE SECOND MODERNITY CELEBRATED ITSELF AND PEOPLE CAME IN DROVES, FURNITURE BY WALTER KNOLL WAS REPRESENTED AS A MATTER OF COURSE.

The institutions that brought life to the Second Modernity and also gave visibility to the avant-garde were the State Trade Office and the "Kunstgewerbeschule" (School of Arts and Crafts), old favorites that had already successfully distinguished themselves as agencies of modernity in the early 20th century. At the State Trade Office, with its museum, enormous library and advantageous central location, director Josef Thuma continued to organize trailblazing exhibitions, featuring subject matter that weaved between design, art and industry and where the question of *Wie wohnen?* (How to live?) would long remain in the foreground. Thuma was, of course, also responsible for the joint appearance of Baden-Württemberg's furniture companies at the Cologne fair, which was now held on a regular basis. Another important factor for the milieu and the climate of change was the "Kunstgewerbeschule" (School of Arts and Crafts), which had now been integrated into the Academy and renamed as the "Institut für Innenarchitektur und Möbelbau" (Institute for Interior Design and Furniture Making). Ever since Bernhard Pankok's and Adolf Schneck's days there, innovation had always been right at the top of the curriculum. Now a new generation was following in their footsteps.[34] In 1952, it made a double appointment of two interior designers who set the course and secured the institute its leading role: Herbert Hirche and Herta-Maria Witzemann received their professorship. The newly arrived pair – him from Berlin, her from Vienna, both around 40 years old – would secure Stuttgart's reputation as a location of furniture innovations for the coming decades. Although their names have since fallen into oblivion and are nowadays only known to insiders, they undoubtedly deserve a place of honor in the virtual Hall of Fame of design. And not only as the creators of items of furniture that would become icons, but also as university professors and as combative representatives of their profession. The fact that these two protagonists of the Second Modernity also worked for Walter Knoll during those years was all but inevitable in the greenhouse climate of Stuttgart. However, the fact that Walter Knoll was the manufacturer that both worked for initially and for many years to come says a lot about his special status.

Whether in 1957 at the "Internationale Bauausstellung" (International Building Exhibition), the IBA in West Berlin, or in 1958 at the World's Fair in Brussels, whenever the Second Modernity celebrated itself and people came in droves, furniture by Walter Knoll was represented as a matter of course. The subject of the IBA '57 was the *Hansaviertel* (Hansa Quarter) in West Berlin's Tiergarten district; a model estate that also contained model dwellings, though this was not the only parallel that could be drawn with Stuttgart-Weissenhof exactly 30 years prior. Once again, an illustrious circle of international architects – 53 in total – was responsible for the buildings and their furnishings. And this time too, furniture from Herrenberg was among the selection. The pioneer Herbert Hirche, lecturer in Stuttgart, architect, co-founder of the "Verband der deutschen Industriedesigner" (Association of German Industrial Designers) and one of the initial protagonists in the design revolution triggered by the radio business Braun, designed a lightweight kitchen stool and a bucket seat with a high backrest for Walter Knoll's appearance in Berlin. Naturally, Walter Knoll, by now 81 and still head of his company, attended the major event in the divided metropolis on the river Spree: the western part now lay – as yet without a wall – like an island within the GDR (German Democratic Republic) and was outfitted as the "window display of the West."

One year later, the senior boss went on his travels again. He also attended the World's Fair in Brussels and, of course, went inside the Atomium, the icon of the exposition, which attracted an incredible 41 million visitors to the Belgian capital. The building's symbolic crystalline structure of metal represented the age of prosperity that was supposedly fast approaching. The West German pavilion, naturally Walter Knoll's main goal, was also an attraction. Over the three light-filled stories of this house of glass, designed by the Stuttgart-based architect Egon Eiermann, only objects meeting the strict criteria of *Gute Form* (Good Design) were exhibited. Unsurprisingly, this also included furniture from Walter Knoll, which the visitor from Herrenberg inspected especially thoroughly.

Restrained simplicity was by now the official style, and not only in Brussels, with which the young Federal Republic presented itself as a future-oriented country. One person who had been pulling the strings in the background to achieve this was Heinrich König, new chairman

---

33 ▶ In light of this development, which shapes the cityscape to the present day, no small number of them switched sides. One example of many is the Stuttgart-born architect Adolf Carl Rüdenauer, a traditionalist who turned into a moderate modernist.

34 ▶ Pankok, born in 1872, who retired as director of the "Kunstgewerbeschule" (School of Arts and Crafts) in 1937, died in 1943. Schneck, who had been a professor throughout the Nazi era and the war, took his leave in 1949, and remained an honorary member of the academy. He died in 1971, aged 87.

AVANT-GARDISTS

Typical for the 1950s are unusual lines and dissolving forms. The overlaps between art and design are unmistakable: just like the portrait of the Stuttgart-born painter Willi Baumeister, taken by Franz Lazi, the chair also appears to consist of separate parts.

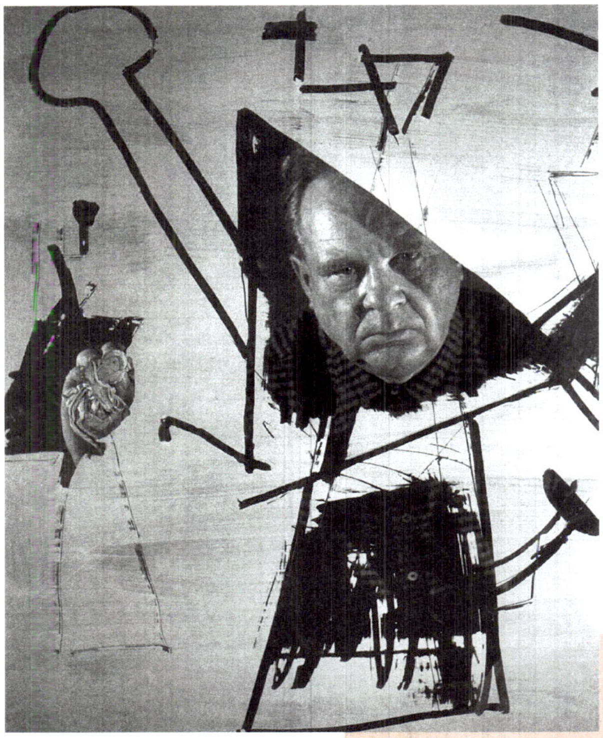

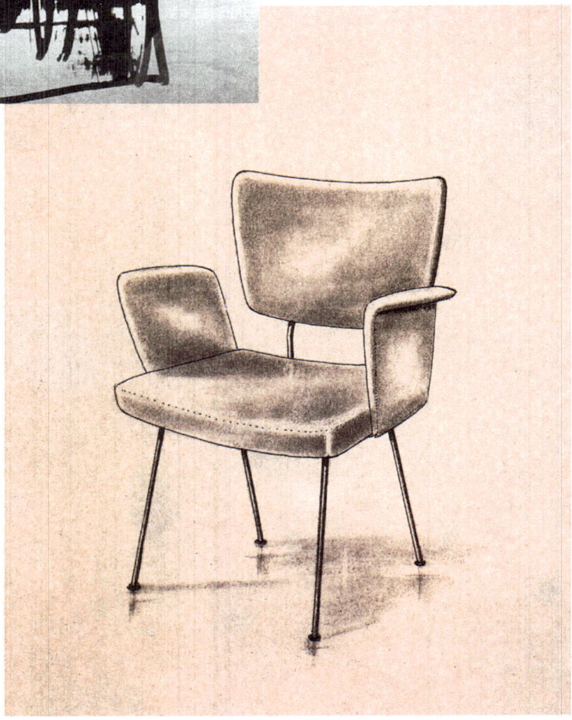

Willi Baumeister, photograph by Franz Lazi, Stuttgart, 1949

Model drawing, armchair 338, Walter Knoll, Herrerberg, around 1955

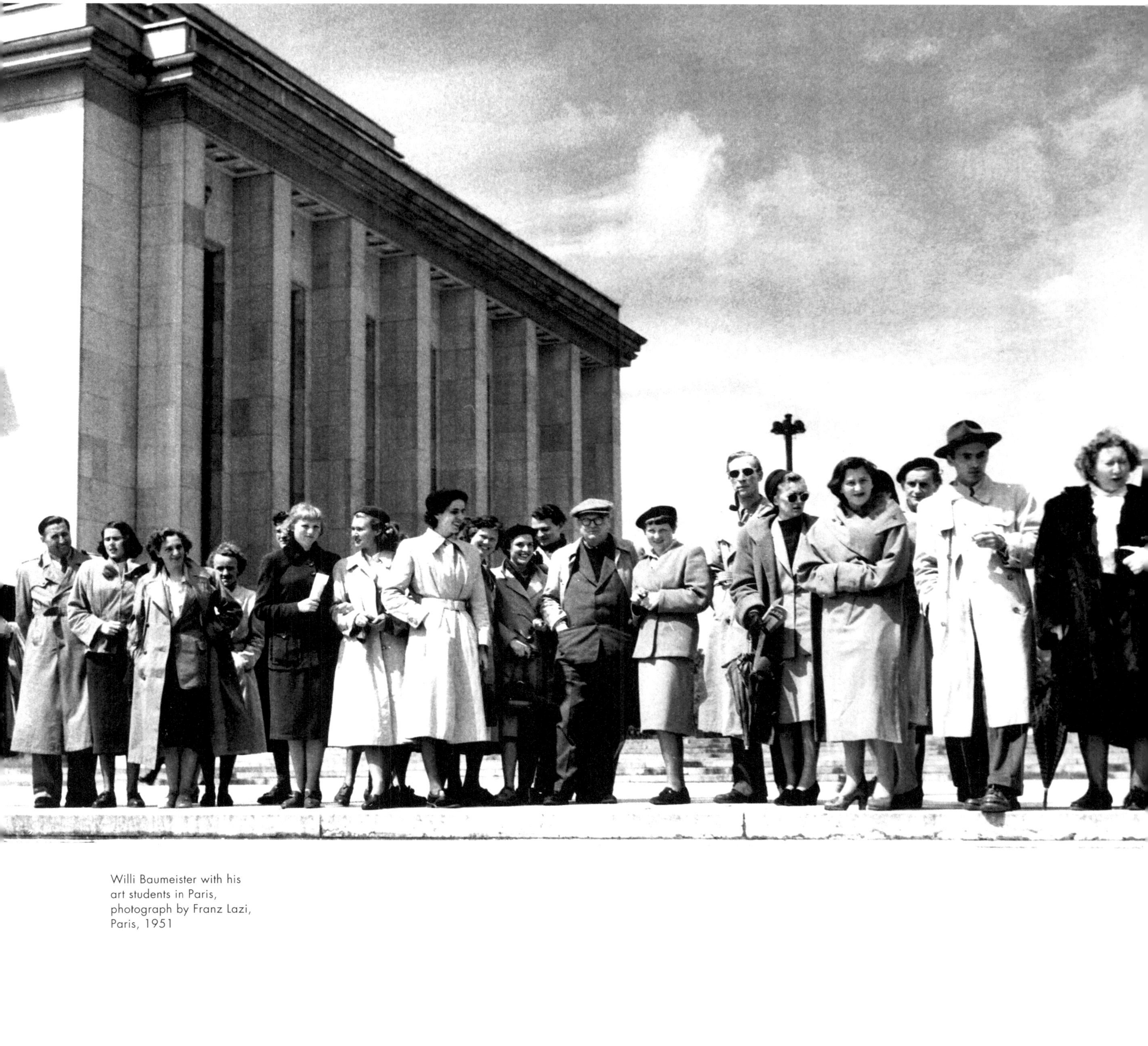

Willi Baumeister with his
art students in Paris,
photograph by Franz Lazi,
Paris, 1951

of Württemberg's "Werkbund" (Association of Craftsmen) who had previously been active in Cologne as director of the 1949 home exhibition. König had connections in the new capital city of Bonn. There, the reform pioneer, former "Werkbund" (Association of Craftsmen) secretary and Swabian, Theodor Heuss was still Federal President. The fact that the Federal Parliament had moved into the former Pedagogical Academy in Bonn, a building on the banks of the Rhine in the "white modernity" style from the time of the Weimar Republic, was by no means mere coincidence, but must be understood as an unequivocal signal.[35] The architect Hans Schwippert, also from Stuttgart's milieu of modernity, was chosen to carry out the conversion from a small teacher's academy into West Germany's parliament building. As was to be expected, he ensured *Gute Form* (Good Design) for the new seat of government from the outset, including when furnishing the parliamentary chambers. The fact that Walter Knoll, as a brand of modernity, was also involved, can hardly come as a surprise. For example, the "smoking room", in those days one of the most popular meeting points of the House, was fitted with upholstered items of "Herrenberg furniture". Heinrich König, a tireless fighter for the ideas of the "Werkbund" (Association of Craftsmen), ultimately advised the government to set up a bureau that would specifically deal with the issue of *Gute Form* (Good Design). He managed to convince Ludwig Erhard, the Minister of Economic Affairs.[36] Ehrhard, not really known as an expert in matters of design, had the "Rat für Formgebung" (German Design Council) established in 1953, the central state institution for the promotion of design to the present day, and would eventually offer one of the first, and today still important design awards: the "Bundespreis Gute Form" (German National Prize for Good Design).[37]

Among the first products to be honored in 1969 was the FK chair (see p. 206). This elegant bucket seat, which can be unhesitatingly referred to as a classic, is still part of the product range of Walter Knoll today. In the 1960s, it was produced by competitor Alfred Kill in Fellbach, which was in a process of expansion and belonged to the group known in the upholstery industry as "the big Ks:" the two Knolls, Kaufeld in East Westphalia, and Kill. During a visit to the Copenhagen furniture fair in the mid-1960s, founder Alfred Kill and his son Peter had gotten to know Jørgen Kastholm and Preben Fabricius and brought them to Fellbach as employed designers – the beginning of a success story that would also involve the aforementioned German National Prize for Good Design. Inspired by functionalism and the resoluteness of Scandinavian design, which had a considerable influence on the aesthetics of the 1960s, interior designers Fabricius and Kastholm devoted themselves to optimizing form, material and ergonomics. In 1961, they founded a studio together that would become the birthplace of numerous classics in furniture history. Their main concern was to clearly state the function of an aesthetic form. In the mid-1990s, the Kill company ran into trouble and was taken over by Walter Knoll, complete with its Danish-influenced product range, which included the FK bucket seat.

IN THE COURSE OF THE 1950s, THE COMPANY WALTER KNOLL ATTAINED A SPECIAL POSITION WITHIN ITS SECTOR, AND WAS CONSIDERED A FLAGSHIP OF MODERNITY.

Back to the "Rat für Formgebung" (German Design Council): in all likelihood, this important authority in Federal Germany's design landscape would not have existed without the networks of the Southwest. It would eventually be headed by Mia Seeger, the publicist and "Werkbund" (Association of Craftsmen) member from Stuttgart, whose passion for modernity had been ignited in her younger years at Weissenhof. She was also familiar with Stuttgart's exemplary policies for promoting the economy and design, not least those of the "Landesgewerbeamt" (State Trade Office). And it was precisely these methods for success that Seeger then carried over to the federal level. She organized top-class exhibitions and selected only top talents to be involved. Under her leadership, the Federal Republic made its mark at the Milan Triennale in 1957, to pick out one example, with a stand that was designed by Arnold Bode. Bode, an artist, curator, university professor and reformist educator, also a brilliant universalist, had launched the documenta exhibition in Kassel two years earlier.[38] Incidentally, Herta-Maria Witzemann, the interior designer from

Stuttgart, also won a silver medal at that same Milan event, at the time Italy's most significant art and design showcase.

Seeger and Witzemann were rare examples in the man's world of the 1950s. What is even more amazing is that there was yet another exceptional woman in Stuttgart. Like Seeger and Witzemann, Margret Hildebrand, manager of the design studio of the "Stuttgarter Gardinenfabrik" (Stuttgart Curtain Factory) since 1948, and soon also the company's managing director, was not only a proven expert who won international prizes. She also, like the other two, fought with vehemence for both *Gute Form* (Good Design) and recognition for her profession. At the end of the war, the "Stuttgarter Gardinenfabrik" had moved its headquarters to Herrenberg. In one of those coincidences of design history, the business was now also just a short walk away from Walter Knoll, a tremendous stroke of luck for both sides. The name "SG," the initials of the textile company, was widely known for its high-quality fabrics and sophisticated patterns, which reached an especially high artistic level in the 1950s and 60s. The company, which produced upholstery and curtain fabrics, practically became the external textile department of Walter Knoll. The fruitful partnership between the like-minded companies continued until into the 1980s. That three female creatives were simultaneously in the foreground to such an extent, at a time when women were not at all envisaged in leading positions, is extraordinary, and a singularity of the Stuttgart milieu of the Second Modernity. The three grandes dames of *Gute Form*, as they were sometimes referred to at the time, were all linked with the Walter Knoll company in different ways. No wonder, given that it was already attracting the best talents back then.

In the course of the 1950s, the Walter Knoll company attained a special position within its sector, similar to that achieved by neighboring company Erwin Behr in the area of modern cabinets and wall units. The two Swabian family companies, which had maintained an aesthetic course since the 1920s and cooperated with each other (for example with the London company of Serge Chermayeff), were by now already considered flagships of modernity. Now competition was on the rise. In the course of the Second Modernity, rivals emerged that were, however, not necessarily newly established companies. A new type of company came into existence, namely the model of manufacturers of modern furniture arising out of Swabian wood workshops. One such example is the Stuttgart-based company Wilde & Spieth. This joinery, established in the mid-19th century and specializing in roller shutters, was visited in the late 1940s by Egon Eiermann, one of West Germany's greatest post-war architects[39], and part of the Stuttgart milieu (his house photographer was Franz Lazi). In Esslingen, Eiermann inquired whether Wilde & Spieth was also capable of making a chair. It was one of those coincidences that have already been mentioned, almost fateful encounters between designers and entrepreneurs who, as in this case, come together at just the right moment, namely at a time of great change. The first two years alone saw the development of over half a dozen models made of plywood, one of the new materials that enabled organic forms and is associated with international designers such as Arne Jacobsen and Charles and Ray Eames. Curved plywood became a design hit of the 1950s. Of course, the companies of Wilhelm and Walter Knoll also worked with it. What was now happening at Wilde & Spieth was a transformation from a pretty normal joinery into an extremely successful manufacturer of modern chairs. Under the banner of *Gute Form*, the economic miracle also spawned an early design industry that thrived particularly well in Stuttgart, and the surrounding area. That furniture, as before in the First Modernity, would be in the foreground, is a phenomenon that runs like a thread through design history. Seating furniture was, is, and continues to be the supreme discipline. Among the companies that reinvented themselves in a similar way to Wilde & Spieth during this period were Bofinger and Holzäpfel. Both also arose out of Swabian wood workshops. In both cases, it was the junior bosses – in the first case, Rudolf Baresel-Bofinger in Ilsfeld, in the second Christian Holzäpfel in Ebhausen – who proved themselves as furniture entrepreneurs and managed to stand out from the bulk of the industry. This, of course, is reminiscent of Walter and Wilhelm Knoll, and also – not to forget – Hans Knoll. All Knoll sons who, in one way or another, managed to step out from the shadows of their fathers to go down in the annals of furniture modernity as pioneers. Two other names from the Stuttgart environment, whose rapid ascent in the post-war era followed a similar pattern, were Rolf Benz and Alfred Kill, who both wrote their success stories with design. Stories that, incidentally, would intersect and blend with the company history of Walter Knoll in differing ways nearly half a century later. In the 1950s and 60s, the new generation of design-obsessed furniture pioneers from Swabia would give new impetus to the already existing infrastructure of modernity. Although hardly any of the newcomers would survive the coming economic storms unscathed and have largely been forgotten, German furniture modernity is inconceivable without them. Only in Swabia did the company addresses, where advanced furniture ideas were in high demand, lie so close together.

---

35 ▶ The former Pedagogical Academy in Bonn on the river Rhine was planned as a teacher training academy by Cologne government building officer Martin Witte in the late 1920s, and was opened in 1933, already under the National Socialists.

36 ▶ Ludwig Erhard's constituency was in Ulm, meaning he was often in the Stuttgart area. In 1949, still non-party affiliated, he was nominated for the Bundestag by the Württemberg CDU party. The fact that Darmstadt, the original seat of the German Design Council, lies halfway between Bonn and Stuttgart, may just be a coincidence.

37 ▶ It was renamed the "Designpreis der Bundesrepublik Deutschland" (Design Award of the Federal Republic of Germany) in 2001.

38 ▶ documenta 1 took place in 1955, and would develop into one of the most important art exhibitions.

39 ▶ His buildings included the German Pavilion at the World's Fair in Brussels, the Kaiser Wilhelm Memorial Church in Berlin, and the *Langer Eugen* (Tall Eugene), the representatives' office tower in Bonn.

FORM GIVER
The designer, architect and university professor Herbert Hirche, who taught at the Stuttgart Academy, shaped a generation of students. He designed assorted seating furniture for Walter Knoll in the strict style of the late 1950s.

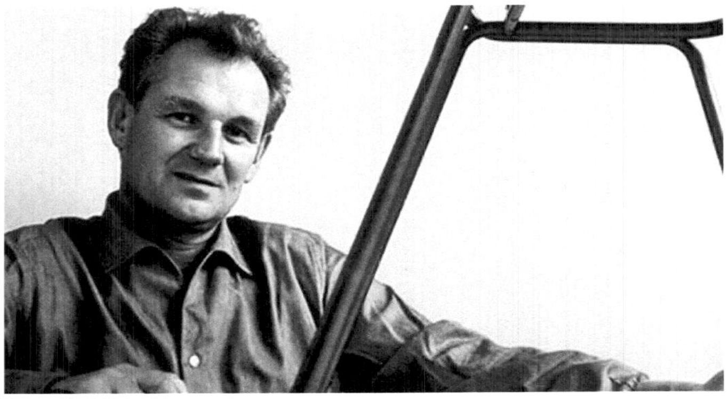

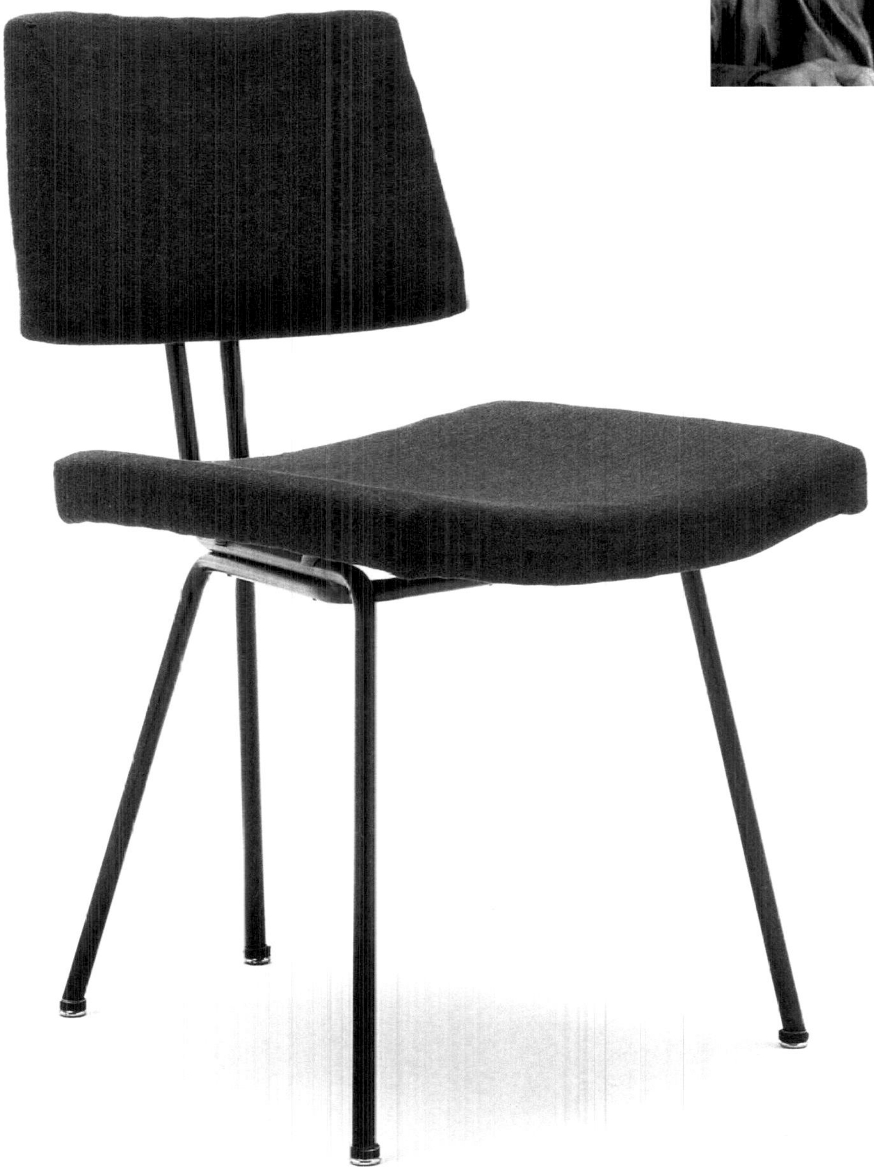

Herbert Hirche, architect and professor at the "Kunstgewerbeschule" (School of Arts and Crafts), Stuttgart, 1953

Original chair 361, Walter Knoll, design by Herbert Hirche, Herrenberg, 1955, restored in 2015

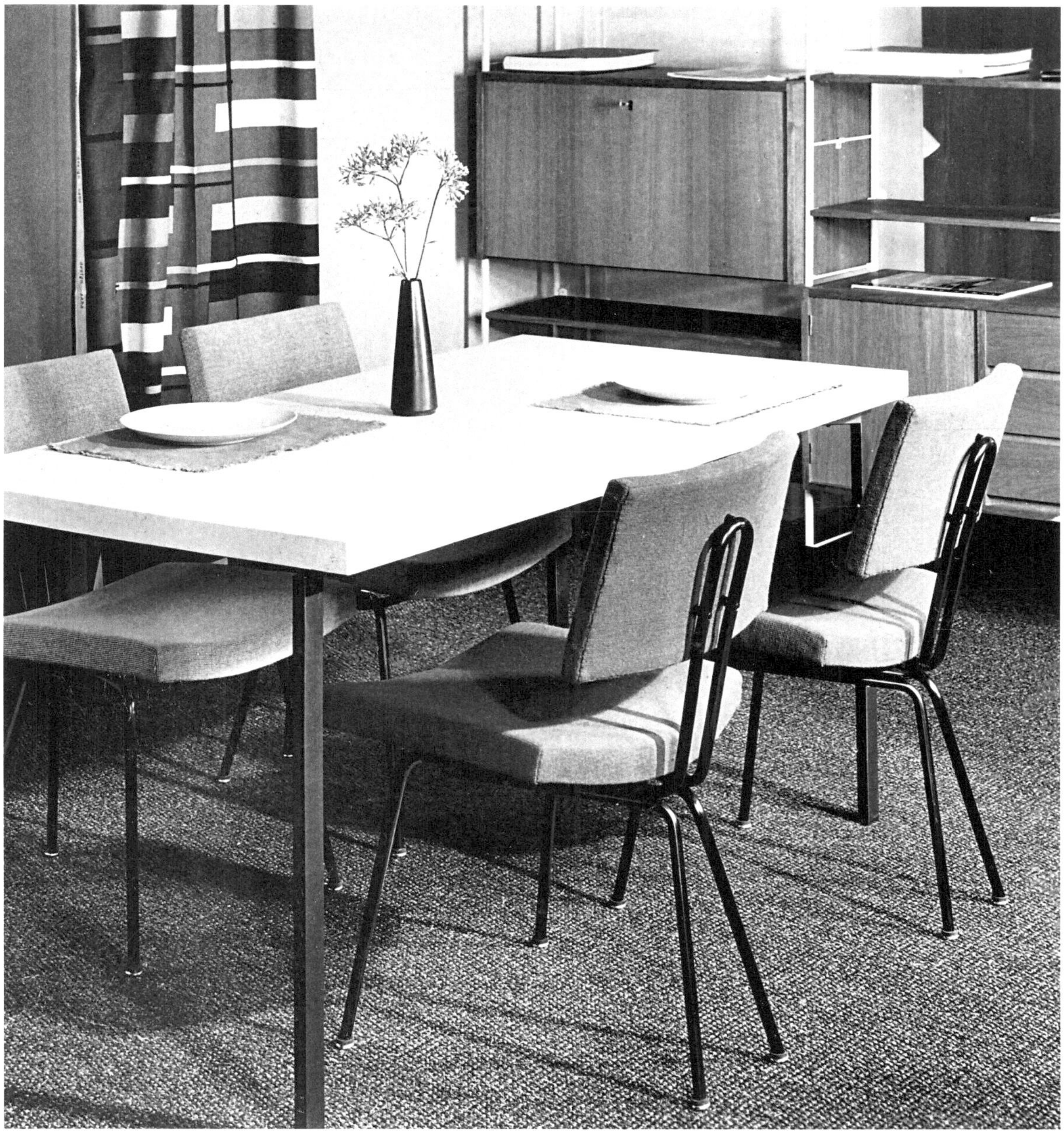

Catalog photo of seating furniture
from Herrenberg,
chair 361, Walter Knoll,
design by Herbert Hirche,
Herrenberg, 1955

WILLY KNOLL'S LAST YEARS

The Wilhelm Knoll company had been severely affected by the Second World War and its consequences. After 1945, the situation looked accordingly gloomy. The factory in Sweden and foreign patents were lost. The English licensee, Parker-Knoll, still bears the family name in its brand to the present day.[40] Nevertheless, the live wire Willy Knoll never doubted that even these major setbacks would be made up for, and probably even outweighed, by reconstruction. As we all know, he was proved right. Seasoned and unperturbed, he did what he had previously learned from his father: he established international contacts again. And success was not long in coming. Back in the early 1950s, half of the at times double-digit sales growth could already be attributed to exports. The lion's share of this rapid development was, as before the war, down to the Antimott spring. It would now also be used in new types of furniture and would evolve into its own brand, which would even take precedence over the company name. Antimott catalogs reached a considerable size and were, in the end, published annually.

When Willy Knoll celebrated his 75th birthday in 1953, everything appeared to be back on track. However, the birthday celebratee, who had by that point already survived several strokes, died the following year. The son of the company founder and brother of Walter Knoll had managed his company over nearly half a century and made it one of the most successful in the industry. The stalwart, who managed his company with a firm hand and drew his moral principles and strong faith from his protestant religion, had lately also been involved with "Sozialhilfe der deutschen Wirtschaft" (Social Assistance of the German Economy), an initiative intended to alleviate the hardships of the post-war era. Somewhat ironically, the enterprising businessman passed away during a rest cure. That he even agreed to it in the first place shows just how bad he was feeling.

One circumstance certainly did not ease the last year of Willy Knoll's life. In 1953, a change in personnel occurred that was a hard blow for him. Walter Combe, his nephew, who had been joint managing director since the 1920s, unexpectedly left the company. And as if the loss of this senior employee, who was nearly irreplaceable and with whom, as his sister's son, he also had a personal connection, had not already been painful enough, Combe went straight to Walter Knoll, Willy's rival brother, of all people. This was surely a family drama that not even the tough Willy Knoll could get over. Walter Knoll signed half of his company over to the defector, making Walter Combe an equal shareholder. Until today, the reasons for this inter-family transfer, which Walter Knoll later referred to as a "turning point of profound significance"[41] are still unknown. The fact that Combe's parents lived in Herrenberg, may have made this somewhat bold step easier for him. At this point in time, Robert Knoll had just become managing director of his brother Hans' branch in Stuttgart and was unavailable. During this phase, in which sales figures rose strongly and the load was increasing, Walter Knoll may have been seeking someone who, in his words, "could stand by my side."[42] And, of course, he still had an old, though rather really old, score to settle with his brother Willy. His solution, which must have hit the family like a bomb, was also reminiscent of the partnership he had with Paul Hahn, and he was perhaps thinking back to those good times.

Willy Knoll had appointed his son Dieter as his successor some time ago. The tall young man in his early thirties, who had studied business administration at the technical university in Stuttgart during the war, had already been granted power of attorney many years earlier. Suddenly, he was left to his own devices. However, he was familiar with the business processes and did not require a familiarization period. He did not

THE DEATH OF THE ENTERPRISING BUSINESSMAN: WILLY KNOLL HAD MANAGED HIS COMPANY FOR HALF A CENTURY AND MADE IT ONE OF THE MOST SUCCESSFUL IN THE INDUSTRY.

bring in a partner. In him, nearly 80 years after the establishment of the company, a representative of the third generation had taken the reins. Needless to say, such unparalleled constancy essentially stems from the particularities of a Swabian family business. Like his father, Dieter Knoll naturally also saw the company as his life's work. Eventually, however, it would slip from his hands.

SEATING REVOLUTION

In August 1953, Walter Knoll made a journey of around 60 miles to Ulm. The reason for the trip was an inauguration ceremony. The "Hochschule für Gestaltung Ulm" (Ulm School of Design) – considered by many as one of, if not the most, important design institutes of the 20th century – was being opened.[43] Its first rector was Max Bill, who had caused such a furor with his promotion of *Gute Form* (Good Design)

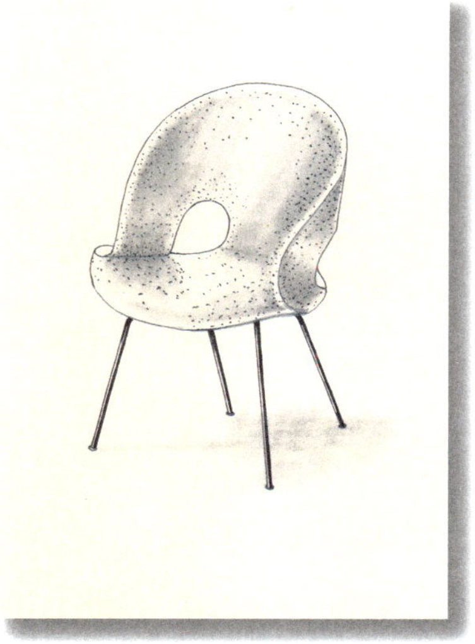

in Cologne in 1949. Now Bill, who had, of course, been a student at the Bauhaus, from which he borrowed the name "Hochschule für Gestaltung" (School of Design)[44], wanted to set up a laboratory for ideal industrial forms, like the one that preceded it in Dessau. Walter Knoll, who had built his company on a foundation of modernity from the outset, had been keenly observing the Bauhaus since back in the 1920s. He had gotten to know Bill in Cologne. He was so taken with the idea that a new kind of Bauhaus would come into being in the immediate vicinity that he even provided financial support for the project. "Dear Mr. Knoll," wrote Inge Aicher-Scholl, co-founder of the "Hochschule für Gestaltung Ulm" (Ulm School of Design), in a letter. "Just as I was brooding over the allocation of our very modest scholarship fund (...), your kind letter, in which you outline to me your intention to make a grant this year, arrived in the afternoon mail. A couple of hours later, a messenger brought me a check to the amount of DM 2000. How can I possibly describe my delight to you?!" (see p. 165).[45] The matter must have been truly close to the heart of the entrepreneur Walter Knoll, whose sense of thrift was well-known. Incidentally, he did not travel alone to Ulm. At the wheel of the car sat Arno Votteler, a young man in his early twenties, who had spent the past year as an interior designer at the company. Interior designers, who were hired as designers at Walter Knoll, although also assigned other tasks, would be an integral part of the staff in the coming decades. A new constellation that was rare, though not unique, in the industry and illustrated the subtle difference that set the company apart from most of the sector. However, the high turnover in this position was in stark contrast to the constancy of the rest of the workforce. Besides working at the drawing table and in the production process, Votteler, who was the first in this post, was also assigned the role of chauffeuring the boss to his duties, including being on-call over the weekend. In the process, the young man was witness to all sorts.

Votteler, a native Swabian from the Black Forest, who would himself later teach as a professor at the Stuttgart Academy, had studied there under Herbert Hirche. Together with him, he was among the founders of the DVID, or "Deutscher Verband der Industriedesigner" (German Association of Industrial Designers). In this way, he followed in the footsteps of Stuttgart's furniture avant-garde as part of its fourth generation. He remained an employed designer in Herrenberg for around two years. A rather short but exceptionally productive period for both him and the company. The early years of his career coincided with the beginnings of the Second Modernity, a time when furniture design, now on a global scale, was undergoing a metamorphosis. Naturally, Votteler, the young professional, inspired and spurred on the feverish climate of change. New, malleable materials such as organic plywood (or plastic) buckets and thin tubular steel, as well as foam instead of traditional upholstery, came into use. Consequently, the upholstered chair was also completely redefined. The "Womb" model was introduced in New York in 1948.[46] This lightweight bucket seat on steel spider legs was deemed a brilliant application of the new paradigms. The flowing lines (with a total absence of edges) were not the only fundamental difference; it was above all distinguished by the blending of all the individual elements of the armchair into a unified overall shape. The design was by Eero Saarinen, architect, son of Eliel and Loja Saarinen, and brother of the adopted Florence Knoll.[47] It is spread that she requested him to do so. Hans Knoll, the commuter between continents, who successfully had his brother-in-law's model produced by his company, naturally reported on this sensation to Herrenberg. Thanks to the direct line between father and son, family connections kept the company one step ahead. This had already worked once before in the case of the Vostra. So well, in fact, that Vostra had in the meantime become its own brand name, like Prodomo before it, with a corresponding logo. The numerous design variants were promoted with their own brochures. And they were even printed in color, which was still quite exceptional at the time.

Walter Knoll took the young fellow Swabian Votteler under his wing. Although the difference in age and experience was substantial, they also had similarities. Both were imposing six-footers, still quite a rarity in those days, and therefore able to look each other in the eye.

---

40 ▶ Companies like the British Parker-Knoll, which has retained the double name to the present day, took over the Antimott patent.

41 ▶ Knoll n.d., p. 101.

42 ▶ Ibid.

43 ▶ Hiesinger and Marcus 1993, p. 177.

44 ▶ Following its relocation to Dessau, the Bauhaus was referred to in a subheading as the "Hochschule für Gestaltung" (School of Design), a very modern choice of words at the time.

45 ▶ Letter (typed), WK archives.

46 ▶ "Low-Cost furniture" was one of the groundbreaking exhibitions of the Museum of Modern Art.

47 ▶ Eero Saarinen was the son of the Finnish architect Eliel Saarinen and director of the Cranbrook Academy where Florence Schust had studied.

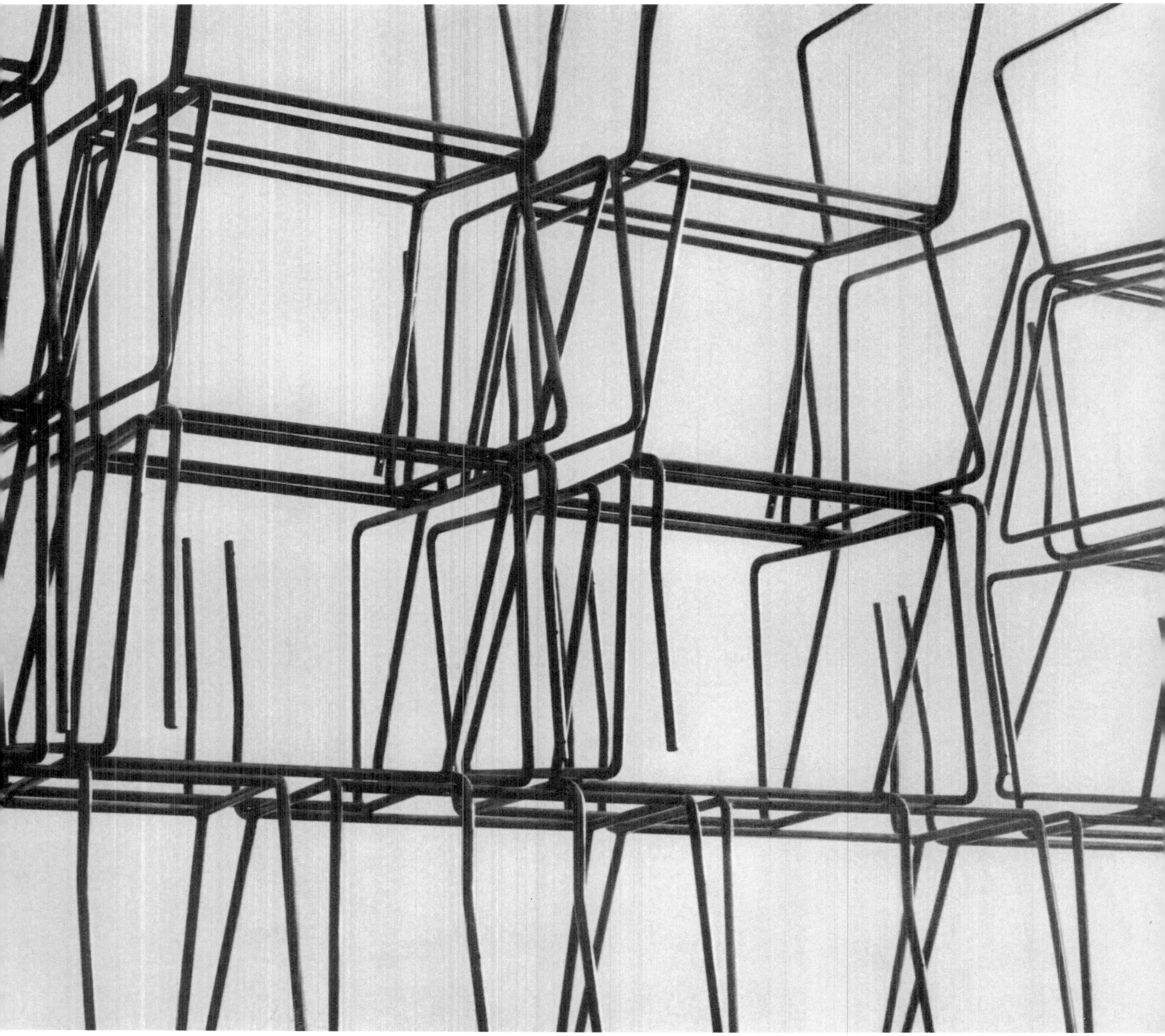

PLANT EXPANSIONS

The Wilhelm Knoll company, which generated a high share of exports, experienced a tremendous boom in the 1950s, built a huge factory hall the length of a soccer field and set up five new wood drying kilns.

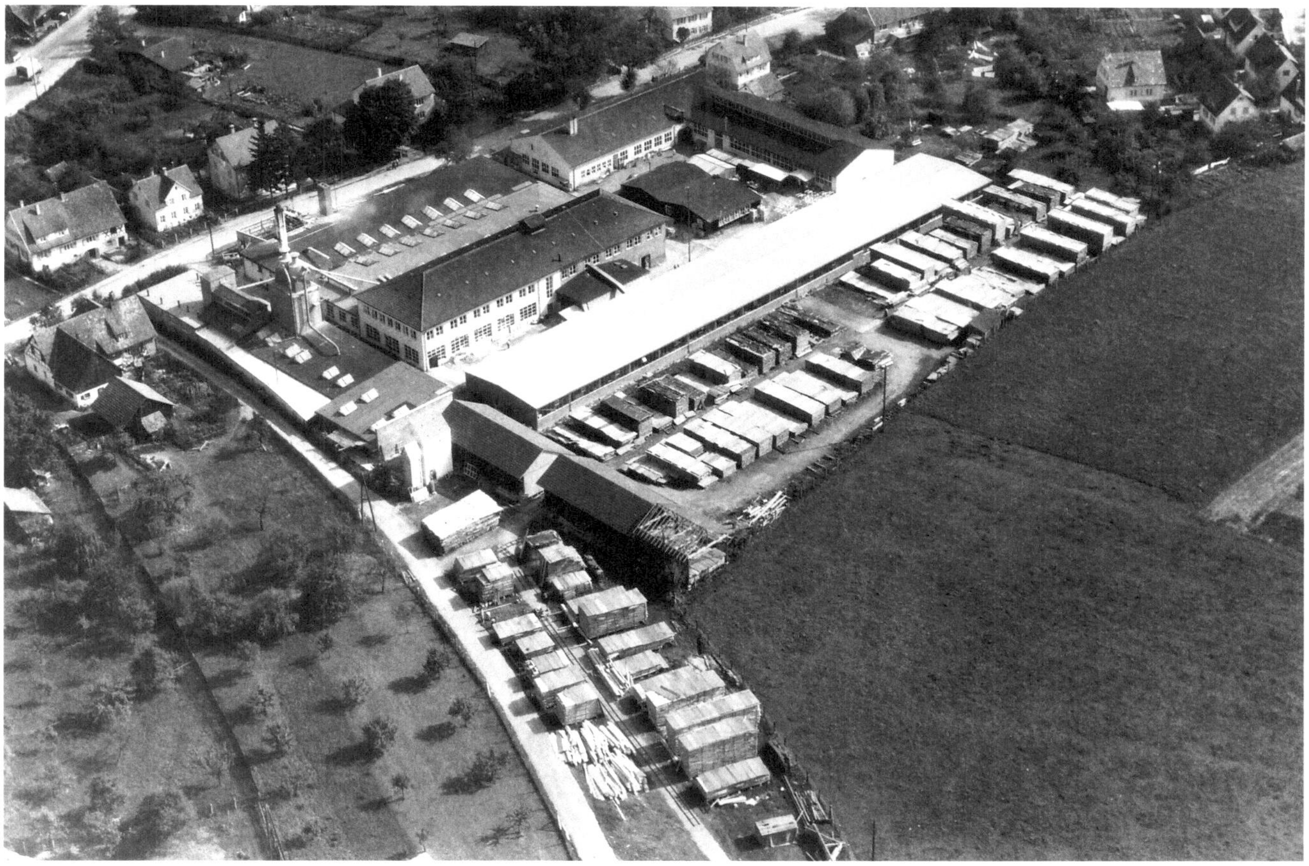

Wilhelm Knoll company, Gaildorf plant, 1959

Antimott catalog photo, tubular steel frames, Wilhelm Knoll, Stuttgart, 1959

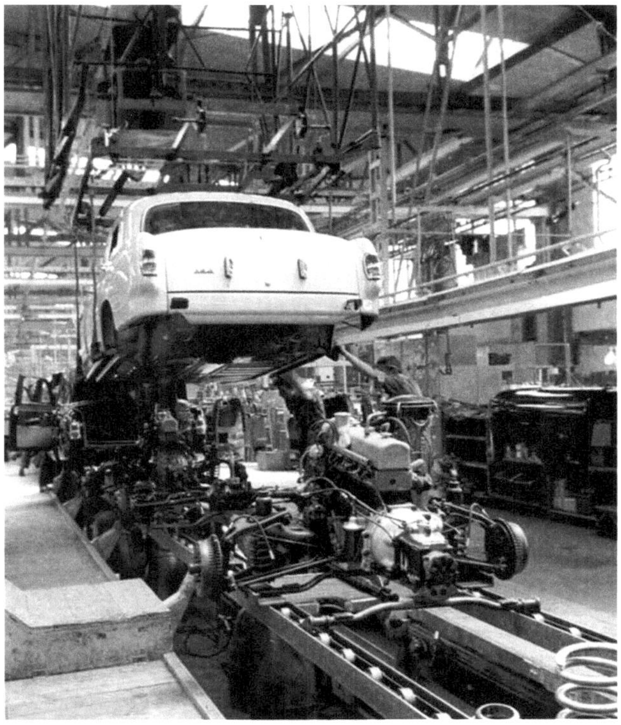

The Stuttgart region was an engine of the economic miracle: here the assembly line at the Mercedes-Benz car factory, Sindelfingen, 1956

And their hearts pounded for modernity. In this spirit, the nearly 80-year-old Walter Knoll and Arno Votteler in his mid-twenties, chatted together late into the evening, after everyone else had already left. The two were made for each other, an entrepreneur-designer pair like those who appear time and again in design history in moments of innovation when – provided the external circumstances are right – something new suddenly arises from a balance of similarity and difference. In that time, Arno Votteler produced several remarkable designs in quick succession, including highly modern bucket seats such as the 350 armchair. It consists of a patented double bucket on four splayed metal legs. It is distinguished by two recesses at seat height, which give the dainty chair a face.[48] This gives it a somewhat cheeky appearance, similar to some of the cartoon characters that were gaining in popularity at the time. However, the holes can also serve as handholds and make the 350 model "see-through" (and even lighter; see p. 138 f.) Much more innovation was hardly possible. By contrast, Votteler's model 368 is essentially a classic relaxing armchair, in other words an upholstered model like those that had a long tradition at Walter Knoll. Admittedly, he skilfully updated them. The high body seems to levitate above the fragile frame. The 368 has an elegant, sleek silhouette. In addition, there is one small, but striking, detail. The armrest, pointed like an arrow, is made of curved plywood, the preferred material of the time (see p. 156). The sleek decorative feature was a worthy

SMALL AND DELICATE, THE BUCKET SEAT 369 WAS ONE OF THE GREAT SUCCESSES OF THE 1950s.

emblem of progress. In the subsequent years, Votteler, who – on Walter Knoll's recommendation – would soon study under Hirche, also designed stands for the Cologne fair for Walter Knoll, at first only on a tiny floor space in a living room format, but with the greatest possible amount of creative energy, care, and precision from the outset.

Though small and delicate, the bucket seat 369 of 1956 was one of the great successes of the 1950s. Here, the individual elements of a traditional armchair blend together so perfectly that it becomes an abstract object, similar to a minimalist sculpture by Henry Moore. The almost circular aperture of the bucket seat and the triangular side silhouette provide a coherent form and a harmonious appearance (see p. 141). This is further underscored by the clear lines of the separately running tubular steel legs. It is possible to slide into the slightly backwards sloping bucket and, thanks

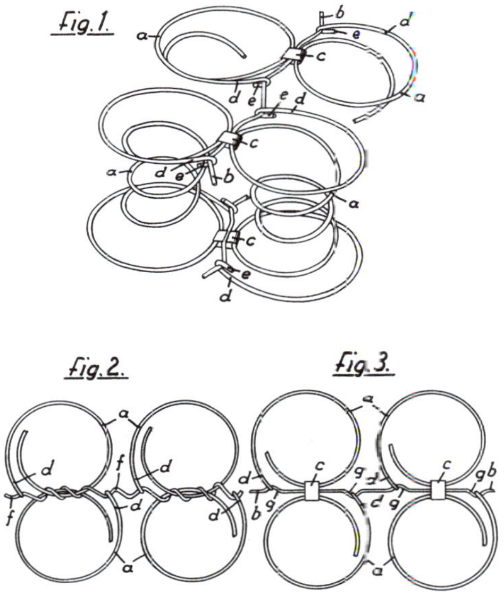

to the front lip, also slide out again. The reduced design, impressive in its coherence, was by Rolf Grunow, Votteler's successor as permanently hired interior designer since 1954. Grunow was employed at Walter Knoll for three years and then established himself as an independent designer in Herrenberg. Close collaboration with Walter Knoll continued until into the 1970s. The model 369, still in the product range today as a re-edition, was a bestseller right from the start, selling by the thousands, a minor sensation at the time. Striking simplicity had always been among Grunow's greatest strengths. The native Westphalian, who was reputedly as sparing with words as he was with his furniture designs, also proved this with his sofa bed 366. With its two upholstered oblongs, it is a quite graphic-looking object that embodied a type and preempted the imminent arrival of minimalism by a couple of years (see p. 157). Grunow was clearly a natural talent of the newly emerging Ulm School.

A handful of employed designers worked for Walter Knoll in succession during the 1950s, none of whom, however, was able to escape anonymity.[49] Even a certain Heinz Vetter, about whom not much is known besides the fact that he supposedly invented the kidney-shaped table in Herrenberg, for which he received no acclaim. Nevertheless, the disputed, but entirely practical, small side table with the iconic curved top was likely the most popular item of furniture during the years of the economic miracle. It would later be denounced as kitsch in purist circles. The catalogs of the mid-1950s mentioned the names of Herta-Maria Witzemann and Herbert Hirche, both academy luminaries, who would, however, also soon become unheard of otherwise.

During this period, Hirche developed rather modest music cabinets and televisions for the Frankfurt-based radio and electronics company Braun. Finally there were radio sets that were appropriate for the Second

Modernity and that architects did not have to conceal – as had been customary until then with the usual radio monstrosities. What was breaking forth here was nothing less than a total upheaval of the aesthetic criteria for everyday objects based on minimalistic principles. In this regard, the alliance that eventually arose between the radio manufacturer Braun and Hans Knoll comes as no surprise. Playing a leading role in the reinvention of objects, which would soon spread like wildfire, was the "Hochschule für Gestaltung Ulm" (Ulm School of Design), which provided comprehensive advice to the company Braun; as is generally known as one of the most fertile cooperations in design history. Herbert Hirche was also on the front lines of this frontal assault on grandpa's radio taking place at Braun. Of course, it was also a matter of resisting conservative sensibilities and the general poor taste that still haunted German homes at the time. Hirche designed lightweight seating furniture for Walter Knoll, all featuring a tubular steel frame, for example the dainty chair 361, whose conspicuously splayed and unusually close together rear legs are reminiscent of an insect (see p. 148 f.). He fitted desk chair 406 with narrow armrests that bent outwards, which subsequently also showed up on other models.[50] Hirche will have welcomed the fact that his furniture bore names consisting of neutral numbers. This was the common tendency during his time at the Bauhaus, after all. Hirche was a dedicated form rebel. For him, the explosive force lay in the clarity with which he intended to create objects that went beyond the ordinary. For this, he needed entrepreneurs who shared the same vision. The close friendship between Hirche and the junior boss Robert Knoll, so close that the families even went on vacation together, was no doubt also due to the fact that they were of roughly equal age. However, it was above all due to their passion for modernity, which could be unashamedly embraced as an ethos at the time.

The fact that Walter Knoll attracted young talents is shown by their origins. Herbert Hirche was a Lusatian, Rolf Grunow a Westphalian, and Herta-Maria Witzemann a Vorarlberger. Among the early works of the newcomers, which brought Witzemann renown in Stuttgart, was the "emergency housing" for Ferdinand Porsche, whose home had been bombed during the war. The young interior designer had a garage and the chauffeur's room at her disposal, where she had a fold-out sofa set up and installed spartan shelving systems in a tiny space. Photographs made this marvel famous. In this way, she made a name for herself. The Stuttgart Television Tower, which she furnished, was her ultimate breakthrough. It virtually raised her to celebrity status in Stuttgart. She was now an in-demand furnisher, including beyond the region. Lastly, she also furnished the official residence of the head of the German government, the "Kanzlerbungalow" (Chancellor's Bungalow) in Bonn. Herta-Maria Witzemann maintained relationships with political leaders. She considered it an aspect of concern of her mission. By contrast, in her numerous publications she stated that she wanted to "raise awareness of the cultural and social significance of the dwelling among broad sections of the population."[51] The Stuttgarter-by-choice had studied in Vienna under Oswald Haerdtl. Haerdtl, in turn, was a student of Josef Hoffmann, the renowned furniture reformer of Viennese Secessionism and pioneer of geometric furniture designs. In this way, Witzemann, who later lived in style in a summer house of the Rococo castle Solitude in Stuttgart, established a connection to another great metropolis of modernity. Her appreciation of the prestigious and the parsimonious, this charming blend of elegance and strictness, is certainly reflected in her works. Perhaps therein also lies the secret of her most successful furniture designs, the Forum 363 model, which she produced for Walter Knoll in 1956 (see p. 168 f.). Whether in concert halls, spa houses or shoe stores, this highly versatile chair could be found virtually everywhere – the workhorse of armchairs. Needless to say, numerous different versions were produced. Custom designs also came into being. For example: because the restaurant in the Stuttgart Television Tower has a round layout, the spacing between the rear legs had to be reduced. Witzemann maintained constant contact with the Knoll furniture family. This took on a quite different quality again when Michael Knoll, son of Robert and grandson of Walter Knoll, enrolled at the Stuttgart Academy in the mid-1960s to study under the grand dame of interior and furniture design.

When annual sales at Walter Knoll broke the four million barrier in 1954, the factory was expanded. There were now around two hundred employees working at the production facilities and the administration department in Herrenberg. At Wilhelm Knoll in Gaildorf, where the workforce had increased by more than half in a few years, there were actually 300. A factory hall longer than a soccer field would soon spring up here. Wilhelm Knoll had no longer been using the full company name since the mid-1920s. The company founder's first name, which evoked the last German emperor, was simply no longer suitable in an era that could be anything but old-fashioned. Instead, the catalogs succinctly referred to Knoll Antimott. Walter Knoll – where use of the family name was, of course, still not permitted – used the initials WK + CO, which were already familiar from the pre-war period.

---

48 ▶ Votteler thus pre-empted a similar design, a bucket seat that Eddie Harlis designed for Thonet, by two years. See: Polster 2008, p. 118.

49 ▶ This principle was maintained up until a few years ago. See Polster 2008, p. 124.

50 ▶ Such as armchair 358 and sofa 392. 392 was offered as the Vostra sofa, and was clearly a top-selling model.

51 ▶ Polster 2008, p. 563.

Catalog photo,
relaxing armchair 368,
now Votteler Chair,
Walter Knoll,
design by Arno Votteler,
Herrenberg, 1954,
manufactured 1956

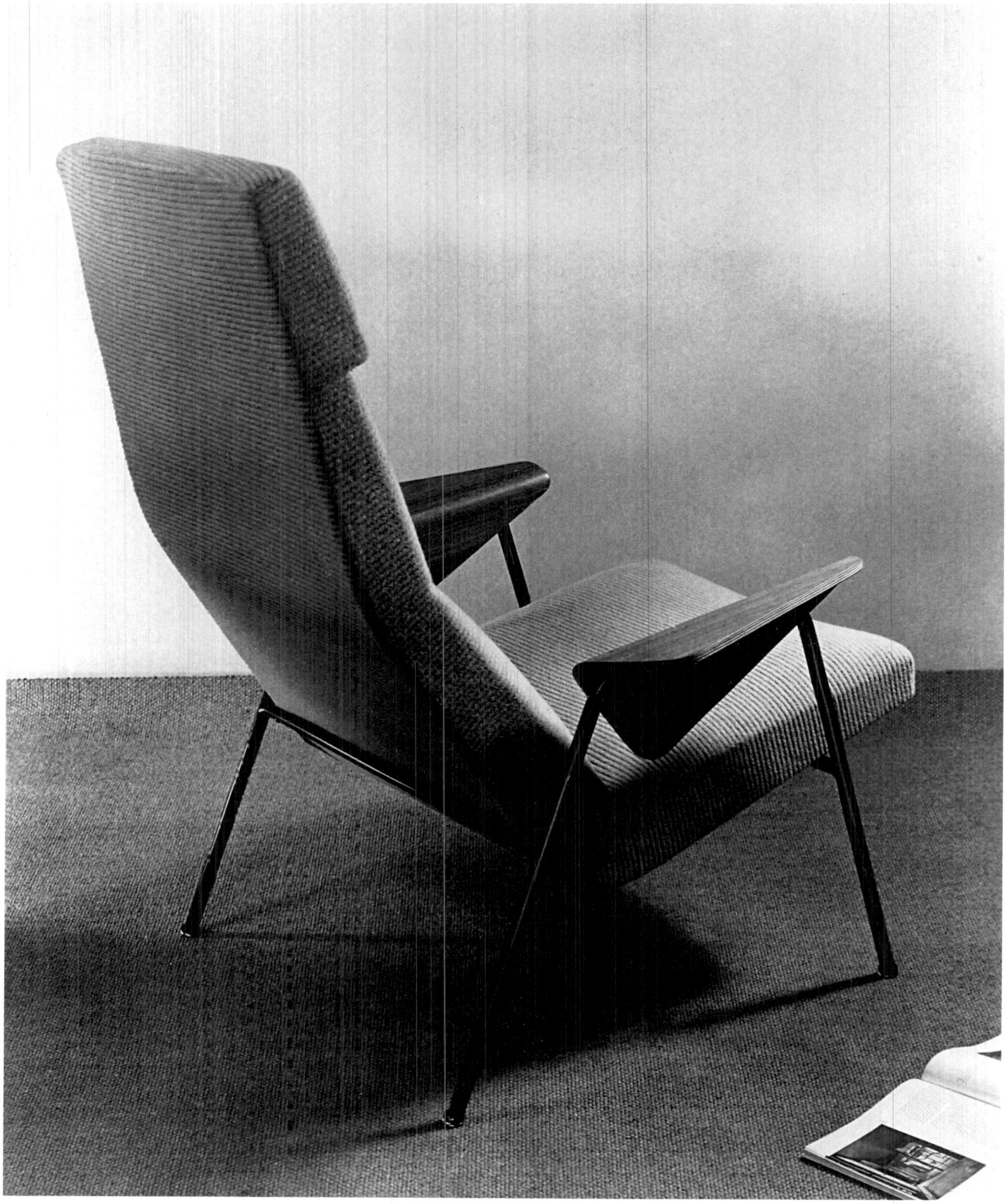

GUTE FORM – GOOD DESIGN

As the principle of *Gute Form* caught on, upholstered furniture was transformed. Walter Knoll developed an unprecedented number of new furniture types, including the model 368, nowadays known as the Votteler Chair, a modern variant of the reading and relaxing armchair.

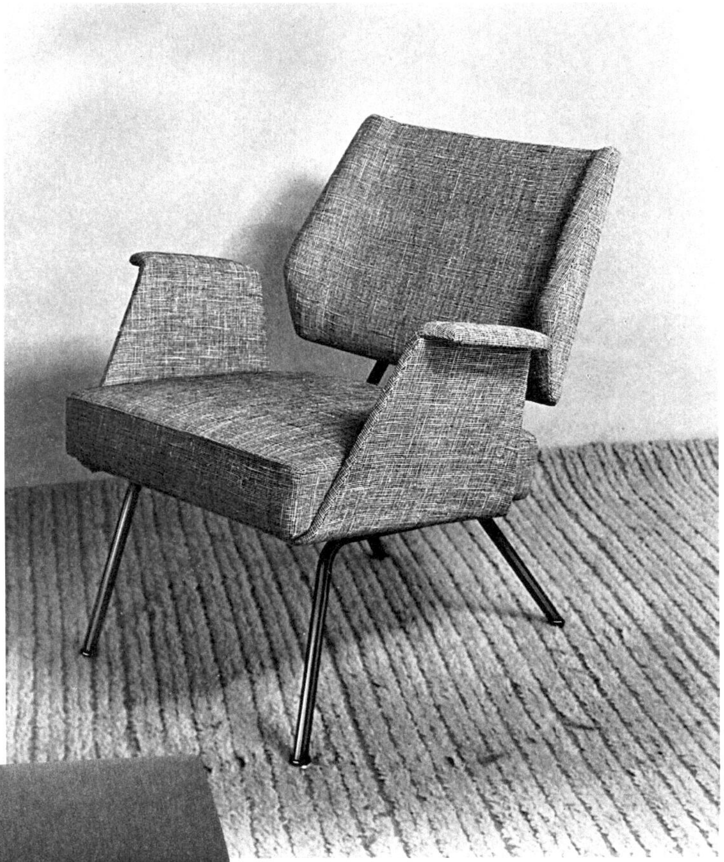

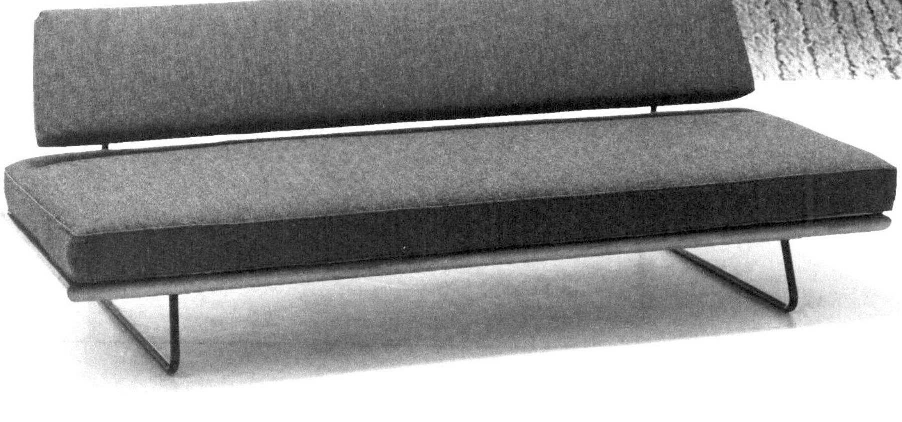

Catalog photo, armchair 358, Walter Knoll, design by Herbert Hirche, Herrenberg, 1954

Sofa bed 366, Walter Knoll, design by Rolf Grunow, Herrenberg, 1956

However, this had one serious disadvantage. It was confusingly similar to the name of the WK-Verband, a sales organization for modern furniture, with which business was even conducted. And that is probably the last thing that a logo should do. The workaround was "Herrenberger Sitzmöbel" (Herrenberg Seating Furniture). Using the site of the company's headquarters as a brand name was an unusual solution that reflected the company's strong identification with the location and the region.

In 1954, Walter and Maid Knoll moved into their new home in Herrenberg's Hildrizhauser Strasse. Until that point, they had always lived in rented premises. The fact that they did not have their home built in Stuttgart was, of course, also a symbolic gesture. The company founder stayed close to his factory and his workforce. The plans for the new construction were produced by Hans Volkart, a Stuttgart-born modernist and architect of the "Schauspielhaus" (Playhouse), a showpiece of the Second Modernity. He was involved in the reconstruction of the completely destroyed inner city of Heilbronn. Volkart, born in 1895 and therefore, like his employer, also a product of the pre-World War I era, had studied at the Stuttgart Academy and was one of those traditionalists who fought on the side of modernity after the war. The furniture patriarch and the successful architect were friends, and regularly met at the Rotary Club, which represented a bridge to Stuttgart and a kind of second home for Walter Knoll. The new home had an open floor plan with a central living area with the other rooms spread around it. This included a private library, which was particularly important to him. Even in those days, the low, single-story construction had a simple and modest appearance, unlike a factory owner's villa and nowhere near as radical as the houses in Weissenhof – although the brilliant white of the facade certainly brought them to mind. In several respects it was similar to the house that Theodor Heuss would have built as a retirement home on Stuttgart's Killesberg a couple of years later and which, owing to its small size and simplicity, would be commonly known as "Heuss's little house".[52] Knoll's little house was just as low-key, unspectacularly shrouded in green in the middle of a meadow orchard and, for precisely this reason, was described as exemplary in an article for the magazine "Architektur und Wohnform" (Architecture and Dwelling Form). "The resulting homely microcosm", enthused the specialist journal, was a "Tusculum of contemplative tranquility."[53] Thanks to "Papa Heuss", the human dimension was clearly in fashion at the time. The magazine was an institution, and for half a century had acted as a mouthpiece for the movement of modernity, appearing in the Reform Period before the First World War under the title "Innen-Dekoration" (Interior Decoration). "Architektur und Wohnform" (Architecture and Dwelling Forms) had by now turned into a compendium of the Second Modernity with the familiar blend of art, architecture and living. Readers of the magazine and customers of Walter Knoll were largely the same people. Unsurprisingly, its subscribers included members of the "Deutscher Werkbund" (German Association of Craftsmen), and also Walter Knoll. That the bookshelves of former "Werkbund" secretary Heuss contained every issue goes without saying. Naturally, he also had a private library in his little house. The magazine was published by Alexander Koch Junior, owner of the Stuttgart publishing house of the same name, a journalistic complement to the already close-knit infrastructure of modernity.[54] Koch was friends with Robert Knoll, with whom he had a lot in common. Besides a great deal of culture and the associated ideals of modernity, the two sons of strong founding fathers also shared the sometimes bitter experiences of a world war generation whose early years had been marked by the two major catastrophes of the 20th century.

DEATH OF A VISION

1955 saw the establishment of the "Verbundkreis" (Network Circle), a now largely forgotten initiative of committed companies that regarded themselves as a lobby for *Gute Form* (Good Design). Exemplary products were selected by a jury, consisting of the bosses of the involved companies, and sent on an annual traveling exhibition around the country. Knoll International also participated in this awareness-raising campaign. This fitted right into Hans Knoll's overall strategy, and his identity shaped in Germany. Among the jurors were distinguished entrepreneurs such as Philip Rosenthal and Erwin Braun, leading figures of the *Gute Form* movement and sons of entrepreneurs, like himself, who were pursuing their own paths. When Braun AG made an appearance at the Düsseldorf Radio Exhibition under the aegis of the "Hochschule für Gestaltung Ulm" (Ulm School of Design) in the same year, which the press and the competition perceived as the storming of the Bastille of kitsch and would go down as a turning point in the annals of design history, its sensational trade fair stand was furnished with Knoll furniture. This collaboration, largely forgotten today, was later continued in the showrooms that Braun established in various large German cities. A key contributor to this – with both his furniture for Walter Knoll and his phonographs for Braun – was Herbert Hirche. The Knoll furniture family was also present in this great moment in design history. Hans Knoll evidently also saw his company Knoll International as a part of the newly emerging German design scene. As successor to his brother Robert in the role of managing director in Stuttgart, he appointed a certain Toby E. Rodes, a Frankfurt-born cosmopolitan and shrewd public relations expert who had spent several years living in the USA. After 1945, Rodes, now employed by the U.S. government, was assigned the responsible task of bringing home the blessings of the Marshall Plan to the Germans. Which was not too difficult. The fact that this public relations pro did not get on particularly well with his employer's father in Herrenberg, would likely have remained just a footnote. However, as other apparent trivialities coincided, misfortune took its course.

Hans Knoll, who, due to the furnishing of the American embassy, was staying in the Cuban capital of Havana in October 1955, died there in dramatic fashion in a traffic accident. A tanker truck that had lost control on a steeply sloping road rolled over his open-top sports car and exploded. Hans Knoll was killed immediately – as was his female passenger friend. The causes and exact circumstances of this mysterious chain of happenstances have never been clarified. In any case, the German-American Knoll was operating in a precarious environment. At the time, Cuba, a corrupt dictatorship, was a stronghold of the American Mafia, which maintained contact with the political world. And Hans had personal relationships that extended into the highest circles of government. Naturally, the sudden and violent death of their son was a heavy blow to his parents, and the entire family. However, besides the human tragedy, it also represented a deep caesura in the history of the Knoll furniture dynasty. The close ties between the American and the

THE CLOSE TIES BETWEEN THE AMERICAN AND GERMAN BRANCHES OF THE KNOLL FURNITURE DYNASTY WOULD UNRAVEL ONCE AND FOR ALL FOLLOWING THE DEATH OF HANS KNOLL.

German branches, which had been so crucial for Hans and which he had established so skillfully, would unravel once and for all. There were several reasons for this. The family was now paying a heavy price for Robert Knoll's departure from Stuttgart, which meant they had lost all influence on Knoll International. Due to the troubled relations between Walter Knoll and Toby E. Rodes – the pair fiercely clashed once again immediately after Hans' death[55] – it was only a question of time before Rodes would terminate the collaboration and stop awarding contracts to Herrenberg. When he subsequently relocated the European headquarters to Basel, Stuttgart lost the special position that Hans Knoll had intended for his home city. Florence Knoll, who would be the sole owner of Knoll Associates for some years, did not pursue Hans Knoll's dynastic plans. She had no connection to Stuttgart whatsoever. There were, however, other reasons why she stepped away. Hans and Florence Knoll had by then already been divorced. They had kept it to themselves and

KNOLL ASSOCIATES
INCORPORATED

continued as though nothing had happened. After his death, therefore, Florence did not feel a particularly strong sense of motivction to emphasize the "ideal Knoll legacy" in one way or another, which, of course, was the genesis of her own company. For this reason, the image of Hans Knoll had already begun to fade during her time. The founder, who had been the undisputed protagonist, was now being diminished little by little to the role of an inconsequential secondary character. In 1965, Florence Knoll left the company that she had been running for ten years and sold it to a corporate group. The new management showed no interest in seeking the roots of her expanding company in the modernity that had originated in Germany, nor did they have any profound knowledge of it. The Knoll name was now nothing more but a brand. Some time around 1970, Knoll Associates was renamed Knoll International, with the name of the Stuttgart branch being quietly applied to the whole company.[56] This barely noticed occurrence illustrates the connection that has since disappeared from, or was quite thoroughly written out of, the self-image and company history of the American Knoll branch. The visions and achievements of its founder Hans Knoll were marginalized. What they were based on – his background – and what they consisted of – his personality and his concepts – is only vaguely recognized today.

52 ▶ The fact that furniture by Walter Knoll also stood inside shall only be mentioned in passing here.

53 ▶ "Architektur und Wohnform" (Architecture and Dwelling Form), December 1956 (Volume 56), No. 2.

54 ▶ The publishing company was founded in 1890 by his father Alexander Koch senior, one of the protagonists of the Reform movement, who pushed for and commented on housing reform in his magazines.

55 ▶ Rodes had drawn up a death notice without the father's permission.

56 ▶ In 1967, two years after Florence Knoll's departure, the company was still being promoted under the old name in Europe.

STATE TRADE OFFICE

The Stuttgart "Landesgewerbeamt" (State Trade Office), which developed a new model of economic promotion with cultural underpinnings, also exhibited the new world of furniture.

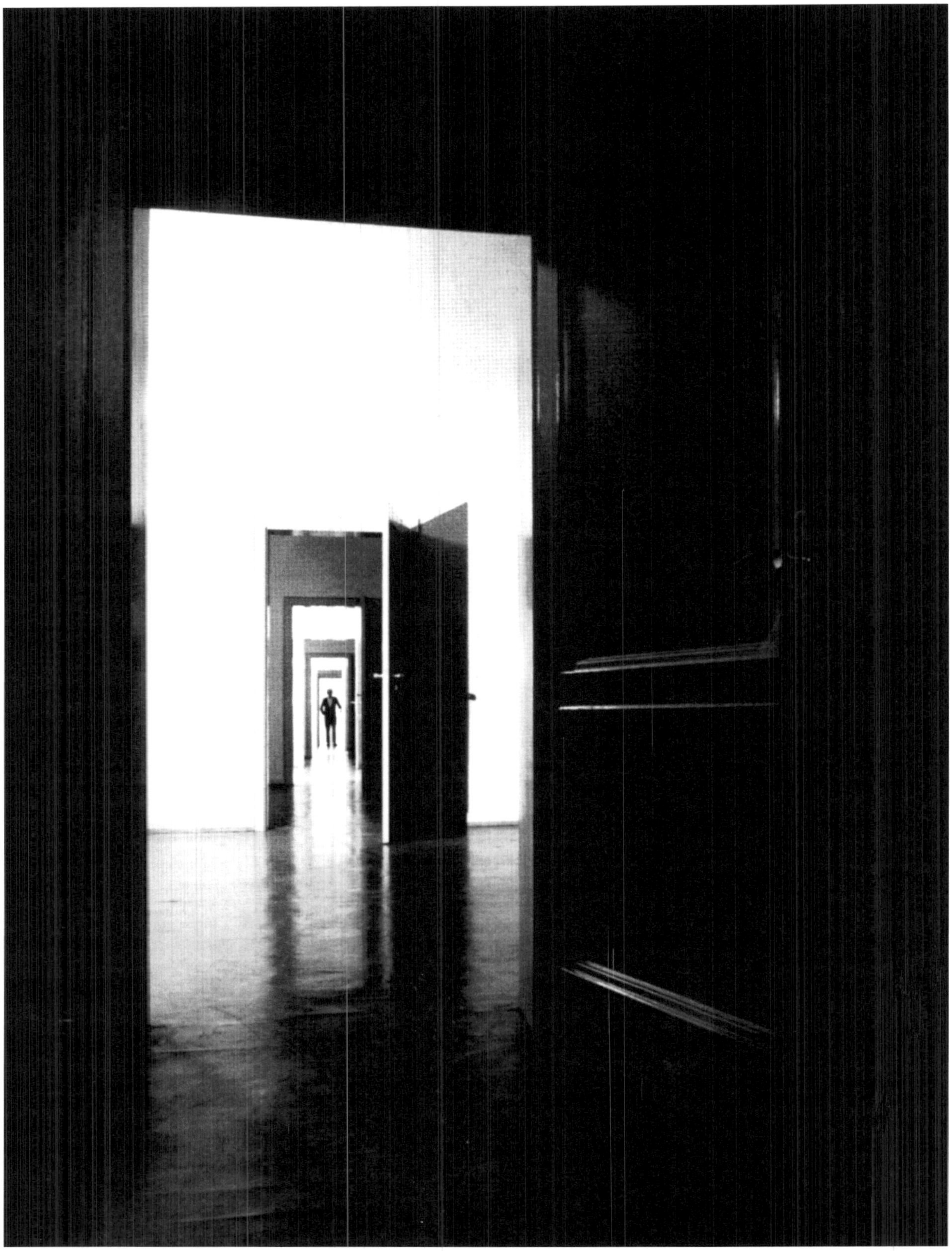

"Landesgewerbeamt" (State Trade Office), photograph by Franz Lazi, Stuttgart, 1951

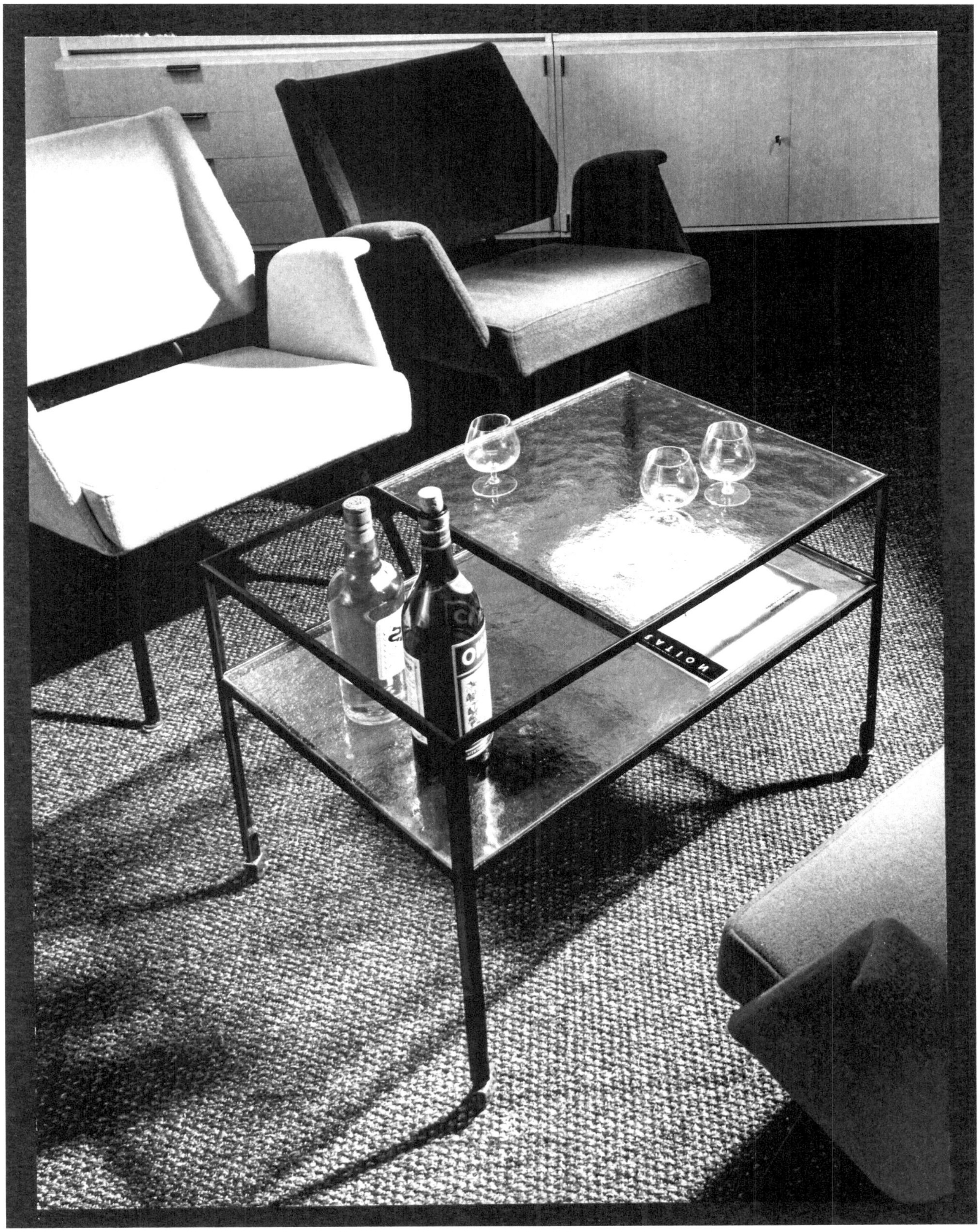

Exhibition at the "Landesgewerbeamt" (State Trade Office), armchair 358, Walter Knoll, bar trolley, Christian Holzäpfel, all designed by Herbert Hirche, photograph by Franz Lazi, Stuttgart, 1956

"Hans had countless stories, but nobody could confirm them,"[57] states an extensive history of the textile division of Knoll Inc., the current name of Hans Knoll's erstwhile company. It continues: "And nobody was really interested."[58] An astonishing statement. After all, it is diametrically opposed to all other contemporaries who knew him and, of course, also to the historical facts. To what extent the extensive exclusion of Hans Knoll, who, on the contrary, was, of course, "the motivating force behind the company"[59] – his company – has systematically distorted perspectives on its history, is unknown. Because nobody has asked this question until now.

At Hans Knoll's funeral in Herrenberg on 11/16/1955, two obituaries were read, one by his father and one by Mr. Woernle, a friend of the family. In his speech Walter Knoll reflected on the principles of success that had been behind Hans' ascendancy. In particular, he referred to the "highly qualified employees from all over the world"[60] and his "personal relationship"[61] with them. The fact that everyone had addressed him as "Hans" must have come as quite a surprise to the old man. Woernle, the second speaker, who briefly outlined the breathtaking ups and downs of Hans' life, also made clear that he had, of course, been "the engine of the company."[62] However, rather unusually, details were also mentioned at this solemn occasion that had been previously unknown to most of the attendees. For example, Walter Knoll alluded to a walk that he had taken with his son on the Schlossberg hill during Hans' final stay in Herrenberg. On this occasion, Hans tellingly informed his father of "grave personal circumstances that cast a shadow on his future life."[63] He – the brilliant achiever – had therefore become a "person living in isolation."[64] Hans had also previously mentioned this several times in his letters to his parents. Hans, the beaming winner, also had a different side. He was lonely and unhappy. How did this go together? Did he tell his father on the walk that he was already divorced from Florence? Two marriages had broken down in short succession. Was his lack of success as husband down to him having other tendencies, namely that he was homophile? And was this perhaps also the reason why he secluded himself? Intimations in Woernle's eulogy mentioning his "fatherly friend" Winthrop and a "devoted circle of friends" hint in this direction. He was a significant entrepreneur who had established modern furniture design in America not only because he knew how to sell it, but also because he attracted an illustrious circle of creatives to his company and bound them to it. To the present day, due to his early death and the new company constellation, his outstanding achievements, his flamboyant personality and his movie-like life have not even begun to be appreciated in all their far-reaching significance, not only for the history of design and furniture, but also for modernity as a whole. As a result, its acknowledgment as an integral part of the Knoll furniture dynasty, in which the DNA of modernity was embedded, also faded from view.

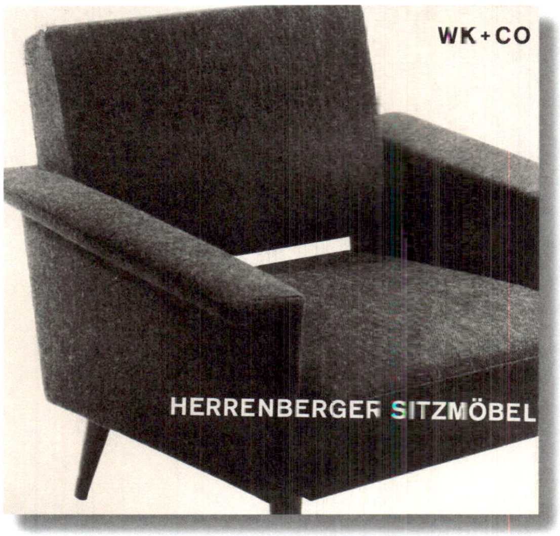

Maja and Peter, the children of Hans Knoll, sometimes still visited their grandparents at the edge of the Black Forest. The following story is told about Peter: his dream car was a former GI Porsche. His grandfather, essentially thrift personified, who never owned a sports car himself, was, however, simply unable to refuse his grandson this not exactly cheap object of his heart's desire. They picked up the sleek 356 model together in Zuffenhausen. The superbly equipped Becker car radio alone cost as much as a small automobile. Afterwards, the proud grandfather introduced his grandson from America to his friends at the Rotary Club. Peter Knoll, who is believed to have later tried his hand as a racing driver, developed no interest in the company whatsoever, just like his sister Maja.

THE GOLDEN YEARS

It was a mild day in the fall of 1956. Above the reddish-yellow leaves of the forests in the Gäu region there was, as if by order, a bright blue sky. On 20th October, Walter Knoll turned 80. The jubilarian celebrated this round date at the "Centraltheater," a large movie theater a short distance from the factory. The guests were put in the mood by a quartet in B-flat major by Mozart for two violins, viola and cello. Then a dozen speakers took to the microphone one after the other, including representatives from the business world and the state government, Herrenberg's mayor, son Robert, and Hans Volkart, the Rotarian and architect of Walter Knoll's new home. As the last speech-giver, Mr. Veigel, Chairman of the Works Council, passed on the gratitude and best wishes of the workforce. Although Walter Knoll deeply rejected all forms of pomp, it virtually inevitably turned into an audience with a furniture monarch. And as his company had just come into full bloom, he had no intention of abdicating yet, despite his advanced age. Right at the end, the patriarch himself rose to speak. "Undaunted by the weight of tributes and praise, but moved to the very depths of his soul by this abundance of faith, the luminary then took to the podium himself," remembered his friend Volkart.[65] "He pledged to pursue the established path and to continue to work hard. With this simple commitment, the 80-year-old revealed his true nature in the most direct way possible." The festivities then concluded with variations on "Haydn's Kaiserquartett" (Emperor Quartet) and the soft tones of the emperor's anthem "Gott erhalte Franz den Kaiser" (God save Emperor Francis). A cocktail party was later held in the new house on Hildrizhauser Strasse. And as it was a mild fall evening, it was possible to celebrate on the terrace and under the apple trees. After all, there was every reason to drink to a highly successful year.

Following a period of rapid expansion, Walter and Wilhelm Knoll both brought out high-quality catalogs for the first time in the mid-1950s, reflecting not only the model development but also their own self-identity. Both used practical spiral binding, but were otherwise significantly

THE PREDILECTION FOR ANYTHING SCANDINAVIAN THAT THE PUBLIC HAD DEVELOPED IN THE MEANTIME, WAS DEMONSTRATED NOT LEAST BY THE STEADY INCREASE IN THE USE OF WOOD.

different.[66] Walter Knoll's "Sitzmöbel für die Wohnung von heute" (Seating Furniture for the Dwelling of Today) catalogs in a small square format look like artistic illustrated coffee table books. They only contain two image formats, portrait and landscape, all in the same size. They were printed in high gloss on thick cardboard. For this reason, the length was restricted to just 20 to 30 pages. Consequently, the selection of models had to be strong. The catalogs are undated.[67] Presumably out of the conviction that they were timeless.

By contrast, the catalogs with black covers that Wilhelm Knoll brought out from 1956 were vintage volumes in a landscape A4 format. They were titled "Knoll Antimott." They provided a comprehensive overview of the furniture range of the time.[68] Their length steadily increased over time, reaching just under 100 pages by 1959. It represented a lavish guide through by far the company's largest and most varied furniture range to date. The company allowed an elaborate design consisting of consistent spot color, full-page illustrative photos, staged interiors featuring pretty young ladies, numerous close-ups, and several technical drawings for furniture with special functions. This included, for example, an extensive range of couches based on the Antimott. Particular emphasis was placec on this modular system, which came with elements such as side parts, seat backs and foot shapes in numerous combinable variants. With its numerous folding mechanisms, extension options and corner solutions, it tied in with old Swabian inventor virtues. It would also turn out to be a building block for business successes of the future.

The ambitious couch range was a system based on wooden frames. The predilection for anything Scandinavian that the public had developed in the meantime, was demonstrated not least by the steady increase in the use of wood. Thanks to numerous exhibitions, the handicraft of the Nordic countries, whose naturalness and charm was greatly admired, had also become popular in America and the rest of Europe.[69] It was already more a lifestyle than a passing trend, especially in Germany, where a soft spot for anything Nordic already had tradition from the days of the *Lebensreform* (Life Reform). The designers, back then either craftsmen or architects, became idols, with names such as Alvar Aalto, Arne Jacobsen, Bruno Mathsson, or Hans Wegner being widely known.

---

57 ▶ Martin, 2011, p. 74.

58 ▶ Ibid.

59 ▶ Fehrmann 2009, p. 66.

60 ▶ Knoll, n.d., p. 112.

61 ▶ Ibid.

62 ▶ Ibid.

63 ▶ Knoll, n.d., p. 107.

64 ▶ Ibid.

65 ▶ Log by Hans Volkart, October 1956; WK archives.

66 ▶ While Walter Knoll focused on individual models, at Wilhelm Knoll the emphasis was on armchairs and sofas, which were almost always offered as a suite. At the time, they were part of the basic furnishings of a middle-class home. Tubular steel frames, which accounted for the main part of the catalog at Walter Knoll, were, by contrast, very rarely used at Wilhelm Knoll (and then usually only as one variant of many).

67 ▶ Judging by the furniture shown inside, the variant shown in the top left may have appeared around 1956. The models produced under license by Cassina from 1958 are not yet included.

68 ▶ The last available volume is from 1961.

69 ▶ See Polster 1999, p. 427.

TRANSITIONS
In the 1950s, Walter Knoll was open to new ideas: it was the first German company to adopt Italian design in its own catalog and supported the "Hochschule für Gestaltung Ulm" (Ulm School of Design), an experimental laboratory of new forms. The model 375 was a modern interpretation of the cocktail chair.

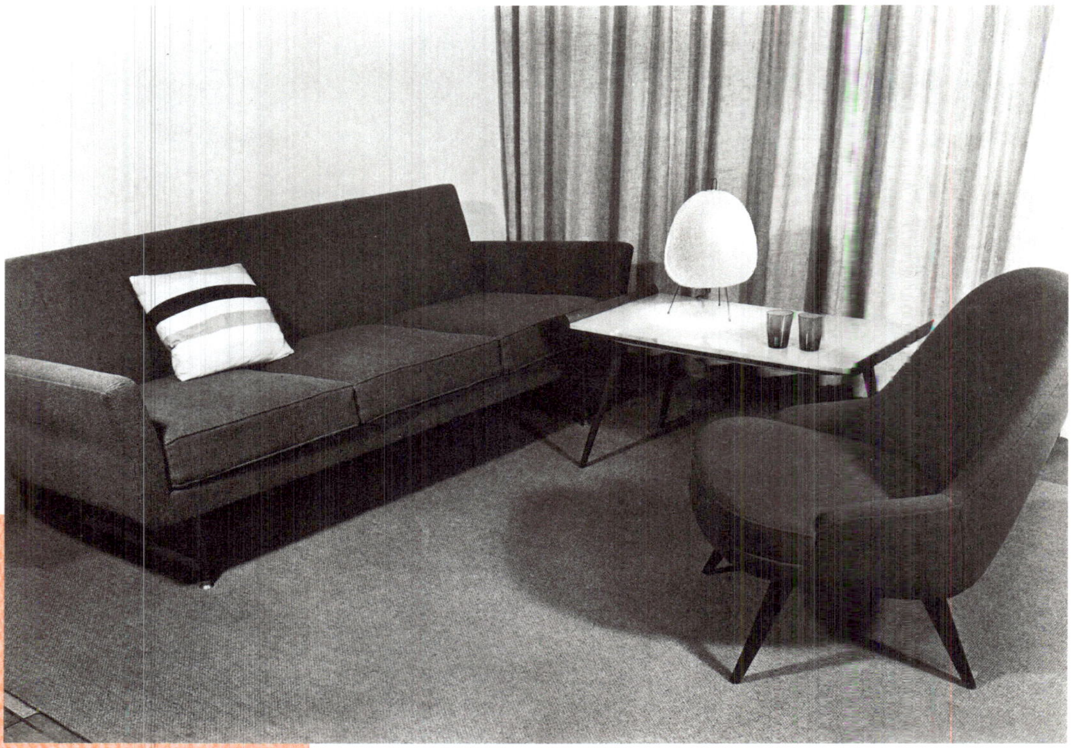

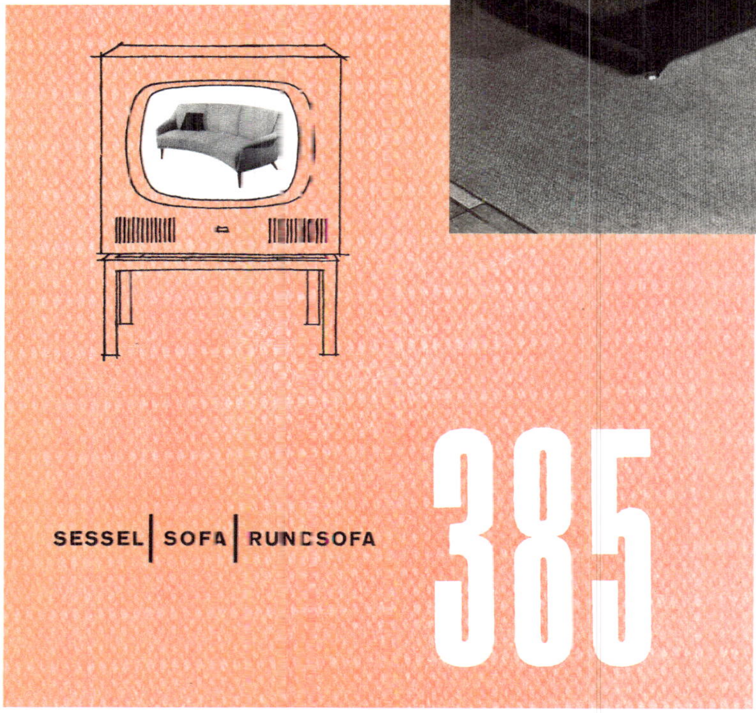

Catalog photo,
sofa 377, Walter Knoll,
design by Friedrich Hill,
Herrenberg, 1960;
armchair 375, Walter Knoll,
Herrenberg, 1957

Brochure cover photo,
Cassina 385, Walter Knoll,
design by Carlo de Carli,
Herrenberg, around 1957

Neue Telefonnummer 68575

Geschwister-Scholl-Stiftung Hochschule für Gestaltung Ulm Telefon 6575

Inge Aicher-Scholl

Herrn
Robert Knoll
i.Fa.Walter Knoll & Co.
H e r r e n b e r g
Württemberg

El[illegible] ,angen
29. DEZ. 1958

22. Dezember 1958

Sehr geehrter, lieber Herr Knoll,

gerade, als ich über der Verteilung unserer sehr bescheidenen Mittel des Stipendienfonds für die zahlreichen Anträge unserer Studierenden brütete, kam mit der Nachmittagspost Ihr liebenswürdiges Schreiben, in dem Sie mich über das Versehen bei der diesjährigen Überweisung Ihres Stipendiums aufklären. Ein paar Stunden später brachte der Bote auch noch den Scheck über DM 2ooo.-. Wie soll ich Ihnen meine Freude schildern?!

Ich habe Herrn Weiss sofort die gute Nachricht und Ihren Wunsch, ihn einmal im Januar in Herrenberg zu sprechen, mitgeteilt. Herr Weiss wird Sie sehr gerne besuchen kommen und dankt Ihnen mit mir und der ganzen Schulleitung für Ihre Hilfe.

Würde Ihnen ein Freitagnachmittag im Januar für den Besuch von Herrn Weiss passen und wären Sie so freundlich, ihm einen Termin zu nennen?

Mit nochmaligem, herlichen Dank und den besten Wünschen für Weihnachten und das Neue Jahr verbleibe ich
Ihre

Inge Aicher-Scholl

(Inge Aicher-Scholl)

Dipl. Ing. Herbert Ohl

P.S. Ich erlaube mir noch, eine Bescheinigung über die Steuerabzugsfähigkeit Ihrer Stiftung beizufügen.

an Herrn Belle am 16.1.59

Anlage

Letter from Inge Aicher-Scholl, co-founder of the "Hochschule für Gestaltung Ulm" (Ulm School of Design), to Robert Knoll, Ulm, 1958

Despite current retro trends, this mass phenomenon is nowadays only remembered by those who experienced it for themselves. New kinds of chairs and armchairs emerged. In particular Danish seating furniture, in which organic forms mixed tradition, elegance and eccentricity, gained absolute cult status.[70] When Wilhelm Knoll offered an armchair by a Finn for the first time, the designer's name was even placed underneath it.[71] Such a great honor had never been bestowed on anyone before (and subsequently never would be again). Though hard to imagine nowadays, the fervor with which the Nordic taste prevailed in those years can be clearly gleaned from the catalogs of the time of both German Knoll companies. Walter Knoll eventually brought out a brochure on the topic, extolling "the diversity and natural beauty of wood".[72] "Scrapes and scratches disrupt a metal surface," it read. "With wood, they look like runes and lovable wrinkles."[73] Both light birch and dark teak, a specialty of the Danes, achieved popularity. Swabian teak was cherry wood. Due to the large number of round bars, additional wood turners had to be hired. The careful polishing of the complex wooden parts with their frequently irregular characteristics was now one of the most perspiration-inducing and time-consuming activities performed at the joineries. The wood boom took on such proportions at Wilhelm Knoll that six new drying kilns had to be set up in Gaildorf. The company now saw itself as a specialist in visible frames made of wood.

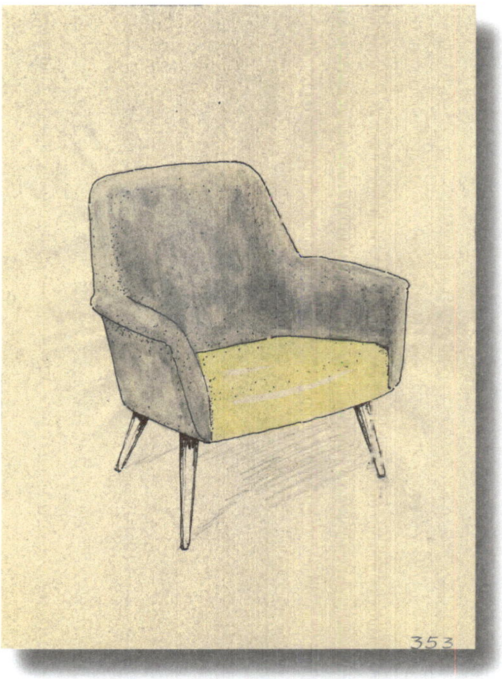

"ESPECIALLY IN THE CASE OF SEATING FURNITURE THE OUTER FORM, THE CONTOURS, ARE OF CRUCIAL IMPORTANCE." WALTER KNOLL

Besides the Nordic countries, there was another nation that caused a sensation at the furniture fair in Cologne on a regular basis. That was Italy. Denmark and Italy would soon provide the largest foreign contingents in Cologne (and still do to this day). New furniture fairs in Copenhagen and Milan competed with the German original. Even though neither Walter nor Wilhelm Knoll exhibited there in those days, annual trips to Italy and Scandinavia were now mandatory events that nobody wanted to miss. During one of his trips to Milan, Walter Knoll established contact with the Cassina company, where brothers Cesare, Umberto and Franco Cassina, along with their sister Adele, were working together at the time. This family business impressed him. As did the lean Superleggera chair by Gio Ponti, which the company from the small town of Meda near Milan had just brought out. It was a worldwide success. However, it was not models by Ponti, rather his student Carlo de Carli and his architect colleague Gianfranco Frattini (both graduates of the Polytechnic University of Milan), that were produced under license in Herrenberg from 1958. In any case, the Germans from the Gäu region were thus the first to begin Italianizing their product range over a number of years. This had long been customary in the European automobile industry by this point in time. In those days, few European brands were willing to pass up on designs by Italian sheet metal virtuosos. A certain Bruno Sacco from Udine, the future chief designer, had just been hired at Mercedes-Benz. Southern flair not only made the collection more interesting, but also ensured internal learning effects. After all, as far as beauty, elegance and finesse were concerned, Italian companies like Cassina were now seen as great role models. However, the learning effect was by no means a one-way street – one of the strengths of Italian design lay in its openness to stimuli from outside.[74] And German role models played a major role on both sides of the Alps.[75] Could it, therefore, not have been Walter Knoll, this committed modernist (who personally knew some of the representatives of the Bauhaus and Weissenhof era), who inspired the Cassina siblings with pre-war modern designs, leading them to produce the I Maestri collection that they would bring onto the market a few years later?

The timing certainly suggests such an exchange of ideas between North and South.

Meanwhile, exciting developments were gaining momentum in Germany. The "Hochschule für Gestaltung Ulm" (Ulm School of Design) had moved into its new building, located outside the city on a hill, that would be seen as a laboratory of things, in the truest sense a stronghold of design. All manner of useful things originated there, such as the van, stackable tableware, the stereo system, and the modular gas station. Lastly, prompted by Inge Aicher-Scholl, there was also an exchange of ideas between Ulm and Herrenberg concerning upholstered furniture. Herbert Ohl, one of the numerous creative figures that had been drawn to Ulm (he was the last rector of the "Hochschule für Gestaltung Ulm"), sent Walter Knoll his ideas about seating in general and, in particular, upholstered furniture. Under the not merely academic sounding heading "Grundsätze: Industrielle Fertigung, Integrale Konstruktion, Universale Anwendung" (Principles: Industrial production, Integral design, Universal application), he developed a modular seating system, using 3D line drawings over 48 pages, that was as systematic as it was complicated (see p. 178). "It is clear to us that innumerable variants of the modular system – as you have outlined – can be built using such structural elements," responded Walter Knoll.[76] Only then to object: "However, it is unclear how such elements can be used to develop forms that appeal to a large part of the buying audience and enable a step back from purely structural and functional aspects."[77] Walter Knoll was in his early eighties, Herbert Ohl in his late twenties. Design galaxies separated the two. However, not only were a moderate modernist and an analytical world changer coming into conflict here, but also a person who had as yet never had anything to do with upholstered furniture and another who knew it from top to bottom. "Especially in the case of seating furniture," the expert explained to the novice, "the outer form, the contours, are of crucial importance and are the deciding factor, as has been proven around the entire world by the successes of the Scandinavian chairs, for example. The structural elements are more or less interesting for the technician and the manufacturer, while regular buyers are primarily interested in pleasant lines and comfort." The experienced pragmatist was highly skeptical, but did not shut the door. Rather, he inquired "whether, before we continue our discussion, you do not see an opportunity to sketch out how good formal solutions can be developed using your sandwich panels." Whether the lateral thinking Ohl, who soon became one of the first in his profession to relocate to Italy, later developed the mesh-covered armchair and eventually became professor of Automobile Design in Pforzheim, replied again, is unknown. Is it possible that the exchange between the two antagonists might actually have brought about revolutionary innovations? In fact, the rationalism cultivated in Ulm would soon gain widespread acceptance, including in the realm of upholstered furniture, and, like a storm, would sweep away all traces of decoration and cosiness.

Abb.1.

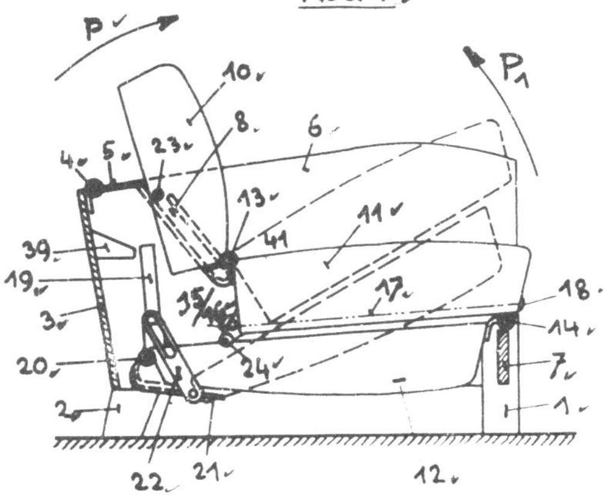

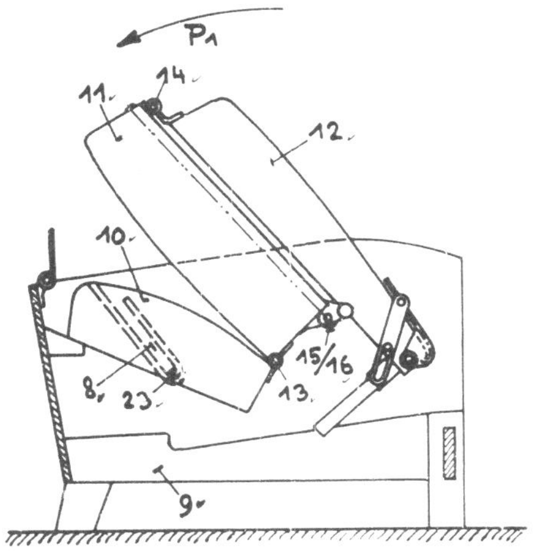

Abb.2.

70 ▶ Alongside many others, the Danes Finn Juhl and Hans Wegner were masters of the artfully shaped chair. However, the Swede Bruno Mathsson and the Finn Alvar Aalto were also popular.

71 ▶ See Wilhelm Knoll catalog, 1960.

72 ▶ Wooden seating furniture, undated, WK archives.

73 ▶ Ibid.

74 ▶ The Scandinavian influence on Italian design is an, as yet, largely unexplored subject.

75 ▶ Tubular steel furniture from Germany was already in high demand in Italy prior to the Second World War.

76 ▶ Walter Knoll, Letter from 5/12/1959, WK archives.

77 ▶ Ibid.

FORUM

When the Stuttgart Television Tower was opened as a first of its kind in the world in 1956, seating furniture by Walter Knoll was also premiered. The versatile Forum chair, with which the tower restaurant is furnished, became a bestseller.

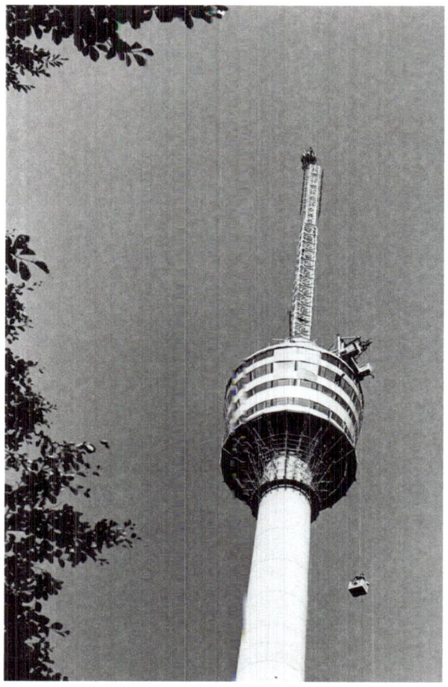

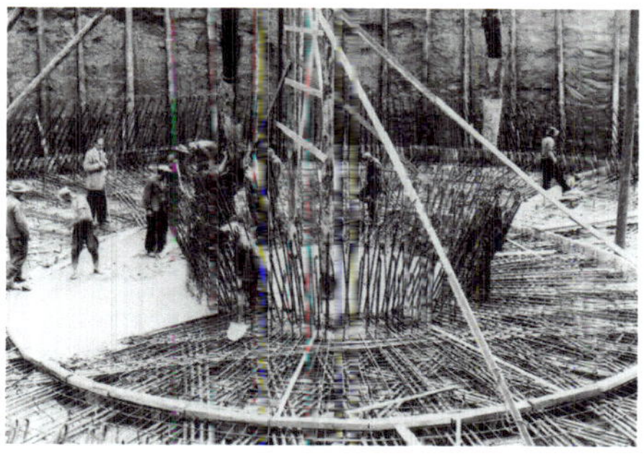

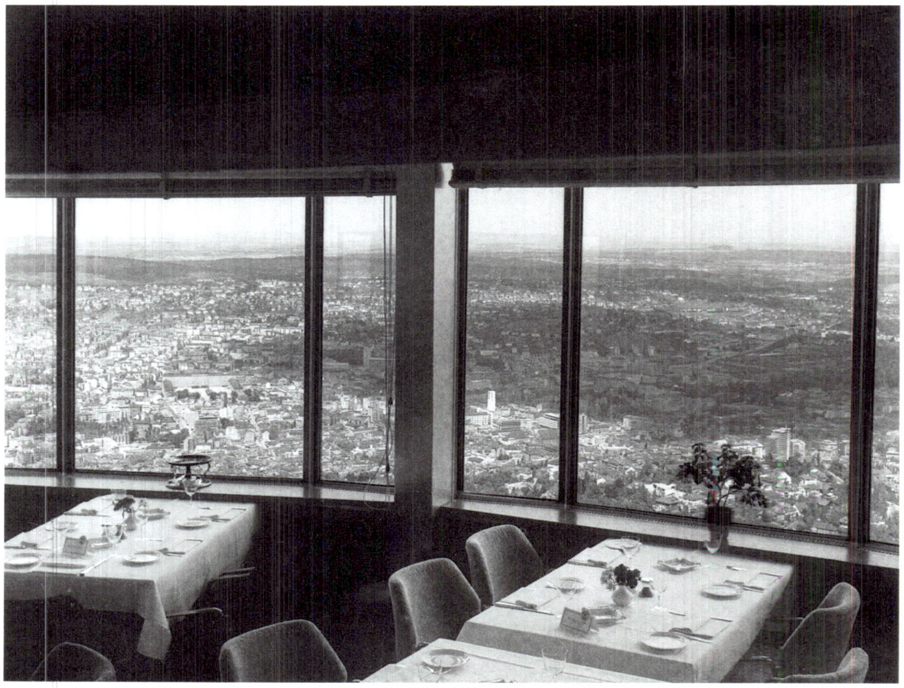

Television Tower, Stuttgart, 1956

Concreting of the foundation, Television Tower, Stuttgart, around 1955

Television Tower restaurant, chair Forum 363, Walter Knoll, design by Herta-Maria Witzemann, Stuttgart, 1956

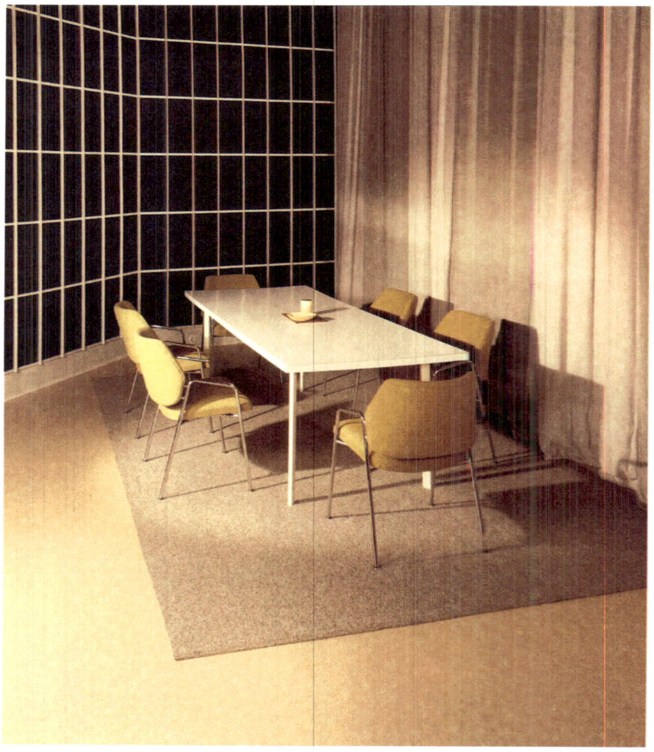

Exhibition at the "Landesgewerbeamt" (State Trade Office), chair Forum 363, Walter Knoll, design by Herta-Maria Witzemann, photograph by Franz Lazi, Stuttgart, 1956

BROADCASTING HALL

The Forum chair by Walter Knoll was used in the new "Süddeutscher Rundfunk" (South German Broadcasting) studio, an acclaimed feat of architecture by Egon Eiermann.

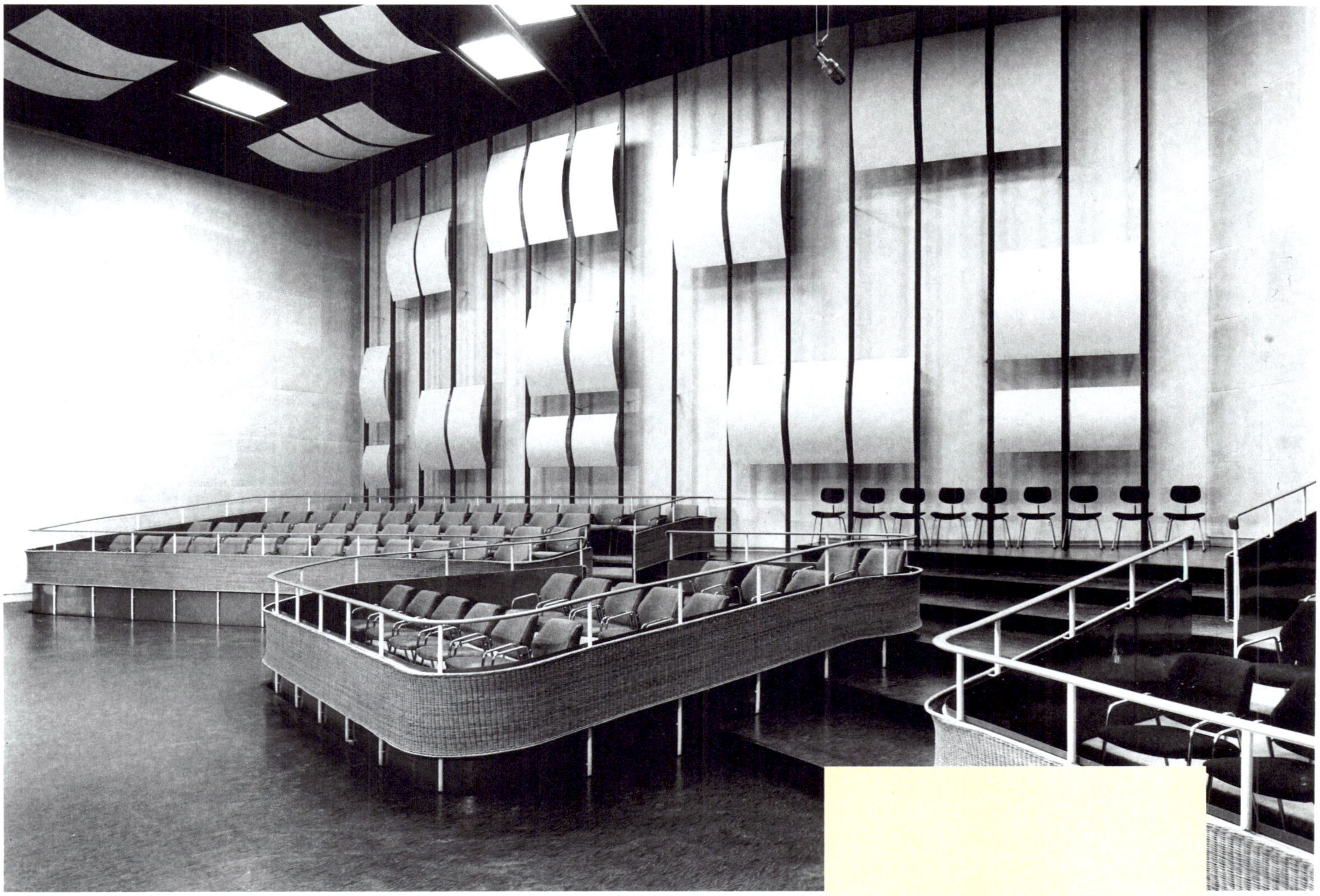

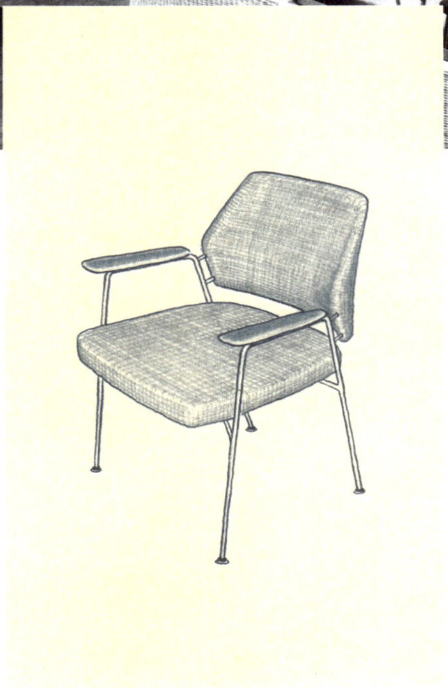

"Südwestfunk" studio at the Villa Berg, seating with the Forum 363, Walter Knoll, design by Herta-Maria Witzemann, architect Egon Eiermann, Stuttgart, 1953

Model drawing, Forum 409, Walter Knoll, design by Herta-Maria Witzemann, Herrenberg, 1956

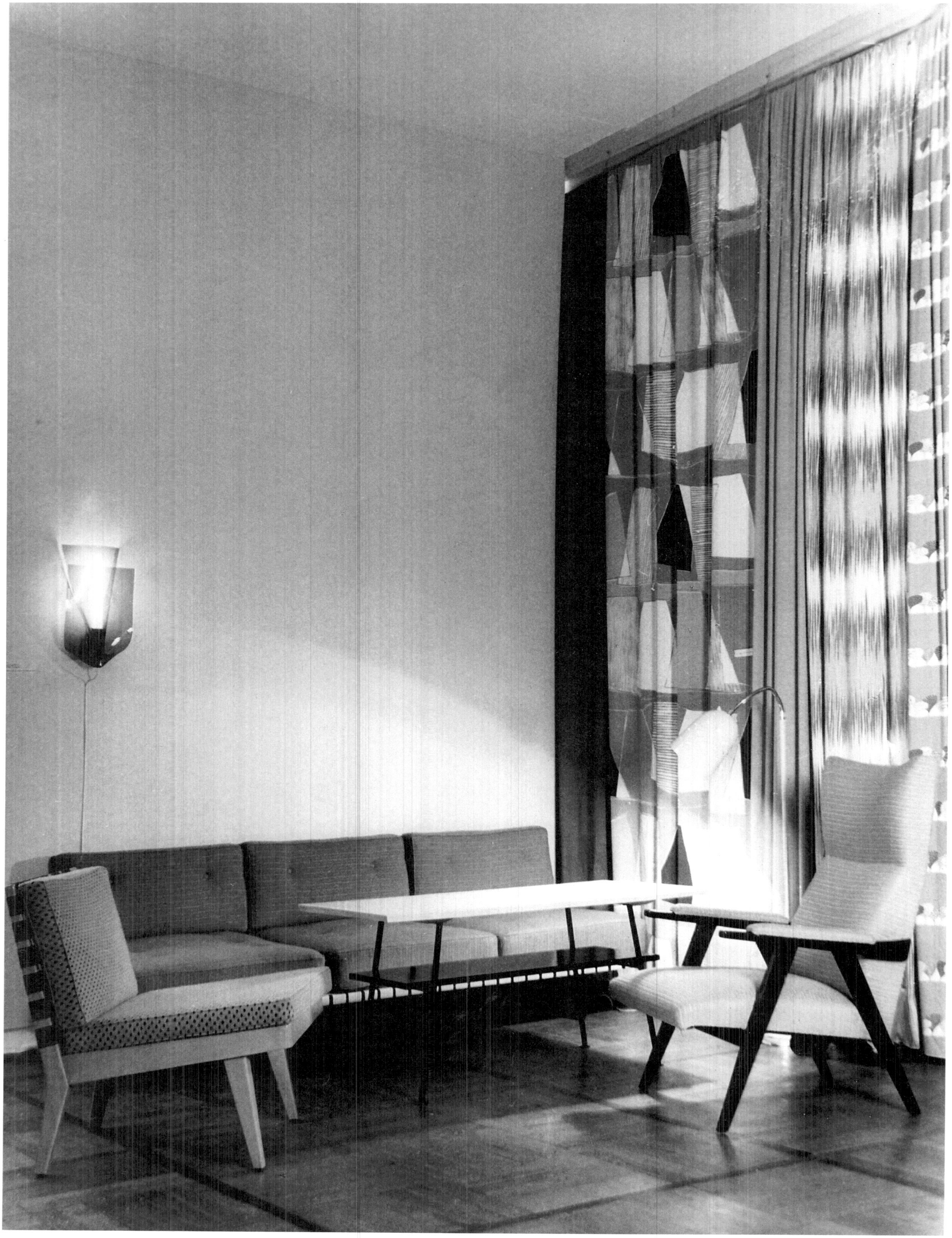

MATERIALS

A close partnership developed with the "Stuttgarter Gardinenfabrik" (Stuttgart Curtain Factory) company from Herrenberg, renowned for the high quality of its designs. New synthetic materials, such as the imitation leather Napa Flex, were also used.

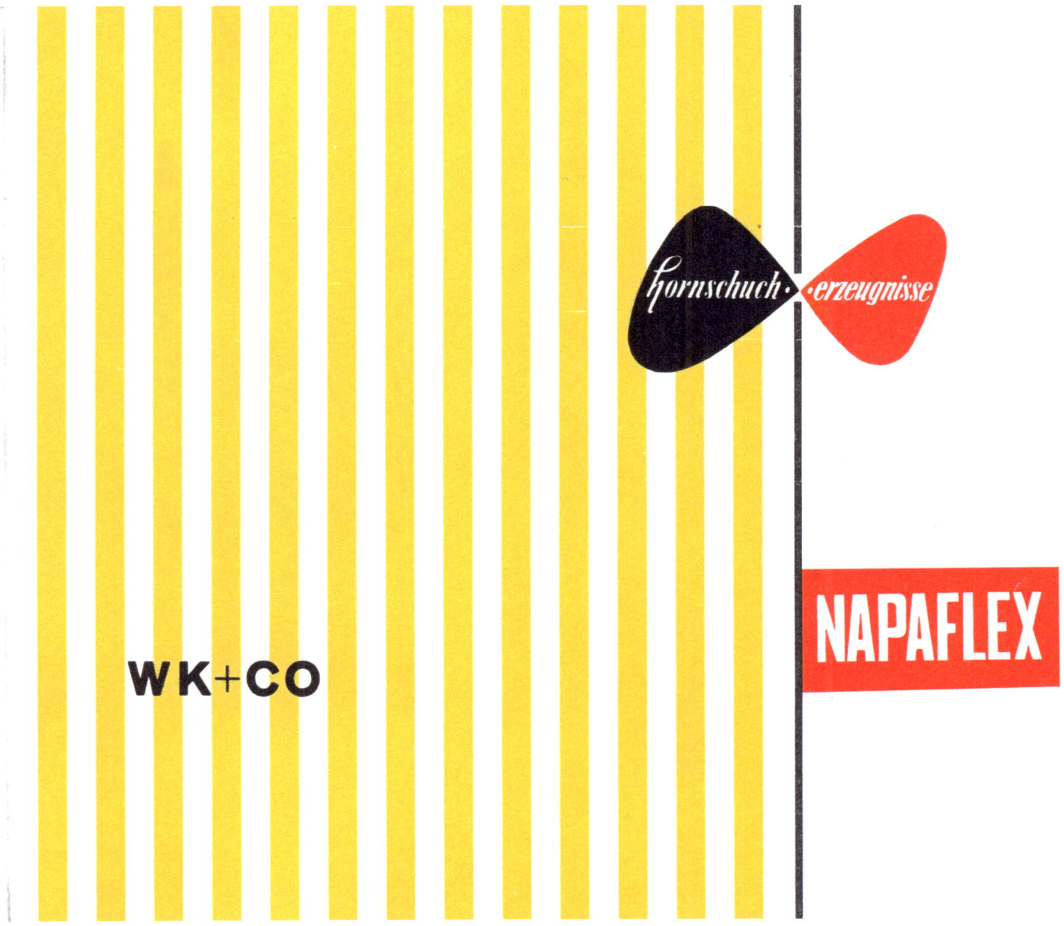

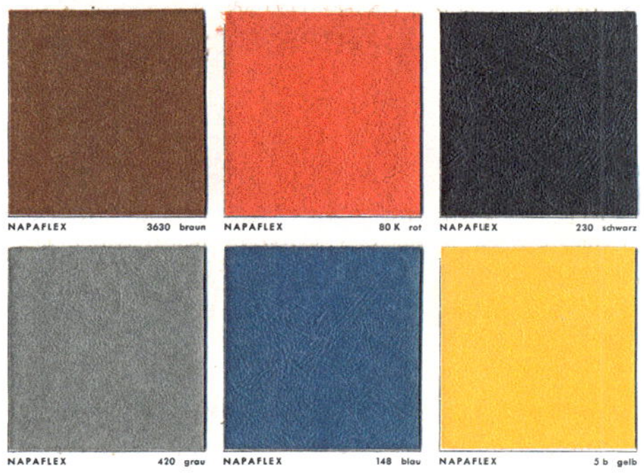

Catalog photo, armchair 319 and chaise longue 322, Walter Knoll, Herrenberg, 1955

Brochure cover page and centerfold, imitation leather Napa Flex, Walter Knoll, Herrenberg, around 1955

EXHIBITION OFFENSIVE

Stuttgart's "Landesgewerbeamt" (State Trade Office) retained its pioneering role with interesting exhibition topics, whether modern poster art or the geometry of new seating furniture.

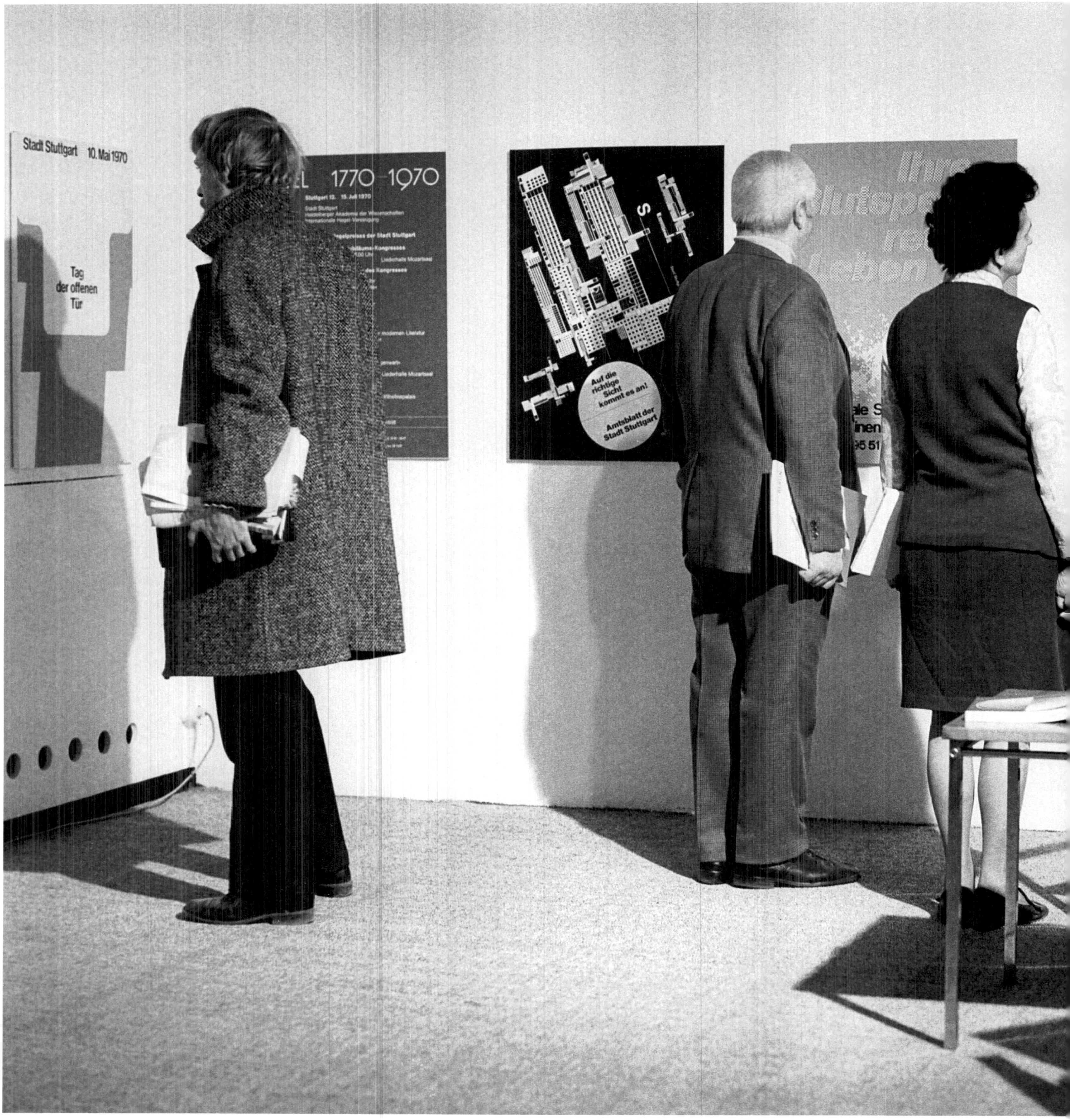

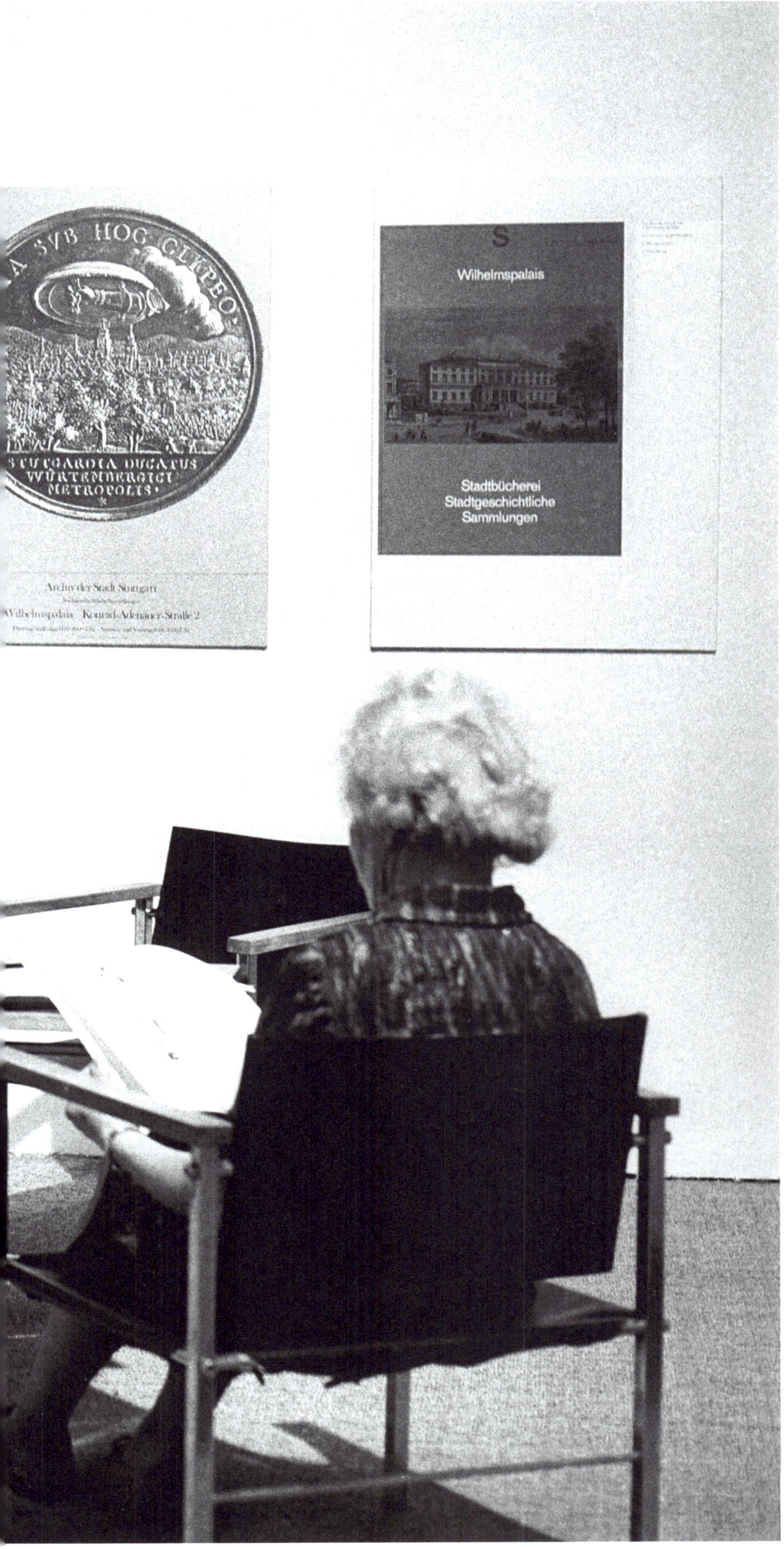

Exhibition at the "Landesgewerbeamt"
(State Trade Office),
Stuttgart, 1960

Poster,
"Landesgewerbeamt"
(State Trade Office),
design by
Herbert W. Kapitzki,
Stuttgart, 1957

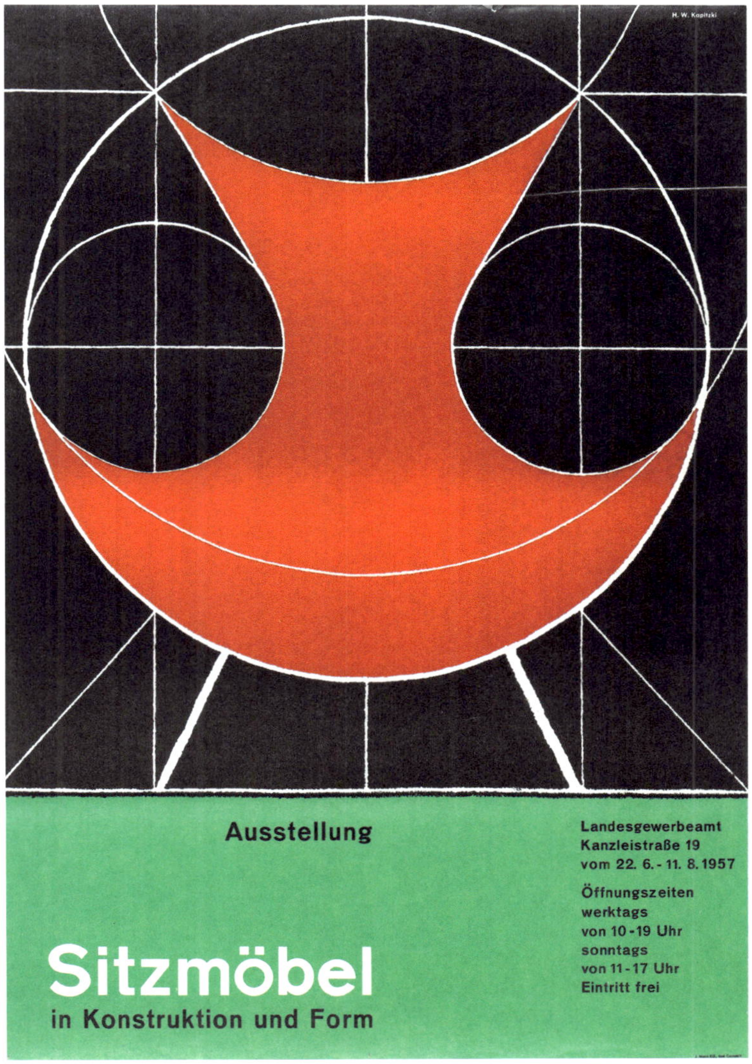

SCANDINAVIA

During the Scandinavian wave of the 1950s, Wilhelm Knoll became specialists in wooden frames, gentle shapes, and a restrained aesthetic. Minimalism was on its way.

Catalog photo,
armchair Antimott 518,
Wilhelm Knoll,
Stuttgart, 1954

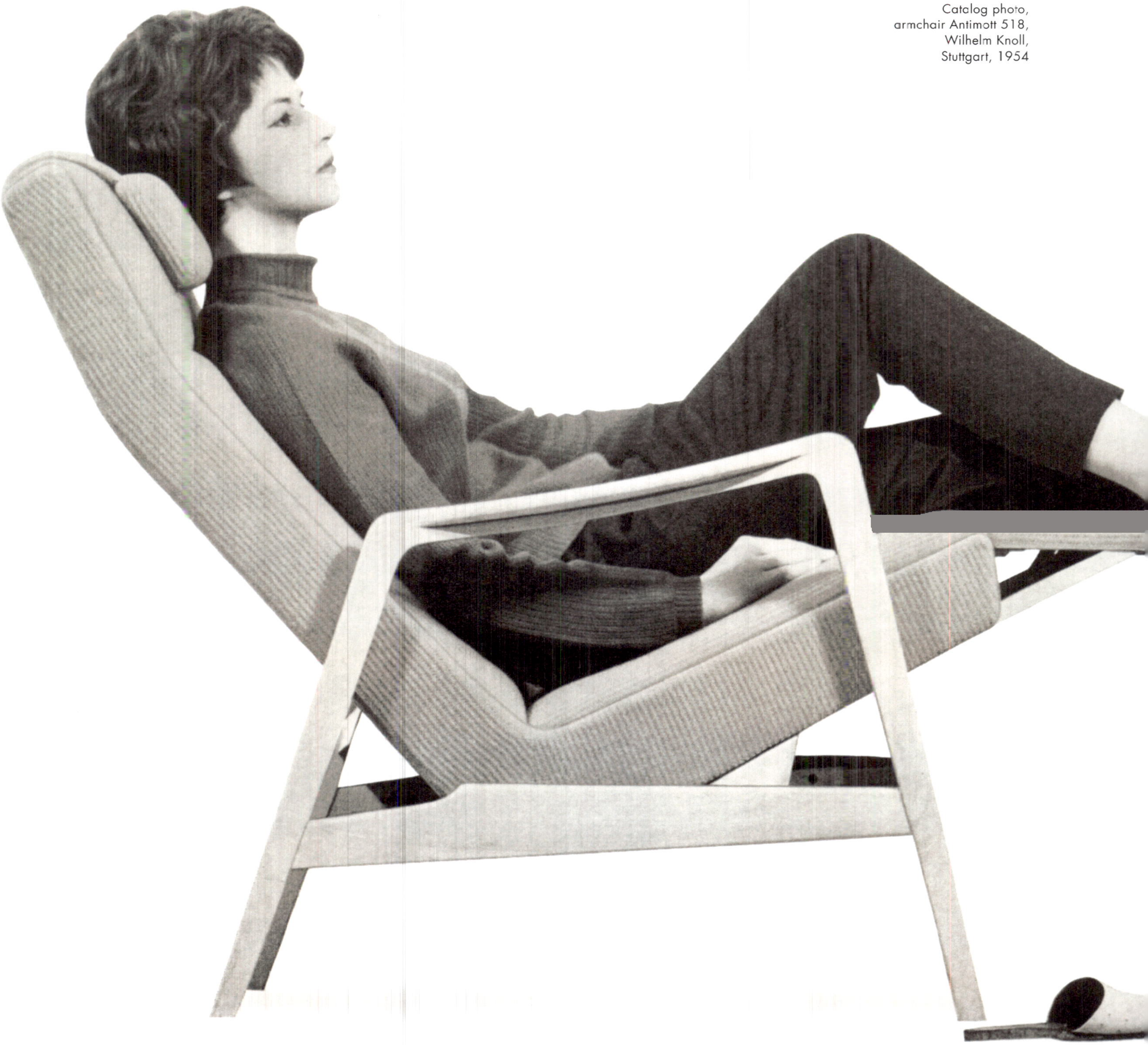

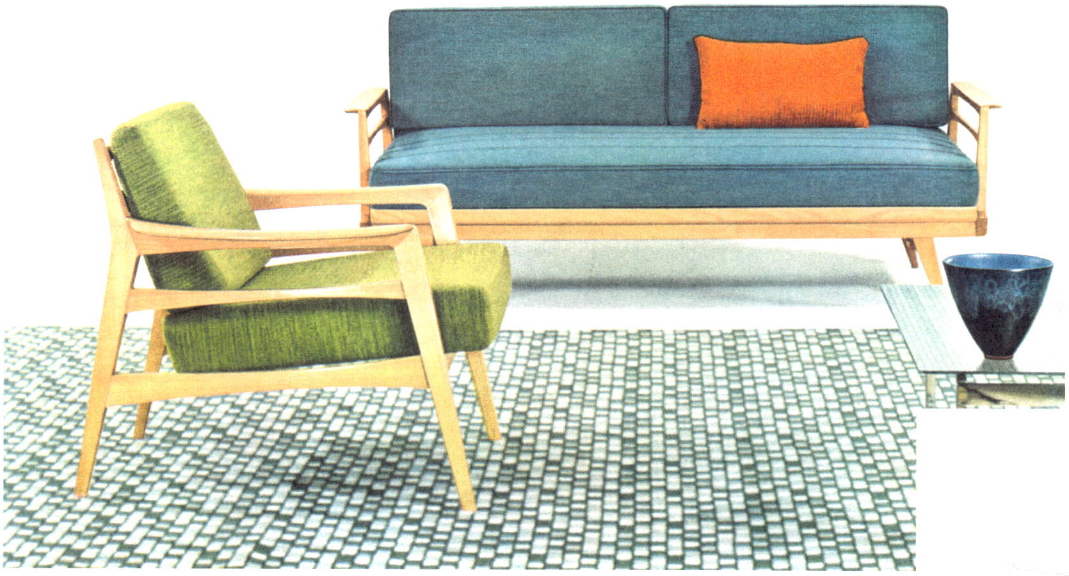

Catalog photo,
sofa Antimott 160/9/PM and
armchair Antimott 219, Wilhelm Knoll,
Stuttgart, 1958

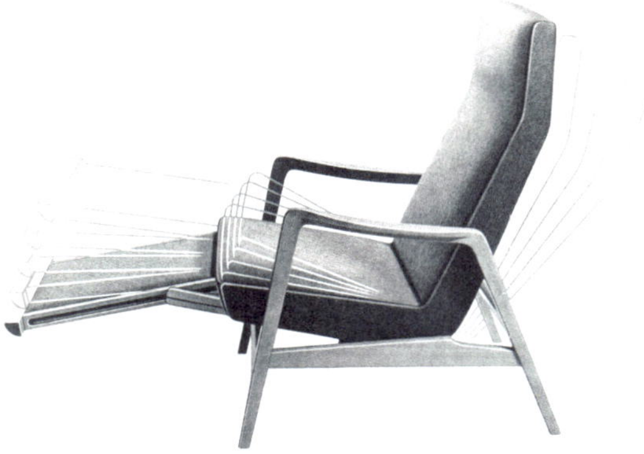

Catalog photo,
adjustable relaxing and television armchair
Antimott 518, Wilhelm Knoll,
Stuttgart, 1957

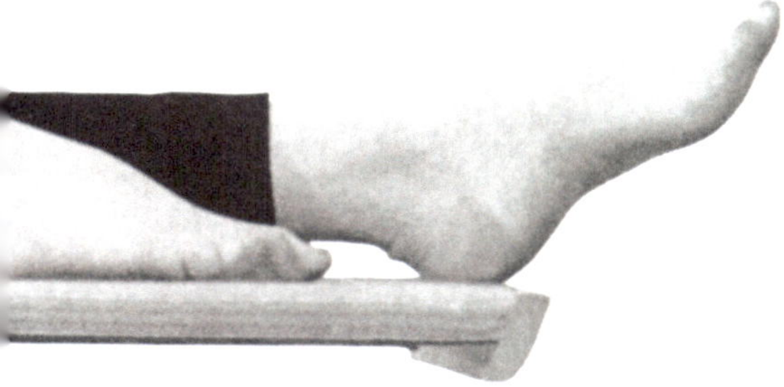

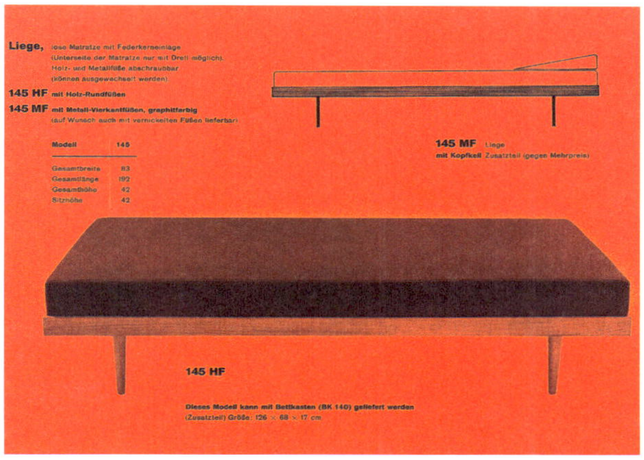

Liege, lose Matratze mit Federkerneinlage
(Unterseite der Matratze nur mit Drell möglich).
Holz- und Metallfüße abschraubbar
(können ausgewechselt werden).

145 HF mit Holz-Rundfüßen

145 MF mit Metall-Vierkantfüßen, graphitfarbig
(auf Wunsch auch mit vernickelten Füßen lieferbar)

Modell	145
Gesamtbreite	83
Gesamtlänge	192
Gesamthöhe	42
Sitzhöhe	42

145 MF Liege
mit Kopfkeil Zusatzteil (gegen Mehrpreis)

145 HF

Dieses Modell kann mit Bettkasten (BK 140) geliefert werden
(Zusatzteil) Größe: 126 × 68 × 17 cm

Catalog page,
chaise longue
Antimott 145,
Wilhelm Knoll,
Stuttgart, 1959

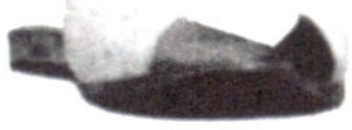

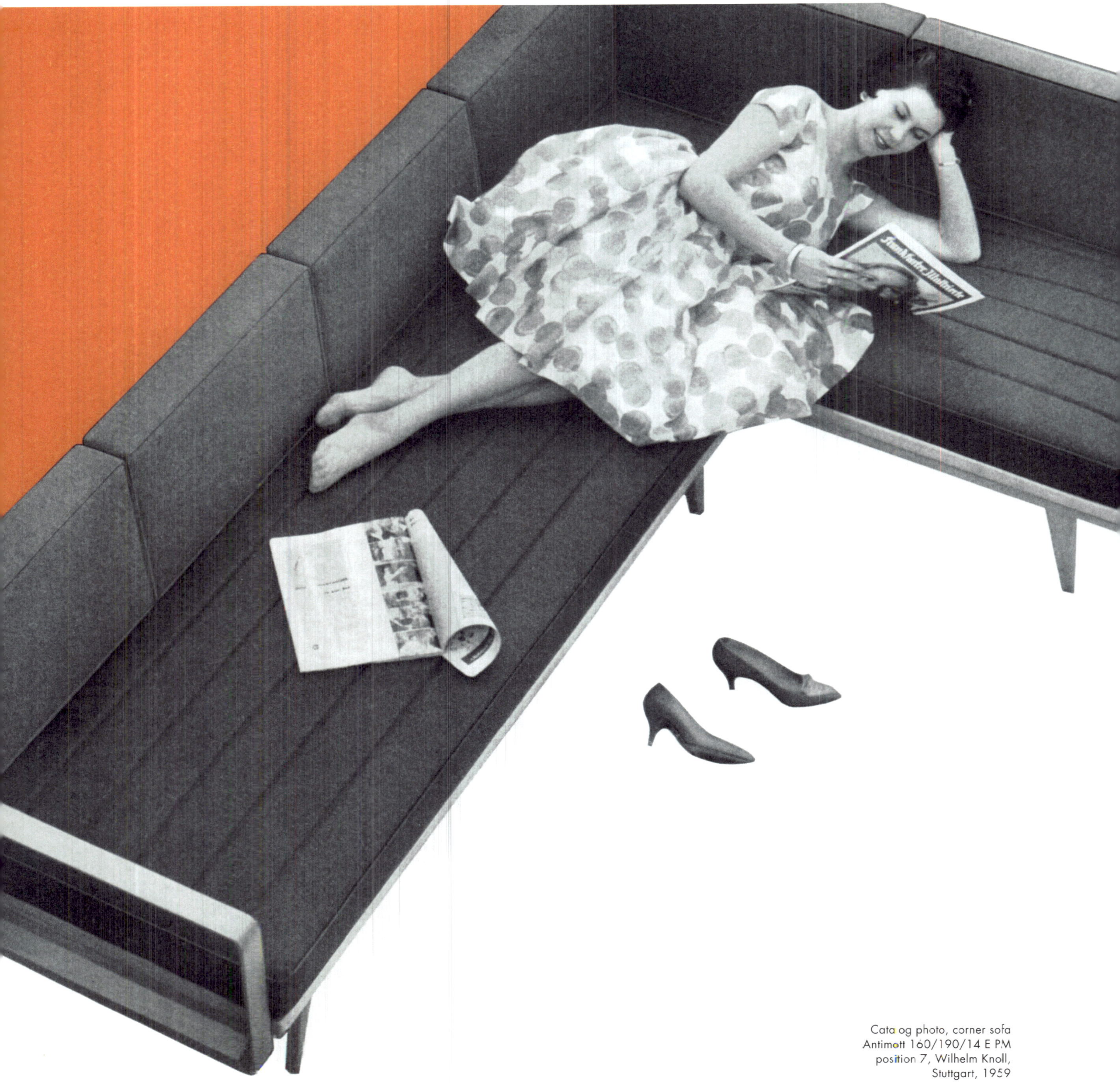

Catalog photo, corner sofa
Antimott 160/190/14 E PM
position 7, Wilhelm Knoll,
Stuttgart, 1959

Antimott catalog,
Wilhelm Knoll,
Stuttgart, 1959

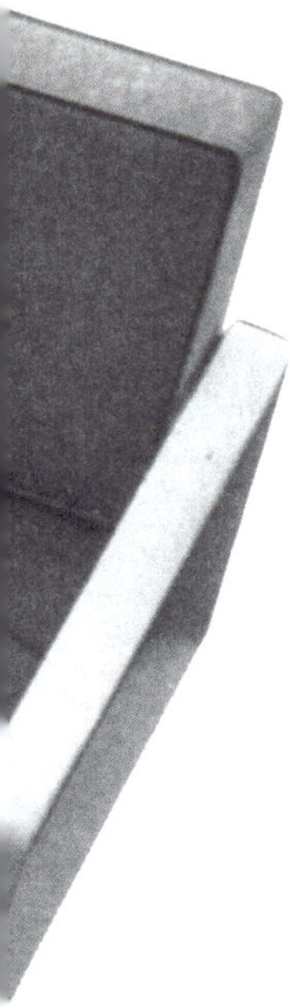

REVIVAL
One invention of the First Modernity was still in great demand: Wilhelm Knoll turned Antimott into its own brand and developed numerous new variants.

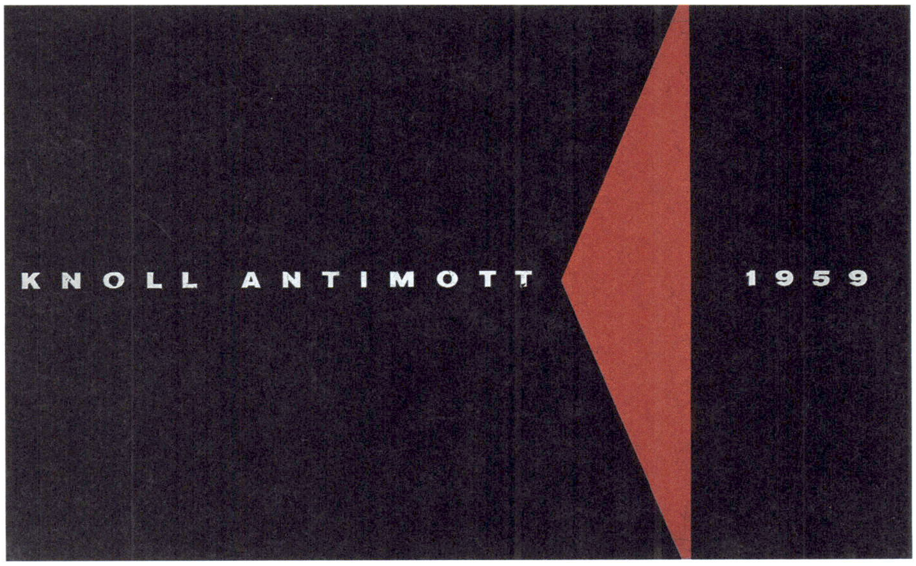

SYSTEM PEOPLE

The innovators of design at the "Hochschule für Gestaltung Ulm" (Ulm School of Design) got to the bottom of things and thus changed them. Herbert Ohl, the last director of the "Hochschule für Gestaltung Ulm," developed a complex modular armchair system that he offered to Walter Knoll. In this case, however, it remained merely a utopia.

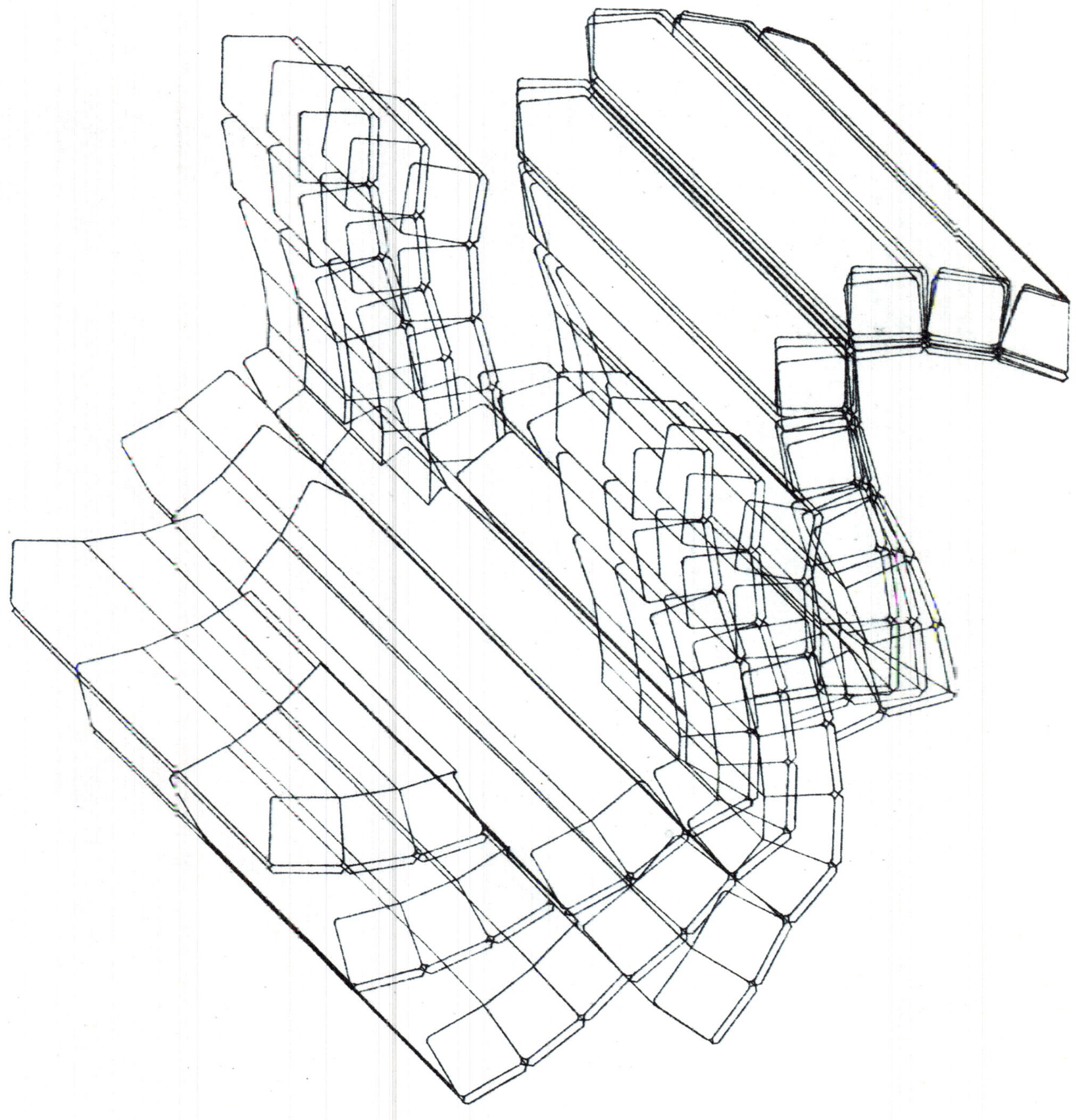

Drawing,
"Flexibilität eines Polstermöbels"
(Flexibility of Upholstered Furniture),
design by Herbert Ohl,
Ulm, 1958

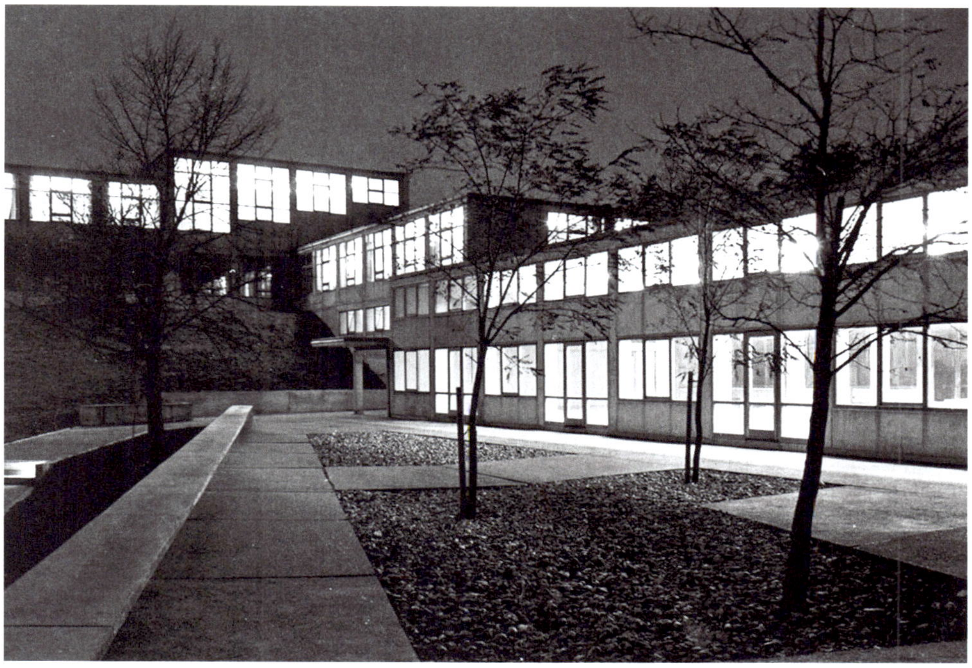

"Hochschule für Gestaltung"
(School of Design),
architect Max Bill,
Ulm, 1954

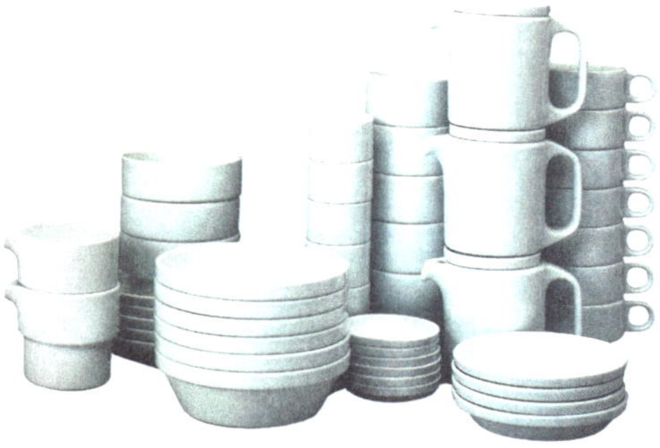

With the stackable tableware
TC 100, system design
reached the kitchen.
Hans (Nick) Roericht, 1959

ORGANIC DESIGN

Or | ga | ni | c de | sign, compound; the dominance of soft forms inspired by nature coincided with the triumph of Scandinavian and Italian design. The latter was also initially referred to as *Bel Design* (beautiful design). The organic paradigm in architecture and design drew great attention for the first time at the 1939 New York World's Fair, in particular as a result of the Finnish pavilion by Alvar Aalto and the Swedish pavilion by Josef Frank, the originator of Swedish Modern. The Italian "Carrozzieri", including sheet metal cutters such as Bertone and Pinin Farina, dominated the field of car design in the mid-20th century with their thrilling curved surfaces. Although organic design would soon be imposed on products of all kinds, furniture design – and not least upholstered furniture – was once again the true pinnacle. Vostra chairs by Jens Risom, which he designed for the company of his partner Hans Knoll and which he, in turn, made available to his father, introduced the organic design paradigm to Germany. The curved bucket seat, whether made of plywood or plastic, took on iconic significance in this extremely productive era and became a symbol of the Second Modernity as a whole – like tubular steel did in the First Modernity. Early designs by Arno Votteler and Rolf Grunow and, eventually, also the FK bucket seat by the Danes Fabricius and Kastholm turned out to be highlights of this genre in the product range of Walter Knoll. Nowadays, the British designer duo PearsonLloyd is continuing the story of the bucket seat into the future.

I WANTED TO CLEAR UP THE SLUM OF LEGS. I WANTED TO MAKE THE CHAIR ALL ONE THING AGAIN.
EERO SAARINEN

1939
The Finnish and Swedish pavilions attract great attention at the New York World's Fair.

1949
Foundation of the Federal Republic of Germany.
Walter Knoll flies to the USA, and visits Ludwig Mies van der Rohe.
The Vostra causes a sensation at the exhibitions "Wie Wohnen?" (How to live?) at Stuttgart's "Landesgewerbeamt" (State Trade Office) and "Neues Wohnen" (New Living) in Cologne's fair halls.

1952
Arno Votteler becomes the first employed interior designer at Walter Knoll.
Lightweight chairs with a plywood bucket and a thin tubular steel frame are established as a new type.

1954
The "Design in Scandinavia" exhibition tours through the USA, triggering a wave that spills back over to Europe.
Record sales at Wilhelm and Walter Knoll (nearly 5 million marks).

1955
The restaurant of the Stuttgart Television Tower (architect Fritz Leonhardt) is furnished with Walter Knoll furniture.

1956
The bucket seat 369 by Rolf Grunow for Walter Knoll sets new standards for the new category of furniture.

1957
Walter Knoll acquires licenses from Cassina.
Open wooden frames in Scandinavian style dominate at Wilhelm Knoll.
"Sitzmöbel in Konstruktion und Form" (Seating Furniture in Design and Form) exhibition at Stuttgart's "Landesgewerbeamt" (State Trade Office).
The "Internationale Bauausstellung" (International Building Exhibition) in West Berlin.

1965
New plastics enable organic forms in product and furniture design.

1969
The first "Bundespreis Gute Form" (German National Prize for Good Design) for the FK bucket seat (design by Preben Fabricius and Jørgen Kastholm).

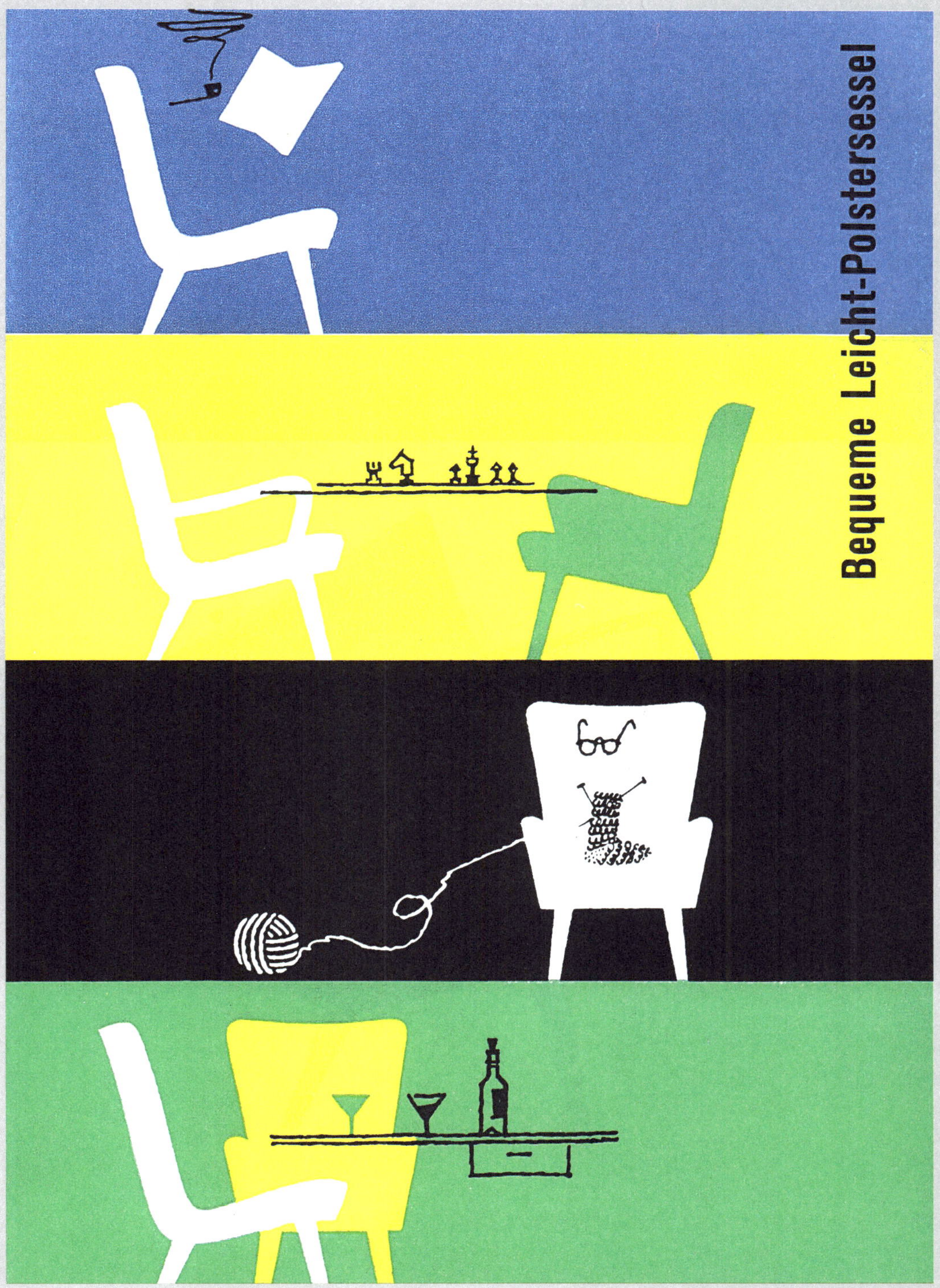

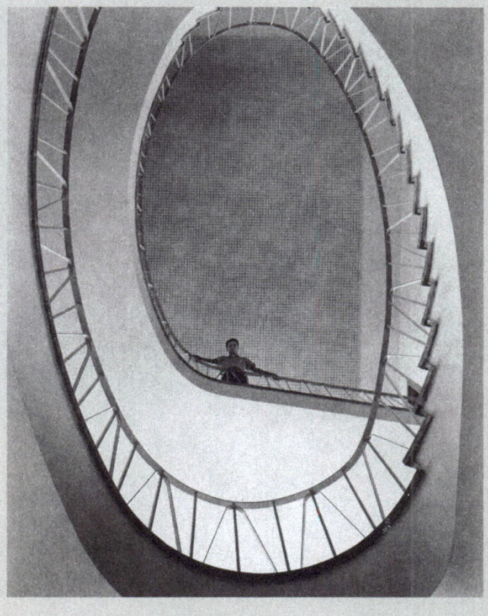

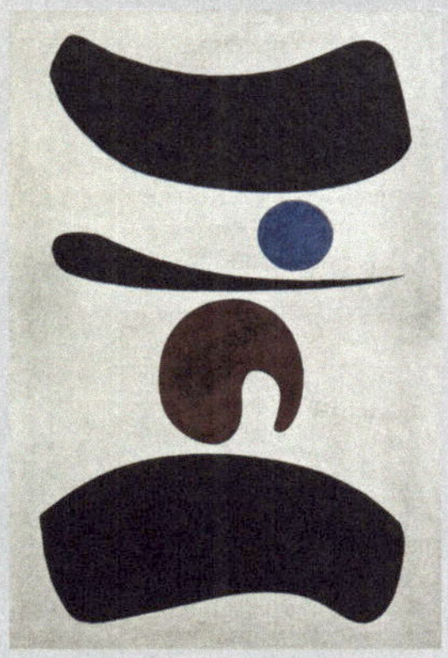

Brochure cover photo,
armchair Vostra 351, Walter Knoll,
Herrenberg, 1951

Stairwell at the Villa Berg,
architect Egon Eiermann,
photograph by Franz Lazi,
Stuttgart, 1951

Oil painting "Tori mit blauem Punkt"
(Tori with blue spot),
Willi Baumeister,
Wuppertal, 1937

THE 1960S

FULL EMPLOYMENT

"Our divisions are fully occupied once again," rejoiced the "Echo aus Herrenberg" (Echo from Herrenberg), the monthly company newspaper, in late 1960.[1] A "battle to comply with delivery dates" was being fought. After all, "we are perfectly inundated with orders and, in these days, even a few major projects have been ruled in our favor."[2] And this ultimately represented not only lucrative business, but also "a matter of prestige for our Herrenberg seating furniture".[3] In fact, it was a "matter of honor for every responsibly thinking employee – from the head of department down to the errand girl – not to jeopardize the good reputation of our company and to do his or her best."[4] This appeal to the workforce was not without reason. In the Federal Republic, the number of unemployed people had again halved to around a quarter million compared to the previous year. The unemployment rate was now approximately one percent. In the Stuttgart region, it approached zero. However, more or less full employment also entailed new problems. "Additional manpower is hard to come by these days," lamented the "Echo aus Herrenberg."[5] Additionally, a glance in the pay packets, which were still placed in workers' hands every week like in old times, was a significant cause for reflection for many. Significantly higher wages were being paid in the metal industry, and especially at Daimler. A migration took place. Even the training department had to be closed due to a lack of apprentices. For Walter Knoll, who saw good job training as valuable in itself, this was naturally a great source of regret.

In 1960, around 200 employees – after all, almost twice as many as in 1950 – had to cope with order quantities that had increased roughly fivefold over the same period. No wonder that "REFA" was introduced during this phase of scarce workforce, with the intention of measuring working time to streamline production processes and fix piecework wages. The REFA people would increase productivity with their stopwatches. The situation was exactly the same at the sibling company Wilhelm Knoll too, which still had its headquarters in Stuttgart. At this time, nearly 300 employees at the main plant in Gaildorf were also well and truly occupied. When a branch was opened in Steyr in 1962, around 100 Austrian "Knollians" were added.[6] As before, Dieter Knoll counted on foreign business. These were the tentative beginnings of globalization, which would soon lead him to exotic locations. Consequently, during a visit to the first furniture fair in Tehran in 1961, he had the opportunity to welcome a high-ranking visitor to his stand. Ludwig Erhard, the Minister of Economic Affairs and soon-to-be Federal Chancellor, guided through the fair by Mohammad Reza Shah Pahlavi, the ruler and future Emperor of Iran, stopped by at the Stuttgart company's stand. A group photo with a lady came into being. This was thanks to the presence of the pretty, young consort Farah Diba, a favorite subject of the German tabloid press at the time. Dieter Knoll went on another great trip a year later. During his first stay in the USA, he also knocked at the door of Knoll Associates in East Greenville, Pennsylvania, to explore "the chances of a close collaboration."[7] However, Florence Knoll, who had been running the company since Hans Knoll's death, was friendly but reserved. Nothing more than a non-binding agreement not to harm each other was secured. However, the home comer declared it a "global contract" upon his return.[8]

Walter Knoll came up with two innovations for the Cologne furniture fair in early 1962 and both had the attributes to be a sensation. Firstly, a bucket seat with a conical column base and a seat base that opened out like a flower. The concise design, which was more reminiscent of a sculpture than an ordinary chair (nor did it resemble the bucket seats of the 1950s), was by Hans Theo Baumann. He was actually a glass specialist and a ceramist. Baumann was, for example, the creator of the trend-setting, cylindrical Berlin coffee service, which he designed for Rosenthal in 1959.[9] Born in Basel, he had worked for the

WALTER KNOLL CAME UP WITH TWO INNOVATIONS FOR THE COLOGNE FURNITURE FAIR IN EARLY 1962 AND BOTH HAD THE ATTRIBUTES TO BE A SENSATION.

Stuttgart-based architect Egon Eiermann and lived a double life as an artist and product designer. He worked for numerous German companies and soon also in the supreme discipline of seating design. The highly versatile designer is one of the many universal personalities of the Second Modernity, such as Max Bill, Hans Gugelot or Herbert Hirche, who gave impulses in completely different fields and were incidentally often also geographic design vagabonds.[10] "The fundamentals of a design are solely the result of human ability," asserted Baumann, who believed in intuition rather than formulas.[11] With this bud-like chair creation for Walter Knoll, he had created a new category of furniture.

That year's second trade fair innovation was very nearly not ready on time. By October 1961, only a single prototype existed. Robert Knoll consequently wrote a densely typed two-page letter in the friendly, obliging tone that was so typical of him. "I have a very bad conscience," he begins, "because I have taken so long to reply to you and have not even thanked you for the card from Holland."[12] A lack of upholstery fabric was to blame. "Your chair is ready to go and is just waiting for the moment that we – 'the management' – make a decision," he continued. There was namely "some resistance", given that it was, after all, an "extraordinary model". Its creator was Otto Kolb, an architect who lived in the vicinity of Zurich. Robert Knoll then described to him, and not without pride, how he eventually resolved the gridlock caused by the lack of decisiveness. "I took it with me to our photographer in Stuttgart in the last week, and hired an equally attractive model and, lo and behold, everyone is delighted." Particularly noteworthy: "My father" – clearly a member of the resistance – "is just as surprised as we all are that your chair took on such an exceptional, charming character when accompanied by a live model."[13]

Otto Kolb, an avant-gardist in his early fourties, already had an impressive career behind him. In addition, his credentials were perfect for Walter Knoll. As a young man, the German-Swiss had already come into contact with the Zurich art scene, which had been given fresh impetus by German exiles during the Second World War, just like in the First World War. Kolb belonged to a circle around the art historian Sigfried Giedion, who saw a considerable number of prominent representatives of "Classical Modernity" come and go, including artists such as Hans Arp and architects like Walter Gropius. The creative spirit that prevailed there never let go of the young Kolb. Eventually, he was hired by Johannes Itten, the wise head of the Bauhaus education model, as a lecturer at the "Werkkunstschule Zürich" (Zurich School of Applied Arts). From there, he soon made his next significant career step, this time right across the Atlantic. On the recommendation of Giedion, a friend of Gropius, he moved to Chicago to join the Institute of Design, formerly the New Bauhaus, which was under the directorship of Serge Chermayeff. There, as head of the product design department, Kolb dealt with innovations of all kinds, developing innovative furniture designs and, together with his wife Ridi, his own collection of lamps. His teaching, in the spirit of Itten and Chermayeff, was based entirely on "creative restlessness." In 1960, after twelve years in the USA, the tireless experimenter returned to Switzerland, built himself a circular glass house in the foothills of the Alps and furnished it with his own furniture creations. The intended outcome soon came to pass. The press raced to the house, and the industry took notice. The home comer was an insider tip.

"Chicago Kolb", as his friends called him, of course, had also offered something unusual to the men from Herrenberg: the model 457 (see p. 188 f.). The form inventor from the mountains combined a lightweight, short-legged steel frame with a no less sophisticated upholstery arrangement. The most striking aspect is the bent and widely protruding armrests. Depending on the perspective, the armchair with wings looked either like an invitation to sit down or a bird just about to take flight. In any case, it was an unusual form of seating furniture that

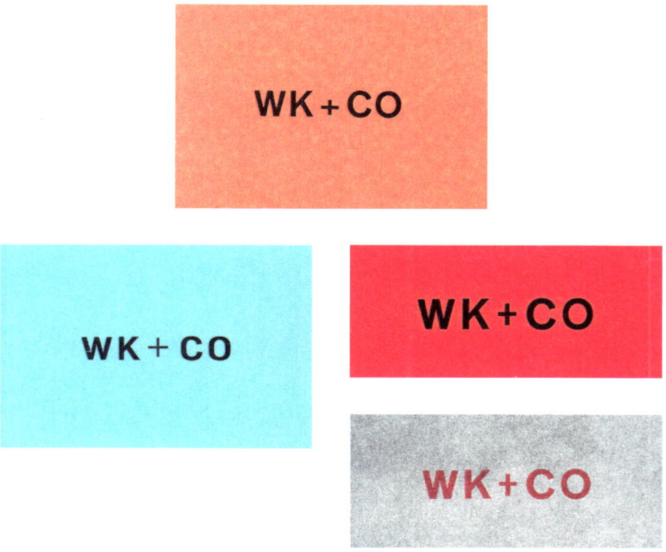

stimulated the imagination. Additionally, the trapezoidal armrests of the 457 provided extra deposit space and encouraged unconventional sitting positions. This may well have been the reason why "Playboy" magazine declared the rare bird as a "Love Chair". Kolb's standalone piece caused a stir but did not turn out to be a bestseller. Like Baumann's tulip, it differed considerably from the models of the 1950s. Both were complex sculptural designs that were perhaps a little too far ahead of their time. At the beginning of the 1960s, a completely different aesthetic was being prescribed.

---

1 ▶ "Unsere Monatsbetrachtung" (Our Monthly Review), in: "Echo aus Herrenberg," magazine supplement "Wir vom Holz" (We from the Wood Industry), November 1960.

2 ▶ Ibid.

3 ▶ Ibid.

4 ▶ Ibid.

5 ▶ Ibid.

6 ▶ From 1962, the plant in Steyr produced "Antimott couches, chaise longues, armchairs and sofas", but almost exclusively for the Austrian market. See: Knoll, 1965, p. 48.

7 ▶ Ibid.

8 ▶ Knoll, 1965, p. 16.

9 ▶ Polster 2008, p. 132.

10 ▶ Bill was Swiss like Baumann, Gugelot was Dutch. Hirche was from Lusatia.

11 ▶ Polster 2008, p. 391.

12 ▶ Designer correspondence, WK archives.

13 ▶ Ibid.

DEMOCRACY

The "Landtag in Stuttgart" was the first newly constructed state parliament building in the Federal Republic. A simple box shape, rather than representative forms, was the order of the day and set standards on the search for an "architecture of democracy," that would not be stately, but functional. The modern upholstered furniture of Walter Knoll, which was strikingly minimalistic at the time, was also in tune with this.

Stuttgart's state parliament building
built in 1961,
photo from 1968

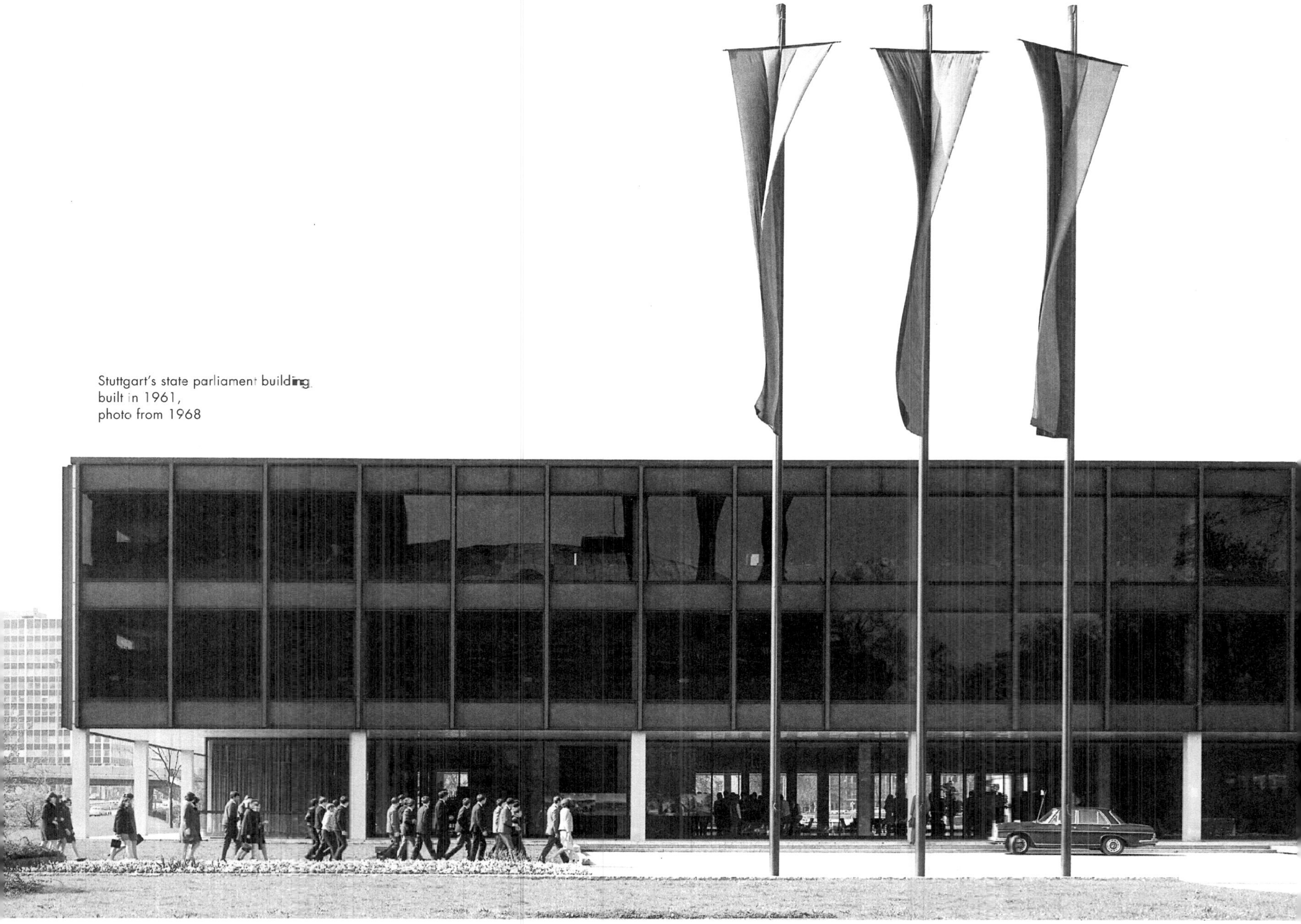

ANGULAR BACKLASHES

Corners and edges, right angles and obtuse angles created simple but visually striking geometry in the living room.

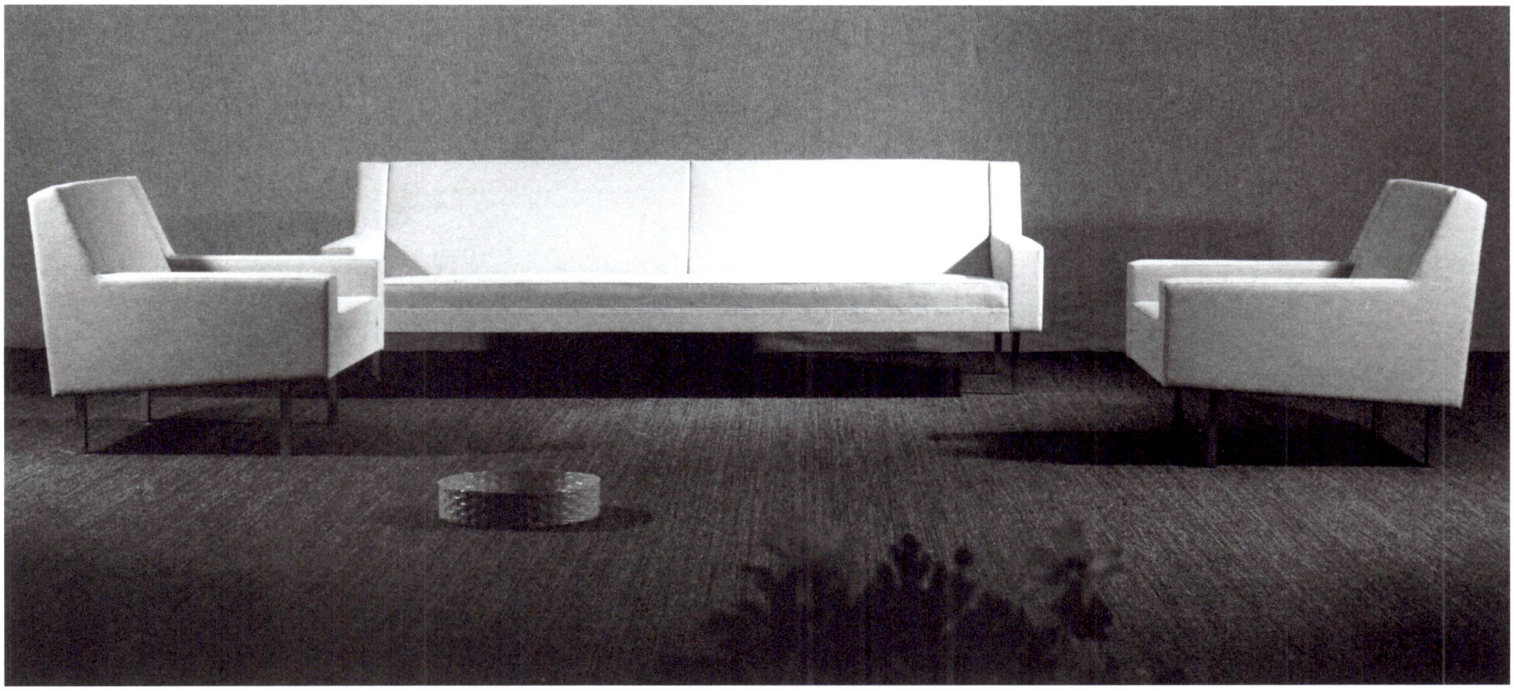

Catalog photo, armchair Antimott 540 and sofa Antimott 541, Wilhelm Knoll, Stuttgart, 1961

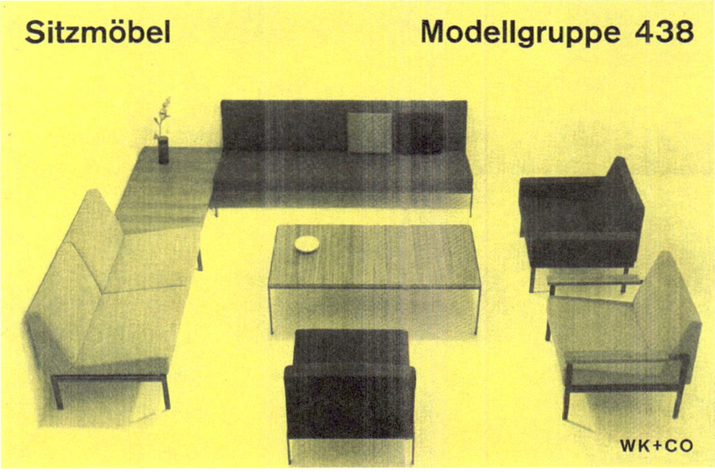

Brochure cover photo, Walter Knoll, design by Rolf Grunow, Herrenberg, 1958

SEATING MINIMALISTS

The model W 54, which came onto the market in 1960, was the simplest chair that had ever been constructed at Walter Knoll: an homage to straight lines and right angles. On a frame of black square steel, resembling scaffolding, lie two cubical foam cushions that are slightly offset and thus protrude a little over the frame. There is a flat, square seating surface on the one hand, and a backrest made of a small foam strip on the other. If the chairs are stood side-by-side, the cuboid upholstery forms columns and rows. The home is transformed into a geometric space. The W 54 was conceived as a "dining room set". This strikingly simple design was by Dieter Waeckerlin, a Swiss native like Baumann and Kolb. Waeckerlin, born in 1930 and thus ten years younger than his compatriots, apparently also avoided grand gestures during his lifetime. The Basel-born designer had already made a name for himself with his company Idealheim (ideal home). The company name said it all. For him, the ideal clearly consisted in omission and a focus on the essential.

The purist Waeckerlin was a trained carpenter and actually specialized in wardrobes. He now also adopted their box shape in his seating furniture. And so successfully, in fact, that the name of a creator was printed on a brochure for the first time at Walter Knoll: "waeckerlin-sitzmöbel" (waeckerlin seating furniture), written in lower-case letters in the style of the Bauhaus, was the name given to this small collection. The cabinets and sideboards also pictured inside are, as stated there, "behr waeckerlin maßmöbel" (behr waeckerlin made-to-measure furniture). Here, Walter Knoll and the Wendlingen-based cabinet specialists Behr – companies that had already cooperated back in the Weissenhof era – joined forces once again, this time in the context of unprecedented furniture minimalism.

One person who had already been designing minimalist furniture back in the 1950s – including a series of folding sofas – was Rolf Grunow. Walter Knoll's former employed designer, who now lived in Herrenberg, was also developing alternatives to traditional suites of upholstery around 1960. "Similar to a modular system, initially there is a basic model, a chair without armrests whose upholstery can be used to group a row of two or three seats or various corner solutions," it was said about Grunow's model set 438, which was in no way inferior to Waeckerlin's purism, but took a slightly more systematic approach (see p. 185, 192 f.). It was a complete living room ensemble featuring square tables that could be hooked onto the steel frames of the seats. Or, just like the chairs, sofas, armchairs and stools, they could float above a thin, black, steel base. This was, of course, all based on right angles – with the exception of the seat and back cushion, which were wedge-shaped for the sake of comfortable sitting and thus gave 438 an even more distinctive visual character. In his living building blocks

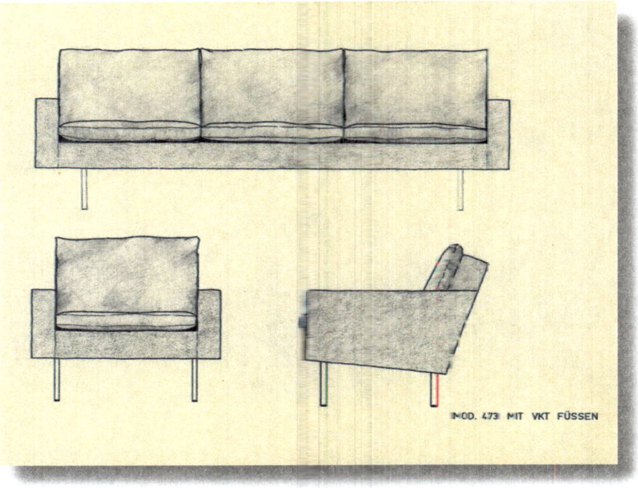

(which were already occasionally referred to as "modules"), the purist Grunow adopted the ideas of the Ulm School of Design. Or did he anticipate them? After all, simplification was not the only principle in Ulm. There was also a desire to break things down into their essential components, first in the mind and then in reality, in order to then innovatively put them back together as building blocks. A triumph of this dissection method was the collaboration between Ulm and the radio company Braun, whereby grandpa's radio was taken to pieces and transformed into the stereo system.[14] More famous, however, is the SK 4 record player, also known as "Snow White's coffin" thanks to its Plexiglas cover, and also because it was a simple box. Its designer, the Dutchman Hans Gugelot, was head of the Department of Product Design in Ulm, and acted as an advisor to Braun through the years. The Ulm-Braun project was crucial to the general acceptance of rationalism, which would quickly take hold in all industries, first in Germany and then worldwide. The cube, in all its variants, was deemed the ideal shape. It is pretty astonishing that, under these conditions, seating furniture continued to serve as a design role model. In the "Ulmer Hocker" (Ulm stool), the wooden seat of Ulm School of Design students, which they sat on and dragged around with them, the cubic maxim found its early academic symbol. Soon, however, different objects altogether also transformed into cubes, including automobiles. From the tiny compact car NSU Prinz 4 to the state carriage, the Mercedes 600, the box shape was now the non plus ultra. In the process, the styling departments at Daimler-Benz and NSU in Neckarsulm became trendsetters. And because all other automobiles also soon had edges and flat surfaces, cubic upholstered furniture was beginning to slightly resemble the new automobiles.

In a photo in the Wilhelm Knoll catalog of 1961, an SK 4 is on the bedside table. The record player, an icon of rational design, was being used as a prop for a new Antimott product: chaise longue 145 (see p. 175). This minimalist design, a cross between a bed and a chaise longue, consisted of only the bare essentials, namely the frame, rails, mattress, and legs. The cuboid on four poles was therefore clearly quite similar to sleeping furniture.[15] The model 145 with wooden feet was also available in a square steel variant. At Wilhelm Knoll, the interior designer Bert Lieber was assigned primary responsibility for adapting the product range to be in line with the now prevailing design asceticism.[16] Never had the catalogs of Walter and Wilhelm Knoll been as similar as during this minimalistic era when everyone, including the Ulm School of Design itself, was hoping to stumble across the philosopher's stone of design by means of a radical reduction to the type in itself.

Like the chrome-plated tubular steel of the 1920s and its considerably thinner version in the 1950s, square steel had now become the preferred material for frames. The preference for right angles went right down to the last detail. And just like its malleable predecessors, angular steel was also loaded with symbolism. It contained the essence of *Gute*

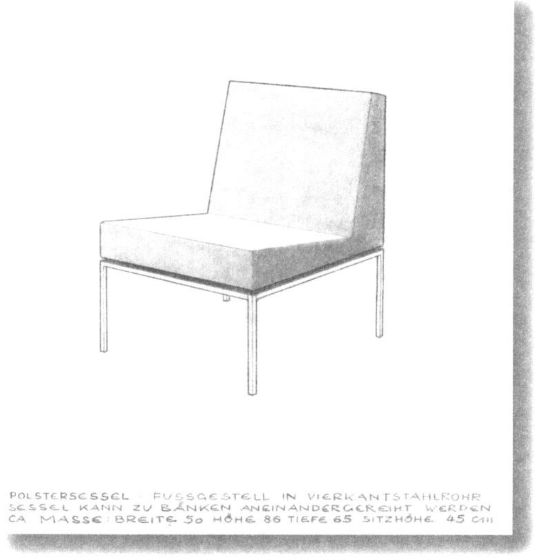

SQUARE STEEL HAD NOW BECOME THE PREFERRED MATERIAL FOR FRAMES. THE PREFERENCE FOR RIGHT ANGLES WENT RIGHT DOWN TO THE LAST DETAIL.

Form (Good Design). The cubic frames, reduced to the bare essentials just like the furniture body, would at best become invisible. For this reason, existential black was the preferred color. Addiform, the first product from Rolf Benz, a young upholsterer from Nagold, also stood on square steel runners.

The newcomers to modern Swabian furniture – from Bofinger, Holzäpfel and Kill via Wilde & Spieth to Rolf Benz – were now also on the search for the final, definitive *Gute Form*. They found designers who were capable of putting this purism into practice among the architects, not least at Stuttgart's art academy and, naturally, also directly at the source itself in Ulm. A couple of examples: Bofinger brought the universal cabinet system M 125 by Ulm lecturer Hans Gugelot – who also developed an armchair with a demountable metal frame for Kill[17] – onto the market.[18] Architect Helmut Bätzner, a Black Forest native, created the first fully plastic chair made from a single section, which was named the Bofinger Chair after its manufacturer. The architect Egon Eiermann and the all-round designer Hans Theo Baumann worked for Wilde & Spieth. Herbert Hirche and Herta-Maria Witzemann, the academy lecturers who had produced important designs that were in production at Walter Knoll, now also provided designs for Holzäpfel. Hirche's glass bar trolley turned out to be a quite programmatic, though not particularly widespread piece of furniture. With its cubic shape and framework made of black steel profiles, this rolling servant looked like an object out of a geometry textbook. Stuttgart's infrastructure of modernity spawned a lively scene with results that needed not fear comparison with other major design centers like Copenhagen and Milan. Here too, was one of the secrets: close and enduring partnerships between entrepreneurs and designers, which, admittedly, only succeeded in exceptional cases.[19]

---

14 ▶ Herbert Lindinger worked for Braun from 1955 to 1958, as part of Gugelot's working group at the "Hochschule für Gestaltung Ulm" (Ulm School of Design). See Polster 2005, p. 76.

15 ▶ Did the catalog designers perhaps know that Hans Gugelot, the creator of the pictured SK 4, had himself designed a bed, a dead-ringer for the 145?

16 ▶ Lieber remained an employed designer at Wilhelm Knoll for a quarter century, even after the takeover by Walter Knoll. See: Votteler 1990, p. 67.

17 ▶ Armchair 4065 was introduced at the 1964 international furniture fair in Cologne. It is an element system: a chrome-plated, demountable metal frame with four corner supports.

18 ▶ Polster 2008, p. 106.

19 ▶ Further examples of such collaboration occurred between the as of recently Ulm-based Max Bill and the Black Forest watch manufacturer Junghans as well as between the as of recently Stuttgart-based Wilhelm Wagenfeld and WMF.

LOVECHAIR

Welcome to the 1960s: this expressive armchair is a bold design by Otto Kolb. For the first time, Walter Knoll placed ads for the trade fair sensation of 1961.

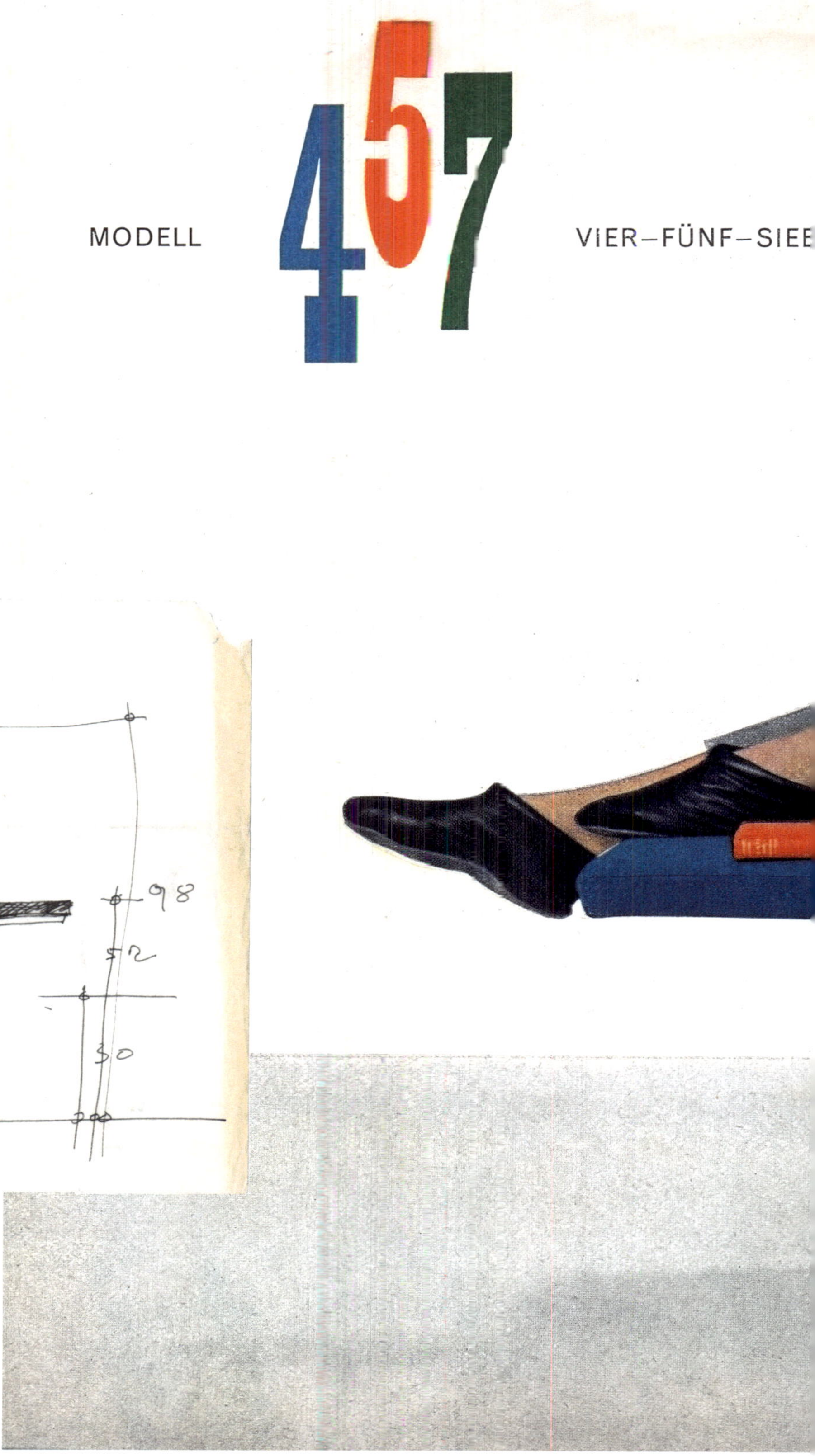

Advertisement,
armchair 457, Walter Knoll,
design by Otto Kolb,
Herrenberg, 1961

Sketch,
armchair 457, Walter Knoll,
design by Otto Kolb,
Herrenberg, 1961

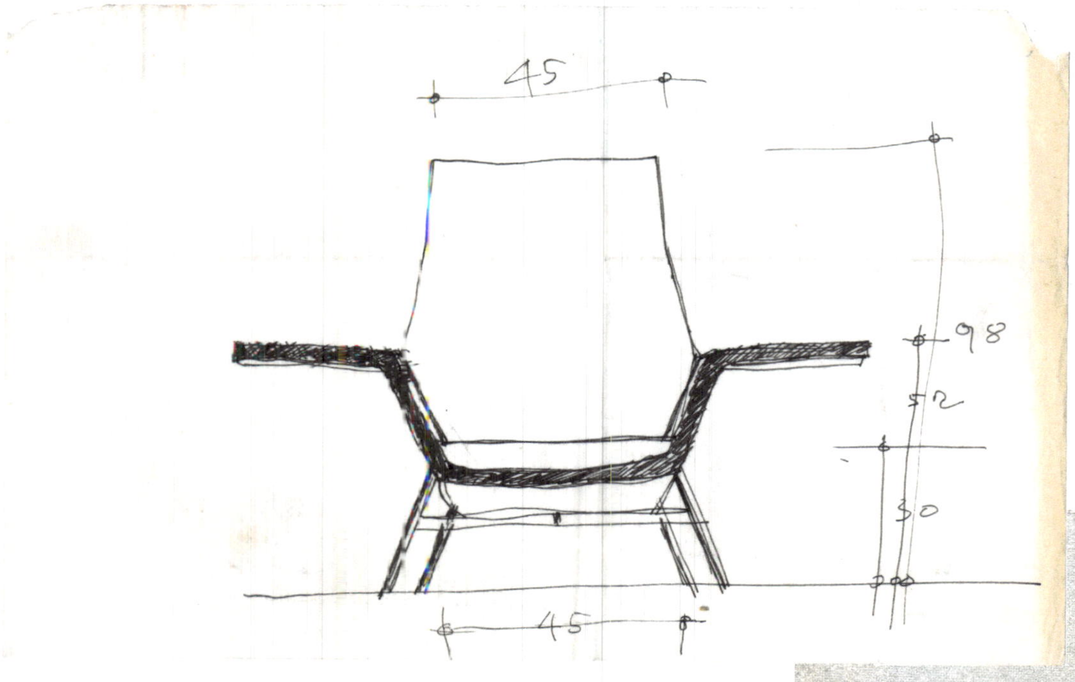

Private residence of Otto Kolb,
architect Otto Kolb,
Zurich, 1961

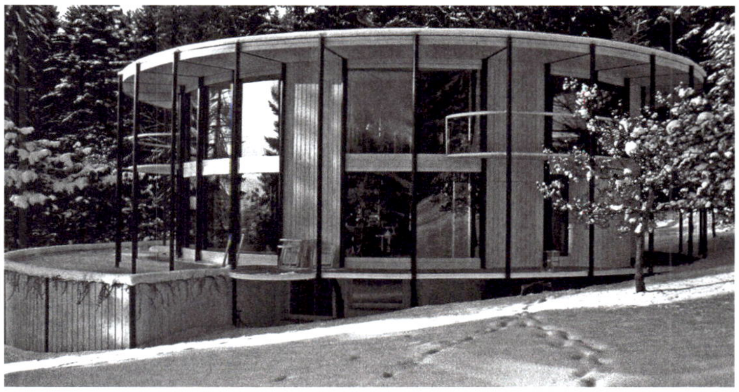

WK + CO

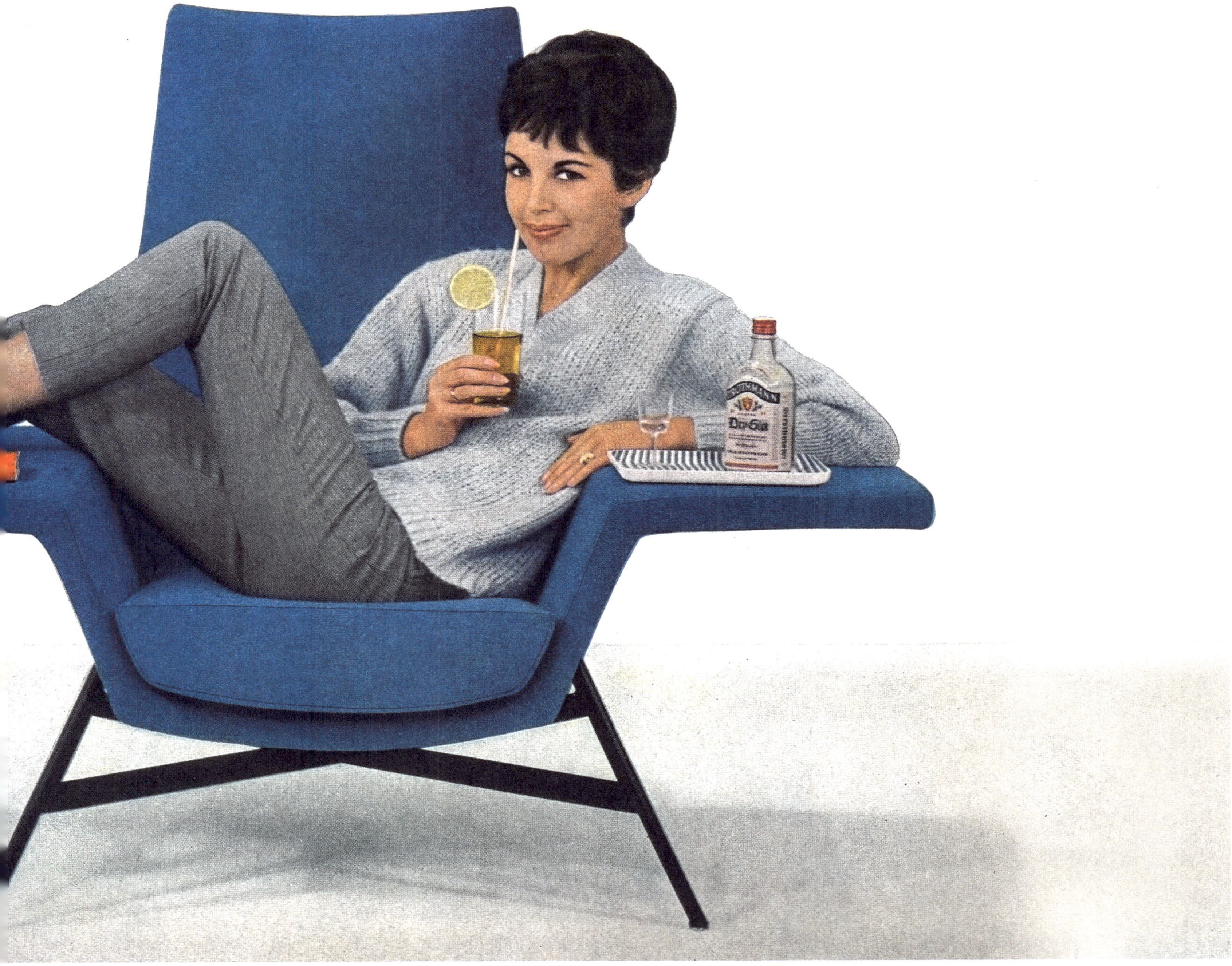

As if the masters of seating minimalism had wanted to prove that they were not only capable of using a ruler, but also a pair of compasses, they produced designs based on circles, that other basic shape that had previously been worshiped at the Bauhaus. This included Waeckerlin's diminutive round chairs, which had a tubular steel frame based on three delicate poles of equal length. They were actually semicircular chairs, just like Grunow's round sofa[20], which had rounded armrests, likewise his round chair (see p. 198). By contrast, in 1962, the Swiss designer duo Trix and Robert Haussmann actually designed a circular chair for Wilhelm Knoll, to which the contrast between the dark leather and the light wooden frame lent extra charm. In the same year, the pair designed an armchair for the Swiss Design Collection, which can still be found in the collection of Walter Knoll to the present day under the name Haussmann 310. The modular suite produced by Walter Knoll in 1963 consisted of a combination of rectangles and circles – round on the inside and angular on the outside. The sitting area, which curves at the back, is incorporated into the waist-high upholstered cube as if it had been cut out of a block. With their straight lines, the cube-shaped seats can be combined, edge to edge, with tables of differing height. System design had reached the living room.

GENERATIONS

After Walter Knoll, now 88 years old, had attended the Cologne furniture fair in the spring of 1964, he insisted on dictating a five-page report for his secretary to type out on the manual typewriter. There was good news to tell. This was because "when entering the stand (his own), the visitor immediately experienced an atmosphere of cultural endeavor and thorough planning," he observed with satisfaction. It was therefore "not a 'trade fair', but a show of well-presented pieces of furniture and carefully selected colors."[21] A total of 28 models were exhibited (including seven by Grunow). The enclosed cost sheet showed a total of around 26,000 Marks. A substantial investment that corresponded to several years' salary. This showed what great importance was now attached to an appearance in Cologne. All developments were critically noted, for example that "with the extraordinarily large offer of upholstered furniture from Germany and abroad, the proportion of sales for the individual manufacturer naturally (had to) shrink." He did not even rule out the "collapse of individual companies."[22] At the end, the senior also made an appearance at the representatives' meeting. He brought his grandson Michael along to this hugely important gathering, which dealt with serious matter but then, in the end, also became quite merry. The recent high school graduate had just completed an internship within the company, and would himself later become a savvy trade fair expert.

At the Christmas party of the same year, a piece by Brahms was played as a prelude, before those celebrating anniversaries were honored according to good custom. Afterwards, Walter Knoll rose to give a speech, in which he recalled how he had founded the company four decades earlier and how everything had begun with a carpenter and five upholsterers in Stuttgart-Feuerbach. Lastly, he announced his formal retirement and urged trust in the co-partners Dr. Walter Combe and his son Robert, who was taking his place. "I myself," disclosed Walter Knoll, "will continue to be part of the company as a limited partner and will be available with my advice and experience in all crucial matters."[23] In this way, the founder remained within the company. The question of who would be calling the shots in "crucial matters" in future therefore remained open. Although Walter Knoll had vacated his executive chair, he continued to be present in the background. And he still had an "executive chauffeur" at his disposal, whose job also included presenting him with important mail at precisely 11 o'clock every morning.

Behind the wheel of the automobile, a Mercedes 220 with tailfins, now sat Josef Czimmer, a young carpenter and frame maker, who had started at the company in the mid-1950s at the age of 15 and would remain loyal to it until his retirement and beyond for over 60 years. His chauffeur service followed a fixed weekly schedule. Among the important appointments was Tuesday lunch when the Rotary Club would meet in the restaurant of the "Stuttgarter Liederhalle" (Stuttgart Concert Hall). The boss then did the shopping, at Feinkost-Böhm or the Föhl pâtisserie, for example. When Czimmer was drafted into the military and faced a medical examination, Walter Knoll sent a letter to put in a good word for him. The examination had then been "very short", pondered the summoned Czimmer.[24] The chauffeur was indispensable. Of course, Walter Knoll also dealt with company matters during private trips, such as a detour he took to Bad Dürrheim

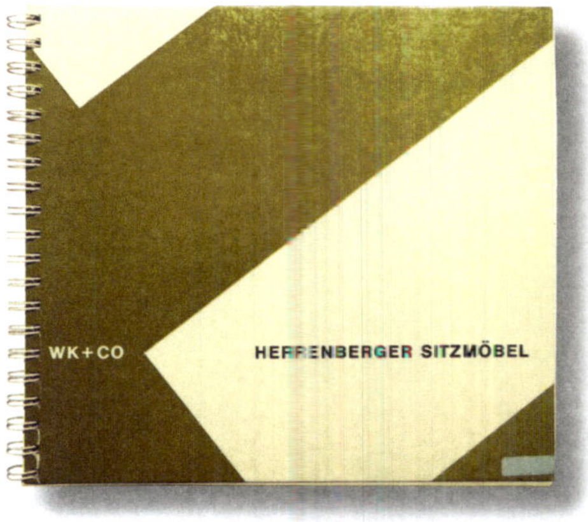

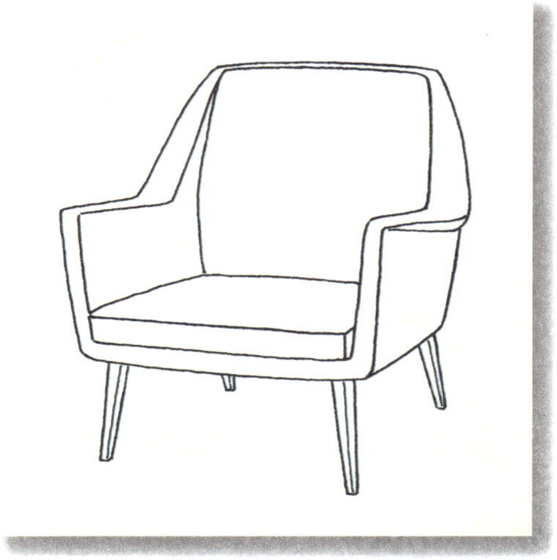

where he inspected the 400 Forum chairs that had just been set out in the great hall of the spa house. As usual, the boss and his chauffeur then spent the night in separate hotels. Josef Czimmer had to be reachable by telephone at all times, including on public holidays. Each year on Christmas Eve, he would bring Robert's family, who lived in Stuttgart, to the grandparents' house in Herrenberg. The return journey must have usually been quite entertaining. After all, that is when the gifts were judged again. And Robert's children, teenagers Kristina and Michael, would comment on grandpa's thrift.[25]

The handover of responsibility from Walter Knoll to his son Robert took place in stages. The founder remained within his company as a gray eminence throughout the 1960s. At the same time, the generation of his grandchildren was already being prepared for its future role. Michael Knoll, son of Robert and Bruni, received an unusually comprehensive education, but not in a commercial direction as had been the rule until then. Michael, who had a talent for drawing and was a frequent visitor to his grandfather's private library with its rich collection of art books, studied at the Merz School in Stuttgart. Originally established as a craft school, an education in the fine arts takes center stage at the reformed secondary school, although – following Stuttgart's special path – great importance is also placed on technical skills. In this respect, Michael Knoll, who had completed internships in various departments of his family's company, was certainly well prepared. At the beginning of the 1960s, he then went to London for a few months, like his uncle Hans had once done, to work for the furniture manufacturer Parker-Knoll and gain his first experiences abroad. Finally, in 1964, the year in which his father took charge of the company, he became a student at the "Freie Kunstschule" (Independent Art School) in Stuttgart. The private institution was founded by Adolf Hölzel, the pioneer of abstract painting, whose circle also included Willi Baumeister.[26] To the present day, this technical college for all things creative, the oldest of its kind in Germany, follows the Bauhaus education model in the spirit of Johannes Itten, who, of course, was also a student of Hölzel. Michael Knoll had also wanted to become an artist but then changed his mind. Already in the

THE HANDOVER OF RESPONSIBILITY FROM WALTER KNOLL TO HIS SON ROBERT TOOK PLACE IN STAGES. THE FOUNDER REMAINED WITHIN HIS COMPANY AS A GRAY EMINENCE.

following year, at the age of 21, he enrolled for a course in interior design at the Stuttgart Academy. He was now in the place where, ever since the days of Bernhard Pankok and Adolf Schneck, the focus had been on reinventing living. The institution, where Arno Votteler had also studied and would later become a lecturer, was a think tank for modern furniture. The sensitive Knoll Junior's teacher was none other than Herta-Maria Witzemann. The Stuttgarter-by-choice, now Germany's most successful interior designer, who had designed a bestseller for Walter Knoll in the form of the model 363 (see p. 168 f.), acted as an outspoken advocate of *Gute Form* (Good Design) there.

---

20 ▶ It is a geometrized further development of the same sofa type by Gianfranco Frattini from 1957.

21 ▶ WK archives, 1964.

22 ▶ Ibid.

23 ▶ "Unsere Monatsbetrachtung" (Our Monthly Review), in: "Echo aus Herrenberg" (Echo from Herrenberg), magazine supplement "Wir vom Holz" (We from the Wood Industry), February 1965.

24 ▶ Interview with Josef Czimmer on 11/17/2014.

25 ▶ Ibid.

26 ▶ Hölzel's circle also included artists such as Johannes Itten, Oskar Schlemmer, Lily Hildebrandt, and Ida Kerkovius.

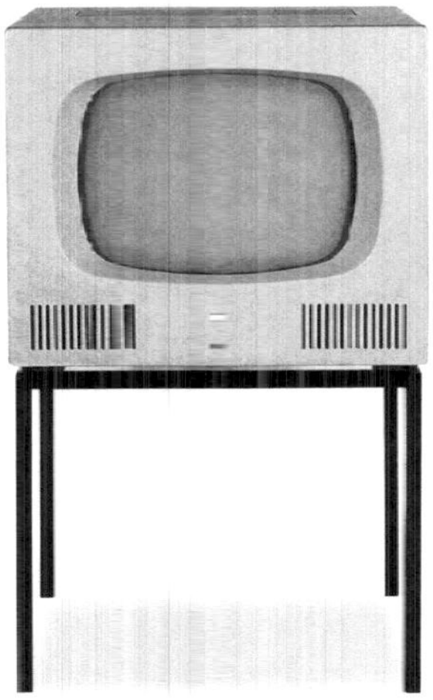

The television that Herbert Hirche designed for Braun at the end of the 1950s was no longer a TV set, but almost a perfect cube.

MINIMALIST

Some believed they had found the archetype of upholstered furniture. The minimalist furniture of the early 1960s worshiped the cube and the modular system.

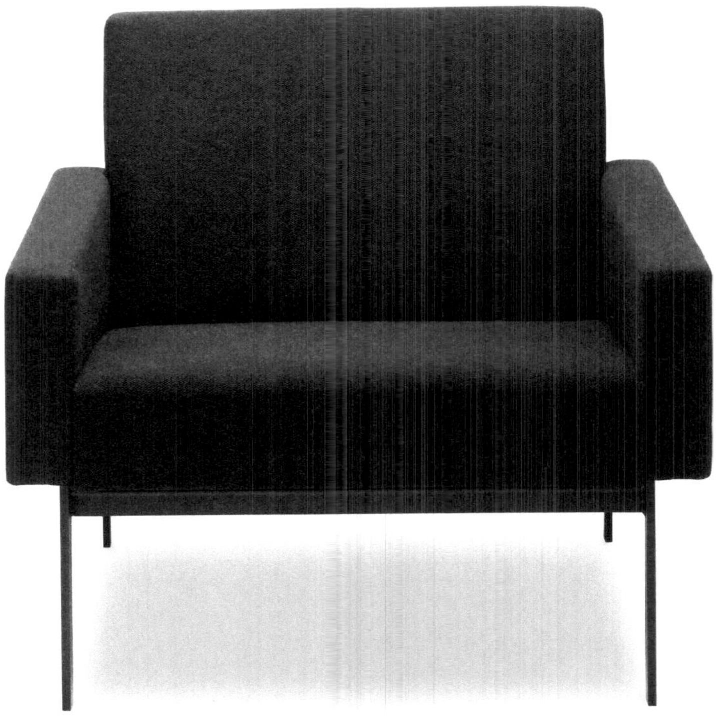

Armchair 438 A, Walter Knoll, design by Rolf Grunow, Herrenberg, 1960

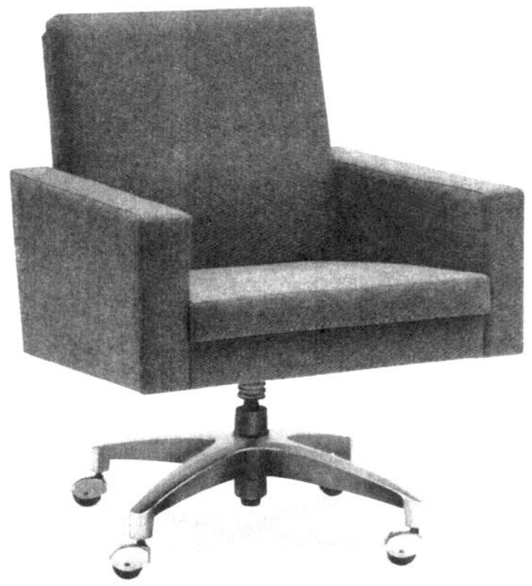

Armchair 496 DV, Walter Knoll,
Herrenberg, 1960

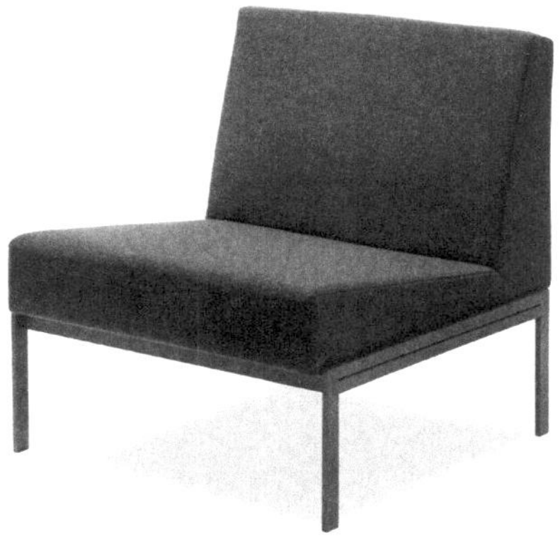

Armchair 438, Walter Knoll,
design by Rolf Grunow,
Herrenberg, 1960

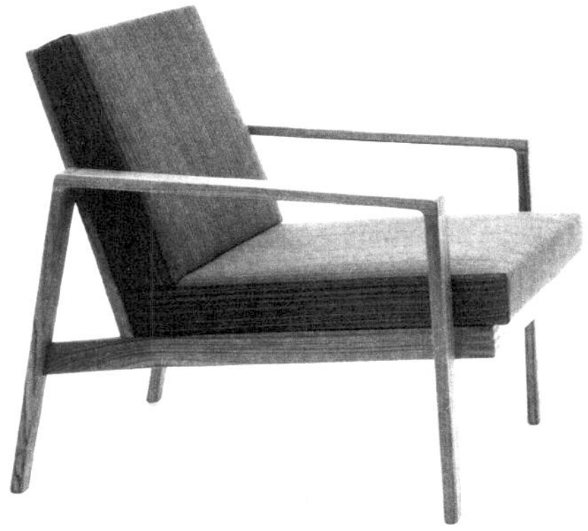

Armchair Antimott 201,
Wilhelm Knoll,
Stuttgart, 1958

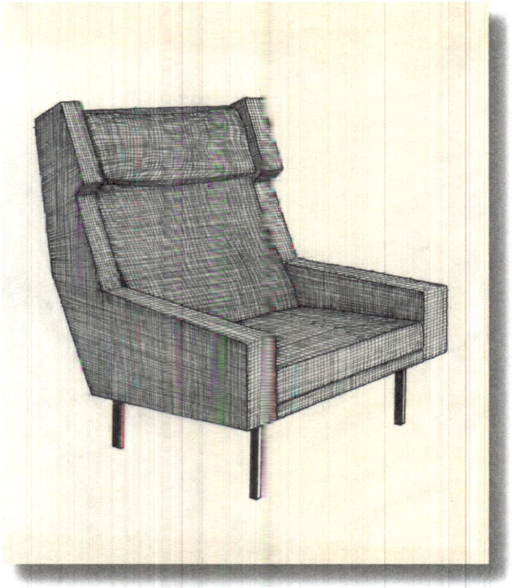

In this respect, she resembled her colleagues at the institute, the architects Herbert Hirche and Rolf Gutbrod, who were, incidentally, also on informal terms with the freshman's father and grandfather. This was also part of Stuttgart's infrastructure of modernity.

The student Knoll was therefore sipping directly from the sources of modern furniture. And this was in the fervid climate of the late 1960s when not only hair, but also ideas, were growing wild. At the time, a whole gang of innovators was giving fresh impetus to a wide variety of fields in Stuttgart. Here, the next generation of architects, among them Günter Behnisch, Frei Otto and Wilfried Beck-Erlang, were developing their own unconventional concepts. The philosopher Max Bense became a thought provoker and pioneer of computer art. Meanwhile, the choreographer John Cranko was leading the ballet company at the "Staatstheater Stuttgart" (Stuttgart State Theater) to worldwide fame. The fact that this has persisted until now is not least down to the ballet school that he eventually founded, at the time the only one with a state diploma and still one of the most acclaimed ballet schools today. Cranko was a welcome guest at the house of Michael Knoll's parents. The Briton, who also appreciated the fact that his host spoke fluent English (still a rarity in those days), was invited round many a time for *Zwiebelrostbraten mit Spätzle* (fried beef and onions in gravy with spaetzle pasta). On such occasions, he naturally also discussed his ideas for a school. Regarding the need for a professional education in dance, the famed choreographer was only ever met with unequivocal support. Ultimately, there was also general agreement as far as an appreciation of good eduction was concerned. Perhaps, if Mrs Witzemann had also joined in, the circle of kindred spirits would have extended even further. After all, she was also vigorously battling for recognition of her study program and, in the end, pushed through the diploma for interior designers for "her boys", as she called her students. Michael Knoll happily and intensively studied under Herta-Maria Witzemann. The fact that it took a good five years for him to graduate as an interior designer in 1970 was, however, also down to a severe automobile accident that forced him to take a break.

Never before had successive employed interior designers been coming and going so quickly. In the 1960s, at least a dozen of them worked at Walter Knoll. The average length of stay was therefore less than a year. The plastic chair produced in one piece was introduced at the 1966 Cologne furniture fair. The Finnish Ball Chair and the Bofinger Chair – which also emerged from the new Swabian design valley and of which well over a hundred thousand were sold[27] – were clear signals that the end of simple angularity was being announced. What followed

IN THE 1960s, SUCCESSIVE EMPLOYED INTERIOR DESIGNERS CAME AND WENT MORE QUICKLY THAN EVER BEFORE.

was a new aesthetic blending pop and plastic. In its review of the trade fair, the chronicler of the company newspaper also reported on "the retail's desire for fancier objects."[28] The review declared that "the struggle among the thousand companies exhibiting in Cologne was very tough, far tougher than in previous trade fair years."[29] In this period of transition and reorientation, during which annual sales figures stagnated at around five million, a few designs for individual pieces of furniture emerged that stood out for their originality and elegance, but never made the rank of bestseller or design classic. The rediscovery of flowing lines yielded a hitherto barely acknowledged variety of new forms.

This eventful time saw an extraordinary project: a lightweight metal chair that was designed according to a principle patented by the architect Bodo Rasch (see p. 204) – the same Rasch, now in his late

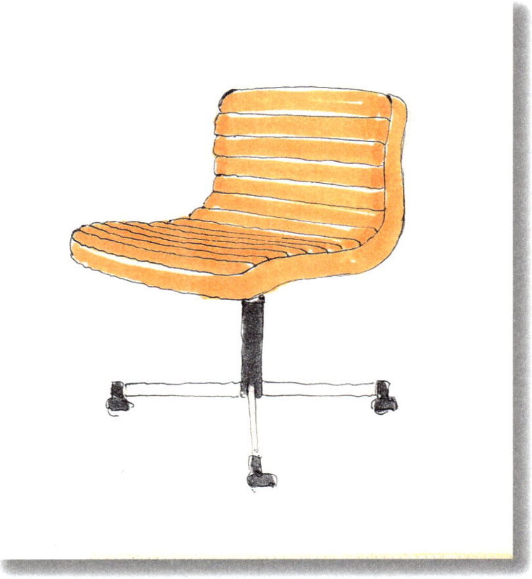

sixties, who as a young man had been involved in the Weissenhof exhibition and had signed up his friend Mies van der Rohe for the project. He had since become friends with the Knoll family. Together with Robert Knoll, he now intended to get a futuristic-looking upholstered chair made of aluminum ready for production. To this end, contact was established with a metalworks factory in the vicinity of Geislingen and the Aluminiumwalzwerke Singen (Aluminum Rolling Mills Singen), one of the largest and most experienced companies in the aluminum industry, which developed the Alucobond composite panels, among other things. A prototype of Rasch's design was produced and then exhibited at the 1969 furniture fair in Cologne. Nevertheless, "although there is certainly interest, the price of the chair in question (had) become much too expensive."[30] A common problem, though it did not cause Robert Knoll to abandon the project in this case. "dear robi, what do you think about the chair that you had made with the aluminum parts according to my idea," cautiously inquired Bodo Rasch eventually. "i believe that my model fills a genuine gap. i could try to establish contact with knoll international. they are lacking new models."[31] This broad hint was also no use. Ultimately, three years had passed, the year was 1972. The aluminum chair was eventually completely forgotten. This seems to have been the fate of a professional visionary like Rasch, who spent his entire life always being ahead of his time – usually too far ahead.

---

27 ▶ Once again, an inspired designer and an inspired entrepreneur had found each other: the architect was Helmut Bätzner, born in Nagold and a colleague of Rolf Gutbrod; the entrepreneur was Rudolf Baresel-Bofinger from Stuttgart.

28 ▶ "Echo aus Herrenberg" (Echo from Herrenberg), April 1966, p. 4.

29 ▶ Ibid.

30 ▶ Letter from Robert Knoll to the Heuer metalworks factory in Schlierbach dated 09/01/1972, WK archives.

31 ▶ Letter from Bodo Rasch to Robert Knoll dated 02/13/1970, WK archives.

FUNCTIONALITY
Folding and combining were old virtues in the Knoll dynasty – thrift likewise, such as the quiet transportation of furniture using electric delivery trucks.

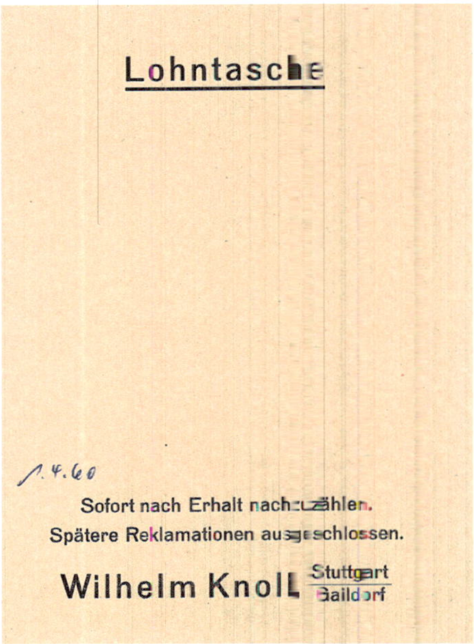
Lohntasche

1.4.60

Sofort nach Erhalt nachzuzählen.
Spätere Reklamationen ausgeschlossen.

Wilhelm Knoll Stuttgart / Baildorf

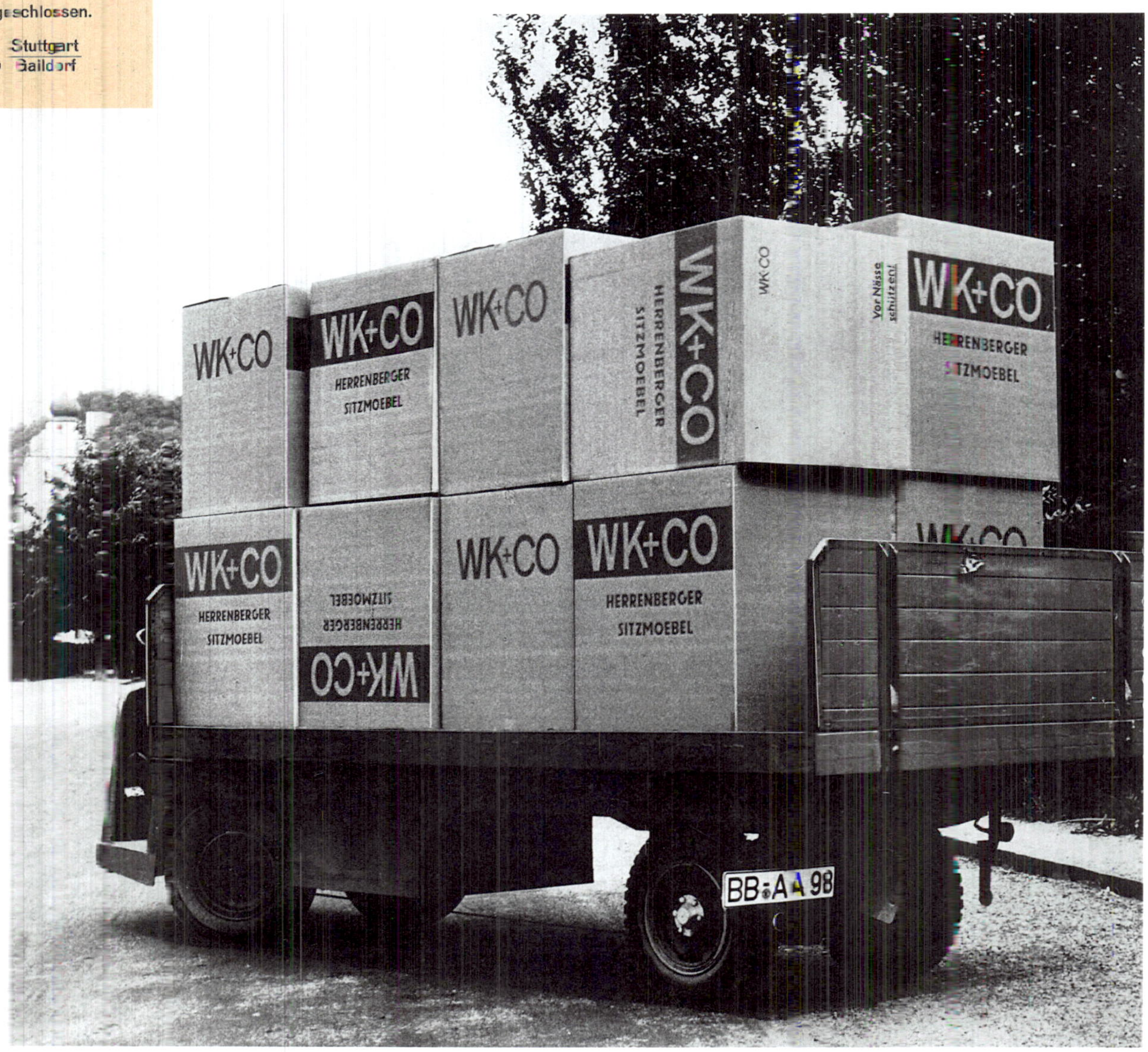

Pay packet,
Stuttgart, around 1960

Furniture transport with
an electric truck,
Walter Knoll,
Herrenberg, around 1955

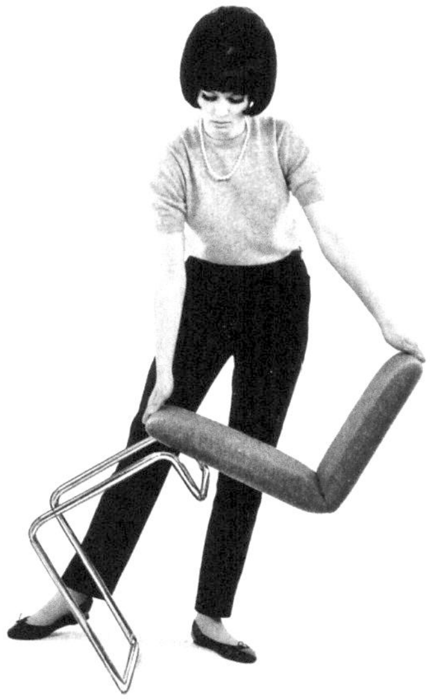

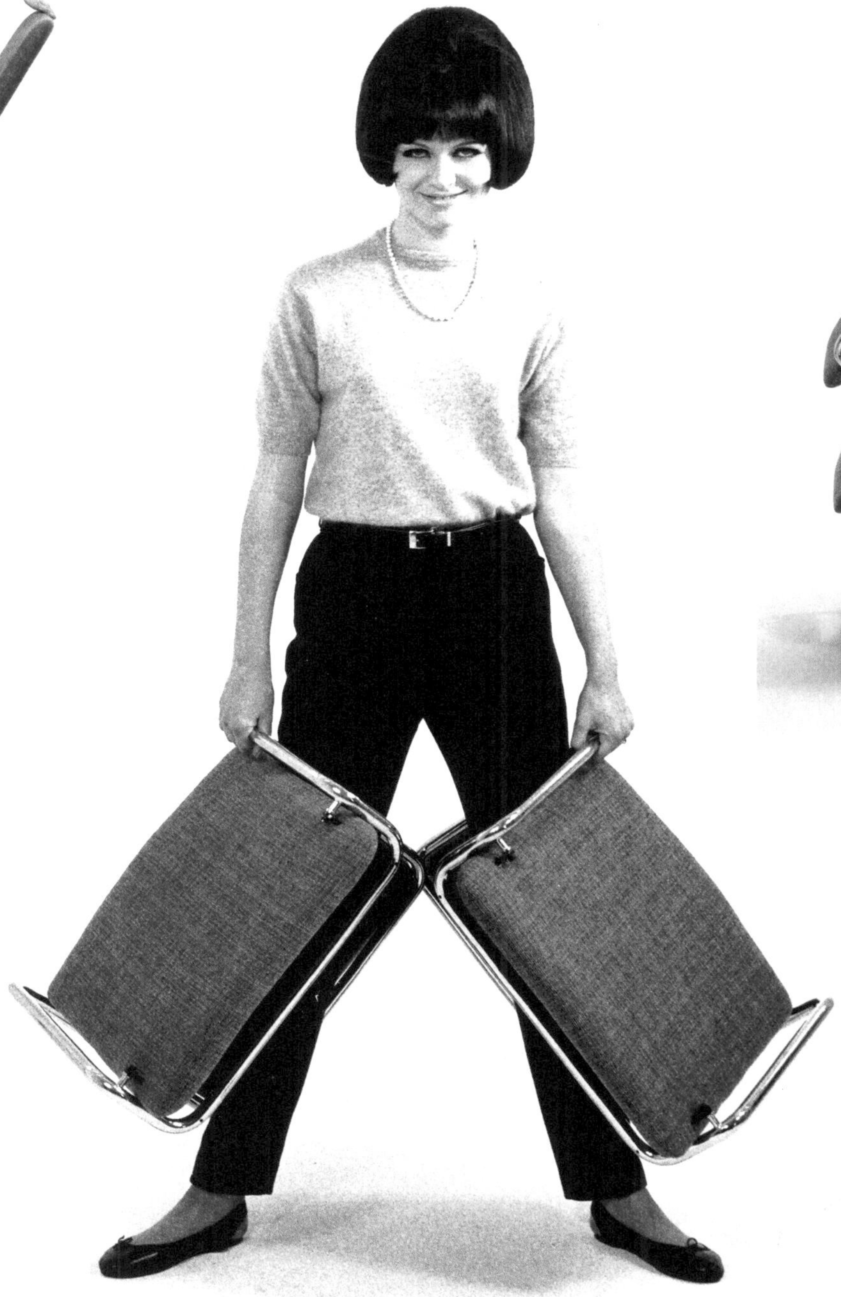

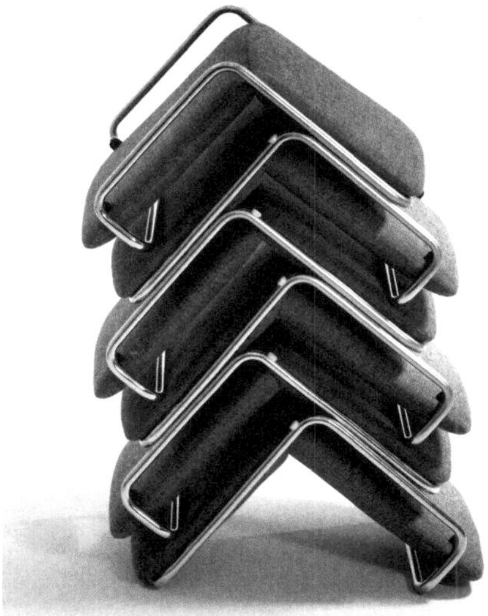

Folding chair 538,
Walter Knoll,
Herrenberg, around 1960

ROUND FORMS

A pair of compasses was also a tool of minimalist furniture geometry. The new circular forms at Walter Knoll were of German, Italian and Swiss origin.

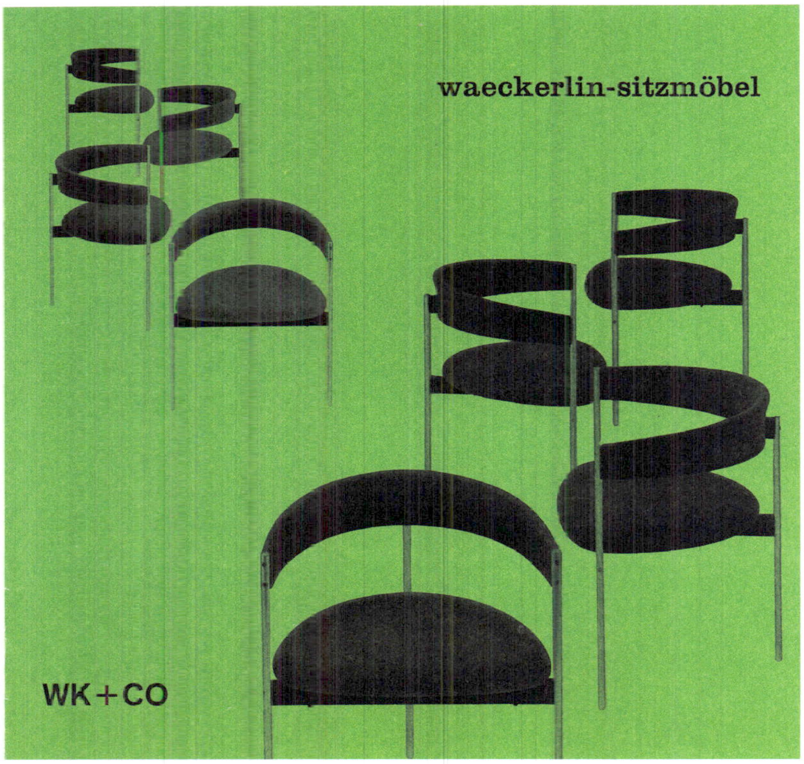

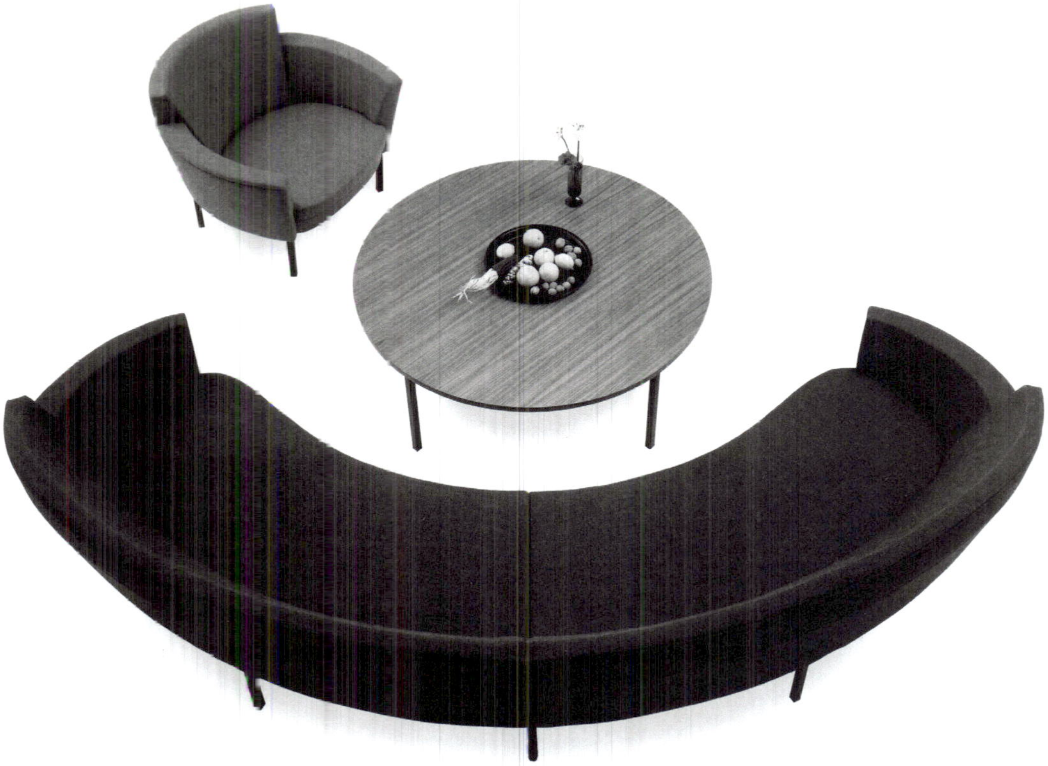

Brochure cover photo, round chair W 55, Walter Knoll, design by Dieter Waeckerlin, Herrenberg, 1961

Round sofa and armchair 470, Walter Knoll, design by Rolf Grunow, Herrenberg, 1962

CHANGING FORMS

In the stylistic no man's land of the 1960s, a few original and, simultaneously, austerely shaped designs emerged, such as an open bucket seat and an office chair with a slim silhouette.

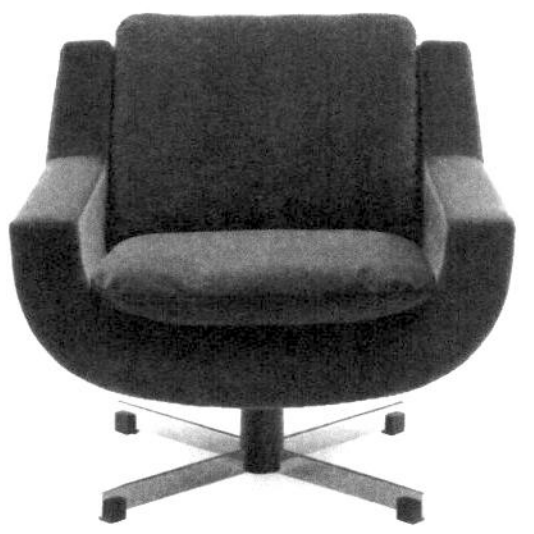

Armchair 508, Walter Knoll,
design by Volker Laprell,
Herrenberg, 1964

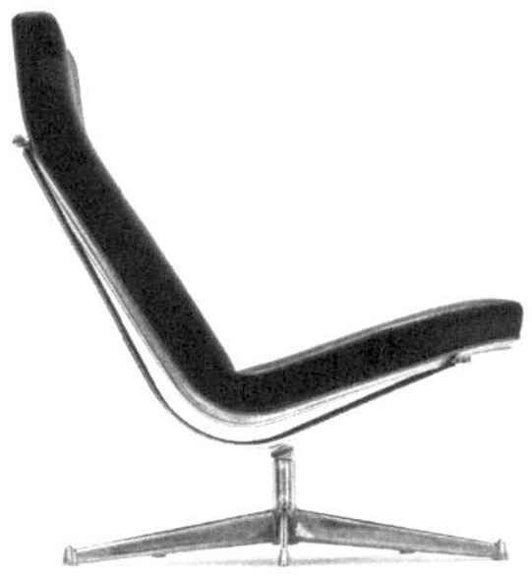

Armchair 567, Walter Knoll,
design by Urs Borer,
Herrenberg, 1966

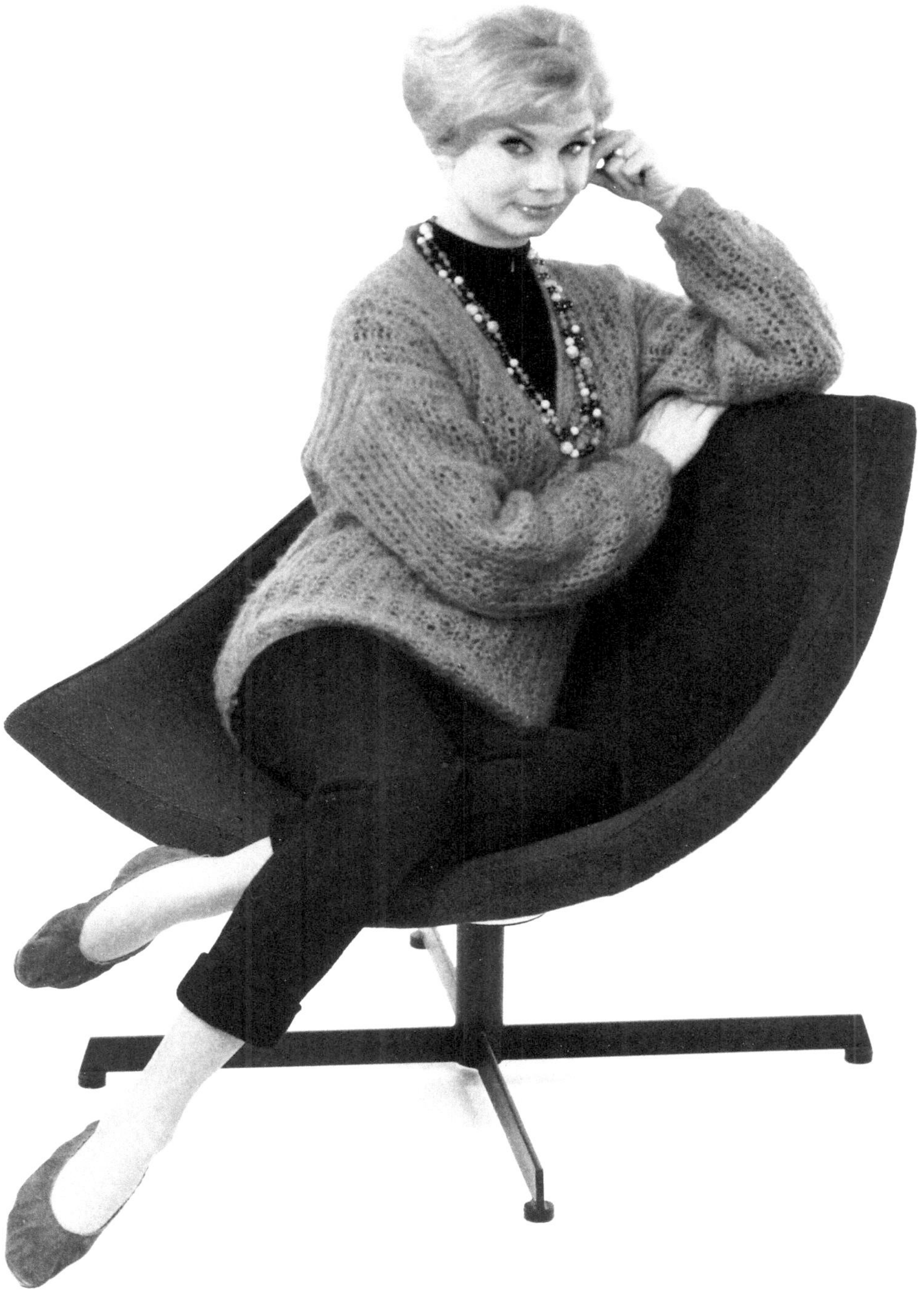

Armchair 430, Walter Knoll,
design by Rolf Grunow,
Herrenberg, 1960

FURNITURE SHOW

The Cologne furniture fair developed into a truly international event. Walter Knoll presented a new product line there, the office furniture range.

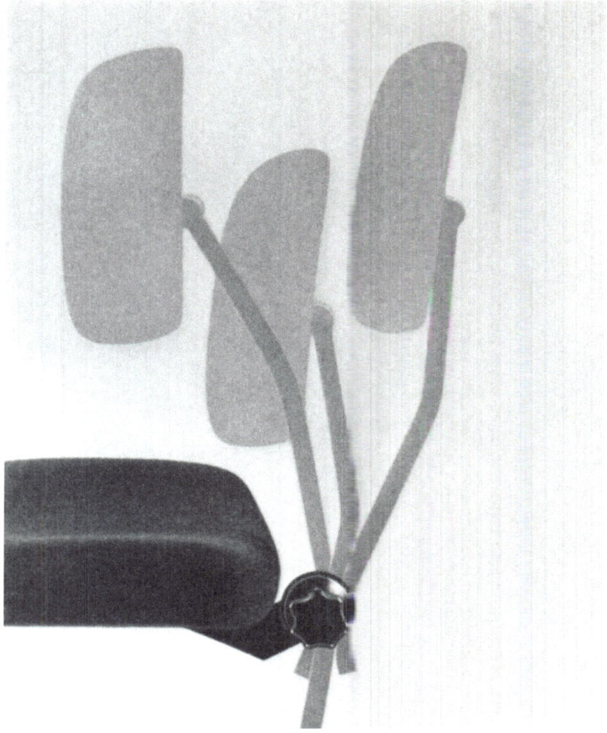

Chair 800 DF 4, Walter Knoll,
design by Urs Borer,
Herrenberg, 1969

Brochure cover photo,
chair 364 DV, Walter Knoll,
Herrenberg, 1965

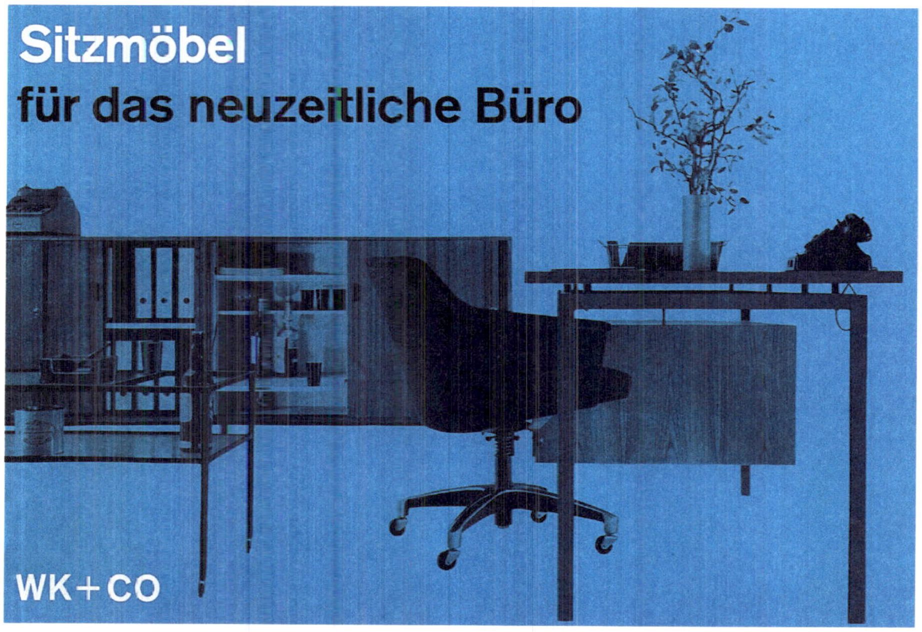

Leaflet for the furniture fair,
Cologne, 1960

SALON INTERNATIONAL

DU MEUBLE

Tous les deux ans,
venant du monde entier, les professionnels du meuble se rencontrent à Cologne, centre commercial et siège d'une foire renommée.

Les avantages décisifs
que présente l'offre internationale: chaque visiteur peut se documenter avec précision et prendre ses dispositions à coup sûr. Cologne est la place privilégiée où de nouveaux contacts peuvent être pris en toute objectivité.

J'expose à
hall IX
stand No. 9567

WILHELM KNOLL
meubles rembourrés
STUTTGART W
Forststraße 71
Tel. 6 91 41 - 43
succursale Gaildorf

Dans 10 halls avec une superficie de 90 000 m²
les fabricants allemands et étrangers montrent leurs productions:

Salles de séjour
Chambres à coucher
Bibliothèques
Salles à manger
Chambres d'enfants
Cuisines
Meubles garnis
Meubles à éléments
Meubles divers
Petits meubles
Ensembles de vestiaire
Tables
Sièges
(chaises, fauteuils, tabourets)
Meubles en vannerie
Meubles en tube d'acier
Matelas

COLOGNE
11-15 FEVRIER 1960

13-1.60

TRADE FAIR STANDS

The stands of Walter and Wilhelm Knoll were established constants at the rapidly expanding furniture fair in Cologne. The selection of textiles was an art in itself.

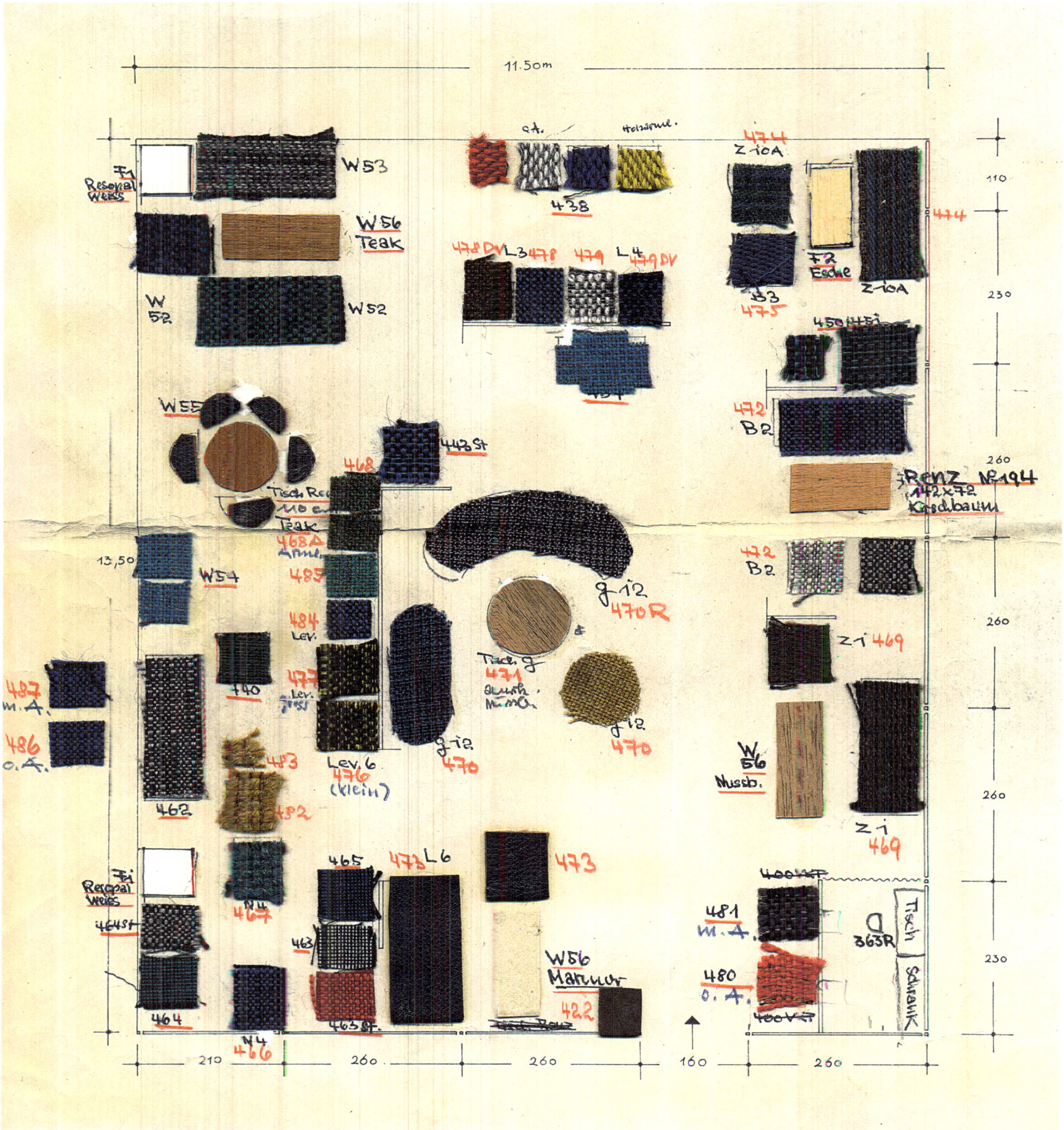

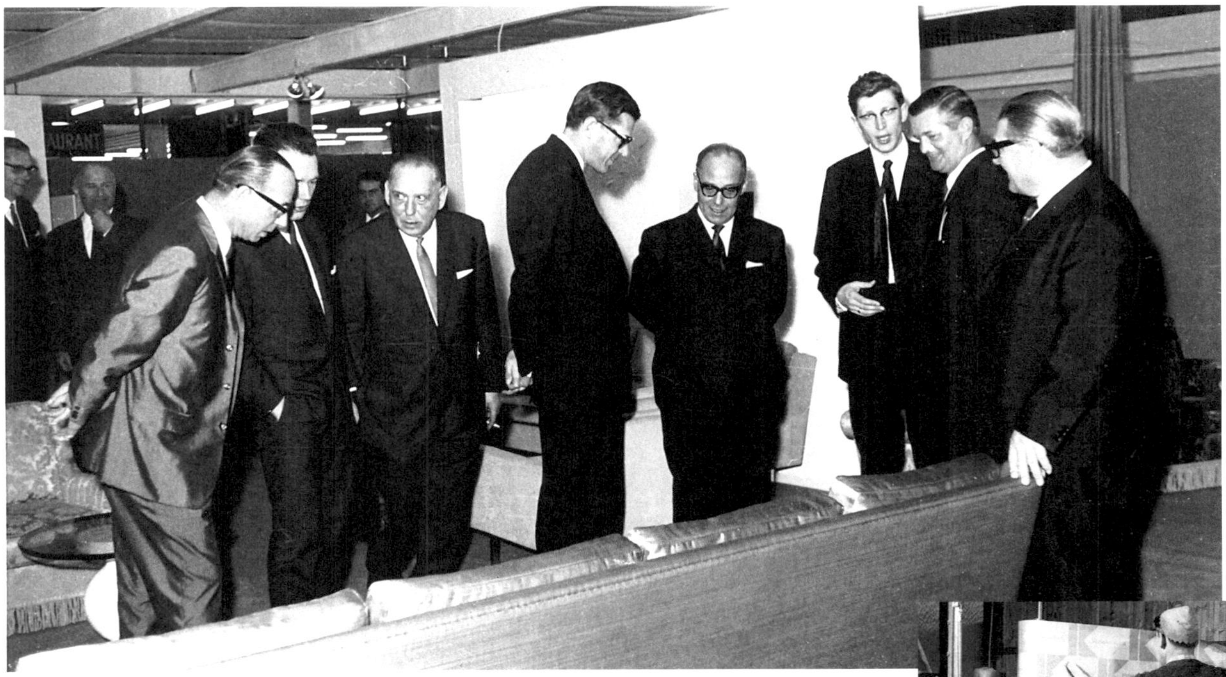

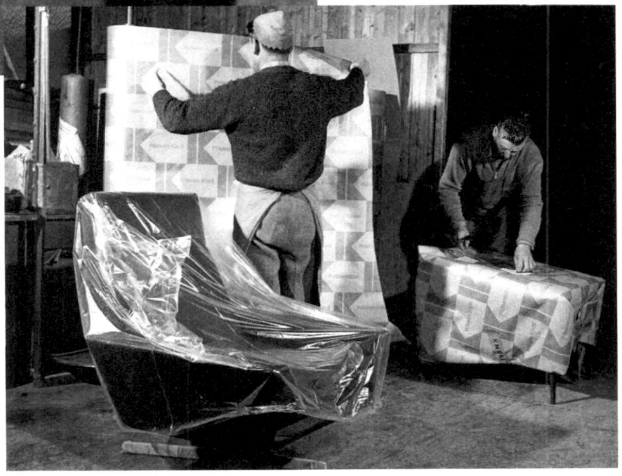

Presentation at the fair stand
of Wilhelm Knoll,
owner Dieter Knoll
(4th from left),
Cologne, 1960

Setting up the fair stand,
Cologne, 1964

Design sketch with fabric samples
for planning the trade fair stand,
Walter Knoll,
Herrenberg, 1959

PROTOTYPE

An aluminum chair by the architect Bodo Rasch was developed through to the prototype stage but, for reasons of cost, was not produced.

bodo rasch

architekt bodo rasch stuttgart oberaicher höhe im wispelwald tel 78 02 74

8-11-1969

Eingegangen
10. NOV. 1969
Erl. am ....

lieber robert knoll ,

die lichtpause wurde von mir angefertigt , weil alu-singen von allen krümmungen die radius-masse gebraucht hat . herr gitter glaubt , dass die in meinem plan festgehaltenen materialquerschnitte ausreichen . an quertraversen ist diejenige bei der schraubverbindung notwendig . je nach steifigkeit der polsterunterlage kann vielleicht auf die traverse an der oberkante rückenlehne verzichtet werden, - vielleicht auch auf diejenige an der vorderen sitzkante . das gewicht dieser beiden traversen ist mit dem gewicht der steifen polsterunterlage zu vergleichen , um zu entscheiden .

bei verwendung von stahl verringert sich der materialquerschnitt um 1/3 , nach angabe von herrn gitter .

beste grüsse

bankkonto: stuberbank stuttgart 5314

Letter from Bodo Rasch to Robert Knoll, Stuttgart, 1969

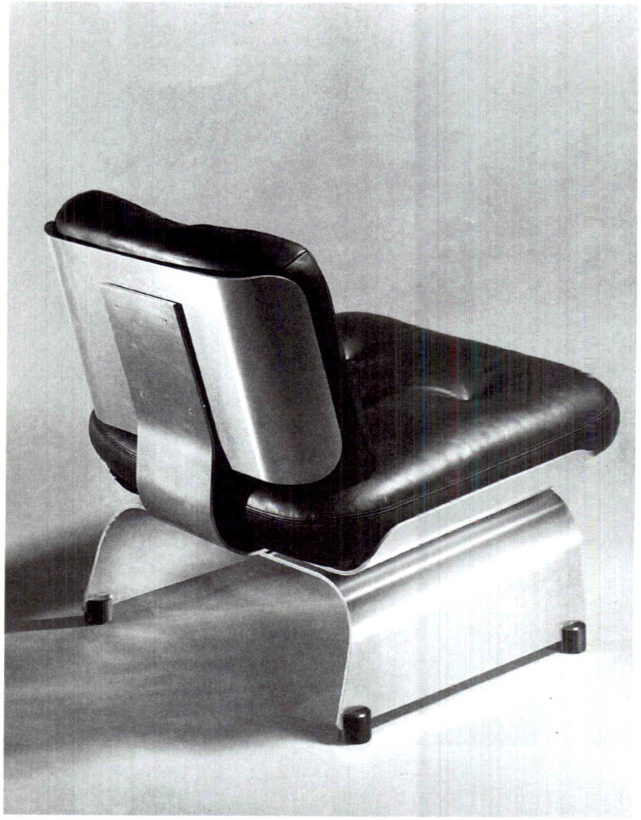

Prototype aluminum chair, Wilhelm Knoll, design by Bodo Rasch (not produced), Stuttgart, around 1965

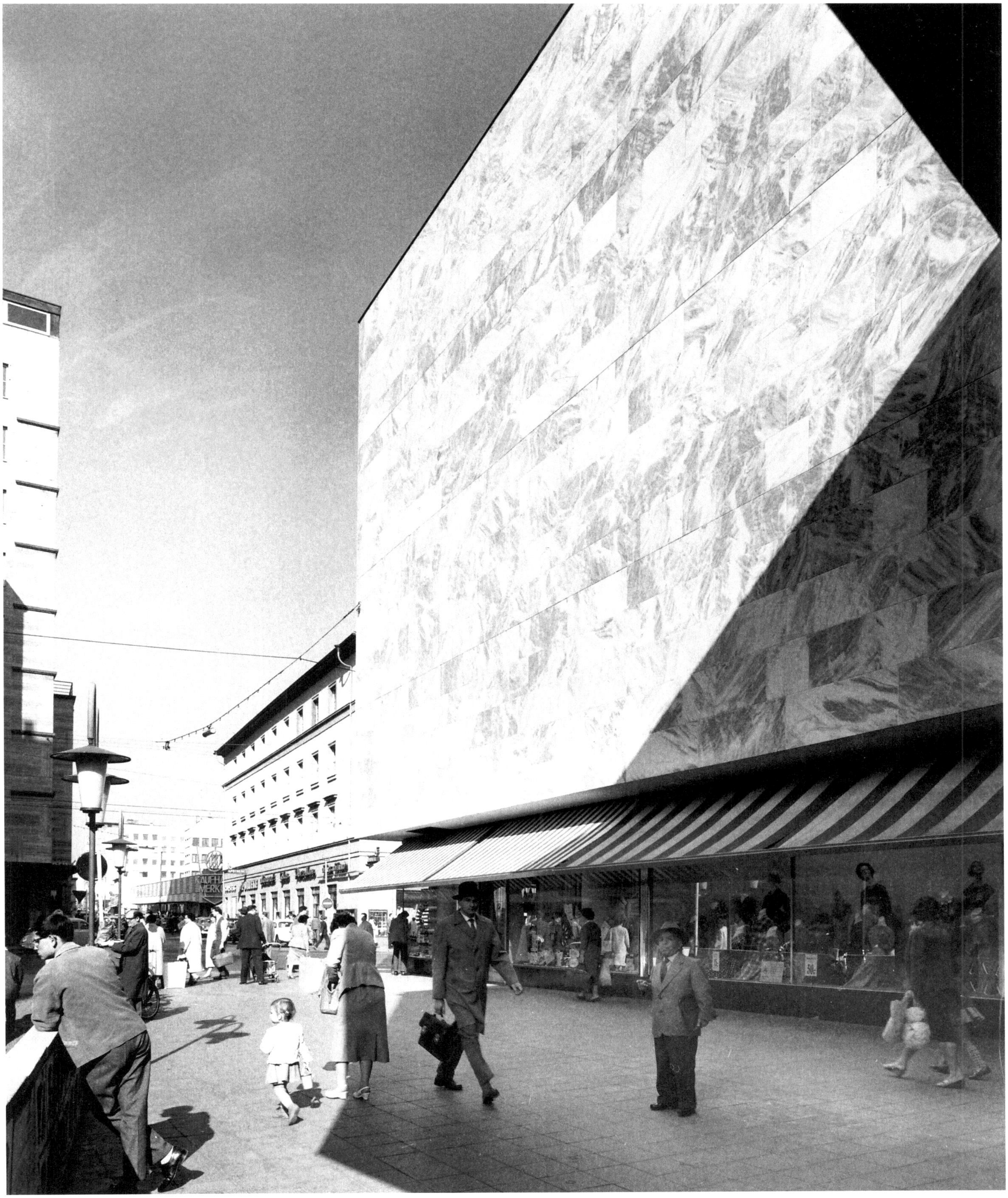

Breuninger department store,
architect Egon Eiermann,
built in 1962,
photograph by Franz Lazi,
Stuttgart, 1962

DANISH CONNECTION

The perfect designs of Jørgen Kastholm and Preben Fabricius were among the most successful of their time. The pair of high fliers also worked for two Swabian manufacturers: Alfred Kill and Walter Knoll.

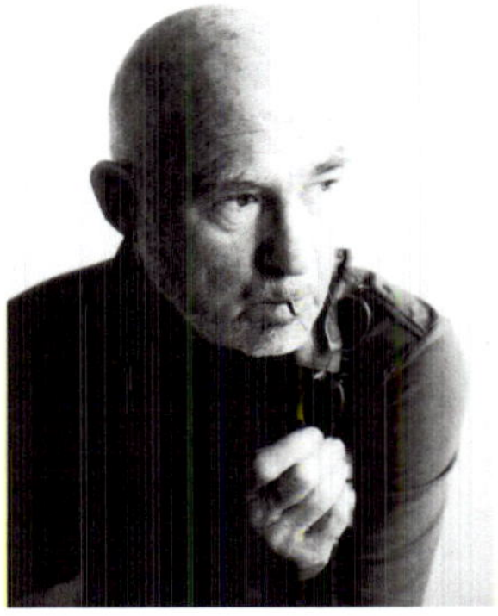

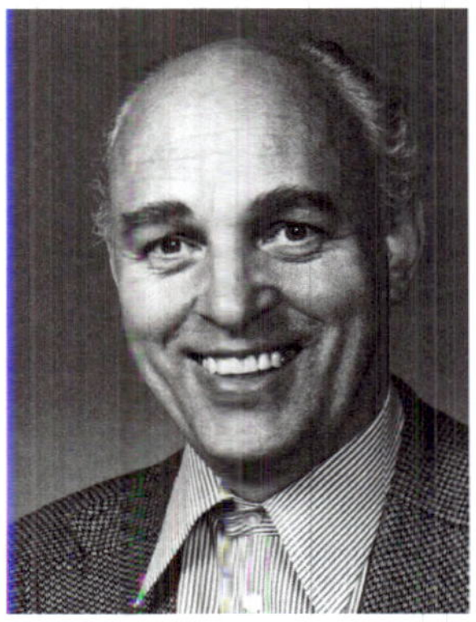

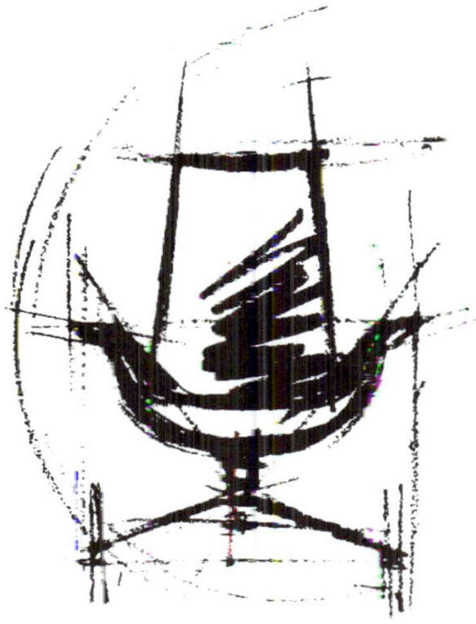

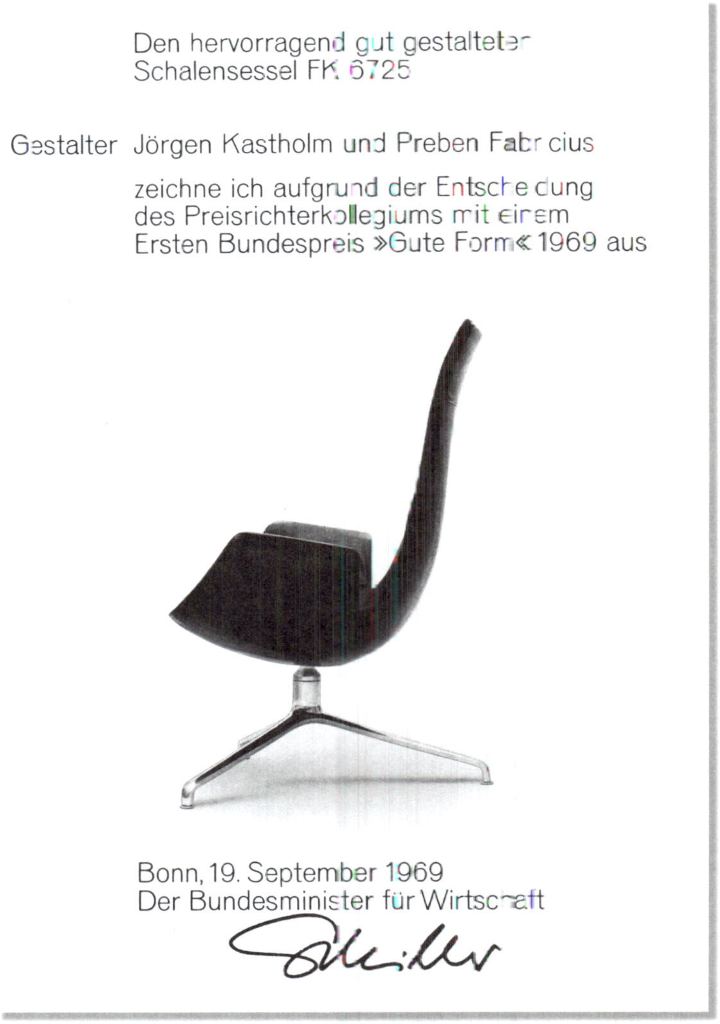

Den hervorragend gut gestalteten
Schalensessel FK 6725

Gestalter Jörgen Kastholm und Preben Fabricius

zeichne ich aufgrund der Entscheidung
des Preisrichterkollegiums mit einem
Ersten Bundespreis »Gute Form« 1969 aus

Bonn, 19. September 1969
Der Bundesminister für Wirtschaft

Certificate for the first "Bundespreis Gute Form" (German National Prize for Good Design) awarded for the bucket seat FK.

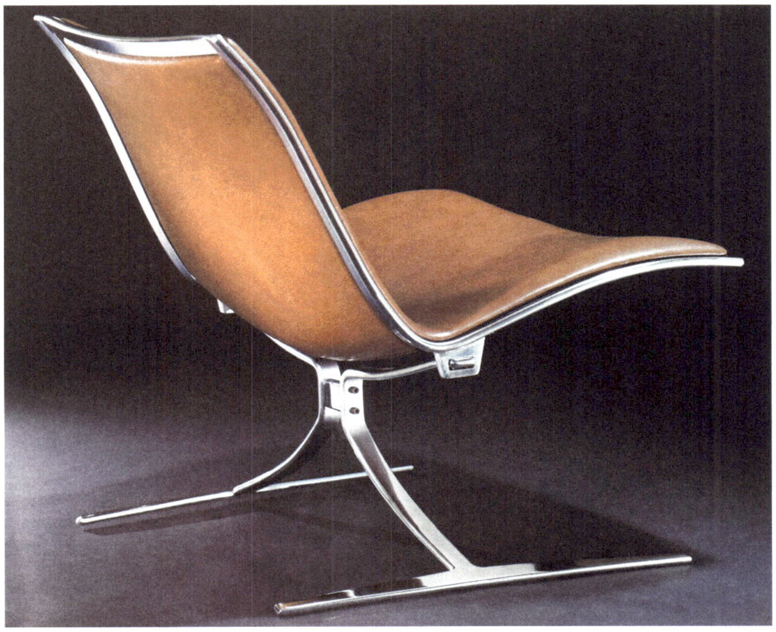

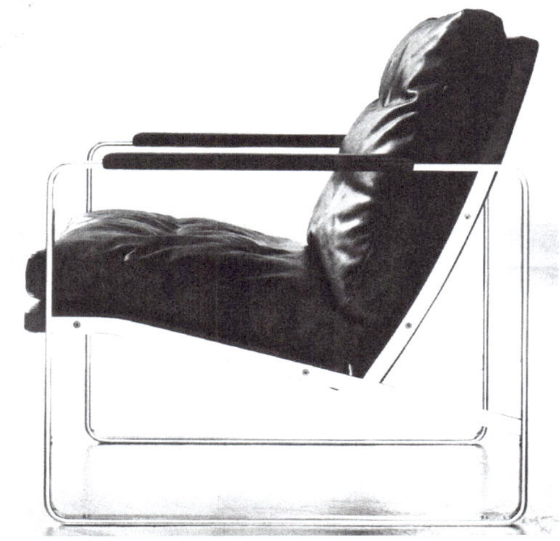

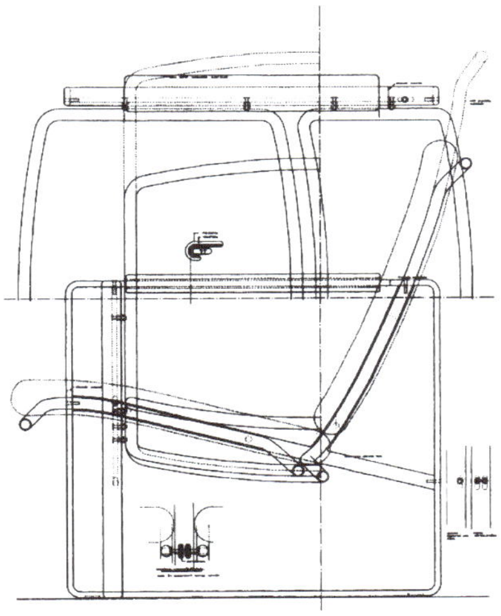

Chair 710,
Kill International,
design by Preben Fabricius,
Fellbach (near Stuttgart), 1976

Company logo,
around 1970

Armchair and design drawing
Conversation Chair, now Fabricius,
Walter Knoll,
design by Preben Fabricius,
Herrenberg, 1972

POP PROFILES

New interpretations of a classic theme: upholstery and steel frames nestle up against one another.

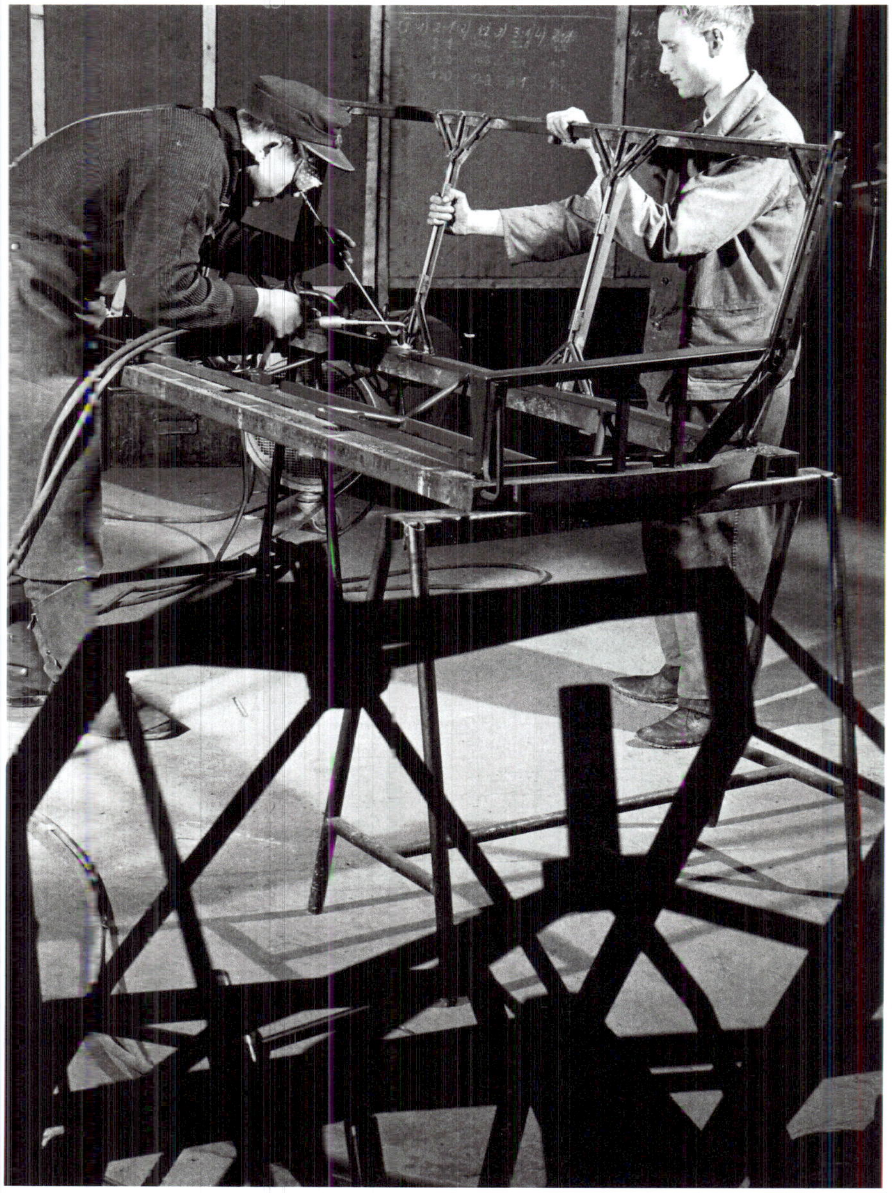

Production at Wilhelm Knoll, Gaildorf, around 1970

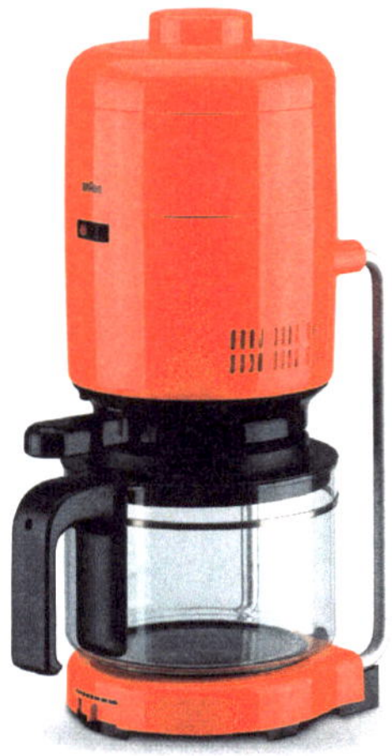

The first modern coffee machine from Braun, the KF 20 designed by Florian Seiffert, was also a tubular steel construction.

TUBULAR REVIVAL

The 1960s and 70s were an era of experimentation. The malleability of metal frames accommodated the climate of change. This produced a fascinating relationship between upholstery and the substructure.

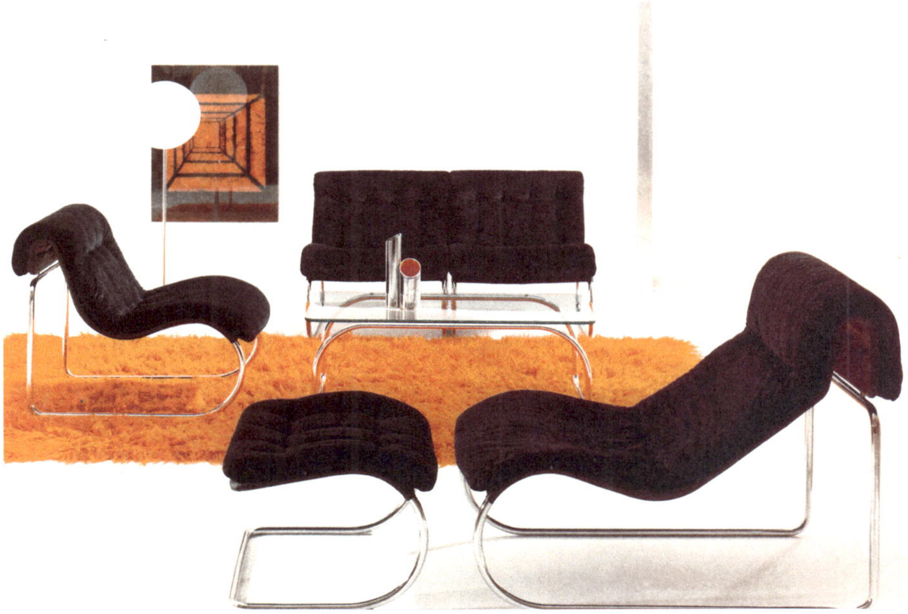

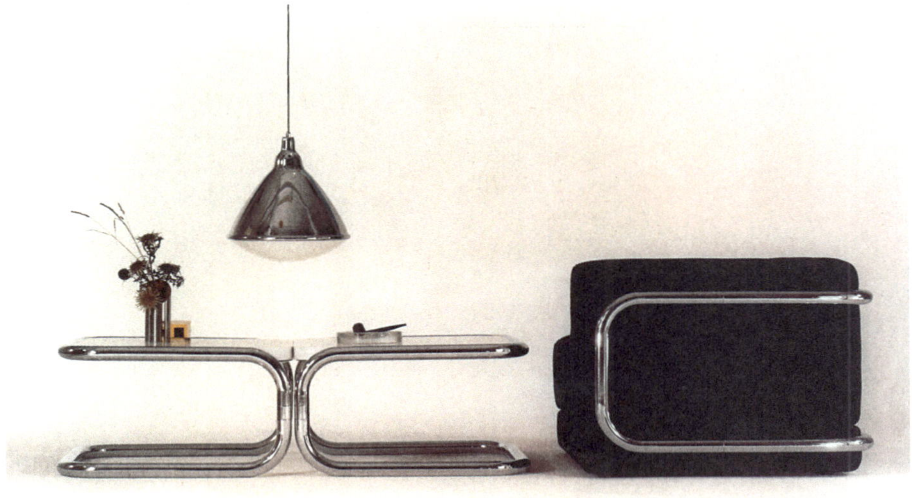

Catalog photo, armchair 147 and 148, stool 148 H and table 148 T, Walter Knoll, design by Bernd Münzebrock, Herrenberg, around 1970

Catalog photo, armchair and table 156, Walter Knoll, design by Bernd Münzebrock, Herrenberg, 1970

GENERATION CHANGE

From the mid-1960s Robert Knoll, son of the company founder, managed the business together with Walter Combe. His approach was to combine innovation with the elegance of "Classical Modernity".

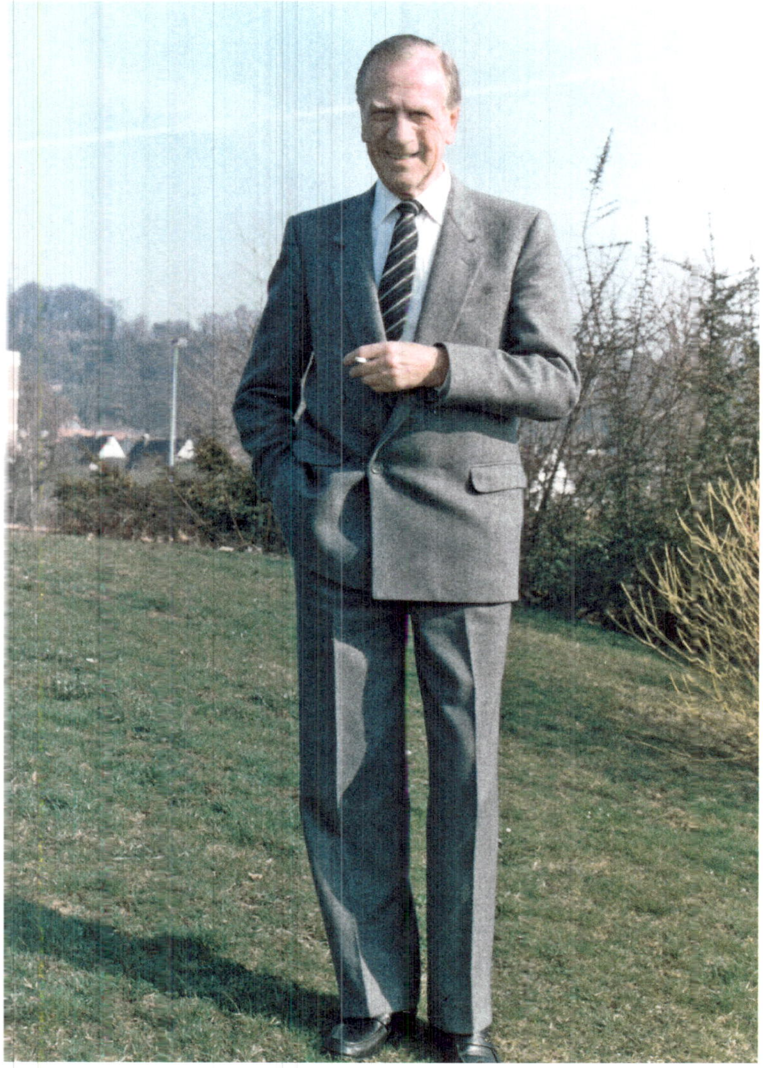

Robert Knoll, son of Walter Knoll, Herrenberg, around 1970

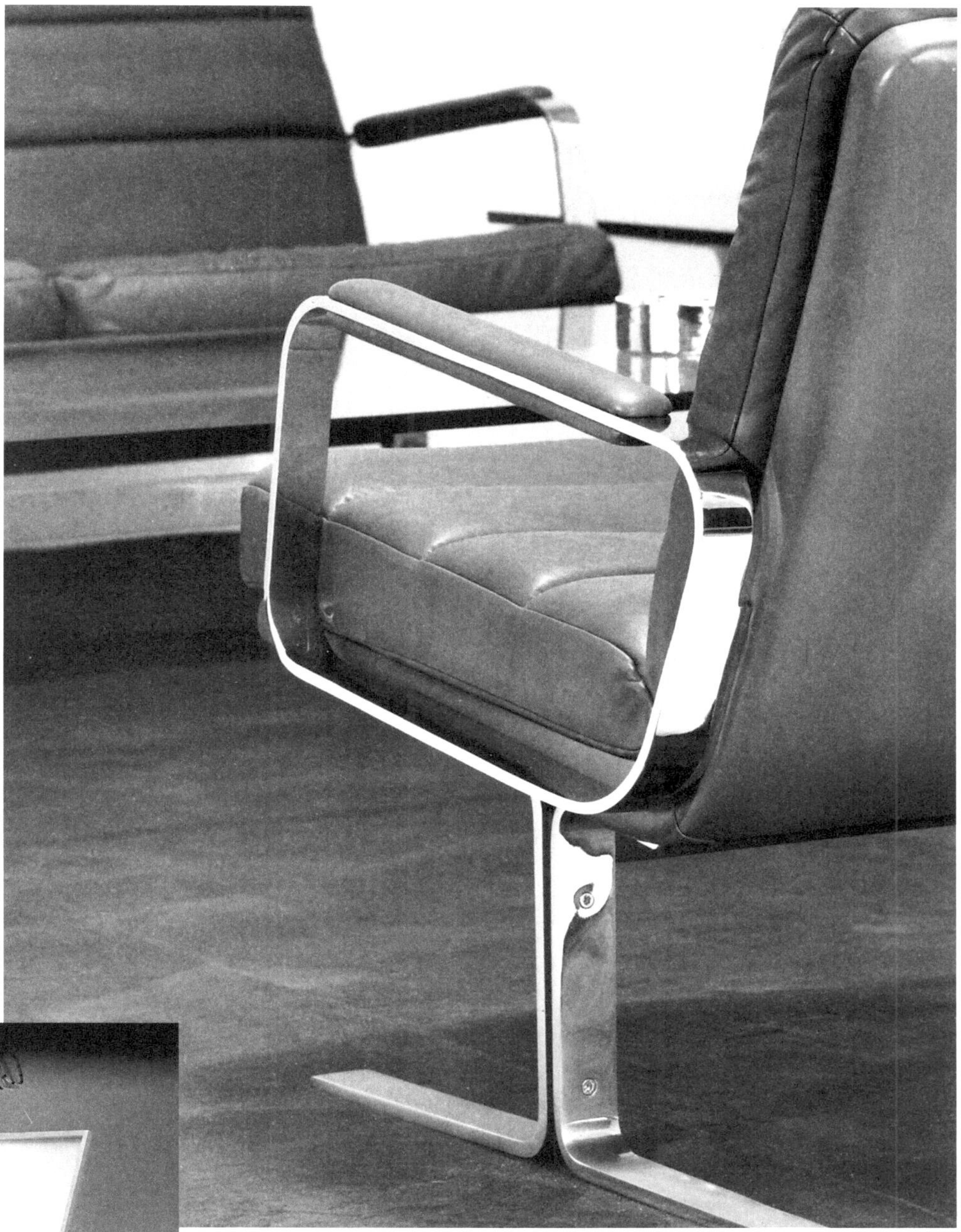

Catalog photo,
armchair 822, Walter Knoll,
Herrenberg, around 1970

Catalog photo,
sofa KN 196, Walter Knoll,
Herrenberg, 1968

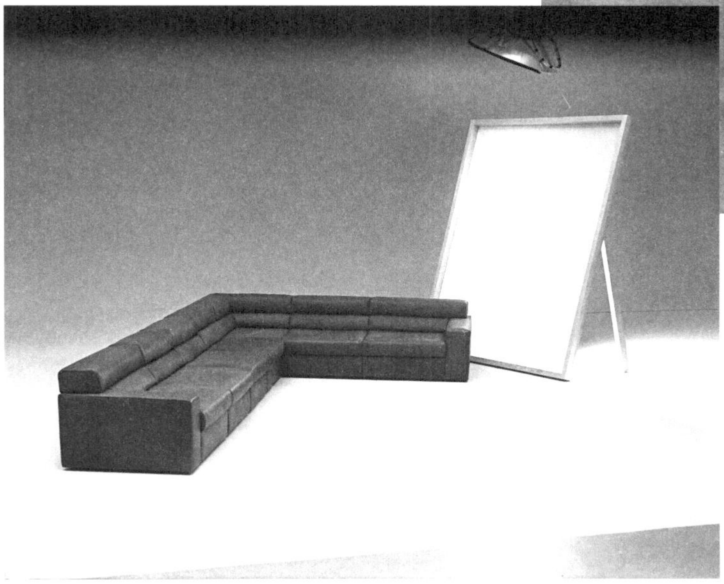

FUNCTIONALISM

Func | ti | o | na | lis | m, noun. In architecture and design, functionalism is understood as a perspective according to which aesthetic principles take a back seat to purpose, often through a reduction to the simplest, frequently cubic, forms. Consequently, it considers that the modern beauty of the designs is a direct result of their simplicity. The perfect cube became a symbol of functionalism, just as it had caught on for the first time in the *Neues Bauen* (New Building) of the 1920s, not least at Weissenhof in Stuttgart and at the Bauhaus in Dessau. Minimalistic, modular and multi-functional: this triple imperative, which originated at the "Hochschule für Gestaltung Ulm" (Ulm School of Design) and centered around Germany, shaped functionalism to a great extent after 1945. Seating furniture systems like those that Rolf Grunow and Dieter Waeckerlin designed for Walter Knoll are prime examples of this – and of system design in the Ulm spirit. Nowadays, designs such as the Together bench by EOOS embody this puristic ethos.

DESIGN IS THINKING MADE VISUAL.
SAUL BASS

1961
"waeckerlin-sitzmöbel" (waeckerlin seating furniture) (Walter Knoll) with minimalistic system design.
New state parliament building with a square floor plan opened in Stuttgart (architect Horst Linde).
Construction of the Berlin Wall.

1962
New Walter Knoll factory hall in Herrenberg opened.

1963
John F. Kennedy is assassinated.
"Modular system" by Rolf Grunow for Walter Knoll.

1964
Walter Knoll hands over control of the company to his son Robert Knoll and Dr. Walter Combe.
Michael Knoll, son of Robert Knoll, studies at the Stuttgart Academy under Herta-Maria Witzemann.

1966
Over 200 well-wishers show up for Walter Knoll's 90th birthday.

Sofa bed 366,
Walter Knoll,
design by Rolf Grunow,
Herrenberg, around 1960

Typeface,
design by Gui Bonsiepe,
Ulm, around 1960

Drawing,
Suspended Houses,
design by Heinz Rasch,
Stuttgart, 1960

ulm

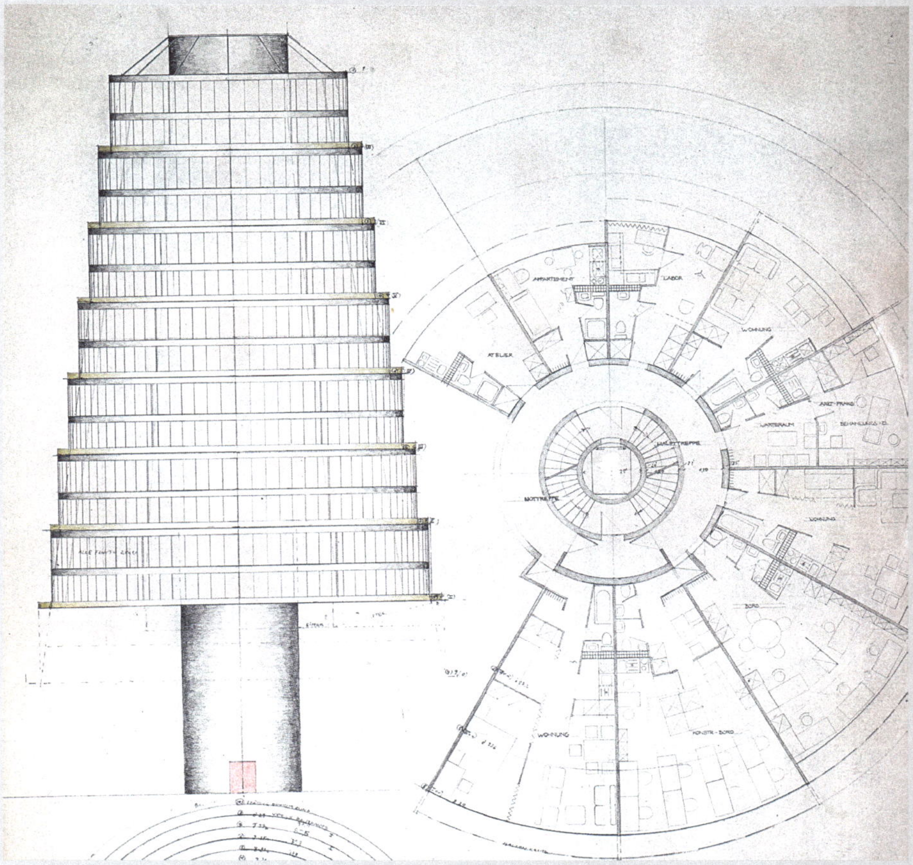

THE 1970S

END OF AN ERA

"You know that the Wilhelm Knoll company has gone bankrupt," said the letter to "my dear business friend," getting straight to the point in the very first sentence.[1] The news of the collapse of the prestigious Swabian furniture company spread throughout the industry like wildfire. "With effect from 3 September 1973," the circular letter addressed to customers and suppliers continued, "the receiver has, in agreement with the previous owners, transferred the production facilities, the company logo, the company name and all rights to continue the current upholstered furniture collection to Messrs Adolf and Gert Oppenländer."[2] The two brothers, who owned a furniture factory in Waiblingen, now continued the "Fabrik exquisiter Polstermöbel" (Factory of Exquisite Upholstered Furniture) – the name under which the insolvent Wilhelm Knoll OHG had been most recently operating – alone.

Dieter Knoll, son of Willy and nephew of Walter Knoll, who had taken over the company founded by his grandfather – the original nucleus of the Knoll furniture dynasty – from his father and had been running it until that point, is not mentioned by name in the circular letter. He was one of the "previous owners."[3] Dieter Knoll had to go. He was 50 years old, the age at which Walter Knoll had founded his company. Dieter Knoll's life had also been intertwined with the family company until then. Its headquarters had been at Forststrasse 71 in downtown Stuttgart ever since the days of Kaiser Wilhelm. His parents' residence was also located at the same address. Dieter Knoll, a graduate business economist and, like his father, a shrewd furniture expert, was a personality known all over town, and was impossible to ignore because of his height alone. The towering man, an avid golfer, tennis player and, among other things, also an active member of the "Württembergischer Automobilclub" (Württemberg Automobile Association), held numerous honorary posts. Some years prior, he had, somewhat unswabian-like, acquired the title of "Consul of Costa Rica". He passed away shortly before the turn of the 21st century at the age of 74. Meanwhile, his name is taking on a posthumous life of its own. The rights to the Dieter Knoll Collection, which did not exist during his lifetime, at some point belonged to a major German furniture corporate group, which, in turn, passed them on to another department store chain. There it is one brand name among many. Furniture can also be purchased online. Consequently, the name Dieter Knoll, void of all meaning, still wanders through the infinite expanses of the Internet like a ghost.[4]

The reasons for the company's collapse are also mentioned in the letter quoted above. It had apparently come to pass "because the prices of a large share of the models had been significantly too low," it declares.[5] However, it does not go into the reasons why the furniture could no longer be sold at profitable prices. One mistake was putting all the company's eggs in a single basket for too long. At the heart of the strategy was the once highly successful Antimott suspension, for which lavish catalogs had been published over the years. In this respect, the drama of Wilhelm Knoll shares parallels with a renowned and far larger company, which found itself in a similarly precarious situation at roughly the same time, and had been holding tight to a successful model for all too long. The company in question is Volkswagen AG, which was struggling to develop alternatives to the Beetle and, for a long time, did not even consider it necessary to do so. Due to an inability to renew itself, Volkswagen also ended up in severe difficulty during that time.[6] At some point, Antimott was no longer a draw. Innovative strength, the core of the company under Willy Knoll, Dieter's father, had also diminished. Furthermore, a price was being paid for the fact that neither Willy nor Dieter Knoll had sought a link with the movement of modernity, which not only served as an ideal compass for the sibling company of Walter Knoll, but also provided creative replenishment. Wherever this was in short supply, a clear focus would sooner or later be lost. "Although production is currently predominantly headed in a timeless modernist direction," a company history stated in 1965, "this does not mean that style compromises cannot be made at any time."[7] And continuing in this spirit: "Some interesting experiments can already be seen as far as period furniture is concerned, e.g. bringing Biedermeier style onto the market in a modern form. The Knoll company is also prepared for such changes."[8] Biedermeier and arbitrariness did not bring salvation. The future of the Wilhelm Knoll company, which had lost its independence, was now entirely uncertain.

FURNITURE WITH A SYSTEM

In 1973, in what was a bad omen for the Wilhelm Knoll company, a contingent from Herrenberg traveled to West Berlin. The four-person team would install seating furniture on site in the largest commission of its kind up to that point. In Berlin's Tegel quarter, a new, state-of-the-art airport was nearing completion. The plans originated in the office of the architect Meinhard von Gerkan and partners.[9] Tegel, a distinctive structure made of exposed concrete, is circular. This makes orientation simpler and, at the same time, shortens arrivals and departures, an example of the intelligent coordination of traffic flows. A similarly ingenious solution was found for the seating areas in the waiting halls, for which Walter Knoll had been awarded the contract. It was a system of bucket seats that could be put together to form L, U and V shapes (see p. 216 f.). The bucket shape, the scratch-proof plastic, the powerful yellow, and the virtually unlimited combinability – it all came from the recipe book of the Second Modernity. Here, the public furniture merged with the functional architecture to form a coherent whole. The flexible seating system could also be easily transferred to other waiting rooms, as occurred at the spa center in Wildbad, for example. A kind of follow-up project was the Berlin Chair, which was designed for the VIP lounge area and emerged somewhat later from the collaboration with von Gerkan's firm. With its frame made of strip steel, the elegant armchair demonstrated that the possibilities for this material, which had been discovered for furniture design in the 1920s, had in no way been exhausted in terms of structure and aesthetics (see p. 222). In this case, an innovative, consistent arrangement of parallel strips proved a success.[10] When the installation work in Tegel was complete after around a month, spouses were permitted to join their husbands and spend a weekend together sniffing the Berlin air at the company's expense.

Tegel became a signal. Walter Knoll had now managed to gain a foothold in the highly promising market for major clients. IBM, the American computer corporation with a monopoly position, which concentrated its German activities in the Stuttgart region, could already be

WALTER KNOLL MANAGED TO GAIN A FOOTHOLD IN THE HIGHLY PROMISING MARKET FOR MAJOR CLIENTS WITH THE ESTABLISHMENT OF THE CONTRACT DIVISION.

considered a long-term customer by this time. At some point, the chemical giant BASF ordered 2,000 Witzemann chairs of the 363 model for its headquarters in Ludwigshafen. That was a company record and an enormous challenge. Such successes were made possible not least by a focus on the office furniture sector with the establishment of the Contract division. Here, the virtues of the First and the Second Modernity lived on. The surest sign: a renewed revival of tubular steel. This was brought about, above all, by Rolf Grunow, a functionalist with heart and soul, a partner since the post-war period and still a resident of Herrenberg. He now also had a like-minded colleague. Bernd Münzebrock, interior designer and trained carpenter, had been employed as a designer and factotum for the management since 1970. Grunow and Münzebrock were virtually equals in terms of formal austerity. At Münzebrock's drawing table emerged designs such as the model 253, a chic minimalist chaise longue on skids, Logos, an extra-slim swivel chair, and, one of the greatest successes of its time, Don, an early executive chair, which was not only visually impressive thanks to its sumptuous upholstery, but also offered a degree of comfort seldom known before (see p. 223, 228 f.). Don – like the club chair before it – was a type unto itself and, like the everyday chair 363, was now also setting new standards in the high-end segment. A giant by the proportions of the time, this chair ultimately turned Walter Knoll into a leading brand of high-quality office furniture.

The triple comeback of full upholstery, tubular steel and leather also resulted in a significant change in aesthetic for household furniture, which, with a sales share of around 75 percent, was still the main line of business. Large volumes of individual furniture items in conjunction with a closed body and simple silhouettes, which already stood out in purely visual terms thanks to their lack of hard edges, now defined the product range. Large radii were used for the tubular steel, which influenced both the strength and the bending of the tube. Another acclaimed phenomenon was combinable upholstered furniture, the so-called "living landscapes". A concept that was completely in line with the Ulm system doctrine, but also comprised a good deal of youth and protest culture. In this context, contact was established with Roswitha Ronkholz-Tölle, an artist from Düsseldorf, who had designed a new kind of upholstered furniture of the by now incredibly popular living landscape for Bofinger. A sample piece was presented at the 1968 furniture fair in Cologne and quickly caused a furore.[11]

---

1 ▶ Letter dated 9/4/1973, WK archives.

2 ▶ Ibid.

3 ▶ According to the industry newspaper "Inside," the development transpired as follows: after the grandson of the company founder had sold the family company to the Oppenländer brothers at the end of the 1950s, Dieter Knoll still held shares and, as managing director, continued to be the face of the company. See: Knoll, 1965, p. 1.

4 ▶ The Dieter Knoll Collection brand dates back to the former branch in the Upper Austrian Steyr, the now no longer existing Wilhelm Knoll Polstermöbelfabrik. It bore the name of Dieter Knoll from the 1960s. In 2001, ownership of the rights to the brand were transferred to the German Steinhoff Group, one of Europe's largest furniture corporations, which eventually sold them to the Austrian company Lutz based in Wels, which claims to be the second largest furniture dealer after Ikea, and is known for its XXXL furniture stores.

5 ▶ Letter dated 9/4/1973, WK archives.

6 ▶ The Italian automobile designer Giorgio Giugiaro designed the Golf, which brought about a turnaround that saved Volkswagen in 1974.

7 ▶ Knoll, 1965, p. 46.

8 ▶ Knoll, 1965, p. 47.

9 ▶ Now Marg und Partner.

10 ▶ Cf. the Barcelona Chair, 1929.

11 ▶ Roswitha Ronkholz-Tölle later took on the pseudonym Tata. See: Polster 2008, p. 170.

RICH IN VARIANTS

The bucket seats for the waiting hall of the new Berlin-Tegel Airport were an innovation. They could be combined in numerous ways and thus adapted to the room. For this reason, they were also used in other waiting areas. The bold colors reveal their origin in the pop era. For Walter Knoll, it was the beginning of contract business.

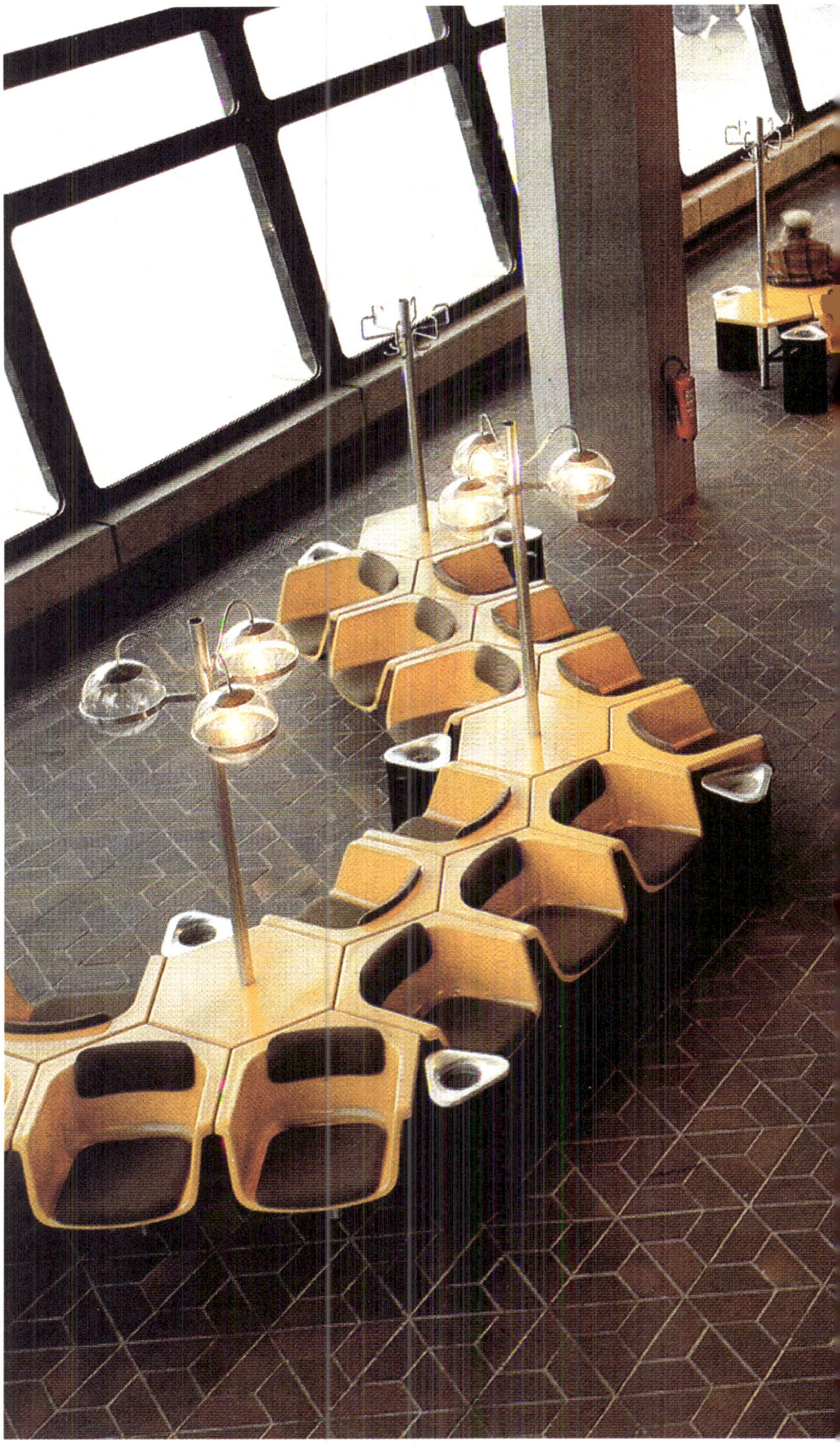

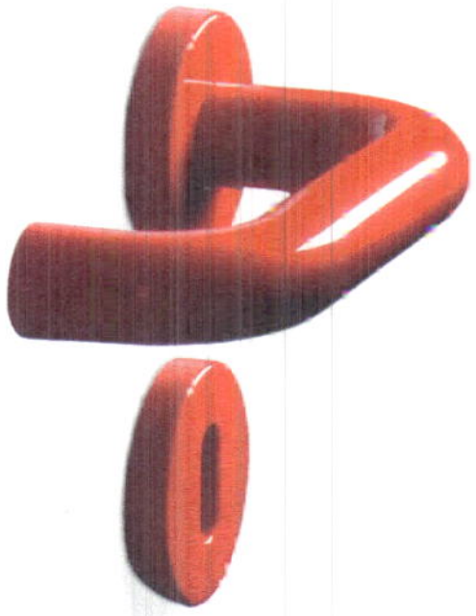

Functional plastic handle in shocking colors: the series 111, a design by Rudolf Wilke for HEWI, 1970

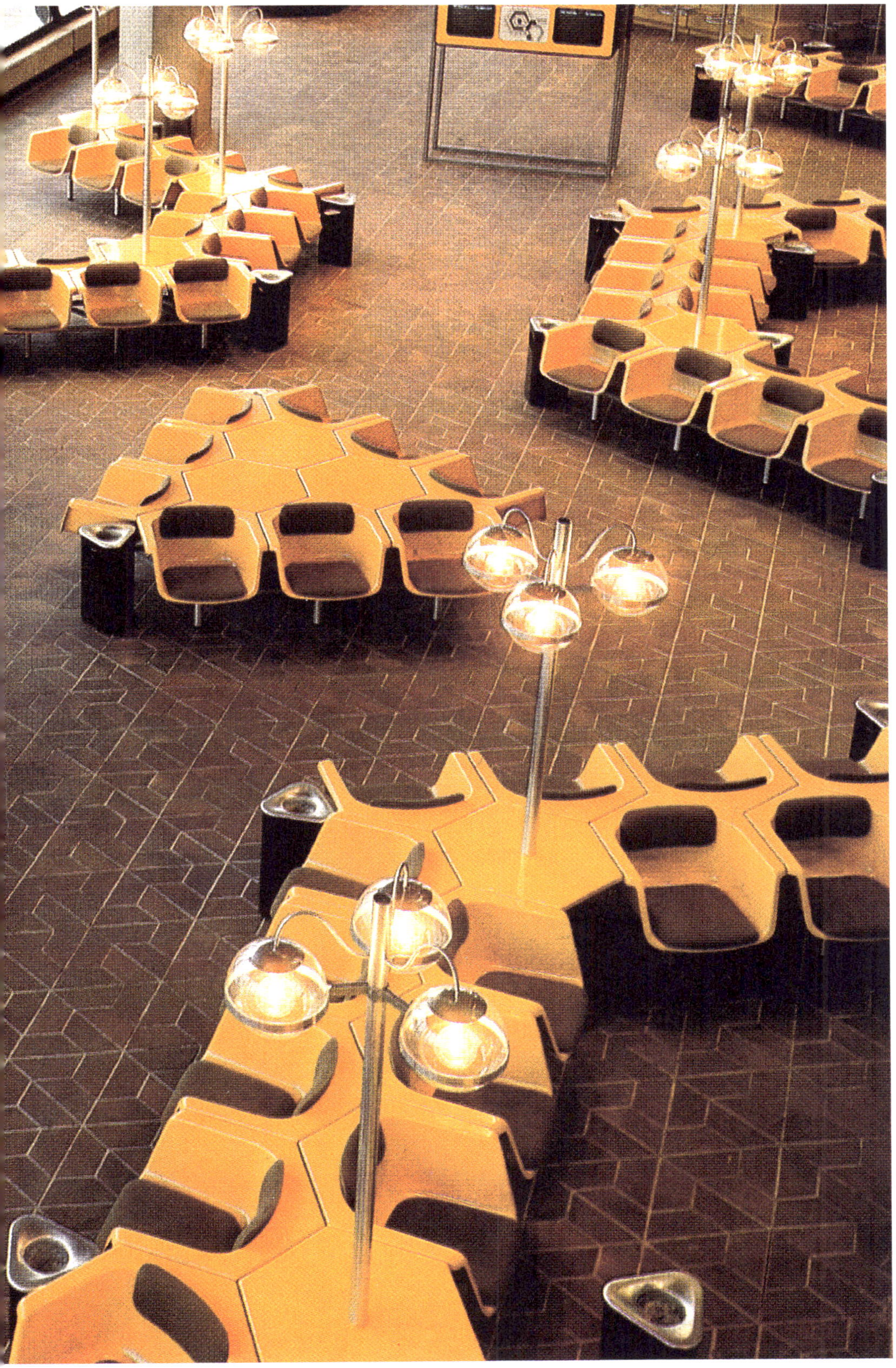

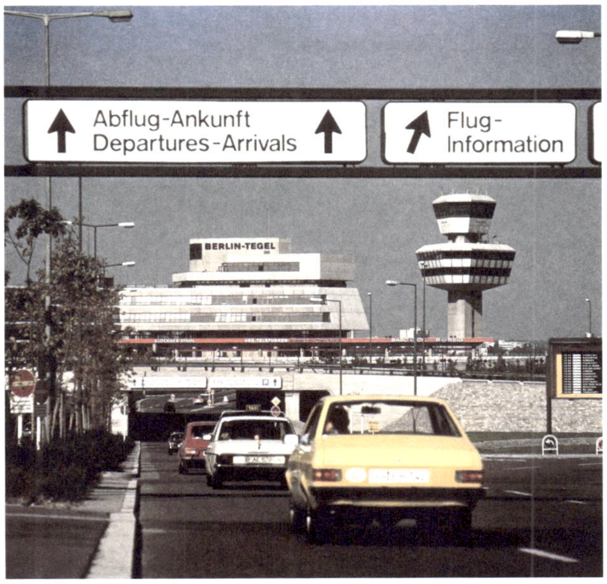

Waiting area of the
Berlin-Tegel Airport,
modular system airport,
Walter Knoll,
design by Meinhard von Gerkan,
Volkwin Marg and Damir Perisic,
Berlin, 1973

Berlin-Tegel Airport,
around 1975

WRITING STYLES

English names signifying internationalism, combined with lower-case letters, which were reminiscent of the Bauhaus. In this way, a fusion of the First and Second Modernity was created. This also included an attempt to develop a new, distinctive architecture of upholstered furniture.

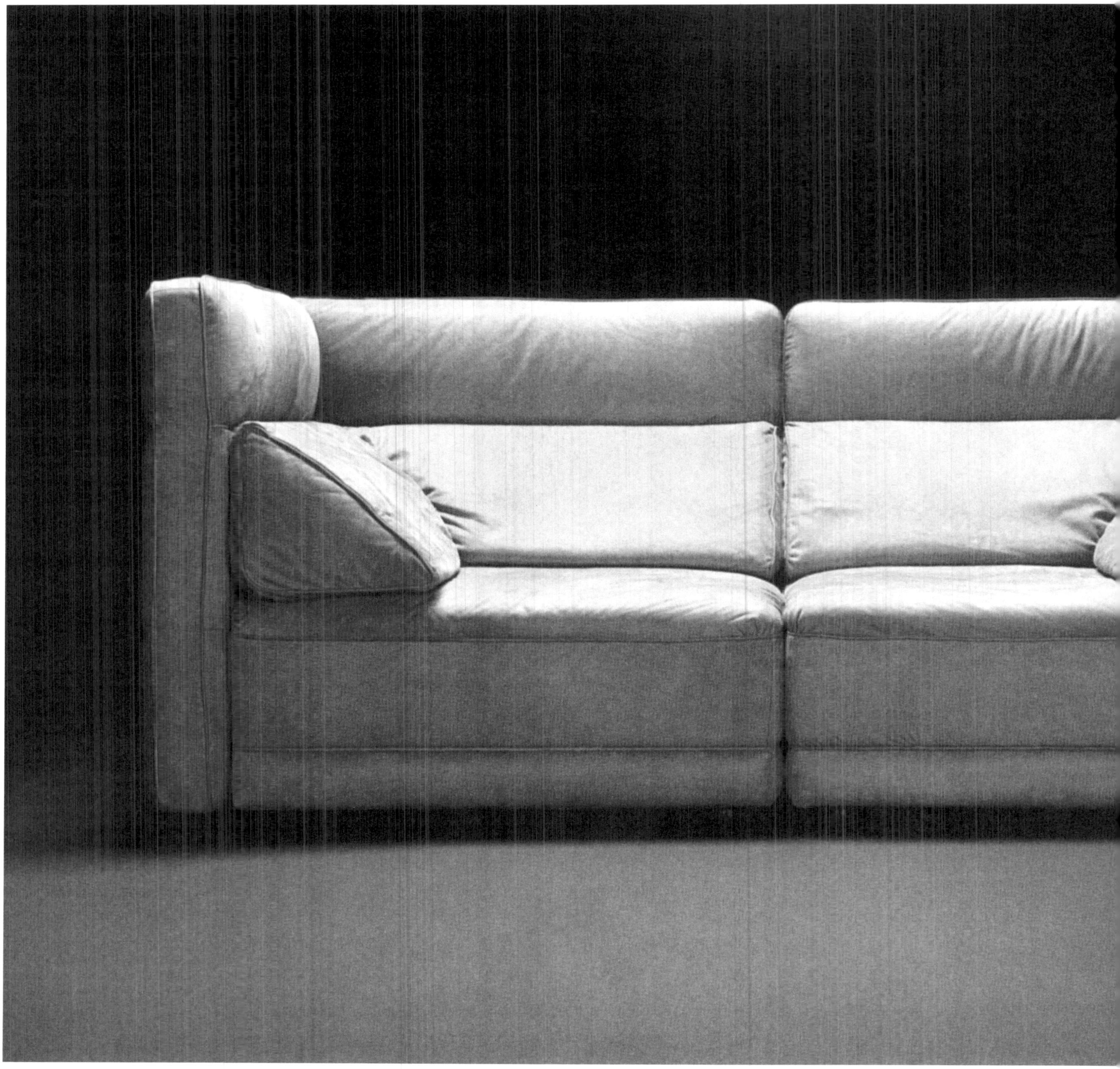

Catalog photo,
sofa Arena 180, Walter Knoll,
Herrenberg, 1974

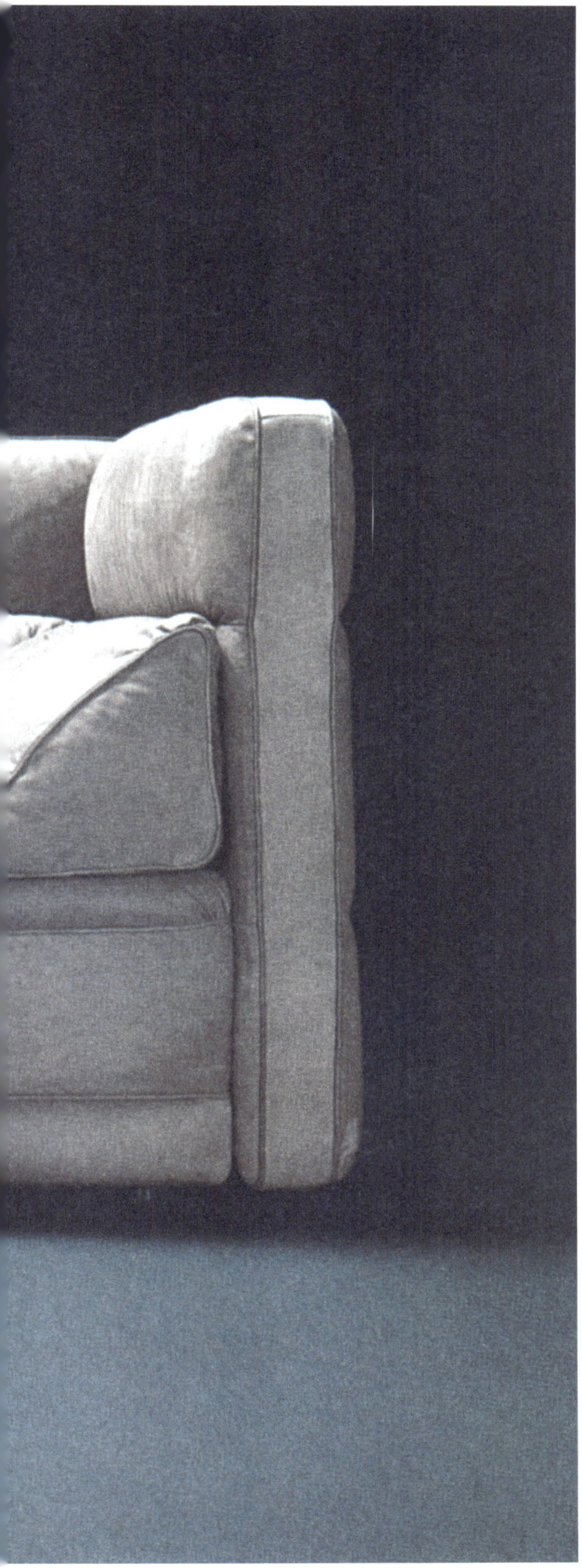

Logo around 1970

collection
walter
knoll

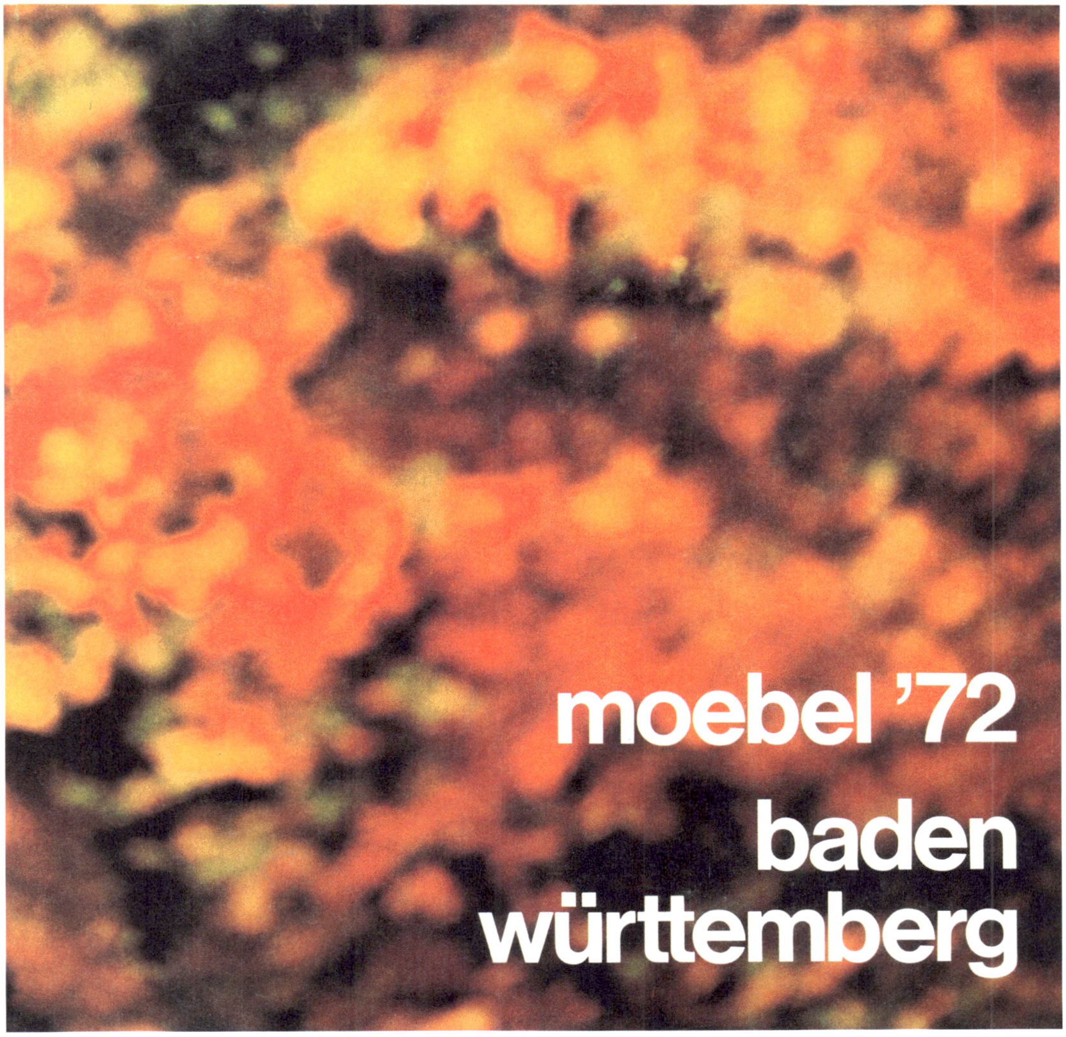

Cover of the "Gemeinschaftskatalog vom Verband der Württembergischen Holz- und Kunststoffindustrie" (Joint Catalog of the Association of the Württemberg Wood and Plastic Industry), catalog for the Cologne furniture fair, Stuttgart, 1972

After this, it was virtually inevitable that Ronkholz-Tölle, who had founded the product design agency Systeam, would also turn to the Walter Knoll company. A conversation took place at the following year's trade fair. The independent designer, who had studied at the "Werkkunstschule" (School of Applied Arts) in Krefeld and would later become a photographer[12], emphasized the observation "that my ideas for new products do not correspond with conventional seating furniture."[13] The living landscape not only eliminated the distinction between armchairs and sofas, but also abolished all existing seating conventions. Nevertheless, a collaboration with Systeam did not materialize. Walter Knoll would, however, soon make its own contributions to this highly topical subject at the time. These included models such as Carré (by Friedrich Hill), which was based on standardized structural elements and a 30-centimeter grid, and Arena (by Bernd Münzebrock, see p. 218), which was lauded as the first high-backed variant of the new furniture type, and was promoted with a series of original studio photographs. In one shot, for example, a bumper car drove into the seating landscape.

CRISIS AND CONSISTENCY

Walter Knoll passed away in July 1971 and, although foreseeable due to his advanced age, the death of the company founder was naturally a decisive event for the family and the company. Obituaries poured in. In him, not only had a major entrepreneurial personality left the stage, but also one who had devoted himself to modernity and redefined upholstered furniture. Despite his almost biblical age of 94, Walter Knoll never withdrew entirely until the end when an operation eventually robbed him of his strength shortly prior to his death. Just like his brother Willy, he had no intention of severing himself from the company, his life's work, while he was still alive. Consequently, the

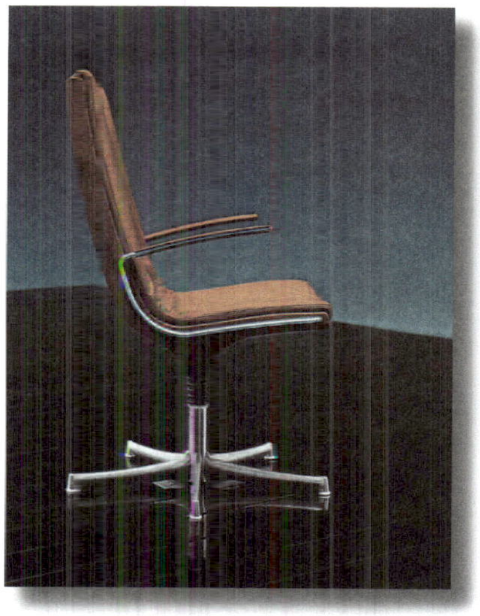

leadership duo of Robert Knoll and Walter Combe, who had, of course, already occupied executive positions throughout the difficult 1960s, now finally had the opportunity to step out of his shadow. However, their age alone – one around 60, the other around 70 – did not exactly suggest a fresh and vibrant new beginning.

The subsequent generation was still waiting in the wings. When his grandfather died, Michael Knoll, now an interior designer, had spent a year working at a classy furniture store in Munich, where the bohemian quarter of Schwabing had not yet reached legendary status and preparations were underway for the Olympic Games. Like Stuttgart, the Bavarian metropolis also benefited from the shift from east to west and the influx of companies such as Siemens and BMW. Once Germany's art capital, it was in the process of transforming into a stronghold of the movie, TV and advertising industry. All this

IN WALTER KNOLL, NOT ONLY DID A MAJOR ENTREPRENEURIAL PERSONALITY LEAVE THE STAGE, BUT ALSO ONE WHO HAD DEVOTED HIMSELF TO MODERNITY.

produced a quite special environment that would go down in film history in Federal Germany.[14] Of course, the Knoll grandson – now in his mid-twenties with his whole life ahead of him – also witnessed plenty of this. After all, it was not just any furniture store that he worked in. "Die Einrichtung" (The Furnishings) – as the store was simply named – was among the most famous of its kind throughout Europe. Directly opposite were the "Vereinigte Werkstätten" (United Workshops), the source of the Reform movement at the beginning of the 20th century, from which a whole string of major designers emerged. Among them was Bernhard Pankok, who would later cause a sensation in Stuttgart. It was certainly also no coincidence that the "Deutscher Werkbund" (German Association of Craftsmen) was founded in Munich. Michael Knoll spent five years full of experiences on the banks of the Isar, and would have practically become a semi-native of Munich had he not been called back to Herrenberg in 1975.

The 1970s were overshadowed by two oil crises. Modernity set tongues wagging. Fears of "no future" badly dampened the mood.

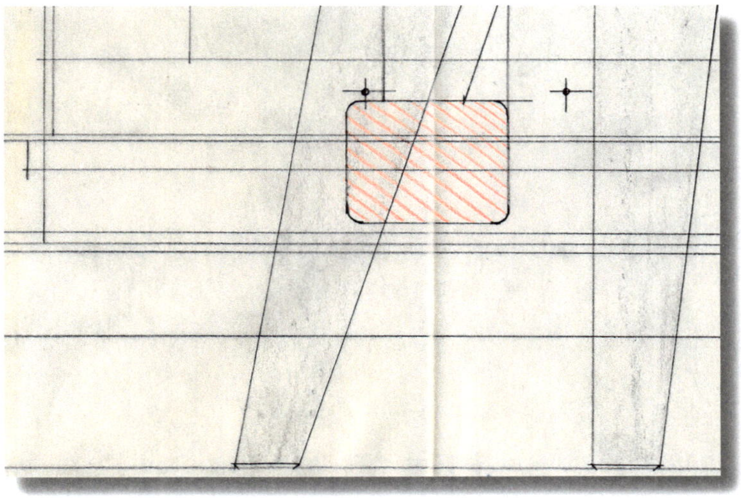

Stuttgart, however, experienced somewhat more continuity than elsewhere. In 1974, the sudden death of mayor Arnulf Klett, who had been continuously in charge of urban matters since 1945, brought the longest period of office of a German municipal leader to an end. However, his successor, Manfred Rommel, would largely emulate him.[15] Collectively, the pair governed Stuttgart for more than half a century. A degree of reliability that was not only unique, but with reasonable certainty, also one of the secrets behind the city's success. With Klett having already distinguished himself as a pronounced pragmatist, as well as an art lover and promoter of modernity, his successor now also proved to be not quite the average politician. Rommel, an excellent orator, host and lover of sound fiscal policy, served as a unifying figure – a kind of "philosopher at city hall," as he was also called – who allowed himself to be guided by values in his work. When, at the end of the decade, Lothar Späth became Minister President and evolved into the father figure of the state over the course of multiple re-elections, the barometer of stability rose even further in the Swabian region.

In 1975, the Walter Knoll company celebrated its 50th anniversary. Reason enough for a ceremony at Herrenberg's town hall and a proud look back. In his speech, Robert Knoll talked at length about the history of the company. And it sat in front of him in person in the form of numerous guests of honor. In the first row sat Herta-Maria Witzemann and Mia Seeger, once Stuttgart's champions of *Gute Form* (Good Design), who had both, as the speaker expressed, long since become its grandes dames. Erwin Behr, the furniture reformer and fellow businessman from Wendlingen, was also in attendance. As was Bodo Rasch, the Weissenhof inspirer and incessant visionary. The man at the lectern greeted Walter Schneider, the creator of Prodomo especially warmly, as he was returning to Herrenberg for the first time since his pioneering days there. Of course, Ernst Josef Auer also had to be present. The new director of the "Landesgewerbeamt" (State Trade Office), the institution without which Stuttgart's rise to a center of modernity would have been inconceivable, was following in the footsteps of his predecessor, for example by founding the Design Center, which exists to this day. Lastly, tribute was also paid to Rolf Gutbrod, a prominent post-war architect and, like the others, a close friend of the Knoll family. The list of distinguished guests, all leading figures of the First and Second Modernity, made it all too clear how inextricably linked the company Walter Knoll was with those eras. However, the fact that the majority of the veterans of modernity in attendance were already well over retirement age also showed that the times were changing.

At the end of his remarks, Robert Knoll then moved on to another aspect of company history: employees celebrating an anniversary. "A family company like ours relies on long-serving employees, who dedicate a lifetime of labor to their company and go through thick and thin together with the management."[16] For him, that was the foundation upon which everything else was based. "I can report that our oldest employee has been a part of our company for 47 years and has worked her way up from commercial apprentice to secretary, earning a great deal of trust along the way."[17] Here, he was talking about Mrs Erna Würth, his right hand, as the headline of the "Gäubote" (Gäu Herald) had it, who had "been absent only once in five decades".[18] Nevertheless, she was just one of many stalwarts. "Nine employees have now been with us for 30 or 40 years. Five employees over 25 years. This amounts to 10 % of our entire workforce. And I am deeply grateful today to be able to thank all of these people, for whom performance of their duty has become a purpose in life."[19]

---

12 ▶ She was among the first of Bernd Becher's students.

13 ▶ Letter from 3/10/1971, WK archives.

14 ▶ Helmut Dietl expanded his portrayal of Munich into a kind of trilogy. This includes the television series "Monaco Franze" (1982) and "Kir Royal" (1986), as well as the feature film "Rossini" (1997).

15 ▶ Arnold Klett was mayor of Stuttgart from 1945 to 1974; Erwin Rommel's son Manfred was mayor from 1974 to 1996.

16 ▶ Manuscript of Robert Knoll's speech of 12/22/1975, WK archives.

17 ▶ Ibid.

18 ▶ "Gäubote," 12/27/1978.

19 ▶ Manuscript of Robert Knoll's speech of 12/22/1975, WK archives.

BERLIN CHAIR

Meinhard von Gerkan's gmp architects' practice developed a design icon, the Berlin chair, for the VIP lounge of the Berlin-Tegel Airport, which itself was a design masterpiece.

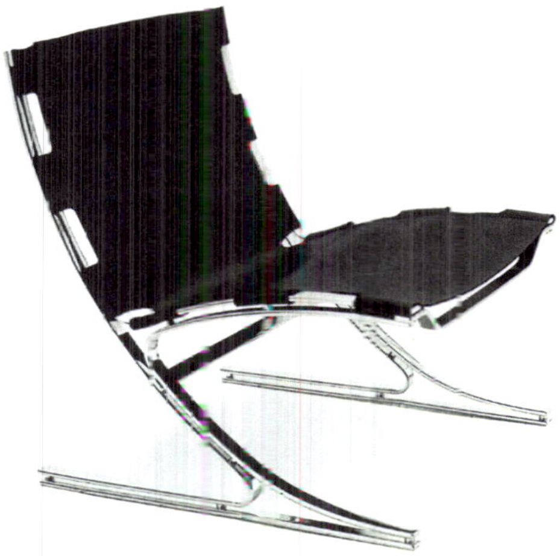

Catalog photo,
Berlin chair 184, Walter Knoll,
design by Meinhard von Gerkan,
Volkwin Marg and Damir Perisic,
Herrenberg, 1975

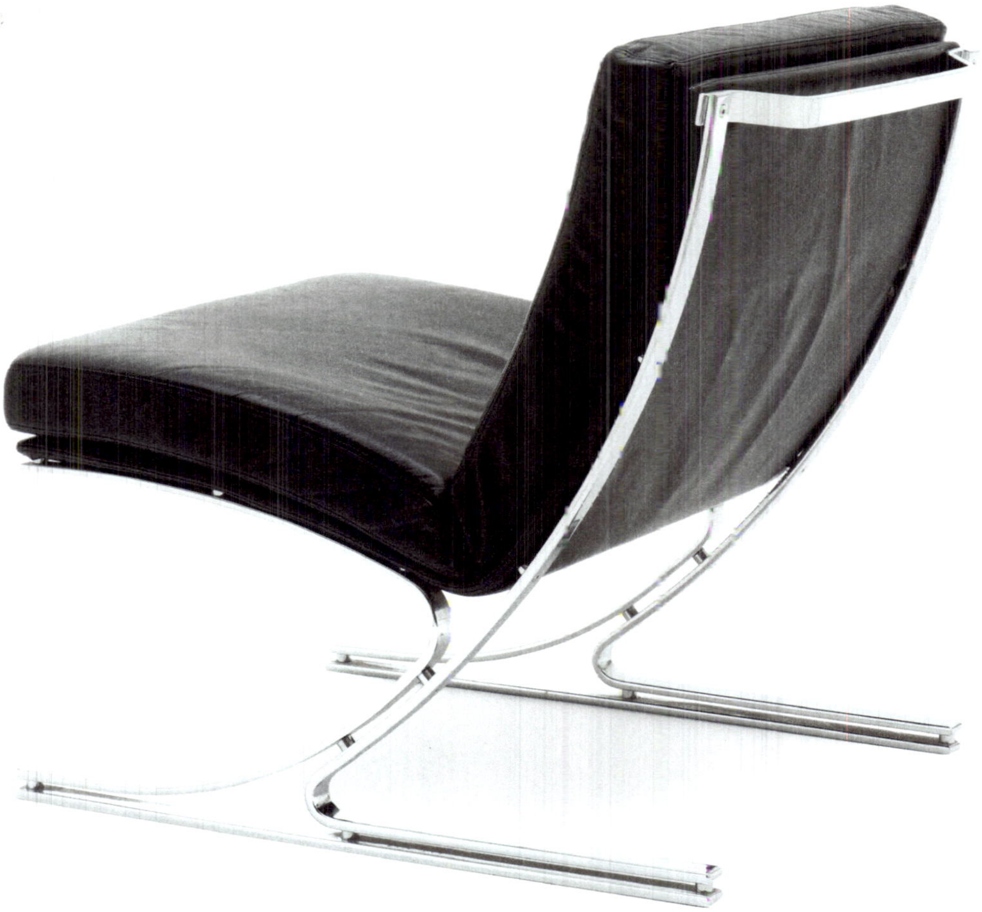

Original Berlin chair 183, Walter Knoll,
design by Meinhard von Gerkan,
Volkwin Marg and Damir Perisic,
Herrenberg, 1975,
Restored in 2015

GOVERNMENT LEVEL

The Federal Cabinet in Bonn sat on upholstered chairs from Herrenberg for decades. Herta-Maria Witzemann, Stuttgart's grande dame of design, exerted influence on political leaders.

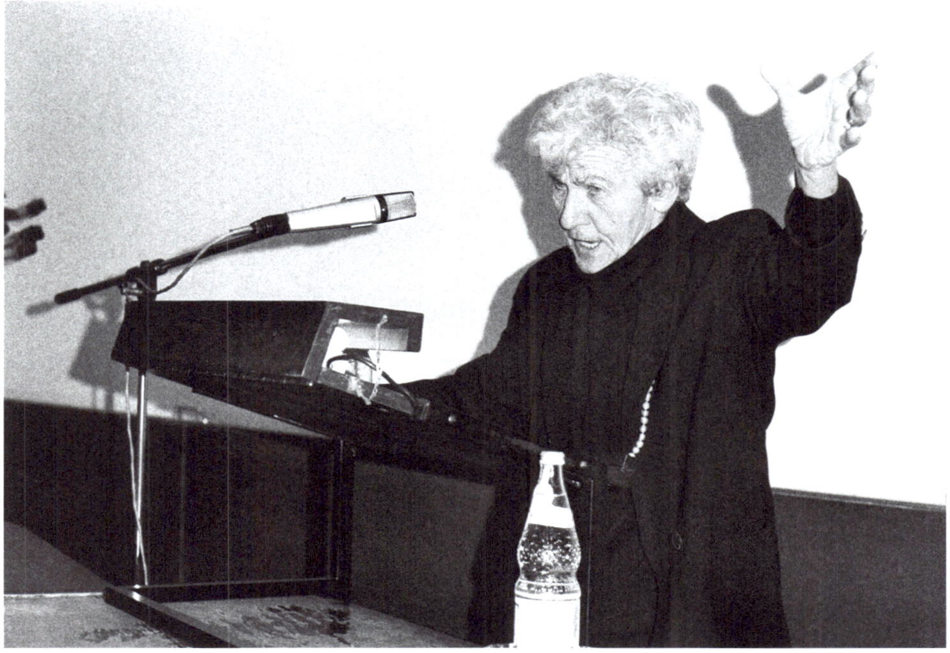

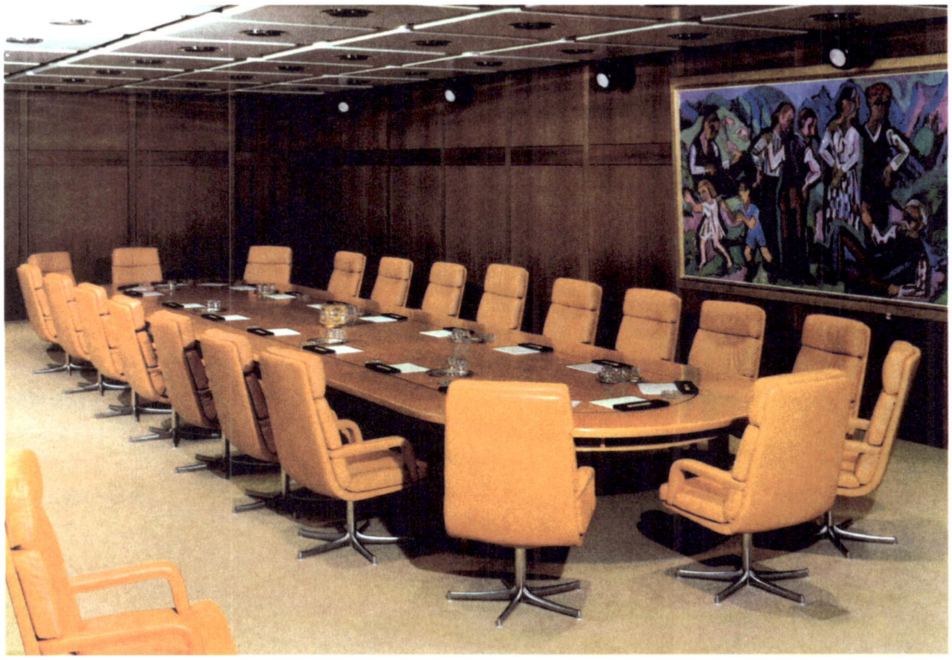

Herta-Maria Witzemann, "Staatliche Akademie der Bildenden Künste" (State Academy of Art and Design), Stuttgart, around 1975

Don armchair 841, in the cabinet's conference room at the Federal Chancellery, Walter Knoll, design by Bernd Münzebrock, Bonn, around 1977

Among the mainstays of the workforce was the upholsterer Otto Veigel, who had already been present in Stuttgart-Feuerbach before the move to Herrenberg, as well as the chair maker Günther Bruckner, who, having spent nearly 25 years in the position of Chairman of the Works Council, would go on to celebrate another quite rare anniversary, for which he would eventually receive the Federal Cross Of Merit. This extremely high degree of loyalty was likely above average even for Swabia. The fact that, at the same time, the company cared about maintaining a balance between young and old was demonstrated by the reintroduction of an apprentice training department in the same year.[20]

THE UPHOLSTERED FURNITURE OF THE 1970s RADIATES THE SAME SORT OF TASTEFULNESS THAT HAD ALREADY PREVAILED ONCE BEFORE IN THE EARLY DAYS OF THE COMPANY.

Another important guest was present at the ceremony: Michael Knoll was not celebrating an anniversary, but an extraordinary debut. As a fourth-generation Knoll, he had been the crown prince from birth who was being prepared for the role of successor from the outset. However, instead of commercial aspects, as had been customary, he gave priority to artistic standards. In this way, he was an exception in the entire industry. Michael Knoll, 31 years young and equipped with the best prerequisites, occupied a position that precisely matched his comprehensive education, although it is difficult to give it a name. Chief designer? Art director? Advertising manager? These were all part of his role, as was the overall planning and execution of trade fairs. Having grown up with the ideas of modernity and having learned design as a student of Herta-Maria Witzemann, developing products and product ranges was particularly close to his heart. The upholstered Casa suite, which emerged on his drawing table, typified the direction that he would pivot to (see p. 238). He pursued the cautious further development of what already existed. Above all, this meant full upholstery with a clearly proportioned body and a largely invisible frame. Sofas and armchairs now often wore dark leather like a fine suit. In this period, collaboration began with Burkhard Vogtherr and Jürgen Lange, two furniture designers from the generation of their new employer, who were at the beginning of their careers and would quickly rise to the top. Designs such as Lario or Studio are typical models of those years in that they largely forgo effects and therefore offer few moments of surprise at first glance, though, for precisely this reason, it seemed as if the ultimate form of classic upholstered furniture was on its way (see p. 243). However, towards the end of the 1970s, there was yet another new emphasis, which, of course, also tied in with modern classics. The Conversation Chair and sofa by Preben Fabricius, who had already proven himself as a specialist in sophisticated steel frames with his designs for Kill, appear exceptionally light (see p. 207). With their slim upholstery, they evoke the days of Prodomo. It was a masterly update on the early Second Modernity and, at the same time, also reminiscent of the work of his brilliant Danish compatriot Poul Kjærholm.

The upholstered furniture of the 1970s radiates the same sort of tastefulness that had prevailed once before in the early days of the company when the club chair was invented. By contrast, a previously unknown degree of coolness found its way into the advertising. It was almost as if Michael Knoll had brought a good deal of Munich flair with him from the Isar to the Neckar. For the first time, elaborate photo shoots took place, often in the open air, during which new creative ideas were put into practice. For example, when the luxury swivel chair Don floated by on a raft, a bumper car swerved through the living landscape, or large canvases such as a circus tent served as a backdrop. Fashion models were used, including – besides the obligatory female beauties – cowboys, sailors and a bullfighter. It was all reminiscent of hip magazines such as "Twen," which were setting new

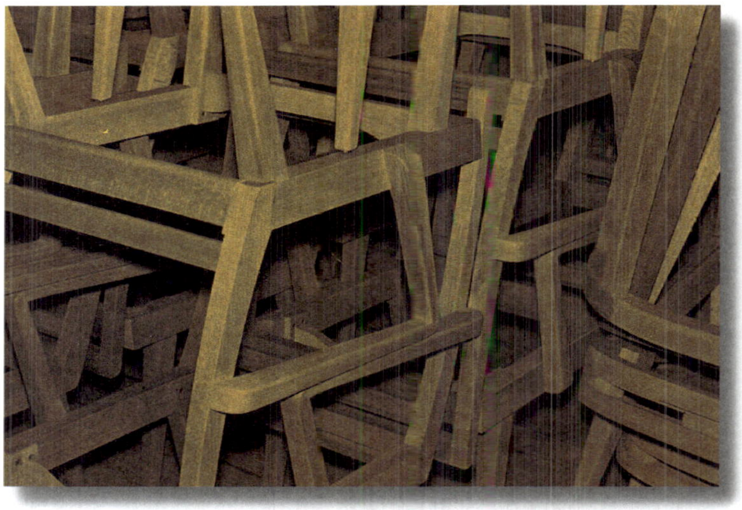

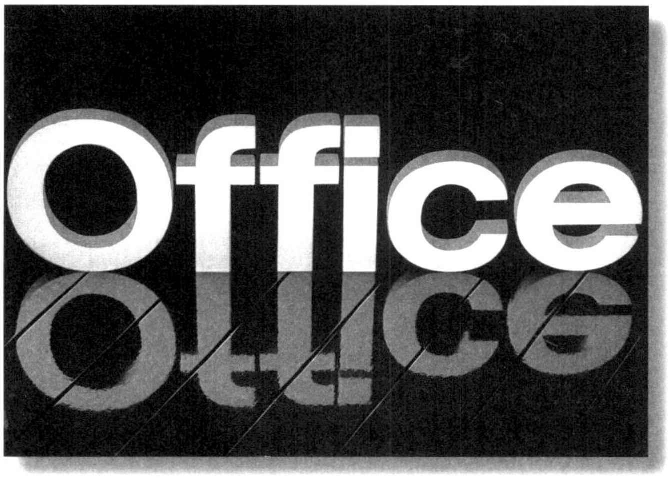

standards in photography and graphics in those days. Never before had the catalogs been so daring. The names "collection walter knoll" and "walter knoll office", which clearly identified the two main product lines, were also introduced during this period. Now that competitor Wilhelm Knoll had fallen into irrelevance, the full name of Walter Knoll could also be used as a brand for the first time.[21] While the use of lower-case letters should probably be understood as a tribute to the Bauhaus and Weissenhof eras, the English names now emphasized the desired internationality.

In fact, during this time, an old, temporarily buried tradition was revived and relations with America were re-established. In 1976, a licensing agreement was entered into with Brayton International, a furniture company with its headquarters in High Point, North Carolina. Two years later, Robert Knoll paid a two-week visit to the new partner, which also took him to New York and the furniture fair in Chicago. There, he did not miss the opportunity to take the lift up to the roof of the Sears Towers, which, with 110 stories, was the tallest building in the world at the time. From Chicago, he headed 600 miles south to High Point, a provincial backwater with an airport, which, in the USA, is dubbed the "Furniture and Hosiery Capital of the World" with a certain degree of pride and irony. This gave rise to business relations that were lucrative for both parties and are developing gratifyingly to this day. Furthermore, from the encounter between Robert Knoll and his counterpart, company owner Paul Brayton, a warm friendship developed.

In Herrenberg, there would soon be an empty chair in the executive's office. Walter Combe, Robert's cousin and executive co-owner since 1953, took his leave in 1979, when he was already 80 years old. According to contract, the successor to this incredibly experienced furniture man, who had been working for Walter's brother Willy since the early 1920s, was his own son Stephan, who had already worked for Bosch and, at the time, was the director of a woolen blanket factory in the Swabian town of Heidenheim. He did not take up his future post in Herrenberg until 1982. It would not turn out to be an ideal configuration.

And then there was yet another small but glamorous event that was the talk of the town in Herrenberg, not least because it contrasted with the agitated mood of the oil crisis. In the summer of 1979, Uschi Obermaier, a fashion model and the personification of the hippie generation, paid a visit to the city in the Gäu region. Accompanied by her partner, the beautiful woman from Munich, who was in her early thirties, was traveling in a Mercedes Superbus that had been converted into an apartment on wheels, which the pair wanted to furnish with comfortable armchairs from Walter Knoll – a truly difficult project, at least to begin with. However, for Uschi Obermaier, the gates opened in a miraculous ways. Michael Knoll, a former resident of Munich and of Obermaier's age, was happy to advise her.

---

20 ▶ The apprentice training departments had been done away with in 1961 "as, at this time, the craft profession no longer seems so attractive, and almost all young people have been drawn to and absorbed by metalworking shops, especially in the automobile industry," "Gäubote" (Gäu Herald), 8/18/1979, WK archives.

21 ▶ In Stuttgart, or rather Gaildorf, a "wilhelm knoll collection" with the same writing style had now also been launched by the rival sibling company.

OFFICE REVOLUTION
This iconic, yet unknown, office chair was designed by Rolf Grunow, who was among the most innovative designers at Walter Knoll for many years.

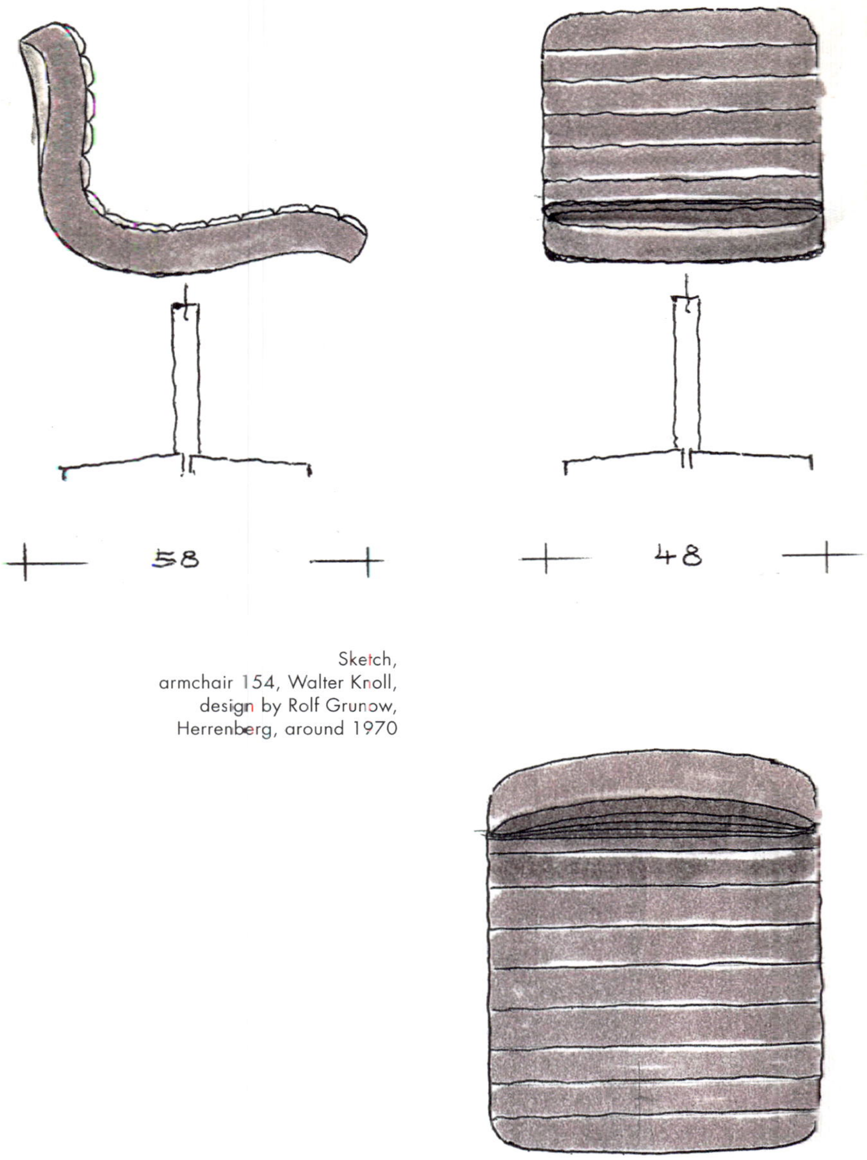

Sketch,
armchair 154, Walter Knoll,
design by Rolf Grunow,
Herrenberg, around 1970

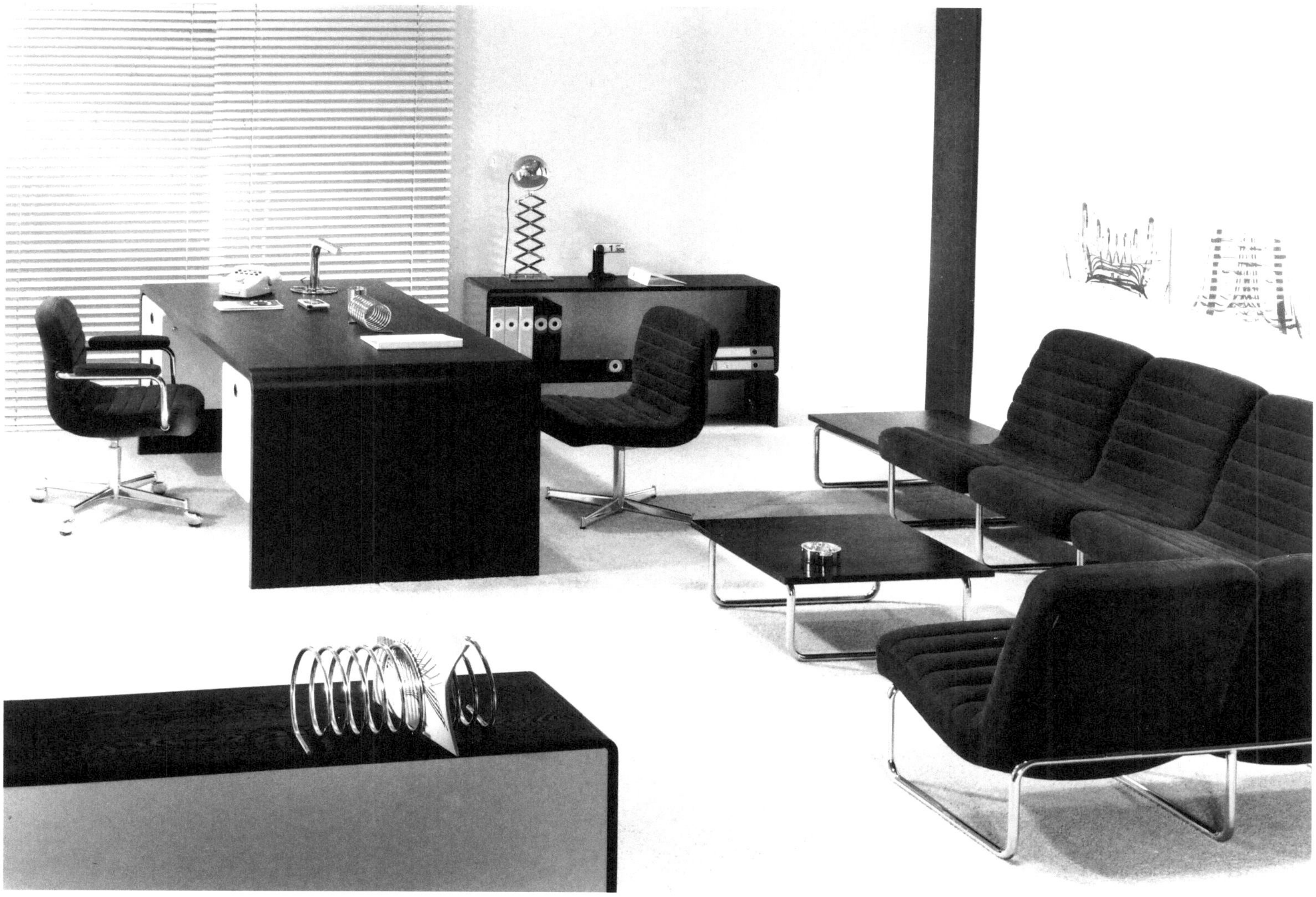

Catalog photo,
armchair 154, Walter Knoll,
design by Rolf Grunow,
Herrenberg, around 1970

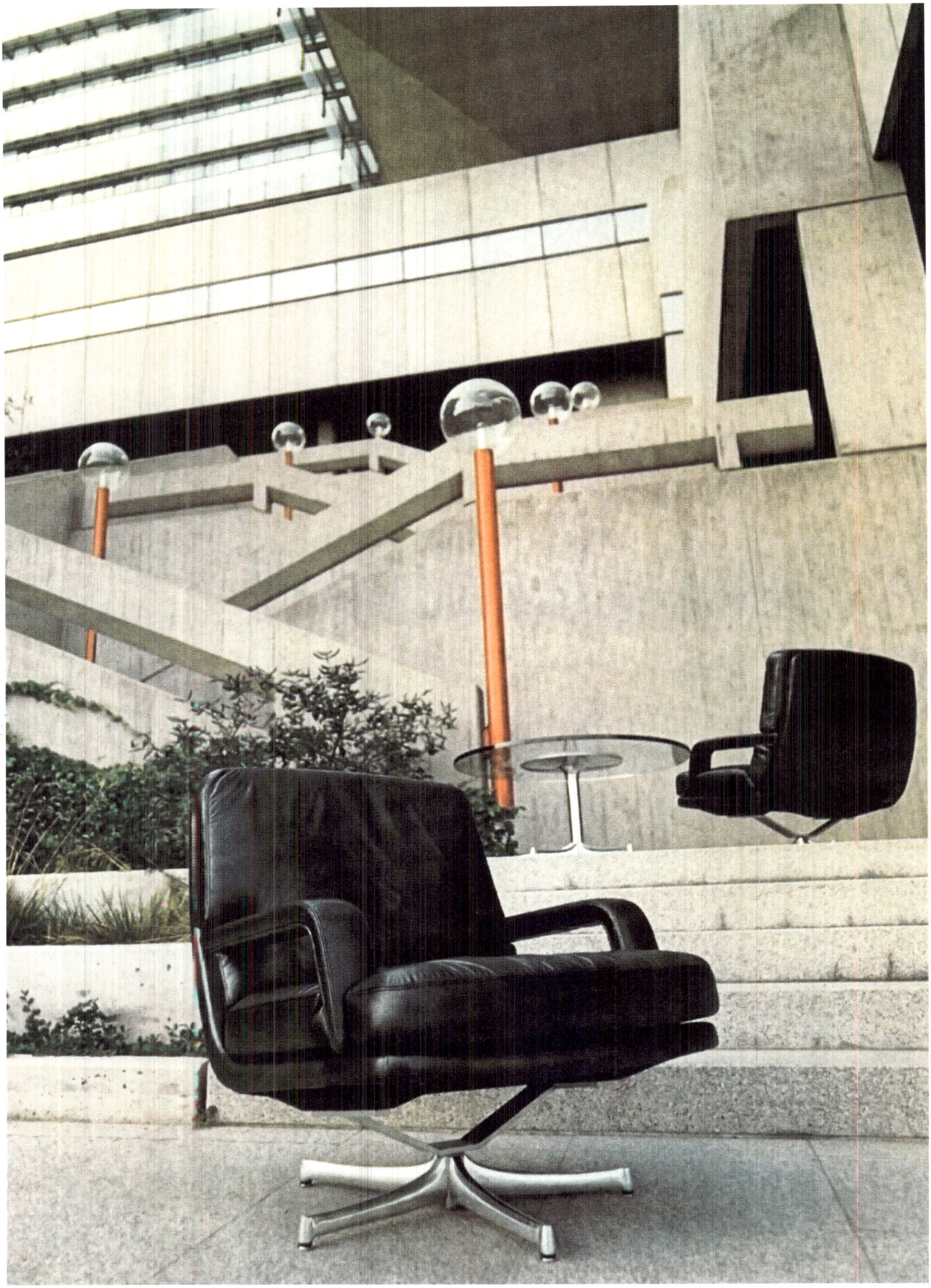

LUXURY CLASS
With the Don executive chair, Walter Knoll once again redefined a genre and converted an item of seating furniture into a status symbol.

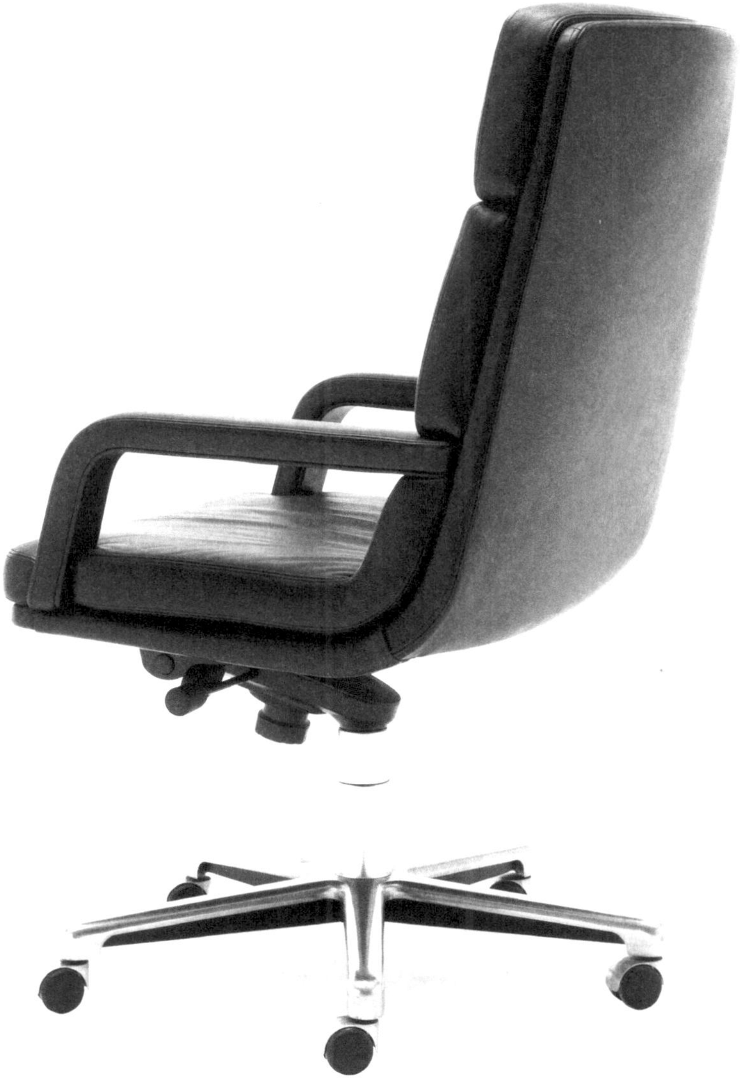

Catalog photo,
armchair Don 839, Walter Knoll,
design by Bernd Münzebrock,
Herrenberg, 1976

Original Don armchair 841, Walter Knoll,
design by Bernd Münzebrock,
Herrenberg, 1976,
restored in 2015

CULTURAL MILIEUS

In the 1970s, Stuttgart was once again a center of modernity – in a wide variety of fields. For example, the architect Günter Behnisch "refurnished" Königstrasse (the city's pedestrian zone), and the choreographer John Cranko, who was often a guest of Robert Knoll, made a big name for himself in the dance scene.

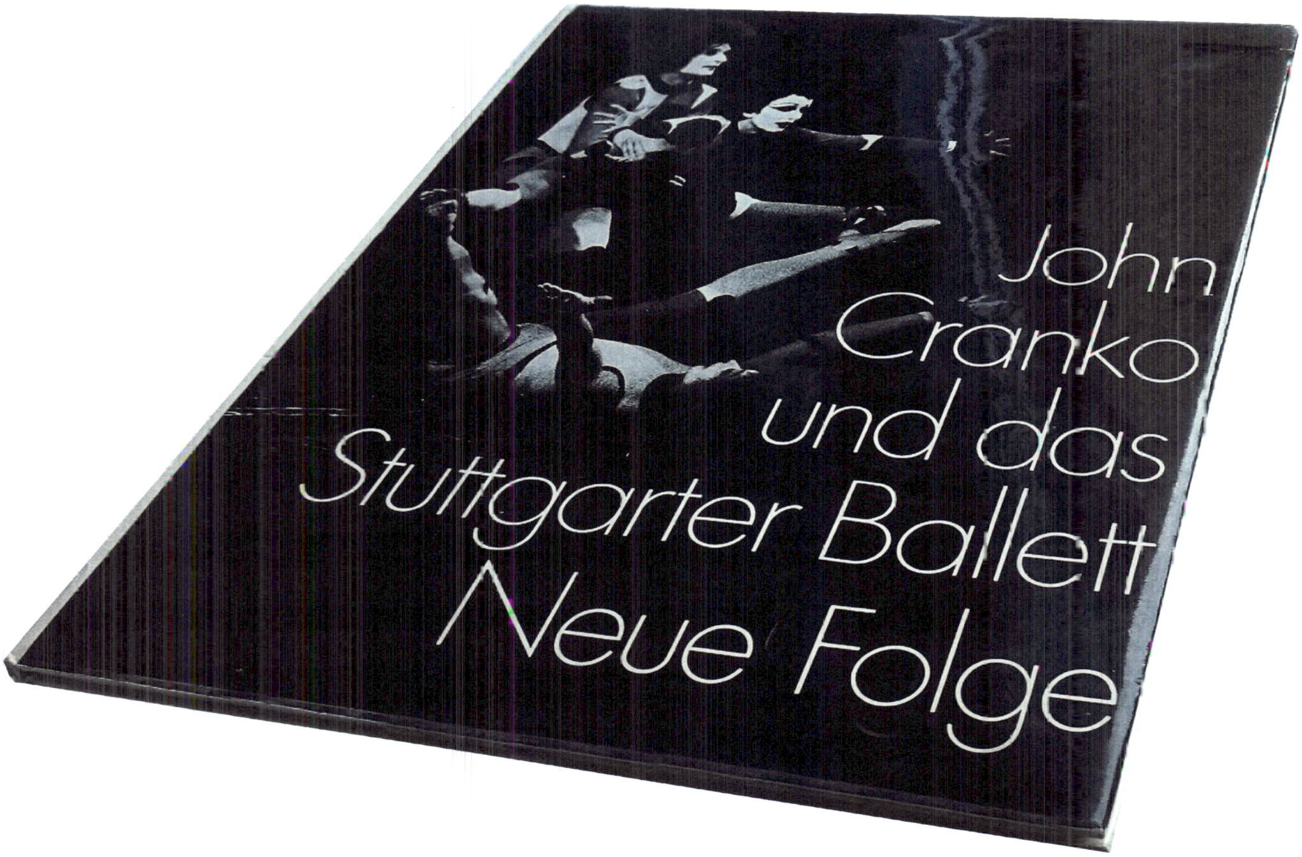

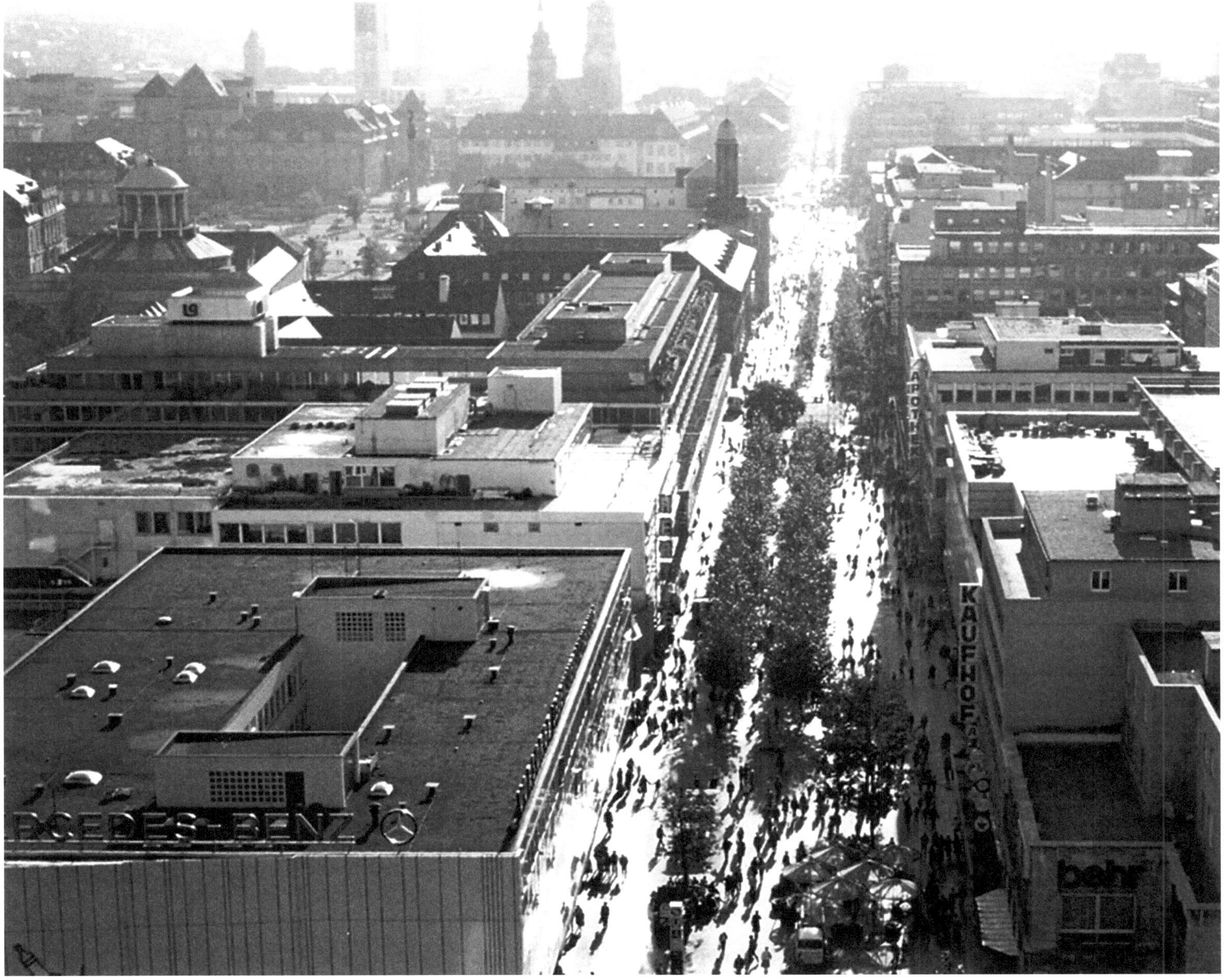

Königstrasse pedestrian zone, designed by the Behnisch architectural practice, Stuttgart, around 1970

THE 1980s

THE KNOLL LEGACY

The 1980s was the decade in which the shock of the oil crises was shaken off and which ultimately ended with the fall of the Iron Curtain and German reunification. Walter Knoll in Herrenberg could look to the new decade with a sense of optimism. Just as it had begun, the "Frankfurter Allgemeine Zeitung" profiled the company in the newspaper's famous business section. Despite the generally subdued mood, revenue had now increased to 15 million marks in Herrenberg. It had therefore trebled since the 1960s. Every fifth item of upholstered furniture was now destined for export. However, the people from the "FAZ" likely marveled at one thing in particular, namely "Walter Knoll's long reference list" – as it was called in the article's headline. This list, which, naturally, was proudly shown around, was a remarkable document. It contained over a hundred major clients, including famous names from the industrial aristocracy, such as Adidas, Henkel, IBM, Krupp, Salamander and WMF, to name just a few. Furthermore, at almost every radio and television broadcasting corporation, everyone was now sitting on seating furniture from Herrenberg. In addition, there were also spa houses, clinics and sanatoriums, as well as schools, universities, and theaters. Walter Knoll was leading in that area that promises large batch sizes, and which is now referred to as contract business. In those days, the prestigious contracts included the German embassies in Madrid and Moscow, and naturally – as was virtually a tradition by that point – the workplace of the head of government, the Federal Chancellery in Bonn, which was still the federal capital. The man of the house Helmut Schmidt, famous for making hard decisions, also had another, aesthetic side. He not had only the bronze sculpture "Large Two Forms" by the English sculptor Henry Moore, a specialist in perfect curves and proportions, installed in front of the door to his office, but his preferred seat for daily use was also a swivel chair with sculptural qualities. He had opted for the Don model from Walter Knoll (see p. 223). Consequently, assembled ministers discussed and, at times, also sat out many a problem on this extra-soft Herrenberg upholstery for a quarter century.

A significant rupture in West German history took place in 1982. Not only did the coalition government of the SPD and FDP collapse. But, as a result, the social-liberal era had also come to an end, and Helmut Kohl was elected as Schmidt's successor as chancellor. A new epoch had begun. In the same year, a break also took place at Walter Knoll in Herrenberg, whose importance for the company history has, as yet, attracted little interest. "This is a black day for me."[2] With these words began a letter that Robert Knoll sent to his son Michael on 4/2/1982. "I thank you for all that we've shared over the years of cooperation," he continued. "I have often been more delighted about it than I have shown. Though I sometimes didn't reveal this out loud, you shouldn't hold it against me. Just like you, I am also quiet and reserved on the outside. Then all the more strongly the emotions rage on the inside!" This frank confession, signed off with "Your papa," likely described the situation and the emotional state of the persons involved quite aptly. However, it came too late. The "black day" referred to here is the day that Michael Knoll resigned. He himself quit the task that he had been so systematically and comprehensively prepared for and that he had taken to with heart and soul. This certainly cannot have been an easy decision. His father took it as a painful "amputation."[3]

The unexpected departure of his son brought an end to seven productive years, a period in which Michael Knoll, advertising manager, product developer and chief designer in one, had been responsible for all design and communication matters. In this intensive period, he further developed the company's product range and image entirely in the spirit of a resolute but always moderate modernist, as had been the guiding principle practiced ever since the company's founding by his grandfather. However, the chemistry between Robert and Michael, who greatly admired his grandfather and had a close relationship with his mother Bruni, had not been right for a long time already. A major reason for this was undoubtedly the fact that Robert had separated from his first wife and remarried back in the 1960s.

Robert Knoll, a gentleman from head to toe, was highly engaging and had many friends. But he also had a different, a hard side. His

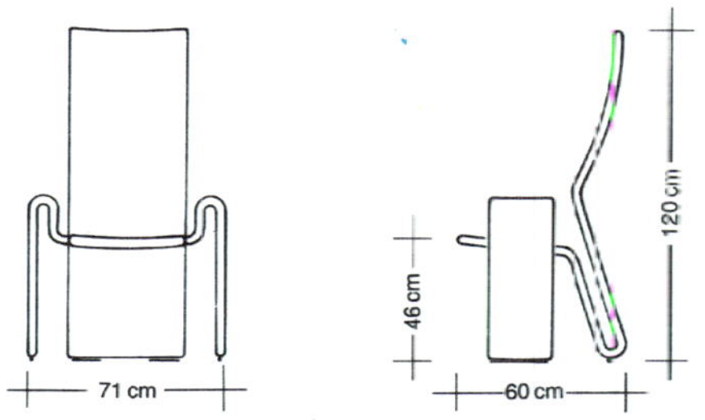

221 Sessel

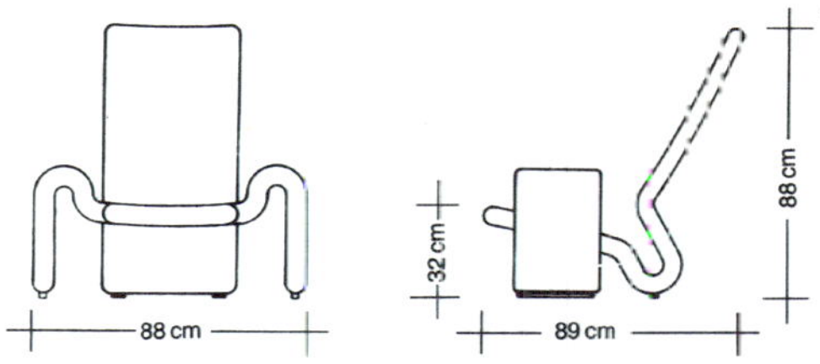

222 Ruhesessel

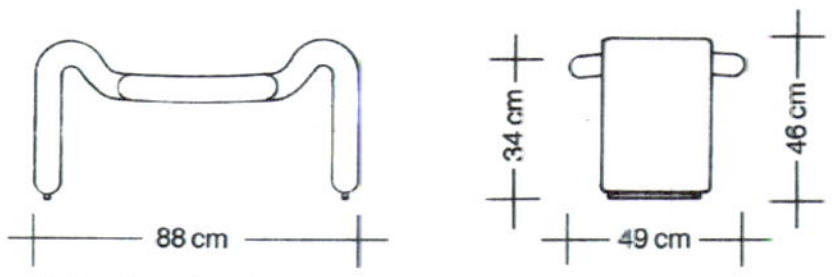

222 H Hocker

son Michael often considered his father's attitude towards him to be cold and unfair. The family and dynastic entanglements, which clearly formed a Gordian knot here, could not be resolved on this occasion either. At some point, Michael, who felt abandoned, could no longer bear the situation.[4] His father retrospectively expressed it in exactly the same way in the quoted letter. In the year that Stephan Combe joined the company as partner and co-decision-maker, Michael Knoll, who had been shaping the image of the company until then, left it. A most unfavorable situation. In that moment, when the break had been made between father and son, Robert Knoll then evoked precisely the mission that Michael had been concerned with. At the end of his letter, somewhat awkwardly but appropriately, he brought up "his ideal vision of the Knoll legacy,"[5] the modern guiding principle of the company. The 70-year-old Robert Knoll greatly doubted whether this ideal was at all feasible without his son. He saw his lifework in jeopardy, and not without reason.

Michael Knoll, like his grandfather and his uncle Hans, gave his notice to his own father. And he had quite similar reasons for this. The father-son conflict set the dynamic of the dynasty in motion. Michael too above all wanted to be free and independent. And, in fact, he did exactly the same as the other two, Walter and Hans, had done before him when they were still the sons of entrepreneurs, and which, as we already know, can be considered a Swabian specialty. Michael Knoll left his homeland and crossed the Atlantic. He went to the USA where he had connections that would also prove helpful in this case. No longer the old Vollmöller contacts, but new relationships, in particular with the company Brayton International, which had already been a licensee of Walter Knoll for several years. Michael Knoll moved to North Carolina in the hot south of the USA. And given that he was a versatile furniture and design expert and enjoyed an excellent professional and personal relationship with his hosts, who were also able to teach a few things to the young German, now in his late thirties, it was a deal based on reciprocity. In this way, the stranger, whose position was very similar to the one he held in Herrenberg and involved a workload that was just as extensive, additionally received a crash course in American business methods – including how to engage in aggressive marketing with dozens of representatives who are also in fierce competition with one another. The fact that he was constantly on the road between the east and west coasts made his stay a real adventure. What's more, he was making very good money. Whenever possible, the young explorer cruised through the vast country in his Plymouth estate car. Already a passionate music lover, he discovered black blues artists there and laid the foundation for a record collection that would quickly swell to several thousand black disks. The *Ländle* back home now seemed very distant.

Michael kept in touch with his mother Bruni the whole time (and was similar to Walter and Hans in this respect too). Mixed news came from home. The plans for the new factory, which was going to be built on the outskirts of the city, came to a halt. In the end, in 1983, even Interior Minister Roman Herzog was invited to the Herrenberg city hall in an endeavor to secure the approval of state funds. However, the future Federal President, who was elected to the Federal Constitutional Court of Germany in Karlsruhe in the same year, could not bring himself to make any concrete commitments. It was a matter of around six million marks, which the company was unable to procure itself. Consequently, the new construction, which was considered to be urgently needed, was delayed until the twelfth of never.

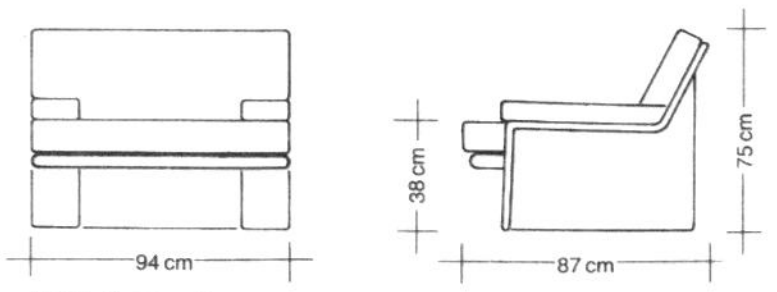

217 Sessel
Sitz: Nosagfederung. Rücken: Gummigurtfederung.
Sitz-, Rücken- und Armlehnkissen:
Superflex mit Polsterdaunenauflage.

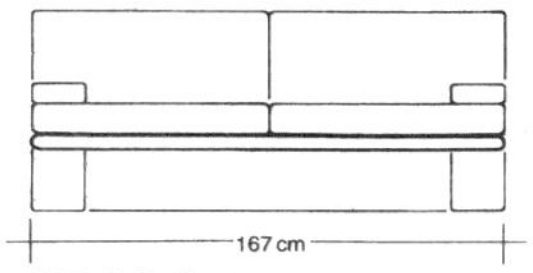

217-2 Sofa 2-sitzig

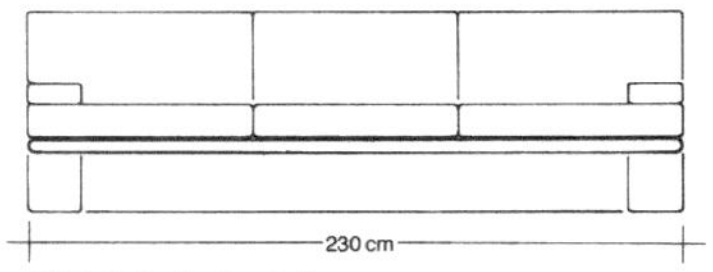

217-3 Sofa 3-sitzig

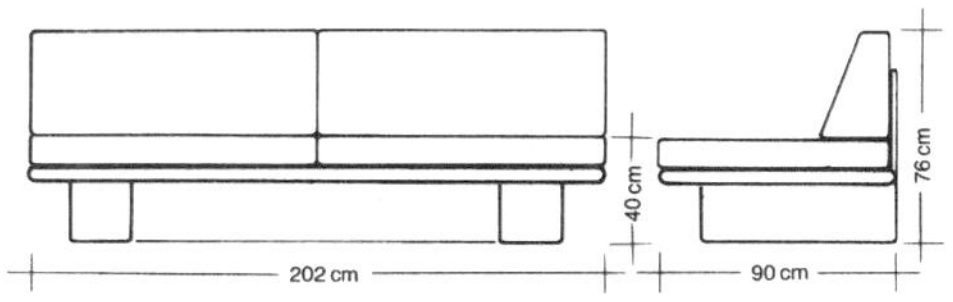

217 L Liege

1 ▶ "Frankfurter Allgemeine Zeitung," 10/23/1980.

2 ▶ Letter from 4/2/1980, WK archives.

3 ▶ Ibid.

4 ▶ Interview with Josef Czimmer on 11/17/2014.

5 ▶ Letter from 4/2/1980, WK archives.

Whether cantilever chairs or full upholstery, the tradition of modernity was a source of inspiration.

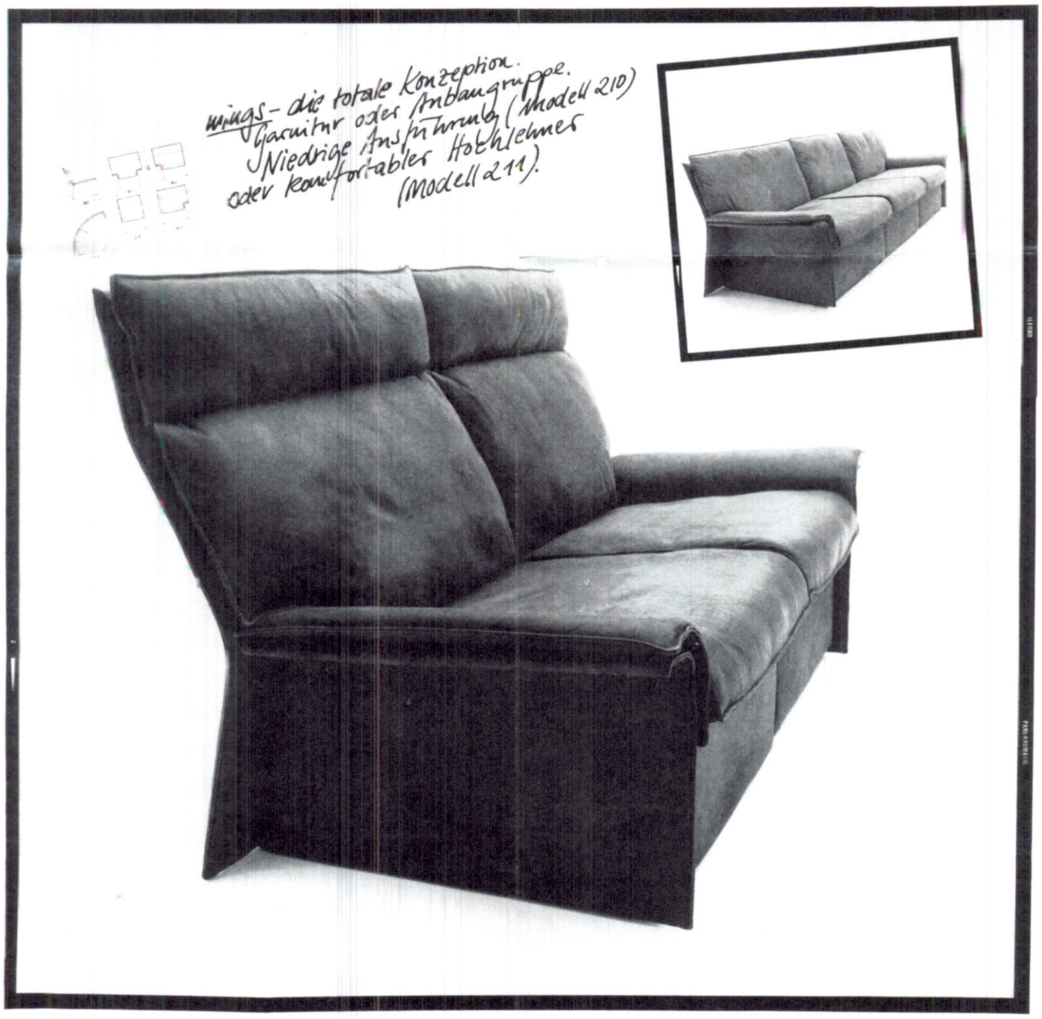

Advertising leaflet,
sofa 211, Walter Knoll,
Herrenberg, around 1980

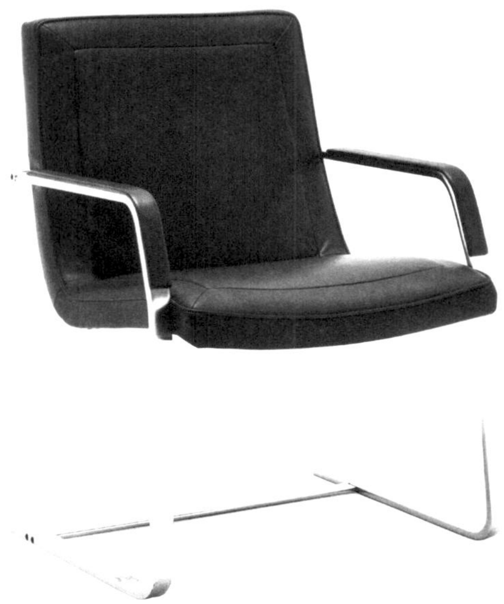

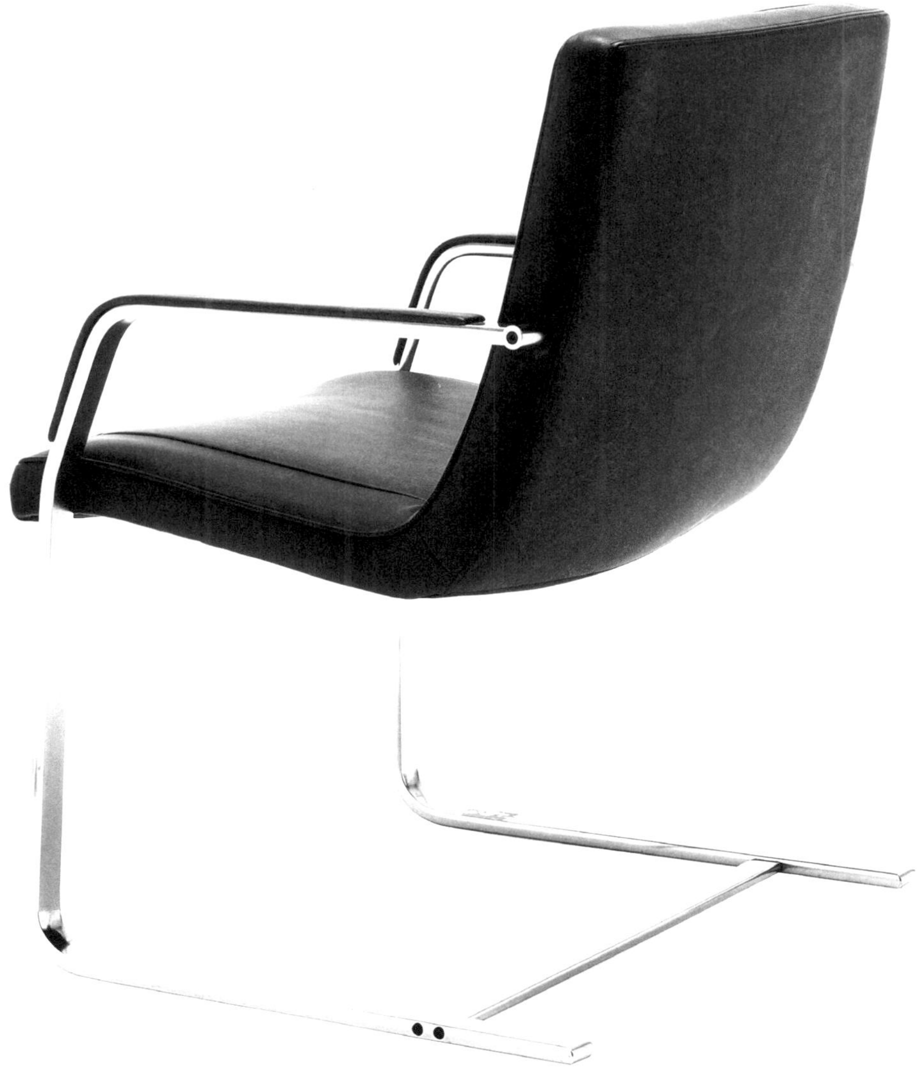

Original armchair Lord 2100,
Walter Knoll,
design by Michael Knoll,
Herrenberg, 1984,
restored in 2015

While in faraway North Carolina, Michael Knoll also learned of a quite fairytale-like story that had taken place in the same year. It sounded a bit like one of the "Thousand and One Nights." In March 1983, his father Robert embarked on a journey to the Middle East. After a flight of 3,500 miles, he landed in Riyadh, the capital city of Saudi Arabia. The report that he drew up about the trip and sent home reveals bright enthusiasm. Which was rather unusual for him. As was the personal, even warm, relationship that he enjoyed with Muhammad Al-Agil, his new business friend, whom he referred to exclusively by his first name. "Muhammad has studied in the USA, by the way," he added, "and knows everyone and his brother."[6] This Muhammad Al-Agil, one of six brothers in a widely distributed family company and ranking number 43 on the list of the richest Saudis at the time, was in the process of building up a furniture business on a grand scale. He held serious discussions with the likable and competent German. And the latter was enthralled: "Muhammad has his headquarters in an elegant villa with a large conference room (furnished with our 839 armchairs in leather)."[7] Why the Swabian-Arabic desert fairytale, which had started so promisingly, ultimately did not have a happy ending and was not resumed until present times, is not understood in detail. However, the fact is that of the 2,000 ordered armchairs, several hundred had already been built but would never be delivered.[8] This was a moderately severe disaster for business.

THE FURNITURE WORLD WAS TURNED UPSIDE-DOWN: POST-MODERNITY HAD BEGUN AND WAS TRIUMPHANT, ESPECIALLY IN THE FEDERAL REPUBLIC OF GERMANY.

At the first works meeting in January of the following year, Robert Knoll, who always came across as authoritative and never patriarchal, offered his apologies to his workforce. "My desire is that will you will largely be spared from unpleasant short-time work in 1984," he said in his frank introductory remarks.[9] Then the company director, now 72 years old, apologized for his absence. "For I know only too well that my absence from day-to-day in-house activities here in recent months has been perplexing for you."[10] Robert Knoll, who, of course, only lived a stone's throw away in the house of his parents, had only made sporadic appearances at the company in the previous six months. He explained this as follows: "After the company vacation, I had decided to tackle some work at home that I had not got round to doing for decades in the hustle and bustle of everyday life. This work, which, besides the 58-year history of the company, also includes an extensive archive collection, seemed important to me. Who else will manage to get this done later on?" He then announced that his research and also his absence would last until at least the summer. It was, of course, no coincidence that he was delving into the history of the company at this time. After all, he was on the search for the Knoll legacy that he believed to be fundamental and that he, and thus also the company itself, now saw in jeopardy. He sensed that gaping cracks were appearing in the dynastic structure and that he was incapable of giving it a greater degree of stability. Robert, always the weak one after his unassailable father, fell into a deep crisis. Hence the desperate flight into the company's history, which, after all, was also his own history; a course of action that was clearly counter-productive in the extreme. In the meantime, he had handed over control of the company to his partner Stephan Combe, a newcomer to the industry, who, now left completely to his own devices, struggled to rescue the company's legacy. Robert Knoll was a tragic case. What must his employees have thought about their boss in this moment? He must have induced astonishment, perhaps dismay, though certainly also a great deal of respect for this Shakespearian performance of a despondent king. Conscientious as ever, he produced a report about it.

MODERNITY OR POST-MODERNITY?

At some point, the news about his father, who had withdrawn – gone into hiding even – reached his son Michael in faraway North Carolina. He would have all too happily turned his stay in America into a permanent arrangement. But now, after just a year and nine months, he returned to his Swabian homeland out of a sense of duty, as his grandfather Walter had once done. He too, of course, would have all too gladly stayed in America. Only now, unlike back then, the possibilities of a new start were very limited for Michael Knoll. The aesthetic coordinates that he now discovered had shifted significantly in the meantime. Once the Memphis group had swept all previous conventions off the flecked Resopal table with its quirky designs in Milan in the early 1980s, the mood had turned. Cast-iron design principles began to waver. By now, virtually anything seemed possible. And the furniture world, which would once again undergo a style revolution, was truly turned on its head. Post-modernity had begun and was triumphant, especially in the Federal Republic of Germany. Young guns, including many art students, rehearsed a joyous break from their

functionalist fathers under the banner of *Neues Deutsches Design* (New German Design). Although this predominantly took place in newspaper columns and galleries and rarely made its way into the living room, they were, in fact, the opinion leaders of the time. New names, such as Michael Graves, Philippe Starck and the Alessi company, also emerged in premium design. And with them, an almost magic word found its way into everyday speech, which had only been used as a technical term, if at all, in most languages until then: design. Many a modernist, frightened by the wind that was blowing at the time, crossed over to the new design vanguard, as is so common during rebellions. For a while, it seemed as if it was now only possible to make it as a gravedigger of modernity. Architecturally, post-modernity had already arrived in Stuttgart. The "Neue Staatsgalerie" (New State Gallery) by James Stirling, one of the early groundbreaking museum buildings in Germany, was hailed as an eclectic masterpiece (see p. 249).

In this turbulent atmosphere, Michael Knoll resumed his work, which was not made easier by the fact that it had now doubled in scope. He now not only assumed his previous all-rounder role as chief designer and advertising manager. As managing partner, he also took on managerial responsibilities. As far as household furniture was concerned, which still accounted for a virtually unchanged three quarters of sales, the home comer continued where he had left off before his brief USA interlude. He resorted to that network of independent designers who knew exactly where Herrenberg was, and were generally also experts in upholstered furniture. Among others, those who now produced models included Jan Armgardt, Peter Maly, and Anita Schmidt. Without exception, they belonged to Michael Knoll's own generation, were interior designers like him and, Memphis notwithstanding, each dyed-in-the-wool functionalists in their own way. In their new old chief designer, they found a competent contact partner and comrade-in-arms, who was also a colleague. After all, Michael Knoll also contributed his own models. In his dual role as manager and designer, he was an extremely rare case in the entire furniture profession. And Walter Knoll now had an in-house design studio, which was also a novelty in the industry.

A stylistic idiom dominated, which – like in the 1970s – was generally based on full upholstery, made use of simpler proportions and, in the process, renounced experimentation. The models fluctuated between refined variants of traditional upholstered furniture and a strictness reminiscent of the days of *Neues Wohnen* (New Living). They were therefore swimming against the tide. The models generally radiated the same sort of tastefulness that had been deemed the guiding principle of the Reform Period prior to the First World War. Here, at the end of the Second Modernity, the pendulum had swung back to the First. This impression is confirmed by the fact that the club chair, the original Knoll furniture innovation, came to enjoy renewed popularity and along with it, of course, also leather.[11] The company pitted itself against the pretentious zeitgeist, though it was not entirely alone in this attitude. It was evident in a wide range of fields in Germany. For example, Jil Sander, a German fashion designer who "appreciates traditional forms, but rejects conservative limitations," enjoyed great success during that time.[12] In automobile design, another pioneering sector, chief designers (Bruno Sacco at Mercedes, Claus Luthe at BMW, or Hartmut Warkuß at Audi) proved their aesthetic staying power. With lasting success, as would become evident. "Design free of gimmicks" would ultimately prevail and was a significant factor in the triumph of premium German automobile brands.

The work of Michael Knoll can also be placed within the stylistic context of a well-tempered modernism. Especially if office furniture is also taken into account, an area that now comprised six product families and was, as before, a preserve of classical objectivity. Besides the core business, other respectable achievements were produced. For example, Susanne Rövenstrunck, the first woman in the position of employed designer, produced a coffee table with Mondrianesque primary colors under a square glass top (see p. 247). She received multiple awards for her wall-mounted coat racks made of painted tubular steel, including from the Stuttgart Design Center. There would never be another employed designer after her, neither male nor female.

---

6 ▶ Log by Robert Knoll, undated, WK archives.

7 ▶ Ibid.

8 ▶ Interview with Josef Czimmer on 11/17/2014.

9 ▶ Statement by Robert Knoll, works meeting, 1/9/1984, WK archives.

10 ▶ Ibid.

11 ▶ In 1987, the Club chair was re-issued on the basis of a design by Ernst M. Dettinger.

12 ▶ Polster 1999, p. 290.

HOMEWORK
As chief designer and art director, Michael Knoll renewed the collection and communication of Walter Knoll.

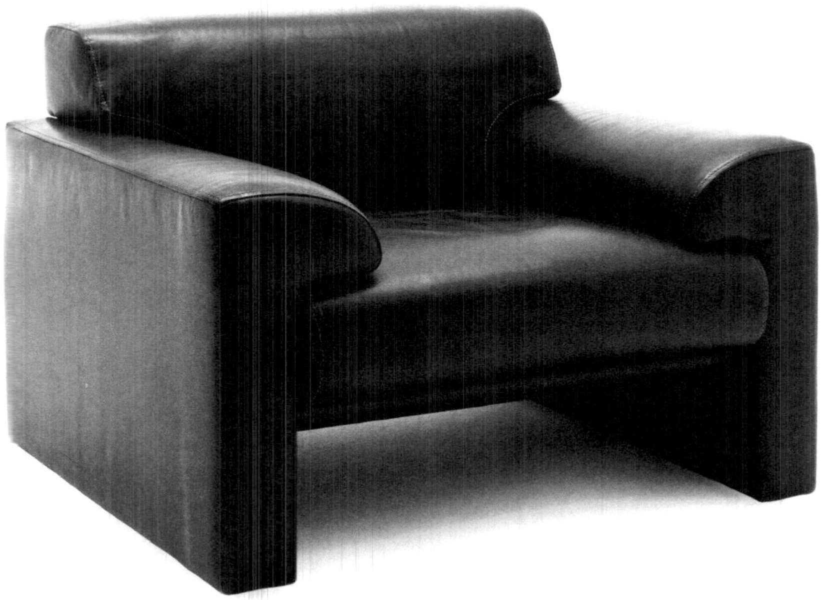

Catalog
Collection Walter Knoll,
design by Michael Knoll,
Herrenberg, 1980

Original armchair
Casa 203-10,
Walter Knoll,
design by Michael Knoll,
Herrenberg, 1984,
restored in 2015

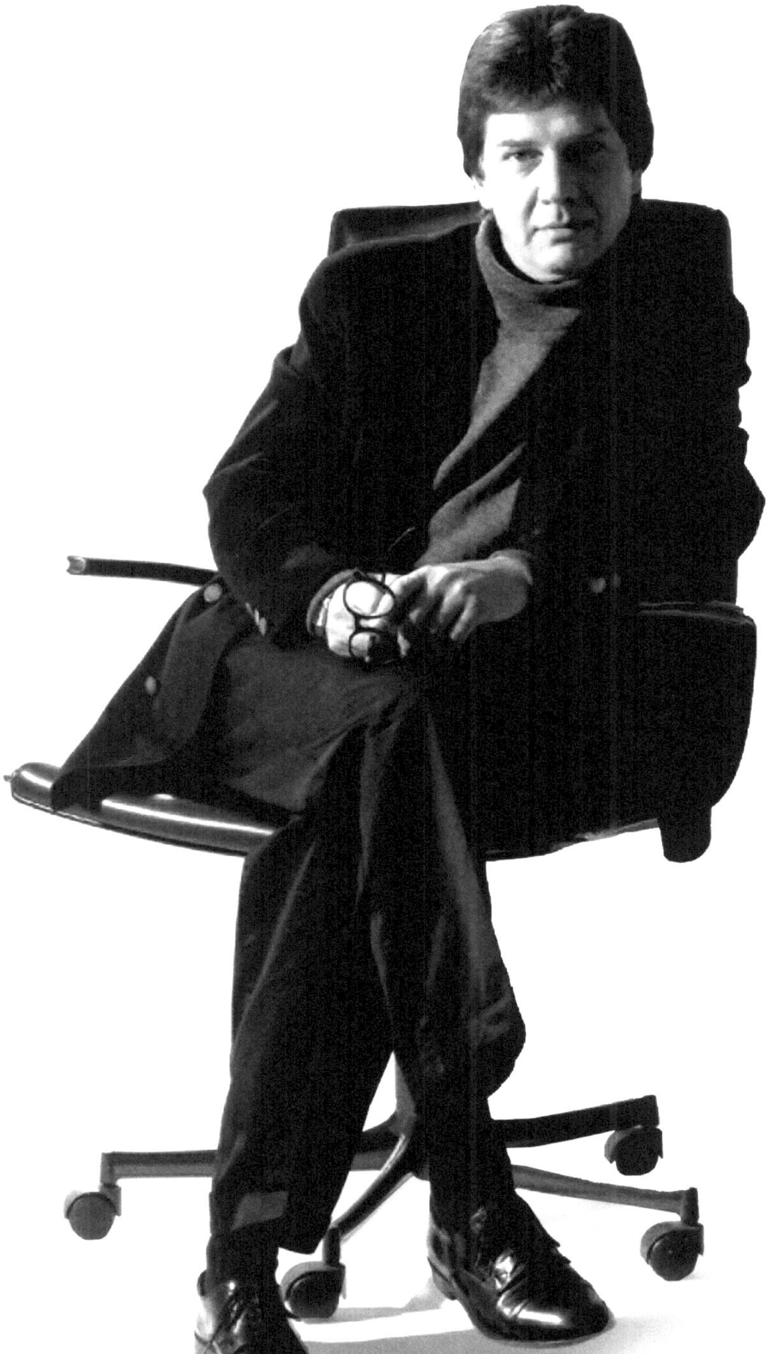

Michael Knoll, son of
Robert Knoll,
partner, designer and
art director

As the dark economic clouds cleared, the consumer climate also picked up again. In addition, latent social change resulted in rising demand. The average area of homes had steadily increased and was now already over 80 square meters. Within a few years, the number of single-person households grew considerably and was approaching eight million by 1983. In the preceding year, the number of building permits had increased by 20 percent. This was good news for the furniture industry. In 1984, like virtually every other year, the Cologne furniture fair once again set a new record. 1,440 companies from 35 countries were showcased on a phenomenal total area of 212,000 square meters. However, the seemingly unstoppable path of expansion also had drawbacks. The gigantic show tended to consist of an unclear "hodgepodge of styles, furniture types and countries,"[13] where it was difficult to separate the wheat from the chaff. In this difficult environment, the Walter Knoll company attempted to fly the flag of modernity.

WITH IMMEDIATE EFFECT, THERE WAS NO LONGER ANYTHING PREVENTING THE OFFENSIVE USE OF THE BRAND NAME WALTER KNOLL, WHICH HAD BEEN BLOCKED FOR 60 YEARS.

The 1984 trade fair was the last time that Walter and Wilhelm Knoll, the famous sibling companies from Swabia, would be represented by separate stands in Cologne. Incidentally, this was the place where the paths of Walter Knoll and Markus Benz, the law student who was at a trade fair for the first time and was earning some money serving at the bar, first crossed. In the same year, Walter Knoll was also present at the burgeoning furniture fair in Milan, but not alone. Shoulder-to-shoulder with four quality brands from Württemberg, including Rolf Benz, the company ventured into the lion's den of post-modernity.[14] The Salone del Mobile, a new kind of annual designer fair unveiling visions of the future, was now an absolutely unmissable event – at least for ambitious manufacturers. The foray of the Swabians, who organized their bold campaign under the fashionable Anglicism of "Five," would, however, remain a singular event. The principle of the joint stand, successfully implemented by Stuttgart's "Landesgewerbeamt" (State Trade Office) ever since the first furniture fair in Cologne, was clearly not so easily transferable to unfamiliar and highly competitive terrain. The rules of globalization that were now being played by still had to be learned.

In 1985, when Michael Knoll had been back from America for a year, his father died at the age of 73. He was followed the year after by former co-owner Walter Combe, who was 87 years old. Both Robert Knoll and his cousin Walter Combe had worked for the company for decades, including a quarter century side-by-side from 1953 to 1979. In the 1960s and 70s they had been equal partners. Now, in Michael Knoll and Stephan Combe – Walter Combe's son who had succeeded him in 1982 – the fourth generation had assumed responsibility. From a dynastic perspective, they were both great-grandsons of company founder Wilhelm Knoll, but had little else in common. Stephan Combe was an old-school manager who did not have a background in the furniture industry and, furthermore, was eleven years older. Questions of modernity and its development, the centerpiece of the ideal Knoll legacy, were not in his DNA. Many a discussion between the mismatched pair reportedly continued right into the early hours of the morning. In an interview with a specialist furniture journal, Michael Knoll once offered the theory that within a company "there must be tension between the divisions," from which a productive culture of dialog could then arise. This is a wise perspective that was based on his own earlier experiences. It may also have been a subtle allusion to the somewhat difficult relations between the two contrasting counterparts in the executive chair.

THE END OF THE FURNITURE FAMILY KNOLL

In these already strained circumstances, a bombshell occurred that made the situation even more complicated. The death knell for the Wilhelm Knoll company, which had already been looming and led to bankruptcy in 1985, presented the new leadership duo with difficult decisions. The collapse of the ancestral company of the Knoll dynasty, which for all too long had wanted to make its mark as a specialist in exposed wood and, in the process, got bogged down in niches outside its field, such as its own line of bath furniture, left behind the shattered remains of a business. Although Dieter Knoll had bowed out of running the company long ago, meaning it was no longer possible to speak of a family business, Walter Knoll took over the company anyway. It was a matter of machines, including those used to produce the legendary Antimott springs. The main incentive, however, was brand rights. The name Wilhelm Knoll was to be prevented from falling into the clutches of outsiders at all costs. The attempt to integrate and refloat[15] the stranded vessel of a company in the form of a "Wilhelm Knoll Collection" was, however, doomed to failure and cost time, energy and money.

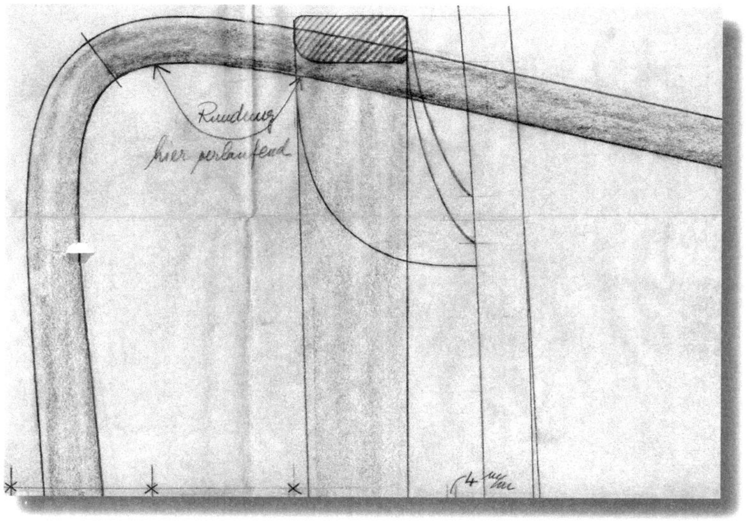

It would not take long until not only the products of Wilhelm Knoll, but also the company name, would disappear from the market for good. Which, in turn, also meant that, with immediate effect, there was no longer anything preventing the offensive use of the brand name Walter Knoll, which had been blocked for 60 years. That was certainly cause for celebration.

The merging of the two German Knoll companies had yet another wondrous knock-on effect. In 1990, just five years after the 60th anniversary of Walter Knoll, it was now possible to look back on 125 years of joint company history. Michael Knoll seized the opportunity with both hands. He had an exhibition set up, which, conceived in the form of a narrative, proudly placed the Knoll upholstered chair on the museum pedestal. This event, which was quite unprecedented in the industry, took place at the "Landesgewerbeamt" (State Trade Office), that legendary Valhalla of Stuttgart modernity, whose huge significance for the development of the region was still known at the time, although it had already been renamed the "Haus der Wirtschaft" (House of Commerce). To provide the necessary expertise, Arno Votteler was brought on board. He had once been a young professional at Walter Knoll as well as professor and director of the Institute for Interior Design and Furniture Design at the Stuttgart Academy.[16] This was the institution where Bernhard Pankok and Adolf Schneck had once heralded the start of modern furniture and Votteler's teacher, Herbert Hirche, had carried it over to the Second Modernity together with Herta-Maria Witzemann. Michael Knoll also studied there later when it was once again a powerhouse of renewal under Hirche and Witzemann. The Knoll exhibition, accompanied with a catalog, was opened quite ceremoniously. Dignitaries from Stuttgart turned up, including Mrs Witzemann. Once again, it seemed as if things had come full circle. And then the whole excitement had yet another not entirely insignificant side affect. On the invitation cards for the exhibition, the name of the company was set in a typeface called Bodoni. This elegant type with its distinctive serifs, whose creator was an Italian, subsequently became a hallmark of Walter Knoll that is now known all around the world.[17]

The keynote speech at the launch of the exhibition was given by the Stuttgart-born art historian Hans Höger. As his topic, he selected an issue of importance for the future: Bauhaus and Memphis: the 1990s? And who would not have wanted to know how the battle between modernity and post-modernity – in which Walter Knoll had taken such a clear position – would likely be settled? There was also another subject that was of burning interest to those in attendance but would, of course, only be brought up behind the scenes. The hall was rife with rumors that serious problems were being experienced in Herrenberg. However, very few people would likely have anticipated that, at the time of this celebratory event, which appeared to be a high point, there were already signs of a crisis that threatened the existence of the company. Just three years later came the next dramatic moment in the company's history. In 1993, it had to be sold. This resulted in the departure of the owners at the time.[18] With Michael Knoll, the last representative of the Knoll furniture dynasty left the company. It was therefore its definitive end. But not the end of the company Walter Knoll. Incidentally, it remained both a family company and in Swabian hands. And the ideal Knoll legacy also survived.

---

13 ▶ Toby E. Rodes, International Furniture Fair Cologne '84, in: md 4/84, p. 51.

14 ▶ The other comrades-in-arms were the companies Draenert, Haiges, and Rausch.

15 ▶ Interview with Michael Knoll, in: "büro" 2/89.

16 ▶ The curators were Alex Müller-Schöll and Susanne Stihl, two employees at the Institute for Interior Design.

17 ▶ The typeface, classed as a classical design, was created by Giambattista Bodoni in 1790.

18 ▶ After an article about the resurrected Walter Knoll company had been published in the "Stuttgarter Zeitung" in 2001, a rebuttal appeared in the same place a week later. It had been obtained by Michael Knoll and contained the following wording: "Contrary to the account given in the article of 21 September 2001, the Herrenberg furniture manufacturer Walter Knoll was not taken over by the Benz family out of insolvency. According to previous shareholders from the Knoll family, the reasons for the sale were succession problems and differences of opinion within the management and the various shareholders." The perception of his life's work was tremendously important to him. "Stuttgarter Zeitung," 9/27/2001, p. 16.

LOCATIONS

Fashion models and furniture models: visual concepts were now being developed for photo shoots and, in the style of the time, furniture was shown in unusual and sometimes absurd situations.

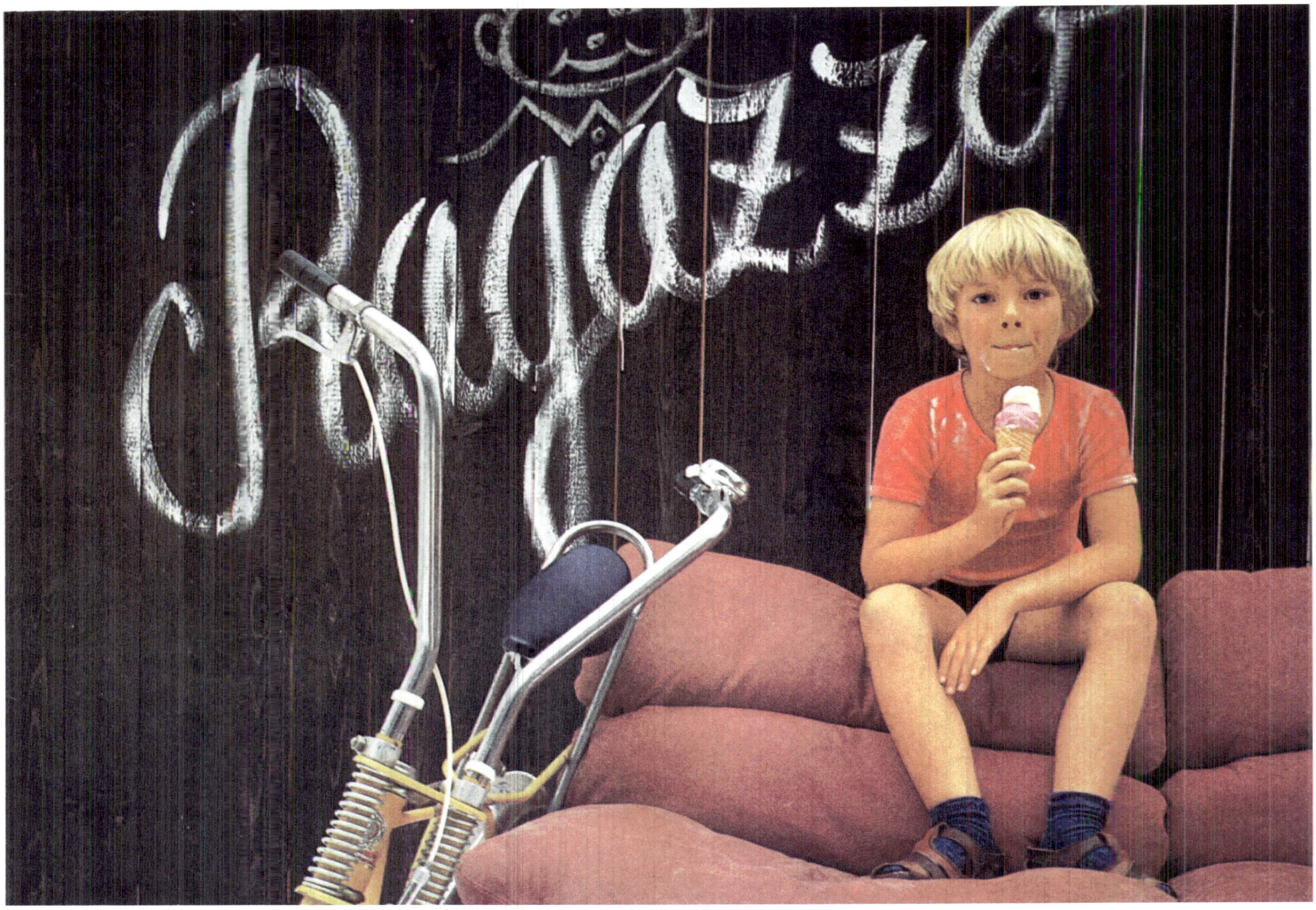

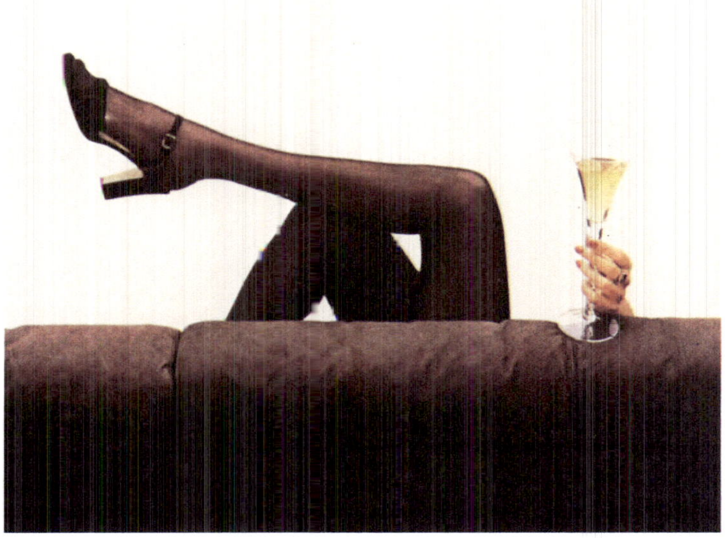

Advertising leaflet,
sofa Ragazzo 185-3,
Walter Knoll,
design by Bernd Münzebrock,
Herrenberg, around 1980

Pro brochure page,
Walter Knoll,
design by Bernd Münzebrock,
Herrenberg, around 1980

TASTEFUL

On the search for the archetypal sofa. Top priority now seemed to be given to exploring the basic shapes of upholstered furniture.

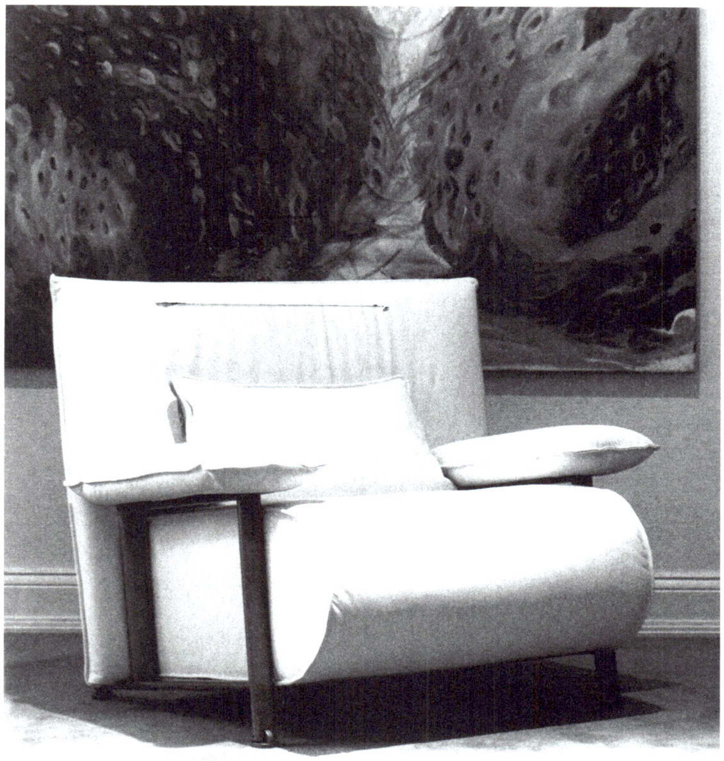

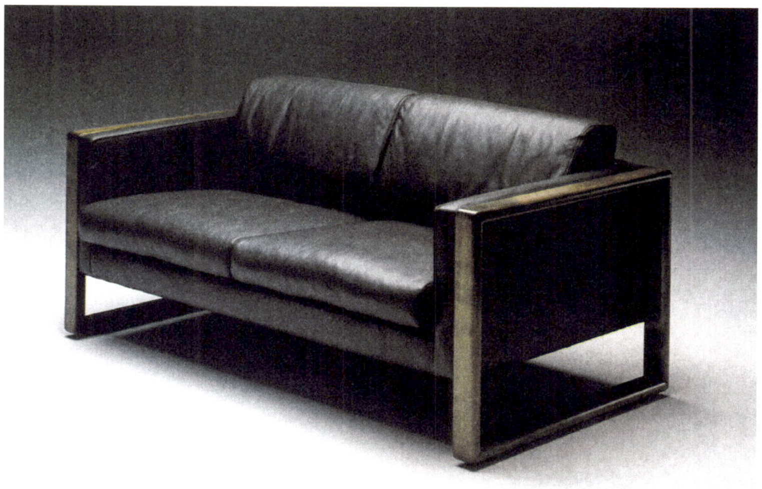

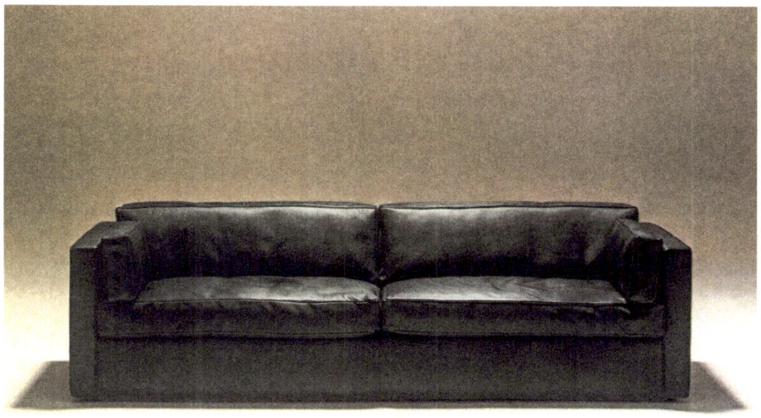

Sofa Studio,
Walter Knoll,
design by Jürgen Lange,
Herrenberg, around 1985

Sofa Mondial,
Walter Knoll,
design by Michael Knoll,
Herrenberg, 1985

Sofa Impuls, Walter Knoll,
design by Peter Maly,
Herrenberg, 1984

WATERSHED MOMENTS

In the 1980s began the era of post-modernity, which challenged all existing conventions and spread the word "design" around the world. A new generation of freelance designers now worked for Walter Knoll.

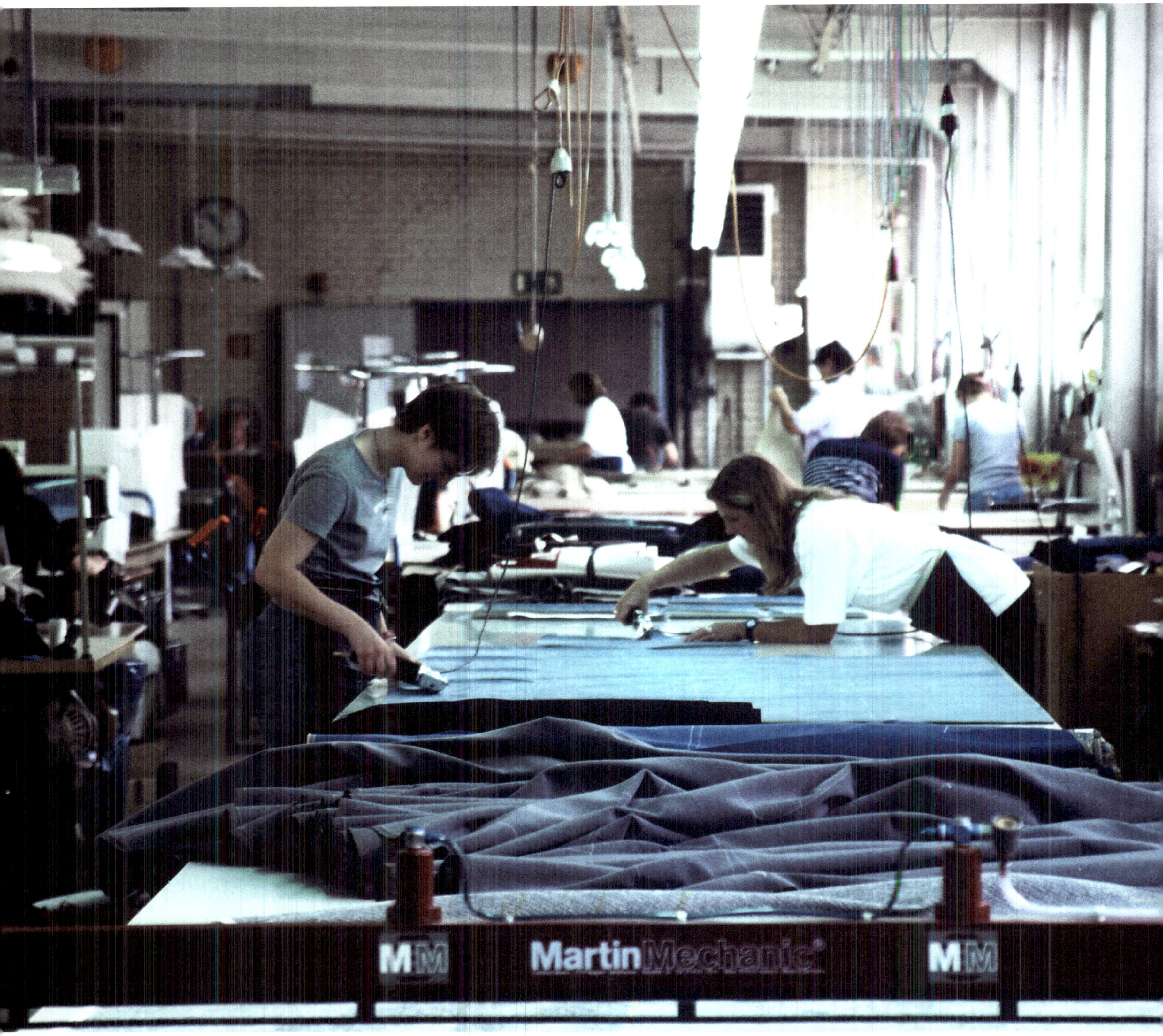

Production, Walter Knoll,
Herrenberg, 1983

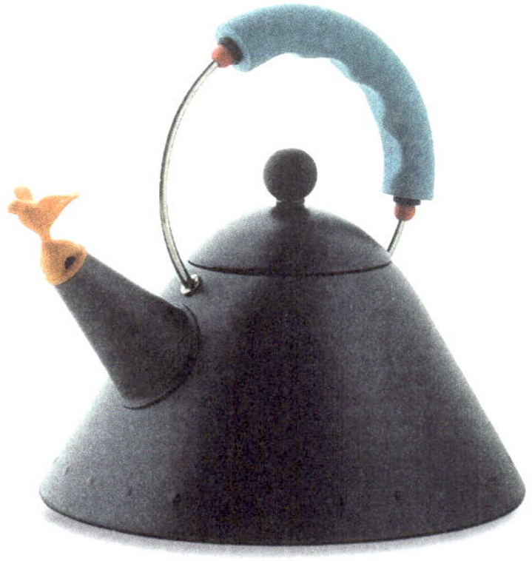

One of the first design objects – and also one of the first to be referred to as such – was a chic kettle.

Armchair Quadriga, Walter Knoll, design by Jochen Hoffmann, Herrenberg, 1984

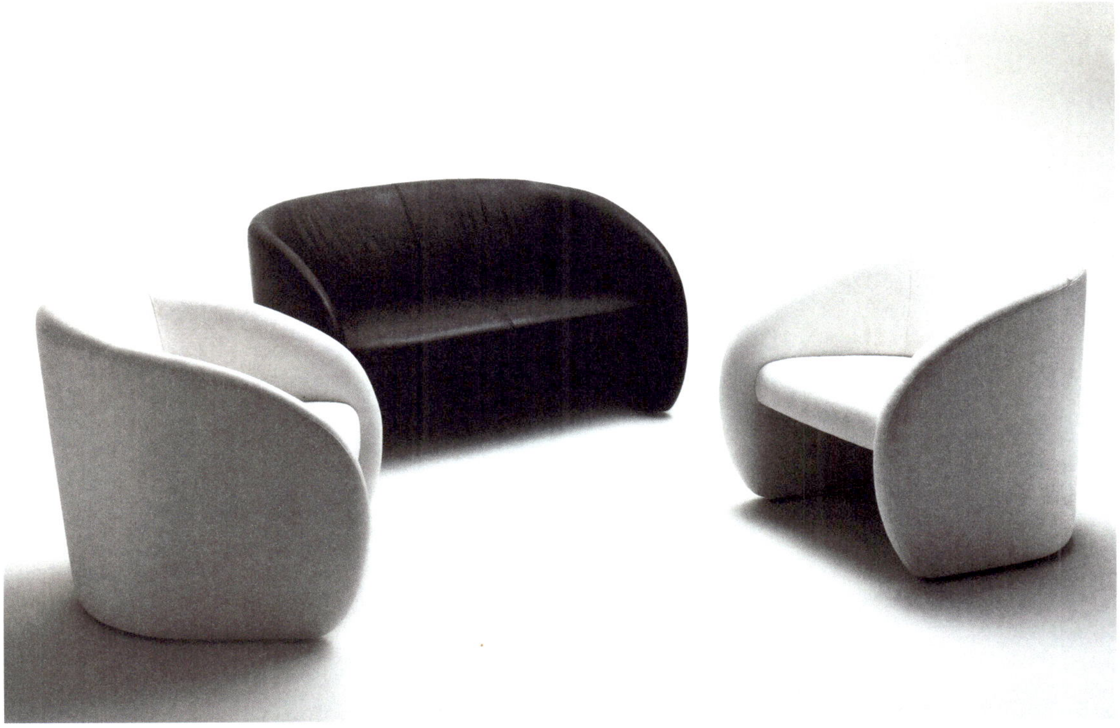

CELEBRATIONS

An exhibition was held for the 125th anniversary of Walter Knoll. The former "Landesgewerbeamt" (State Trade Office) – nowadays known as the "Haus der Wirtschaft" (House of Commerce) – a birthplace of Stuttgart modernity, served as a suitable venue. Many of its representatives were in attendance, including professor Arno Votteler, who organized the exhibition.

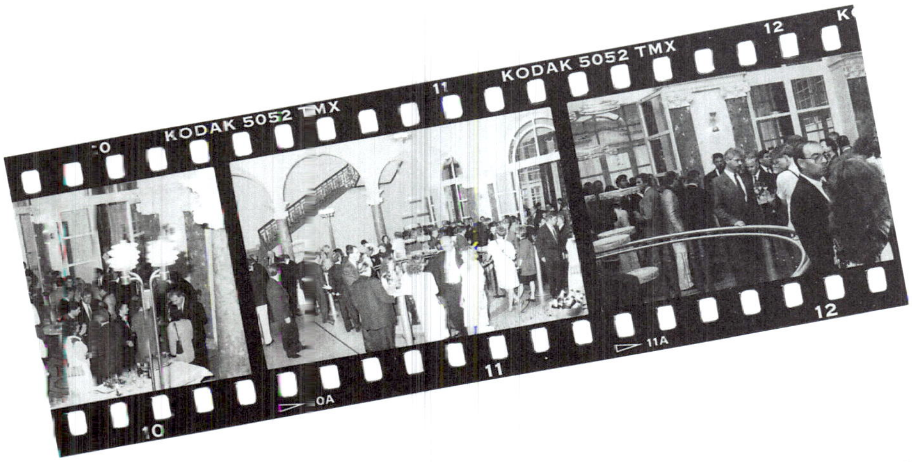

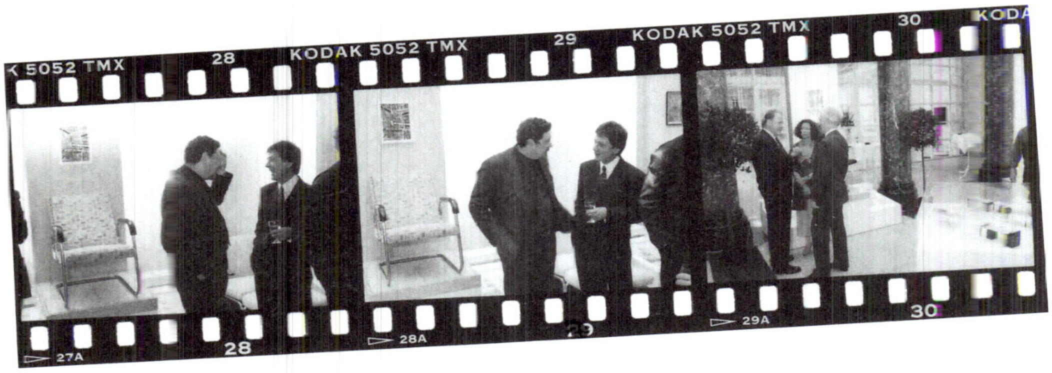

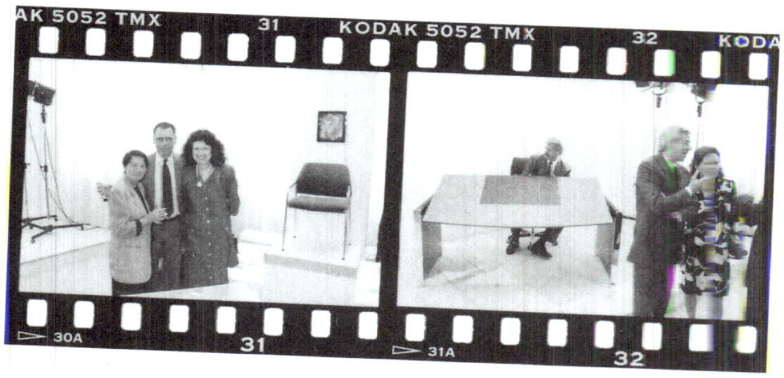

Contact prints, company celebration in the "Haus der Wirtschaft" (House of Commerce), 125 years of Walter Knoll, Arno Votteler talks with Michael Knoll (28–29), Stuttgart, 1990

Tavolo 101, Walter Knoll,
design by Susanne Rövenstrunck,
Herrenberg, around 1990

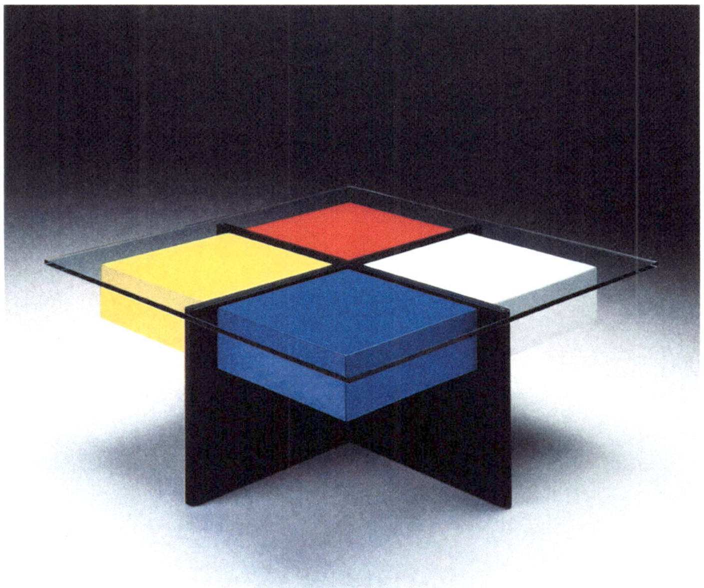

Poster and cover of the catalog
for the anniversary celebration,
Herrenberg, 1990

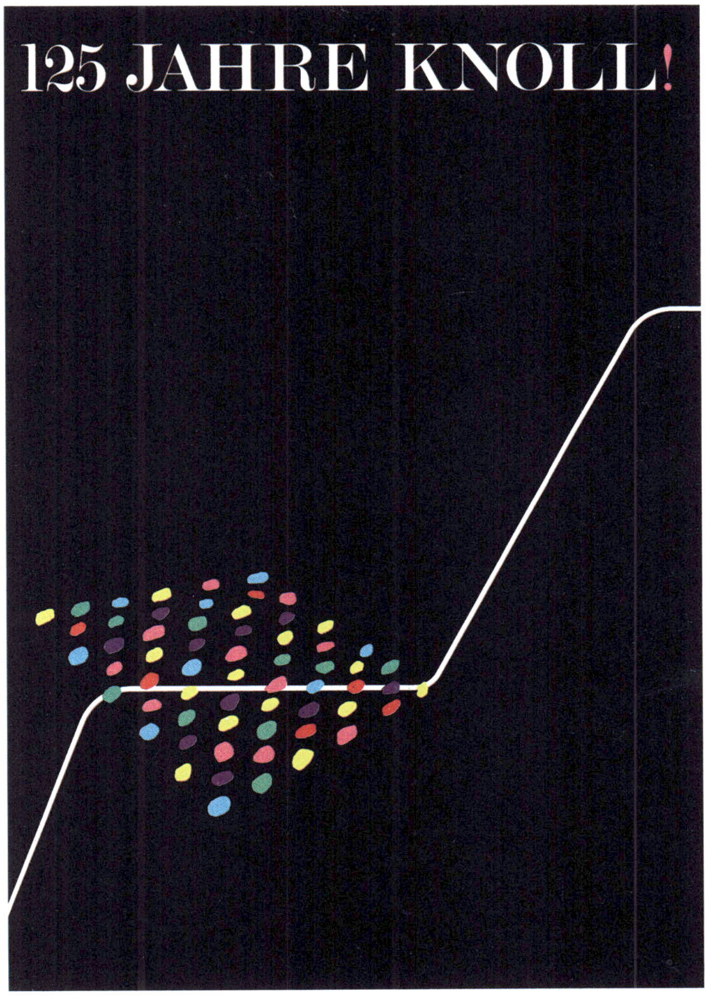

POST-MODERNITY

Post- | mo | der | nity, noun; with the introduction of this epochal term, modernity is considered to be over for the first time and begins to paraphrase itself. As a label for a style, it caught on above all in architecture. The belief that nothing fundamentally new could be created, but that anything was possible, causes the use of quotations to be a key stylistic feature of post-modern design. The Tavolo table series from Walter Knoll, which is based on the colors and forms of the painter Piet Mondrian, is a striking example of this. The Memphis group – pioneer of the new lack of direction in terms of product lines – challenges all existing furniture conventions. Milan is now the leading design metropolis. A kettle with a little bird that whistles on its spout becomes a bestseller and, at the same time, the first popular design object to be referred to as such. The anthropomorphic armchair M2 by David De Mayo, which the Israeli designed for Walter Knoll, was also a pioneering feat.

LESS IS A BORE.
ROBERT VENTURI

1972
The book "Learning from Las Vegas" by the architect Robert Venturi is considered a key work of post-modernity.

1980
Armchair M2 by David De Mayo for Walter Knoll.

1981
First Memphis collection presented in Milan.

1984
Walter Knoll participates in the Milan furniture fair together with four other Swabian companies under the title "Five". Michael Knoll runs the company together with Stephan Combe.

1985
Wilhelm Knoll is taken over by Walter Knoll.

1986
Designs by Jan Armgardt, Ernst Dettinger, Peter Maly and Anita Schmidt are included in the Walter Knoll product range.

1987
Neues Deutsches Design (New German Design) is exhibited at documenta 8.

1988
"125 Jahre Walter Knoll" (125 years of Walter Knoll) anniversary exhibition in the "Haus der Wirtschaft" (House of Commerce – formerly the "Landesgewerbeamt" (State Trade Office) in Stuttgart – accompanied by a catalog with new company lettering. Annual sales of 20 million marks (100 employees).

1990
Table Tavolo by Susanne Rövenstrunck.

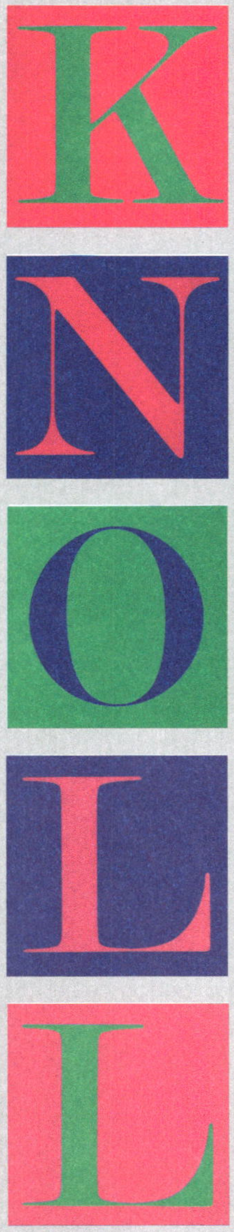

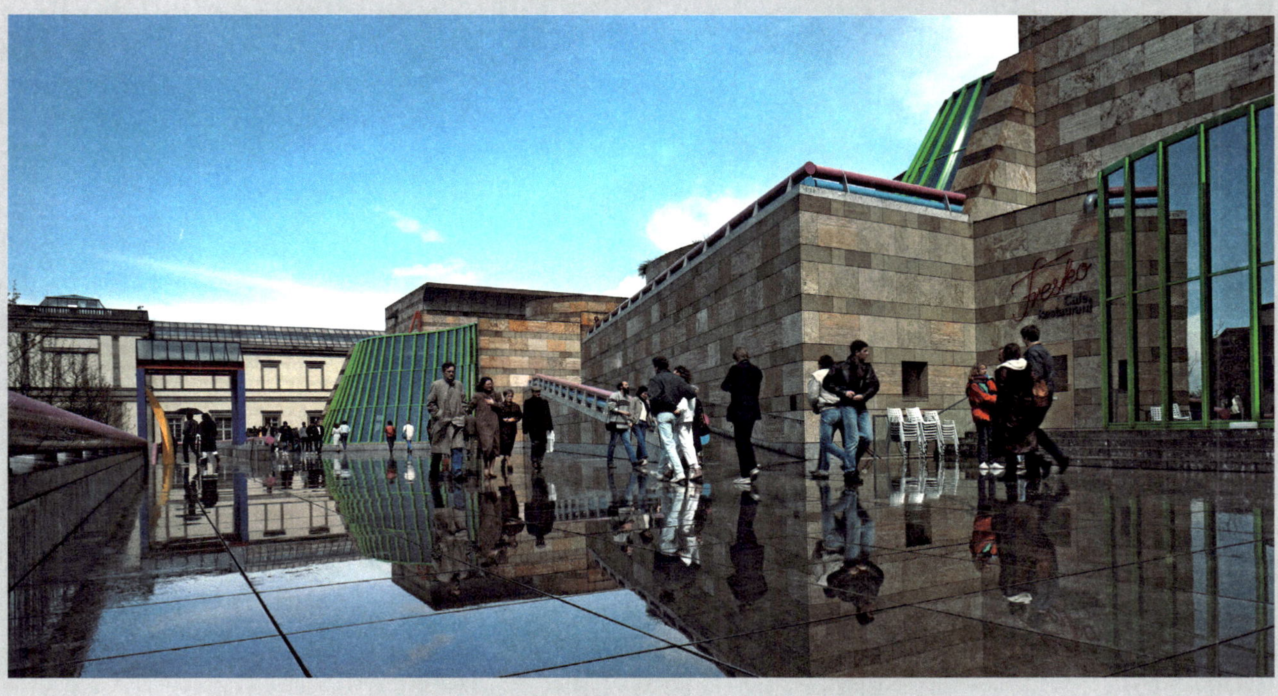

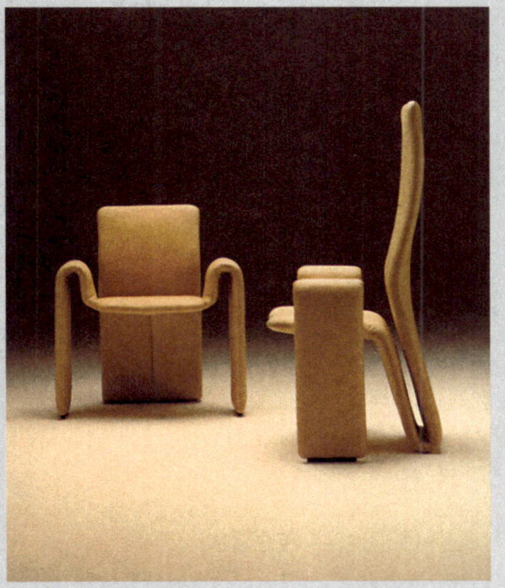

"Neue Staatsgalerie" (New State Gallery),
Architect James Stirling,
Stuttgart, 1982

Bodoni typeface in the catalog for the
anniversary celebration,
Herrenberg, 1990

Armchair M2, Walter Knoll,
design by David De Mayo,
Herrenberg, 1980

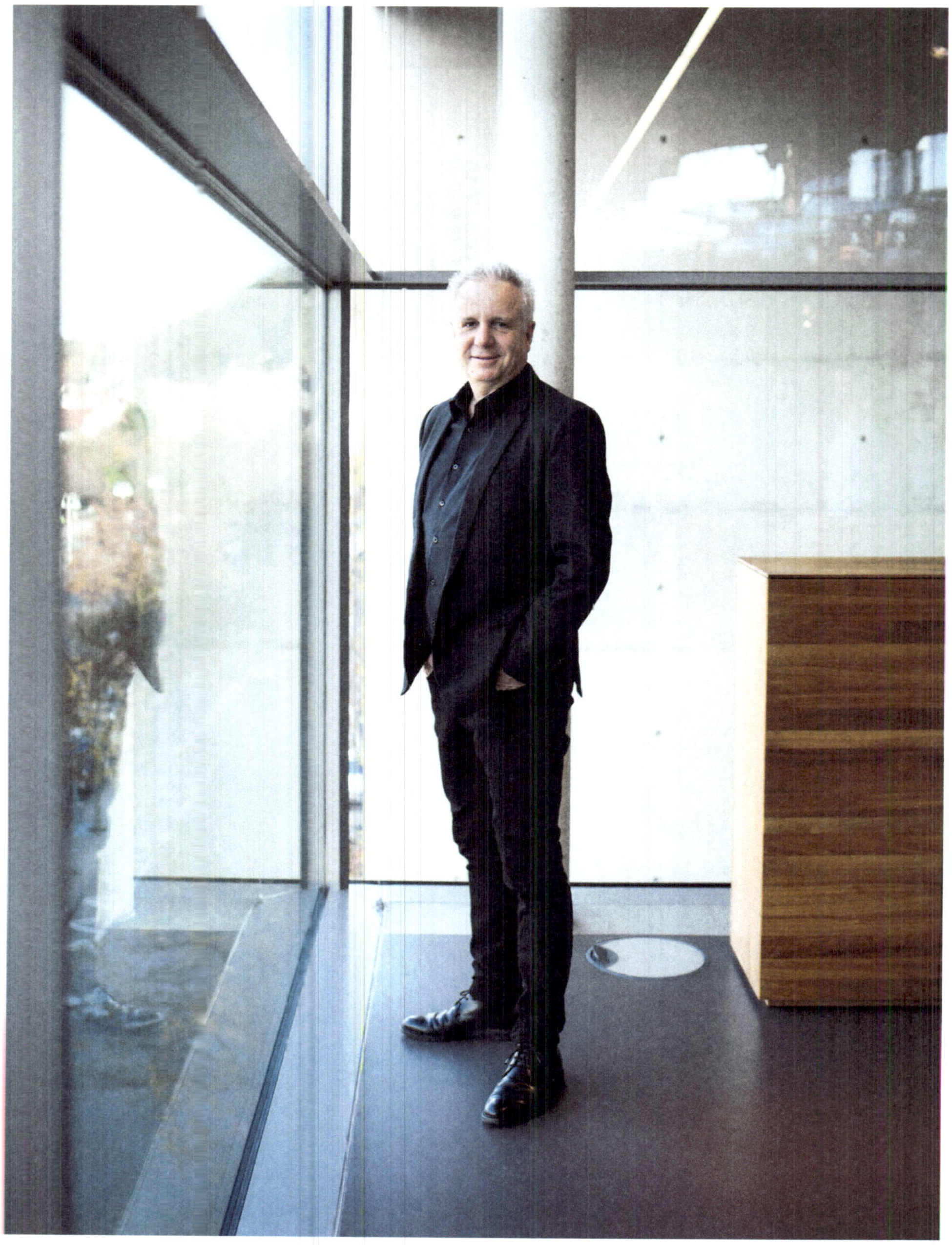

In 1993, the Benz family purchased the Walter Knoll company and Markus Benz took over management of the firm.

THIRD **MODERNITY**

1993 TO PRESENT

THE 1990s

THE *WENDE*

The wrapping of the Reichstag in Berlin in 1995 – an action that was executed with military precision by the New York artist duo Christo and Jeanne-Claude and enclosed the block from the imperial period in 100,000 square meters of bright, silvery fabric – became a world event. The grandiose spectacle that transformed the historic architecture into a monumental sculpture only a few years after Reunification drew attention to the former and future German parliament. The fabric panels had scarcely been rolled up again when conversion was begun of the 101-year-old building which had once been the largest building site in the German Empire. Following heated public discussions, the total renovation that followed was finally crowned with an accessible glass cupola that became a new Berlin landmark. It was the work of the extraordinary British architect, Norman Foster. Lord Foster, showered with architectural awards and knighted by the queen, once again succeeded at what he managed to achieve with surprising regularity: he created an icon. The new Reichstag, which opened in 1999, became a complete synthesis of the arts, including seating furniture by Walter Knoll. As in the case of the Weissenhofsiedlung in the First Modernity and the Stuttgart Television Tower in the Second Modernity, epoch-making architecture was again combined with furniture by Walter Knoll in the Third Modernity to produce a compelling symbiosis. All this was in turn an indication of how contemporary history and furniture design were intricately interwoven. Walter Knoll, the company that had honed its craft in all phases of modernity, was able to point the way at the points of transition. But shortly before the dawn of the new century, there were still several deep-rooted problems to be solved and decisions to be made.

On a cold winter's day in January 1993, as Rolf Benz and his son Markus wandered together through the snow-covered Black Forest overlooking Kälberbronn, the conversation kept circling back to a single subject. Rolf Benz, who had founded the furniture company bearing his name and had managed it for over a quarter of a century – although he no longer owned it – had never given up hope that one day, he would again direct a family-owned company.[1] Father and son were now discussing the Walter Knoll company in Herrenberg, the town neighboring their hometown of Nagold. The prestigious company whose name they respected had entered into hard times and, like so many of its competitors, no longer had the resources to carry on. The Benz family was now considering whether to take over the tradition-rich company in a move that was bound to cause a slight tectonic shift in the furniture landscape. The merger of two such renowned furniture families would cause a sensation and preserve the Knoll dynasty. Rolf Benz ultimately yielded his place to the younger generation. His oldest son Markus would direct the company in what turned out to be a decision with far-reaching consequences. It was the reason the two men had sought the peace and tranquility of the Black Forest.[2] It was obvious that substantial risks were involved. At the time, no one could predict whether the company had enough substance to stand up on its own two feet in a highly competitive market. All the experts who were consulted advised against it. There was, however, one great advantage, in that Markus Benz – who was originally educated as a commercial lawyer – had already become familiar with the industry and gained valuable experience at Wilkhahn, a manufacturer of high-end office furniture. The father and son also recognized other positive factors. They saw a unique opportunity in the excellent reputation of Walter Knoll and the comprehensive craftsmanship ability that the company possessed. They believed in the brand's potential. No one standing in the gray light beneath that cloudy winter sky could ever have predicted the heights to which the Walter Knoll brand was about to rise. Rolf Benz's dream of continuing the family legacy was fulfilled.

The early 1990s were a time of optimism in Germany. The fall of the Berlin Wall in 1989 and the simultaneous rending of the Iron Curtain that had divided Europe into East and West seemed like only yesterday. The two German states that were so different from one another had been united as one country for two years. The East's euphoria spread, especially to large areas of the economy. As we now know, the vision of "flourishing landscapes" associated with Reunification was never fulfilled, or only much later. Nevertheless, the landscape had shifted for all time and the new, expanded Federal Republic was once again a sovereign member of the international community. The Cold War was over. Due to the profound political upheavals – the *Wende* that was on everyone's lips – other changes that were happening on a much larger scale often went unnoticed. The world was about to enter a new Industrial Revolution based on the power of microchips and containers crossing the oceans. The fall of the political blocks boosted world trade. The Third Modernity had begun. Only those who recognized the changes and made their decisions accordingly were prepared for what came next. Soon there was a PC on every desk. A little later, it was even possible to travel with your office on a laptop. The digitization of business processes was only a matter of time. In the mid-1990s, the first digital system for product planning was introduced at Walter Knoll.

As a leading sector, the automotive industry had long begun to distribute their design centers across the globe. The furniture industry, once again a reliable indicator of the spirit of the age, became increasingly globalized. The word "design" now referred to Milan, where the furniture fair – the "Salone del Mobile" – was the measure of all things relating to style and aesthetics. Although Walter Knoll had made a hesitant appearance there in the mid-1980s, the international mindset that had been part of the Knoll dynasty's very DNA had at some point been lost. When Markus Benz carried out his family's plan and became the new director in Herrenberg in October 1993, the company was a sort of "Sleeping Beauty." What was beautiful and valuable was hidden under a layer of dust and thorns. According to the 1994 balance sheet – the first to be prepared under the new owners – sales were still at 14 million marks. Three years later in 1997, they had risen to 20 million marks.

IN THE SNOW-COVERED BLACK FOREST, ROLF AND MARKUS BENZ REACHED A MOMENTOUS DECISION.

RARE COINCIDENCES

In addition to an intelligent and consistent brand strategy, Markus Benz attributed his successful rescue operation to a series of external circumstances that occurred more or less by chance – those rare coincidences that have often been spoken of in the history of design and furniture and that can give developments a tremendous boost. In such times of transition, it's a matter of recognizing the risks while taking hold of the unique opportunities. We have only to remember Hans Knoll, the transatlantic traveler of the Knoll dynasty whose international, creative staff were the result of a wave of immigration that happened to take place just as he was successfully establishing his business in the U.S. He was about the same age as Markus Benz when Knoll Associates became a model, polyglot company – just one of several parallels between the two entrepreneurs. Like Markus Benz, Hans Knoll sought a human connection with his employees and, along with the visions that fueled his passion, also displayed the necessary degree of charm. But in addition to a dynamic personality that drove the project forward and a long series of correct decisions, his tremendous success was also due to a coming-together of fortunate circumstances. These lucky coincidences came to his aid more than once, says Benz. They appeared to him in the form of a variety of exceptional people. One of these "happy coincidences," as he calls them, was a young woman with whom he began a permanent relationship while still a student. She had emigrated from Poland in the late 1980s and imparted to him, the legal expert, an appreciation for beautiful things. This woman, whose areas of expertise included art, handicrafts, and fashion, and who was herself an artist with a studio near Cologne, opened him up to a world far beyond the intricacies of the law. This free training in stylistic and aesthetic sensibility also had its highly pragmatic aspects. For example, he helped her with her sewing and repaired the sewing machine whenever it broke down.

Yet another "happy coincidence" was of a very different nature. In the early 1990s Markus Benz, who was getting ready to change careers, was working in Bad Münder near Hanover for Wilkhahn, one of the world's foremost office furniture companies. The younger Benz, now 30, completed a training program. This was when Fritz Hahne, the guiding light behind the Wilkhahn brand, was still working at the company. Hahne, then in his early 70s, was one of those post-war-period personalities who, similarly to Erwin Braun and Philip Rosenthal, developed new visions, forged new paths in product design, and thus became pioneers of the Second Modernity.

Along with Braun, Wilkhahn pursued what was probably the most rigorous design concept of that period. Like others named here, Hahne directed a family business and considered his work to be more than just an economic undertaking. For him, a company wasn't just an organization. Hahne introduced the young Benz to the idea of a social and cultural organism – a concept that he continued to pursue and develop further. Since the 1960s, the design staff at Wilkhahn had mainly been recruited from the "Hochschule für Gestaltung Ulm" (Ulm School of Design), which was then the premier location for the new generation of designers.[3] The analytical and critical spirit of Ulm, with its love of experimentation combined with methodologies of the Second Modernity that so strongly influenced design in Germany and spawned a radical new product culture, formed the undercurrent that was embraced by both companies in the mountainous regions of Swabia and northern Germany. Markus Benz described Fritz Hahne – who, like Walter Knoll, had his rough edges – as one of his most important "teachers."

---

1 ▶ Two years earlier, an unsuccessful attempt had been made to take over the Kill company.

2 ▶ Just such a reflective and meaningful walk by a father and son had already taken place once before in the history of the Knoll dynasty, but under very different auspices. In 1955, Walter and Hans Knoll had taken a walk on the Schlossberg hill in Herrenberg to discuss the future of the Knoll furniture dynasty.

3 ▶ Walter and Robert Knoll were also known to be among its supporters.

A CASE OF RESTRUCTURING

In the early 1990s, the Walter Knoll company in Herrenberg was in an extremely precarious state. To save the tradition-rich company, all areas had to be tackled at once.

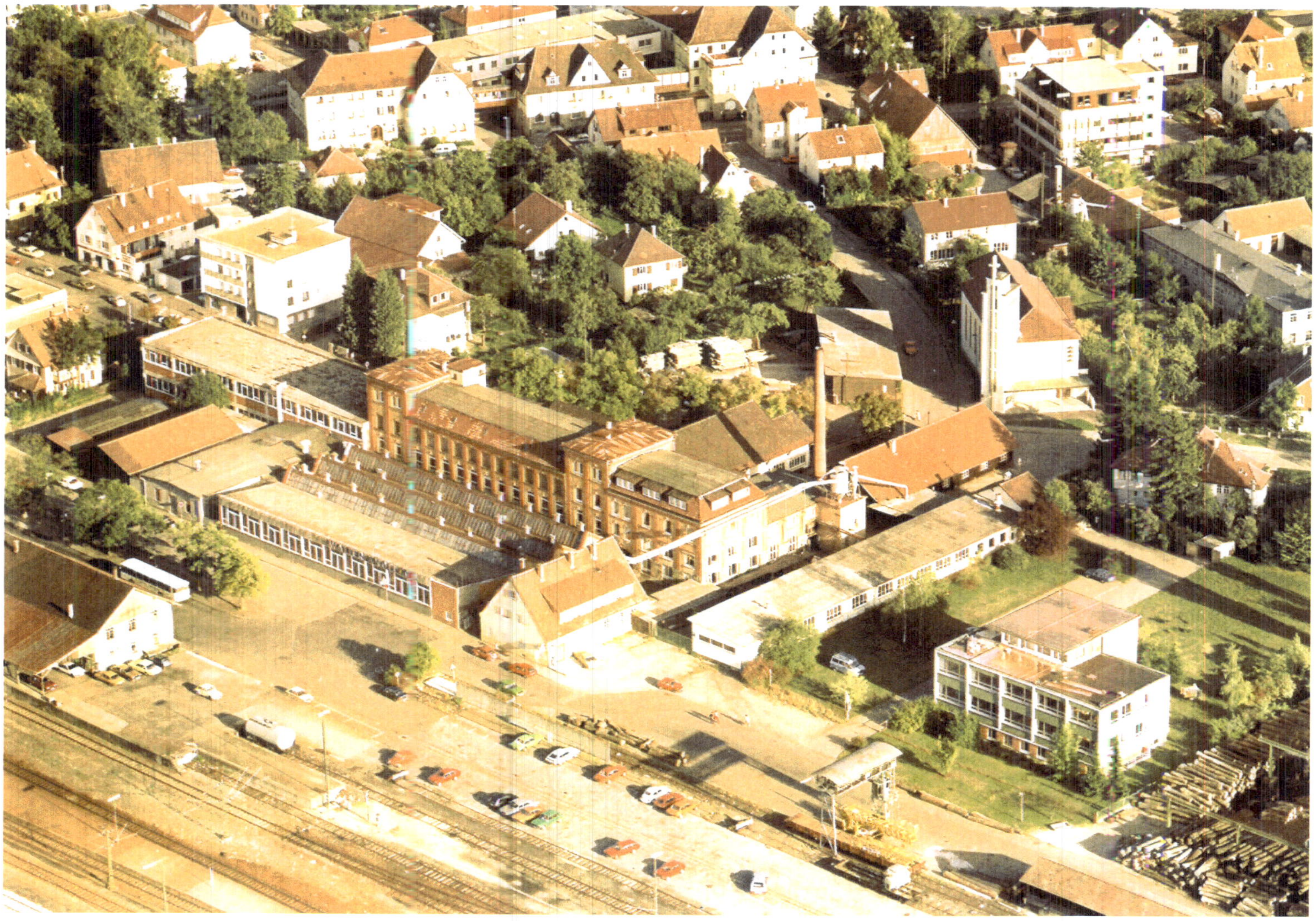

Factory premises before the conversion,
Herrenberg, 1993

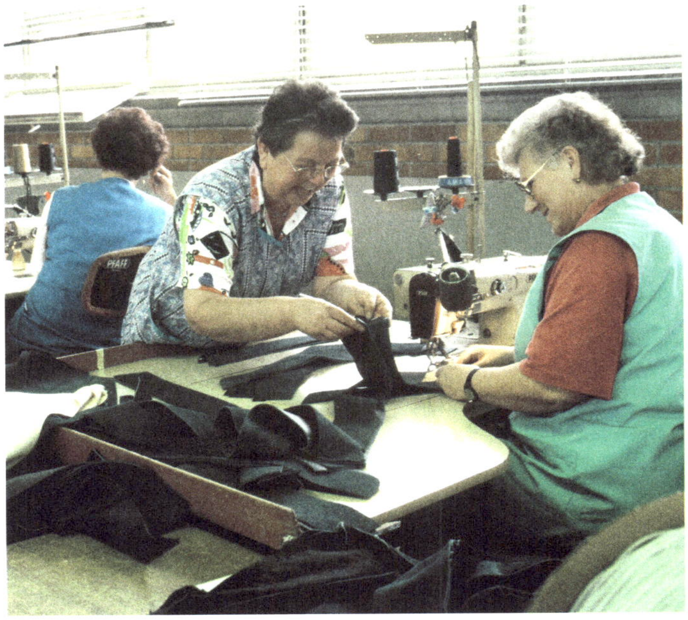

Seamstresses around 1995

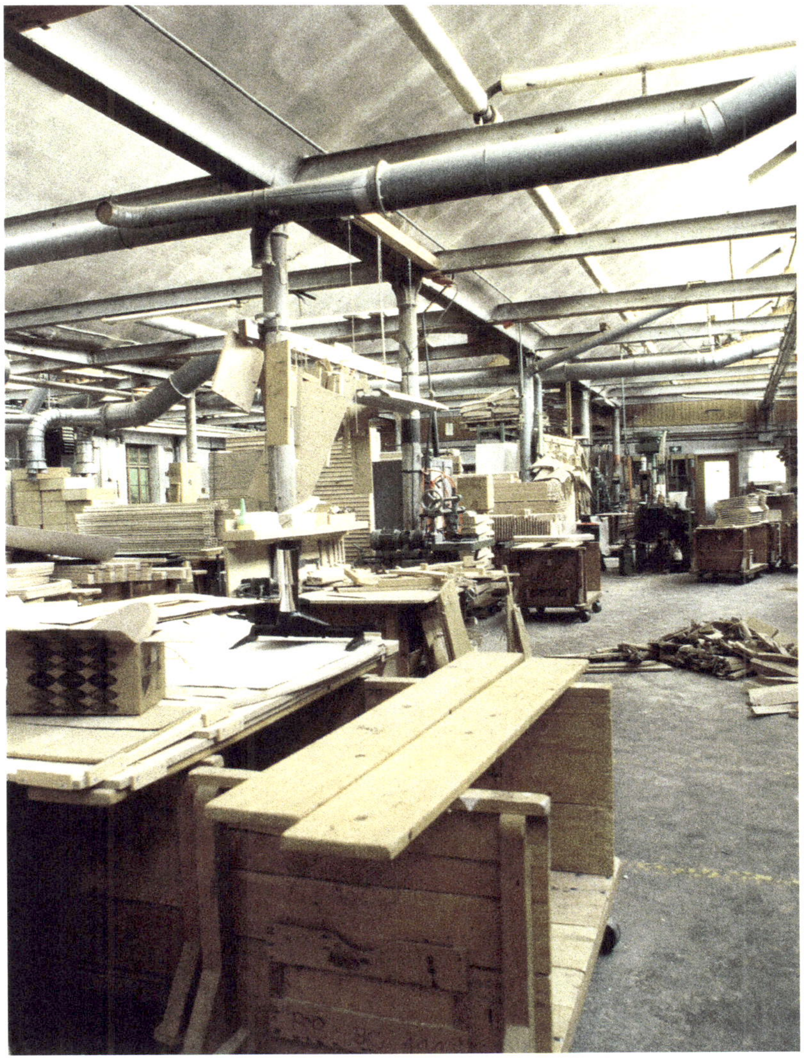

Carpenters' shop around 1995

He also valued Hahne's commitment to *Gute Form* (Good Design), which continues to be his standard for perfection and, equally important, for the coherence of the overall design. Under Hahne's auspices, the unwavering search for the internal logic and timelessness of a project, and its pursuit to the very end, experienced a golden age. Benz, who was at the very center of it all, clearly recognized this. It became the central goal of his activities. He also recognized that it was only achievable if the company's management, technicians, designers, and the entire team maintained a close dialog. Thus the budding entrepreneur was handed the spiritual tools of his trade, which were none other than the instruments of the Second Modernity. In addition, a large portion of the missionary zeal that makes such feats possible was probably due in part to that Protestant ethic, whose Lower Saxon and Swabian versions were very similar in their purism.[4] Examining these circumstances, it's clear that they would be difficult to recreate. There is a subtle but immensely effective factor behind them.

HAHNE INTRODUCED THE YOUNG BENZ TO THE IDEA OF A SOCIAL AND CULTURAL ORGANISM – A CONCEPT THAT HE CONTINUED TO FOLLOW AND DEVELOPED FURTHER.

The events that unfolded show how critical personal interactions can be. Theodor Diener, then CEO of Wilkhahn, transferred Markus Benz to the sales department in Berlin where he worked under Michael Blank, head of Wilkhahn's Berlin office. "You need a good teacher," said Diener. That was his most profound conviction and the reason he sent Markus Benz to Berlin, even though the budget for doing so had already been cut. It was Blank who would later develop and implement the model for the new Walter Knoll company – in a congenial partnership with Markus Benz.

Michael Blank was originally from East Berlin. The degreed architect, design connoisseur, fast-talker, and rigorous thinker was an extraordinary person who had also followed an extraordinary career path. What then occurred serves as a prime example of how German-German experiences can complement one another and how reunification can work on a practical level. Michael Blank, thirteen years older than Markus Benz, had for some years worked for an institution with the old-fashioned name of "Amt für industrielle Formgestaltung" (Office of Industrial Design). In 1987, AIF opened a design center for public outreach that was headed by Blank. The "Office" bore a not so coincidental resemblance to Stuttgart's "Landesgewerbeamt" (State Trade Office). Both agencies were dedicated to developing business, and particularly export – well known to be a central focus of the chronically currency-strapped GDR – through high-level public relations. AIF's ambitious goal was to raise East-German goods to a "world-class level" by deliberately associating them with modernity. Marianne Brandt and Mart Stam, both of whom had strong ties to the Bauhaus, were part of this ambitious establishment early on in their careers.[5] Michael Blank worked at AIF as department head of the "Designzentrum Neue Industriekultur" (Design Center for New Industrial Culture) and was specifically responsible for visual communication, which was for him a veritable Shangri-La in the midst of the gray, real-socialist monotony. Astonishing feats were accomplished, although the showpiece products created there very rarely made it onto the shelves in the East German economy of scarcity. Blank, a universalist with expertise in architecture, photography, graphics, and much more, organized exhibitions – reminiscent of Stuttgart's "Landesgewerbeamt" – in the tradition of the First and Second Modernity. So it was probably no coincidence that following the dissolution of the GDR, the country in which he had always lived, he sought to restart his professional career at Wilkhahn.

Blank met Hahne at the 1989 World Design Expo in Japan when Hahne was looking for someone who knew Berlin and East Germany and also knew sales. That Blank met Markus Benz, of all people, at his new company was yet another of these happy coincidences. In this way, two very different people who both happened to be planning a new beginning found one another. The communications expert, with his extensive and highly specialized pool of experiences, had no fixed plans and was fascinated by the zeal of the young Swabian entrepreneur in the making. From the very start, they complemented and understood one another. This became crystal clear after they'd been working together for two years at Wilkhahn's Berlin sales office. They were able to achieve record sales – no doubt also buoyed by the transitional climate of the new German capital. But that was only one reason why the coincidental acquaintanceship soon grew into a friendship and, finally, a twenty-year professional partnership. What mattered to Markus Benz was that he had someone by his side who had a great deal of expert knowledge and was also on his same wavelength. And for the Berlin-born Blank, talking and discussing were absolute, unmistakable priorities. His wife, Annette Blank, accompanied her husband from Berlin to the southwest and guaranteed high-level PR for Walter Knoll with her agency, Büro Blank.

Michael Blank was a philanthropist. He put people at the center. Without him, the corporate culture at Walter Knoll could never have evolved to where it is today. For Markus Benz, Blank was a mentor – similar to what Karl Gustav Vollmöller, Walter Knoll's brother-in-law, was to Walter. He strongly advocated cultural infusions from the outside and relied on international designers. As co-chairman in charge of sales and marketing, Blank was a driving force behind the reinvention of the Walter Knoll brand.

For all this to come to pass, however, another happy coincidence was necessary – the most fundamental in every person's life – the family into which they are born. The Benz family and the Benz family business shaped Markus Benz as a person from his youth. He automatically inherited the entrepreneurial perspective, although his professional orientation was initially very different. His father, Rolf Benz, a Swabian self-made man, had a career that was remarkable even during the years of Germany's economic miracle. When he founded his own company in 1964, Markus was three years old. For a long time Nagold – situated on the edge of the Black Forest and today an agile, up-and-coming small city – was seen as a remote site in the midst of a desolate region. Nevertheless, the town was strongly influenced by a tradition of craftsmanship. It was there that Rolf Benz was born into humble circumstances in 1933 as one of eight children. His ancestors were mainly artisans. One of his grandfathers ran a locksmith's shop and a winch workshop. He was also descended from cloth-makers and oil merchants. To this day, the family still owns an oil mill. His parents ran a textile business. When salesmen came, his mother always asked herself whether a material "would appeal more to the pharmacist's wife or to the butcher's wife."[6] Rolf Benz later referred to this as his "training in marketing."[7] After his father took him out of school at the age of fifteen[8], he learned upholstery in his uncle's workshop. When his uncle died in a car accident, he was forced to take over the company at a young age. Although at that time, as he said, he "really wanted to leave," he soon realized that he could better develop his talents in this independent capacity, which included the ability to pitch in and optimally organize the work of others. And because he was a bright young man and was passionately interested in what was happening in the furniture world, opportunities soon came his way seemingly on their own. All he had to do was take hold of them. He also had to be willing to shape his own life and strive for independence – values that he exemplified and later passed on to his son Markus.

The 1950s, the *Sturm und Drang* years of the Second Modernity, offered ideal conditions for a brand-new beginning – particularly in the southwest, the epicenter of the design and furniture revolution. The young entrepreneur simply had to look at what was happening in his immediate vicinity, where a number of companies were producing the counter-models of the heavy, full upholstery that continued to adorn German living rooms. At that time Walter Knoll, where famous designers were constantly coming and going, was the supreme role model and also inspired the young and curious Rolf Benz. As a natural talent, he soon became an enthusiast of "modern living." His Swabian character, in which a will that bordered on stubbornness coexisted with an openness to the new, was an important source of success and was what finally made his advancement possible. Nevertheless, he soon ran up against unforeseen and insurmountable obstacles. Like his own family, the family of his deceased uncle, whose company he was still heading, belonged to the Old Order Mennonites.[9] It was a religious community with strict rules of conduct that tightly governed the lives of its adherents and also mistrusted too much economic success. But Rolf Benz held his ground and did the unthinkable. In order to stay true to himself, he and his wife left the religious community – a step that also meant breaking off from the rest of his family and making himself an outsider. He occupied a similar position in the furniture industry, which wasn't necessarily a disadvantage. Independence strengthened his will and gave him an alert intellect.

---

4 ▶ Also see note 9.

5 ▶ After 1945, Brandt taught at the "Hochschule für Werkkunst" (Academy of Fine Arts) in Dresden, having been brought there by Stam. Together with Stam, she transferred to the "Hochschule für angewandte Kunst Berlin-Weissensee" (Berlin-Weissensee Academy of Art) and at the same time worked at the "Institut für industrielle Gestaltung" (Institute of Industrial Design), which could be considered the predecessor institution to the "Amt für industrielle Formgestaltung" (Office of Industiral Design).

6 ▶ Interview with Markus Benz, Herrenberg, 08/06/2014

7 ▶ Ibid.

8 ▶ There is an obvious parallel here with Walter Knoll, who left school at the age of 15 to begin an apprenticeship – also in accordance with his father's wishes.

9 ▶ The Benz family were Mennonites – a Protestant religious community with roots in the Anabaptist movement, primarily in Switzerland and Swabia.

LOOKING FOR A NEW APPROACH

The fact that the new head of Walter Knoll, Marcus Benz, had also changed careers must have also made the new start easier. After his previous career in the law, he had learned important lessons about modernity at the Wilkhahn company.

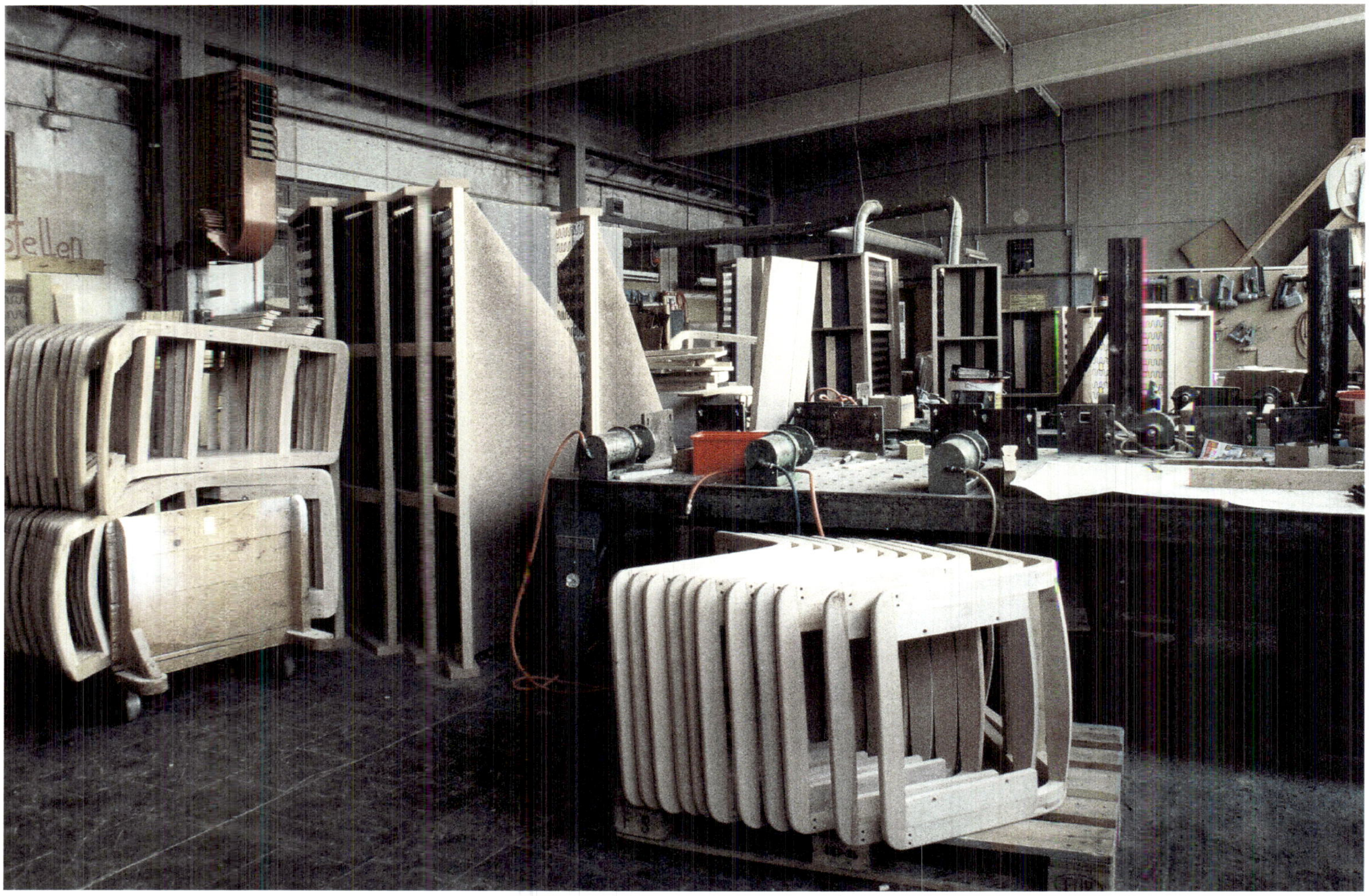

Carpenters' shop around 1995

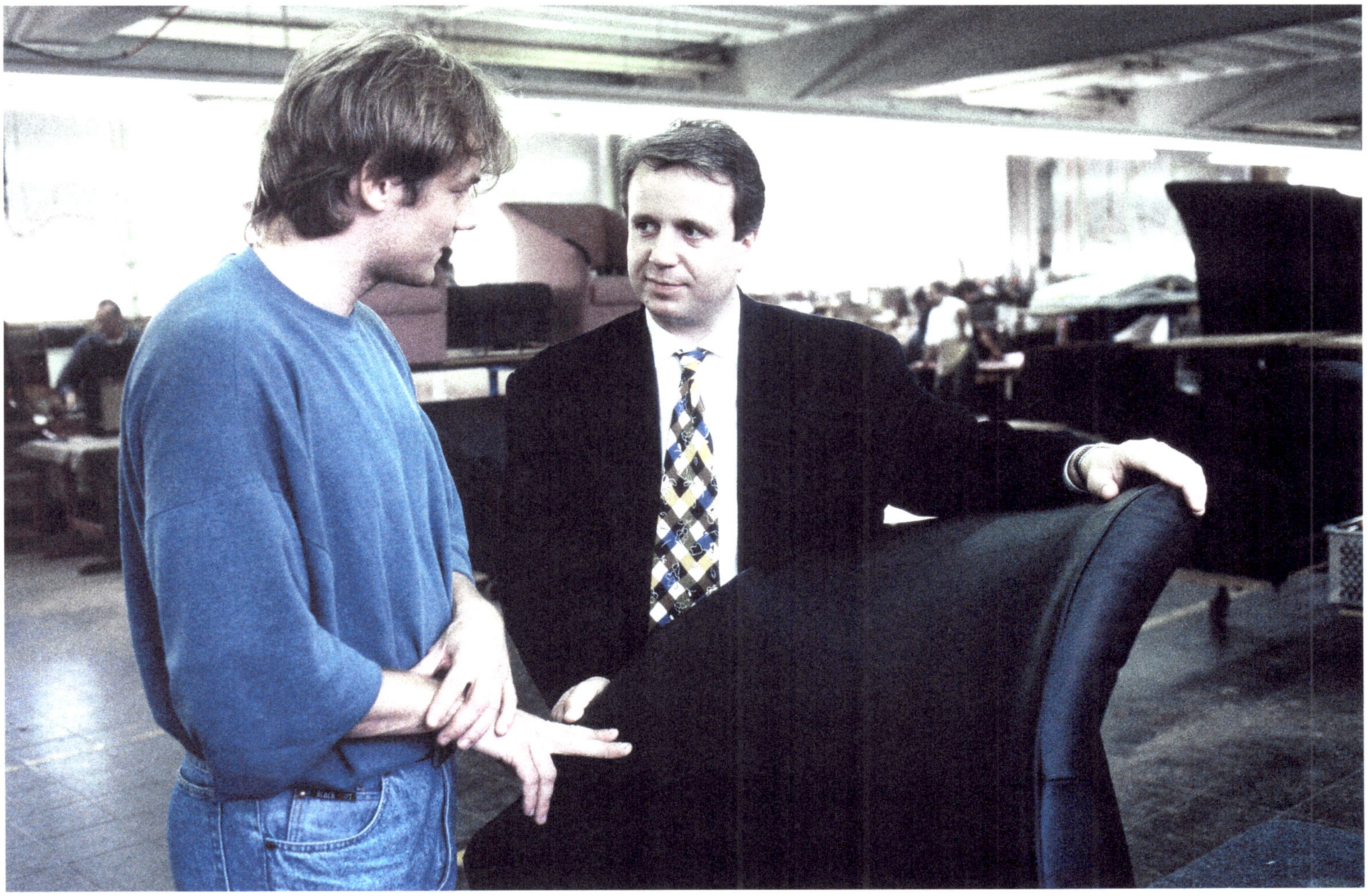

Markus Benz speaking with an employee
in around 1995

Nor was Rolf Benz all alone in the world. His wife Hilde stood by him. She came from the neighborhood of Heilbronn, the northern Swabian region that the Knoll family also left to move closer to Stuttgart. Hilde Benz's strong, socially-minded attitude set the climate in her family and also gave her son Markus character traits such as sensitivity and sociological imagination. Rolf Benz, with his momentous secession at around 30 years of age (which is also the age at which his son Markus would make his new start) now founded his own company, which soon gained a foothold thanks to good design and clever campaigning. But he also had another advantage. Because of the close connection between him as a person and the company, he managed to make the name of Rolf Benz into a strong brand – which is still a rarity in the industry today, especially in Germany. Such a strong emphasis on brand was based on the simple and correct observation that a medium-sized company had nothing to gain from the price wars on the anonymous mass market. This same fundamental insight was already part of Markus Benz's personal makeup when he entered the furniture business. At the end of the 1970s, however, things had progressed a little too quickly for the over-achiever Rolf Benz. Within months, the company emerged from its most successful year ever into a precarious situation from which it was saved only by the sale of the majority shareholding in 1980. Rolf Benz was now a minority partner and CEO of his own company. "It was a profound event," says his son.[10] It was also probably the reason why the Benz children all went their own ways – including Markus, the eldest, who studied law instead of following in his father's footsteps. It was his own decision to cut the cord – a version of the father-son dynamic that never occurred in the Knoll furniture dynasty and which, of course, had significant benefits when dealing with such a successful and naturally dominant father. Nor did Markus allow this rupture to discourage him, but instead used the opportunity to truly apply himself. Actually, during Rolf Benz's time as CEO, the company he led experienced a monumental upward trend. According to a survey, one-third of Germans today recognize the Rolf Benz brand – a fact that speaks for itself.

At the beginning of the 1990s, a fateful meeting took place. Rolf Benz happened to run into Michael Knoll, Walter Knoll's grandson, in Stuttgart. Michael, who then headed the company, told him about his current precarious position. This gave Benz an idea. He had never given up on his goal of again directing an independent, family-owned company. It was no coincidence that Benz, who was himself a social climber, had developed a furniture brand for the upwardly mobile. He now saw an opportunity to explore new territory. The combination of Benz and Knoll, two prominent but very different furniture families, was anything but typical. It marked the fusion of two autonomous cores that was bound to cause noticeable tremors in the furniture landscape. The takeover was a surprise coup.

The prehistories of the two families also reflect the stages of modernity. The roots of the Knoll dynasty extended far back into the 19th century. In the early 20th century, in an almost epic company and family saga, three independent branches were formed under the names of Wilhelm, Walter, and Hans Knoll – each of whom fundamentally revitalized upholstered furniture in his own way. The German Knoll lines were then reunited during the latter phase of the Second Modernity.[11] The Benz furniture family, which was spectacularly successful in the Second Modernity, then rescued Walter Knoll on the threshold of the Third Modernity. This furniture liaison and the brilliantly happy ending were, to put it mildly, an unexpected payoff.

The internal clean-up operation at Walter Knoll lasted into the late 1990s. When the company was first taken over, it was in dire straits. After having served so long as a role model for others, it had lost sight of its original vision. It was not just a matter of a few adjustments. A

FINALLY, THE BENZ FURNITURE FAMILY, WHO WROTE A SPECTACULARLY SUCCESSFUL CHAPTER IN THE SECOND MODERNITY, RESCUED WALTER KNOLL ON THE THRESHOLD OF THE THIRD MODERNITY.

total makeover was required in all areas simultaneously. A large part of the company's problem was due to its over-inflated product range, the depth of production this necessitated, and the correspondingly high inventory. The old ideal and formerly a source of pride – the concept of producing everything in-house, from table legs to springs – had long become outmoded. Selling frames, for example, was considered a sacrilege. These taboos now had to be broken. What was needed was a paradigm shift to an ultra-modern upholstery and assembly operation. It began with an extremely uncomfortable task: the inevitable layoff of employees. Almost one-third of the staff had to go. According to Markus Benz, he did not acquire the tact necessary for the job in a management seminar. He inherited it from his family, and particularly from his mother Hilde. She understood how to keep the six-member

Benz family together through extremely turbulent years, a feat that required a great deal of dexterity and empathy. Thus she also became her eldest son's teacher in the area of people skills. Hilde Benz's role naturally reminds us of the key role that the – one could almost say – great mothers of the Knoll dynasty played with such brilliance.[12] Markus also inherited another essential ability from his family that does not necessarily come naturally to a lawyer – an entrepreneurial mindset. His father Rolf Benz, the entrepreneur who invented himself, was always a tremendous role model for Markus in whatever profession he chose.[13]

THE POETICS OF SEATING DESIGN

Hidden beneath the dust that had settled on Walter Knoll toward the end of the Second Modernity, there were also recipes for success from the Knoll furniture family's own history: for example, the way in which they were able to benefit from regional strengths through synergies.[14] It was these very values – including the explorer mentality and the deliberately planned cooperation with the best – that now had to be revived. The chances of this strategy succeeding were excellent, given that Swabia was now more than ever a unique metropolitan center for highly developed specializations. The region around Stuttgart features a high-tech density that is unrivaled worldwide, all within radius of two- to three-hundred kilometers, where the noble arts of welding, polishing, and soldering are celebrated on a daily basis. It was important to exploit this tremendous local advantage not only in selected and isolated cases but also through systematic networking. Whatever could not be found locally now had to be sought in the greater Milan area, Europe's other El Dorado of sophisticated design, technology, and materials solutions. Ultimately it was a matter of establishing a cluster supply chain, which may sound abstract, but also has extremely concrete as well as very human aspects. The benefits of the geographic proximity of high-tech experts were not just logistical. The relatively short and now well-worn paths also permitted a direct exchange. So it was not at all unusual for an established technological master to visit Herrenberg and offer his wealth of experience in the service of product development.

Another new direction was the expansion of the company's own expertise and training program. Only a few years after the new start, training was again offered, especially in the company's core technical capabilities, such as upholstery and sewing. Another problem, the shortage of workers, once again found a solution in a historic coincidence. In the early 1990s, ethnic Germans living in Russia began migrating by the thousands to the Federal Republic. Recognizing this as an opportunity and acting on it was yet another factor in the company's success. The newcomers from the ex-Soviet Union were out to better themselves and had strong family values – in other words, they were typical immigrants. They included a number of jacks-of-all-trades who had acquired a wide range of practical skills in the economy of scarcity from which they were fleeing that were similar to the proverbial Swabian "tinkering." Thus, the hiring of many Russian Germans who are still on the payroll today can be seen as an excellent example of integration.

One of the most difficult problems in those early days, recalls Markus Benz, was finding a compelling design concept. Here, too, he was able to benefit from his father, whose willingness and ability to engage in discussions with designers made him a role model. Nevertheless, the necessary exceptional personalties were still lacking. In the mid-1990s, following a successful restructuring and several mediocre designs, Markus filled the gap with pioneering models from the Second Modernity. Vostra, 369, and FK, concise iconic chairs from the golden age of organic design, provided an ideal intermediate solution.[15]

---

10 ▶ Interview with the author, 2015.

11 ▶ Founder Wilhelm Knoll was followed by his son Willy and, in 1954 by Willy's son Dieter. Walter Knoll, Willy's older brother, handed the business over to his son Robert in 1964, who was in turn replaced by his son Michael in 1982. Both Dieter and Michael Knoll, grandsons of the founders, had to give up control of their companies at the end of the 20th century.

12 ▶ Had the two mothers, Emma and Maia Knoll, not stood behind their children, this dynasty would probably never have existed.

13 ▶ Nevertheless, his son Markus also considers his training as lawyer to be a significant advantage. Among other things, it taught him to precisely analyze complex issues.

14 ▶ Thus, the revolutionary Antimott upholstery system was developed in collaboration with Hirth Versuchsbau, a Stuttgart company specializing in engines. The alliance with the cabinet manufacturer Behr was also groundbreaking. Behr, like Walter Knoll, was a well-known proponent of modernity.

15 ▶ FK by Preben Fabricius and Jørgen Kastholm, Vostra, and the bucket seat 369 were highly respected and extremly successful designs of their day. The latter was used, for example, in the Hilton Hotel in Berlin.

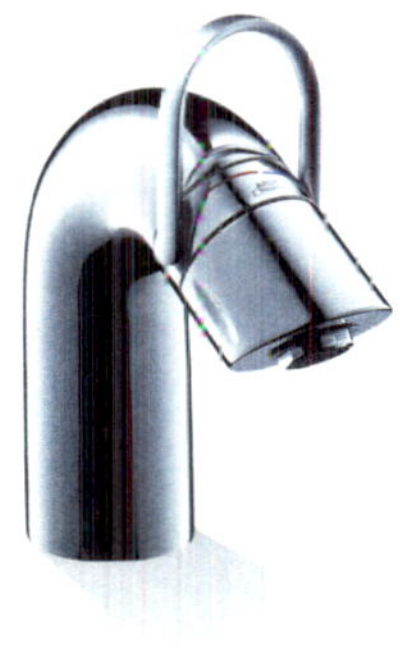

Arco single lever basin mixer,
design by Phoenix,
1991

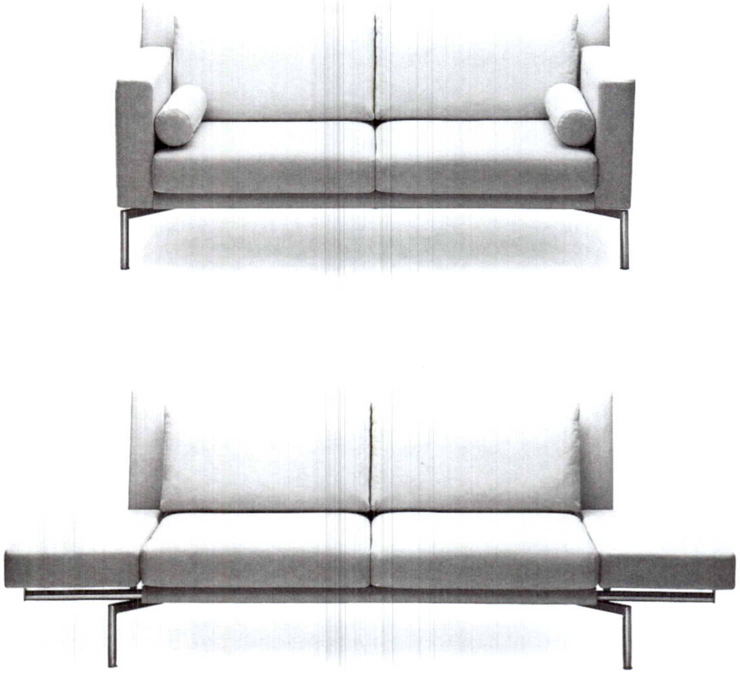

Sofa Jason 390,
design by EOOS,
1997

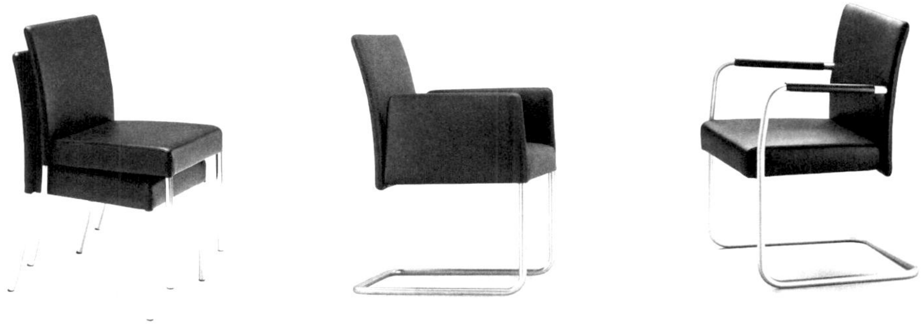

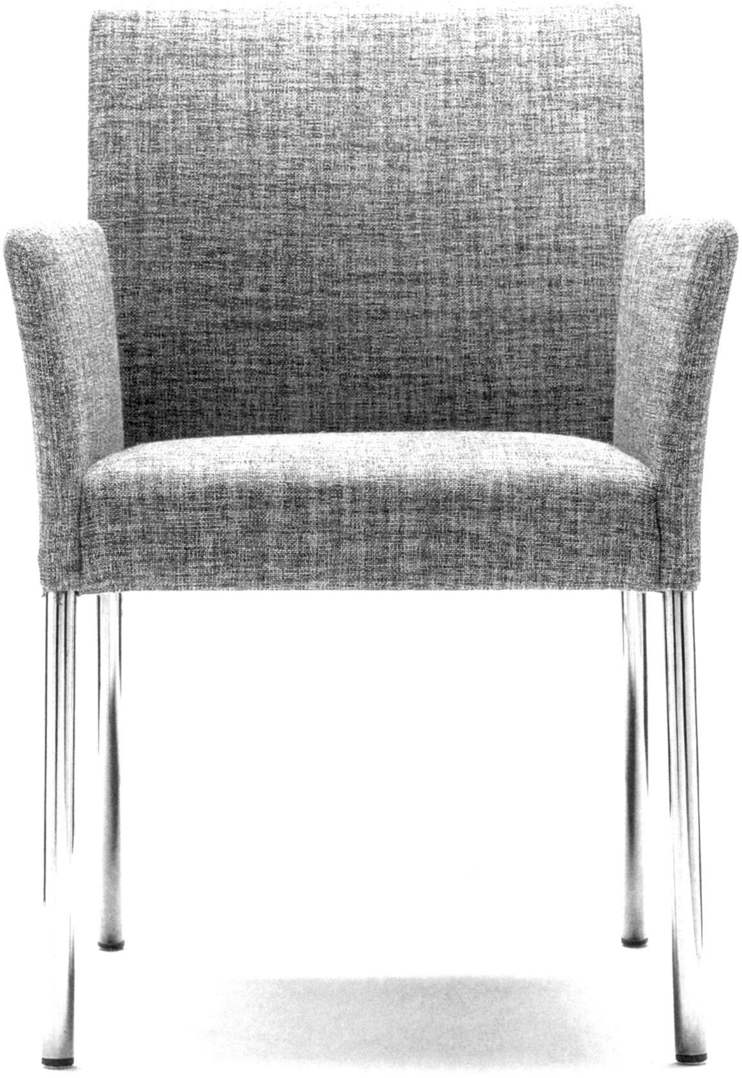

Chairs and cantilever chairs Jason, design by EOOS, 1998

Vostra, the small upholstered chair by Walter Knoll that was based on a design that Hans Knoll gave to his father, and the bucket seat 369 that Walter Knoll designed in the 1950s and was made possible by the advent of new materials, started things off. Thus began what has since become an impressive "Classic Edition." The bucket seat FK, this captivatingly elegant beauty, joined the product range when the Kill company was taken over at the end of 1999. Kill was a nearby company that had enjoyed success with Danish seating furniture since the 1960s and had quickly risen to become one of Walter Knoll's fiercest competitors. The product range, largely designed by Preben Fabricius and Jørgen Kastholm, contained numerous models, most of which were based on metal frames and leather and included a large number of designs whose aesthetic half-life seemed to go to infinity.[16]

The important step of basing the brand on the design had not yet been taken. On the lookout for designers, Markus Benz first began approaching the big names – including Paolo Piva, an Italian maestro who lived in Vienna – at the beginning of the 1990s. Although they never actually collaborated,[17] the turnaround came with a visit by three young Austrians who had studied under Piva in Vienna. "Go to Benz," the maestro advised them. At the time, no one could have predicted that this would be such a historic moment in the company's recent history – especially since the encounter started off with a linguistic misunderstanding. The guests said that they had brought along a "Bankerl" that they had designed. This earned them some puzzled looks, because "benches" were not a specialty of Walter Knoll. But the misunderstanding was soon cleared up: "Bankerl" was Viennese for sofa. A chair, on the other hand, was called a "Sesserl" (normally an armchair).

IN 1997, THE "JASON ERA," AS IT WAS CALLED IN-HOUSE, BEGAN AT WALTER KNOLL AND, TO A CERTAIN EXTENT, THROUGHOUT THE INDUSTRY.

Once the terminology had been clarified, little stood in the way of one of the most astonishing success stories in furniture design history in recent decades. Martin Bergmann, Gernot Bohmann, and Harald Gründl, who presented themselves as a trio – a highly unusual phenomenon in the industry – were in the same class at school and had just completed their studies as furniture and industrial designers. They now called themselves ECOS after one of the heavenly horses that draw the chariot of the Sun God, Helios. Obviously, the newcomers were aiming high. They presented the prototype of a sofa and chair that also bore a name from Greek mythology with a slightly Scandinavian sound – Jason, the hero and leader of the Argonauts who set out to find the Golden Fleece, which was supposed to make them invincible. When we consider what a resounding success this seating furniture range has since become – and how it opened the door to the Third Modernity for Walter Knoll – the grandiose name now seems prophetic. From a technical design point of view, it was particularly derived from the image of a crawn bow as a ritual of protecting. The curved back became the distinguishing feature of a product line that continues to be one of Walter Knoll's most successful to this day. The powerful idea caught on. This was how the young designers and Walter Knoll, their very first industrial customer, came to discover one another. It was undoubtedly yet another of those wonderful coincidences that have often been mentioned and that always have something inexplicable about them.

One clearly recognizable source of their joint success was, however, the fact that both sides enjoyed intensive dialog. The tradition-rich company that was currently experiencing a tremendous upheaval and the studio founders from Vienna were both on the brink of something new, making them a perfect fit, each having something to offer the other. The situation can thus be seen as almost a prime example of one of those great moments when manufacturers and designers find one another – a far from frequent occurrence that can, however, be a quantum leap for both parties if they take advantage of it. In this case as well, it developed into one of those congenial, long-term, company-designer partnerships that occur so rarely.[18] The comparison with Hans Knoll is obvious. He, too, was a communicative, natural talent, one of the first to cross national boundaries, engage closely with his designers, and set in motion a unique creative process more than half a century earlier.[19] A collaboration now began between Walter Knoll and EOOS that has produced numerous unparalleled innovations over a period of two decades. EOOS was Walter Knoll's actual entry into the Third Modernity, which would enable the company to leave its mark on the profession.

1997 saw the beginning of the "Jason era" (as it's now known in-house) at Walter Knoll and, to a certain extent, throughout the industry.[20] This somewhat modest upholstered furniture that's as light-weight as a regular chair but as comfortable as an armchair crossed genre borders, eliminated some of the squareness of upholstered furniture, and was universally usable. In this way, it resembled other, similarly androgynous models that the Knoll dynasty had produced, especially

Willy Knoll's light-weight Antimott model and Forum, the bestseller that Herta-Maria Witzemann designed for Walter Knoll in the 1950s as an early jack-of-all-trades. But Jason far surpasses them all. With its micro-pocket springs, for example, the chair also possesses characteristics from the Swabian development forge, which is constantly working on transforming upholstered furniture. But existing models also continue to evolve. Meanwhile, an extensive Jason family has been created, ranging from the minimalist Lite version to the barstool. The three members of EOOS have since ascended to the virtual design heavens and have produced more designs than they can count. Even the collection that has won almost every famous design award is another point that they have in common with the Walter Knoll company.[21] Both have appeared regularly on various stages where the prizes are handed out.

Naturally, the burning question is whether there's a secret formula behind the steep rise of the successful trio, which sees itself as a sort of rock'n'roll band of design, and what that formula might be. Obviously, they have the necessary power and a successful combination of team spirit and individual virtuosity. But they also have showmanship. The eloquent innovators from Vienna's inner city are driven to present and explain themselves. They've invented a brilliant term to describe their unorthodox methods: "Poetical Analysis," which is itself a kind of poetry to which they hold the copyright. It is a highly specialized method that cannot be learned at a university and signifies that for each design task, EOOS comprehensively and thoroughly analyzes the meaning and function of the object. It goes far beyond the external form and encompasses an in-depth analysis of the practical that is achieved through systematic and unbridled thinking. Once a person is open to it, a wide variety of parameters come into play that include everyday mythology and rituals as well as social and philosophical questions. Perhaps it's that playful treatment of all aspects of design from which "poetry" actually springs. It also enables EOOS to detect hidden needs. They consider the works that are created in this unique way to be a "cultural service to society." Unpredictability is also a constant feature in their creative process, probably because it unavoidably incorporates an appropriate but hard to define measure of snide Viennese humor. This is what Markus Benz especially values about them: EOOS is always good for a surprise. There are no restrictions on thought.

The result is what everyone looks for in a collaboration but is still so difficult to achieve: a creative climate. That fact that they do not necessarily comply with the separation between genres and happily violate the boundaries between chair, armchair, and cabinet is all part of picture. The many designs that EOOS has contributed to the Walter Knoll range are so diverse that, at first glance, no one would attribute them to a single design studio. These include many modern classics such as the sofa Living Platform, the armchair Bao, and the Leadchair, an executive armchair of the new generation. For EOOS, it is always about the human angle. Thus, the Viennese designers contributed to Austria's "Places for People" pavilion at the Biennale Architettura 2016 in Venice. The "places" in question were easy-to-build and easy-to-modify living environments for refugees. In 2004, they already had a bench – think "Bankerl" – in their creative repertoire. This was the first upholstered bench of its kind, another highly innovative, hybrid item of furniture. This innovative form, called "Together," recaptures the archaic tradition of the corner seat and seeks to recover lost rituals such as relaxed get-togethers with family and friends.

---

16 ▶ It might be called the school of Poul Kjærholm, that brilliant minimalist from the early 1960s who, like, Fabricius and Kastholm, was Danish.

17 ▶ A collaboration between them never took place, because it could have endangered Paolo Piva's partnership with Wittmann and B&B Italia.

18 ▶ These long-lasting partnerships are typical of certain countries, such as Denmark and Italy, as the author has mentioned in several of his publications. This apparently regional phenomenon has never been studied.

19 ▶ Hans Knoll was the communicator who established the connections and the network. He was supported by his wife Florence, who mainly functioned as a designer.

20 ▶ The Jason sofas and armchairs, as well as the Jason chair, all came out in the same year.

21 ▶ Vienna's Museum of Applied Arts marked EOOS' 20th anniversary with a retrospective show in 2015. The anniversary of the relationship between Vienna and Herrenberg was also celebrated shortly thereafter.

A MATCH MADE IN HEAVEN

As the history of design teaches us, when designers and companies are a match, their personalities always play a role – but most often, so does coincidence. The design team EOOS from Vienna not only found their way to Herrenberg, but also entered into a long-term partnership.

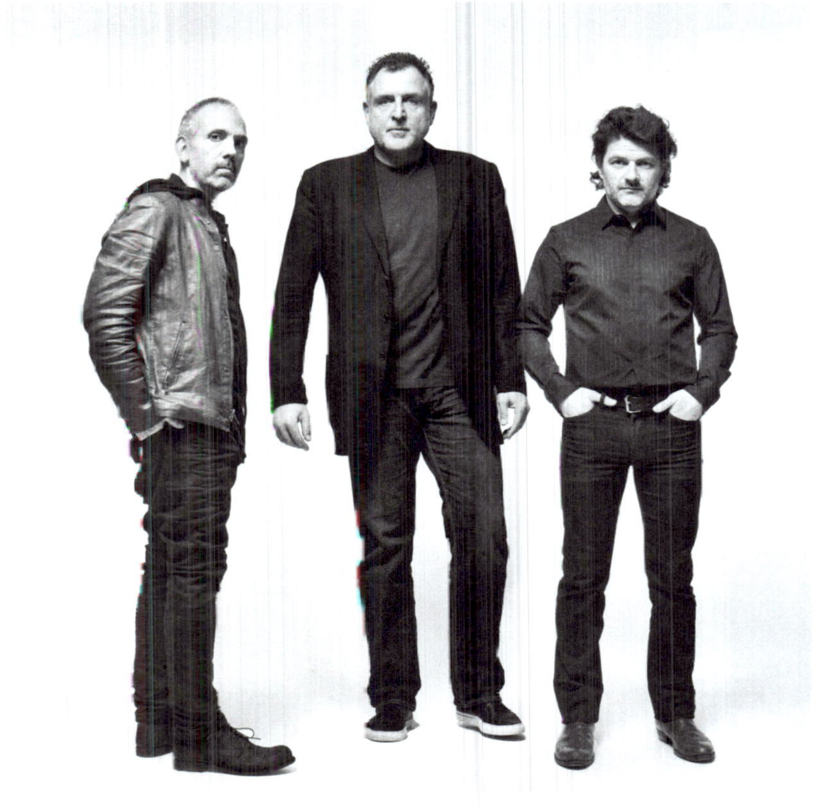

The EOOS team: Harald Gründl, Martin Bergmann, and Gernot Bohmann

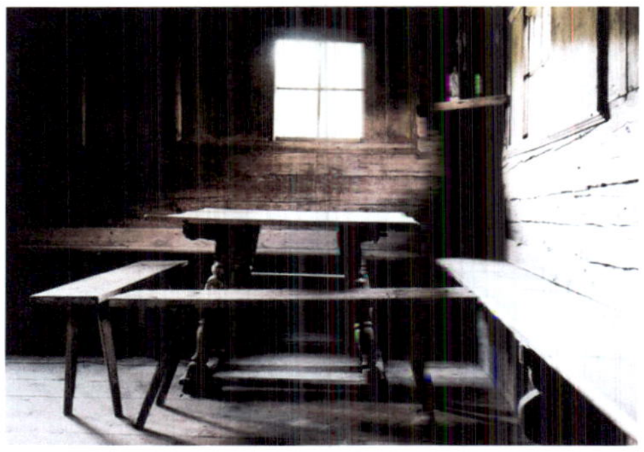

The traditional corner seat

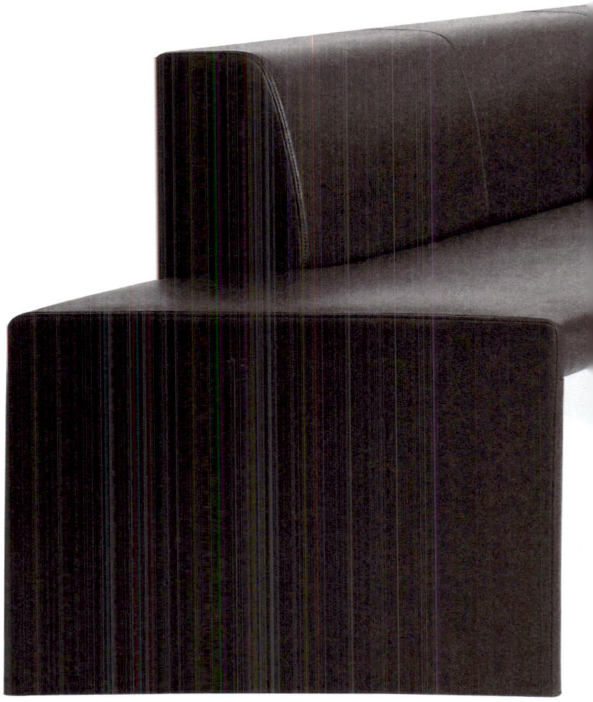

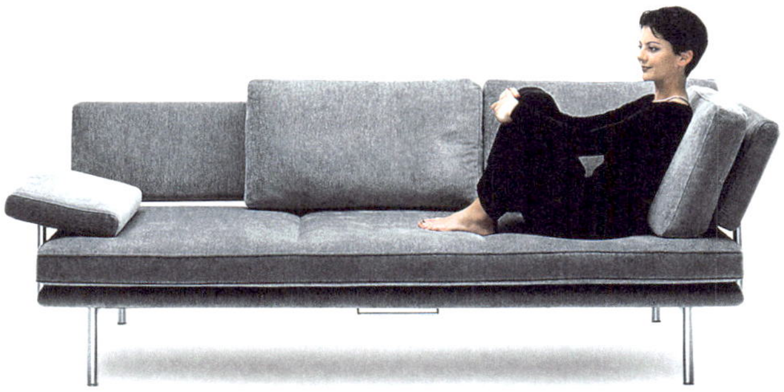

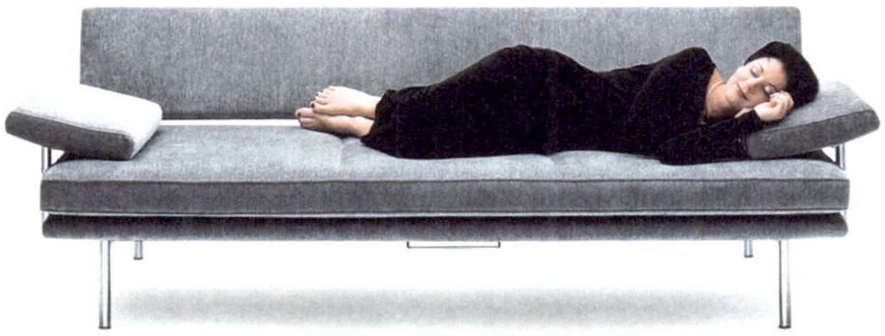

Sofa Living Platform,
design by EOOS,
1998

Corner seat Together,
design by EOOS,
2004

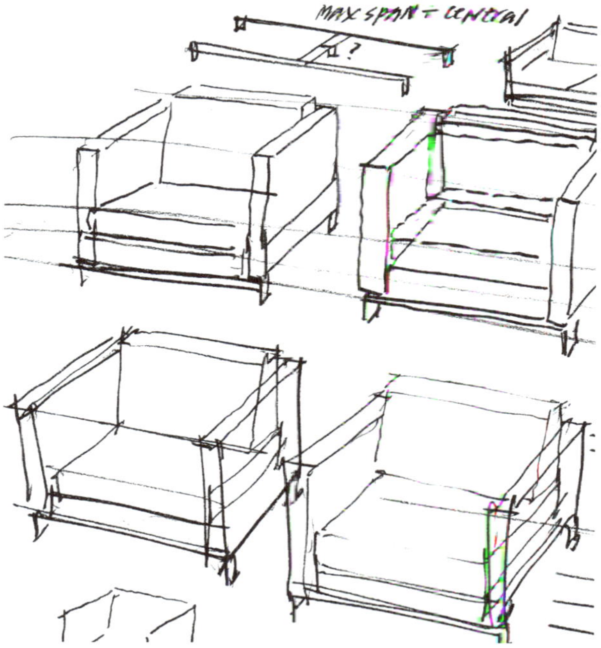

THAT'S BERLIN

By the end of the 1990s, the reorientation stage was over and the contours of the new, modern Walter Knoll had emerged. The Walter Knoll company was now ready to tackle truly monumental tasks. These soon included a lighthouse project that would fundamentally alter the brand's status and position. The qualitative boost came with the inauguration of the new Reichstag in Berlin in 1999. The talent for being in the right place at the right time that was manifested on the eve of the 21st century would contribute to the company's success time and time again. Norman Foster, the architect of the Berlin Reichstag, is one of the most well-known and perhaps the most successful member of his profession. He is always the first choice when it comes to prestigious objects anywhere in the world. When engaged in a major project, Foster + Partners is known for setting up a local office – which is exactly what they did in Berlin. The firm's specialties include administrations, bridges, airport terminals, museums, skyscrapers, and other large projects extending all the way to urban planning. One of the most famous Foster buildings from recent years is the bulbous and pointed 30 St Mary Axe, the "Gherkin," which has become a new London landmark.

Interior architecture has always been a part of the Foster + Partners portfolio as well. Turning up at the firm's headquarters, the Riverside Studio located directly on the Thames, in the runup to the Reichstag conversion project was far from an obvious move. Simply approaching a potential customer without any previous contact was already a courageous step. Markus Benz took it on as a job for management. The young Swabian entrepreneur dared to enter the London lion's den where his company, which had done so little for so long, was barely known.[22] Markus Benz still remembers the seemingly endless staircase and the feeling of the awe that overtook him. Just finding a receptive ear was already a remarkable achievement. But the appointment scheduled for a mere 20 minutes with Foster's partner, interior architect and senior designer John Small, lasted well over two hours.[23] The spark was kindled. They seemed to be able to meet one another openly and on an equal footing – central requirements for any successful collaboration. The idea that Markus Benz was proposing was also compelling. He was able to include the EOOS furniture that was just being developed and that now very obviously represented an unbeatable offer – the Jason series. Later on, Norman Foster and Walter Knoll would jointly develop large "architectural elements" for seating that were approximately 20 meters long. When the opening ceremonies for the parliament building were held in Berlin in 1999, Walter Knoll's upholstered furniture was prominently featured in many places, including the restaurant, lounges, halls, and corridors.

The foundation had now been laid for the mutually beneficial liaison between London and Herrenberg. The Foster 500 armchair and sofa series – typical in its prestigious elegance – was just the beginning. When it was designed by Norman Foster and developed in close cooperation with experts from Herrenberg, it represented a double premier and undoubtedly the strongest of Foster's numerous successful designs. In terms of design type, it was a sort of déjà vu experience, a contemporary reinterpretation of the club chair from the early 20th century – the genre through which the Knoll dynasty had made its impressive entrance into modernity and which was also inspired by England. The Foster 500 model, to which a number of successors have since been added, has meanwhile become an archetype in the Third Modernity as well as – the one follows the other – a reliable sales driver.

Its powerful presence in the political arena had a prior history in the Second Modernity. At least half a century earlier, Walter Knoll's upholstered furniture had provided comfortable seating for selected representatives of the people at the Federal Parliament in Bonn. Later, in the 1970s, the Cabinet of the German Federal Chancellery also relied on executive chairs produced in Herrenberg. Back then, such high-ranking references had boosted contract business and would now do so again – although on a totally different level. The difference was as great as the difference between Bonn and Berlin. The ultimate catalyst was the partnership with Foster + Partners, a development that the furniture industry also took as a sign. This epoch-making event divided the company's history into a before and an after. It was the beginning of its international phase and its entrance into the world of large-scale projects. At the same time, it marked Walter Knoll's debut as the brand of architects. In an interview he gave to an art magazine, Foster, the Lord from London, had the following to say about the job of designer and architect: "The most successful works, whether buildings or musical pieces by Mozart, whom I admire greatly, appear effortless. But creating something that appears effortless and is hopefully long-lasting always takes a tremendous amount of effort."[24] For Foster, intellectual penetration of the task is a prerequisite for a masterpiece. He knows that effortlessness is difficult and that simplicity can usually be achieved only through highly complicated means. What holds true for serenades and symphonies also holds true for superior architecture and design. This fundamental insight applies not only to Foster + Partners as an important working basis, but also to Walter Knoll, with both companies wanting to play first violin in their respective fields.

Moreover, Lord Foster, the "Baron of Thames Bank" and "Knight Bachelor," has never concealed his fascination with Germany's early modernity. *Neues Bauen* (New Building) of the 1920s and the functional thinking which the Bauhaus came to represent have fascinated him from an early age.[25] It was a predilection that especially predisposed him to a connection with the Walter Knoll company. Both sides share the canon of values that include, according to Foster, functionality, durability, and elegance[26] and serve as the guiding principle for their work. When masterpieces are in fact created, says Foster, they're "like children."[27] You have to be extremely careful about how you love them, he warns, whether we are talking about work or life.

In Berlin, which both Markus Benz and his board partner Michael Blank knew intimately from their shared time at Wilkhahn, there was more of a gold-rush feeling than ever. The former and current capital, which was now once again the seat of the government that had moved from the Rhine River to the Spree, was – barely a decade later – Europe's largest construction site and at the same time a playground for the architectural avant-garde. Lots of new embassy buildings had to be furnished. The experienced partners once again succeeded, and this time – with the Reichstag as their dream beginning and reference – immediately upped the stakes with a whole range of additional top-class projects. They made valuable contacts with the architects working in the capital, including Jan Kleihues,[28] who created the winner of multiple architectural prizes, the Sofitel Berlin Kurfürstendamm five-star hotel, formerly the Hôtel Concorde – that echo of Art Deco that rises above the Berlin cityscape like a complete masterpiece by Wagner. For this project, Walter Knoll worked with Kleihues to develop the Elton armchair, and ultimately with Meinhard von Gerkan, whose Swissôtel – also highly praised and award-winning – set a strong tone. The modern rotunda, with its 70 square meter video screen on Kurfürstendamm, brought a touch of Times Square atmosphere to urbane West Berlin. The design for the new central train station, a glass giant, was also created by von Gerkan's firm, which had already worked with Walter Knoll on the Tegel Airport project in the 1970s. The fact that the Berlin Chair created back then was about to appear in a new version can also be considered a tribute to the capital city.[29]

Another spectacular new building appeared on Pariser Platz, the perceived center of Berlin. The DZ Bank headquarters was built by the prestigious American architect, Frank O. Gehry. In this case, Gehry – known for his daring designs that avoid right angles as much as possible – opted for a traditional sandstone facade with a clear orthogonal grid in accordance with strict Berlin design guidelines. The swelling shapes that are normally attributed to him are all on the inside, including a boldly curving glass roof and a large-format sculpture whose puzzling shape has opened it up to numerous interpretations, partly due to the fact that the creator will not supply any information. To find peace in this world of biomorphs, visitors can sink into seating furniture by Walter Knoll that was selected by the client for this prominently situated building attracting crowds of curious sightseers every day. This noble address near the Brandenburg Gate has long been one of the most exclusive in Germany and is steeped in extraordinary history. The images of the fall of the Berlin Wall still linger in our minds. Walter Knoll also experienced an important event here: it was on Pariser Platz that Walter Knoll, the company founder, successfully asked for the hand of his future wife, Maria "Maia" Vollmöller, in marriage in 1909.[30]

---

22 ▶ Walter Knoll had supplied furniture to the HSBC in Hong Kong in the 1980s, but that was a long time ago.

23 ▶ Small was with Foster + Partners from 1985 to 2010 and is now the Director of Design at Steelcase, one of the largest manufacturers of office furniture.

24 ▶ "Gebäude sind wie Kinder" (Buildings are like children), in: *Art. Das Kunstmagazin*, 11/2011

25 ▶ The Levy and Cohen Houses in the London district of Chelsea are a rare example of *Neues Bauen* (New Building) in prewar London. They were jointly developed by architects Walter Gropius and Erich Mendelsohn and implemented in collaboration with their English partners Maxwell Fry and Serge Chermayeff. It was no coincidence that the Cohen House was refurbished by Foster + Partners, although none of the parties involved knew that Hans Knoll was working for Chermayeff at exactly the time these houses were being built.

26 ▶ "Gebäude sind wie Kinder" (Buildings are like children), in: *Art. Das Kunstmagazin*, 11/2011

27 ▶ Ibid.

28 ▶ Son of the equally well-known architect Josef Paul Kleihues. The two founded the joint architectural firm of Kleihues + Kleihues in 1996.

29 ▶ The chair was reissued in 2015 in honor of Walter Knoll's 150th anniversary.

30 ▶ Walter Knoll's brother-in-law, the connoisseur and world traveler Karl Vollmöller, had a luxury apartment on Pariser Platz, where he introduced his friend Walter to his father. It was on this neutral territory that the father assented to the marriage of his daughter Maria to the suitor whose social status was not quite up to par.

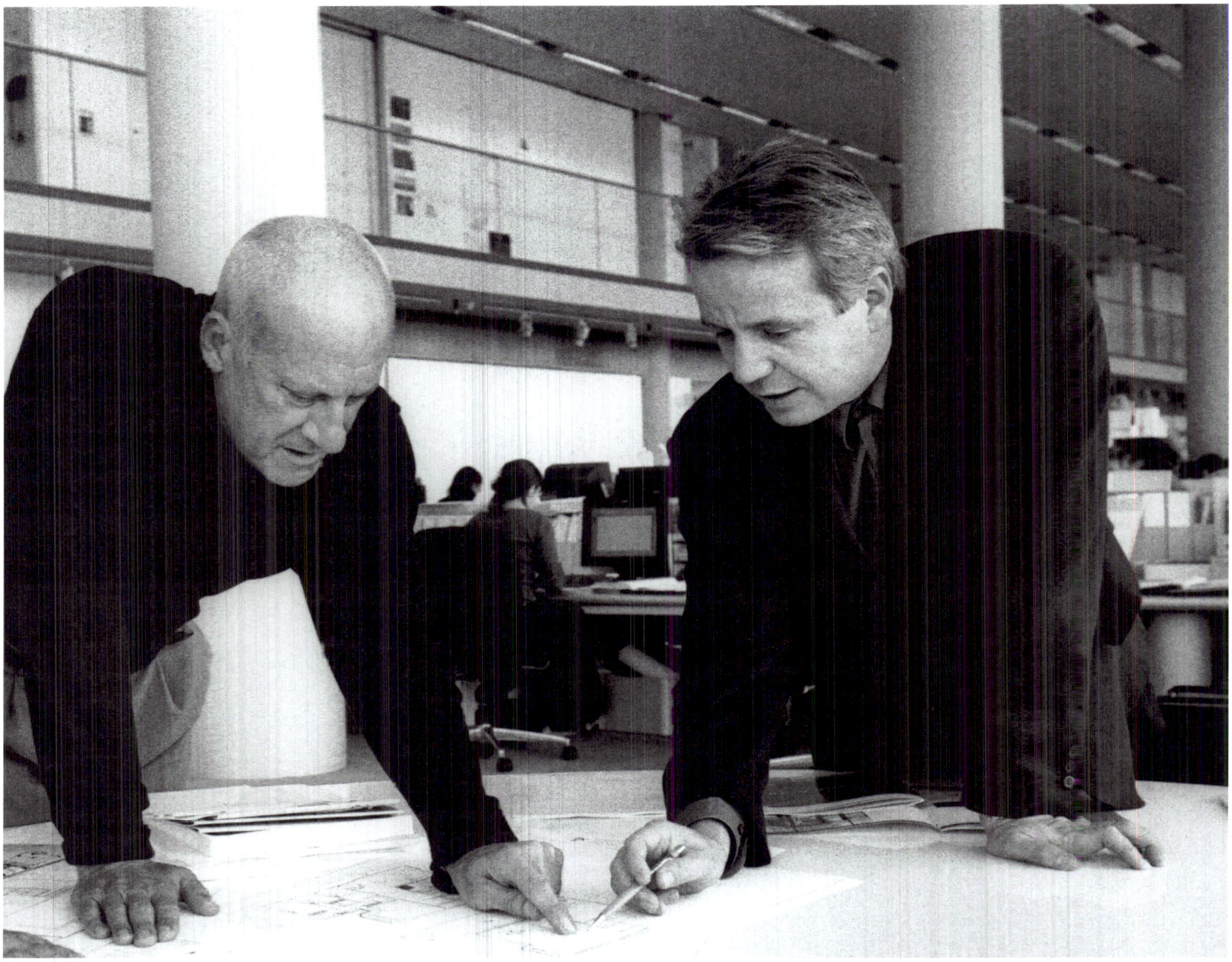

Norman Foster and Markus Benz engaged in the design process, 2002

Dome of the Berlin Reichstag, architecture by Foster + Partners, 1999

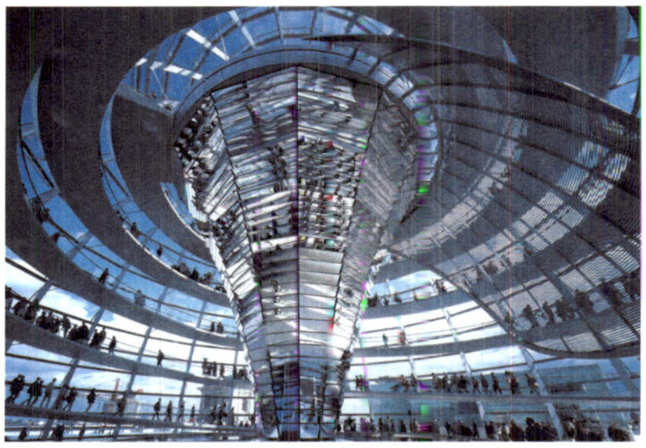

BERLIN

A sense of optimism reigned in the past and present German capital. Collaboration with Foster + Partners on the Reichstag was especially significant. It was a lighthouse project that would alter the course of Walter Knoll.

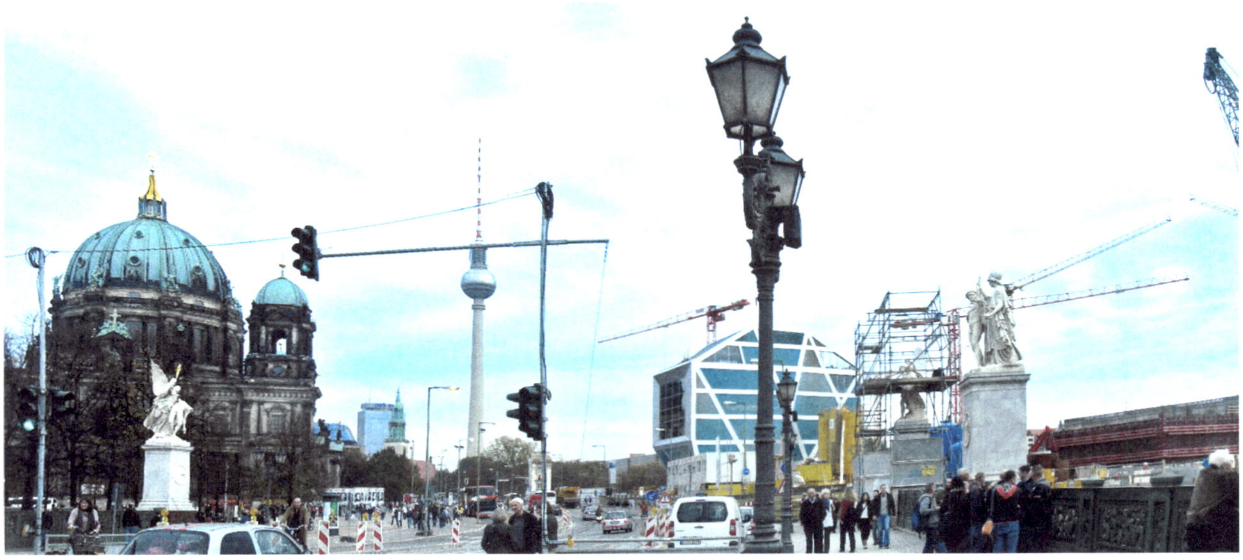

Unter den Linden, Berlin

Armchair Foster 500,
design by Norman Foster,
2002

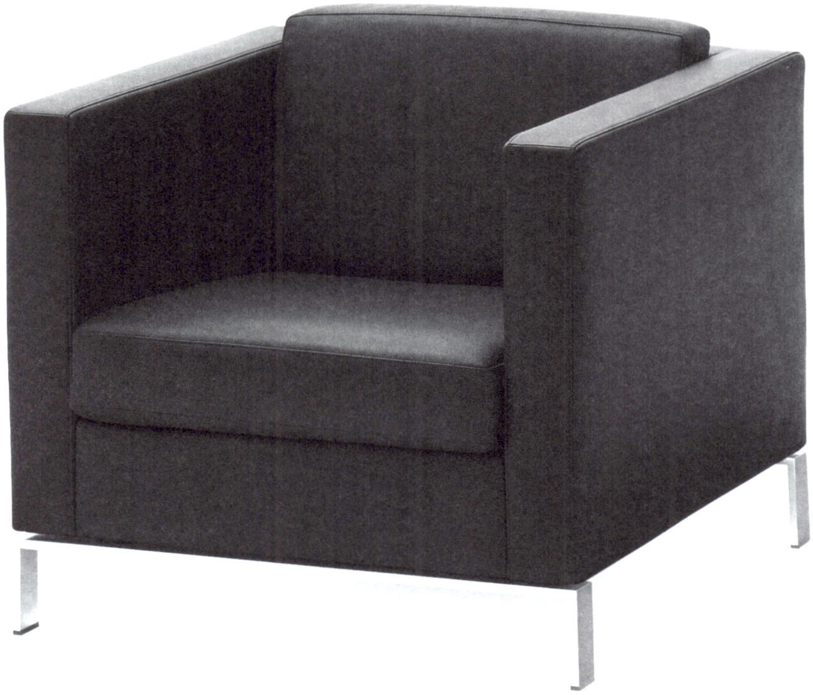

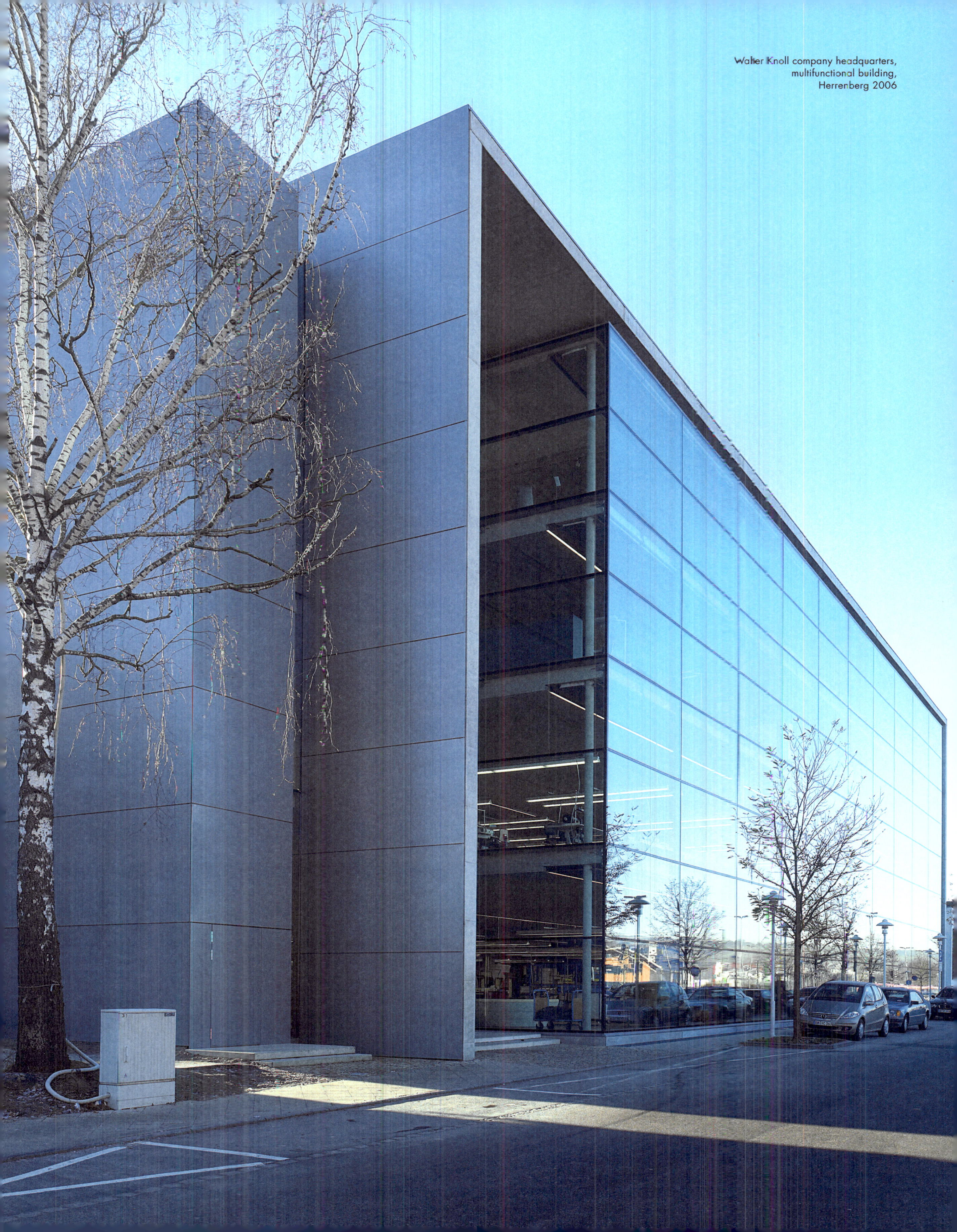

Walter Knoll company headquarters,
multifunctional building,
Herrenberg 2006

A CLEAR VIEW

Walter Knoll's multifunctional building was built in Herrenberg, a historic district town near Stuttgart, in 2006. The modern building interacts with traditional industrial architecture on the expanded premises. Together, they form the Walter Knoll Brandland.

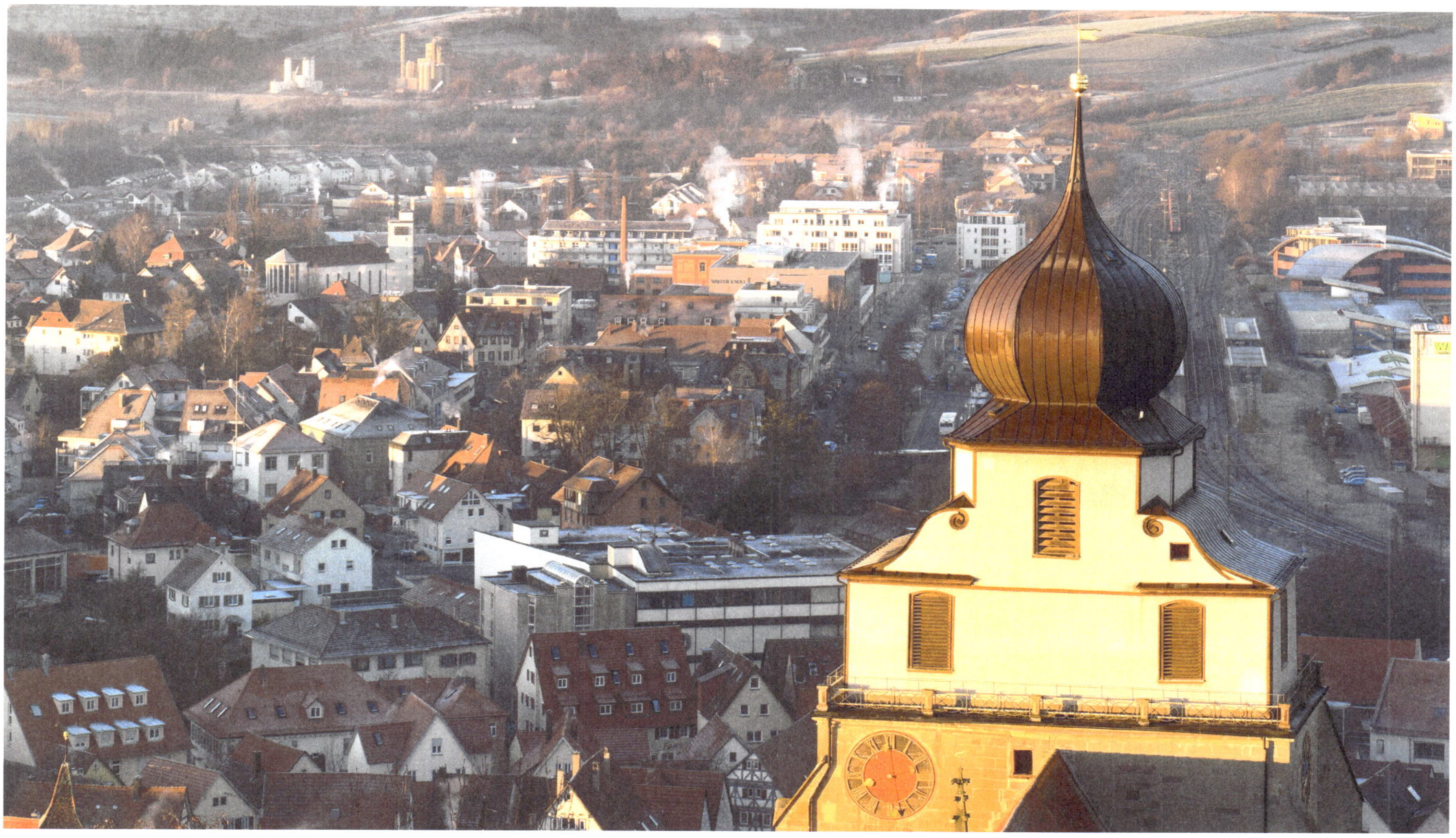

Stiftskirche on Herrenberg's Schlossberg hill

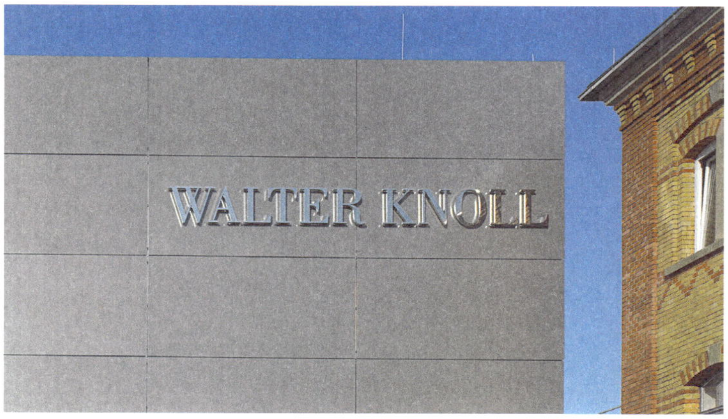

Company buildings, old and new construction

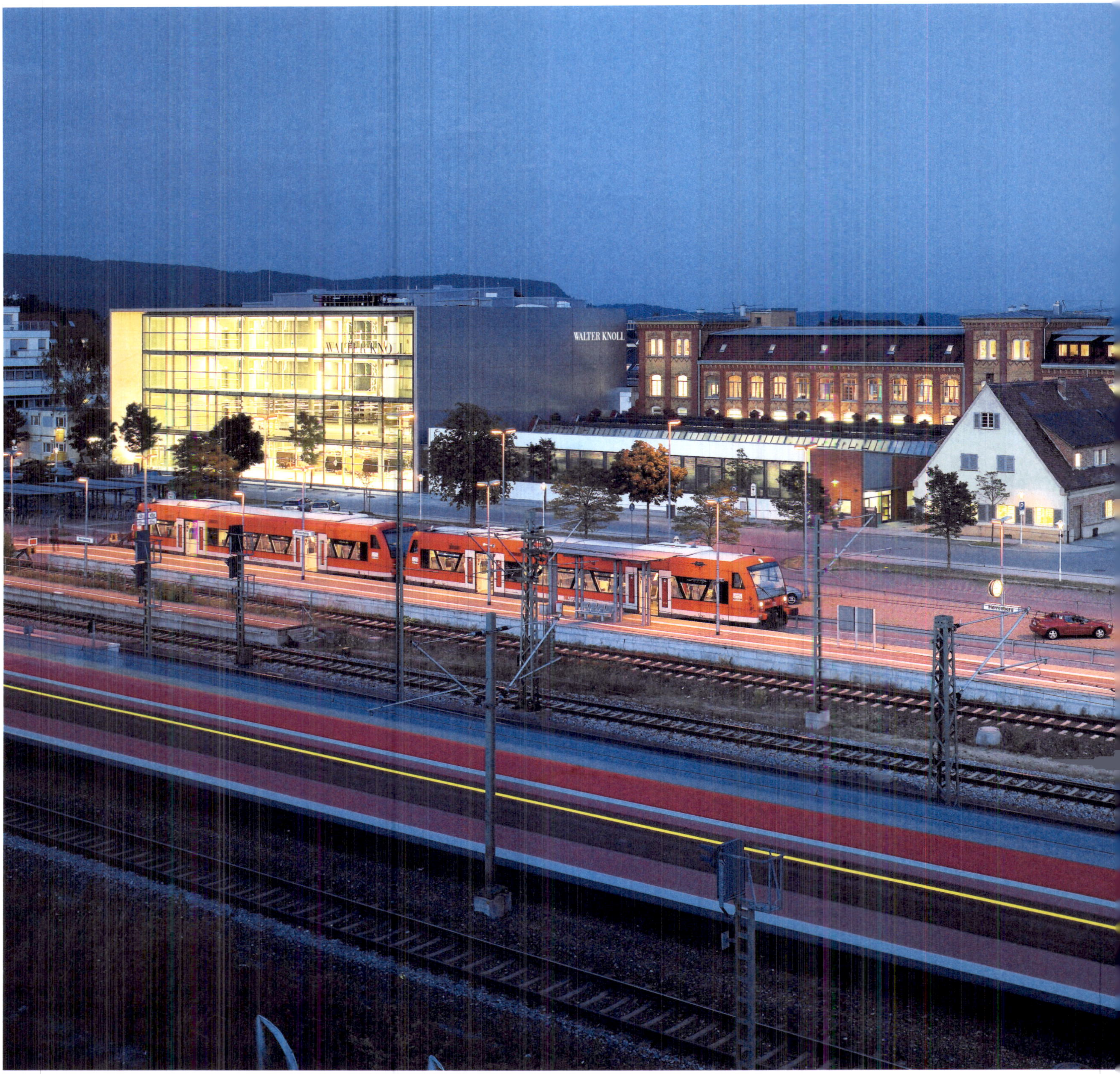
WALTER KNOLL

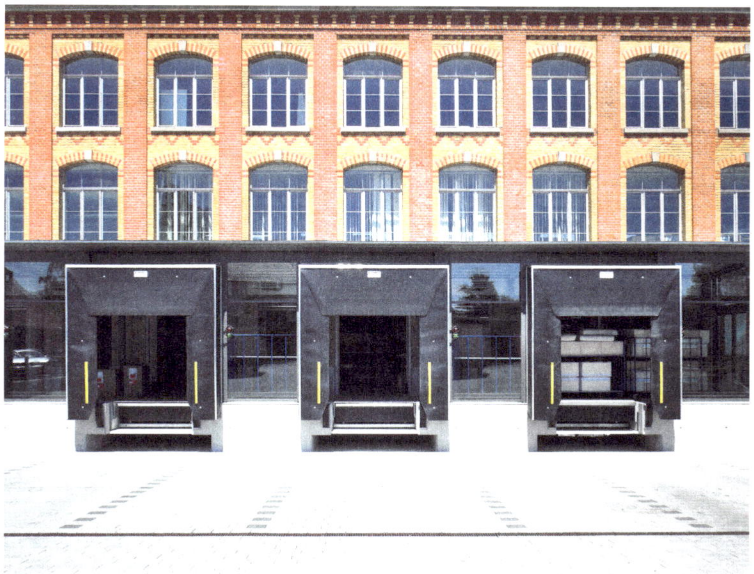

Loading zone

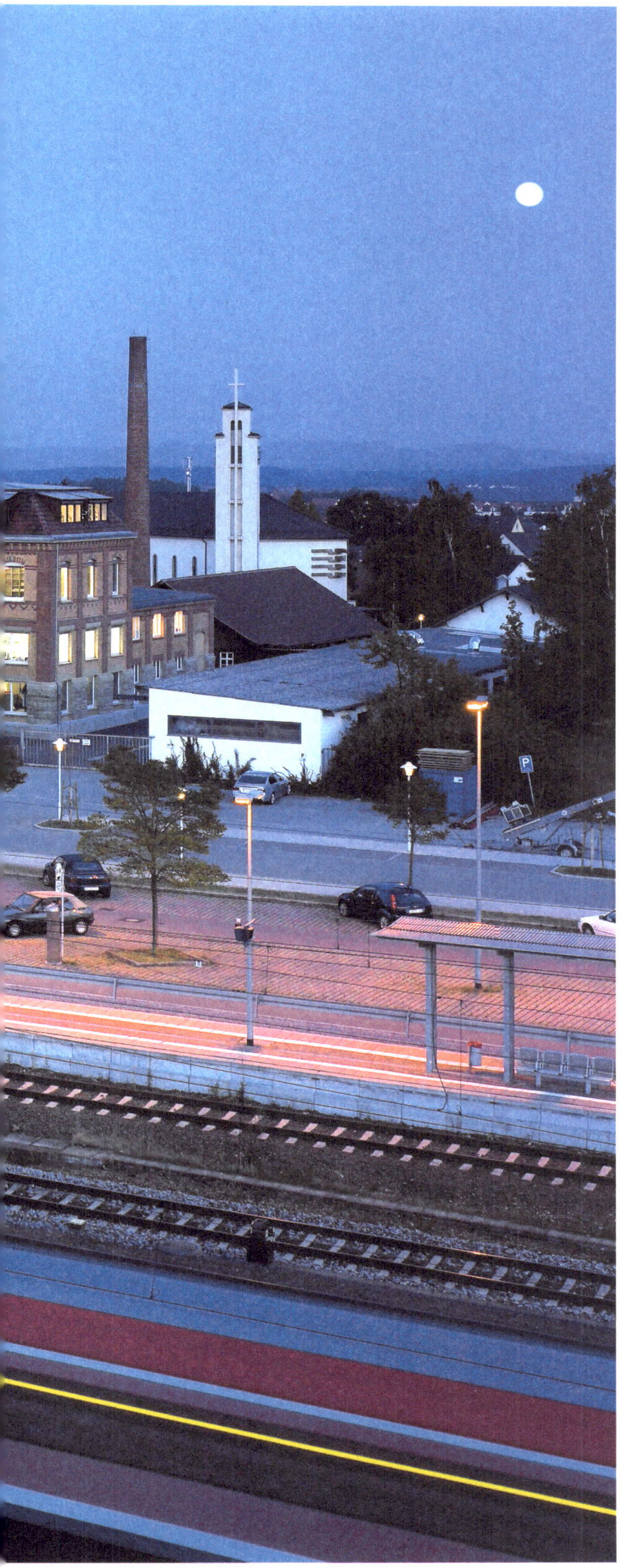

Bahnhofstrasse with company buildings

TECHNICAL REVOLUTION

Tech | ni | cal | Rev | o | lu | tion. In around 1800, new machines, the factory system, and the railroad unleashed an avalanche of unprecedented changes. The process began in England and soon spread to today's industrialized countries. About one-hundred years later, electrification, motorization, and mass production resulted in another tremendous thrust. At the dawn of the 21st century, another technical revolution took place: digitization led to the global networking of data streams and the automation of production and other processes. Today these phenomena seem to be accelerating at an ever faster rate. Whereas Walter Knoll's old factory building, a typical brick structure from the imperial period, can clearly be attributed to the first technical revolution, high-tech is integrated into the modern multi-functional building from 2006 in the form of technological innovation and energy optimization. Thus, the company architecture reflects the phases of the technical revolution. In terms of the products, this is even more the case. The Antimott and Prodomo upholstery systems with their metal springs are prime examples of the innovative upholstery technology of their time. The same applies today to the Leadchair swivel chair. Because of its new type of upholstery in which the leather is applied directly to the foam cushion, the model represents a milestone in Walter Knoll history.

TO CREATE, ONE MUST FIRST QUESTION EVERYTHING.
EILEEN GRAY

1993
The Benz family purchases the Walter Knoll company. Markus Benz, son of Rolf Benz, takes over management at the age of 32.

1995
The internal restructuring phase is completed. The wrapped Reichstag by the artist duo Christo and Jeanne-Claude becomes an international sensation.

1997
The successful imm and Orgatec furniture fairs in Cologne are a turning point for Walter Knoll. Production increases despite a downturn in the furniture industry. With EOOS and the Jason sofa, the new, modern Walter Knoll is born.

1998
The volume of orders has doubled since 1994. Product campaign with around a dozen new developments. Chairs in the Jason range by EOOS become the bestseller.

1999
The redesign of the Berlin Reichstag is the start of collaboration and product development with Foster + Partners. Entry into the international project business.

2001
Inauguration of the new production building in Mötzingen.

Roof of the Allianz Arena, Munich, design by Herzog & de Meuron, 2005

Swivel chair Leadchair Executive, design by EOOS, 2012

WLAN symbol

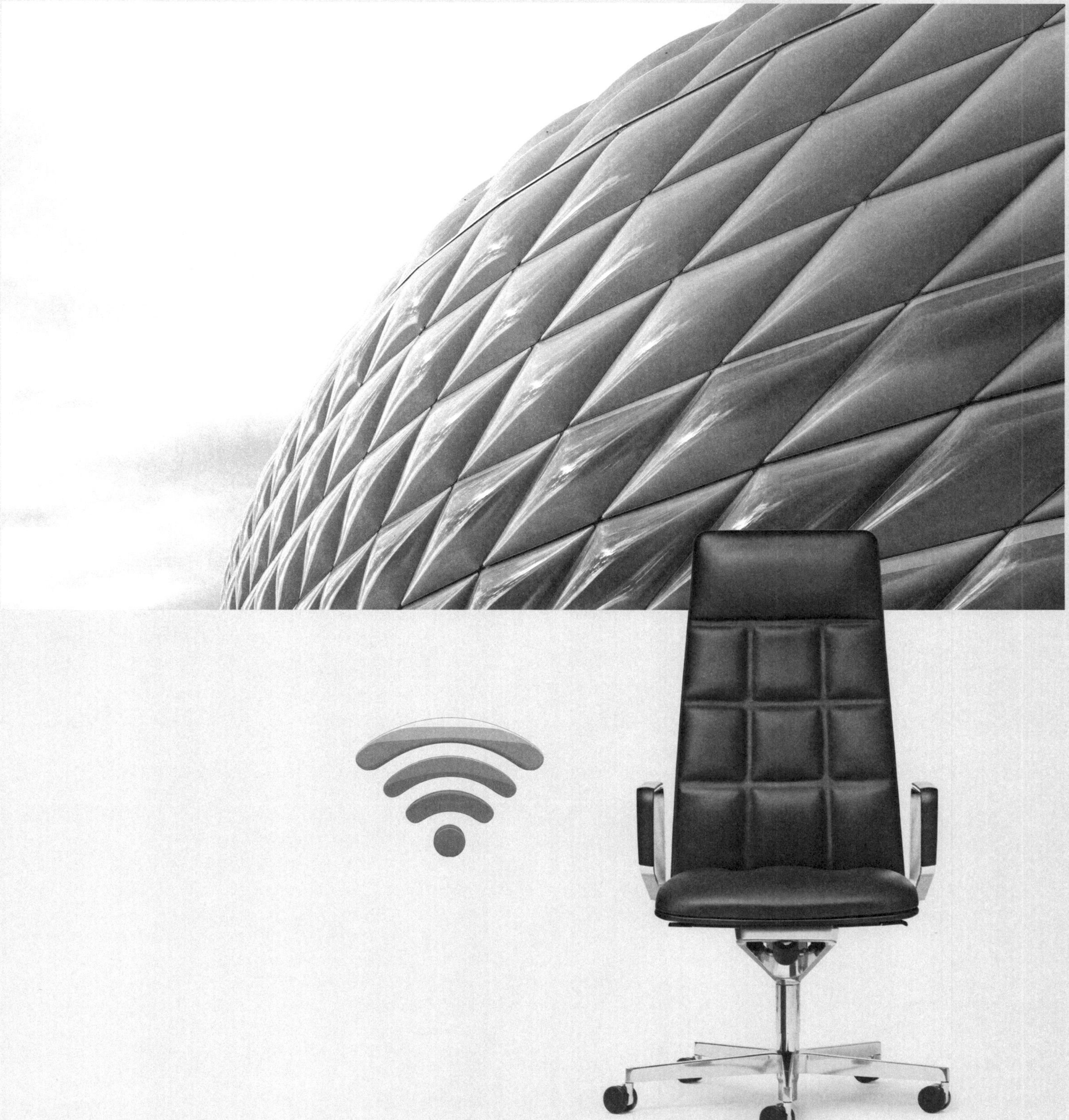

21ST CENTURY

ARCHITECTS AND OTHER JACKS-OF-ALL-TRADES

The activities in Berlin, which was now once again an international cultural metropolis, also accelerated its transformation in a cosmopolitan direction. Markus Benz knew that a medium-sized company like Walter Knoll in particular couldn't survive without exporting. To achieve his goal of a presence on all relevant markets, he had to establish an information network with representative offices on every continent. Soon the company had an opportunity to participate in projects with a European orientation. This included a new grand hotel in Sweden, a historic palace in Vienna, a university in Aberdeen, Scotland, and the International Tribunal for the Law of the Sea in Hamburg established by the United Nations. Thanks to projects at home and abroad, the company made many contacts with the participating architects, for whom Walter Knoll now became a known quantity. It was significant that the seating furniture from Herrenberg had now risen to an elite level and was seen as a professional tool. Playing in the big leagues with the international brands created a positive momentum that has continued to this day.

However, strategists Benz and Blank had an even higher goal in mind – perhaps their most important one ever – inspired by their experiences with Norman Foster and the Reichstag. That project was the blueprint for an ambitious scheme that had never been tried before. They actively sought out collaborations with renowned architects in order to develop a new generation of upholstered furniture. The history of furniture design – and particularly of seating furniture – is studded with designs created by top architects ranging from Alvar Aalto to Frank Lloyd Wright, and from Marcel Breuer to Marco Zanuso. Earlier on, Walter Knoll had also handled designs by architects, such as those by Herta-Maria Witzemann and Meinhard von Gerkan, so the idea was nothing new, except in the way it would be implemented. Walter Knoll would now become the brand of architects. This most resembles the projects of Hans and Florence Knoll, who took a similar step in the mid-20th century in the U.S, gathering around them an international crew of superior talents for Knoll Associates that included architects such as Eero Saarinen and Warren Platner.[1] Most of the members of that mixed crew were – like Hans Knoll himself – immigrants from Europe who had an American passport. This was different from Walter Knoll's current situation, in which one looked for top talents among a cast of global urban nomads.

Consequently, the Englishman Norman Foster was followed by other renowned international architects including Ben van Berkel from the Netherlands and Kengo Kuma from Japan. It was not primarily about big names, but rather about a mindset and approach that the two partners shared and that made the extraordinary possible. It required a creative relationship that flourished only in a favorable climate. Once again, a comparison can be made with Hans Knoll, a charismatic personality who knew how to inspire enthusiasm and how to set the right tone with creative types who had a reputation for being especially sensitive. Markus Benz, who grew up in a large and lively family, and whose first career in the law required that he be a talented speaker, is also an adept and sensitive communicator. Moreover, he had the support of Michael Blank, a universalist, an eloquent fast-thinker, and a dyed-in-the-wool native of Berlin. Their ability to establish relationships and maintain them over the long term was the necessary prerequisite, without which they would not have been able to entice the best of the best collaborate with them.

BENZ AND BLANK ACTIVELY SOUGHT OUT COLLABORATIONS WITH RENOWNED ARCHITECTS IN ORDER TO DEVELOP A NEW GENERATION OF UPHOLSTERED FURNITURE.

This was the only way to achieve design "made in Germany" at the highest level, where the partners were linked to the company and to Markus Benz by a bond of friendship.

Several basic but less spectacular plans were also implemented at this time, such as the gradual conversion of production to greater industrial efficiency and the introduction of quality control. The number of complaints, which was already small, dropped to an impressivley low level. It was amazing how quickly the strategy of making all the adjustments at once paid off in results and figures. Walter Knoll continued to grow, counter to the general trend. Whereas sales in the German upholstered furniture industry dropped seven percent in the year the Reichstag was inaugurated, with the sector experiencing its worst year of the post-war period, two-digit sales increases were now practically a matter of course at Walter Knoll. In just two years, the company more than doubled its revenues to a highly respectable 39 million in 1999, the second-to-the-last year in which calculations were still in Deutschmarks. Six years later, revenues had doubled again, now reaching 38 million euros. With such fantastic results, the Herrenberg company was an exceptional phenomenon among its still primarily medium-sized competitors.

While Germany's Reunification proceeded more or less smoothly, more profound changes were occurring in society that were also significant for the Walter Knoll company. Thus in the 1990s, a shift in values took place that resulted in a fundamental change in lifestyle and buying habits. One effect was that the market polarized into a high an a low end, while the middle eroded. The furniture market, where the giant Ikea was making low prices the norm, was a prime example. At the same time, the start of the new century brought about a growing awareness of quality and an appreciation of luxury. Luxury had long been taboo in Germany. Even the word was out of favor. However, a substitute word was found: design, whose current meaning came from the U.S. and did not become part of the international vocabulary until the end of the last century, when it took on cult status – especially when it was permanently linked with a brand name. Here, again, the furniture and interior design industry played a key role, after having set the tone in terms of form and style throughout the 20th century. According to a study, one-third of all German manufacturers in the high-end segment were from world of home furnishings [2] At Walter Knoll – where the trend was already upwards and where good design and high quality had always been unshakable principles, even during the most difficult times of restructuring – the change had the effect of an added catalyst. The Herrenberg company not only resumed its top position among German manufacturers of high-end upholstered furniture, but also joined the circle of elite brands that had long appeared to be reserved for Italian manufacturers.

The final decades of the 20th century, the German automotive industry celebrated its triumph as a prime example of the shift in values – it might even be called a Germanization of the high end. Until now, commercial travelers returning from Asia have reported their astonishment to hear the phrase "Vorsprung durch Technik" ("progress through technology") that has found its way into standard usage around the world. With this slogan, which has appeared everywhere in its untranslated form since the year 2000, Audi won the hearts and minds of the world's car lovers. The German language – heavy on consonants and somehat harsh-sounding – became the message. It seemed to hold the secret to that perfection and precision that are, with good reason, attributed to the Germans. It was the dawn of a new era for the long-standing "Made in Germany" mythos, referring to a clear and uncompromising line justifiably seen as typically German and representing a bridge between the First and Third Modernity. It was not just about the shape of the vehicles but also about the image of the brand as a whole. So it was inevitable that the automotive industry would discover architecture. In subsequent years, numerous buildings were created for the presentation and self-portrayal of major brands, including showrooms, customer centers and – a novel idea – ambitiously designed museums. Today, every leading brand has a spectacular new museum building that interprets modernity in some architectural form. At the same time, a dialog is always established between architecture and interior design – aspects that must complement one another if the sought-after harmonious image is to be achieved. In this area, Walter Knoll had first-class references. This was already the case during the First and Second Modernity,[3] but it was playing out on a much higher level since the brand's reorientation.

So it was no surprise when Walter Knoll became the preferred partner of leading German automotive brands in their corporate design offensive, once again proving that the company knew best how to express brands in furniture. Ambitious projects were realized on behalf of manufacturers such as Daimler and Porsche. For Walter Knoll, it was the beginning of the corporate business model. The auto industry's new showcase buildings feature such contradictory architectural concepts as that of the Mercedes-Benz Center, with its clearly articulated glass-and-concrete structure and, at the other end of the stylistic spectrum, the jagged, futuristic Porsche Museum – both of them Stuttgart attractions representing the broad spectrum of the Third Modernity. Walter Knoll is the natural counterpart to this advanced automotive culture. Anyone visiting a modern temple of mobility will, of course, also want the seating to be on-brand.[4] But this natural affinity with the automotive elite goes beyond the simple enjoyment of exclusive products.

---

1 ▶ Saarinen's bucket seat and Platner's wire furniture are classics of mid-century design, as the Second Modernity is referred to in America.

2 ▶ "Der Markt der modernen Wohnkultur" (The market of modern living culture), "Focus" Marktanalyse, reprint, January 2006.

3 ▶ This refers only to the Weissenhofsiedlung from 1927 and the Stuttgart Television Tower from 1955, two key buildings from the First and Second Modernity that were equipped with seating furniture from Walter Knoll.

4 ▶ It was similar during the First Modernity when it was still a matter of very different modes of transportation, such as the luxury liner "Bremen" and the "Hindenburg" Zeppelin, but Knoll upholstered furniture also fit perfectly into that highly exclusive framework. Today, it is all about presentation, but in a certain sense, the first-class accommodation on a luxury liner and the gondola of an airship were also a kind of showroom.

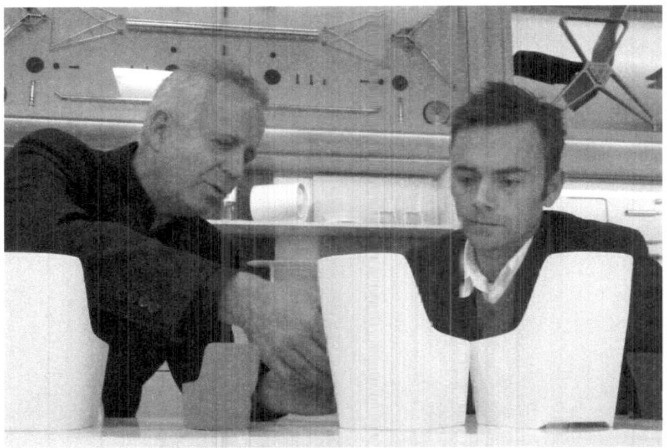

Markus Benz and Mike Holland from Foster + Partners with models of the 520 armchair.

Armchair Foster 520, design by Foster + Partners, 2012

TEAM SPIRIT

At Foster + Partners, Markus Benz now collaborates with Mike Holland, Head of Industrial Design, among others. Holland, who has worked there since 1995, heads a studio in London with 14 designers who are masters of all facets of their genre, from product and interior design, to lighting and transportation, all the way to furniture design.

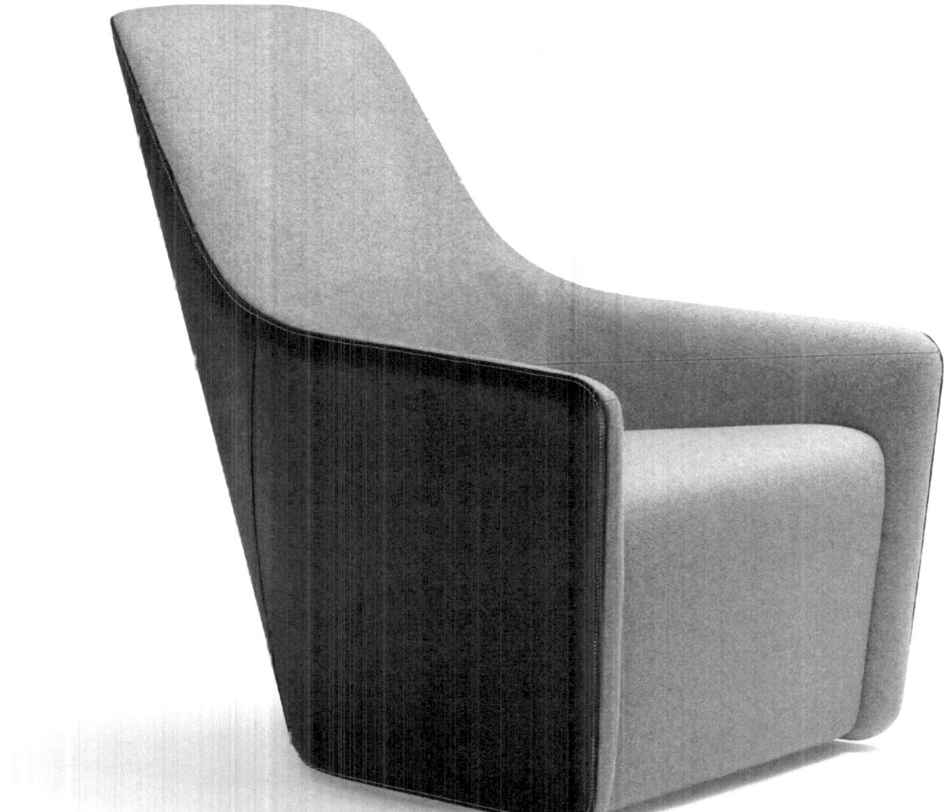

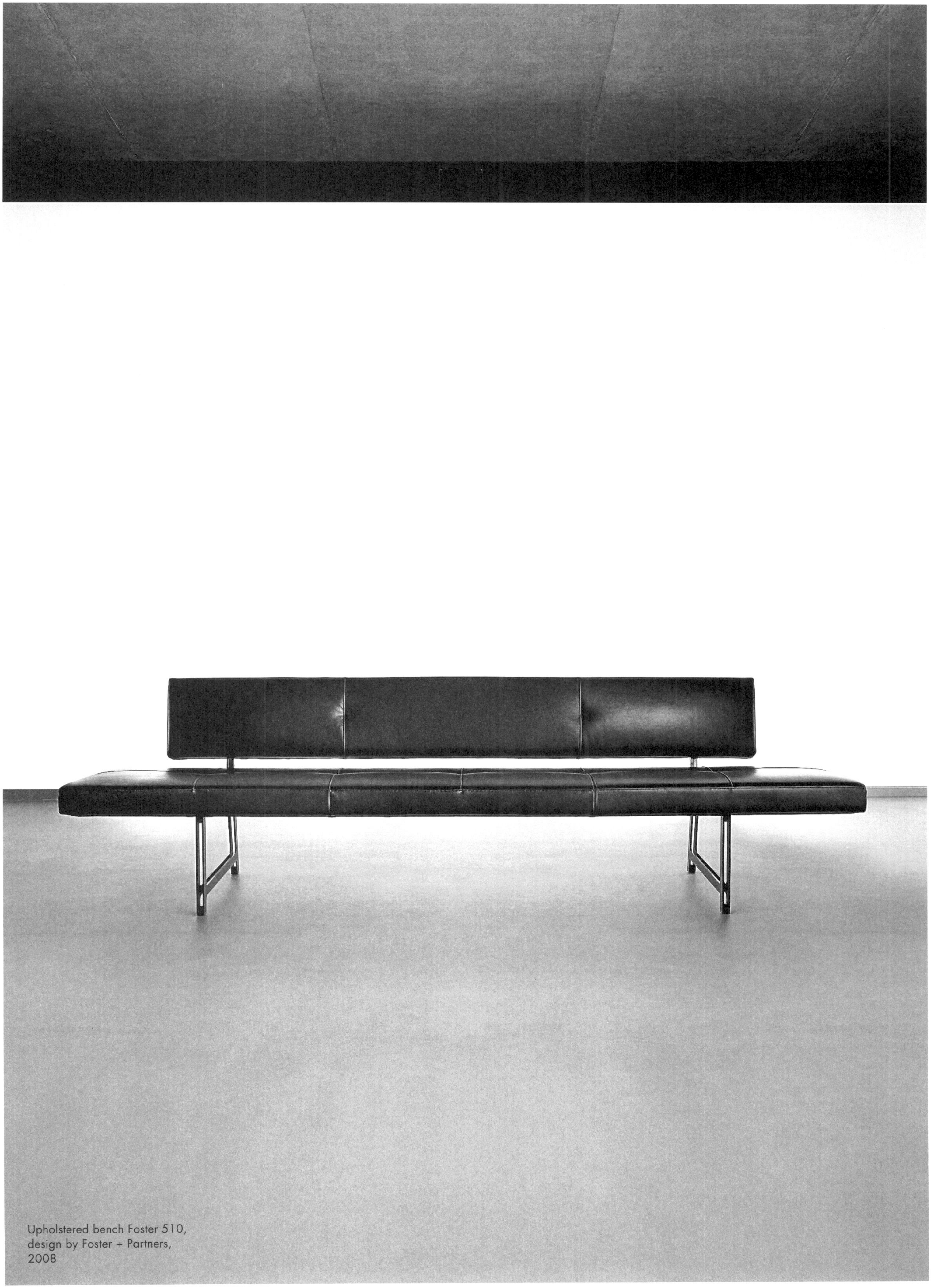

Upholstered bench Foster 510,
design by Foster + Partners,
2008

It also extends to manufacturing and its infrastructures. In other words, the furniture David and the automotive Goliath are also similar in their methods for achieving top quality.[5] The two industries are also among the champions – if not world champions – of export, thus completing this picture of related structures whose essential core is high-level globaliuation.

The furniture and auto industries both possess success genes so typical of the region that originated with the First Modernity and is now more effective than ever.[6] Walter Knoll is part of this complex infrastructure that is unrivaled worldwide. So it was only fitting that the company celebrated the 125th anniversary of the Knoll furniture dynasty at the "Landesgewerbeamt" (State Trade Office) in 1990. That was just before its near-collapse and the elimination of the State Trade Office in its original form, but despite these ruptures, the structures that had been built over decades continue to exist. Today, Walter Knoll is stronger than ever in terms of culture and sees itself as providing an economic and cultural service.

The Mercedes-Benz museum, which is now an integral part of the Mercedes-Benz world, was opened in Stuttgart in 2005.[7] It is an ambitious edifice whose interior comprises a review of the history of the world's premier automotive brand in the form of a double helix. Walter Knoll was able to match it with an ideal furniture design. The sofa Circle, with its bold curves, not only reflected the organic design idiom of the building, but could also hold its own in the spacious single room. The author of this sculpture serving both form and function was the Dutch architect Ben van Berkel, who was also responsible for the design of the museum building itself. Together with his business partner Caroline Bos, he operates the UNStudio architectural firm in Amsterdam, which is known the world over for its visionary designs. The team of van Berkel and Bos specializes in the use of digital CAD technology, which has enabled them to accomplish transformations that have repeatedly and boldly challenged our ideas of how architecture should look. One example is the La Défense building complex situated in Almere, The Netherlands, constructed of customizable modules and with a rainbow-colored façade that changes according to the position of the sun. Then there is the Galleria department store in Seoul, a luxury mall with a glass shell comprising LED lights whose lighting and color effects extend into infinity. Another highly respected project is a new bridge in Budapest, Hungary. Van Berkel once worked in the offices of Santiago Calatrava and Zaha Hadid – an experience that fundamentally shaped him.[8] Hadid, a master of fluidity, used to intimidate clients with the audacity of her designs. Such unusual shapes now greeted visitors to the Mercedes-Benz Museum, where Circle had its spiritual beginnings. This large sofa, simultaneoulsy concave and convex, demonstrates how an extraordinary creation can emerge from the inspired dialog between company and designer. In this case, the exchange between Amsterdam and Herrenberg evolved from a professional partnership into a friendship between Markus Benz and Ben van Berkel.

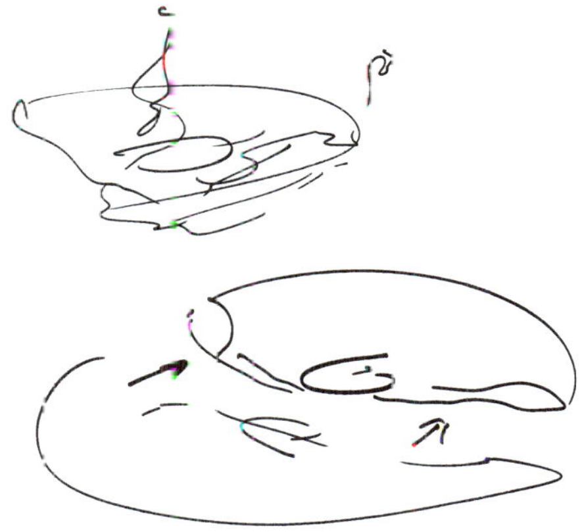

DIRECT CONNECTIONS OVERSEAS

The expansion of Walter Knoll's portfolio was in step with its creative team, which became increasingly international. Among the most productive who were now contributing to the catalog was PearsonLloyd, a design studio in London. This is the company name of Luke Pearson and Tom Lloyd, who express their unity through the orthographic compression of their names. The claim that production in England, the cradle of industry, is not quite what it used to be is not entirely true. In one industry at least, it still leads the world – the creative industry, a term that was invented in England. London supplies the world with cool style, witty ideas, and professional methodologies. The Royal College of Art, one of the leading producers of talent and at least as cosmopolitan as London itself, is constantly infusing the industry with new blood. It is also where Luke Pearson and Tom Lloyd studied in the mid-1990s, before the founded their company in 1997. A short time later when they met Walter Knoll, they – like EOOS before them – still belonged to the untamed, unknown younger generation populating the European design scene. They, too, were discovered by their new client and shared the same spirit of transition. Thus, an international design idiom was established on the imaginary axes between Herrenberg, Vienna, and London that was both new and bound to the tradition of modernity. Meanwhile – in another astonishing parallel to the Austrian trio – Pearson and Lloyd had become known in the most prestigious circles of their industry. At some point, the New York business magazine "Fast Company" ranked the two Brits among the "Masters of Design," which included the top 50 designers "shaping our future." In the interim, Tom Lloyd worked at Pentagram and Luke Pearson was senior designer at Ross Lovegrove. Both were guest lecturers at the Royal College. They joined the successful English studio tradition, taking what design service providers such as Minale Tattersfield and Pentagram once demonstrated and carrying it over into the new century. The name PearsonLloyd stands for absolute professionalism, versatility and, most importantly, an uncompromising customer orientation that focusses on their clients around the world. Their tremendous output alone proved that they are on one and the same wavelength as Markus Benz. They have since contributed more than a dozen models and model series to Walter Knoll's product range. The majority of their designs are based on a single theme: the upholstered bucket seat. The bucket seat was one of the

ON THE IMAGINARY AXES BETWEEN HERRENBERG, VIENNA, AND LONDON AN INTERNATIONAL DESIGN IDIOM WAS ESTABLISHED THAT WAS BOTH NEW AND BOUND TO THE TRADITION OF MODERNITY.

greatest furniture innovations of the mid-20th century, associated with names like Arne Jacobsen, Eero Saarinen, and Charles and Ray Eames. Walter Knoll also numbered among the pioneers.[9] Today, PearsonLloyd is proof that no dust has settled on this accomplishment of the Second Modernity. These British perfectionists use their designs to explore the grammar of the organic form and give new meaning to this supreme discipline of design: sometimes compact, sometimes in a lounge format. For over 20 years, PearsonLloyd has been researching the perfect bucket shape, whose challenge lies in the combination of form, function, and comfort. The bucket is a complex shape that must be mastered both formally and ergonomically: a sculpture in which there are no random points on the curve, but every point is precisely defined. The two Londoners bring to the task their rich experiences from a very different field: the aircraft industry. They are sought-after experts in airplane seating and have designed numerous seats for passenger aircraft, initially for Virgin Atlantic Airways and then for other airlines as well. It is a complex discipline that celebrates the interplay between design and engineering on the highest level, and PearsonLloyd have succeeded at it time after time.

The millennium arrived with much less fanfare than was predicted. Once again, the apocalypse failed to materialize. Instead of crashing, computers continued to operate undisturbed. At the same time, the world witnessed upheavals that caused a veritable sea change. The Earth had become a village. Suddenly globalization was affecting everyone, beginning with their wallets. On January 1, 2002, the euro was introduced. The common currency of the EU, for which the Germans even gave up their beloved marks, became the most important currency after the dollar. The establishment of the eurozone, now the world's largest single market, was perfectly timed for an expansive company like Walter Knoll, which was mainly seeking its future outside its national boundaries. In the coming years, exports would become the engine driving of a steep upward trend.

---

5 ▶ It also applies to the cluster supply chain previously mentioned.

6 ▶ These structures are inseparably linked to the Stuttgart "Landesgewerbeamt," the institution with such a terribly old-fashioned name and totally forgotten today, that once spawned a unique industrial culture in Swabia. From the very start, it was not about being technologically ahead. It was also about a culture in which creative forces were believed to exist. The intersections between business promotion and artistic, design, and building avant-garde was already one of the great strengths of the Stuttgart model in the early 20th century.

7 ▶ Mercedes-Benz Welt is a Daimler customer center in Stuttgart-Bad Cannstatt that opened on May 19, 2006. It consists of the Mercedes-Benz Museum and the Mercedes-Benz Center.

8 ▶ Calatrava, an engineer and artist from Valencia who specializes in bridges, repeatedly created breathtaking structures such as the Samuel Beckett Bridge in Dublin. The same applied to the Iraqi-born Hadid, the first woman to win the Pritzker Prize, the "Oscar of architecture."

9 ▶ Those who supplied groundbreaking designs in this profession included the salaried designers Rolf Grunow and Arno Votteler. Back then, Walter Knoll had a head start based on its American contacts and a familial advantage: Eero Saarinen, a pionner of the bucket seat, was Hans Knoll's brother-in-law.

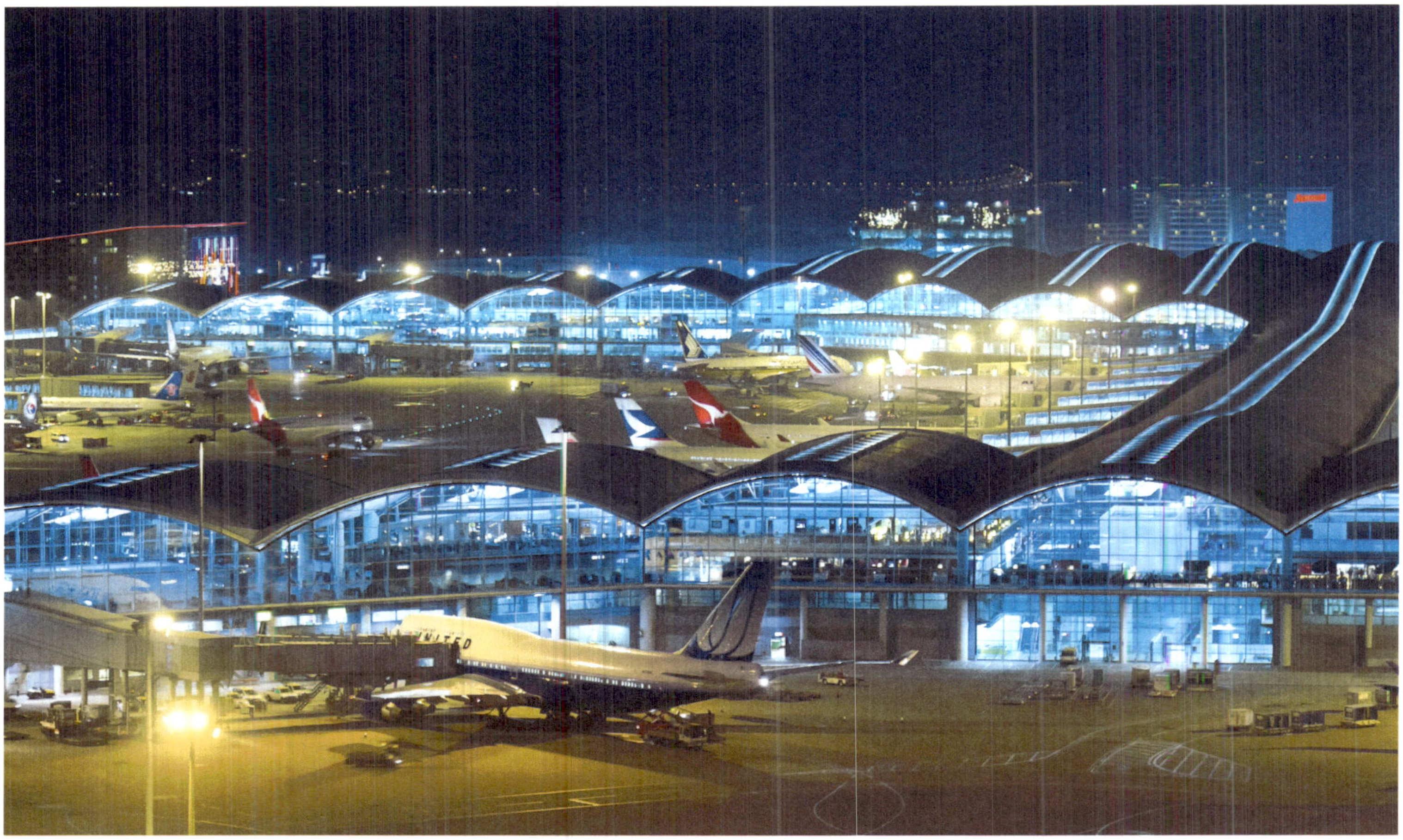

Hong Kong International Airport,
architecture by Foster + Partners, 1998

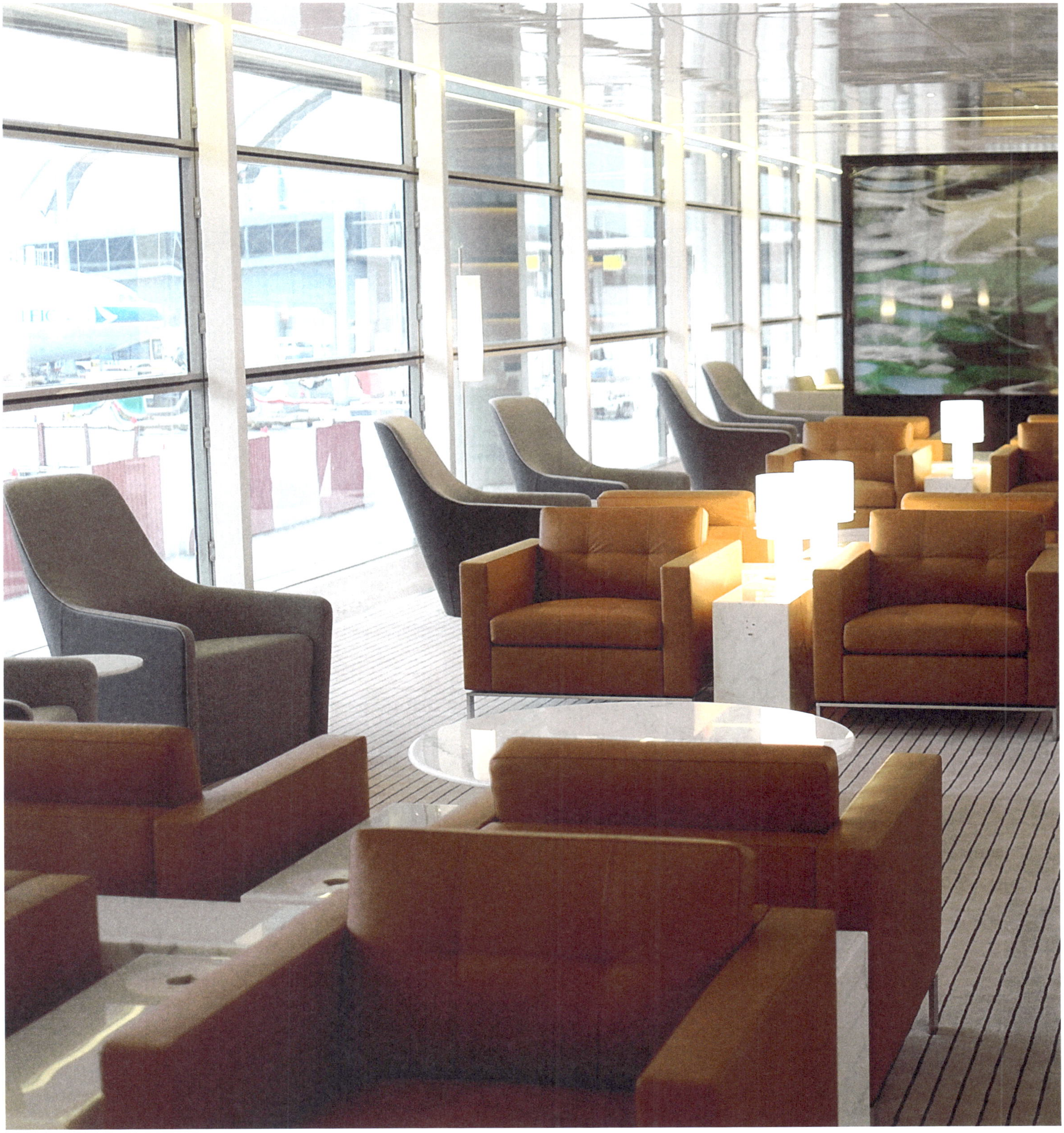

Cathay Pacific Lounge in Hong Kong International Airport,
furnished with armchairs Foster 502 and 520

ONE OF THE SUCCESS FACTORS WAS THE VISION OF ESTABLISHING HIGH-QUALITY PROJECTS WORLDWIDE THROUGH A COMPREHENSIVE NETWORK OF ARCHITECTS, DEALERS, AND THE COMPANY'S OWN EMPLOYEES.

Brand-new markets appeared overseas, primarily in the Middle and Far East. China, which was once the sleeping giant, had finally awakened. Hong Kong, Shanghai, and a number of other cities were transformed into mega-metropolises whose skylines heralded epic growth. Markus Benz now targeted these emerging nations in his travels. He, like many Swabians, had a familial predisposition toward cosmopolitanism. Thus, at the beginning of the 20th century, his grandmother Wilhelmine had also ventured out into the world. At the tender age of 15, she emigrated to the U.S., actually managing to obtain her father's consent. As mentioned before, the travel bug was widespread in the Knoll dynasty and Markus Benz, as agent and ambassador of its furniture brand, was part of a long line that included Wilhelm, Walter, and Hans Knoll. The filled order books spoke for themselves. One of the newly acquired customers was the Shanghai Municipal Electric Power Company, one of the most successful businesses in the People's Republic of China. This power company had ambitious plans, including such daring concepts as a worldwide power grid. In 2003, it opened a new headquarters, a highly modern complex made of concrete, steel and glass in which products from Herrenberg were ubiquitous. From then on, other continents started recognizing Walter Knoll for what it already was: first-class on the international level when it came to upholstered furniture. There were many factors to this success, including the vision of setting up high-caliber projects worldwide implemented by a comprehensive network of architects, dealers, and the company's own employees. It was a matter of acquiring complex setups in foreign countries, placing them under contract, and implementing them. Ultimately it was the beginning of another new business area: furnishing the international headquarters of companies throughout the world.[10]

Essential prerequisites for establishing a suitable presence in these new territories were the thoroughly overhauled and now multi-faceted portfolio and the honed brand image. They also included a minor but not insignificant detail that was thrown in for free: the German heritage. Foreign business partners' strong preference for the "Made in Germany" label is well-known, as is the excellent reputation of German industrial goods – above all the highly-coveted automobiles. But consumer goods such as bathroom fittings, cutlery, and washing machines from Germany also have an excellent reputation worldwide, which is why they are preferred for major projects. Thanks in large part to Walter Knoll, this confidence now extended to products for executive offices, boardrooms, and lobbies. It was extremely fortunate that this promise corresponded to a real and renewed increase in quality that was achieved mainly through a further improvement of production process. The promise of premium quality can be fulfilled only if all the parameters are right.

To seize the new international headquarters business segment, the company had to be represented on site, so a Walter Knoll contact office was established in Shanghai and staffed with its own employees. It was only a matter of time before another booming region would be added. A second office was opened in Dubai. The centers on the Persian Gulf, which had been under construction for decades and were funded by billions of dollars in oil money, were transformed into fantastically surreal cityscapes. One of these hotspots was Dubai, favorite center of trade for business people from other Arab countries that had a corresponding need for banks and hotels. When the Burj al Arab, a superlative luxury resort and new landmark, opened there in 1999,[11] it marked the birth of the boom in modern and postmodern architectures. In Dubai City, the largest city in the United Arab Emirates, the Burj Khalifa Tower has already been reaching to the sky for several years. At a height of 800 meters, it is the tallest skyscraper in the world. So it was no coincidence in this new era of Walter Knoll that the company's first major project in the Middle East was the Commercial Bank of Dubai. A special feature of this particular bank building is the circular assembly room situated directly beneath the cupola, the Majlis, where sofas that can seat a total of 40 people are arranged in a circle (see p. 303).[12]

In 2003, one year after the opening of the bank in Dubai, construction began on another extraordinary highrise on the opposite side of the Atlantic. In the center of Manhattan, a building with a more moderate height of 142 meters was beig built according to the design of the London office of Foster + Partners. It was the company headquarters of the Hearst Corporation, one of the leading American media groups. Inaugurated three years later, as a "signature building" it stands out from the many other anonymous New York highrises. In addition to a sophisticated structure,[13] Foster's tower also has an exceptional environmental footprint for a building of its type, consuming significantly less energy and water. This economical use of resources as demonstrated by such a powerful architectural specimen has its origins in the ethics of Foster + Partners – and of Walter Knoll. But that was certainly not the reason why Norman Foster once again chose upholstered furniture from Herrenberg for this project. For him, it was always about a comprehensive concept of architecture in which the unity of the building and interior spaces is an integral and self-evident part. At the dawn of the 21st century, barely a decade after the company's dramatic upheaval, Walter Knoll – the leading brand of modernity – had become an international player and risen to the pinnacle of its industry. The company's breakthrough was no accident, but was based on a long-term strategy manifested, for example, in the projects in Shanghai, Dubai, and New York.

ENCOUNTERS IN BRANDLAND

As the company continued to grow, it became obvious that it would soon require larger premises. A master plan consisting of three construction phases had been developed early on and was gradually being implemented. Phase one was in Mötzingen, a municipality between Herrenberg and Nagold where a new factory was commissioned in the summer of 2001 that has accommodated pre-upholstery line ever since. In a space of approximately 7,500 square meters distributed over two floors, individual components of the different models are prepared for assembly.[14] The building was designed by Hansulrich Benz, Markus Benz's younger brother, who studied at the Stuttgart academy. His works exemplify the guiding principles of modernity, of which the Academy was a stronghold during the last century.[15] That the architect Benz sees himself as part of this tradition is especially evident from the buildings he designed for Walter Knoll. When it comes to corporate identity, even the company's buildings are a family affair. When a new production hall was constructed in nearby Mötzingen, Hansulrich Benz created a solitary building. The free-standing, and therefore widely visible structure stood in clear contrast to the "Gäu," that gentle rolling landscape above the Black Forest. Naturally, the building was also a symbol of the ancestral location practically unknown outside Swabia. The exposed location surrounded by fields and the formal austerity of this industrial building – differing from a cube only in terms of its recessed, slightly inset entrances – only serve to highlight its culitvated character. Although the emphasis was of course on function, it appears to be more than just a functional building. The structure is clad in a muted gray, titanium zinc sheet metal, carefully crafted to extend its service life as long as possible. This garb, as sophisticated as the leather cover on a Walter Knoll armchair, sends an unambiguous message: the products created here are of the same high-quality as the building itself. The finely coordinated minimalism communicates more than just the codes of modernity. It also expresses essential characteristics of the corporate culture – the ultimate brand architecture.[16]

In 1937, the Walter Knoll company moved from Stuttgart to its present location in Herrenberg, where it could already look back on several decades of often turbulent development. To learn about the character of this medium-sized city,[17] it is best to go to the market square. With its colorful half-timbered buildings and equally photogenic "Stiftskirche" (Collegiate Church), it is the ultimate example of Swabian small-town charm. From there, it's just a few steps to the Schlossberg hill, where Walter Knoll and his son had their last conversation on a winter's day in 1955.[18]

---

10 ▶ Contemporary examples include the Davidoff headquarters "Maison Davidoff" in Basel and numerous boutiques worldwide, as well as the new European Central Bank in Frankfurt.

11 ▶ The Burj al Arab, or "Arab Tower," is one of the world's finest hotels and, at a height of 321 meters, is also one of the tallest. Its unmistakable design in the shape of a sail and its location on an island off the coast make it unique.

12 ▶ Majlis is an Arabic word for a place of sitting or gathering. In this room, people can literally gather in a large circle. Custom-made products such as these are an essential service, especially in non-European cultures where customs, including seating customs, are often very different. In this case, the Lazlo sofa was adopted to specific requirements in order to fully meet the customers' needs.

13 ▶ Diagonal steel supports that trace a graphic pattern of triangles and rhomboids on the facade lend the Hearst Tower its distinctive character. However, the structure is not only striking but also practical. It required less steel than a conventional rectangular lattice construction.

14 ▶ The inner workings of upholstered furniture are the basis for seating comfort. The pre-upholstery creates the conditions for a precise seating of the covering. The structure of the frames and springs is determined by the design. Wooden or metal frames form the foundation for the suspension. Moldings and foams of different densities shape the upholstery. The cushion filling is dictated by use and ergonomically reasonable comfort.

15 ▶ The Stuttgart State Academy, now the "Staatliche Akademie der Bildenden Künste" (State Academy of Art and Design), participated in the specialist discourse of the 20th century. Whereas the architecture department at the technical university took on a conservative, oppositional role as the "Stuttgarter Schule" (Stuttgart School) in the First Modernity, and explicitly took a stand against the Weissenhofsiedlung in 1927, the "Werkkunstschule" (School of Applied Arts) later integrated into the Academy has made its Stuttgart location an important center of the movement of modernity since its founding. In the Second Modernity as well, the powerful ideas on architecture issuing from Stuttgart were highly regarded around the world. This was reflected, for example, in the awarding of the Pritzker Architecture Prize to Frei Otto in 2015, the first of two Germans to receive this distinction. Otto was also influenced by the work of Santiago Calatrava, who in turn was a teacher of Ben van Berkel.

16 ▶ The construction of "Mötzingen I" was from the outset designed for growth and, because all success indicators were clearly pointed upwards, was supplemented with a second building as planned. In 2011, "Mötzingen II" was built, a multifunctional hall for assembly, production, and logistics.

17 ▶ That's why Herrenberg bears the title "large district town."

18 ▶ Hans Knoll, probably one of the most successful furniture entrepreneurs at that time, nevertheless found no personal happiness – which was also one of the topics of conversation on that walk with his father.

ARCHITECTURE AS SYMBOL

A second production site was built in the foothills of the Black Forest, not far from Herrenberg. The plans for the minimalist building were supplied by Hansulrich Benz, the younger brother of Markus Benz, who studied at the Stuttgart Academy. Thus, even the company's architecture remained family affair.

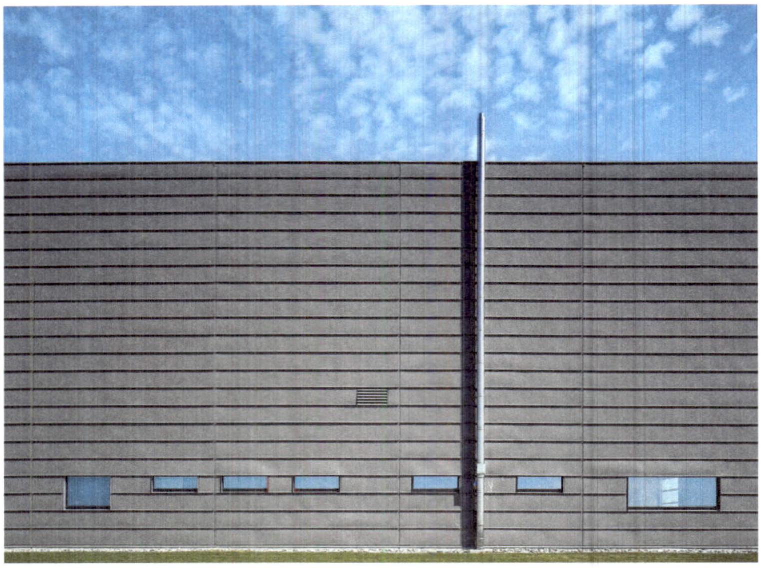

Mötzingen I factory, 2001

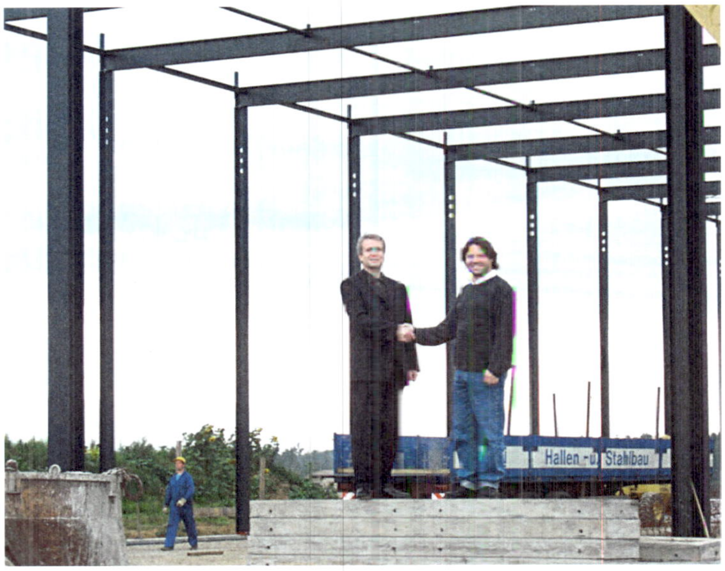

Client and architect at the laying of the foundation stone: Markus and Hansulrich Benz, 2000

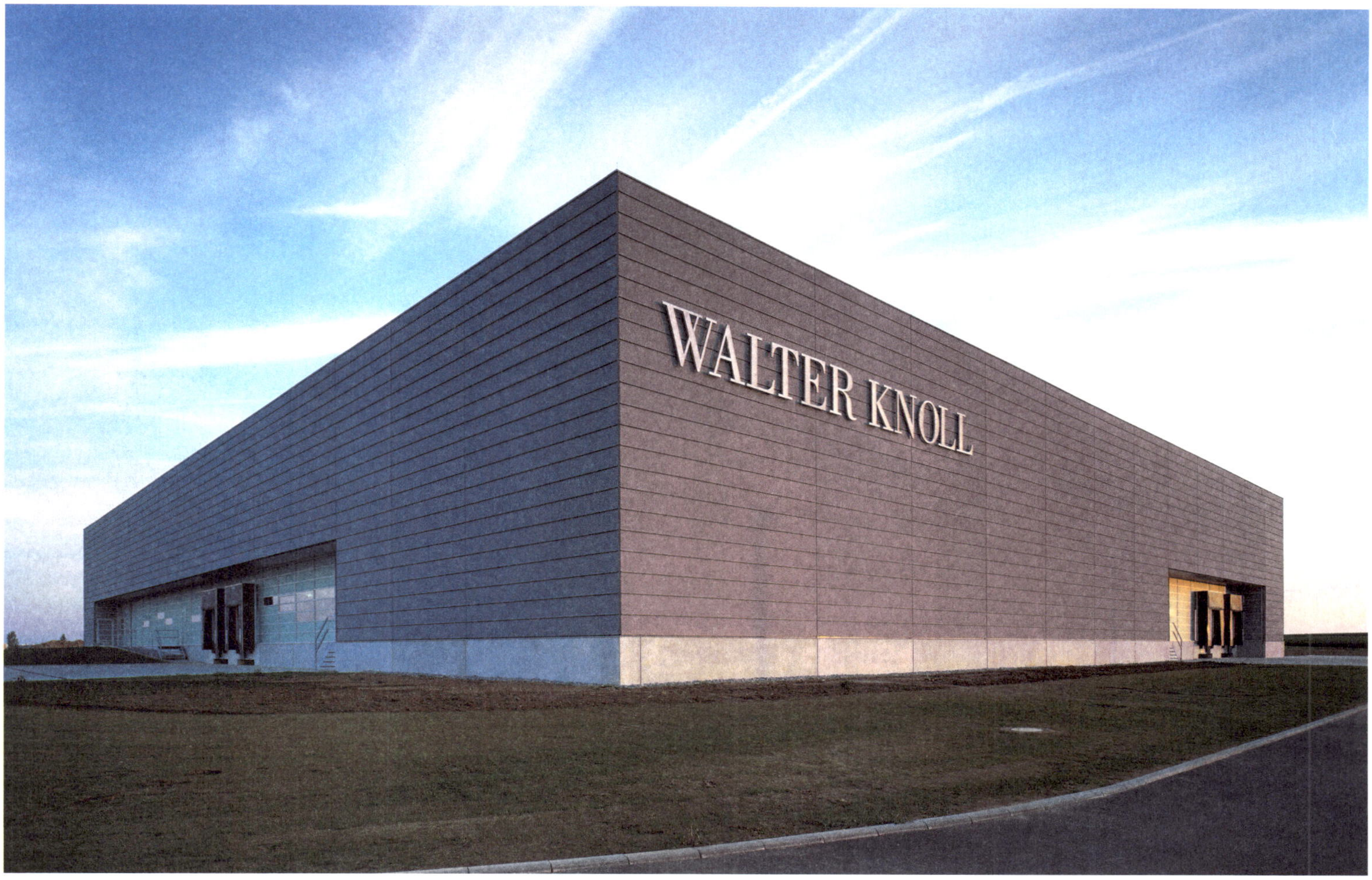

Mötzingen I factory, 2001

Today as ever, visitors are rewarded with a panoramic view over the picturesque roofscape of the old city and the beautiful Gäu. But the idyllic picture postcard soon reveals another side. Herrenberg, situated in Stuttgart's immediate catchment area and grown to an impressive 30,000 inhabitants,[19] excels by the same commercial dynamism for which the region is rightly famous[20] and which is also clearly evident in the industrial parks in the surrounding area. Industry and culture often appear side by side. Sindelfingen, the "car city" and an important factory location for Mercedes-Benz, and Tübingen, with its world-famous university, are Herrenberg's close neighbors. The city's

THIS UNIQUE BUILDING ENSEMBLE ALREADY CREATES A PURELY VISUAL ARC FROM THE FIRST TO THE THIRD MODERNITY AND THEREBY REVEALS SOMETHING OF THE SOUL OF THE WALTER KNOLL BRAND.

days as a sparse, remote area are long gone, as evidenced by the fact that the Stuttgart Airport is a mere half-hour away by car and that the Autobahn has a Herrenberg exit.

From the hilltop, it is possible to see the train station and the tracks that established the connection to Stuttgart and the modern age a little more than 100 years ago. Walter Knoll's company headquarters is located directly across from the station at Bahnhofstrasse 25 – a prominent and impressive glass and concrete structure that clearly stands out from its otherwise unspectacular surroundings. The mere fact that the company has remained in this traditional location is a clear sign of the continuing appreciation for the Knoll legacy. For a long time, there were plans to move the company to an industrial area – the usual story, with obvious advantages. Nevertheless, the idea was rejected, because in an anonymous location, it would have been impossible to realize the other, much loftier intention making the Walter Knoll brand visible in its entirety. That is why the existing factory was not demolished, in contrast to what is frequently the practice. On the contrary, construction work was begun to isolate the older building sections so that they could then enter into a dialog with the modern architecture. The prominent section of the historic building substance is the former Vollmöller textile factory, a handsome building from the imperial period. Its red and yellow bricks form a simple pattern that makes a charming contrast to the gleaming silver facade of the new construction. It is precisely these varied components that give this unique industrial building ensemble the appearance of a mature organism. In this way, it establishes a purely visual arc from the First to the Third Modernity, thereby providing a glimpse of the soul of the Walter Knoll brand.

Hansulrich Benz, who also designed the new multifunctional company building, managed to make differentiated statements about the furniture brand of modernity using very simple means. If you were to examine the exposed concrete more closely or run your hand across it, the smooth surface would remind you of marble, a sign of its high quality. The architect is striving for conciseness. His minimalist credo was summarized as, "It must be possible to describe a powerful architectural idea in a single sentence." In this case that means: "The concrete brace accommodates a recessed glass cube."[21] The most famous glass cube in architectural history, which was also the first, was the Bauhaus in Dessau, which immortalized its then director Walter Gropius. The new 50-meter-long, 16-meter-tall Walter Knoll building follows this exact same tradition of courage and clarity, and contains other references to world architecture as well. Take, for example, the legendary "unsupported glazed corner" that Gropius and his partner Adolf Meyer designed for the Fagus shoe last factory in Alfeld. This stroke of genius that still delights fans of modern architecture today – and a perfected version of which now reappeared in the entrance area of the new building – was also an early example of successful brand architecture,[22] symbolizing transparency and openness. With his "concrete brace," Hansulrich Benz ultimately resorted to a structural element that had caused a furor as part of a building of the Second Modernity, namely the UN Headquarters on New York City's East River – the headquarters of international understanding and the embodiment of international style.[23] What could be more fitting for Walter Knoll, a company that employs people from over two dozen countries and forms its own little polyglot universe?

Meanwhile, a coherent brand architecture came to be considered essential. No large company should be without one. The pioneers of this development were not, however, the economic heavyweights but the medium-sized companies, often family-owned, such as the aforementioned Fagus Factory,[24] the Braun company, which was much more than just a design mill, and also Wilkhahn, the company where Markus Benz learned the basics of brand culture. There he assimilated a principle that – like all simple principles – is difficult only when

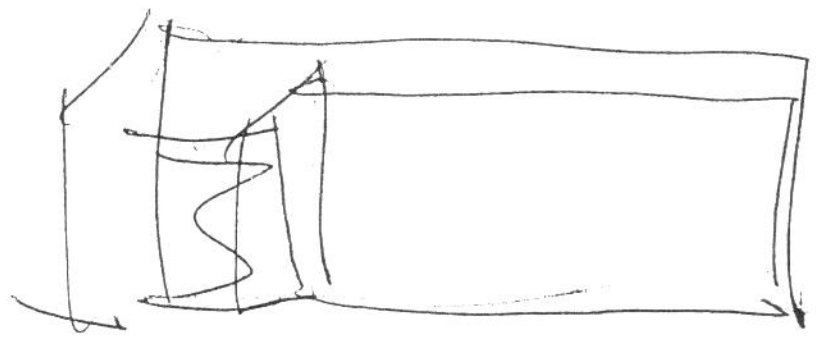

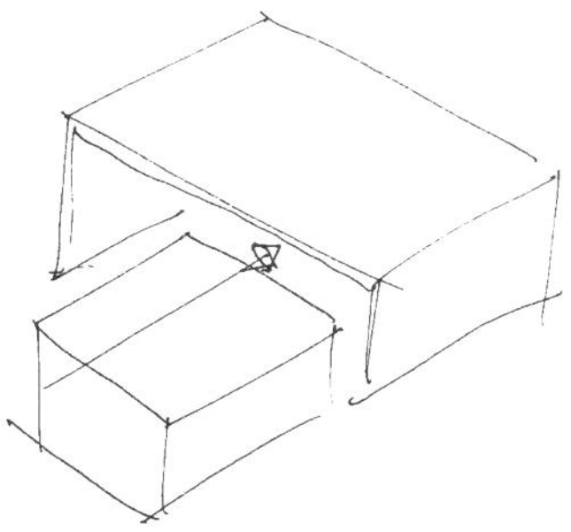

you try to implement it. The principle: all parts are equally important. As in a living organism, they form a balance and are constantly communicating with one another. Naturally, this also applies to the different areas of a company, and in a very literal sense. The transparency of processes between departments was implemented in the architecture. The four stories comprising around 1,000 square meters each were identical in their unfinished state, basically making them equal. There are no fixed walls, only concrete columns – a tribute to Ludwig Mies van der Rohe, who turned the open space in the hall of columns of the First Modernity into a structural world view. In this case, the avoidance of structural barriers was taken to the extreme. All the technical equipment was accommodated in the ceilings, which was itself a technical coup. This extremely versatile structure makes Walter Knoll's headquarters the prototype of a multifunctional building. It permits a flexible exchange in both directions: inward and outward. Markus Benz also invented a name for it: Brandland. It refers to a space where the brand can be experienced, which automatically makes it a space for encounters, where visitors meet the people who generate premium products and find out how they do it.

The glass facade represents the principle of exchange – not just symbolically but on a very practical level through its transparent and reflective properties. The building enters into a mutual relationship with its surroundings through its facade. Anyone who visits the company or walks past it can watch upholsters and other employees hard at work, making the train station forecourt into one of the liveliest spots in the city. On the other hand, the mirror-smooth surface also acts like an outdoor movie screen that reflects the weather and cloud conditions. The fact that the interior is drenched in light and provides an unobstructed view of the wide landscape around it are benefits that are almost too obvious to mention.

The targeted functionality extends to all aspects, including the responsible treatment of natural resources. Not only does the building have an optimal interior climate, but it also has an excellent energy balance, thanks to special climate control equipment on the south facade and other ingenious technical refinements. Sustainability is a central value at Walter Knoll. All new buildings, whether in Herrenberg or Mötzingen, are built to exemplary ecological standards. In fact, the company recently joined the ranks of "climate-neutral furniture manufacturers,"[25] meaning that even its production is also energy and environmentally friendly. It is based on a certain type of enlightened thinking and acting that takes into account as many relevant aspects of a task as possible – a holistic approach that understands the development of objects within their context, whether it is applied to a building, a chair, or the company as a whole. This central and incomparable mindset has been a recurring theme of modernity that has been cosistently adopted by Markus Benz.

---

19 ▶ When Walter Knoll first came to Herrenberg around the middle of the last century, it still had fewer than 4,000 inhabitants.

20 ▶ Several successful medium-sized enterprises and subsidiaries of international groups have settled in Herrenberg, including the American IT company Solectron and the Belgian company Omega Pharma.

21 ▶ Walter Knoll, Design Reloaded, Herrenberg 2006, p. 28.

22 ▶ Whereas the Fagus Factory itself was designed by the architect Eduard Werner, Gropius and Meyer were responsible for the administrative wing's spectacular glass facade. What mattered most to their customer, the entrepreneur Carl Benscheidt, was the visual effect. He deliberately chose the location within sight of the railway line.

23 ▶ The building was designed by an international architectural firm headed by the French-Swiss Le Corbusier and the Brazilian Oscar Niemeyer.

24 ▶ Even AEG which, beginning in 1907, was the first to develop a modern and comprehensive corporate identity and appointed Peter Behrens as its artistic consultant for this purpose, was still a family business run by the Director's son, Walther Rathenau.

25 ▶ See www.moebelmarkt.de/beitrag/dgm-klimapakt-walter-knoll-ist-klimaneutraler-moebelhersteller (04/18/2017)

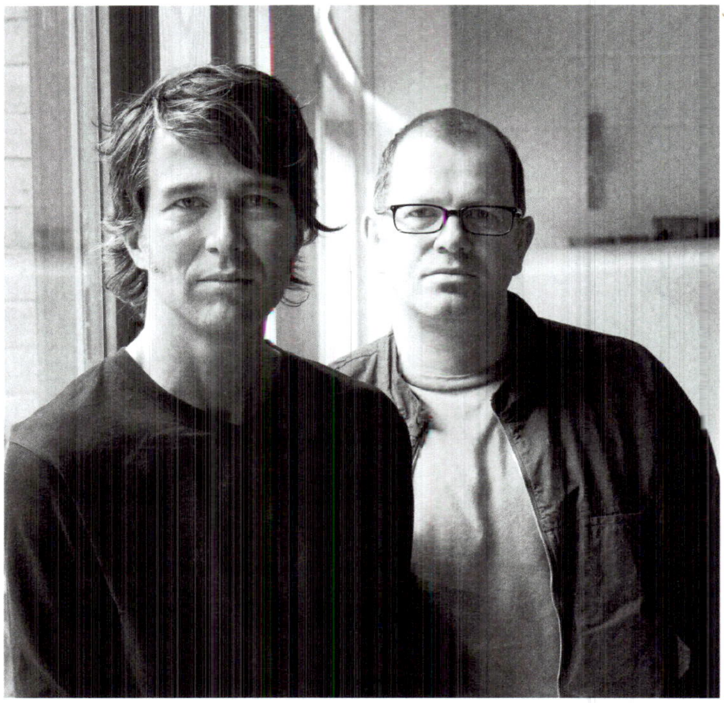

Luke Pearson and Tom Lloyd

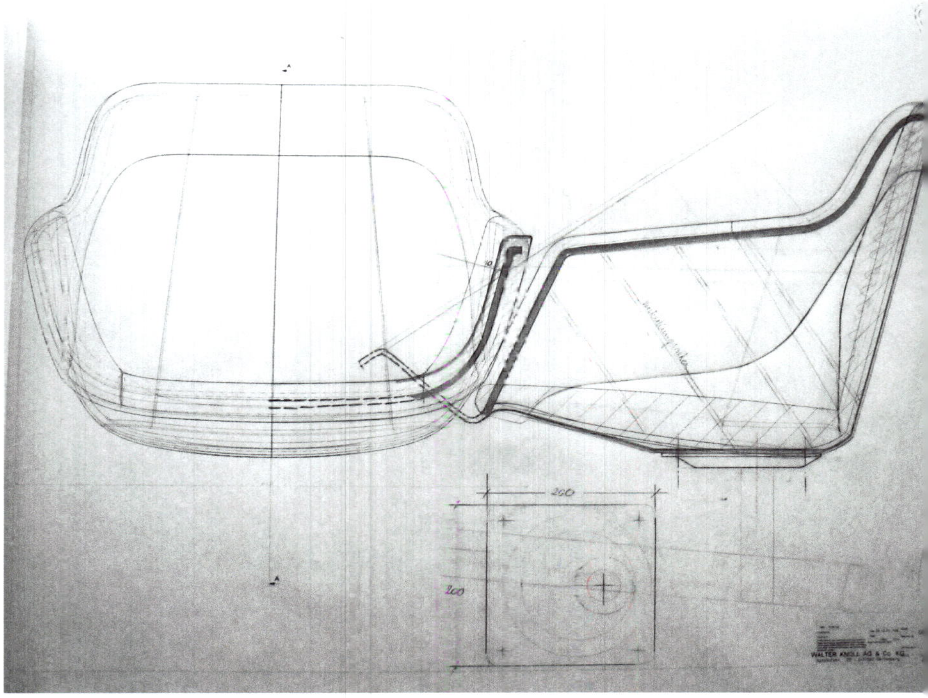

Sketch of the armchair Turtle

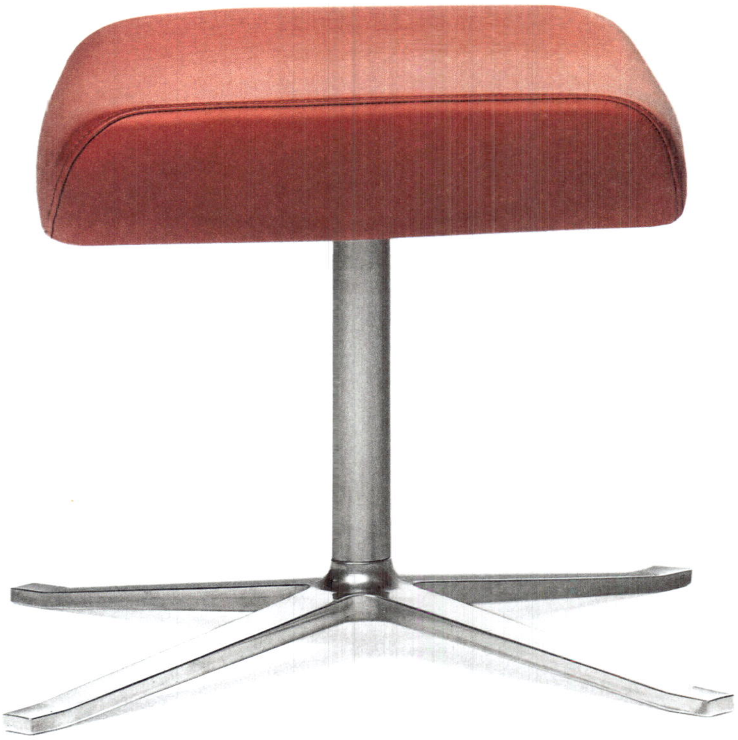

MASTER OF THE BUCKET

PearsonLloyd carries on the great English studio tradition. The London design duo made a name for itself in the aircraft industry and combines technical and stylistic mastery.

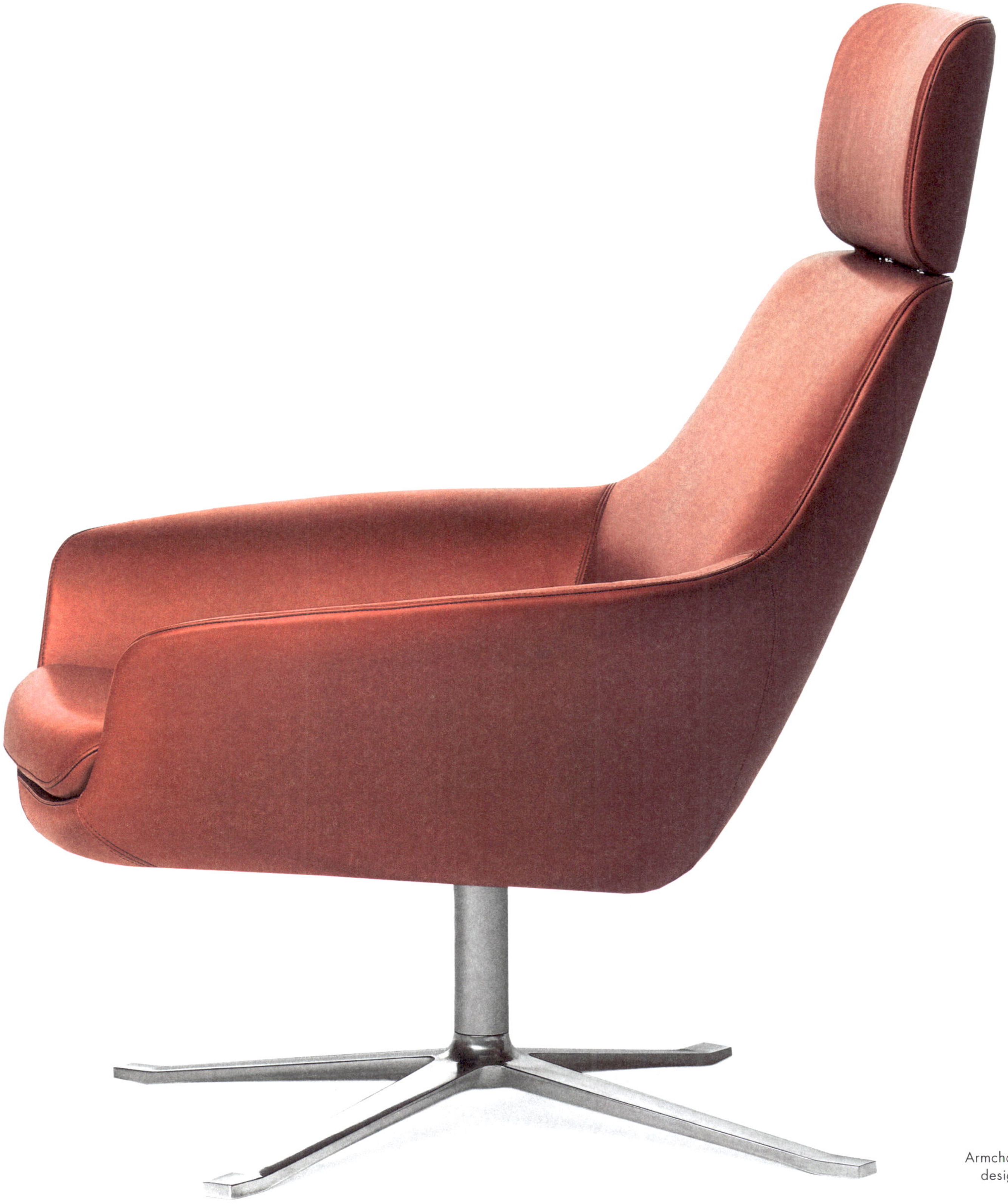

Armchair with stool Oscar, design by PearsonLloyd, 2002

THE BEST OF THE BEST

The summer of 2006 was unforgettable. Although the German national soccer team did not win the World Cup on its home turf, it did manage to turn the tournament into a lively celebration. Overnight, the old clichées disappeared and the image of Germany's brand took a positive turn. It was not just the young team's refreshing playing style or the general good mood that contributed to this impression. The twelve stadiums – all of which had either been completely renovated or newly constructed – showed the Federal Republic in a new light, as a welcoming host, an innovative country, and leading proponent of the Third Modernity. Among the impressive designs, there were a few that stood out, such as the Munich stadium that the Swiss architects Herzog & de Meuron had clad with illuminated foil cushions and, of course, the Olympiastadion in Berlin, whose floating roof lent the powerful structure a lightness of being. The less well-known but similarly spectacular new building in Frankfurt am Main also caused a sensation. With a roof structure consisting of 44 supports, tensioned wire cables, and a video cube suspended above the playing field, it was the epitome of high-tech made in Germany – or, more specifically, made in Swabia. This miracle of stadium and media technology was the work of two former employees of Fritz Leonhardt, creator of the Stuttgart Television Tower – the symbol of that blend of clever architecture and engineering ingenuity so typical of the region.[26]

THE "MEISTERKREIS" HAS OVER 70 MEMBERS, INCLUDING TRADITIONAL COMPANIES SUCH AS MEISSEN, MONTBLANC, AND LEICA. SOON AFTER ITS FOUNDING, WALTER KNOLL BECAME PART OF THIS ELITE GROUP.

Another innovation was introduced inside the World Cup stadiums: VIP areas,[27] a customized feature that stadium operators are offering the clubs. Boxes, also called lounges, are rented out and can be used by companies for entertaining customers and events. It was the birth of the hospitality business model. These enclaves of superior views and sophisticated requirements were, of course, carefully designed. One of the first VIP areas had appeared in Stuttgart a few years earlier in the Gottlieb Daimler Stadium, now the Mercedes-Benz Arena. As part of the expansion and modernization of the grandstand in 2001, business boxes and business seats were installed, along with suitable restaurant and meeting areas. All the boxes were furnished with models from Walter Knoll. In other lounges as well, upholstered furniture from Herrenberg soon provided the VIP seating in almost all the showcase stadiums that were built for the World Cup.

The year 2006 was a turning point for Germany's reputation.[28] But there were other changes during this period that might have been less spectacular but expressed a serious change in mentality. It was no secret that Germany was a top performer in many areas. But within its own borders, people had long found it difficult to be proud of these accomplishments. Although "Made in Germany" was considered a first-class seal of approval worldwide, manufacturers of premium products found no support at home. In other countries, producers took the offensive – for example, France, where the luxury industry had long ago banded together to form its own trade association.[29] As strange as it may seem, the Federal Republic had yet to discover the existence of such a model sector. There is still no commonly used term for it today. So in 2011, it was high time that the "Meisterkreis" (Master Circle) be formed. This association represents high-end German companies in the cultural and creative industries for the purpose of promoting the "culture of excellence" for which it stands. The "Meisterkreis" now has over 70 members, including traditional companies such as Meissen, Montblanc, and Leica. But newer companies are also represented, including the fashion label Talbot Runhof. The bulk of its members are medium-sized companies – for example, Sennheiser, a leading headphone brand and still a family-owned company. Walter Knoll soon became part of this elite group, because the goals of the "Meisterkreis" were in line with the company's own goals. They both stood for constant innovation, but also for the preservation of traditional values, especially in the area of craftmanship – a fine line that everyone has to walk to achieve perfection, and which makes the "Meisterkreis" a club for the inimitable. Markus Benz, a member of the "Meisterkreis" Board of Directors, has expressed it as follows: "We deliver an economic-cultural performance – Made in Germany, at its best." Together with the German Foreign Ministry, the "Meisterkreis" founded the "German Contemporary Excellence" campaign, which launched a first-rate exhibition representing avant-garde businesses. The exhibition has been touring major cities around the world since 2017. Germany's high-end industry, which has received little

AS THE FURNITURE BRAND OF MODERNITY, WALTER KNOLL IS ONE OF THE MOST EXCLUSIVE ADDRESSES FOR HIGH-CALIBER PROJECTS, IN BOTH THE PRIVATE AND PUBLIC SECTORS.

attention for such a long time, is arguably one of the most diverse of its kind.[30] There were good reasons for that. Throughout the previous century, Germany had been one of the most innovative countries, from the First to the Third Modernity. The history of Walter Knoll could be considered a prime example.[31]

As the furniture brand of modernity, Walter Knoll is one of the most exclusive addresses for high-caliber projects, in both the private and public sectors. Walter Knoll understands how to adequately express the identity of its clients in furniture. In the public sector, it is a matter of brand identity; in the private sector, it involves personal identity. With over 150 years of experience in furniture design and development, combined with expertise and a feel for quality, materials, and colors, the company has become the leading provider of high-quality furnishings – for headquarters, showrooms, luxury hotels, and private homes.

One project in particular exemplifies this high level of perfomance and forms a bridge between the tradition of modernity and the future: the "Thomas Mann House" in Los Angeles, which was officially opened by the Federal Republic of Germany in June 2018 as a new cultural meeting place. The house in which the author and Nobel Prize laureate lived with his wife in American exile from 1942 to 1952 was on the point of being demolished when it was purchased and fully restored. At the opening ceremony, Foreign Minister Frank-Walter Steinmeier emphasized its considerable cultural and political significance by calling it "the Oval Office of the émigré opposition"[32] during the Second World War. It was designed in the glazed, "white modernity" style according to plans by Julius Ralph Davidson, a native of Berlin who had settled in Los Angeles as an architect. Even then, the Knoll dynasty was already represented. Davidson included furniture from the new Hans Knoll company in its furnishings. In the course of the restoration work, a deliberate decision was made not to restore the furnishings to their original condition, but instead to translate the cosmopolitan modernity of the original design into the aesthetics of the present. For this ambitious scheme, only companies that guaranteed the highest level of creativity and craftsmanship were considered – including Walter Knoll.[33] "We are pleased to be part of this community of shared values," said Markus Benz, "and to contribute to preserving a monument of recent German cultural history as a bridge."

---

26 ▶ The engineers Jörg Schlaich and Rudolf Bergermann were already involved in the supporting structure of the roof of the Munich Olympic Stadium in 1972. At that time, the Stuttgarters Günter Behnisch and Frei Otto were the head architects.

27 ▶ The concept of "VIP" was used to transfer the box principle to other areas. The term originated in the early 20th century in connection with wealthy Russian emigrants. In 1927, airline tickets for the Paris–London line were sold in the Paris newspaper of the Russian diaspora with the designation "vesima imenitaya persona" (very eminent person). This established a precedent that was then carried over into English as "very important person" and eventually started popping up at train stations, rock concerts, and on many other occasions.

28 ▶ Like any cultural transformation, this was also expressed linguistically. The German term "Mannschaft" was suddenly being used internationally as a synonym for a strong team spirit. As with "Vorsprung durch Technik," its many consonants and the harsh sound were already part of its secret of success.

29 ▶ The exclusive club is called Comité Colbert. Other countries have comparable organizations. In England it is Walpole, in Italiy it is the Fondazione Altagamma, and in Spain it is the Círculo Fortuny.

30 ▶ In terms of figures, the "Meisterkreis" represents a branch of trade with far more than 100,000 employees and an added value estimated at over 80 billion euros.

31 ▶ It is no coincidence that the goals of the "Meisterkreis" are similar to those of the Stuttgart "Landesgewerbeamt" and of the "Deutscher Werkbund," of which Walter Knoll was also a member.

32 ▶ Jürgen Schmieder: "Im Oval Office des deutschen Exils" (In the Oval Office of German Exile), in: "Süddeutsche Zeitung," 06/19/2018

33 ▶ In addition to Walter Knoll, companies like Thonet, Vitra, Jan Kath, and Occhio are also represented.

THE PERFECT SEAT

PearsonLloyd was responsible for the bucket seat's spectacular renaissance at Walter Knoll and fully exploited this classic genre in numerous versions.

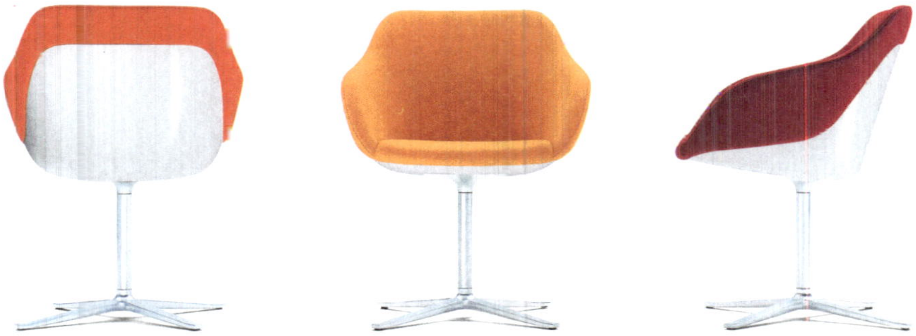

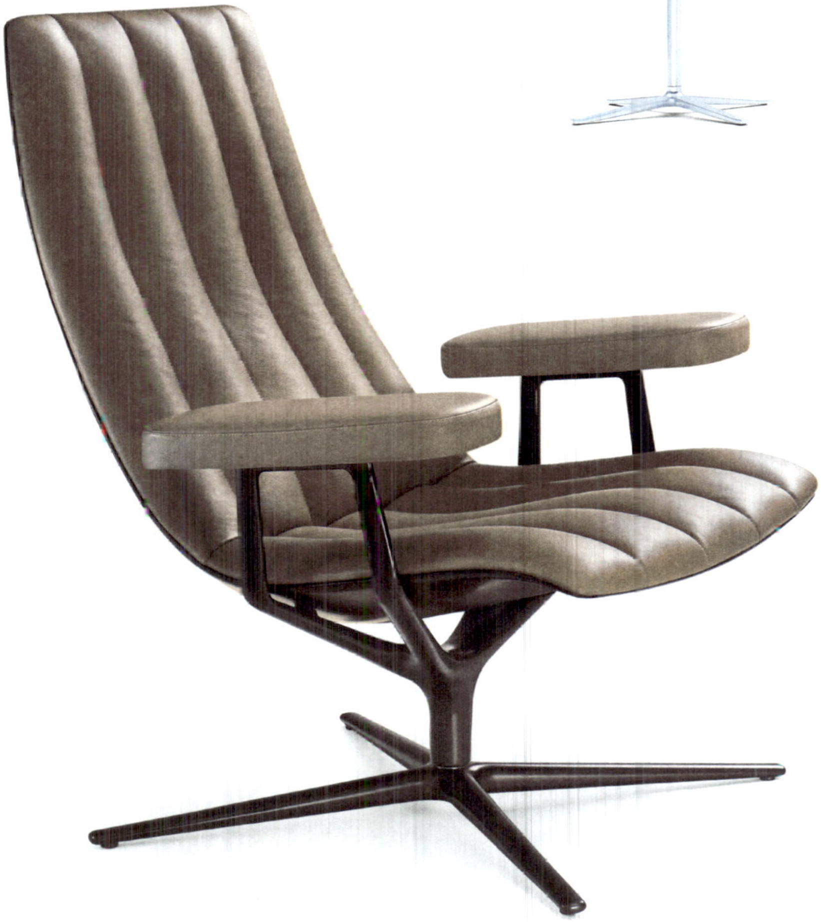

Armchair Turtle,
design by PearsonLloyd,
2004

Armchair Healey Lounge,
design by PearsonLloyd,
2014

Armchair Healey Soft,
design by PearsonLloyd,
2017

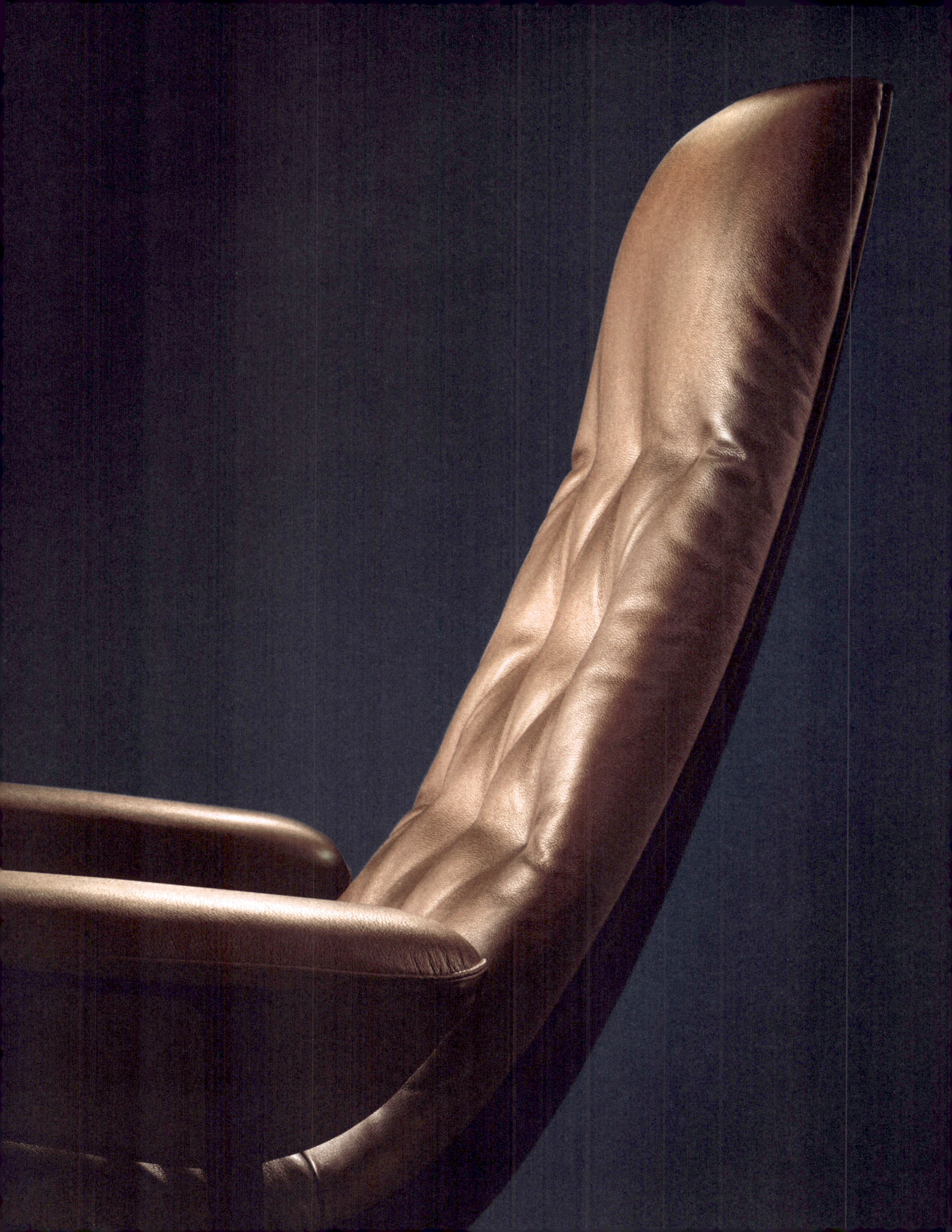

WORK MOTIFS

Excellent training and a pleasant working atmosphere were always among the fundamental principles at Walter Knoll. The company places tremendous value on core technical capabilities such as upholstering and sewing. But in the area of leather-working as well – where the comapny originally got its start – skilled craftsmanship goes hand in hand with state-of-the-art technology.

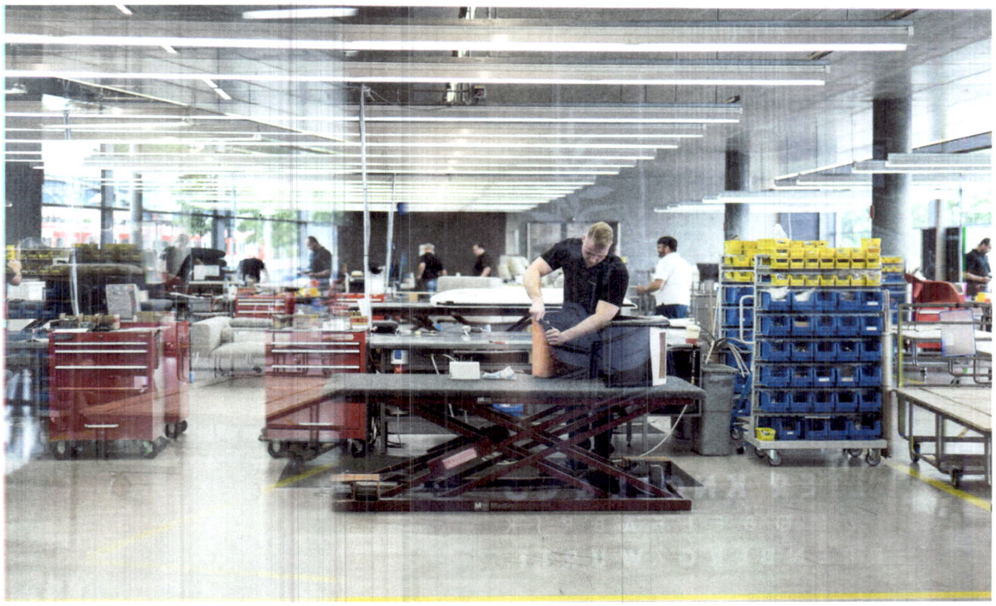

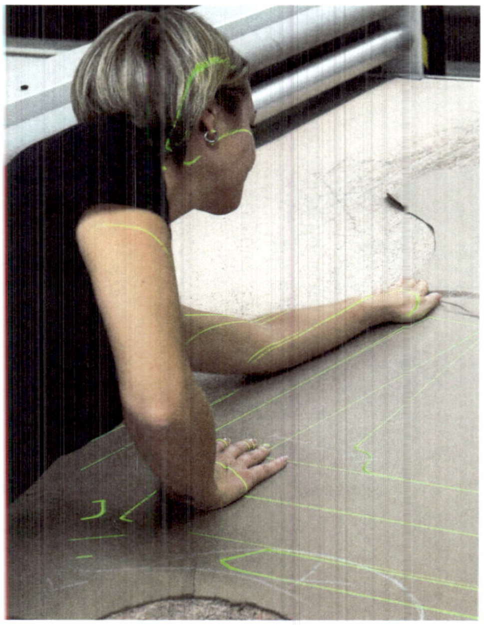

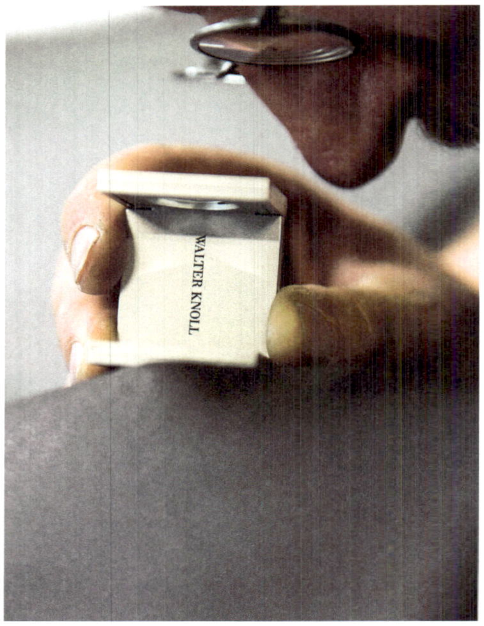

Uphostery workshop visible from the street, Herrenberg

Cutting leather using a laser CAD cutter

Leather inspection

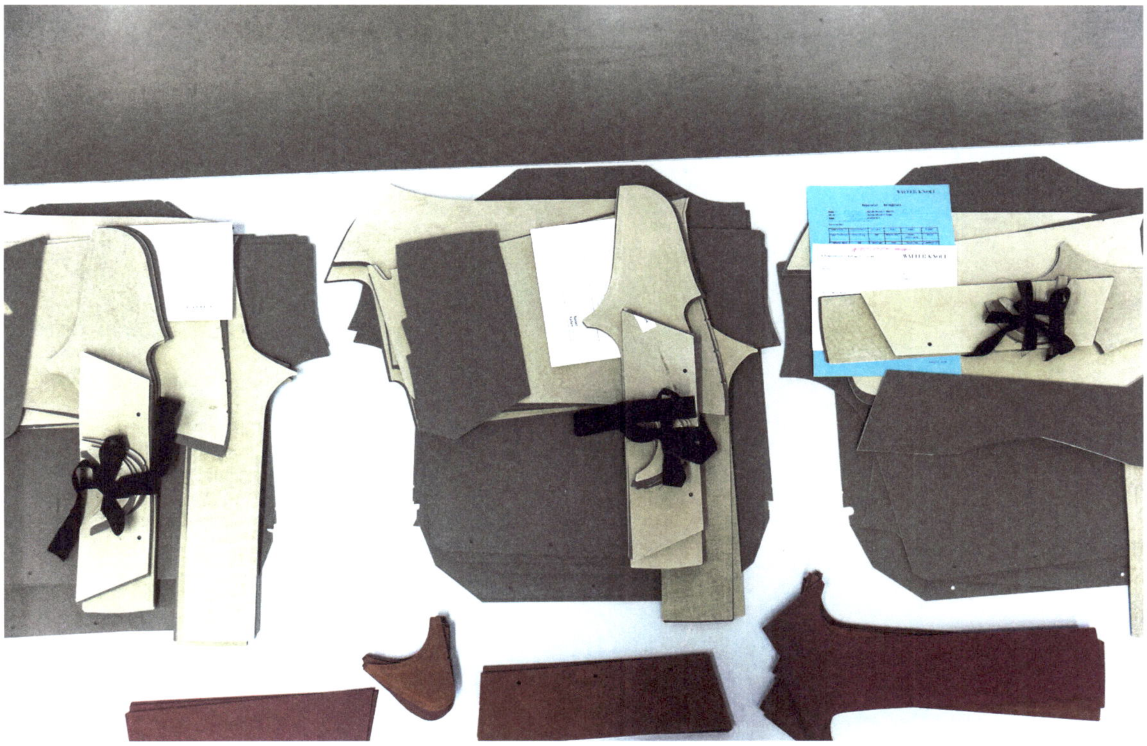

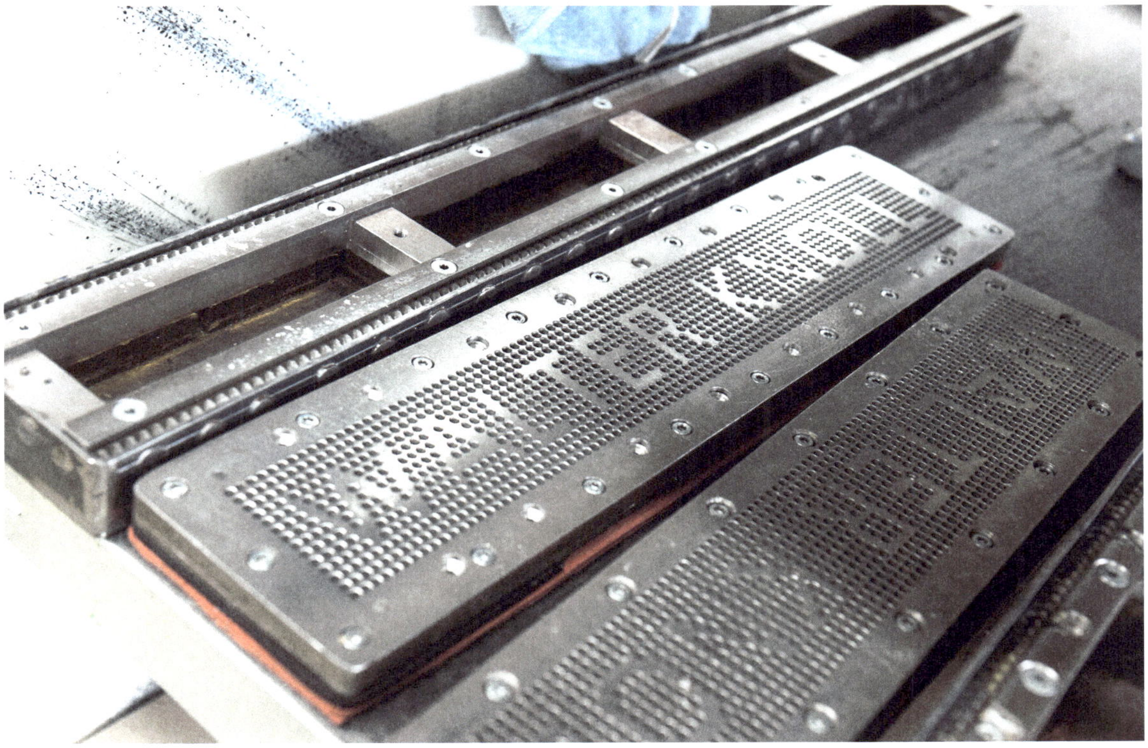

Cut leather

Leather stamps

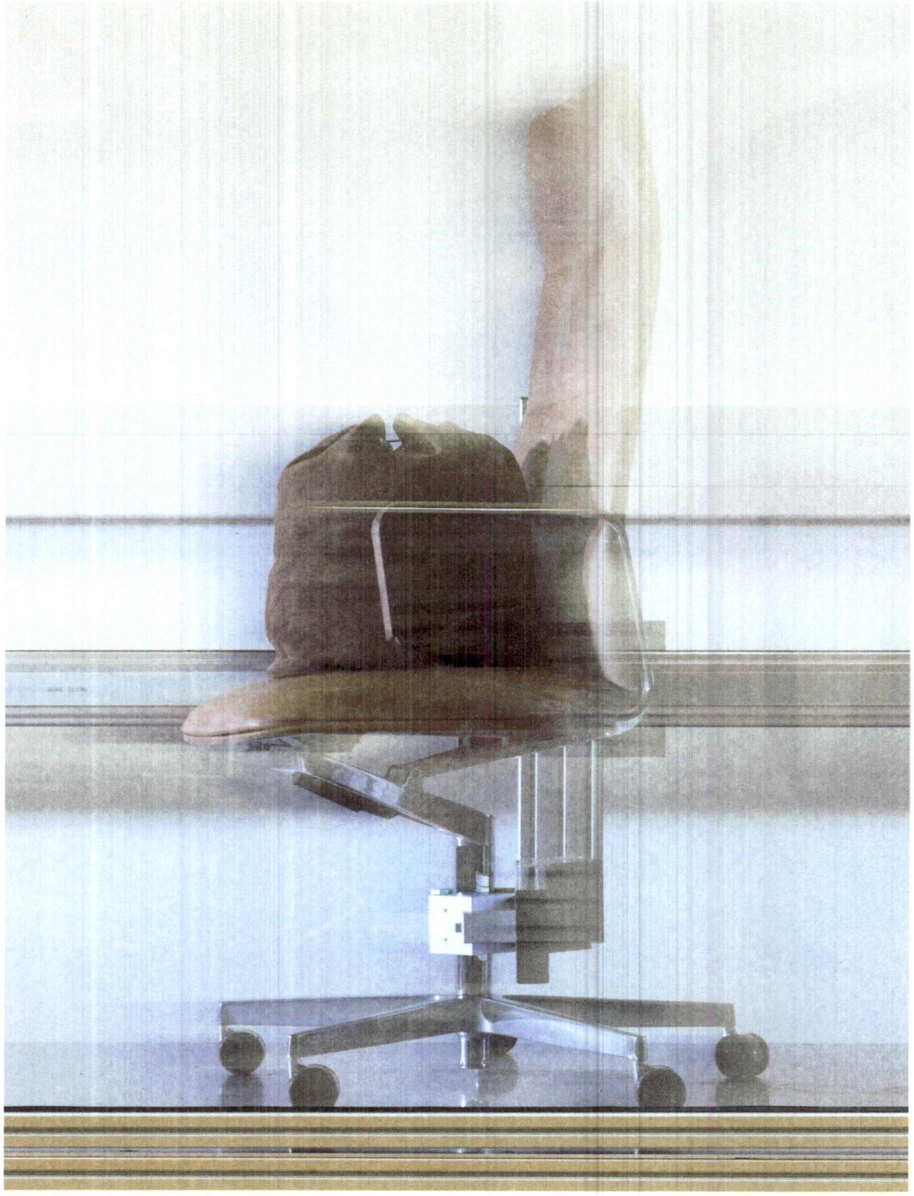

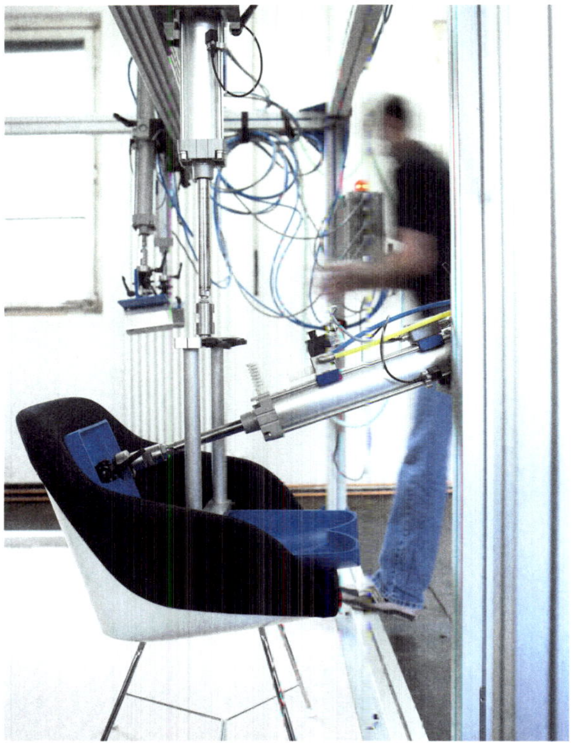

Material inspection: stress tests

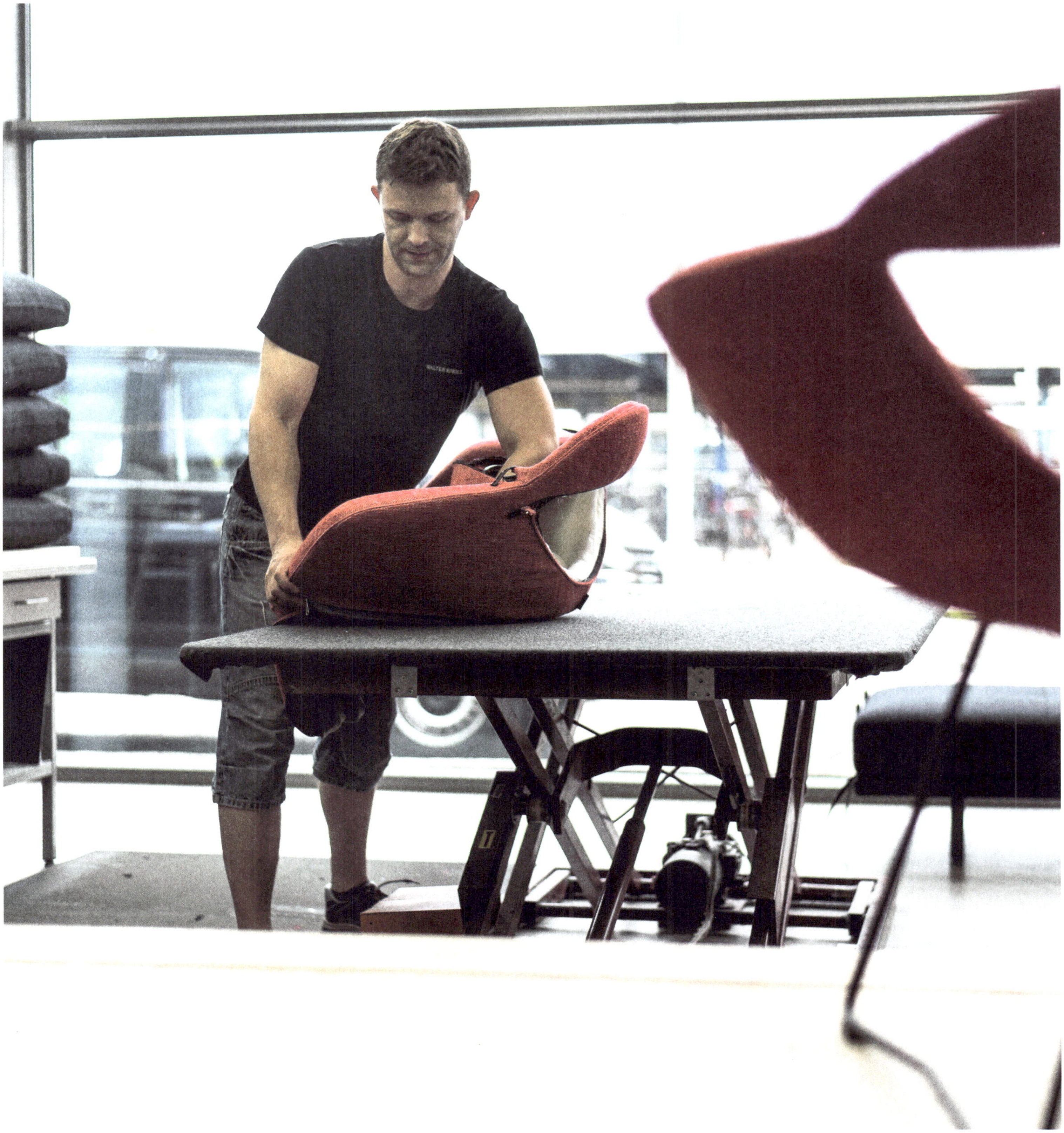

Upholsterer

GLOBAL PRESENCE

The 21st century saw the beginning of the company's globalization phase and its entry into the world of large-scale projects – a new chapter in the history of Walter Knoll as the brand of architects.

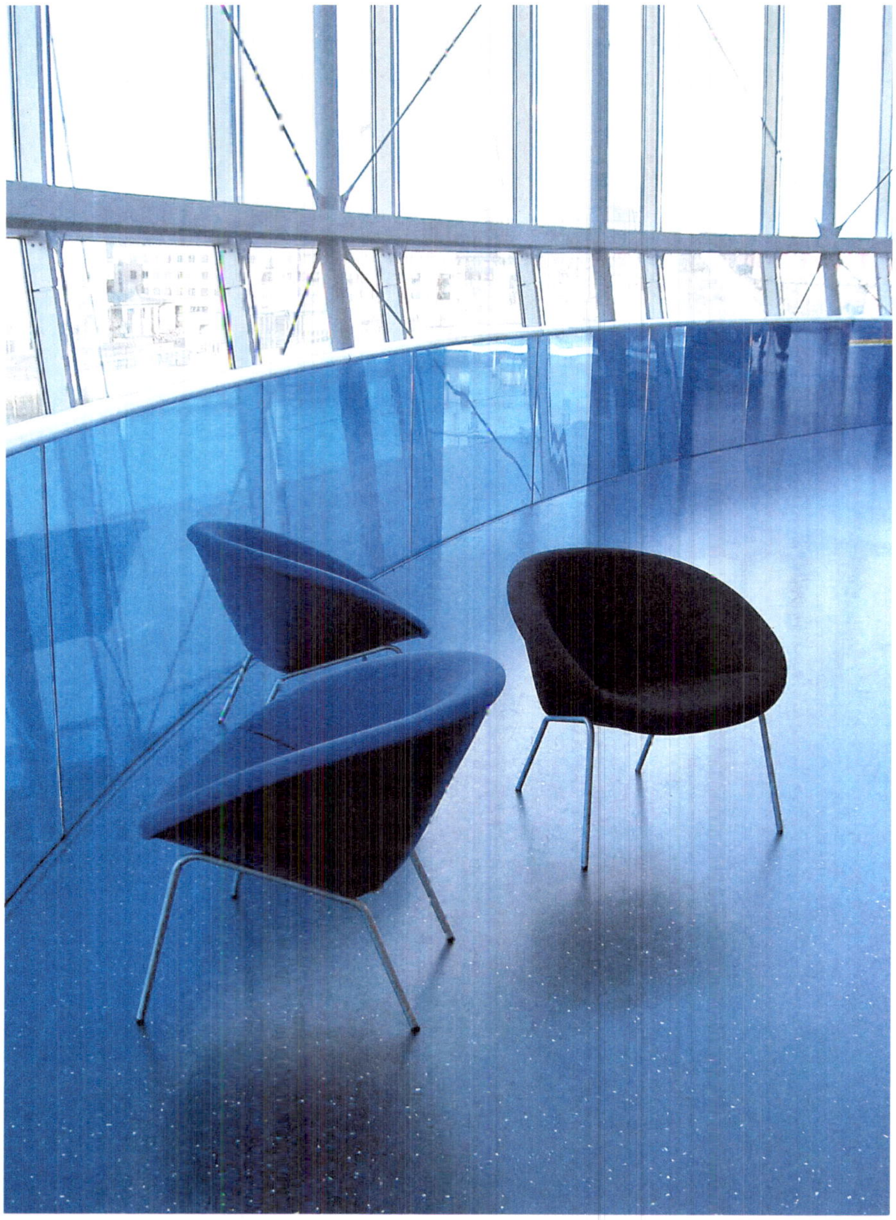

Interior of the concert hall The Sage, Gateshead, furnished with armchairs 369, design by Walter Knoll Team, 1956

The Sage concert hall, Gateshead, architecture by Foster + Partners, 2004

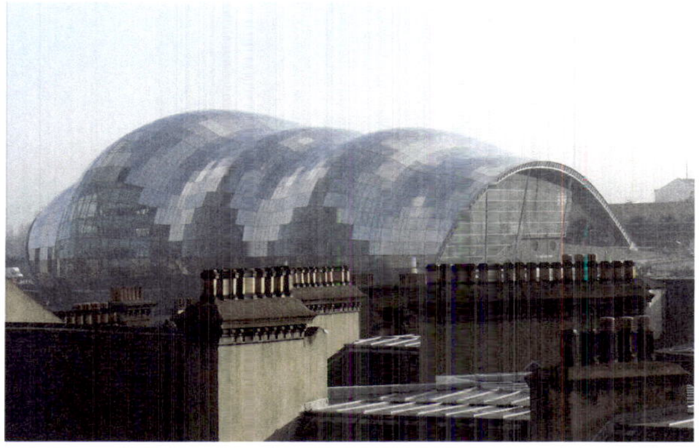

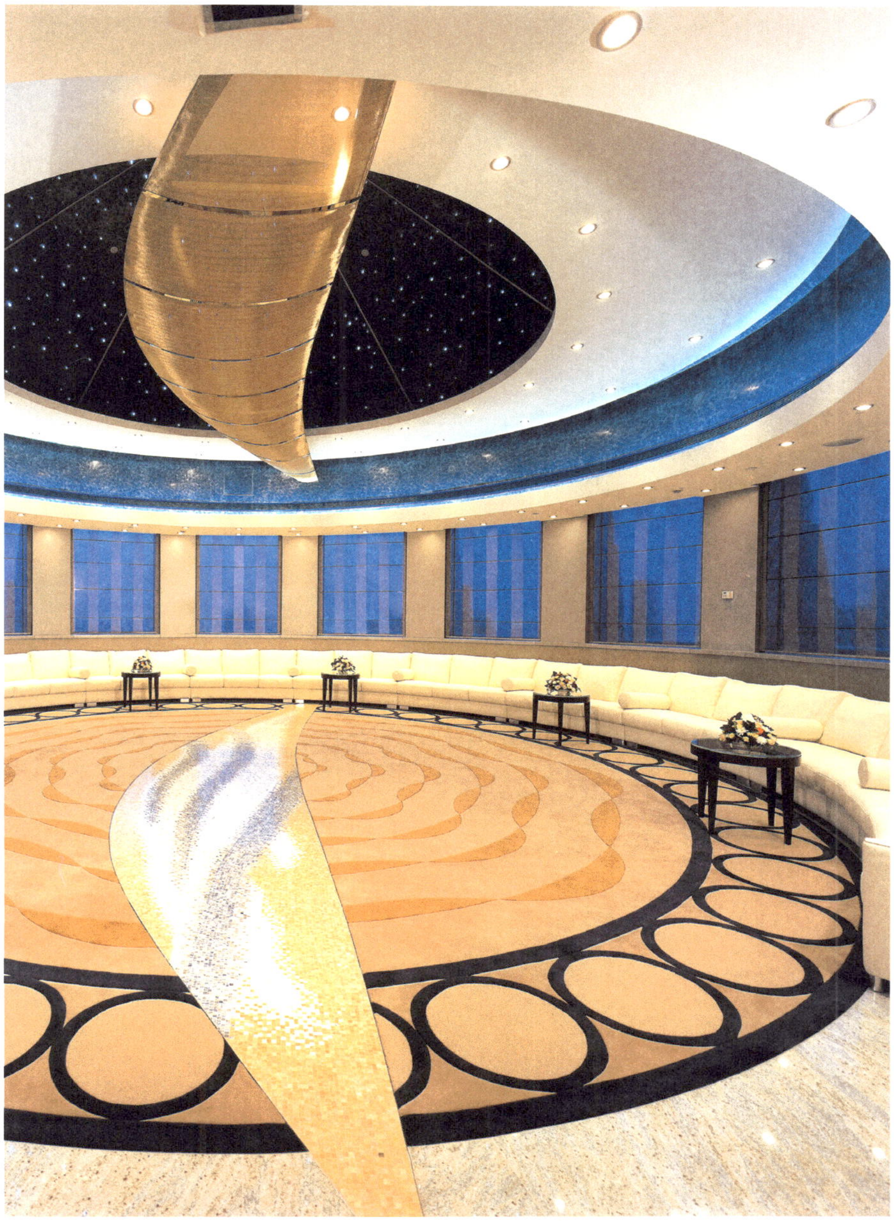

Interior of the Commercial Bank of Dubai,
furnished with specially crafted
round sofa Lazlo,
2000

Commercial Bank of Dubai,
United Arab Emirates,
architecture by Hamilton International LLC,
2002

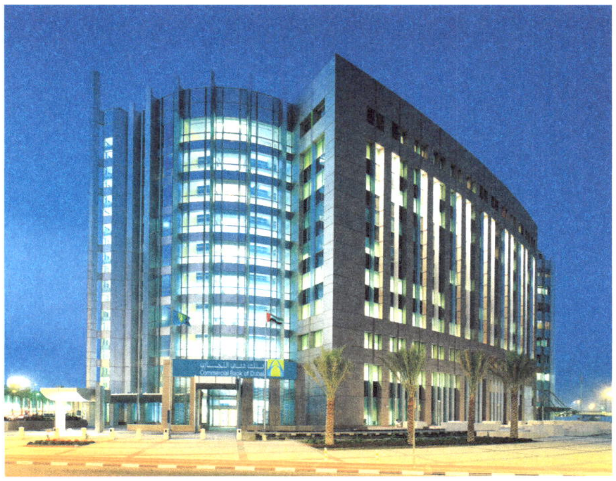

CORPORATE ARCHITECTURE

When the automotive industry created iconic museums dedicated to its own history, Walter Knoll's furniture was the first choice for the interiors.

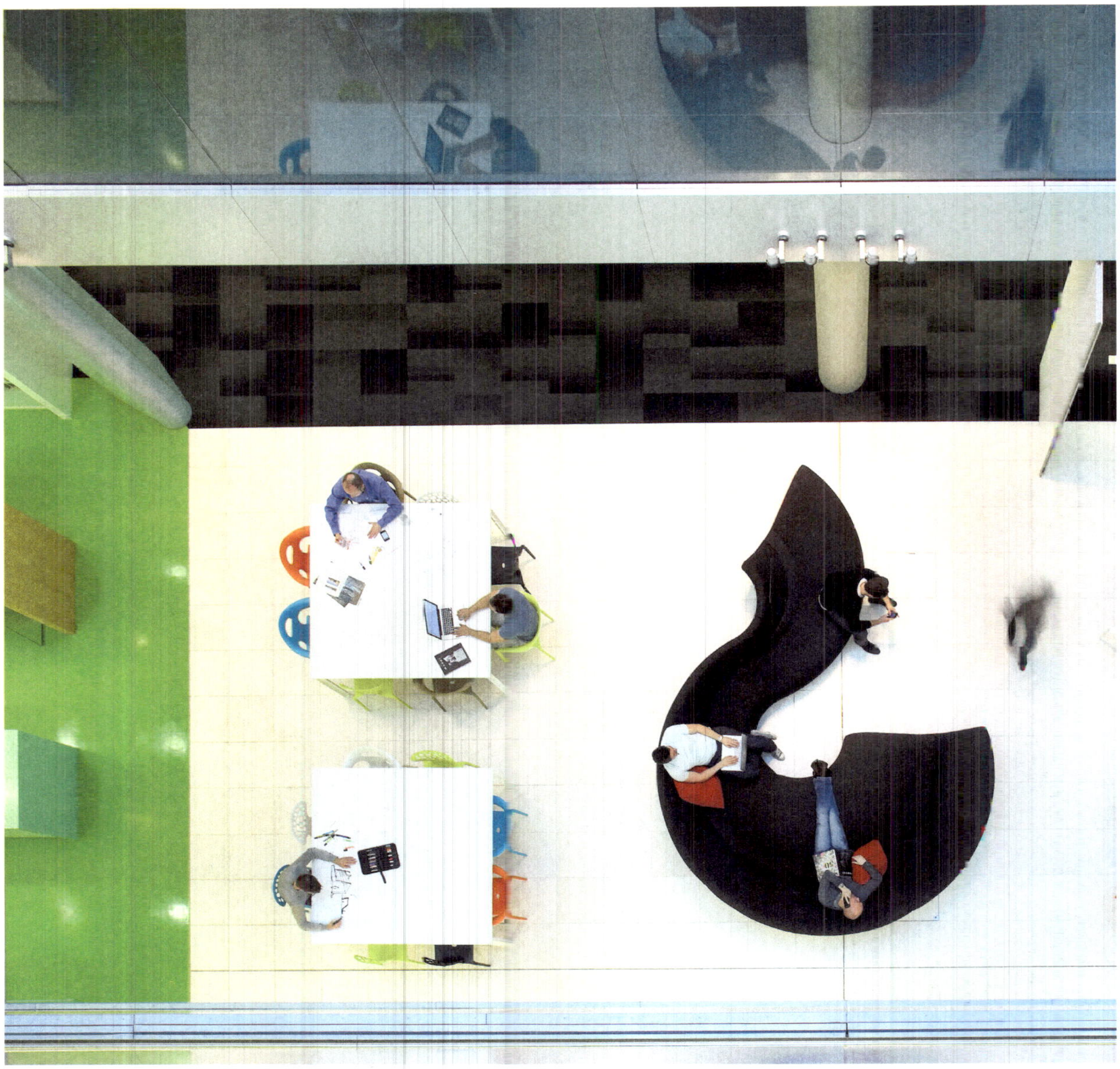

Interior of the HOK architectural firm, London, furnished with a Circle sofa

Mercedes-Benz Museum, architecture by UNStudio/Ben van Berkel, Stuttgart, 2006

Interior of the Mercedes-Benz Museum, furnished with Circle sofa, design by UNStudio/Ben van Berkel, 2005

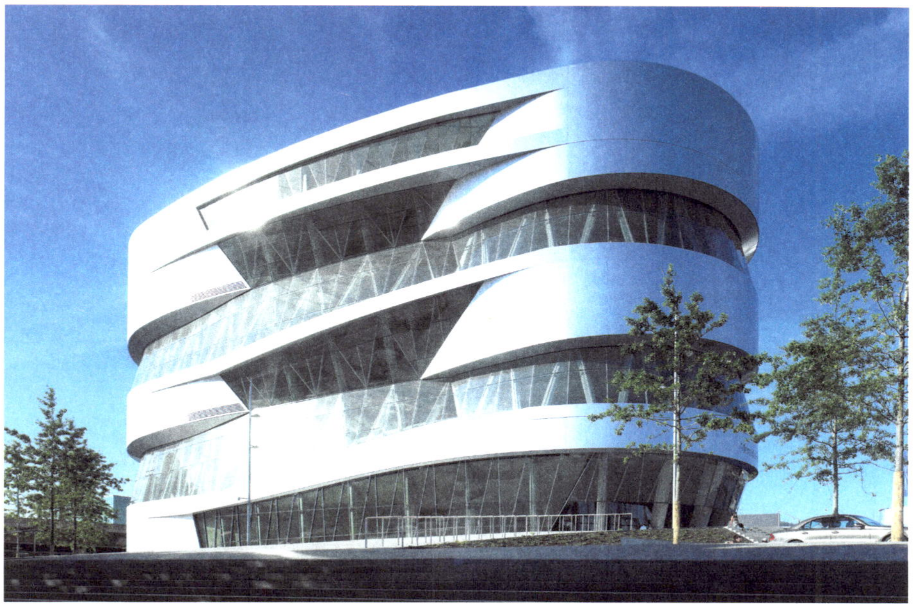

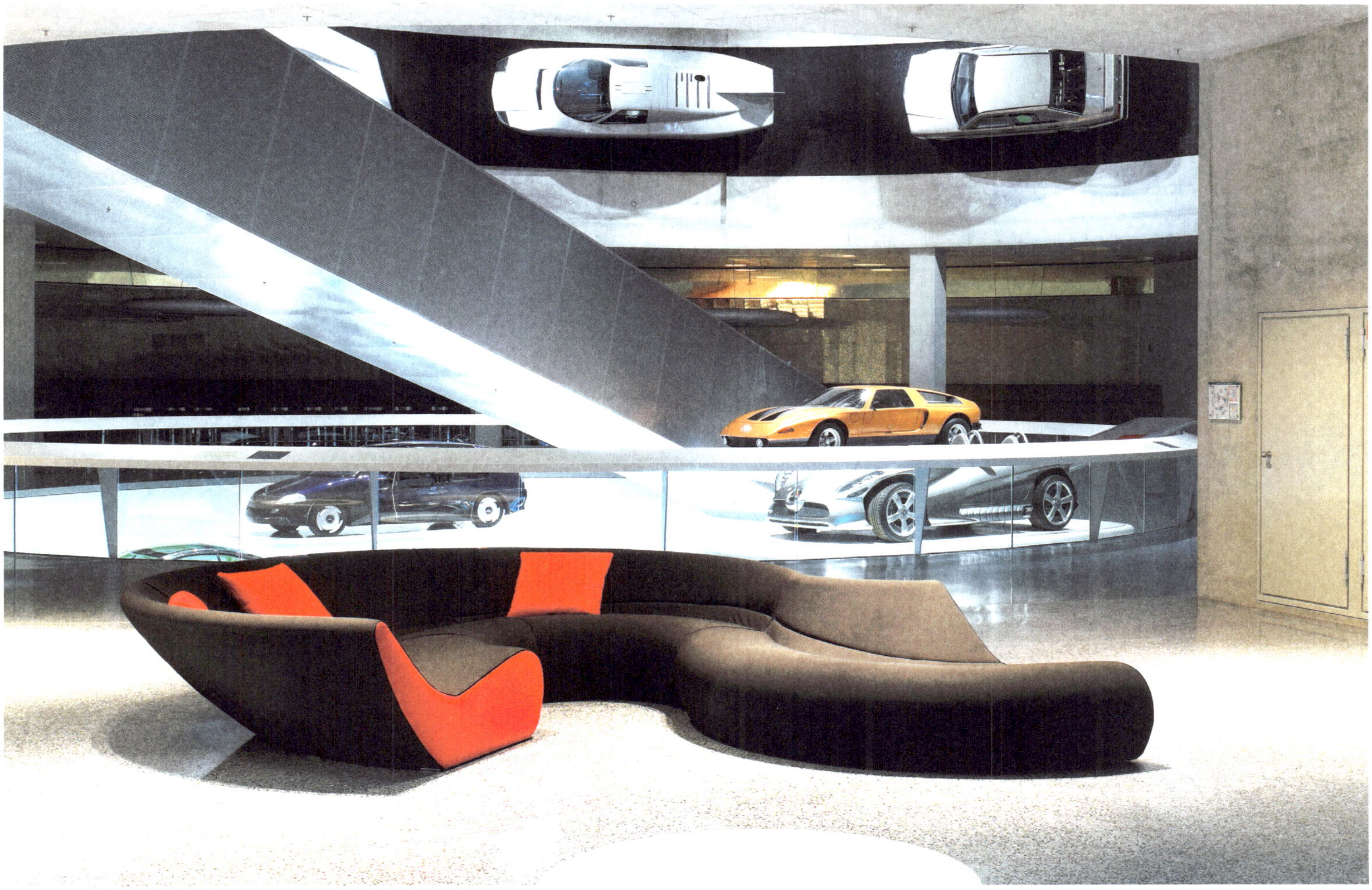

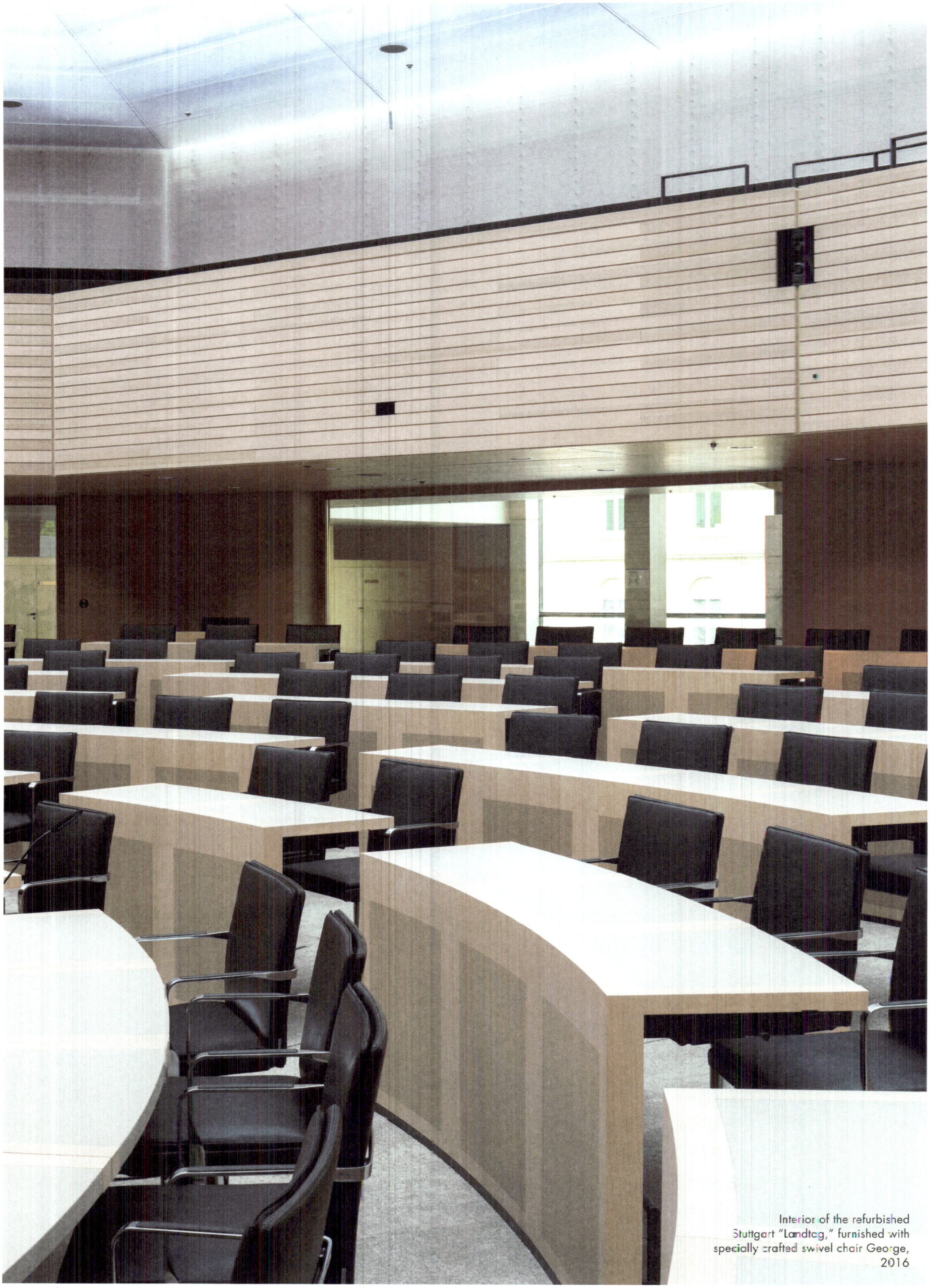

Interior of the refurbished Stuttgart "Landtag," furnished with specially crafted swivel chair George, 2016

SHAPING DEMOCRACY

For the refurbishment of the Stuttgart "Landtag" (State Parliament), an iconic building from the Second Modernity, seating furniture from Herrenberg was used. The furnishing of parliamentary buildings is also a company tradition.

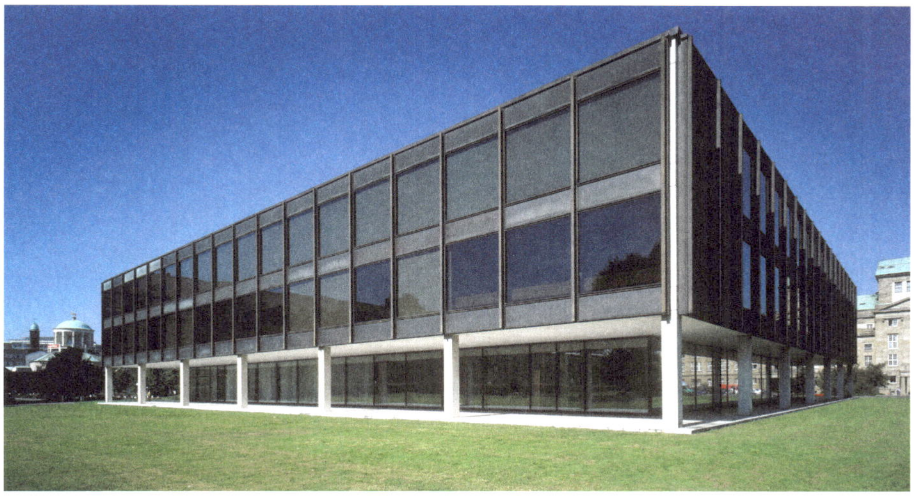

Stuttgart "Landtag" building, architecture by Horst Linde, 1961, architects of refurbished building, Staab Architekten, 2016

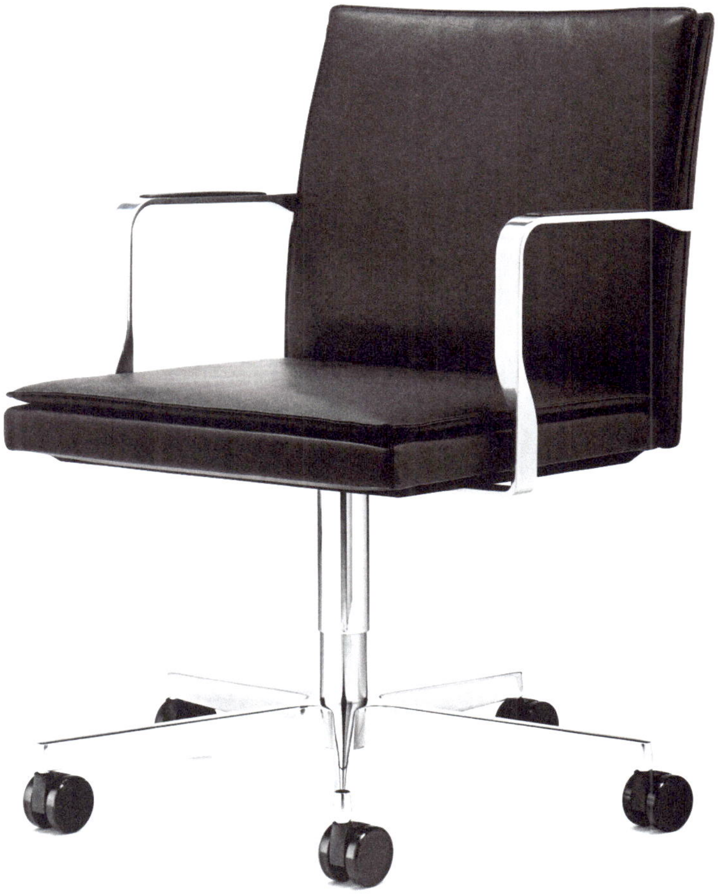

Swivel chair George

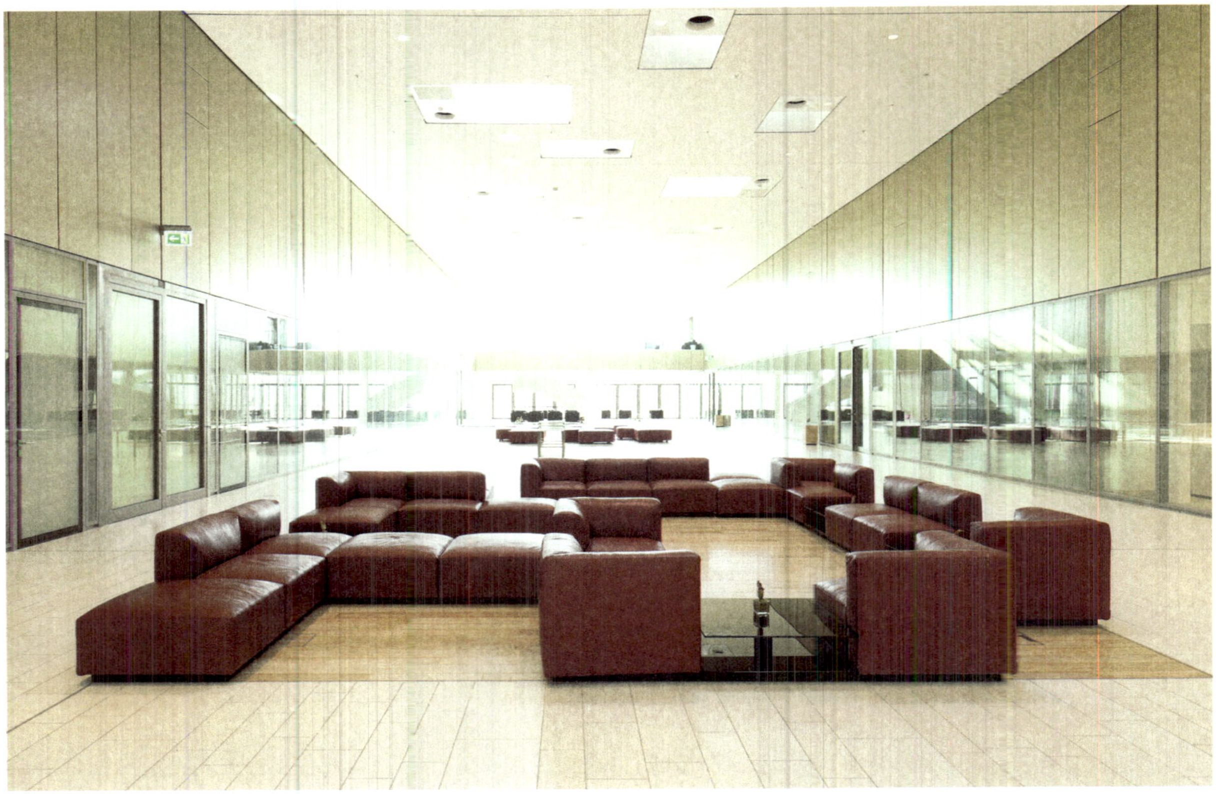

Interior of ThyssenKrupp Quartier, Essen, furnished with sofa Living Landscape 730, design by EOOS, 2008

Interior of ThyssenKrupp Quartier, Essen, furnished with Foster 500

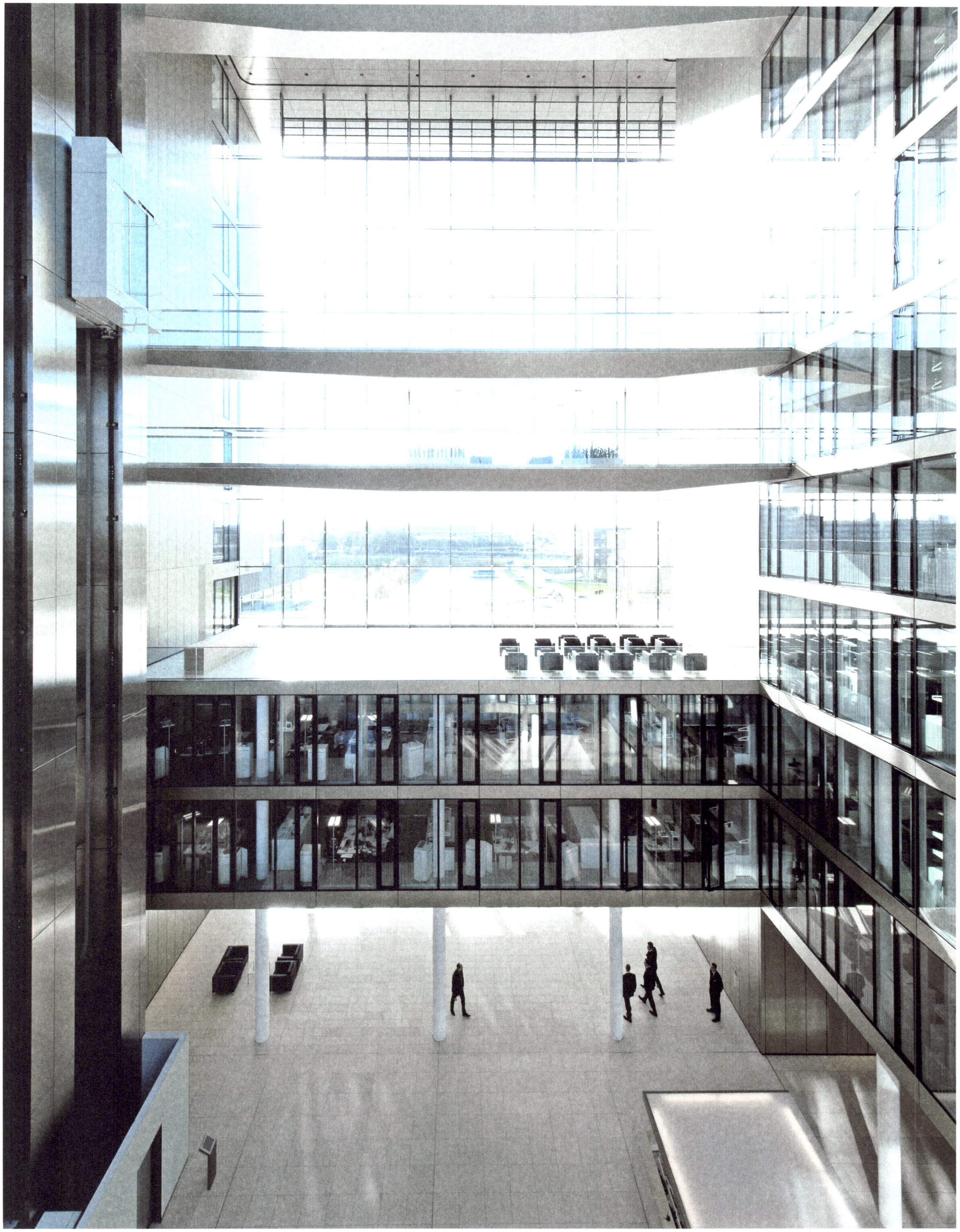

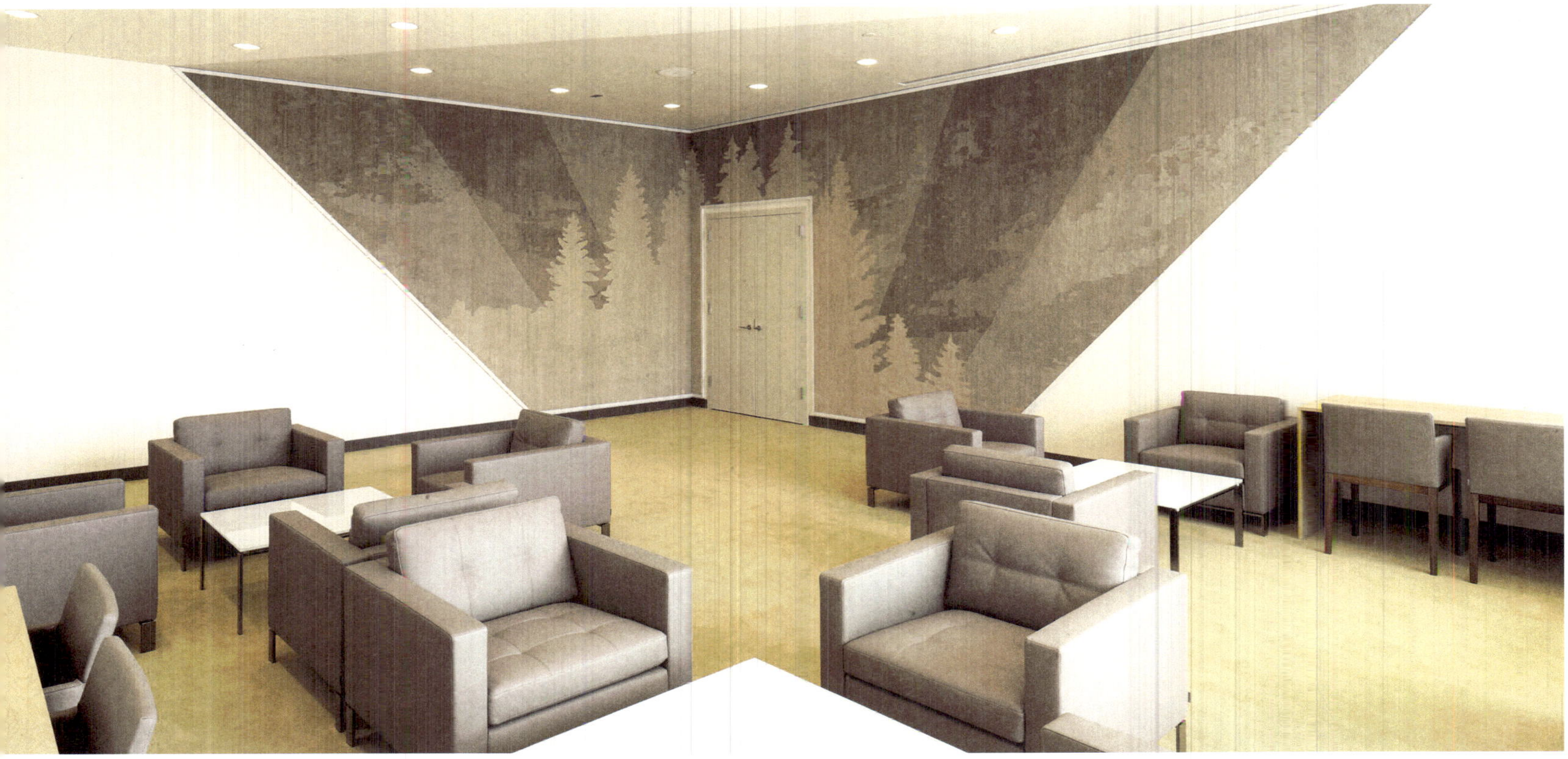

Quiet Room in the UN Headquarters, New York, furnished with armchairs Foster 502 and chairs Andoo

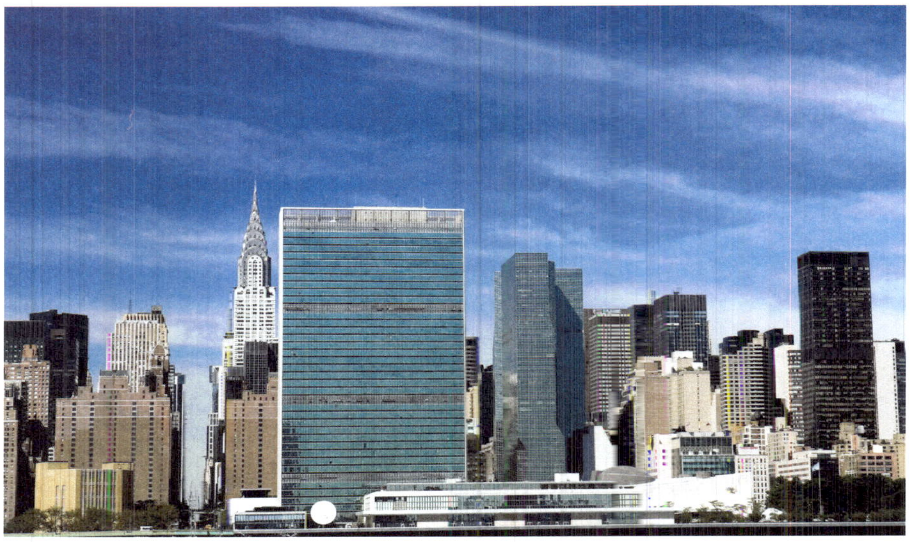

UN Headquarters, New York, principle architects Le Corbusier and Oscar Niemeyer, 1951

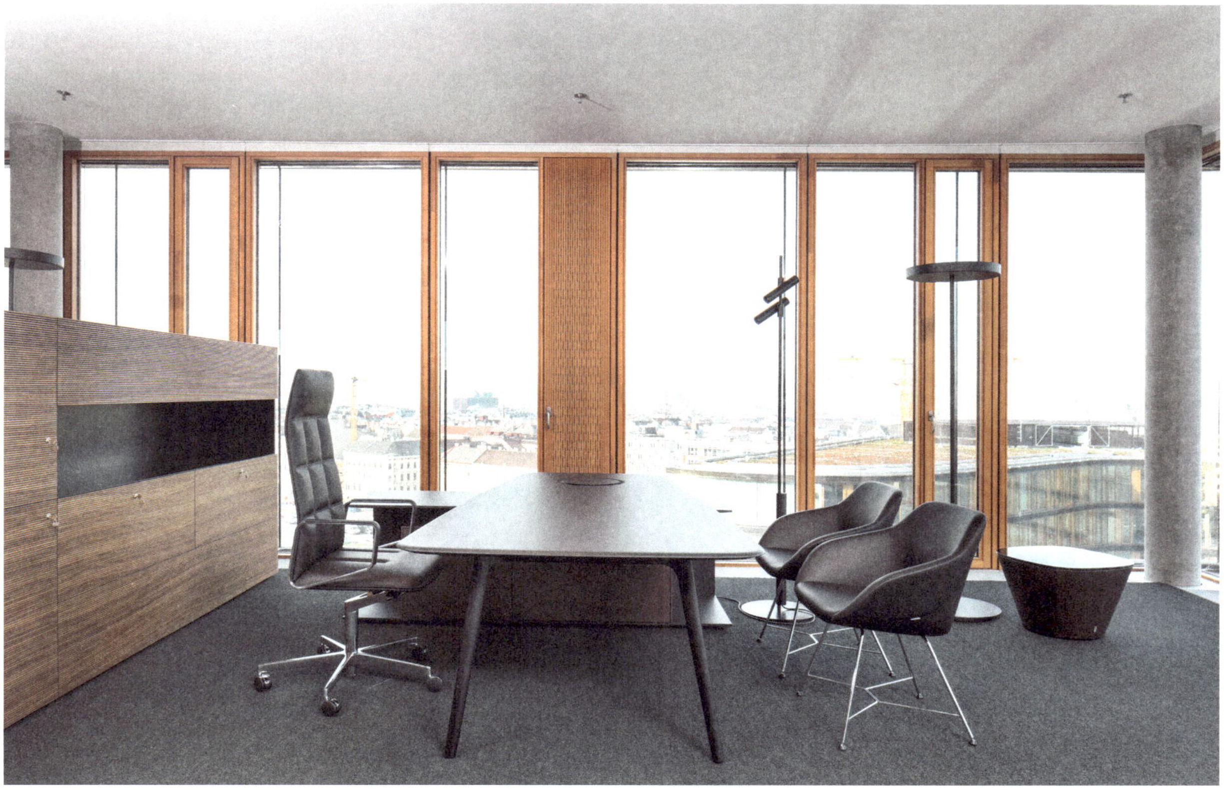

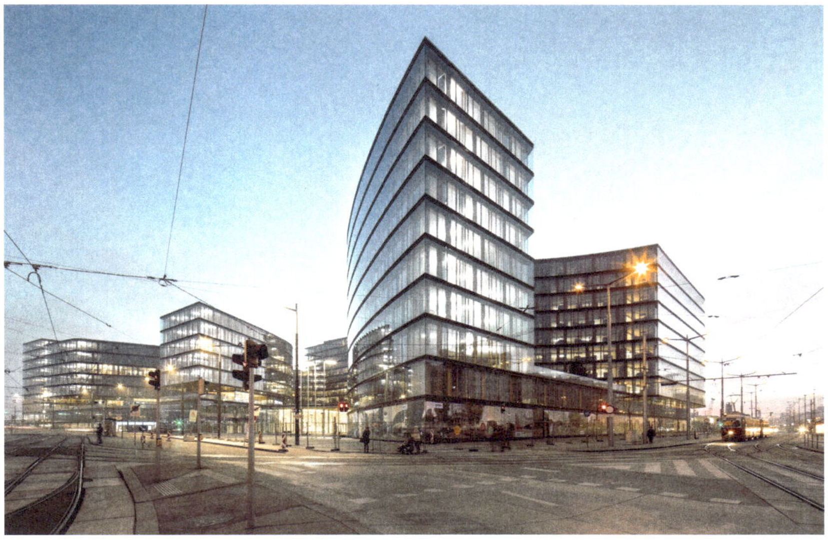

Interior of Erste Campus, furnished with armchair Leadchair Executive, table Keypiece Communication Desk, and chairs Turtle

Erste Campus, headquarters of Erste Group, Vienna, architecture by Henke Schreieck Architekten, 2015

Haus am Weinberg,
architecture by
UNStudio/Ben van Berkel,
Stuttgart, 2011

Interior of Haus am Weinberg,
furnished with armchairs Turtle

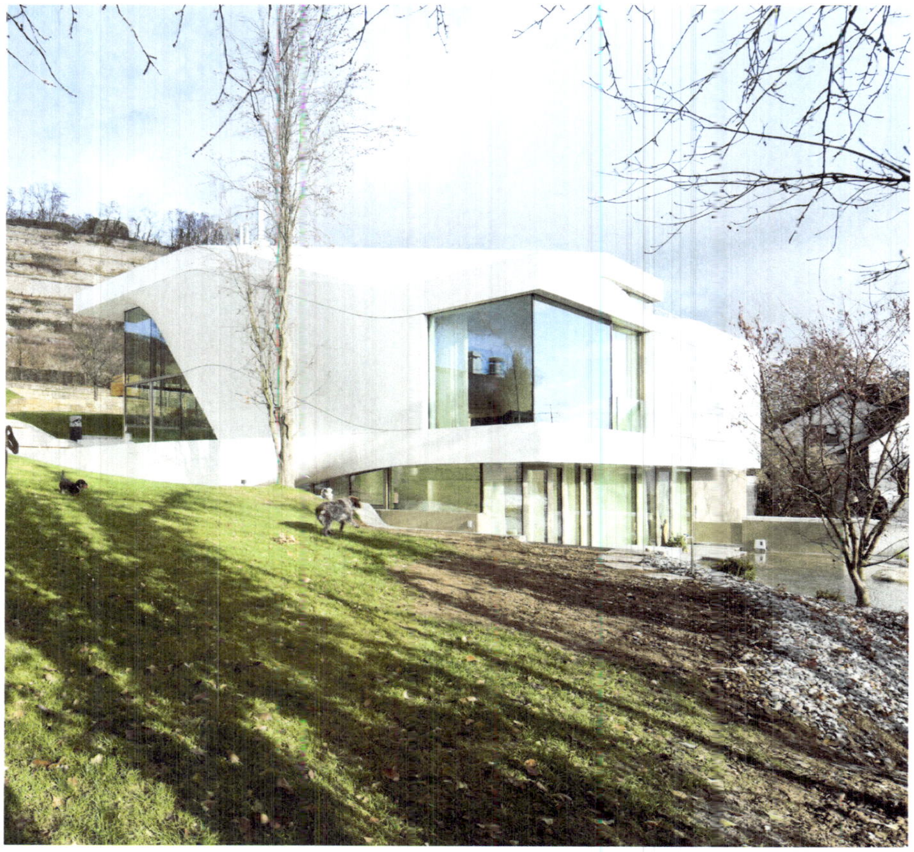

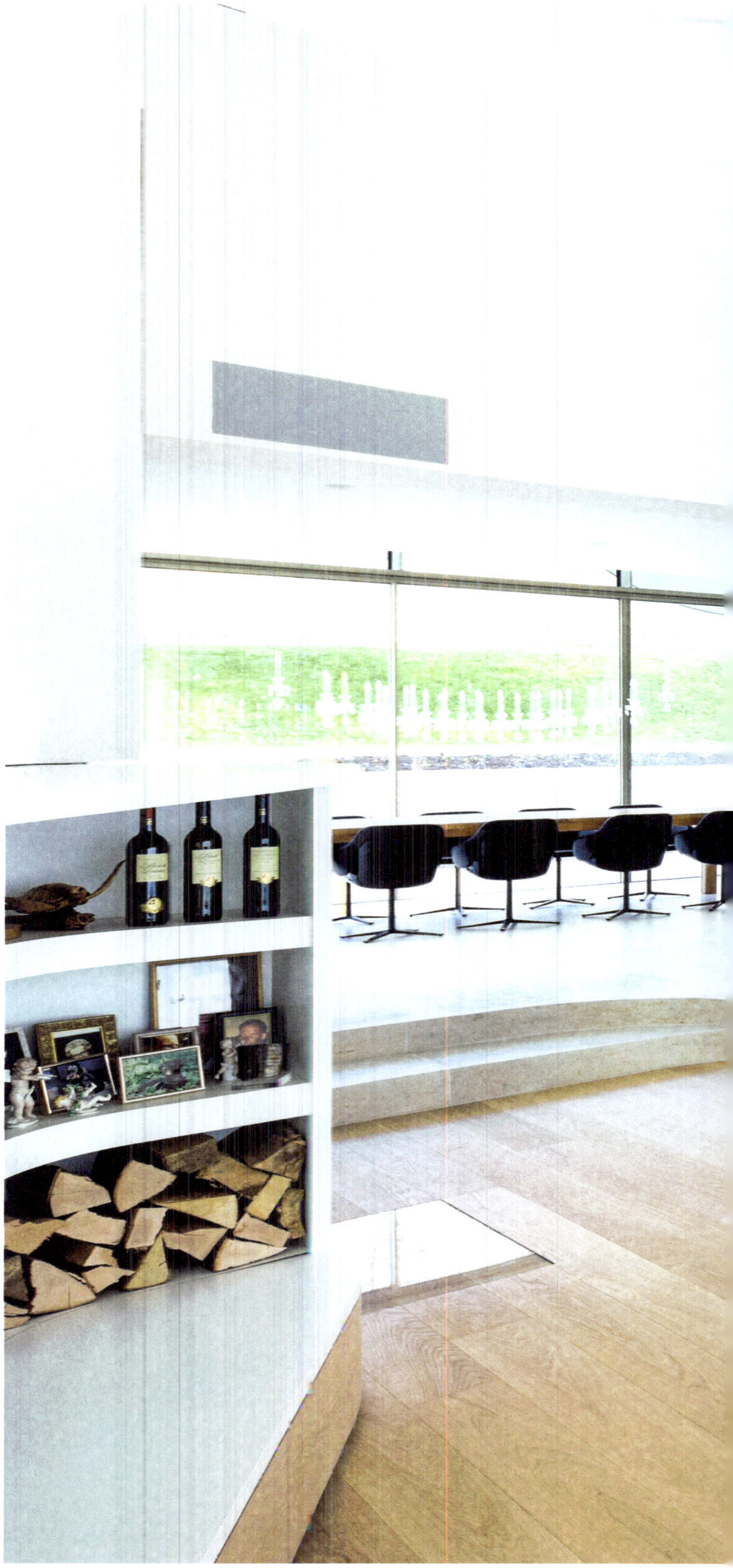

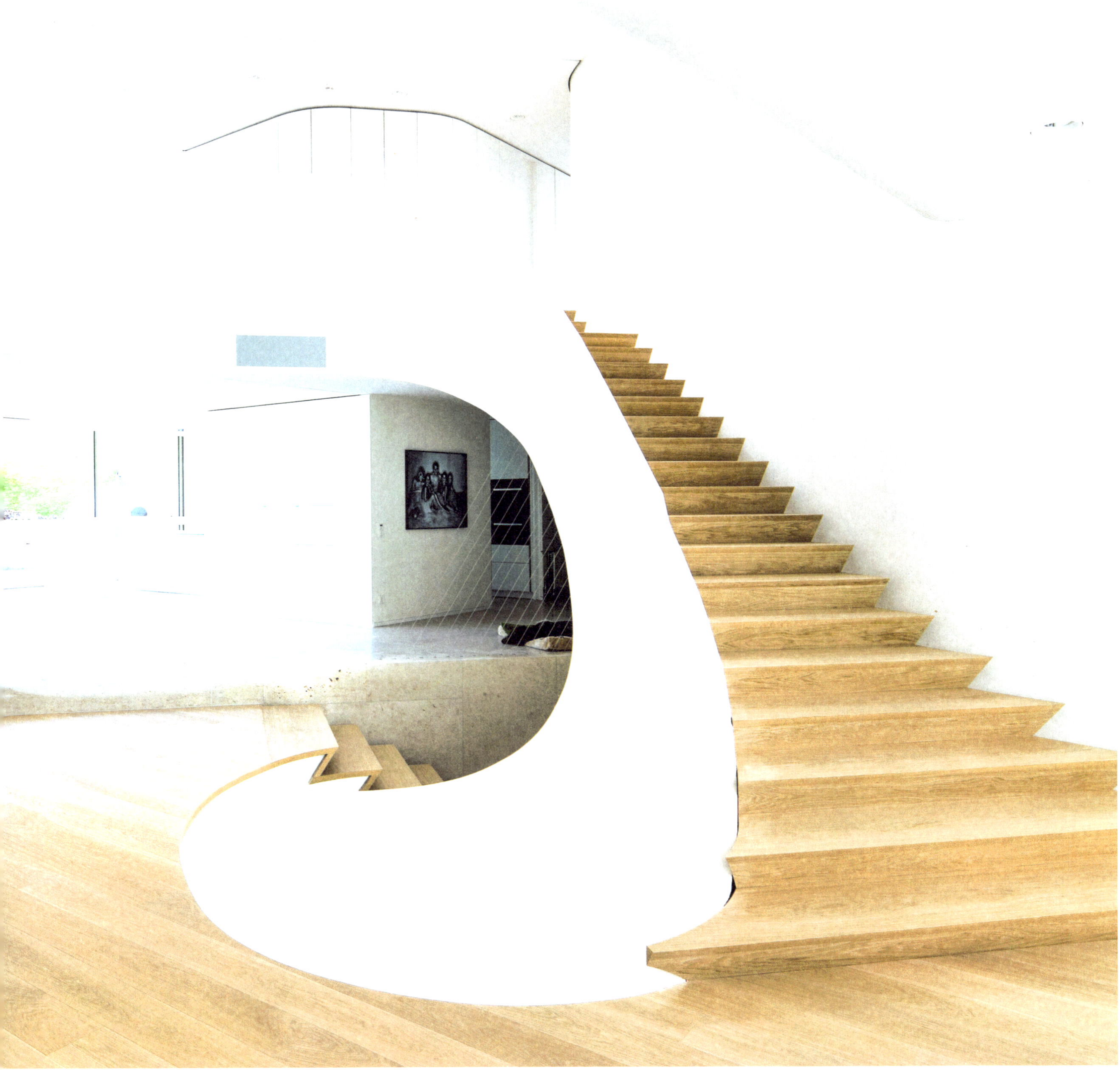

Markus Benz and Meinhard von Gerkan, Herrenberg 2015, armchair Berlin chair, design by Meinhard von Gerkan, 1975

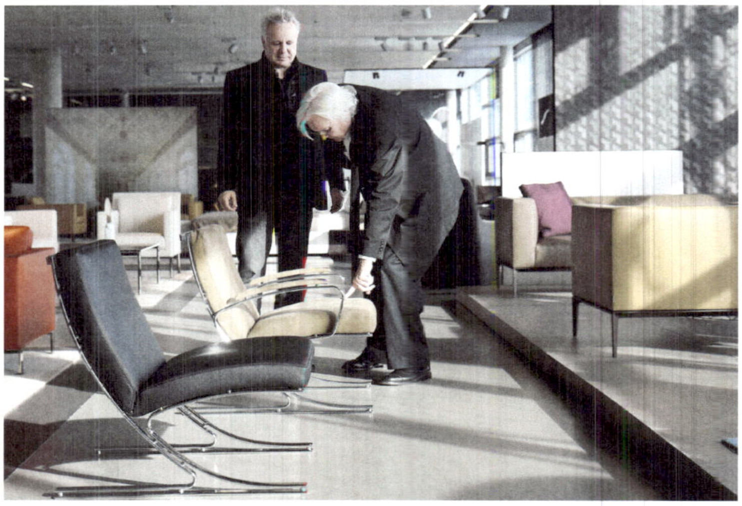

Interior view of Berlin central train station

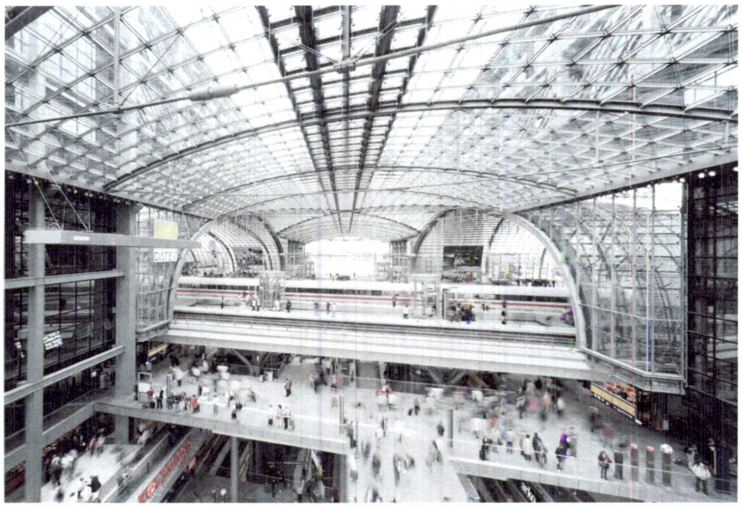

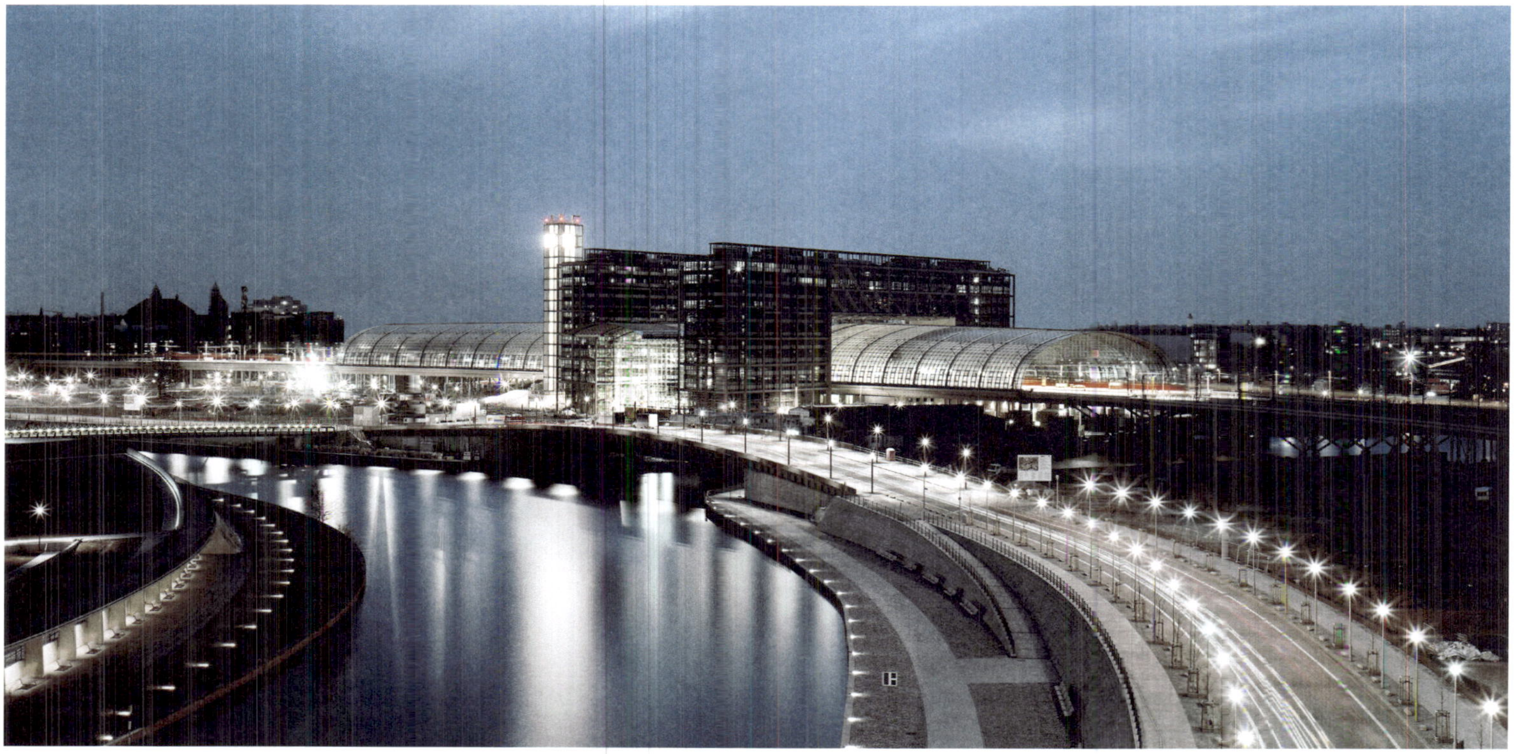

Berlin central train station, architecture by gmp Architekten von Gerkan, Marg und Partner, 2006

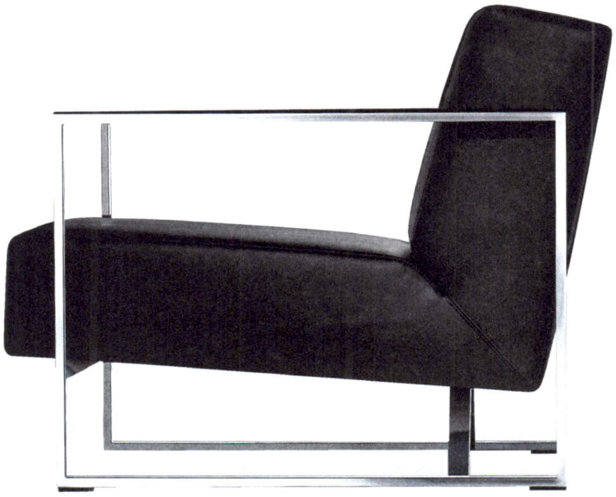

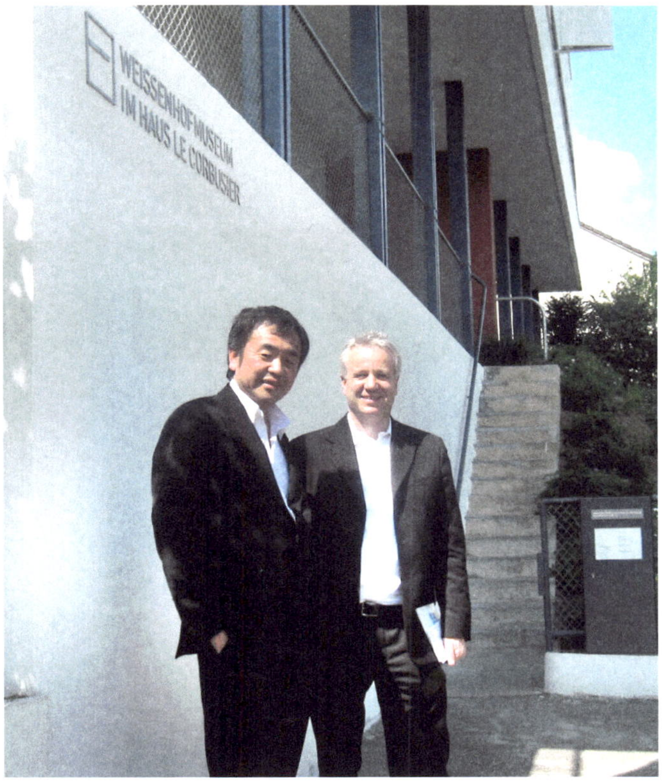

Armchair Sen,
design by Kengo Kuma,
2007

Markus Benz and Kengo Kuma
at the Weissenhofsiedlung,
Stuttgart, 2008

A PIONEER OF HIS DAY

The Turkish designer Sadi Ozis (1923–2012) was one of the formative designers of the Second Modernity. He understood how to combine Middle-Eastern shapes and Western minimalism.

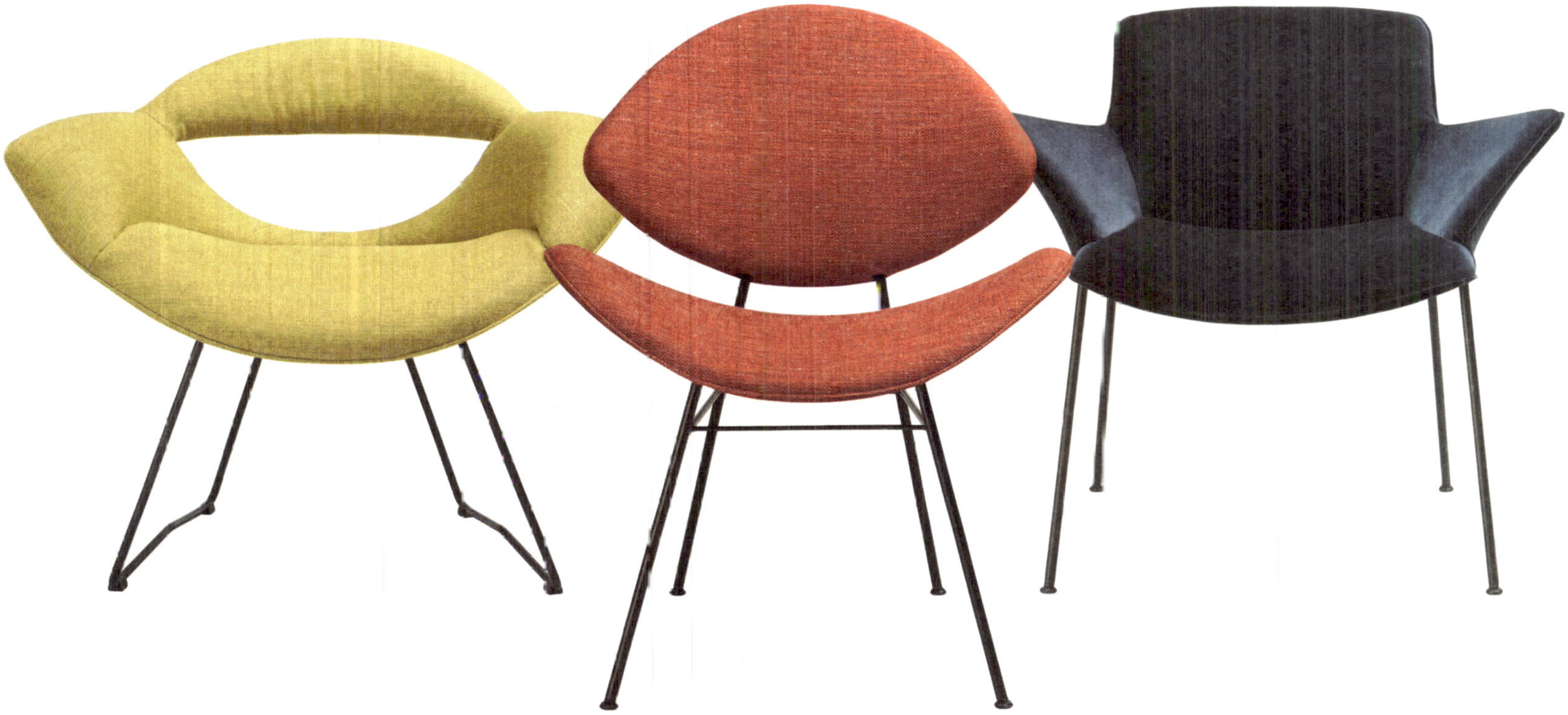

Chair Rumi

Fishnet Chair

Burgaz Chair

Fishnet Chair,
originally made with course-meshed
fishnet woven between a steel frame,
design by Sadi Ozis,
1959

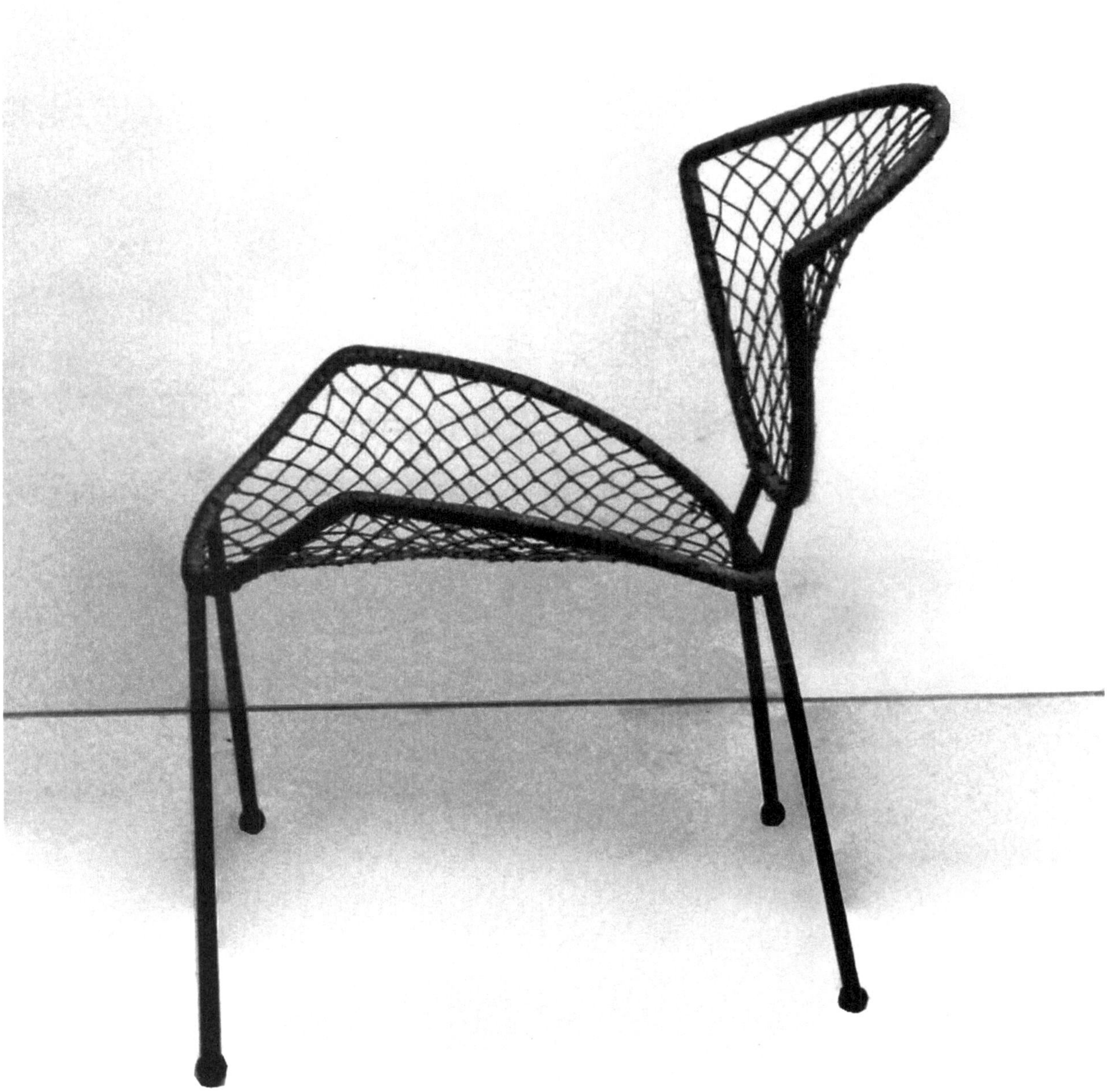

FIFTH CONTINENT
Walter Knoll operates a subsidiary with a production plant on the other side of the globe.

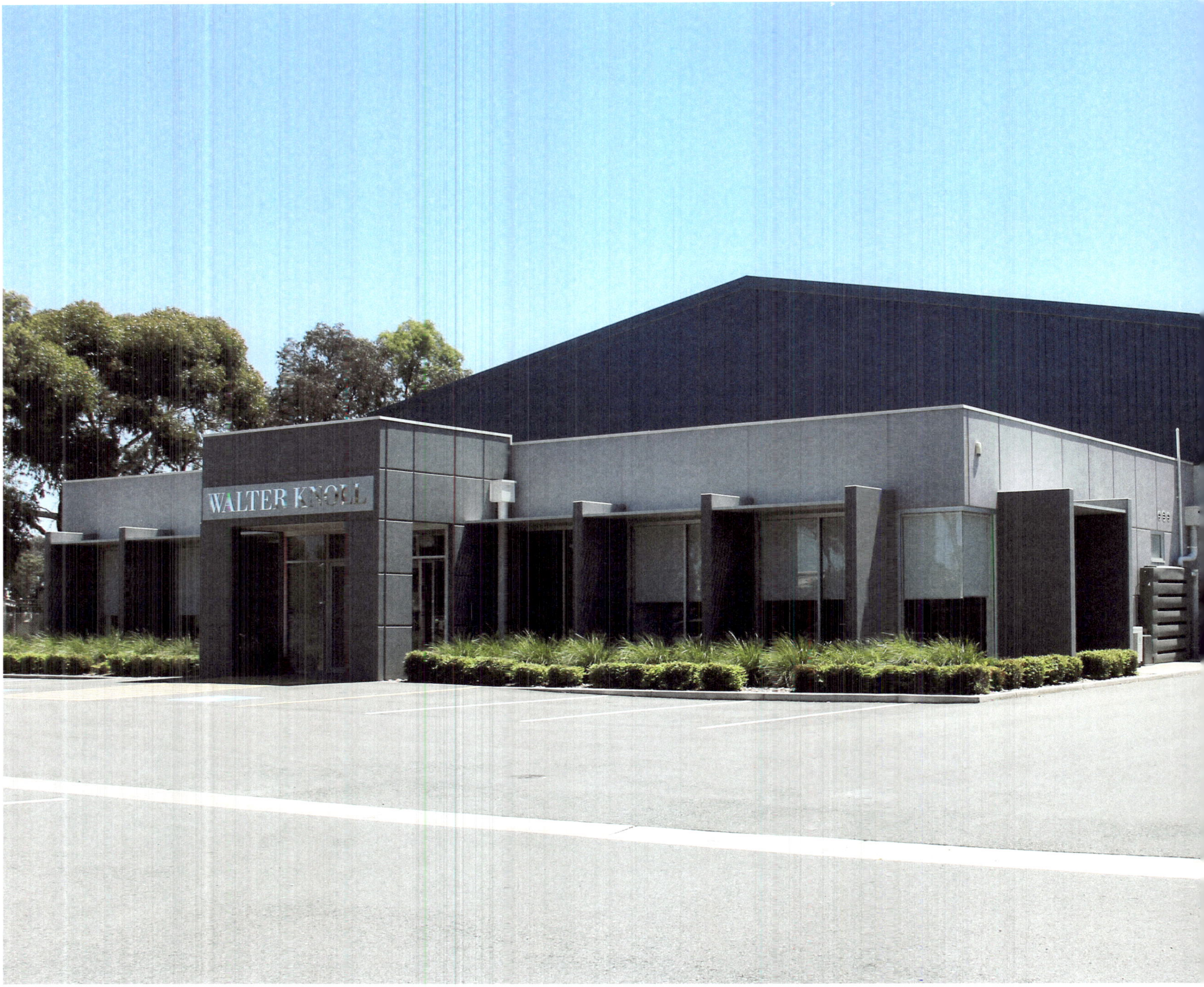

Factory and showroom,
Walter Knoll Australia, 2012

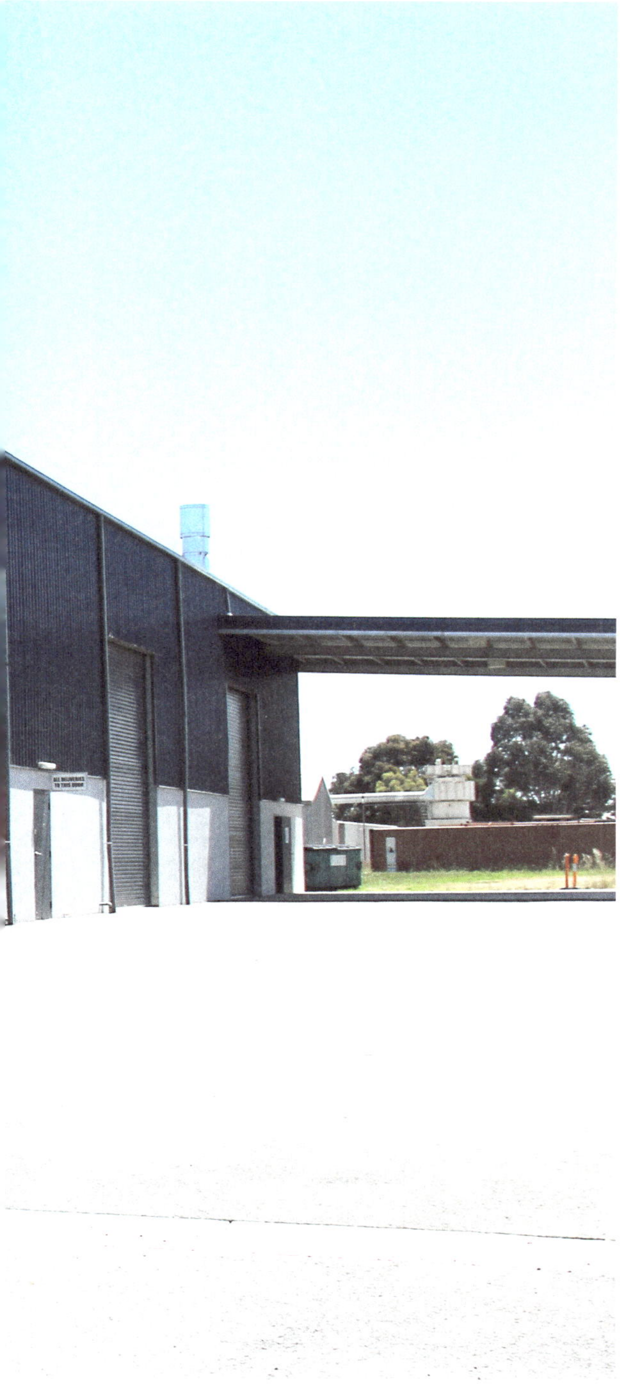

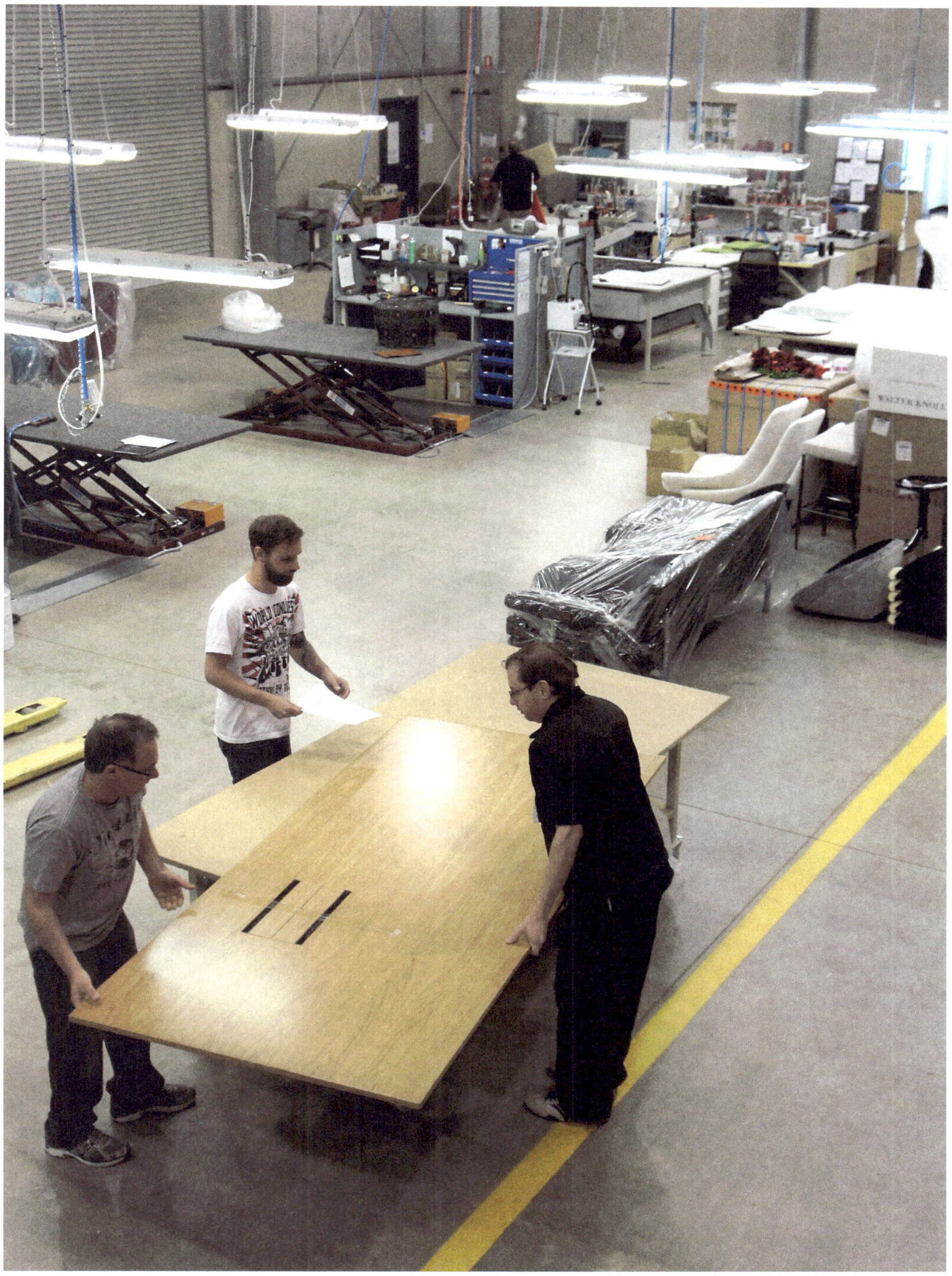

Subsidiary of Walter Knoll in
Salisbury, Australia 2012

STUTTGART, 4.0

The Swabian metropolis is not only a powerhouse of industry, but has also been an important cultural center since the First Modernity. Again and again, it has set the architectural tone.

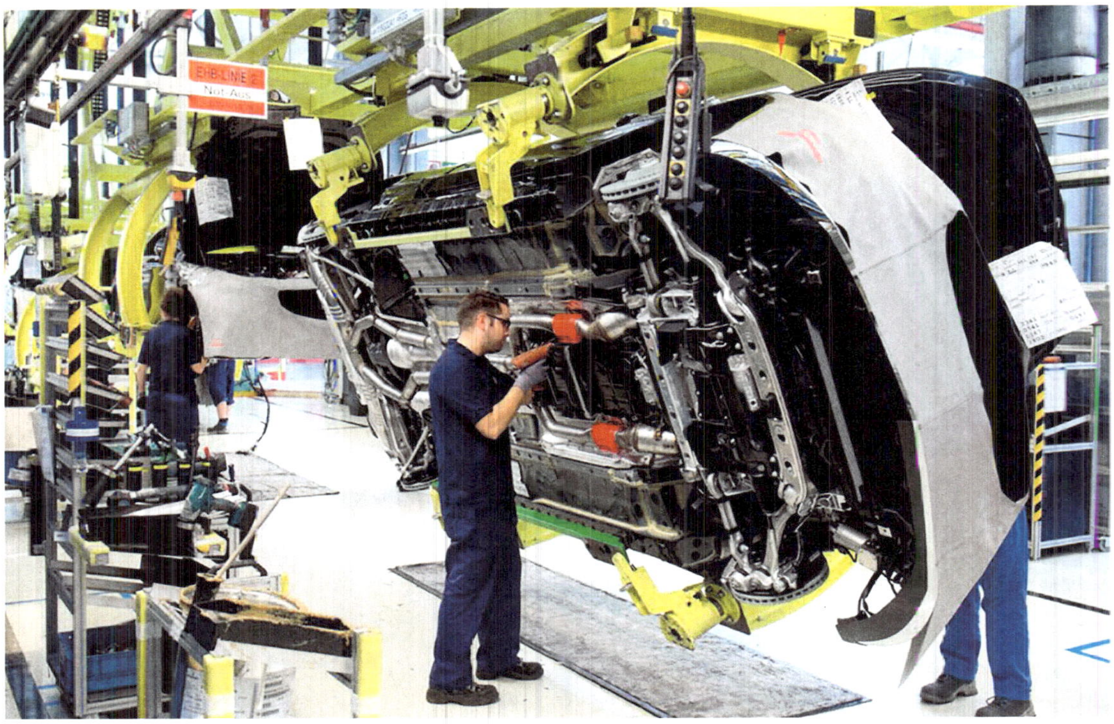

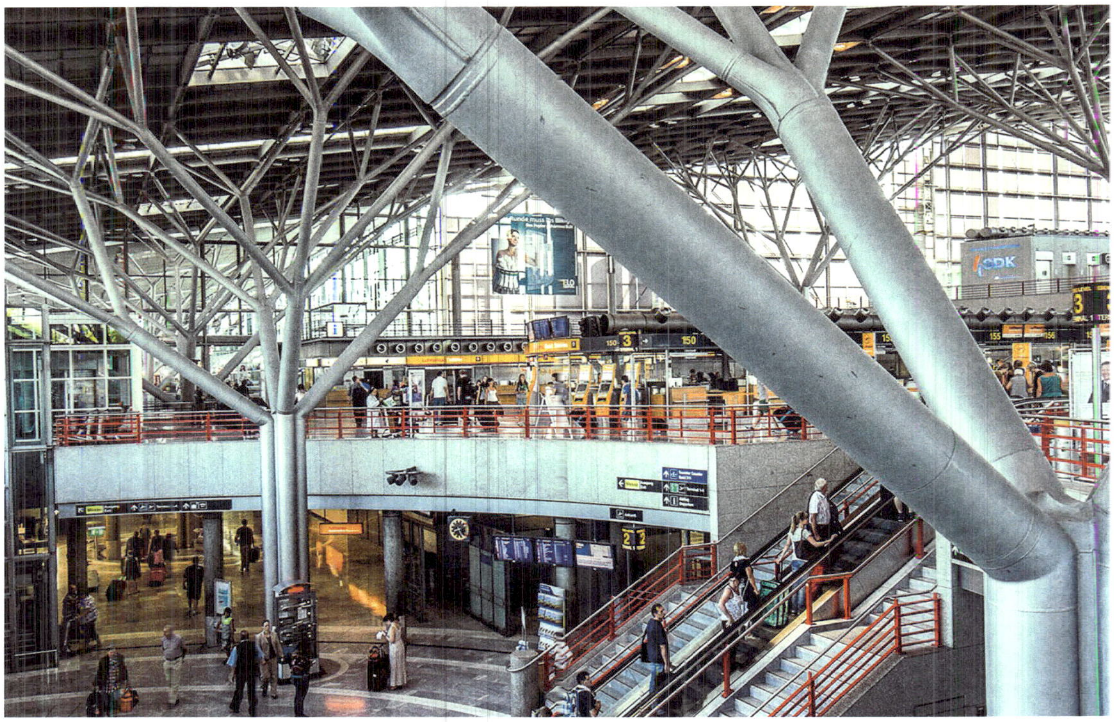

Mercedes-Benz assembly hall,
Sindelfingen

Stuttgart airport departure lounge,
architecture of new construction in part
by Meinhard von Gerkan,
2004

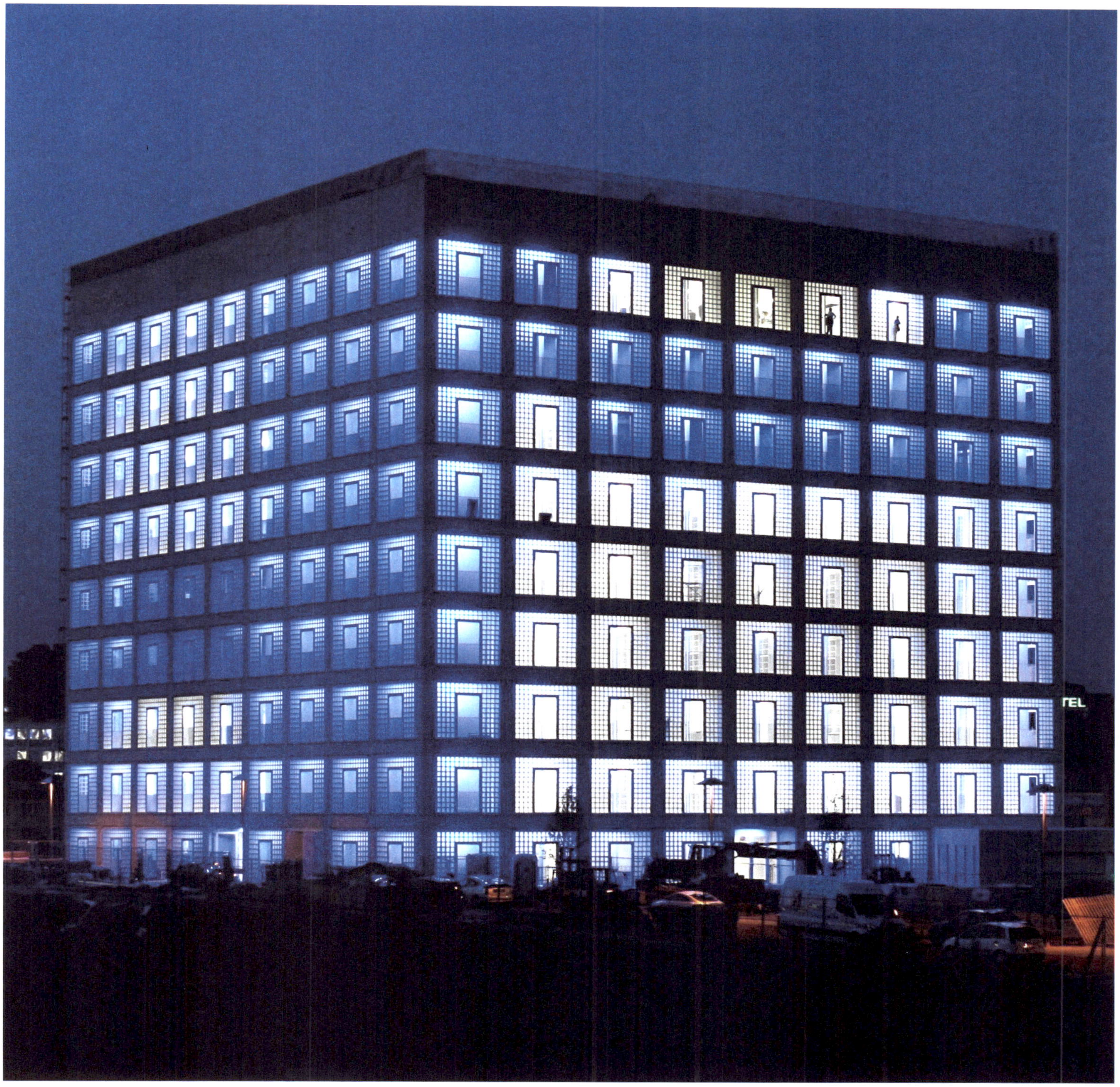

Central library of the Stuttgart "Stadtbibliothek" (Municipal Library), architecture by Eun Young Yi, 2011

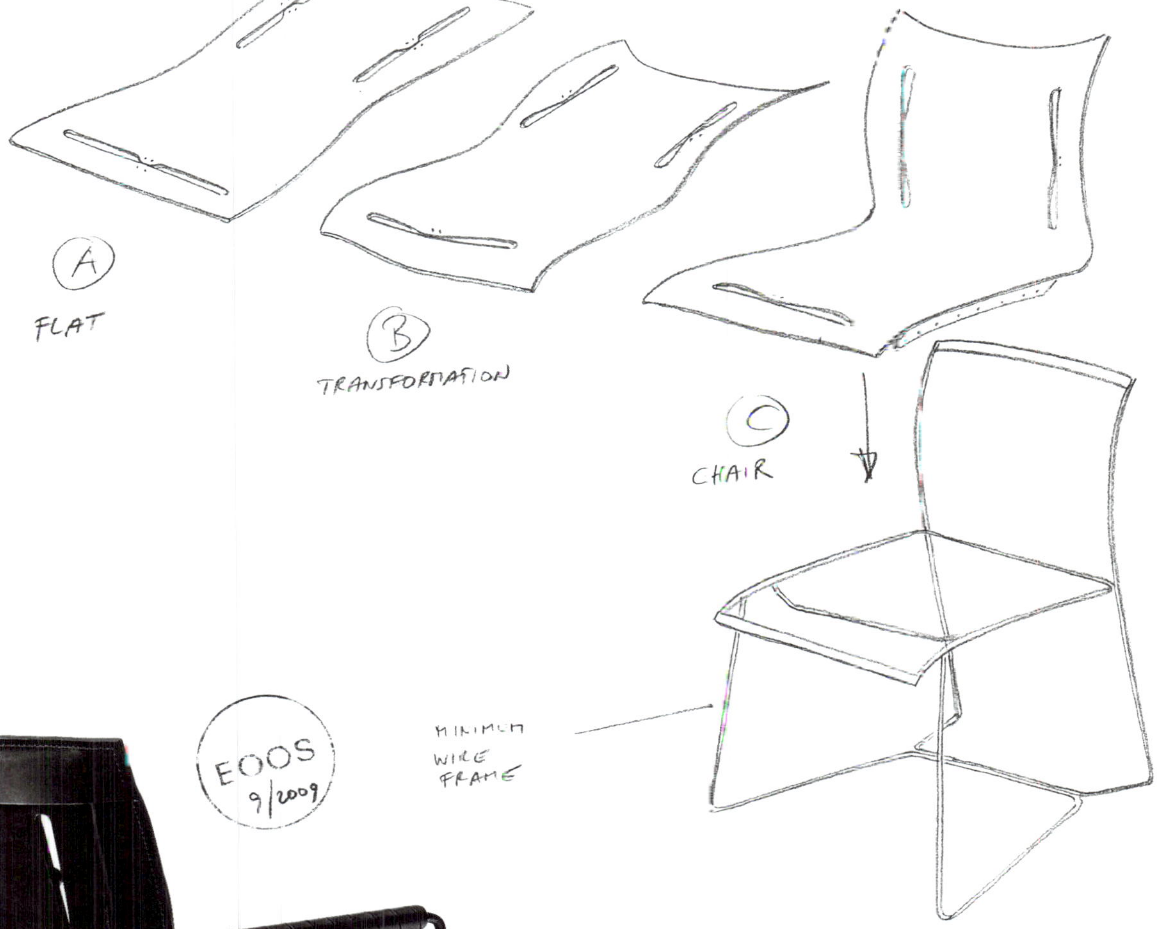

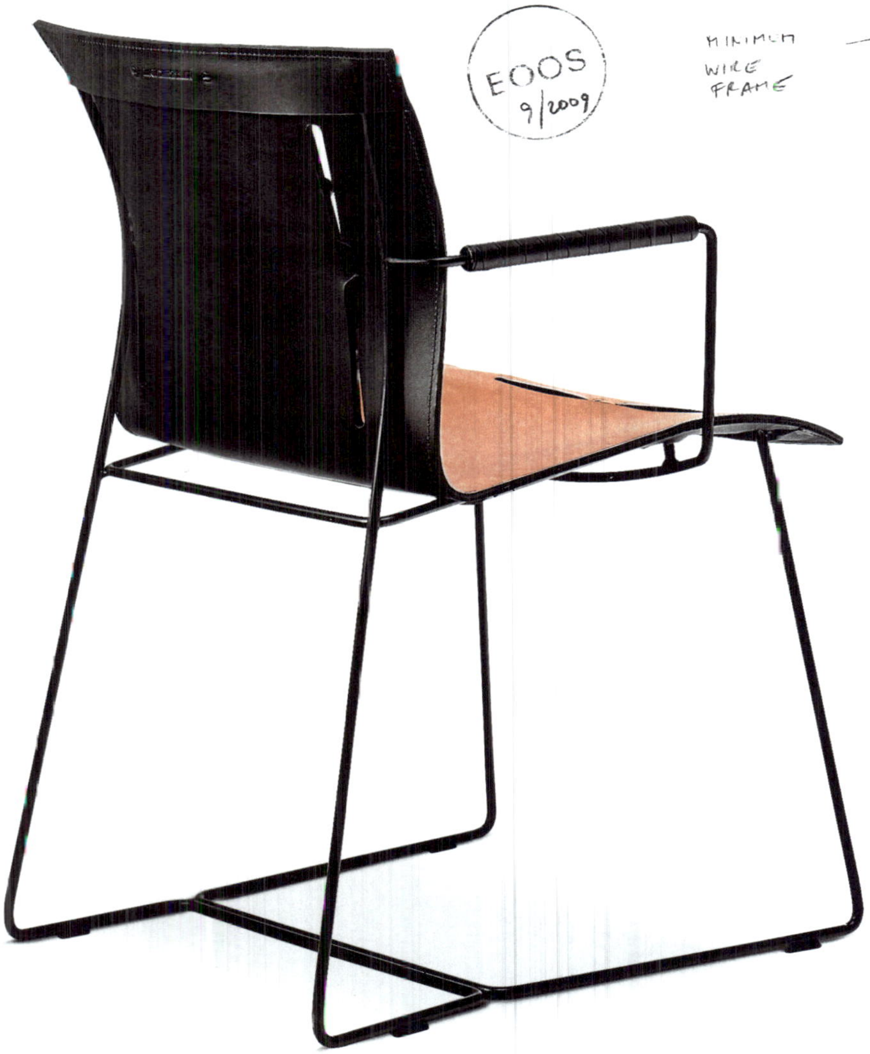

Chair Cuoio,
design by EOOS,
2010

SUSTAINABILITY

The responsible use of resources – whether it is in the materials used for products, in production processes, or in architecture – is embedded in Walter Knoll's corporate ethics and reflected in the spare aesthetics of many designs.

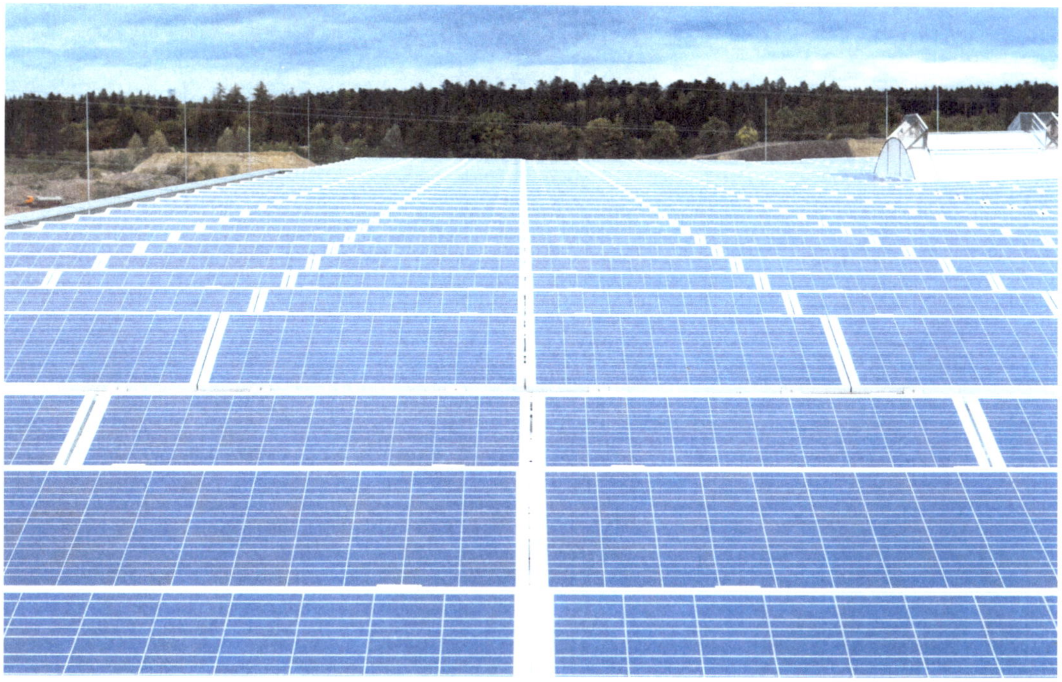

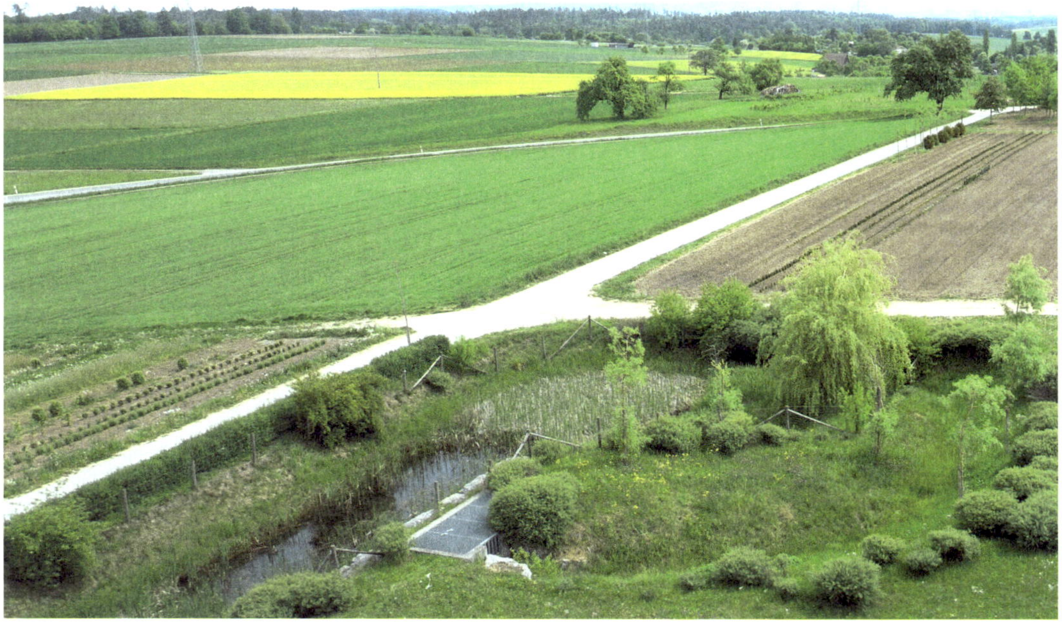

Photovoltaic plant on the roof of the Mötzingen II production hall

Retention basins for water storage at Mötzingen II plant

LIGHTNESS OF BEING

Metal furnishings with a small diameter perpetuate a tradition of the First Modernity. At the same time, an aesthetic of lightness is informally combined with minimalism – sustainability in the best sense of the word.

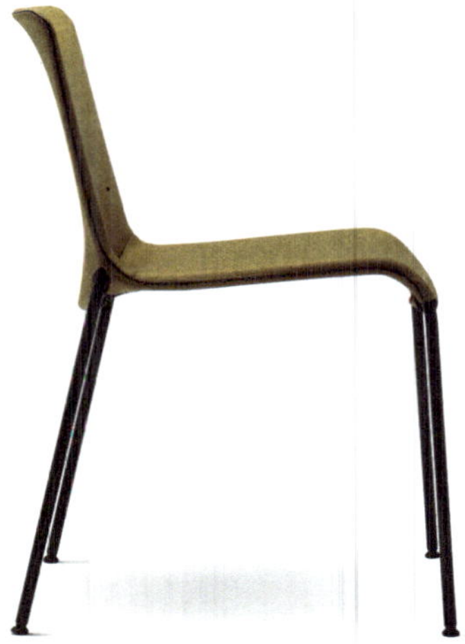

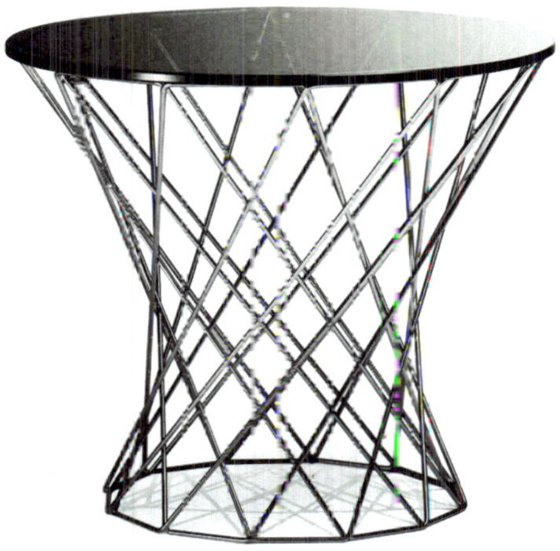

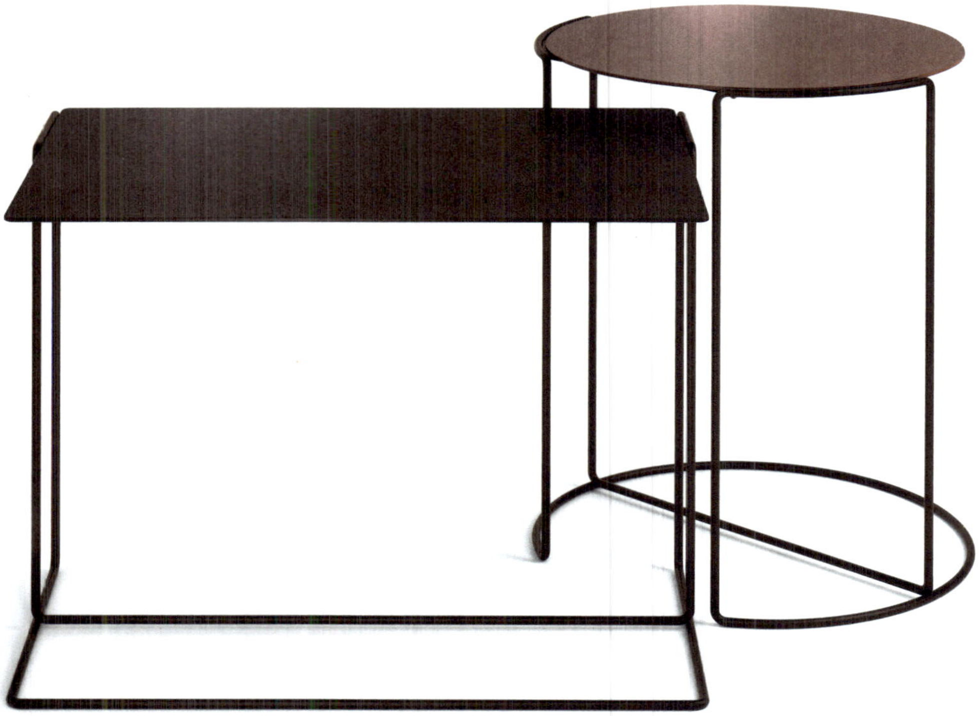

Chair Liz,
design by Claudio Bellini,
2012

Side table Oki,
design by EOOS,
2013

Side table Oota Table,
design by EOOS,
2011

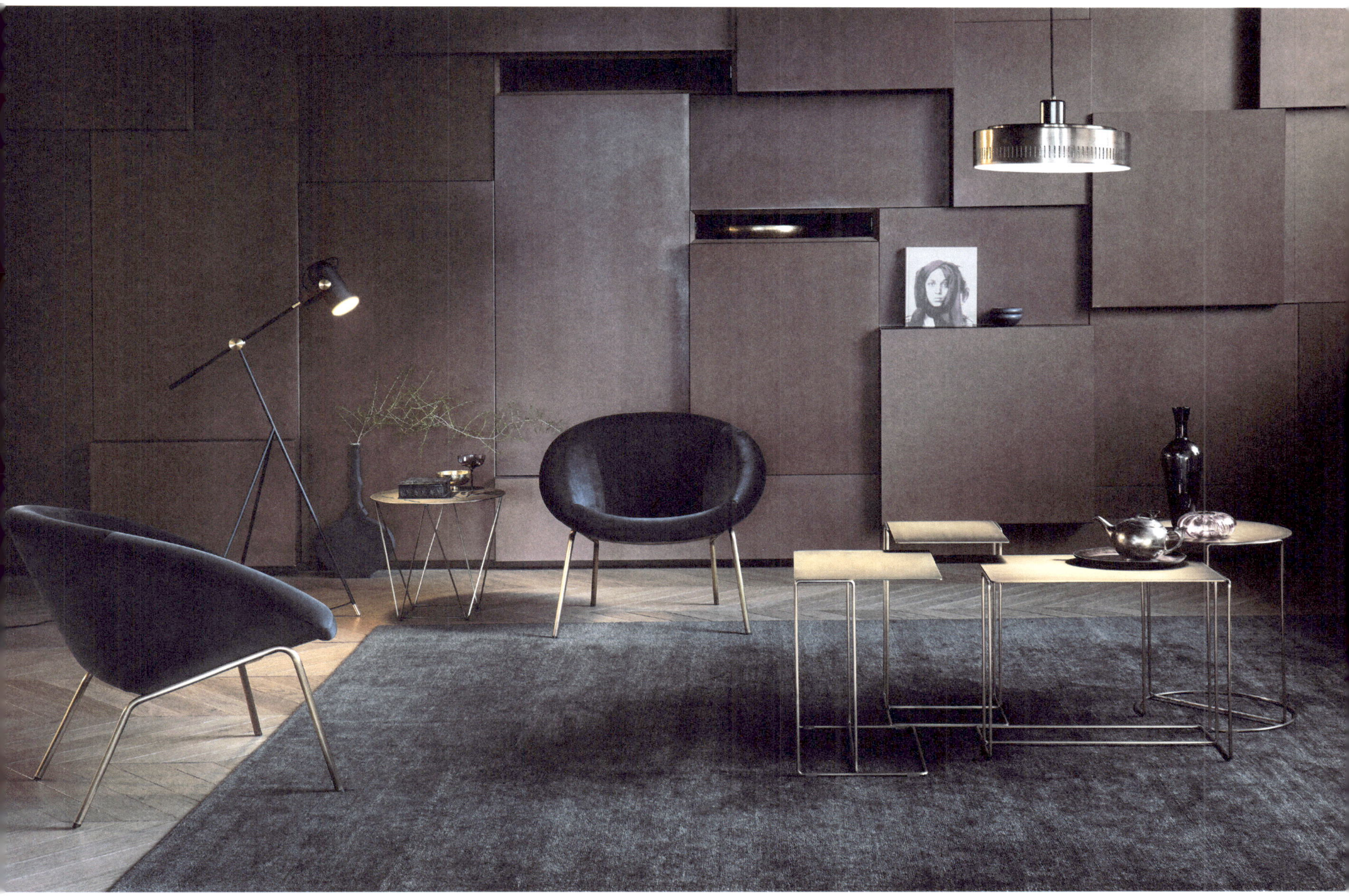

Armchair 369

Side table Oki

Side table Joco,
design by EOOS,
2010

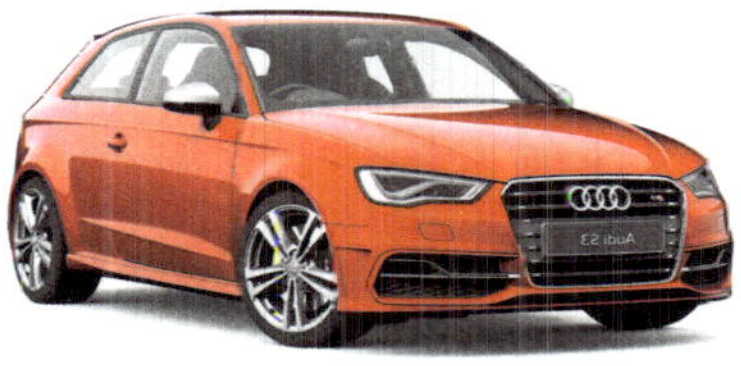

Auci S3,
design by Wolfgang J. Egger,
2007

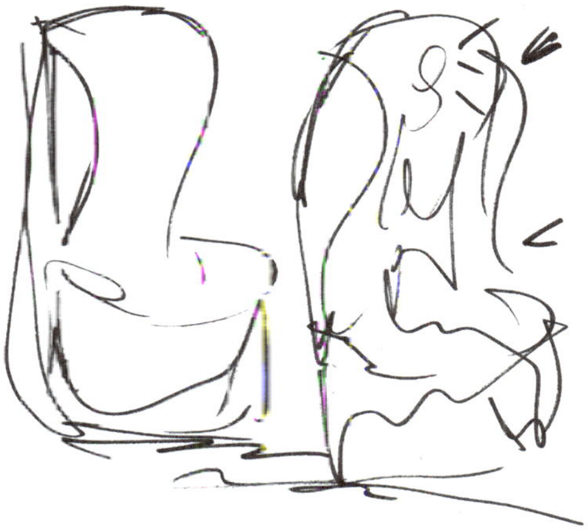

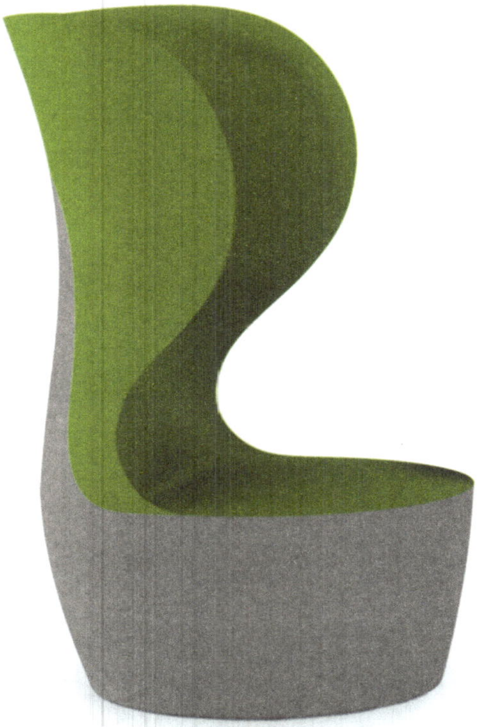

Sketch and armchair
Silent Chair from the
Seating Stones range

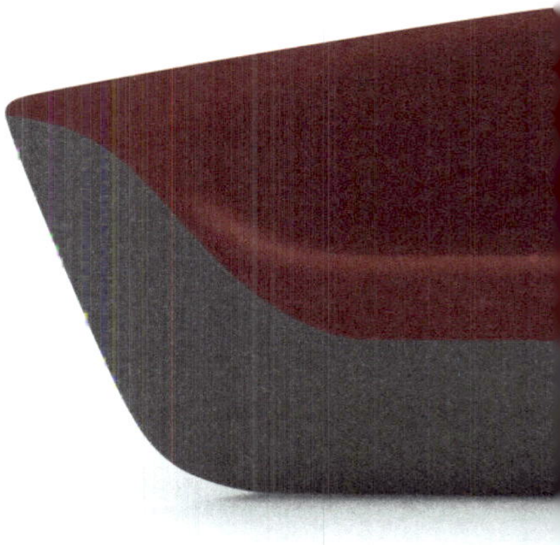

Seating Stones
combination

VISIONS IN 3D
Dutchman Ben van Berkel is a virtuoso of digital CAD technology and the fluid form. He achieves transformations that stretch our power of imagination.

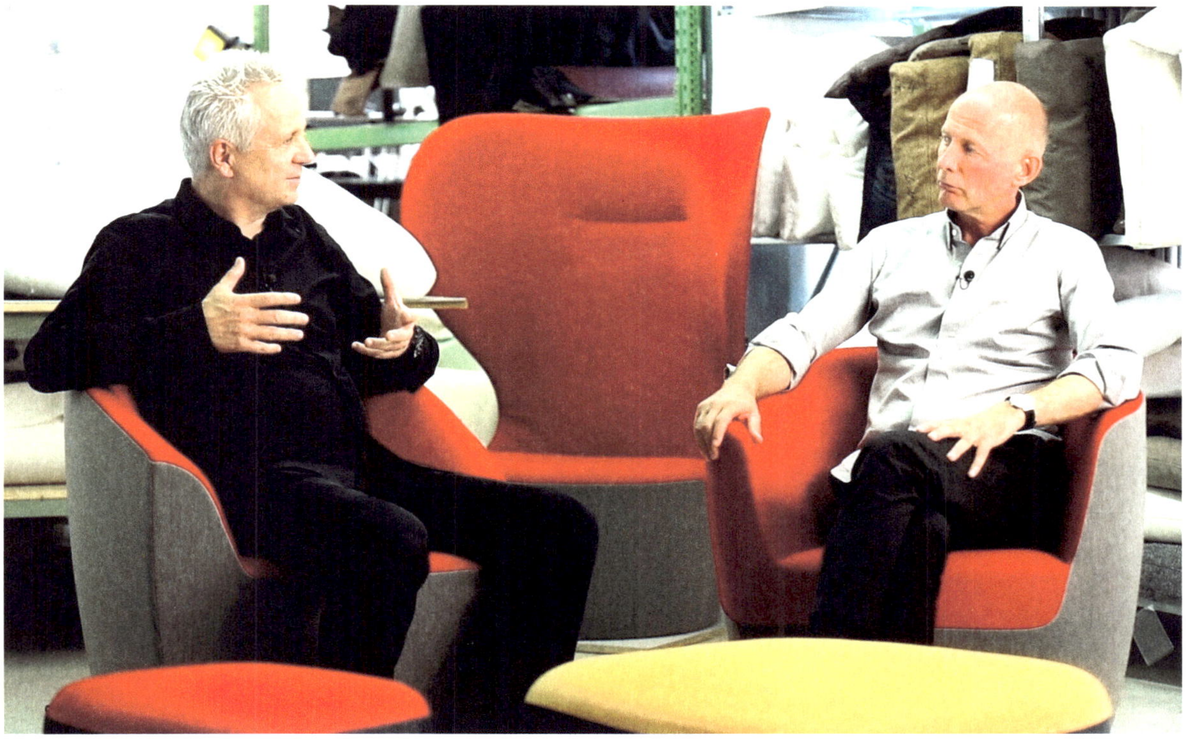

Markus Benz and Ben van Berkel, armchair Seating Stones, design by UNStudio/Ben van Berkel, 2012

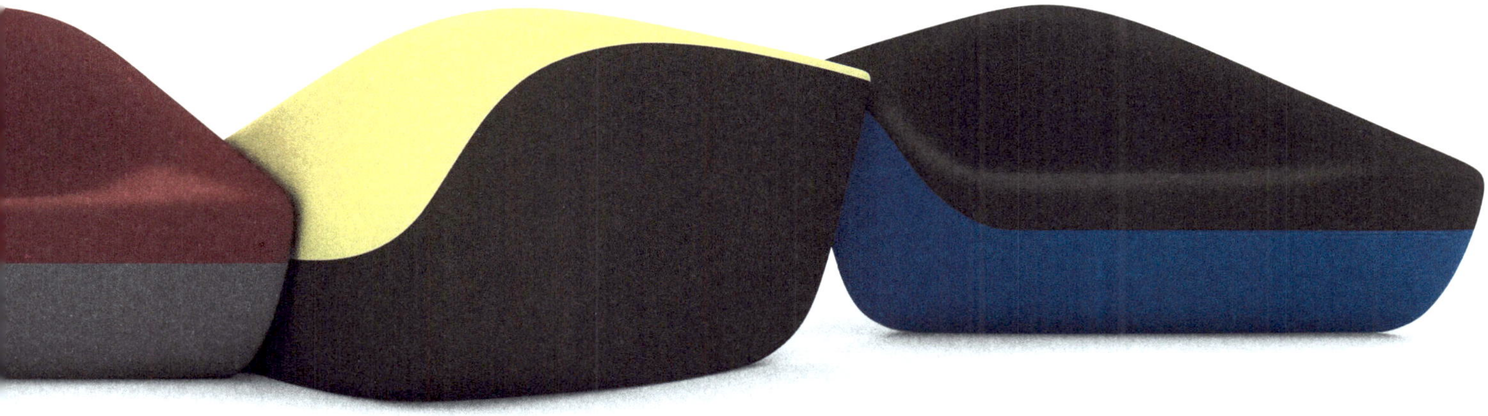

THE WORLD OF WALTER KNOLL
In major metropolises like London, Zurich, and New York, customers can experience the Walter Knoll brand in dedicated showrooms and brand spaces.

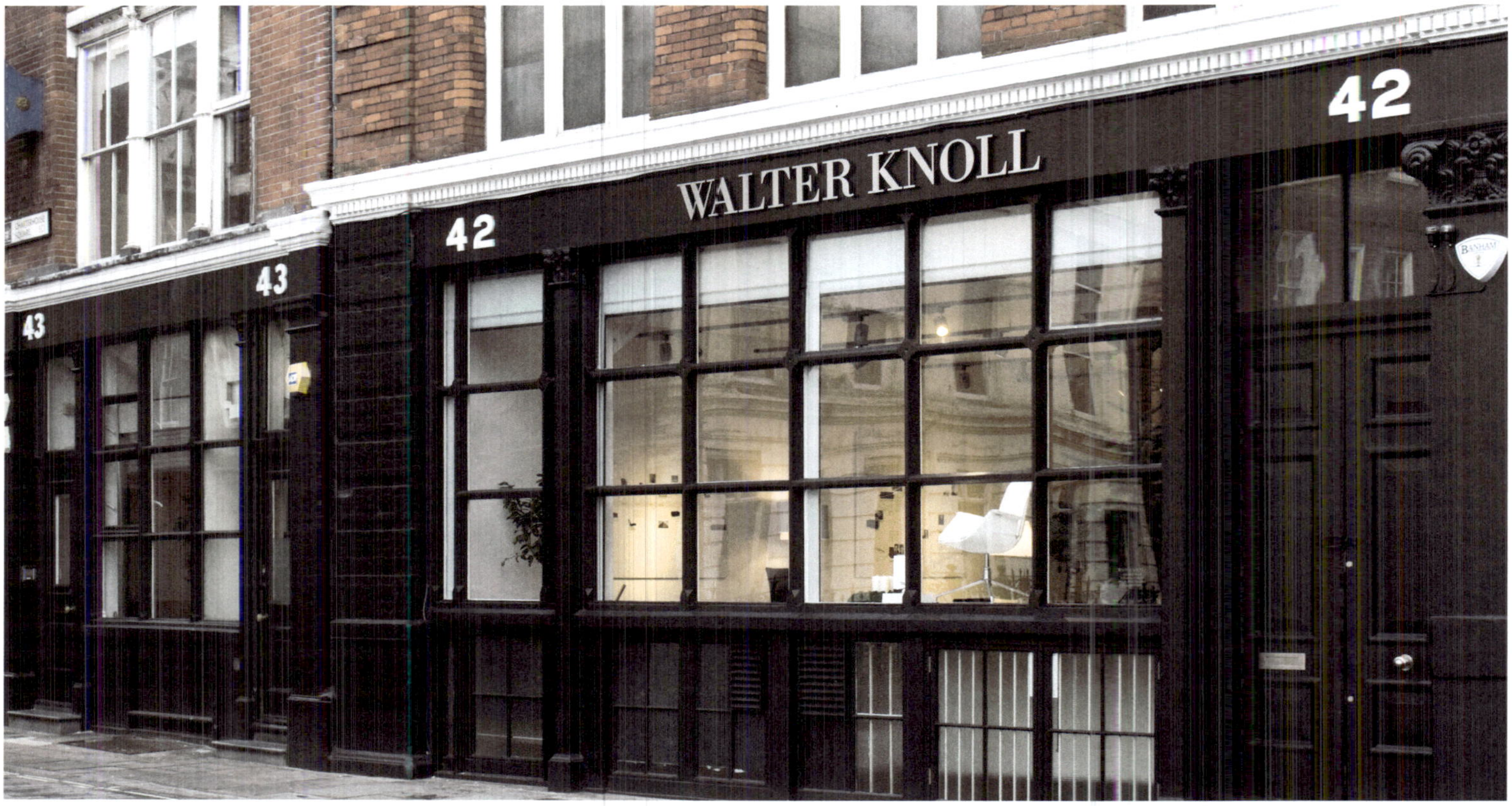

London

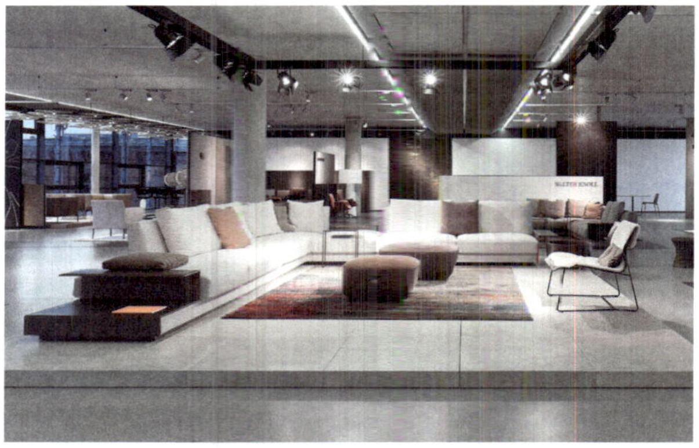

Herrenberg

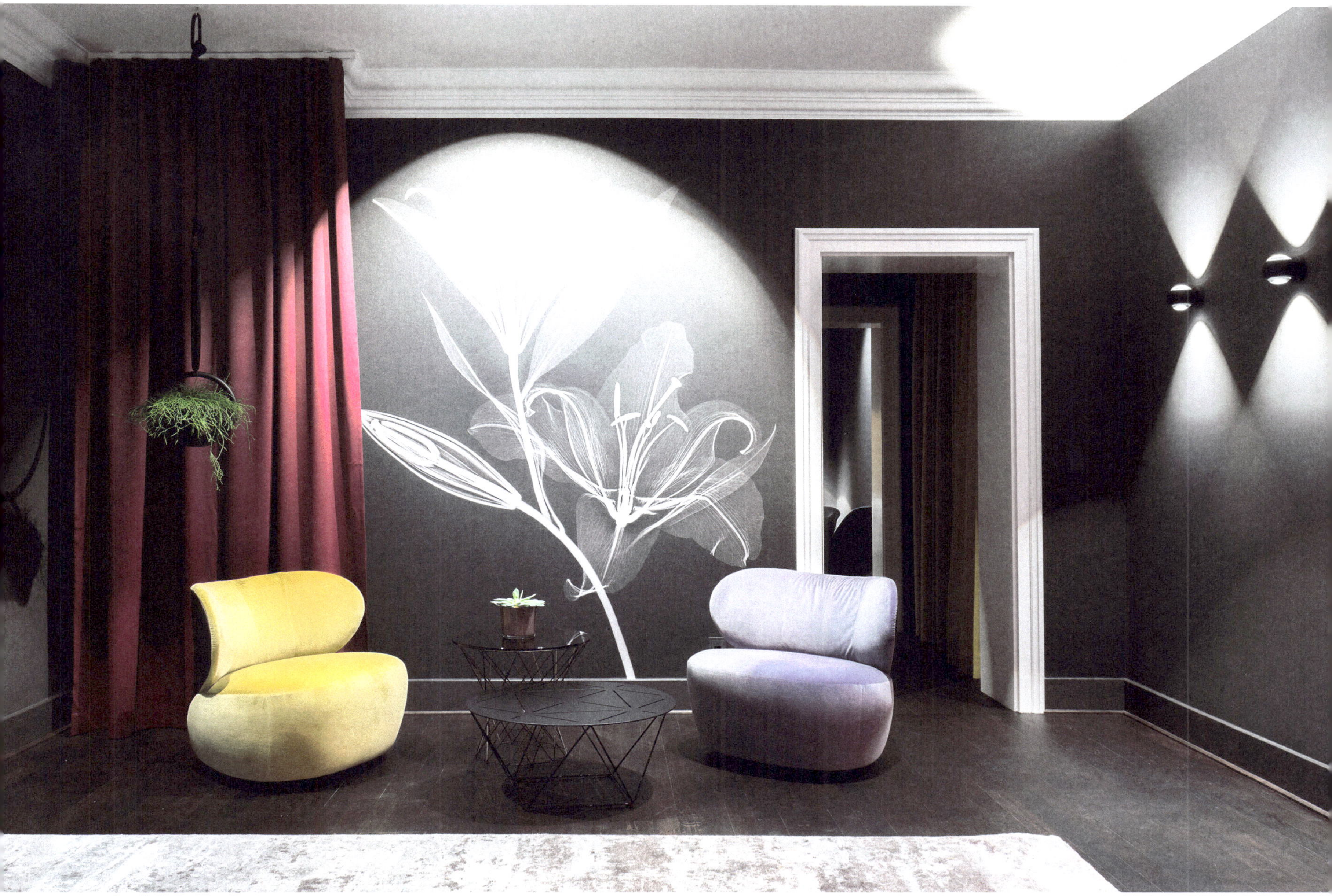

Düsseldorf

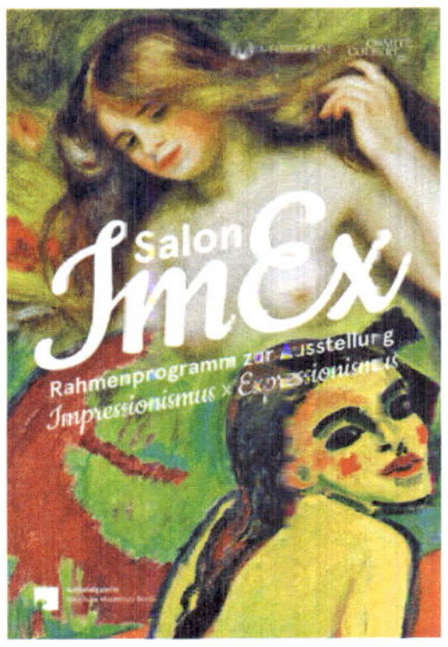

Poster for ImEx exhibition Berlin 2015

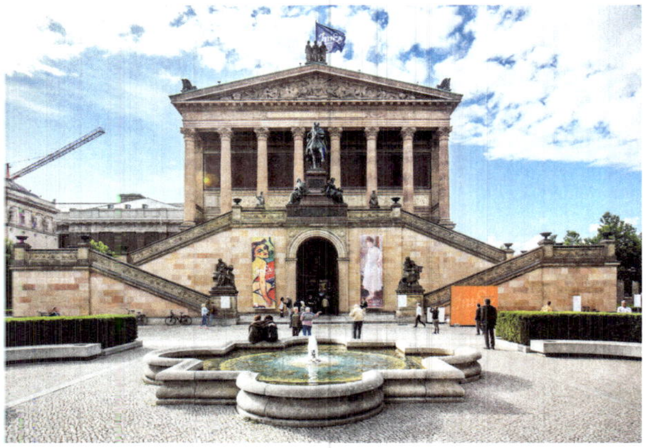

Alte Nationalgalerie, Berlin, architecture by Friedrich August Stüler and Johann Heinrich Strack, under construction from 1867 to 1876

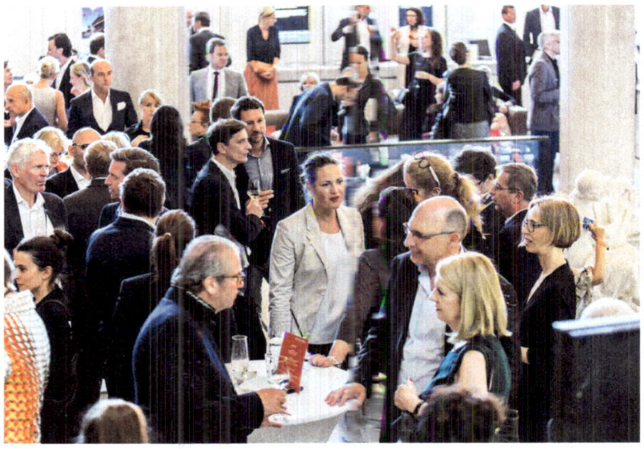

Event at ImEx exhibition celebrating Walter Knoll's 150th anniversary, Alte Nationalgalerie Berlin, 2015

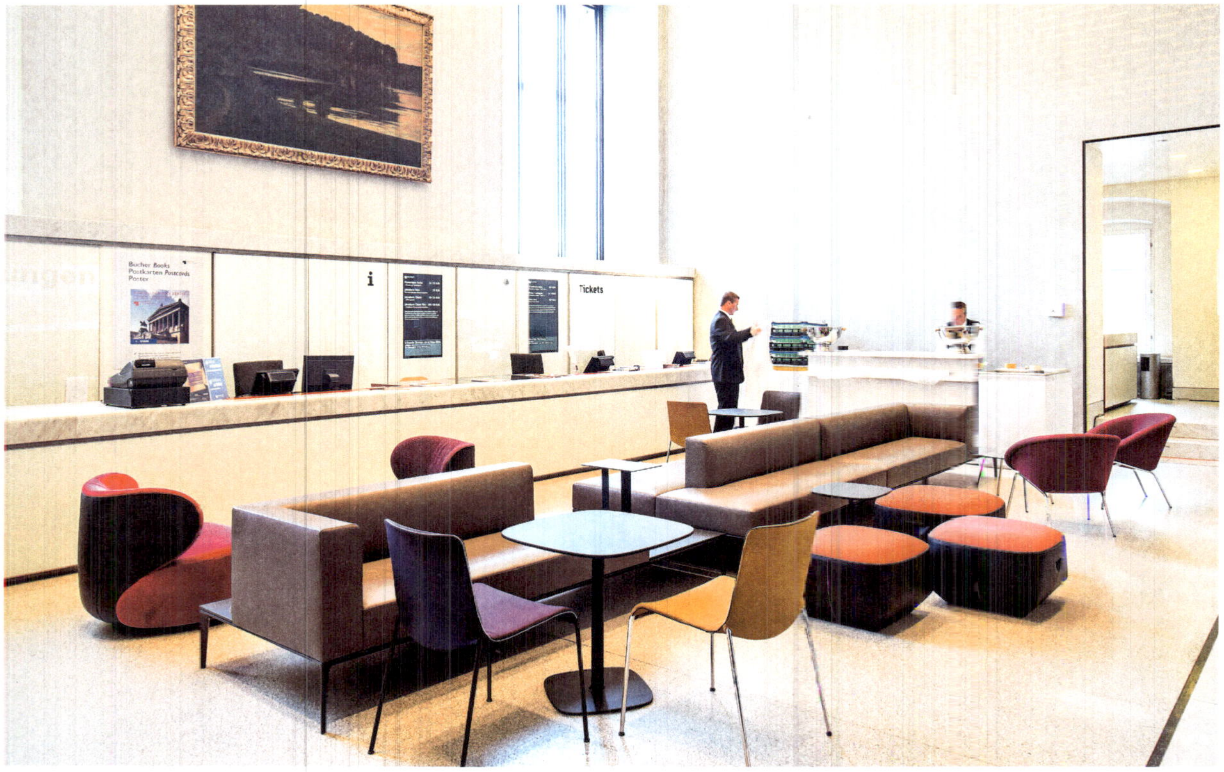

Interior of the Alte Nationalgalerie, Berlin

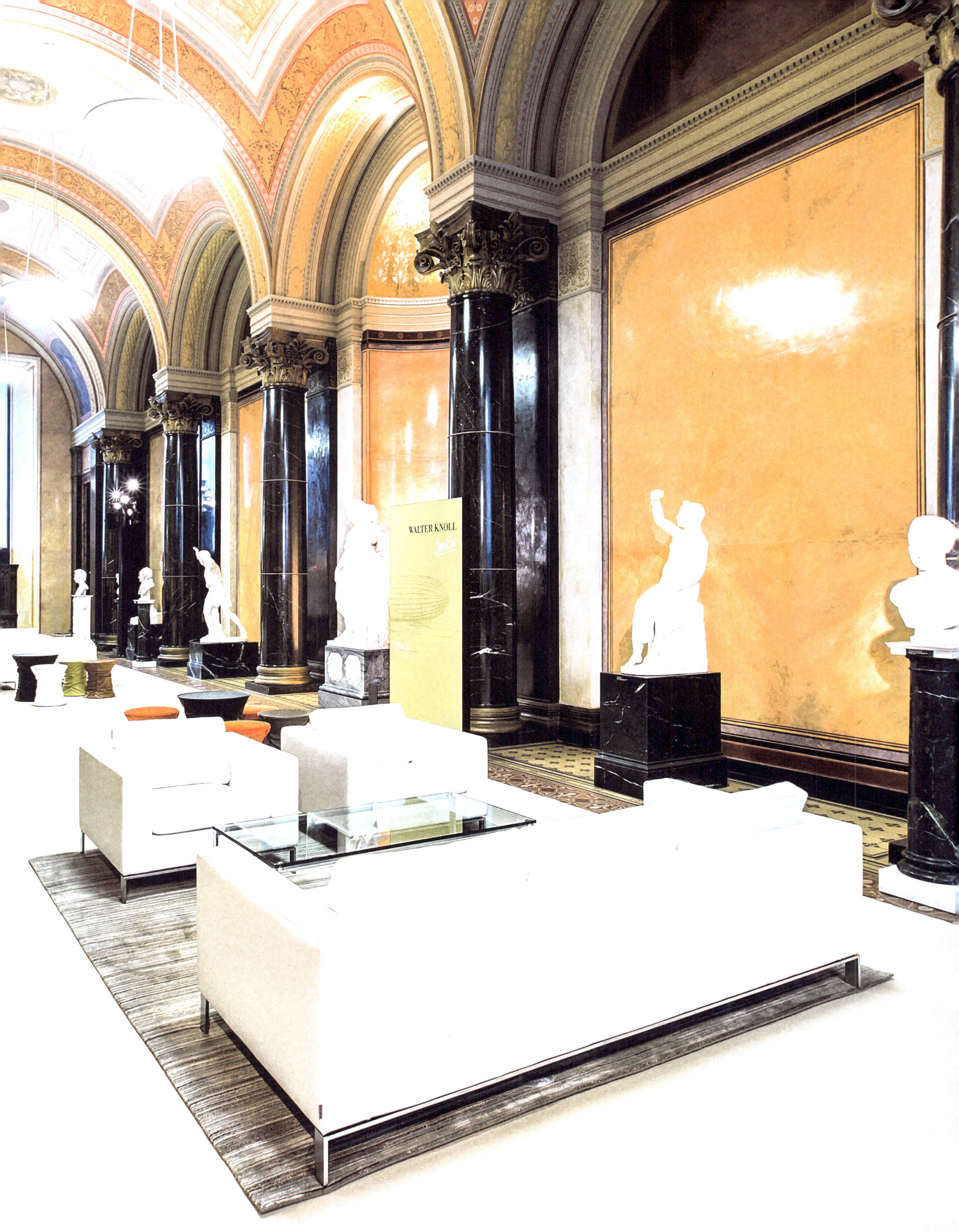
WALTER KNOLL

ONE AND A HALF CENTURIES

The history of Walter Knoll encompasses the First, Second, and Third Modernities.

Celebrating 150 years of Walter Knoll, introduction of the Classic Edition, Herrenberg, 2015

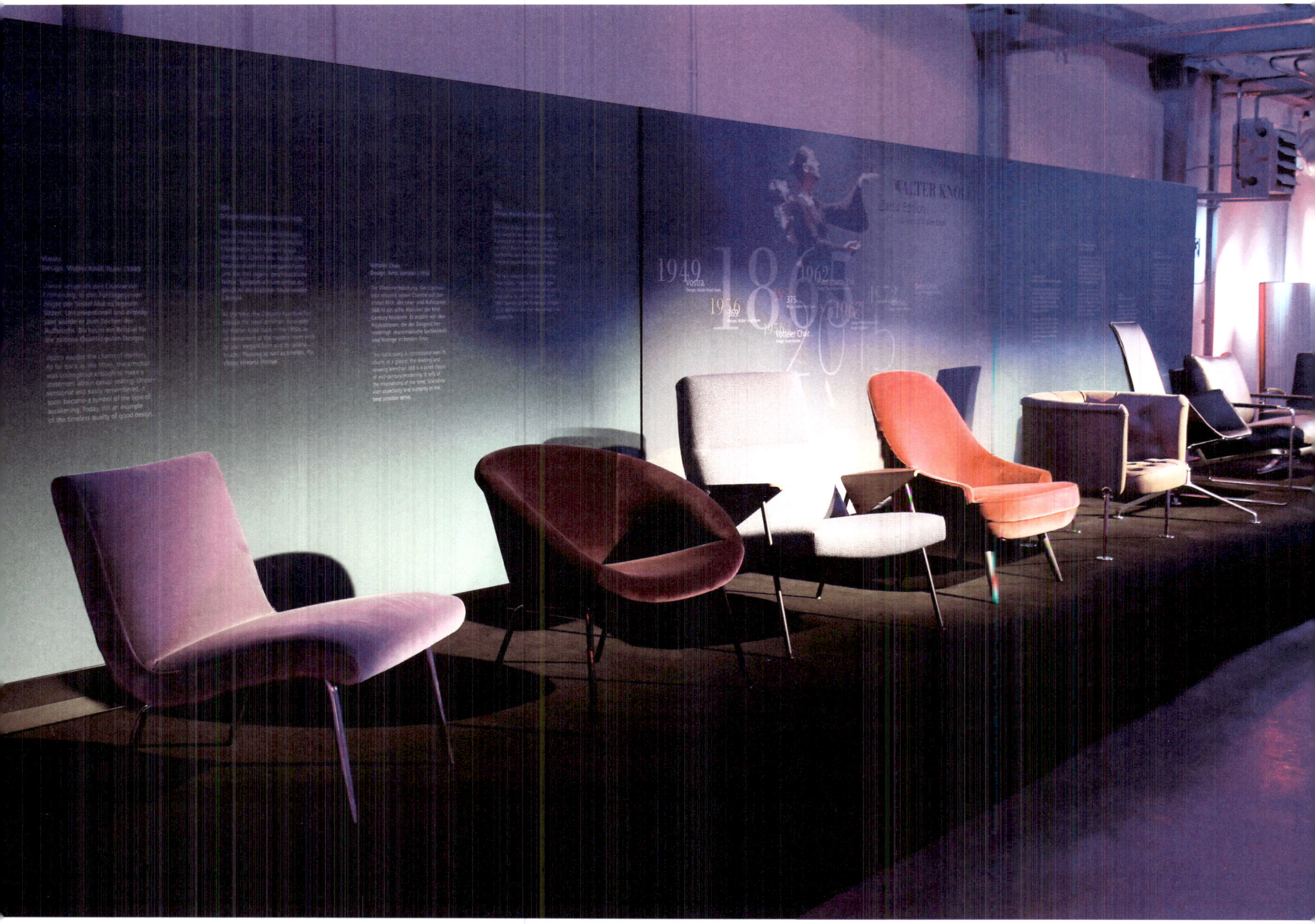

150 YEARS OF WALTER KNOLL

From left to right: Markus Benz with Jean-Remy von Matt, chairman Jung von Matt, moderator Stefanie Anhalt, his father Rolf Benz, chairman of the supervisory board at Walter Knoll, and Gabor Steingart, publisher of "Handelsblatt"

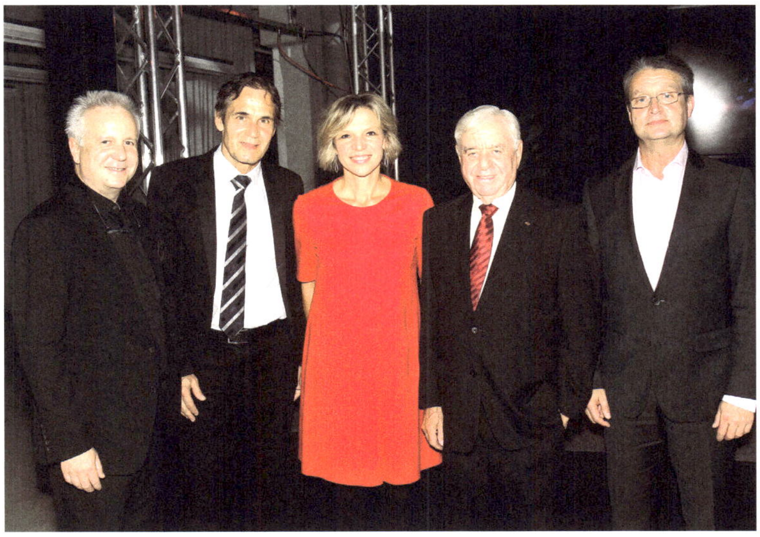

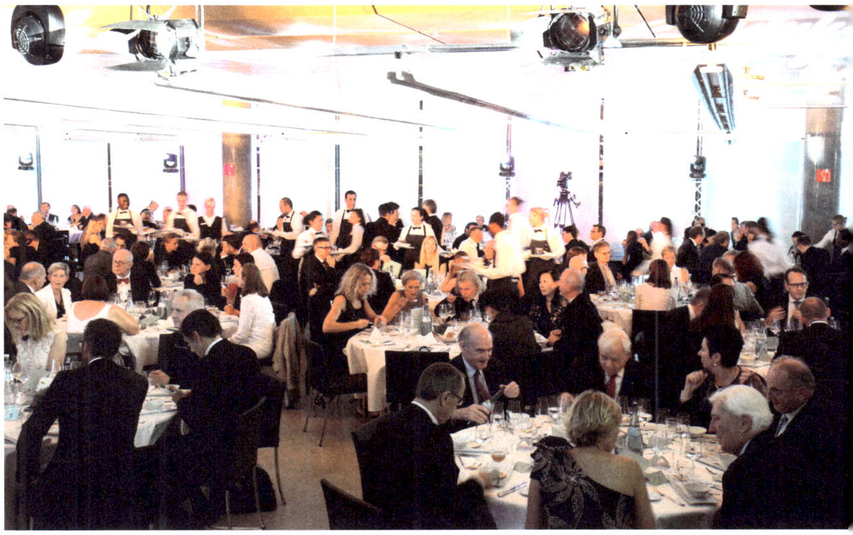

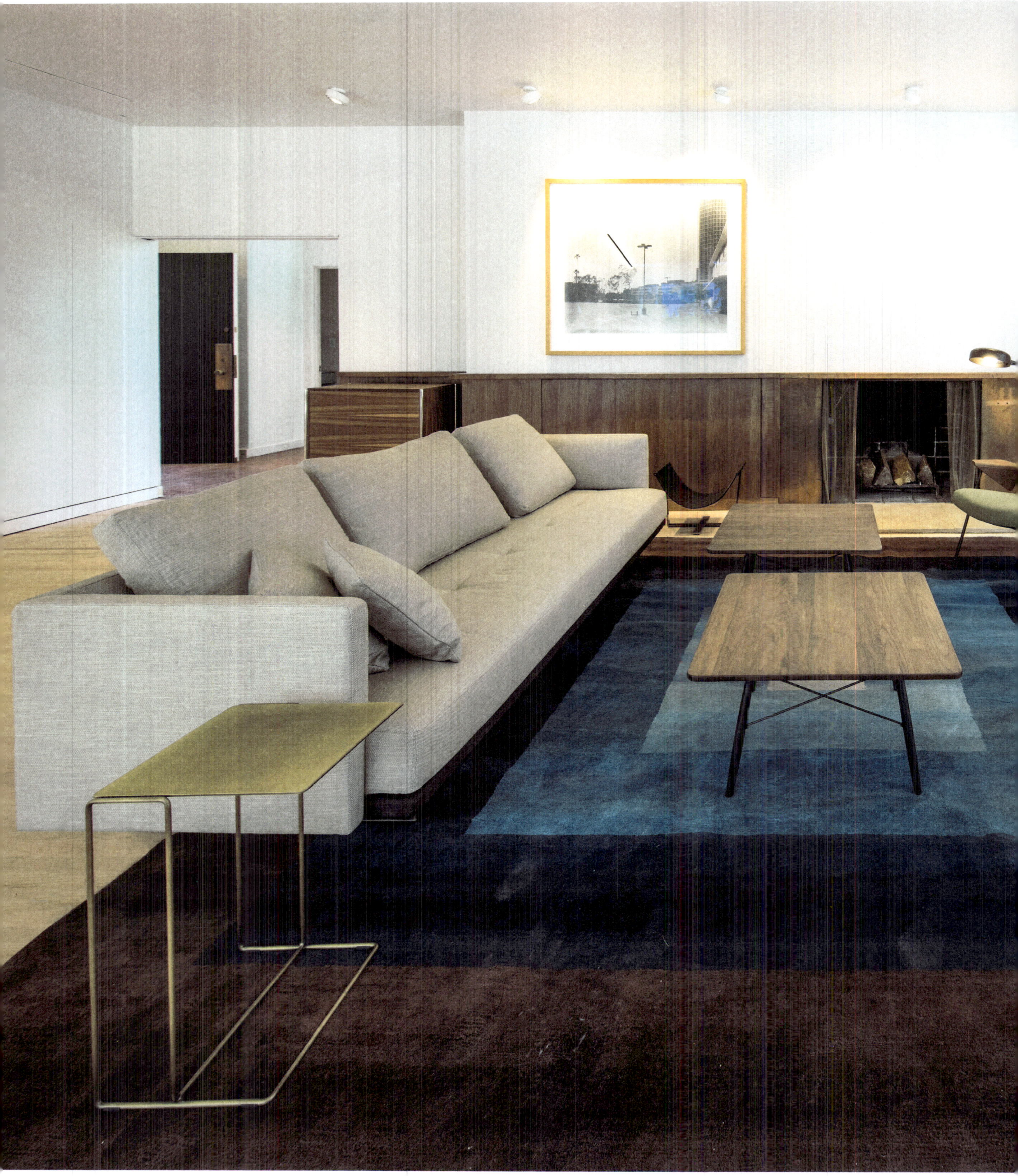

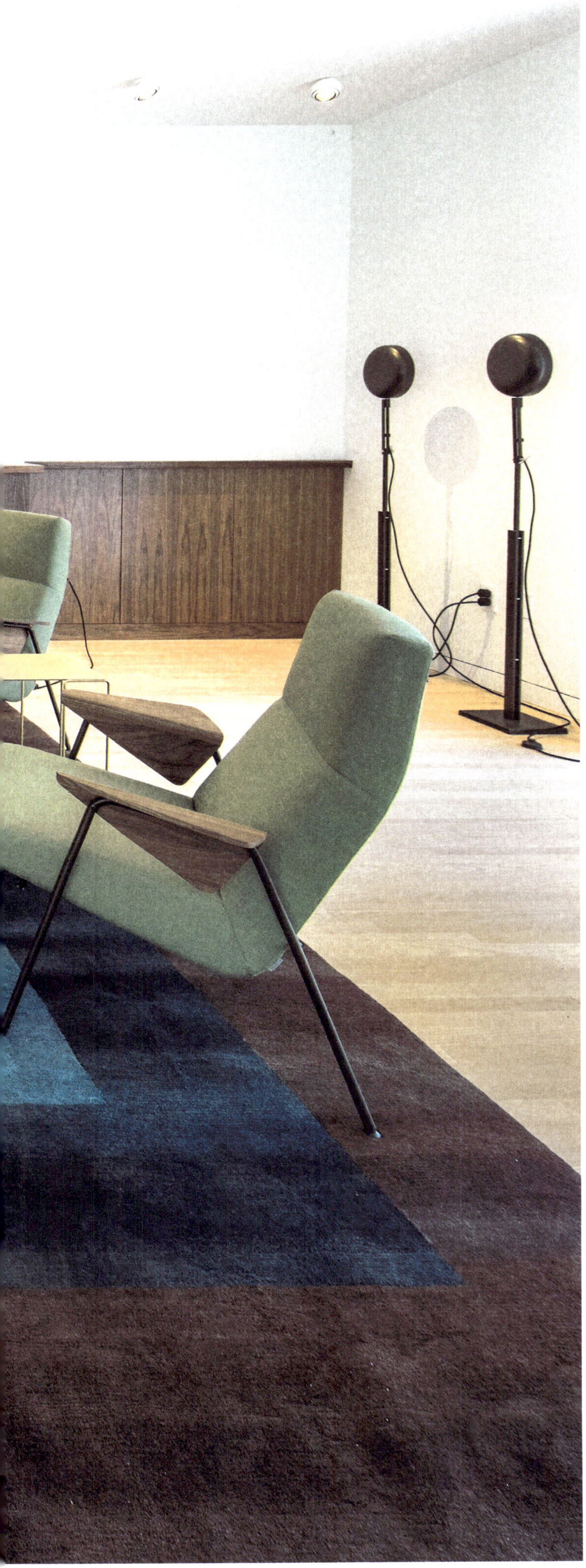

Interior of "Thomas Mann House", furnished with armchairs Votteler Chair, sofa Prime Time, and side table Oki

"Thomas Mann House," architecture by Julius Ralph Davidson (1889–1977), Los Angeles, 2018

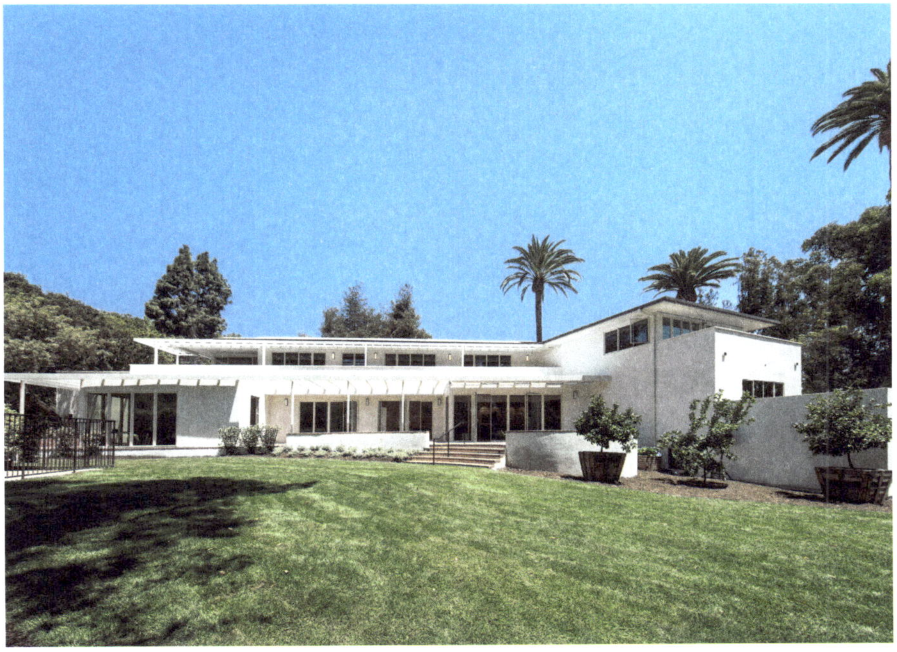

FUTURE

Fu | ture. A smartphone has much more power than NASA did in 1969, the year of the moonlanding. We all know that it will continue to proliferate. In the future, will we be surrounded by computers? Will computer chips connected to the global network be embedded in all our wallpaper, in every eyelash, in absolutely everything? No one has a crystal ball that can tell us the future. Even futurology walks a fine line between science and hoax. But the world does not stand still. It revolves faster and faster. Even fashion and trend are just synonyms for the future that is inevitably coming. Happy are those who can discern its direction. An economic sector like the furniture industry, which has been a finely tuned barometer of social change at least since the last century, needs a direct line to the future. Masters of form and technology, like the PearsonLloyd studio, are engaged in developing an idea of the future every day. But we also need methods such as "Poetical Analysis" – that unorthodox but complex methodology used by the EOOS studio – to predict how we might sit and live tomorrow. We are all heading into a world full of meaning all children so dearly long for. And the adults too.

WE AS DESIGNERS SEE IT AS OUR RESPONSIBILITY TO CREATE THINGS WHICH MAKE LIFE AND THE FUTURE BETTER.
RICHARD SAPPER

2000
Beginning of the collaboration with PearsonLloyd.

2001
The digital encyclopedia Wikipedia goes online.

2003
First projects in the Middle East, including the Commercial Bank of Dubai.

2004
The upholstered furniture Together by EOOS reinvents the corner seat.

2006
The new company headquarters opens in Herrenberg. With the multifunctional building, Walter Knoll's Brandland is created. The book "Design Reloaded," a portrait of the company and the new building, is published. Furnishing of the VIP areas of almost all German stadiums created for the World Cup.

2007
Collaboration with the Japanese architect Kengo Kuma.
Walter Knoll subsidiary founded in Australia. Awarded "Design Management Europe Award."

2008
One of the most successful exhibitions in the company's history. 18 new models are introduced, including Living Landscape. The economic meltdown triggers a worldwide financial crisis.

2009
Walter Knoll brand space opens in London.

2011
The company's highest order intake ever, with 7 million euros in a single month. Stuttgart's cube-shaped "Stadtbibliothek" (Municipal Library), designed by the South Korean architect Eun Young Yi, becomes a new urban icon.

2015
150-year celebration. "Paris Agreement" on climate change.

2016
Furnishing of the plenary hall of the restored "Landtag" in Stuttgart.
Le Corbusier House in Stuttgart's Weissenhofsiedlung is made a World Heritage site.

2017
Opening of the Elbphilharmonie concert hall in Hamburg.

2018
Brand space opens in New York.
Furnishing of the "Thomas Mann House" in Los Angeles.

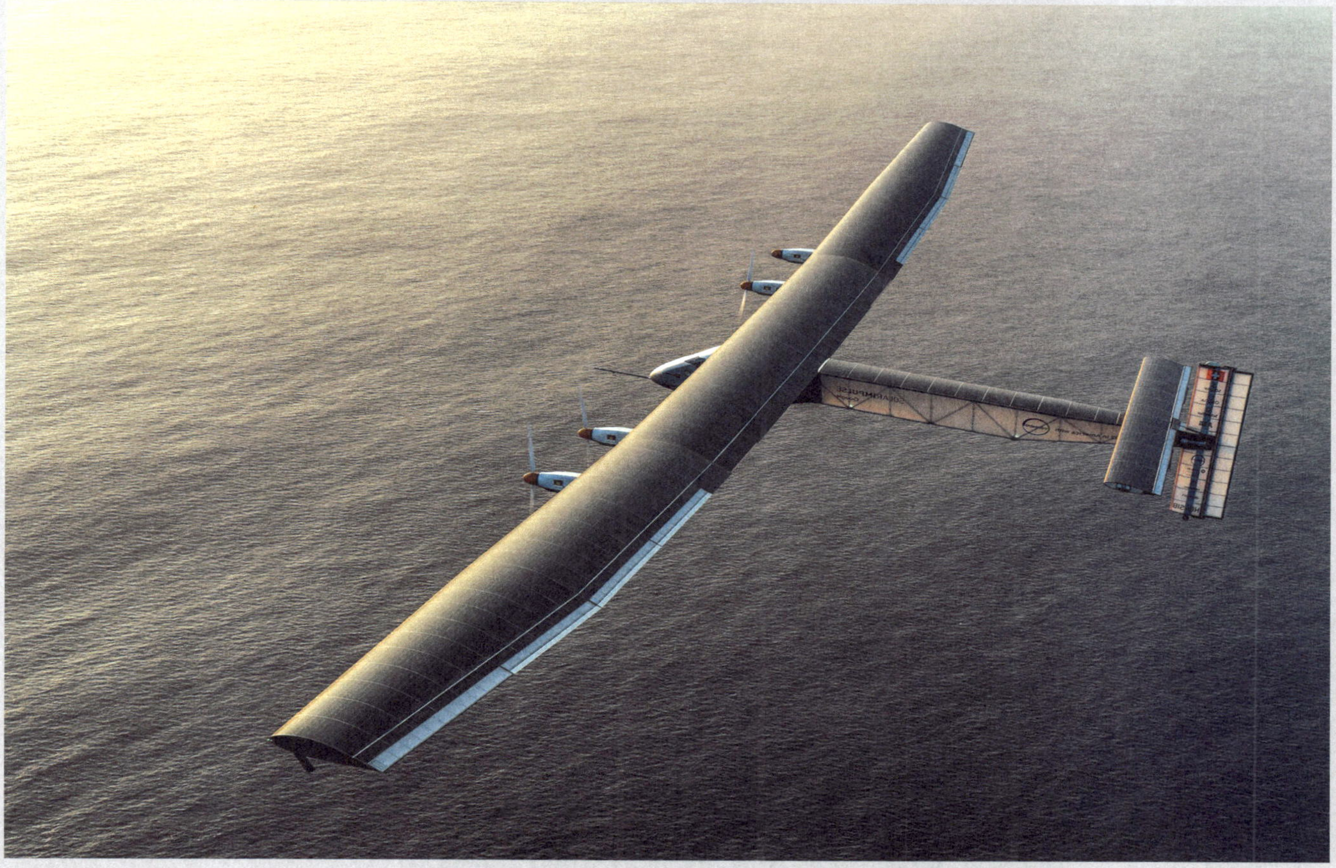

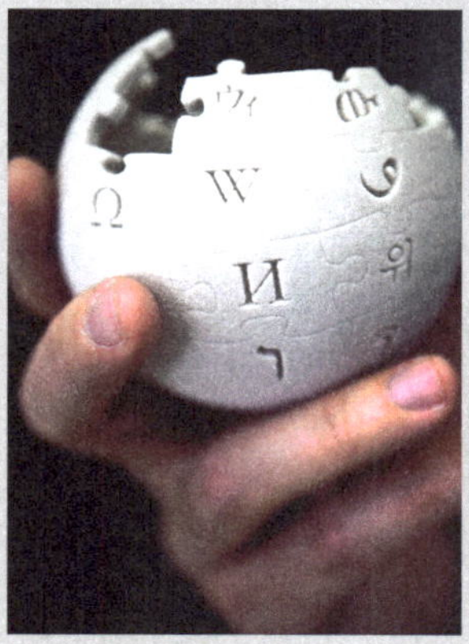

Solar-powered airplane "Solar Impulse"
circling the globe, Egypt

Wikipedia globe,
San Francisco 2009

Sofa Living Landscape 755,
sideboard The Farns,
side tables Oki and Oki Table,
pillow Kiwara from the
Badawi Pillows range,
carpet Suma,
dinig table Tadeo,
chair Saddle Chair

Sideboard The Farns,
standing height table Deen Table,
barstool 375,
carpet Chimbuka

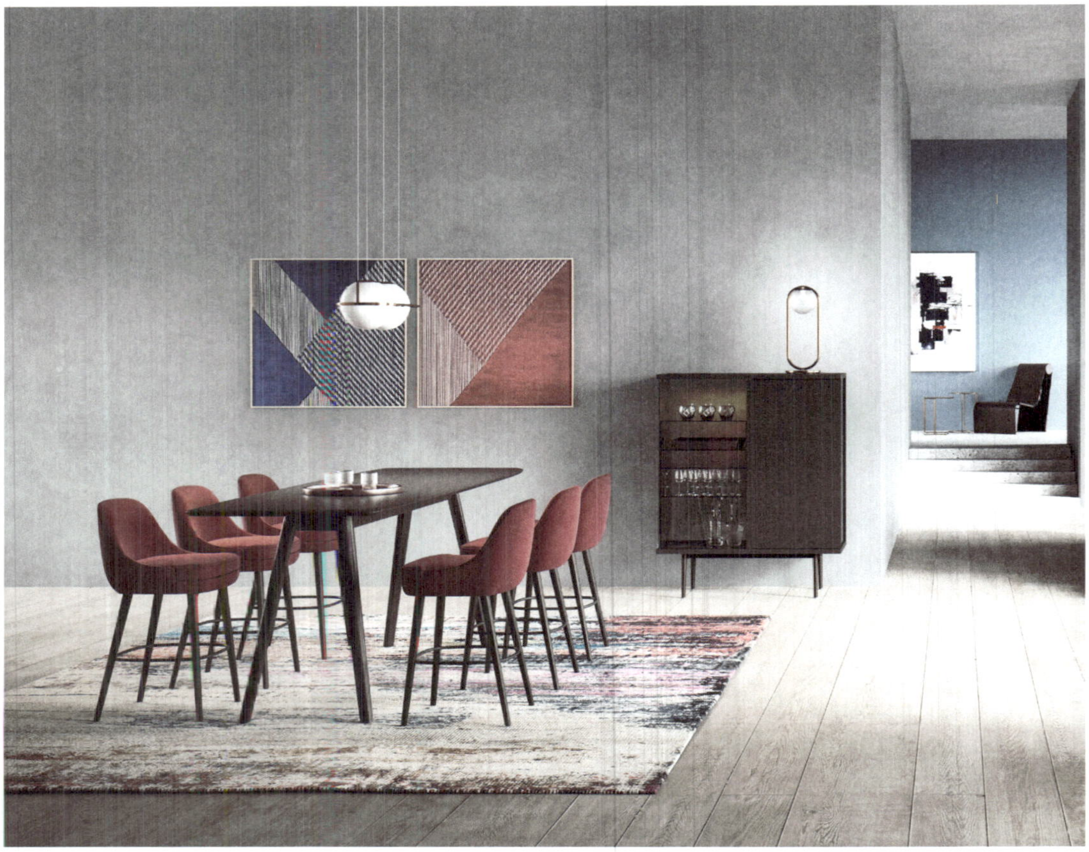

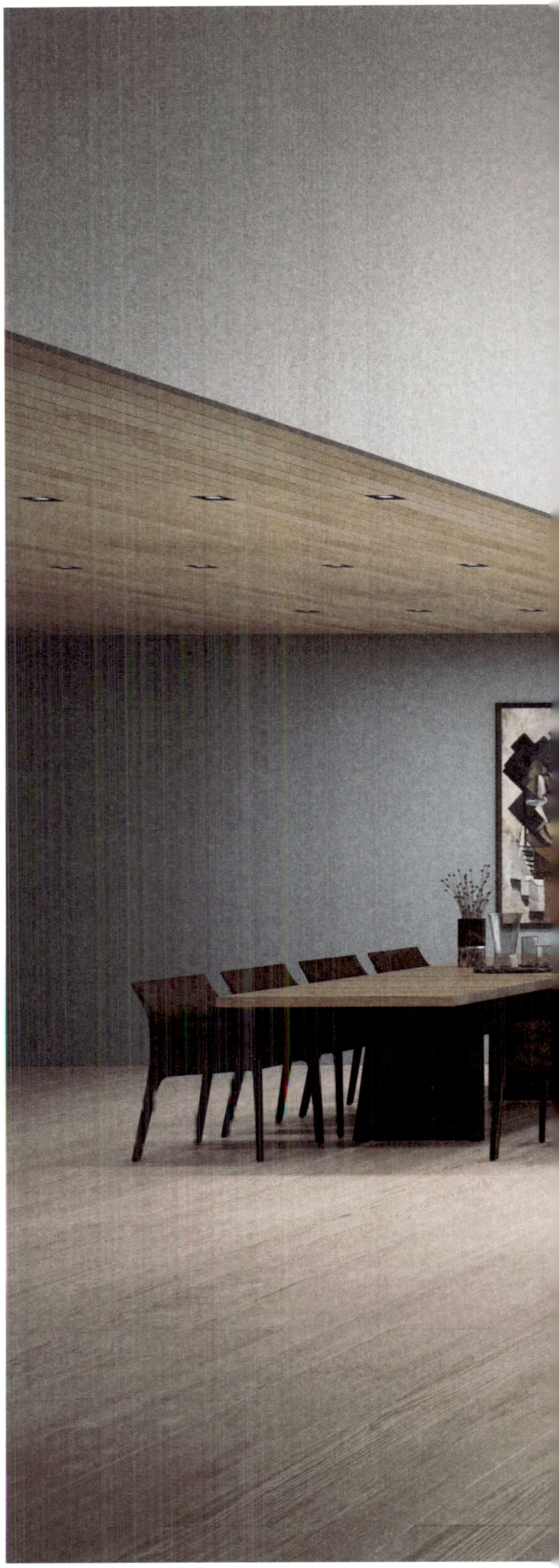

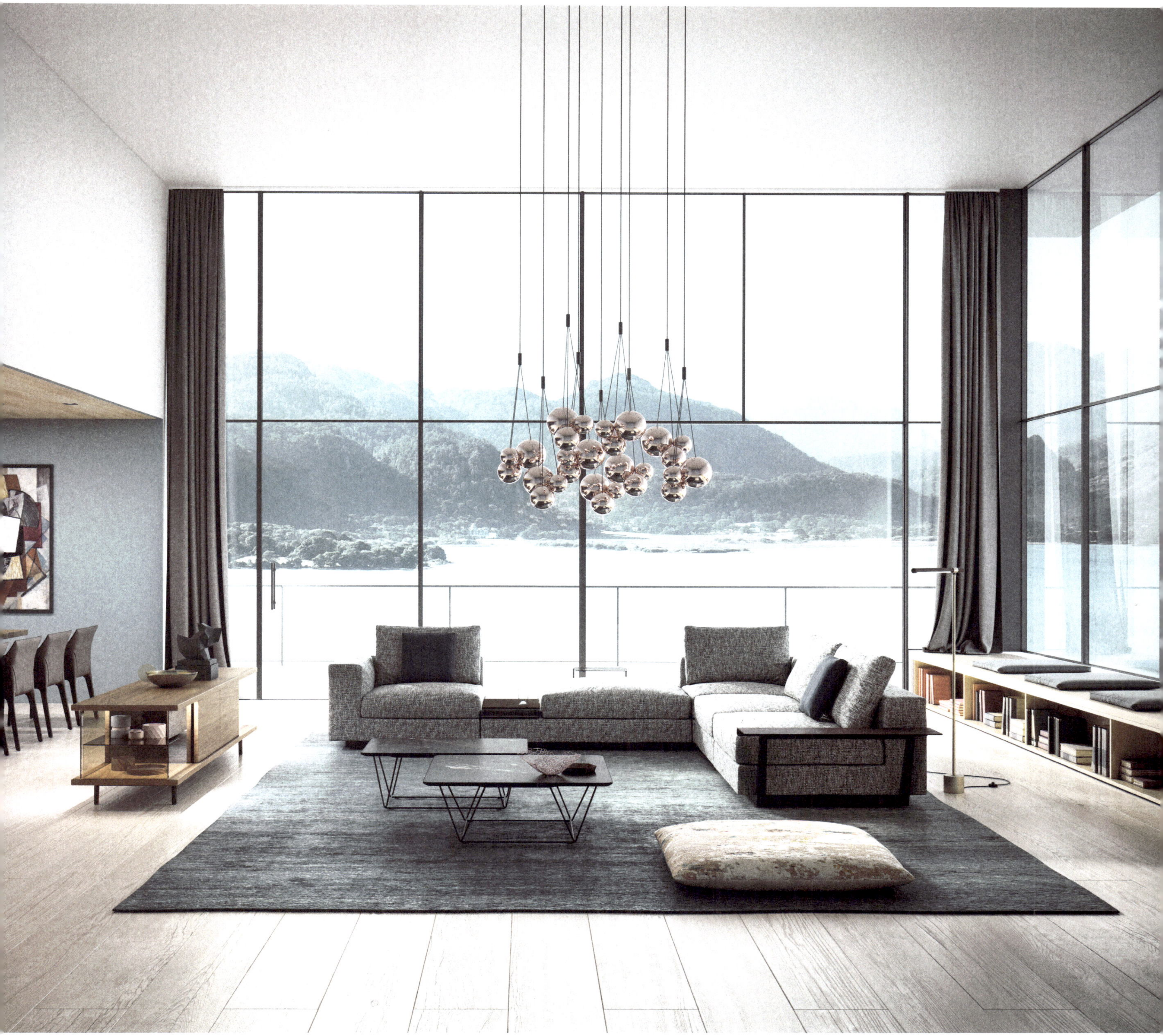

ROBERT AND EMILIE VOLLMÖLLER
1849–1911
Company founder Robert Vollmöller was, like his wife and children, rooted in Stuttgart's milieu of reform.

KARL GUSTAV VOLLMÖLLER
1878–1948
Son of Robert and Emilie Vollmöller. Literary figure, scientist and friend of Walter Knoll, who ran the company until the 1930s.

HANS KNOLL
1914–1955
Son of Walter Knoll. Migrated to the USA in the 1930s and there founded one of the first design-oriented furniture companies, which he ran together with his wife Florence Knoll.

MARIA KNOLL
née Vollmöller
1884–1956
Daughter of Robert and Emilie Vollmöller

⚭

WALTER KNOLL
1878–1971
Son of Wilhelm Knoll. Company founder and pioneer of modernist furniture. Ran his company between the 1920s and 1960s.

ROBERT KNOLL
1912–1985
Son of Walter Knoll who ran the company from the 1960s until the early 1980s.

HERBERT KNOLL
1919–1944
Brother of Robert and Hans Knoll.

DR. WALTER COMBE
1899–1986
Managing director of Wilhelm Knoll from the 1920s; managing partner at Walter Knoll from the 1950s to 1970s.

⚭

HELENE WOERNLE
née Knoll
Sister of Walter and Willy Knoll.

⚭

HEINRICH WOERNLE
Husband of Helene Knoll

TRUDE COMBE
née Woernle
Daughter of Heinrich and Helene Woernle.

ERICH KNOLL
Brother of Walter and Willy Knoll, also active in the furniture industry.

WILHELM KNOLL
1839–1907
Company founder, leather expert and exporter who elevated the company to the status of "Royal Court Supplier".

WILLY KNOLL
1878–1954
Son of Wilhelm Knoll and brother of Walter Knoll. Pushed forward the modernization of upholstered furniture and exports through innovations. Ran the company from 1907 until the 1950s.

DIETER KNOLL
1915–1997
The son of Willy Knoll ran the company between the 1950s and 1980s.

Knoll furniture dynasty

VOLLMÖLLER AG
Founded as a textile factory in Stuttgart in 1881. The hosiery specialist, for a time one of the largest companies in its sector, existed until the 1960s.

FLORENCE KNOLL
née Schust
1917–2019
Wife of Hans Knoll. Designer and owner who ran her company until the mid-1960s following the death of her husband.

KNOLL, INC.
The third company of the Knoll dynasty was founded by Hans Knoll in New York in 1937 under the name Hans Knoll Associates and brought modernist furniture design to America.

MICHAEL KNOLL
1944
Son of Robert Knoll. Studied interior design in Stuttgart. Designer and art director in the 1970s. Managing partner with Stephan Combe in the 1980s and 1990s.

STEPHAN COMBE
1930
Son of Dr. Walter Combe. Managing partner during the 1980s and 1990s as successor to his father.

MARKUS BENZ
1961
Son of Hilde and Rolf Benz. The qualified lawyer took over control of Walter Knoll in 1993 and led the company to the top of the international high-end furniture segment.

DR. MICHAEL BLANK
1948–2016
As co-executive and close partner of Markus Benz, responsible for marketing and sales until 2013 following the takeover of Walter Knoll.

WALTER KNOLL
The second company of the Knoll dynasty was founded in Stuttgart in 1925 and specialized in modern upholstered furniture. Relocated to Herrenberg in the 1930s. Taken over by the Benz family in 1993.

BARBARA BENZ
1966
Daughter of Hilde and Rolf Benz. Managing partner of architare – barbara benz einrichten GmbH + Co. KG.

PROF. DR. STEFAN BENZ
1964
Son of Hilde and Rolf Benz. Chief physician at the Sindelfingen-Böblingen clinical center and partner of the Walter Knoll company.

HANSULRICH BENZ
1963
Son of Hilde and Rolf Benz. Architect of the newer company buildings in Herrenberg and Mötzingen.

WILHELM KNOLL
Original company of the Knoll dynasty. Founded as a leather business in Stuttgart in 1865. Evolved into a leading company for modernist seating furniture after 1900. Was taken over by Walter Knoll in 1986.

HILDE AND ROLF BENZ
1938 and 1933
Rolf Benz founded the eponymous company for modernist upholstered furniture. He ran the company for 35 years as founder, owner, managing director and then as chief executive. The last shares held by the family were sold to the Hüls Group in 1999.

Index

The author

Bernd Polster, a publicist and artist, was one of the first book packagers in Germany, developing and implementing book concepts for German and international publishing houses since 1999. To this end, he founded the büro formweh. One of his main fields of interest is cultural history. Most of his books have been translated into other languages, including the standard work on the design brand Braun. Polster is Germany's best-known design author and Bauhaus expert. New releases: *Der Architekt seines Ruhms* (The Architect of His Own Fame), a biography of Walter Gropius. and the somewhat different book for the 100th anniversary: *Das wahre Bauhaus* (The Real Bauhaus), published by teNeues.
Find more information at www.berndpolster.de

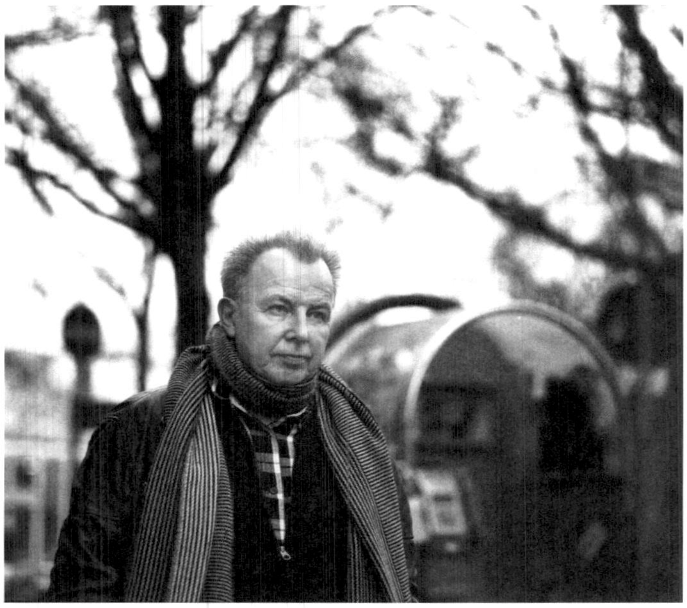

Photo credits

Unless otherwise explicitly specified in the following list of figures, all figures originate from the archives and inventory of the companies Wilhelm and Walter Knoll or are not subject to copyright. We have endeavored to locate all copyright holders. Should this inadvertently not be the case at any point, please notify us.

Alexander Huber, Nagold 308/309
Alte Nationalgalerie, Berlin 330 top left + center left
Archiv formweh, Bonn 12, 22, 42 top left, 67 left, 77 top left
Archiv Franz Lazi, Stuttgart 129, 135, 139, 144 left, 145, 160, 161, 168 bottom right, 181 top right, 205
Archiv Hans Roericht, Ulm 179 bottom left
Archiv Neptun Ozis, Istanbul 317
Basim Ghomorlou, Bonn 348
Bernd Polster, Bonn 271
Bieffe Rendering, Sommacampagna 338/339
Bildarchiv Foto Marburg, Marburg 31 bottom left, 39
Bildarchiv Foto Marburg / Waltraud Krase, Marburg 74 right
bpk / Staatsgalerie Stuttgart, Stuttgart 173
Brigida Gonzales, Stuttgart 79
Bundesarchiv, B 145 Bild-F003564-0004 / Rolf Unterberg / CC-BY-SA 3.0, Koblenz 153 bottom
Christian Kandzia, Altbach 231
Christof Sage, Filderstadt 332/333
Daimler AG, Stuttgart 117 bottom, 153 bottom, 320 top
David Flynn, Sydney 285
David von Becker, Berlin 330 center right + bottom, 331
DEKRA, Stuttgart 300 left
Deniz Saylan, Berlin/Stuttgart 281
Deutsches Architekturmuseum, Frankfurt 213 top right
Didier Descouens / CC-BY-SA-4.0, Bouloc 41
die arge lola, Stuttgart 223 top
Dr. Lossen & Co., Stuttgart-Feuerbach 75, 77 bottom left, 78 top + bottom right
Elfie Semotan 266 top left
EOOS, Wien 322 top
Firmenarchiv Alessi, Omegna 245 top left
Firmenarchiv Arzberg, Selb 106 top left
Firmenarchiv Audi, Ingolstadt 326 top left
Firmenarchiv Braun, Kronberg im Taunus 192 top left, 209 top left
Firmenarchiv Hansgrohe, Schiltach 262 top left
Firmenarchiv HEWI, Bad Arolsen 216 left
Firmenarchiv Porsche, Stuttgart 138 top left
Firmenarchiv Quittenbaum, München 99 top left
Flughafen Stuttgart 320 bottom
Gabriel Büchelmeier, München 311 top + bottom
gmp Archiv, Hamburg 217 top right
Hans-Georg Esch, Hennef/Sieg 5, 270 bottom, 272-275, 288 left, 289, 305 top + bottom
Hansulrich Benz, Weissach 291
Haus der Geschichte Baden-Württemberg, Sammlung Eder, Stuttgart 10/11
Hong Kong International Airport 284
Hufton+Crow, London 304
Iwan Baan, Amsterdam 312/313
Jane Kolb, Wermatswil 189 top right
Kunstmuseum Stuttgart 181 bottom right
Landesmedienzentrum Baden-Württemberg, Stuttgart 14, 122/123, 184, 249
Landesmuseum Württemberg, P. Frankenstein, H. Zwietasch, Stuttgart 34/35
Landtag von Baden-Württemberg, Stuttgart 307 top
Lane Hartwell 337 bottom left
LenzWerk Holding, Berlin 334/335
M Franke 328 top
Marcus Bredt, Berlin 314 top right + bottom
Michael Knoll, Herrenberg 118, 127, 239
Michael Tümmers, Leinfelden-Echterdingen 306
Museum Hochschule für Gestaltung, Ulm 179 top right
Norman Foster, London 268
Nigel Young, London 302 left + right
Olaf Meyer, Köln 70 top left
Oscar Gonzales/NurPhoto via Getty Images, Washington 277 top
PearsonLloyd, London 292
Peter Schumacher, Stuttgart – various product images, Third Modernity
Philipp Meuser, Berlin 310 top
Picture Alliance, Frankfurt am Main 321
Robert Reichel, Stuttgart-Feuerbach19, 23
Sebastian Böttcher, London 250, 298/299, 301
Solar Impulse, Lausanne 337 top
Stadtarchiv Stuttgart 15, 18, 21, 50/51, 58/59, 87, 115, 134, 168 top left + right, 169 top left, 172
UN Photo/Mark Garten 310 bottom
UNStudio, Amsterdam 282, 326 bottom left + top right, 327 bottom
VG Bildkunst, München 31 top right, 181 bottom right
Zeppelin Museum, Friedrichshafen 102 top + bottom, 103
Zooey Braun, Stuttgart 328 bottom

Bibliography

Deutsches Kaiserreich: *Weltausstellung St. Louis Amtlicher Katalog. Ausstellung des Deutschen Reiches*, Berlin 1904.

Deutscher Werkbund: *Werkbund-Ausstellung. Die Wohnung* (catalog), Stuttgart 1927.

Klaus Konrad Dillmann: *Robert Vollmöller – Leben und Zeit eines schwäbischen Textilunternehmers*, Ilsfeld 1999.

Astrid Eichstedt und Bernd Polster: *Wie die Wilden. Tänze auf der Höhe ihrer Zeit*, Berlin 1985.

Cherie und Kenneth Fehrman: *Interior Design Innovators 1910–1960*, San Francisco 2009.

Sigfried Giedion: *Befreites Wohnen*, Zurich 1924.

Sigfried Giedion: *Die Herrschaft der Mechanisierung. Ein Beitrag zur anonymen Geschichte*, Frankfurt/Main 1982.

J. F. Häuselmann: *Entwürfe von Karl Pullich*, in: *Innen-Dekoration*, Juli–Aug., Stuttgart 1917.

Sebastian Haffner: *Geschichte eines Deutschen. Die Erinnerungen 1914–1933*. Stuttgart 2000.

Guido Harbers: *Die schöne Wohnung*, Munich 1951.

Marta Herford: *Der entfesselte Blick – Die Brüder Rasch und ihre Impulse für die moderne Architektur*, Berlin 2014.

Theodor Heuss: *Robert Bosch – Leben und Leistung*, Stuttgart 1986.

Kathryn Hiesinger und George Marcus: *Landmarks of Twentieth-Century Design*, New York 1993.

Charles Higham: *Marlene: The Life of Marlene Dietrich*. W. W. Norton & Company Inc. 1977.

Eric Hobsbawm: *Das Zeitalter der Extreme. Weltgeschichte des 20. Jahrhunderts*, Munich and Vienna 1995.

Eric Hobsbawm und Terence Ranger: *The Invention of Tradition*, Cambridge 1992.

Walter Klein: *Das Württemberger Musikzimmer in St. Louis nach den Entwürfen und Modellen von Professor Bernhard Pankok*, in: *Stuttgarter Mitteilungen über Kunst und Gewerbe*, Edition 1904/05, Stuttgart.

Maximilian Knoch: *Zurichtung*, in: *Handbuch der Gerbereichemie und Lederfabrikation. Dritter Band/2. Teil. Die Lederarten und deren Herstellung*, S. 42, Vienna 1955.

Walter Knoll: *Erinnerungen* (manuscript), Herrenberg n. d.

Company Walter Knoll: *Echo aus Herrenberg. Firmenzeitschrift*, Herrenberg.

Familie Wilhelm Knoll (ed.): *100 Jahre Wilhelm Knoll*, Stuttgart 1965.

Landesgewerbeamt Baden-Württemberg (Hrsg.): *Wie wohnen. Bautechnik, Möbel, Hausrat. Gedanken und Bilder zur Ausstellung.* Stuttgart and Karlsruhe 1949.

Earl Martin (ed.): *Knoll Textiles*, New York 2011.

Peter McMahon und Christine Cipriani: *Cape Cod Modern. Midcentury Architecture and Community on the Outer Cape*, New York 2014.

Hermann Muthesius: *Die Wohnungskunst auf der Welt-Ausstellung in St. Louis*, in: *Deutsche Kunst und Dekoration*, Ill. 9, Darmstadt 1905.

Bernd Polster: *Braun. 50 Jahre Produktinnovationen*, Cologne 2005.

Bernd Polster: *Das Designbuch*, Munich 1999.

Bernd Polster: *Designlexikon USA*, Cologne 2002.

Bernd Polster, Volker Fischer und Katja Simon: *bauhaus design. Die Produkte der Neuen Sachlichkeit*, Cologne 2009.

Bernd Polster: *Wohndesign Deutschland. Die Klassiker*, Cologne 2008.

A. C. Rüdenauer: *Über Wesen und Ziel deutscher Wohnkultur; in: Innendekoration – das behagliche Heim. Die gesamte Wohnungskunst in Bild und Wort*, Vol. 48, pp. 341–345, Stuttgart 1937.

Dieter Schnermann: *Wertvolle Merkmale eines reichen Lebens. Aus dem Leben Walther C. Knolls*, in: Roman Janssen (ed.): *Herrenberger Historische Schriften*, Vol. 6, pp. 391–402, Herrenberg 1999.

Schwäbischer Merkur 1896, Stadtarchiv Stuttgart, archive number 1056/2.

Mia Seeger: *Der Neue Wohnbedarf*, Berlin 1932.

Bernd Sösemann: *Jenseits von Partei und Parlament – W. Rathenaus „aufbauende Ideenpolitik" in der „DG 1914"*, in: Hans Wilderotter (ed.): *Walther Rathenau 1867–1922 – Die Extreme berühren sich*, pp. 169–178, Berlin 1993.

Staatsanzeiger für Württemberg 1896, Stadtarchiv Stuttgart, archive number 1056/2.

Bruno Taut: *Die Neue Wohnung*, Leipzig 1924.

Arno Votteler and Herbert Eilmann: *125 Jahre Knoll. Vier Generationen Sitzmöbel-Design*, Stuttgart 1990.

Max Weber: *Die protestantische Ethik und der Geist des Kapitalismus*, Tübingen 1934.

Württemberger Zeitung, 25/09/1928.

Idea: Markus Benz
Concept: Bernd Polster, büro formweh
Author: Bernd Polster
Project management: Tamara Karcher
Copyediting: Dr. Simone Bischoff
Translations & proofreading: Anja Hemming-Xavier and
Romina Russo Lais, WeSwitch Languages GmbH & Co. KG
Proofreading: Stephanie Rebel,
Inga Wortmann-Grützmacher, teNeues Media
Editing: Carlotta Hoffmann, büro formweh
Text and image research: Carlotta Hoffmann, Bernd Polster
Graphical design: Eva Stadler
Graphical assistance: René Gruszka, Carlotta Hoffmann
Image editing & proofing: Jens Grundei, Robin Hopp, teNeues Media
Production: Alwine Krebber, teNeues Media
Editorial coordination: Pit Pauen, teNeues Media

English edition: ISBN 978-3-96171-179-6

Printed in Italy

Bibliographic information published by the
Deutsche Nationalbibliothek
The Deutsche Nationalbibliothek lists this publication in the Deutsche Nationalbibliografie; detailed bibliographic data are available on the Internet at http://dnb.dnb.de.

Published by teNeues Publishing Group

teNeues Media GmbH & Co. KG
Am Selder 37, 47906 Kempen, Germany
Phone: +49-(0)2152-916-0
Fax: +49-(0)2152-916-111
e-mail: books@teneues.com

Press department: Andrea Rehn
Phone: +49-(0)2152-916-202
e-mail: arehn@teneues.com

teNeues Media GmbH & Co. KG
Munich Office
Pilotystraße 4, 80538 Munich, Germany
Phone: +49-(0)89-443-8889-62
e-mail: bkellner@teneues.com

teNeues Media GmbH & Co. KG
Berlin Office
Kohlfurter Straße 41–43, 10999 Berlin, Germany
Phone: +49-(0)30-4195-3526-23
e-mail: ajasper@teneues.com

teNeues Publishing Company
350 7th Avenue, Suite 301, New York, NY 10001, USA
Phone: +1-212-627-9090
Fax: +1-212-627-9511

teNeues Publishing UK Ltd.
12 Ferndene Road, London SE24 0AQ, UK
Phone: +44-(0)20-3542-8997

teNeues France S.A.R.L.
39, rue des Billets, 18250 Henrichemont, France
Phone: +33-(0)2-4826-9348
Fax: +33-(0)1-7072-3482

www.teneues.com

teNeues Publishing Group
Kempen
Berlin
London
Munich
New York
Paris

teNeues

MIX
Paper from responsible sources
FSC® C016466